A TREASURY OF AMERICAN WRITERS

FROM
Harper's
MAGAZINE

A TREASURY OF AMERICAN WRITERS

FROM *Harper's* MAGAZINE

Edited by

Horace Knowles

Bonanza Books
New York

This 1985 edition is published by Bonanza Books distributed by
Crown Publishers, Inc. by arrangement with Harper & Row.

Printed and bound in the United States of America

LIBRARY OF CONGRESS CATALOGING IN PUBLICATION DATA

Main entry under title:

Treasury of American writers from Harper's magazine.

    Includes index.
    1. American literature—20th century.   I. Knowles,
Horace.   II. Harper's magazine.
PS536.T74 1985   810'.8'005   85-13312
    ISBN 0-517-48074-3

h g f e d c b a

Grateful acknowledgment is made for permission to reprint
the following selections:

Excerpts from *One Man's Meat,* copyright 1939, 1940,
1941, 1942 by E. B. White; "The Coming—and Disciplining—of Industrialism" from *The Big Change,* copyright 1950 by Frederick Lewis Allen; "The Only Woman
in the Lifeboat" from *Atlantic Ordeal,* copyright 1941 by
Elspeth Huxley; "A Platform and a Passion or Two" from
Three Plays, copyright © 1957 by Thornton Wilder;
"Mark Twain Speaks Out" from *The Autobiography of
Mark Twain,* edited by Charles Neider, copyright © 1958
by The Mark Twain Company: "I Will Leave This House"
from *No Traveller Returns,* copyright 1934 by Joseph
Auslander; excerpts from *The Passionate State of Mind,*
copyright 1954 by Eric Hoffer; "The Decision to Use the
Atomic Bomb" from *On Active Service in Peace and
War,* copyright 1947 by Henry L. Stimson; "Merrill's
Marauders" from *The Marauders,* copyright © 1956 by
Charlton Ogburn, Jr. Published by Harper & Brothers.

"Highbrow, Lowbrow, Middlebrow," copyright 1949 by
Russell Lynes.

"Whiskey Is for Patriots" from *The Hour,* copyright 1948,
1949, 1951 by Bernard DeVoto; excerpt from *The Great
Crash,* copyright 1954 by John Kenneth Galbraith; "To
Praisers of Women" by Archibald MacLeish, reprinted as

iv

CONTENTS

Contents

Note to the Reader

by HORACE KNOWLES

You *can* buy the entire bound file of *Harper's*—218 fat volumes. Read them, and you'll acquire a liberal education, a need for bifocals, and a new age reckoning. I am now 109 magazine years old. I feel it.

This book is a selection of the best material published in *Harper's* since its first issue in 1850. Many devoted readers of the magazine will, no doubt, disagree with my choice. For only two criteria have governed the selections here—surpassing interest for today's readers and literary excellence. My aim has been to produce a book which would be stimulating and enjoyable for people of our times. Consequently much material which proved engrossing to earlier generations has been left out.*

Nevertheless there is an extraordinarily wide range of material in this book, as there has been in the magazine since its beginning. It includes the work of writers few people have ever heard of, as well as pieces by authors of international repute. Some articles are so unusual they almost defy classification; others deal with subjects on the mind of the whole world.

The controversial is here. Two Southerners, William Faulkner of Mississippi, and T. R. Waring, a Charleston (S.C.) newspaper editor, slug it out on the integration issue. They are paired under the section "Big Changes."

You'll sympathize with Robert Dean Frisbie in his encounter with the lovely Polynesian, Miss Tern, in the article "The Sex Taboo at Puka-Puka." He says that when, nude, she trips gracefully down the beach, "the innocent and lovely creation of a fairy wand, I am not nearly enough of a Saint Anthony not to feel a warm tremor pass over me."

That article is under "Our Perennial Flirtation," all about girls. Our

---

*Chances are, for example, that I omitted the piece Lizzie Borden was reading in *Harper's* that hot August morning in 1891 when her father and stepmother were whacked to death with an ax. She testified about it at the inquest, though she didn't name the specific story which absorbed her. Anyway, the Fall River (Mass.) trial jury later acquitted *Harper's*-reading Lizzie.

lady readers are likely to react in an entirely different way to John Fischer's famous little essay, "The Loving Care of Determined Women." He writes: "Never before in history has any nation devoted so large a share of its brains and resources to the sole purpose of keeping its women greased, deodorized, corseted, enshrined in chrome convertibles, curled, slenderized, rejuvenated, and relieved of all physical labor."

In the section "Our Love Affair with Culture," you will find criticism and comment on literature, the theater, and music. Mark Twain is represented with some just-published parts of his *Autobiography*. E. M. Forster writes brilliantly on art and the artist in general. Others on their specialties: Carl Van Doren, George Bernard Shaw, Clifton Fadiman, Katherine Anne Porter, Thornton Wilder and Oscar Levant.

Loren Eiseley has what we think is perhaps his finest piece, "The Secret of Life" in the section "Science and Philosophy." It is sublime. In this section, too, is Eric Hoffer, the amazing San Francisco longshoreman, whose book *The True Believer* has won international acclaim, and has fascinated, among thousands of others, President Dwight D. Eisenhower. Aldous Huxley is here, and there's a good scientific detective story, "The Coming Ice Age," which made headlines all over the country last year.

It has been said that history cannot be written without *Harper's*. An indication why is seen in the section "Daguerreotype of America." Horace Greeley writes on his famous trip West, and John Muir on his discovery of the full range of the Sequoia. And in the lovely little piece, "A Bit of Life in Oregon," we understand why the anonymous author gave the shirt off his back to a pretty Indian maid.

You'll also find interesting things from early issues in other sections—the shocking story of child labor in New York City in the 1870's, under "Big Changes"; the famous interview George Ward Nichols had with Wild Bill Hickok, under "Scalawags and Hard Cases"; and, for Civil War buffs, two fine pieces on that conflict under "Fighting Words."

In "An Eye on the Outside World," Arnold Toynbee and D. W. Brogan give us the historian's perspective in analyses of two aspects of the modern world. John Gunther reminds us in that section that the century's madman, Adolf Hitler, was not just something out of a nightmare.

No finer series of personal essays than E. B. White's "One Man's

Meat" ever appeared in *Harper's* or any other magazine. He wrote them during the five critical years beginning in 1938. A selection of the best is included in "An Image of America Since Yesterday." That section also includes Russell Lynes' famous "Highbrow, Lowbrow, Middlebrow."

Three lively scholars, Frederick Lewis Allen, Henry Steele Commager, and John Kenneth Galbraith, have contributed their special talents in "Big Changes." Bertrand Russell, the perennial firebrand, writes on "The Functions of a Teacher" in "Science and Philosophy."

There are many more, and in the story and poetry sections, some of our most gifted artists.

If many famous writers are here, they have earned their places; none is included solely because of his name. *Harper's* has always had name writers. In the 1890's, for instance, it carried the work of such people as Stephen Crane, George Du Maurier, William Dean Howells, Bret Harte, W. W. Jacobs, Henry James, Arthur Conan Doyle, Sarah Orne Jewett, James Russell Lowell, Woodrow Wilson, Theodore Roosevelt, and Carl Schurz. None of these is represented in this book, and a similar list, likewise not here, could be compiled for each of the ten other decades since the magazine was started. There were Dickens and Thackeray, Rudyard Kipling and Joseph Conrad, Willa Cather and Sherwood Anderson. There were outstanding reports on exploration, just to name one category, by Henry M. Stanley, Sven Hedin, Roy Chapman Andrews, Robert E. Peary, Roald Amundsen, and Vilhjalmur Stefansson. Also, it is probably safe to say that no other magazine, outside of scientific journals, carried more early articles on the subject of what we now call atomic physics. In January, 1904, Sir Ernest Rutherford wrote on "Disintegration of the Radioactive Elements," and Sir William Ramsay (both Nobel Prize winners) wrote on "Atoms" in 1913. And there were many others.

But the exploration of Africa, the drive for the Poles, even the unlocking of the atom's secrets, are old stories in a day when the frontier is Space. And the stories of the master fiction writers mentioned above were either mainly curios, have been reprinted in other anthologies, or were not their best work. All were eliminated in the competition with the wealth of quality material available.

Pictures were omitted to make room for more writing, although *Harper's* practically invented the illustrated magazine, and all the best artists were there, including Thomas Nast, Frederic Remington,

Howard Pyle, J. W. Alexander, A. B. Frost, C. S. Reinhart, Howard Chandler Christy, and Charles Dana Gibson.

A few of the articles to follow, particularly the old ones, have been shortened where it seemed justified.

I had much help and guidance in assembling the book. *Harper's Magazine* is the pride and joy—and justly so—of the House of Harper. Never before had the House permitted an inclusive anthology to be assembled from its treasures, which make up the richest storehouse of periodical literature in existence. I am especially indebted to John Fischer, who had much to do with shaping the book; also to Simon Michael Bessie and John Appleton, Harper editors, whose suggestions were invaluable; to Miss Rose Daly, Editorial Secretary of *Harper's Magazine,* who runs it; to Mrs. Dorothy Norton and Mrs. Indra Carnarius, for research; and finally to my wife and son, who let me— whenever I wanted to, nights, Sundays, and holidays for the past two and one-half years—hole up "in that room with all those damn magazines."

Introduction

by JOHN FISCHER

This book has been distilled from a singular kind of magazine, and so carries its special flavor. Some people like it—so much, in fact, that they become lifelong addicts. These often acquire a taste for *Harper's* in adolescence (perhaps from an indulgent grandfather) and soon find it habit-forming. Yet when taken regularly and in moderation it appears to do them little harm. Indeed, the proprietors claim for it a bracing, tonic effect, which is said to whet the palate, stimulate intellectual digestion, and induce sparkling conversation.

In honesty, however, it must be admitted that other readers find it hard to stomach. They complain that it is unsettling—even dangerous—and that its contents are too sharp and pungent for the general taste. Hence this note. It is intended, like the label on a bottle, to give the customer a fair idea of what he may find inside, and where it came from.

Harper's has never been produced for the mass market. Its founders designed it (because they had no other choice) for a small, specific clientele. This was the so-called educated class. A century ago, before the days of universal public education, this was the only group that had the ability, the leisure, and the money to read much of anything. It was, in effect, the governing class of the country—those people in the professions, industry, and public service who largely decided the issues and set the standards of taste for the rest of the population.

The four brothers Harper were themselves representative members of this group. They started life on a farm just outside Brooklyn, then a pleasant pastoral village. None of them had much enthusiasm for the soil, and at the age of sixteen, the eldest—James—rowed across the East River and got himself a job as an apprentice to a printer. In the strict Methodist tradition of the time he lived frugally, worked from daylight till long after dark, and saved his pennies like a Horatio Alger hero. By the time he was twenty-two, in 1817, he was ready to set up a print shop of his own, in partnership with his brother John; as it prospered, the two younger members of the family, Wesley and Fletcher, came in to form the firm of Harper & Brothers.

They were extremely practical businessmen, interested at least as much in money as in literature. They hated to see their presses standing idle, in between book jobs; and they needed some way to advertise their books. A solution to both problems, which they hit upon in 1850, was to start a magazine. As was natural for men with such an acute fiscal instinct, they wanted to get their editorial material as cheaply as possible—and the cheapest way was piracy. Because there was then no international copyright law, they simply appropriated what they liked from British publications, which were then publishing most of the good writing being done in English. As a consequence the early issues of *Harper's New Monthly* were filled almost entirely with the works of British writers—among them Dickens, Thackeray, Coleridge, Lord Chesterfield, Harriet Martineau, and Oliver Goldsmith.

This piratical policy worked so well that within six months the magazine had reached a circulation of fifty thousand copies, a remarkable figure for the time. The editor—a young man named Henry J. Raymond—was encouraged by this success to branch out on his own; he founded the *New York Times* and for five years edited it in what time he had left over from the magazine.

He was also a politician, and his employers were themselves intensely interested in the political life of the period. Another apprentice, who had worked at the same press with James Harper, was Thurlow Weed; he was to become the nation's first great political boss and a founder of the Republican party. Partly through his friendly interest, James Harper became mayor of New York and Raymond went to the state assembly and later to Congress. Naturally enough, their magazine began to devote an increasing share of its space to public affairs —particularly the opening of the West, the growth of Northern industry, and the looming conflict over slavery.

It was treasured by its subscribers; hundreds of them bound their old copies into leather-covered volumes, and carried them across the plains in covered wagons or around the Horn to the gold camps of California. By the light of whale-oil lamps they were read aloud in innumerable family circles from Maine to Oregon. By the time the Civil War broke, *Harper's* was firmly established as the leading national monthly—"a mirror," as a later editor put it, "of American life and ideas."

Whether they lived in sod huts or Newport mansions, many of these readers had certain things in common. They did not read merely for amusement; they believed passionately in culture, for themselves and their children. They felt they had a part in the American mission to civilize a continent and to build a democracy which might serve as a model to the world. They believed it their duty to take a responsible interest in public affairs. Such convictions were both reflected and reinforced in the pages of the magazine they read.

During the succeeding generations *Harper's* has, of course, undergone many changes in format, content, and editorial techniques. Yet its chosen audience remains much the same: those people who assay considerably higher than average in discrimination, intellectual curiosity, and concern for the national well-being. As a result it has developed certain characteristics which show plainly in this book:

1. *It deals primarily in ideas.*

Especially the sort of ideas which will make important news a year —or five or ten years—later. For example, in 1928 it published an article by George Ellery Hale about the possibility of building a telescope much larger than any ever attempted, and the new information it might bring us about the universe. It so impressed scientists at the Rockefeller Foundation that it led directly to the construction of the 200-inch telescope on Mount Palomar. More recently George F. Kennan, perhaps America's foremost authority on the Soviet Union, outlined in *Harper's* a proposal for a drastic shift in foreign policy. At the time it got a chilly reception in Washington—but at this writing, less than two years later, it is being discussed very seriously indeed, in the State Department and every capital in Western Europe.

In other fields—ranging from oceanography to economics, from the theater to religion—*Harper's* tries to find the fresh, seminal thinkers, whose ideas may have a real impact on the future shape of our world.

2. *It provides a highly selective kind of news coverage.*

Harper's makes no attempt to cover the ephemeral happenings which fill about 90 per cent of the space in news magazines and the daily press. What it does attempt to report are those events and personalities that may have a lasting historical significance—and it tries to cover them in a more authoritative, carefully considered, and analytic fashion than daily or weekly publications can ordinarily achieve.

Thus Secretary of War Henry L. Stimson first explained in the pages of *Harper's* the U.S. government's decision to use the atomic bomb against Japan. To cite an instance of a very different kind, John Bartlow Martin—in one of the most widely reprinted articles of recent years, "The Blast in Centralia No. 5"—exposed a scandal that had cost many lives; it shook up a state government, a labor union, a political party, and a whole series of state and federal laws.

(The magazine's editors believe that much of the best writing of our times is being done by highly skilled reporters—such as Martin, Richard Rovere, Russell Lynes, William S. White, Martin Mayer, and a few dozen others—who are developing the magazine article into a new literary form, of a stature not far from that of the short story, poetry, drama or the novel.)

3. *It seeks an independent assessment of public issues.*

As a former editor, Frederick Lewis Allen, said, "We live today in an all-too-organized world of mighty governments, corporations, institutions, associations, parties, and blocs, each with its own publicity machine; wearing its own blinders to all that does not serve its own special ends. . . . Some place there must be where the general interest, as contrasted with each and all of these special interests, can have a hearing; where the attempt is made to balance and adjust their conflicting claims. This, we think, is a job for the independent magazine. It should be just as far-sighted as possible. And it should try to make, now and then, at least an approach to wisdom."

To this end, *Harper's* keeps apart from any party, pressure group, or commercial interest. It endorses no candidates, peddles no ideology, grinds no private axes. Instead it tries to reflect the widest possible spectrum of responsible opinion—including many opinions with which the editors personally disagree. It is skeptical of the public relations counselor and the official pronouncement; and—to quote Allen again—it has a special respect for the sharp-eyed individual observer "who sits all by himself, unorganized, unrecognized, unorthodox, and unterrified."

4. *It welcomes controversy.*

The mass media usually have to shun controversial subjects, because they dare not risk offending any substantial number of readers. *Harper's* does not try to woo everybody—and it assumes that its kind of reader is tough-minded enough to enjoy a lively argument, even when it rubs him on a raw spot. Consequently it is able to examine the behavior of Sacred Cows—for example, U.S. Savings Bonds, the veterans' and farmers' lobbies, the giant charity fund-raising outfits, and the F.B.I.—with a candor not often found elsewhere. But it tries to deal with such subjects responsibly, not sensationally; and to the aggrieved—who are many—it offers space for uninhibited rebuttal.

5. *It provides a vehicle for the artist in literature.*

The short story writer, the poet, the essayist, the critic, and the humorist find here a welcome for their best work—uncramped by popular formulas or conventional forms. And the work of an entirely unknown writer is considered just as eagerly as that of a William Faulkner or Arthur Miller.

All too often these five standards measure the aspirations rather than the accomplishments of the editors. To them, nearly every issue of the magazine is a disappointment, because it falls short of what they hoped to create. Yet now and then they feel that they come somewhere near the mark, and that a proportion of the things they publish may have a permanent value. This book is a sampling of such items, submitted in the hope that at least some of those who try it will find the flavor robust, well matured, and a pleasure.

A TREASURY OF AMERICAN WRITERS

FROM

Harper's

MAGAZINE

I

An Image of America Since Yesterday

One Man's Meat

by E. B. WHITE

AUGUST, 1939—JULY, 1942

For nearly five years, beginning in October, 1938, E. B. White wrote a monthly department called "One Man's Meat" for the magazine. He was living on a farm in Maine at the time, and from that quiet, rural vantage point he turned a discerning eye on a world plunging into war. He set the peaceful life he was leading against the backdrop of the earth-shaking events around him in some of the most beautiful prose of this century. Mr. White is famous for his brilliant contributions to The New Yorker. *He is the author of several books of essays and poems and two children's classics—*Charlotte's Web *and* Stuart Little.

The first sign of spring here is when the ice breaks up in the inkwell at the post office. A month later the ice leaves the lakes. And a month after that the first of the summer visitors shows up and the tax collector's wife removes the town records from her Frigidaire and plugs it in for the summer.

———◆———

See that the ewe has milk, that her udder is all right, her teats open, and that the lambs get the milk.

That's what my bulletin said. Stern advice for a city-bred man who came late to shepherd's estate. The ewes and I went through a joint pregnancy; they carried the lambs, I carried the bulletin and the worry and the wonder. I was pretty sure that no matter how closely I watched I would finally be caught off my guard. On a Sunday morning in February, just at daylight, my hour came. The little boy burst into the bedroom and cried: "Wake up, you got a lamb!"

I pulled on some cold clothes and stumbled out toward the barnyard. Before I got down to the shed where the sheep were I could hear a lamb blaring. The sound seemed artificial, almost as though some-

5

body were blowing short blasts on a cheap horn. I slowed my step and looked in at the door of the fold. On the frozen ground just over the threshold a lamb lay dead. A coating of frost had formed on its stiff yellow fleece. The ewe stood just beyond, her stern showing traces of blood, her eyes full of bewilderment. A few feet away there was another lamb, staggering about in small spasmodic jerks, its little dung-smeared body about the size of a turnip, its woeful voice strangely penetrating in the biting wind that blew in through the open door. Here was my lamb all right, waiting to be wrapped warmly in the nearest bulletin.

It lived through the morning, lying in a carton by the stove, but it was a weak lamb and never recovered from the first awful chill. Shortly after lunch, having nursed twice and received our blessings, it died. It was one of the briefest and most popular visitors we ever had, being loved by all and particularly by the dachshund, who showed a deep gripping appreciation of its lovely aromatic newness— the dung in its fleece warmed by the kitchen heat gave it a heavenly intensity quite in keeping with its Biblical connotation. There is something about a lamb you don't get over in a hurry. It's been gone quite a while now, and others are on the way, but the dachshund and I still tremble all over when we think of it.

———◆———

Miss Nims, take a letter to Henry David Thoreau. Dear Henry: I thought of you the other afternoon as I was approaching Concord doing fifty on Route 62. That is a high speed at which to hold a philosopher in one's mind, but in this century we are a nimble bunch.

On one of the lawns in the outskirts of the village a woman was cutting the grass with a motorized lawn mower. What made me think of you was that the machine had rather got away from her, although she was game enough, and in the brief glimpse I had of the scene it appeared to me that the lawn was mowing the lady. She kept a tight grip on the handles, which throbbed violently with every explosion of the one-cylinder motor, and as she sheered around bushes and lurched along at a reluctant trot behind her impetuous servant, she looked like a puppy who had grabbed something that was too much for him. Concord hasn't changed much, Henry; the farm implements and the animals still have the upper hand.

I may as well admit that I was journeying to Concord with the deliberate intention of visiting your woods; for although I have never knelt at the grave of a philosopher nor placed wreaths on moldy poets, and have often gone a mile out of my way to avoid some place of historical interest, I have always wanted to see Walden Pond. The account which you left of your sojourn there is, you will be amused to learn, a document of increasing pertinence; each year it seems to gain a little headway, as the world loses ground. We may all be transcendental yet, whether we like it or not. As our common complexities increase, any tale of individual simplicity (and yours is the best written and the cockiest) acquires a new fascination; as our goods accumulate, but not our well-being, your report of an existence without material adornment takes on a certain awkward credibility.

My purpose in going to Walden Pond, like yours, was not to live cheaply or to live dearly there, but to transact some private business with the fewest obstacles. Approaching Concord, doing forty, doing forty-five, doing fifty, the steering wheel held snug in my palms, the highway held grimly in my vision, the crown of the road now serving me (on the righthand curves), now defeating me (on the lefthand curves), I began to rouse myself from the stupefaction which a day's motor journey induces. It was a delicious evening, Henry, when the whole body is one sense, and imbibes delight through every pore, if I may coin a phrase. Fields were richly brown where the harrow, drawn by the stripped Ford, had lately sunk its teeth; pastures were green; and overhead the sky had that same everlasting great look which you will find on Page 144 of the Oxford Pocket Edition. I could feel the road entering me, through tire, wheel, spring, and cushion; shall I not have intelligence with earth too? Am I not partly leaves and vegetable mold myself?—a man of infinite horsepower, yet partly leaves.

Stay with me on 62 and it will take you into Concord. As I say, it was a delicious evening. The snake had come forth to die in a bloody S on the highway, the wheel upon its head, its bowels flat now and exposed. The turtle had come up too to cross the road and die in the attempt, its hard shell smashed under the rubber blow, its intestinal yearning (for the other side of the road) forever squashed. There was a sign by the wayside which announced that the road had a "cotton surface." You wouldn't know what that is, but neither, for that matter, did I. There is a cryptic ingredient in many of our modern improvements—we are awed and pleased without knowing quite what we are enjoying. It is something to be traveling on a road with a cotton surface.

The civilization round Concord today is an odd distillation of city, village, farm, and manor. The houses, yards, fields look not quite suburban, not quite rural. Under the bronze beech and the blue spruce of the departed baron grazes the milch goat of the heirs. Under the porte-cochère stands the reconditioned station wagon; under the grape arbor sit the puppies for sale. (But why do men degenerate ever? What makes families run out?)

It was June and everywhere June was publishing her immemorial stanza: in the lilacs, in the syringa, in the freshly edged paths and the sweetness of moist beloved gardens, and the little wire wickets that preserve the tulips' front. Farmers were already moving the fruits of their toil into their yards, arranging the rhubarb, the asparagus, the strictly fresh eggs on the painted stands under the little shed roofs with the patent shingles. And though it was almost a hundred years since you had taken your ax and started cutting out your home on Walden Pond, I was interested to observe that the philosophical spirit was still alive in Massachusetts: in the center of a vacant lot some boys were assembling the framework of a rude shelter, their whole mind and skill concentrated in the rather inauspicious helter-skeleton of studs and rafters. They too were escaping from town, to live naturally, in a rich blend of savagery and philosophy.

That evening, after supper at the inn, I strolled out into the twilight to dream my shapeless transcendental dreams and see that the car was locked up for the night (first open the right front door, then reach over, straining, and pull up the handles of the left rear and the left front till you hear the click, then the handle of the right rear, then shut the right front but open it again, remembering that the key is still in the ignition switch, remove the key, shut the right front again with a bang, push the tiny keyhole cover to one side, insert key, turn, and withdraw). It is what we all do, Henry. It is called locking the car. It is said to confuse thieves and keep them from making off with the laprobe. Four doors to lock behind one robe. The driver himself never uses a laprobe, the free movement of his legs being vital to the operation of the vehicle; so that when he locks the car it is a pure and unselfish act. I have in my life gained very little essential heat from laprobes, yet I have ever been at pains to lock them up.

The evening was full of sounds, some of which would have stirred your memory. The robins still love the elms of New England villages at sundown. There is enough of the thrush in them to make song inevitable at the end of day, and enough of the tramp to make them hang round the dwellings of men. A robin, like many another American, dearly loves a white house with green blinds. Concord is still full of them.

Your fellow-townsmen were stirring abroad—not many afoot, most of them in their cars; and the sound which they made in Concord at evening was a rustling and a whispering. The sound lacks steadfastness and is wholly unlike that of a train. A train, as you know who lived so near the Fitchburg line, whistles once or twice sadly and is gone, trailing a memory in smoke, soothing to ear and mind. Automobiles, skirting a village green, are like flies that have gained the inner ear—they buzz, cease, pause, start, shift, stop, halt, brake, and the whole effect is a nervous polytone curiously disturbing.

As I wandered along, the toc-toc of ping-pong balls drifted from an attic window. In front of the Reuben Brown house a Buick was drawn up. At the wheel, motionless, his hat upon his head, a man sat, listening to Amos and Andy on the radio (it is a drama of many scenes and without an end). The deep voice of Andrew Brown, emerging from the car, although it originated more than two hundred miles away, was unstrained by distance. When you used to sit on the shore of your pond on Sunday morning, listening to the church bells of Acton and Concord, you were aware of the excellent filter of the intervening atmosphere. Science has attended to that, and sound now maintains its intensity without regard for distance. Properly sponsored, it goes on forever.

A fire engine, out for a trial spin, roared past Emerson's house, hot with readiness for public duty. Over the barn roofs the martins dipped and chittered. A swarthy daughter of an asparagus grower, in culottes, shirt, and bandanna, pedaled past on her bicycle. It was indeed a delicious evening, and I returned to the inn (I believe it was your house once) to rock with the old ladies on the concrete veranda.

Next morning early I started afoot for Walden, out Main Street and down Thoreau, past the depot and the Minute Man Chevrolet Company. The morning was fresh, and in a bean field along the way I flushed an agriculturalist, quietly studying his beans. Thoreau Street soon joined Number 126, an artery of the State. We number our highways nowadays, our speed being so great we can remember little of their quality or character and are lucky to remember their number. (Men have an indistinct notion that if they keep up this activity long enough all will at length ride somewhere, in next to no time.) Your pond is on 126.

I knew I must be nearing your woodland retreat when the Golden Pheasant lunchroom came into view—Sealtest ice cream, toasted sandwiches, hot frankfurters, waffles, tonics, and lunches. Were I the proprietor, I should add rice, Indian meal, and molasses—just for old time's sake. The Pheasant, incidentally, is for sale: a chance for some nature lover who wishes to set himself up beside a pond in the Concord atmosphere and live deliberately, fronting only the essential facts of life on Number 126. Beyond the Pheasant was a place called Walden Breezes, an oasis whose porch pillars were made of old green shutters sawed into lengths. On the porch was a distorting mirror, to give the traveler a comical image of himself, who had miraculously learned to gaze in an ordinary glass without smiling. Behind the Breezes, in a sun-parched clearing, dwelt your philosophical descendants in their trailers, each trailer the size of your hut, but all grouped together for the sake of congeniality. Trailer people leave the city, as you did, to discover solitude and in any weather, at any hour of the day or night, to improve the nick of time; but they soon collect in villages and get bogged deeper in the mud than ever. The camp behind Walden Breezes was just rousing itself to the morning. The ground was packed hard under the heel, and the sun came through the clearing to bake the soil and enlarge the wry smell of cramped housekeeping. Cushman's bakery truck had stopped to deliver an early basket of rolls. A camp dog, seeing me in the road, barked petulantly. A man emerged from one of the trailers and set forth with a bucket to draw water from some forest tap.

Leaving the highway I turned off into the woods toward the pond, which was apparent through the foliage. The floor of the forest was strewn with dried old oak leaves and *Transcripts*. From beneath the flattened popcorn wrapper (*granum explosum*) peeped the frail violet. I followed a footpath and descended to the water's edge. The pond lay clear and blue in the morning light, as you have seen it so many times. In the shallows a man's waterlogged shirt undulated gently. A few flies came out to greet me and convoy me to your cove, past the No Bathing signs on which the fellows and the girls had scrawled their names. I felt strangely excited suddenly to be snooping around your premises, tiptoeing along watchfully, as though not to tread by mistake upon the intervening century. Before I got to the cove I heard something which seemed to me quite wonderful: I heard your frog, a full, clear *troonk,* guiding me, still hoarse and solemn, bridging the years as the robins had bridged them in the sweetness of the village evening. But he soon quit, and I came on a couple of young boys throwing stones at him.

Your front yard is marked by a bronze tablet set in a stone. Four small granite posts, a few feet away, show where the house was. On top of the tablet was a pair of faded blue bathing trunks with a white stripe. Back of it is a pile of stones, a sort of cairn, left by your visitors as a tribute I suppose. It is a rather ugly little heap of stones, Henry. In fact the hillside itself seems faded, browbeaten; a few tall skinny pines, bare of lower limbs, a smattering of young maples in suitable green, some birches and oaks, and a number of trees felled by the last big wind. It was from the bole of one of these fallen pines, torn up by the roots, that I extracted the stone which I added to the cairn—a sentimental act in which I was interrupted by a small terrier from a nearby picnic group, who confronted me and wanted to know about the stone.

I sat down for a while on one of the posts of your house to listen to the bluebottles and the dragonflies. The invaded glade sprawled shabby and mean at my feet, but the flies were tuned to the old vibration. There were the remains of a fire in your ruins, but I doubt that it was yours; also two beer bottles trodden into the soil and become part of earth. A young oak had taken root in your house, and two or three ferns, unrolling like the ticklers at a banquet. The only other furnishings were a DuBarry pattern sheet, a page torn from a picture magazine, and some crusts in wax paper.

Before I quit I walked clear round the pond and found the place where you used to sit on the N. E. side to get the sun in the fall, and the beach where you got sand for scrubbing your floor. On the eastern side of the pond, where the highway borders it, the State has built dressing rooms for swimmers, a float with diving towers, drinking fountains of porcelain, and rowboats for hire. The pond is in fact a State Preserve, and carries a twenty-dollar fine for picking wild flowers, a decree signed in all solemnity by your fellow-citizens Walter C. Wardwell, Erson B. Barlow, and Nathaniel I. Bowditch. There was a smell of creosote where they had been building a wide wooden stairway to the road and the parking area. Swimmers and boaters were arriving; bodies splashed vigorously into the water and emerged wet and beautiful in the bright air. As I left, a boatload of town boys were splashing about in mid-pond, kidding and fooling, the young fellows singing at the tops of their lungs in a wild chorus:

> Amer-ica, A-mer-i-ca, God shed
>   his grace on thee,
> And crown thy good with brotherhood
> From sea to shi-ning sea!

I walked back to town along the railroad, following your custom. The rails were expanding noisily in the hot sun, and on the slope of the roadbed the wild grape and the blackberry sent up their creepers to the track.

The expense of my brief sojourn in Concord was:

Canvas shoes...............	$1.95	
Baseball bat...............	.25 }	gifts to take back
Left-handed fielder's glove....	1.25 }	to a boy
Hotel and meals............	4.25	
In all.................	$7.70	

As you see, this amount was almost what you spent for food for eight months. I cannot defend the shoes or the expenditure for shelter and food: they reveal a meanness and grossness in my nature which you would find contemptible. The baseball equipment, however, is the sort of impediment with which you were never on even terms. You must remember that the house where you practiced the sort of economy which I respect was haunted only by mice and squirrels. You never had to cope with a shortstop.

◆

In the cities (but the cities are to be destroyed) lights continue to burn on into the morning, in the hotel bedrooms that open into the dark court, in the little sitting rooms off the bedrooms, where the breakfast things linger, with the light gleaming on the half grapefruit and the bright serving covers and the coffee thermos, the ice melting around the grapefruit rind all through the morning and shades going up across the areaway where the other people in dressing gowns and bathrobes and pajamas are lifting the receiver from the hook and calling room service and ordering the half grapefruit and the toast and marmalade and running the water behind the shower curtain. The city wakens, but to its own internal suns, each lamp with its parchment shade and the cord, dusty twisted, that connects it to the center of light and of power, the umbilicals of the solar system. (But they tell me the cities are all to be destroyed and that people will no longer live in the impractical cities, but the time has not yet come.) Nevertheless I must begin keeping green the memory of the cities, the ferns and tiger plants in the boxes under the lights in the dining rooms and the restaurants and the grills, the opening and closing of the doors of the elevators, and the finger always on the button summoning the elevator, waiting silently with the others (there are always others in the city) and the ascent and descent always with the others, but never speaking. In the bookshops the clerks, wanting to know if they can help, but you say no you are just looking around, and the terrible excitement of so great a concentration of books in one place under one roof, each book wanting the completion of being read. Under the marquee, after the show, huddling out of the rain with the rain on the roofs of the cabs and the look on the faces of the city people desperate in the rain, and the men in their black coats and hats darting out into the withering fire of raindrops to seek the turbulent headwaters of the stream of taxis, and the petulance and impatience and desperation of the women in their dresses waiting for the return of the men who are gone so long into the fierce bewildering night, and the mass urgency, there under the marquee, as though unless they all escaped safely into a cab within five minutes they would die. (You must leave the key at the desk when you go out. Even though the cities are to be destroyed, don't forget to leave the key at the desk when you go out.)

———◆———

On the first morning after this latest fall of snow, we went out early, my wife and I, to hunt for a sleigh and a horse. The plow had been along the road and left a perfect surface for sleighing. At the crack of day, in a six-cylinder sedan, we sallied forth to look for all our yesterdays. I knew of several barns where I thought the past might lie.

This quest will long remain in my mind—the great beauty of the morning, with the trees loaded with quiet snow, the special luster of earliness and the purity and expectancy of new day, the sharp air, and the low cold sun promising the continuance of wintry pleasures, and in our memory the jingle of bells. We went from farm to farm (the ones we knew had horses), rapping on kitchen doors, stirring up the wives who would tell us where the men were. Everywhere the same answer: either there was no sleigh or there was a sleigh but it was buried under six tons of hay or the horse was unshod. But what surprised us was the enthusiasm which our request aroused—the wives standing in the doorway with the cold in-draught of air chilling them, saying they too would like to take a sleighride on a morning like this. Into the faces of some of them a queer look of wistfulness came. It wasn't just the sleighs that were buried; it was the sense of the past, something of merriment gone, a sound of bells over snow. In the faces of one or two a look of exquisite longing, a memory of love somehow associated with sleighriding.

Nothing ever came of this quest. We got on to the back roads finally, but the day grew older and the morning began to get shoddy the way it does about eleven. A man can go round just so long hollering for the past, then he quits and gets on with the present. We did come across a sleigh on the way back, but the owner had arrived at his destination, taken the horse out, and was paying a call. We didn't have the crust to intrude.

There is a stanza in Robert Frost's poem "Two Tramps in Mud Time" which describes an April moment when air and sky have a vernal feeling, but suddenly a cloud crosses the path of the sun and a bitter little wind finds you out, and you're back in the middle of March. Everyone who has lived in the country knows that sort of moment—the promise of warmth, the raised hope, the ruthless rebuff.

There is another sort of day which needs celebrating in song—the day of days when spring at last holds up her face to be kissed, deliberate and unabashed. On that day no wind blows either in the hills or in the mind; no chill finds the bone. It is a day which can come only in a northern climate, where there has been a long background of frigidity, a long deficiency of sun.

We've just been through this magical moment—which was more than a moment and was a whole morning—and it lodges in memory like some old romance, with the same subtlety of tone, the same enrichment of the blood, and the enchantment and the mirth and the indescribable warmth. Even before breakfast I felt that the moment was at hand, for when I went out to the barn to investigate twins I let the kitchen door stay open, lazily, instead of closing it behind me. This was a sign. The lambs had nursed and the ewe was lying quiet. One lamb had settled itself on the mother's back and was a perfect miniature of the old one—they reminded me of a teapot we have, whose knob is a tiny replica of the pot itself. The barn seemed warmer and sweeter than usual, but it was early in the day, and the hint of spring-burst was still only a hint, a suggestion, a nudge. The full impact wasn't felt until the sun had climbed higher. Then came, in a rush, the many small caresses which added up to the total embrace of warmth and life—a laziness and contentment in the behavior of animals and people, a tendency of man and dog to sit down some-where in the sun. In the driveway, a deep rut which for the past week had held three or four inches of water and which had alternately frozen and thawed, showed clear indications of drying up. On the window ledge in the living room, the bare brown forsythia cuttings suddenly discovered the secret of yellow. The goose, instead of coming off her nest and joining her loud companions, settled down on her eleven eggs, pulled some feathers from her breast, and resigned her-self to the twenty-eight-day grind. When I went back through the kitchen I noticed that the air that had come in was not like an in-vader but like a friend who had stopped by for a visit.

The passionate love of Americans for their America will have a lot to do with winning the war. It is an odd thing though: the very patriotism on which we now rely is the thing that must eventually be in part relinquished if the world is ever to find a lasting peace and an end to these butcheries.

To hold America in one's thoughts is like holding a love letter in one's hand—it has so special a meaning. Since I started writing this column snow has begun falling again; I sit in my room watching the re-enactment of this stagy old phenomenon outside the window. For this picture, for this privilege, this cameo of New England with snow falling, I would give everything. Yet all the time I know that this very loyalty, this feeling of being part of a special place, this respect for one's native scene—I know that such emotions have had a big part in the world's wars. Who is there big enough to love the whole planet? We must find such people for the next society.

Although internationalism often seems hopelessly distant or im-practical, there is one rather encouraging sign in the sky. We have, lately, at least one large new group of people to whom the planet *does* come first. I mean scientists. Science, however undiscriminating it has seemed in the bestowal of its gifts, has no disturbing club affiliations. It eschews nationality. It is preoccupied with an atom, not an atoll.

There will be a showdown on internationalism after this war. The bitter debate between isolation and intervention (a debate ended abruptly last Sunday morning on an island in the Pacific) was really an extension of the fundamental conflict between the national spirit (which is in practically everyone) and the international spirit (which is in some but not in all). Nationalism has two fatal charms for its devotees; it presupposes local self-sufficiency, which is a pleasant and desirable condition, and it suggests, very subtly, a certain personal superiority by reason of one's belonging to a place which is definable and familiar, as against a place which is strange, remote.

Before you can be an internationalist you have first to be a naturalist and feel the ground under you making a whole circle. It is easier for a man to be loyal to his club than to his planet; the by-laws are shorter, and he is personally acquainted with the other members. A club, moreover, or a nation, has a most attractive offer to make: it offers the right to be exclusive. There are not many of us who are physically constituted to resist this strange delight, this nourishing privilege. It is at the bottom of all fraternities, societies, orders. It is at the bottom of most trouble. The planet holds out no such inducement. The planet is everybody's. All it offers is the grass, the sky, the water, and the ineluctable dream of peace and fruition.

Clubs, fraternities, nations—these are the beloved barriers in the way of a workable world, these will have to surrender some of their rights and some of their ribs. A "fraternity" is the antithesis of *fraternity*. The first (that is, the order or organization) is predicated on the idea of exclusion; the second (that is, the abstract thing) is based on a feeling of total equality. Anyone who remembers back to his fraternity days at college recalls the enthusiasts in his group, the rabid members, both old and young, who were obsessed with the mystical charm of membership in their particular order. They were usually men who were incapable of genuine brotherhood, or at least unaware of its implications. Fraternity begins when the exclusion formula is found to be distasteful. The effect of any organization of a social and brotherly nature is to strengthen rather than to diminish the lines which divide people into classes; the effect of states and nations is the same, and eventually these lines will have to be softened, these powers will have to be generalized. It is written on the wall that this is so. I'm not inventing it, I'm just copying it off the wall.

I find, on rigid introspection, that my feeling for internationalism, and my trust in it, are intuitive rather than reasonable. It is not so much that I have faith in the ability of nations to organize themselves as that I mistrust what will happen if again they fail to do so.

—◆—

The mechanics and spirit of a capitalistic press and radio are both comical and beautiful today. The first words I heard after the news came of Japan's attack in Hawaii were: "Give Mother foot comfort for Christmas." It was in the voice we all know so well—as though the speaker had marshmallows in place of tonsils—but it had that thoroughly cockeyed quality for which in the long run we are fighting. It makes a man suddenly realize his strange and wonderful indebtedness to the cosmetic industry and the tobacco trade and all the rest which are supplying us with capsules of news every few moments.

I was in Washington a while ago, sniffing around and annoying people by looking into their wastebaskets; and while I was there I went over one morning to a Senate committee hearing where Mr. LaGuardia was testifying. The committee was investigating the problem of small businessmen who were being squeezed out of business by defense rulings. It wasn't big news by a long shot, but a couple of cameramen showed up and maneuvered into position quietly, crouching, one on either side of the Little Flower. They were well behaved, for photographers, but now and again one of them would explode a flash. Finally one of the committeemen spoke rather sharply, asked them to quit and let the hearing proceed in peace. They seemed not to hear this request. They just crouched, motionless. Then the Mayor asked them to go away and wait for him outside. The boys crouched and smiled. A newspaper correspondent sitting next to me said, proudly: "They won't pay any attention to those guys." Nothing was done. The hearing proceeded. It was a familiar pantomime—the free press, deplored yet admired. Under their vests the senators were secretly glad that they were unable to dislodge a couple of American photographers. It was what the hearing was about really—the photographers, squatting imperturbably in front of the men who were plotting to win a war which would preserve for photographers the right to squat imperturbably.

It is hard to believe now that Washington was ever the way I saw it a week or so before the outbreak of war. I had been told that I should find Washington a madhouse, but I remember it as a quiet place that managed somehow to give the impression of stability and peace, no matter how rapidly the bureaus were proliferating. Nobody seemed worried. The taxi driver who took me from the station to the hotel said he was on his way the next morning to apply for a time-keeping job on a defense project, which would pay fifty dollars a week; and he reported with considerable enthusiasm that some of the laborers on the job had made as high as one hundred and six dollars in one week. Not even a collapsing world looks dark to a man who is about to make his fortune. The President, when he received the press in his Oval Study, gave little sign of tension and went out of his way to capture a joke or a pleasantry in mid-air. The weather was soft and agreeable; in the parks the oaks still held their leaves, releasing one now and then, indolently. Young girls on their hard high heels tapped home from the offices through the warm benign parks, and the squirrels and the pigeons deployed in the sunlight. In the Maryland countryside, where I visited for a week-end, there was the same hazy beauty, somnolence, and security—the little firm hills and the valleys between, friendly and warm as a mother's lap, the cornstalks in the still green pastures, the big barns, the winter wheat, and the honeysuckle and the cedars and the holly. In the morning the birds struck up almost as cheerfully as in the deep South, and on the air was the skunky smell of box. Here and there the physical signs of war, nowhere the conviction of reality.

The whole history of the war so far has been the inability of people in the democracies to believe their eyes and ears. They didn't believe the Rhineland or the persecution of the Jews or Poland or France or any of the rest of it. That phase of the war is over. Now, at least, we can see and hear.

—————◆—————

Walt Whitman should be around today to see how the boys are regenerating his stuff. For a long time I kept wondering where I had heard all this singing before—the radio programs dramatizing America, the propaganda of democracy, the music in the President's chats, the voices of the poets singing America. Then it came to me. It is all straight Walt. The radiomatics of Corwin, the sound tracks of Lorentz, the prophecies of MacLeish and Benét, the strumming of Sandburg, the iambics of Anderson and Sherwood. Listen the next time you have the radio tuned to the theatrics of the air—you will hear the voice of old Walt shouting from Paumanok. If there were any doubt about where he stands in the literary ladder this decade has put an end to it. He is right at the top. He must be good or he wouldn't be heard so clearly in the syllables of our contemporaries.

There is a certain something about this sort of writing which is unmistakable: the use of place names, the cataloguing of ideas, the repetition of sounds, the determination to be colloquial or bust, the celebration of the American theme and the American dream, the appreciation of the man in the street and the arm round the shoulder, the "song of the throes of democracy." You can't miss it when you hear it. Sometimes, when one is jittery or out of whack, it seems as though one heard it too much—so much that it loses its effect. But Walt unquestionably started it. He was the one who heard America beating on a pan, beating on a carpet, beating on an anvil. He heard what was coming, and he said the words.

The Men from Mars

by JOHN HOUSEMAN

DECEMBER, 1948

Here is the fascinating, behind-the-scenes story of the 1938 CBS radio dramatization of H. G. Wells' novel The War of the Worlds *which panicked the country. John Houseman was co-founder with Orson Welles of the Mercury Theater, which put on the show. Mr. Houseman was born in Rumania in 1902, educated in England, and came to the United States in 1925. He has produced many movies and Broadway plays, and has been a director, writer, and teacher. Recently he has been artistic director of the American Shakespeare Festival in Stratford, Connecticut.*

RADIO WAR TERRORIZES U.S.—N. Y. *Daily News,* October 31, 1938

Everybody was excited I felt as if I was going crazy and kept on saying what can we do what difference does it make whether we die sooner or later? We were holding each other. Everything seemed unimportant in the face of death. I was afraid to die, just kept on listening.

—*A listener*

Nothing about the broadcast was in the least credible.—Dorothy Thompson

The show came off. There is no doubt about that. It set out to dramatize, in terms of popular apprehension, an attempted invasion of our world by hostile forces from the planet Mars. It succeeded. Of the several million American citizens who, on the evening of October 30, 1938, milled about the streets, clung sobbing to one another or drove wildly in all directions to avoid asphyxiation and flaming death, approximately one-half were in terror of Martians—not of Germans, Japanese, or unknown enemies—but, specifically, of Martians. Later, when the excitement was over and the shadow of the gallows had lifted, some of us were inclined to take credit for more deliberate and premeditated villainy than we deserved. The truth is that at the time, nobody was more surprised than we were. In fact, one of the most remarkable things about the broadcast was the quite haphazard nature of its birth.

In October 1938, the Mercury Theater, of which Orson Welles and I were the founding partners, had been in existence for less than a year. Our first Broadway season had been shatteringly successful—*Julius Caesar, The Cradle Will Rock, Shoemaker's Holiday,* and *Heartbreak House* in the order of their appearance. In April, Orson, in a straggly white beard, made the cover of *Time* Magazine. In June, the Columbia Broadcasting System offered him a radio show—The Mercury Theater on the Air, a series of classic dramatizations in the first person singular with Orson as master of ceremonies, star, narrator, writer, director, and producer. He accepted. So, now, in addition to an empty theater, a movie in progress, two plays in rehearsal, and all seven of the chronicle plays of William Shakespeare in preparation, we had a radio show.

We opened on July 11. Among our first thirteen shows were *Treasure Island, 39 Steps, Abraham Lincoln, Three Short Stories* (by Saki, Sherwood Anderson, and Carl Ewald), *Jane Eyre, Julius Caesar* (with running commentary by Kaltenborn out of Plutarch), and *The Man Who Was Thursday*. Our second series, in the fall, began with Booth Tarkington's *Seventeen, Around the World in Eighty Days,* and *Oliver Twist*. Our fifth show was to be *Life with Father*. Our fourth was *The War of the Worlds*.

No one, as I remember, was very enthusiastic about it. But it seemed good programming, between the terrors of Dickens' London slums, and the charm of Clarence Day's New York in the nineties, to throw in something of a contrasting and pseudo-scientific nature. We thought of Shiel's *Purple Cloud*, Conan Doyle's *Lost World*, and several others before we settled on H. G. Wells' twenty-year-old novel, which neither of us, as it turned out later, remembered at all clearly. It is just possible that neither of us had ever read it.

II

Those were our golden days of unsponsored radio. We had no advertising agency to harass us, no client to cut our withers. Partly because we were perpetually overworked and partly because that was the way we did things at the Mercury, we never seemed to get more than a single jump ahead of ourselves. Shows were created week after week under conditions of soul- and health-destroying pressure. On the whole they were good shows. And we *did* develop a system—of sorts.

It worked as follows: I was editor of the series. With Welles, I chose the shows and then laid them out. The writing, most of it, was done by Howard Koch—earnest, spindly, six-foot-two—a Westchester lawyer turned playwright. To write the first draft of an hour's radio script took him about five days, working about fifteen hours a day. Our associate producer was Paul Stewart, a Broadway actor turned director. His function was to put the broadcast through its first paces and preliminary rehearsals. Every Thursday, musicless and with rudimentary sound effects, a wax record of the show was cut. From this record, played back later that night, Orson would give us his reactions and revisions. In the next thirty-six hours the script would be reshaped and rewritten, sometimes drastically. Saturday afternoon there was another rehearsal, with sound—with or without Welles. It was not until the last day that Orson really took over.

Sundays, at eight, we went on the air. Beginning in the early afternoon—when Bernard Herrmann arrived with his orchestra of twenty-seven high-grade symphony players—two simultaneous dramas were regularly unfolded in the stale, tense air of Studio Number One: the minor drama of the current show and the major drama of Orson's gargantuan struggle to get it on. Sweating, howling, disheveled, and single-handed he wrestled with Chaos and Time—always conveying an effect of being alone, traduced by his collaborators, surrounded by treachery, ignorance, sloth, indifference, incompetence and—more often than not—downright sabotage! Every Sunday it was touch and go. As the hands of the clock moved relentlessly toward air time the crisis grew more extreme, the peril more desperate. Often violence broke out. Scripts flew through the air, doors were slammed, batons smashed. Scheduled for six—but usually nearer seven—there was a dress rehearsal, a thing of wild improvisations and irrevocable disaster. (One show was found to be twenty-one minutes overlength, another fourteen and one-half minutes short.)

After that, with only a few minutes to go, there was a final frenzy of correction and reparation, of utter confusion and absolute horror, aggravated by the gobbling of sandwiches and the bolting of oversized milkshakes. By now it was less than a minute to air time. . . .

At that instant, quite regularly week after week—with not one second to spare . . . the titanic buffoonery stopped. Suddenly out of chaos, the show emerged—delicately poised, meticulously executed, precise as clockwork, and smooth as satin. And above us all, like a rainbow over storm clouds, stood Orson on his podium, sonorous and heroic, a leader of men surrounded by his band of loyal followers; a giant in action, serene and radiant with the joy of a hard battle bravely fought—a great victory snatched from the jaws of disaster.

In later years, when the Men from Mars had passed into history, there was some bickering among members of the Mercury as to who, exactly, had contributed precisely what, to that particular evening's entertainment. The truth is that a number of us made a number of essential and incalculable contributions to the broadcast. (Who can accurately assess, for instance, the part played by Johnny Dietz's perfect engineering, in keeping unbroken the shifting illusion of imperfect reality? How much did the original old H. G. Wells, who noisily repudiated us, have to do with it? Or the second assistant sound man? Or individual actors? Or Dr. Goebbels? Or Charlie McCarthy?) Orson Welles had virtually nothing to do with the writing of the script and less than usual to do with its preliminary rehearsals. Yet first and last it was his creation. If there had been a lynching that night, it is Welles the outraged populace would have strung up—and rightly so. Orson was the Mercury. *The War of the Worlds,* like everything we did, was his show.

Actually, it was a narrow squeak. Those Men from Mars barely escaped being stillborn. Tuesday afternoon—five days before the show —Howard Koch telephoned. He was in deep distress. After three days of slaving on H. G. Wells' scientific fantasy he was ready to give up. Under no circumstances, he declared, could it be made interesting or in any way credible to modern American ears. Koch was not given to habitual alarmism. To confirm his fears, Annie, our secretary, came to the phone. She was an acid and emphatic girl from Smith College with fine blond hair, who smelled of fading spring flowers. "You can't do it!" she whined. "Those old Martians are just a lot of nonsense. It's all too silly! We're going to make fools of ourselves! Absolute fools!"

For some reason which I do not clearly remember our only possible alternative for that week was a dreary one—*Lorna Doone.* I tried to reach Welles. He was at the theater and wouldn't come to the phone.

The reason he wouldn't come to the phone was that he was in his thirty-sixth successive hour of dress-rehearsing *Danton's Death,* a beautiful, fragmentary play by Georg Buechner out of which Max Reinhardt, in an augmented form, had made a successful mass-spectacle in the twenties. Not to be outdone, Orson had glued seventeen hundred masks on to the back wall of the Mercury Theater, and ripped out the entire stage. Day after day actors fell headlong into the rat-ridden basement, leaped on and off erratically moving elevators, and chanted the "Carmagnole" in chorus under the supervision of Marc Blitzstein.

Unable to reach Welles, I called Koch back. I was severe. I taxed him with defeatism. I gave him false comfort. I promised to come up and help. When I finally got there—around two the next morning —things were better. He was beginning to have fun laying waste the State of New Jersey. Annie had stopped grinding her teeth. We worked all night and through the next day. Wednesday at sunset the script was finished.

Thursday, as usual, Paul Stewart rehearsed the show, then made a record. We listened to it rather gloomily, long after midnight in

Orson's room at the St. Regis, sitting on the floor because all the chairs were covered with coils of unrolled and unedited film. We agreed it was a dull show. We all felt its only chance of coming off lay in emphasizing its newscast style—its simultaneous, eyewitness quality.

All night we sat up, spicing the script with circumstantial allusions and authentic detail. Friday afternoon it went over to CBS to be passed by the network censor. Certain name alterations were requested. Under protest and with a deep sense of grievance we changed the Hotel Biltmore to a nonexistent Park Plaza, Trans-America to Intercontinent, the Columbia Broadcasting Building to Broadcasting Building. Then the script went over to mimeograph and we went to bed. We had done our best and, after all, a show is just a show. . . .

Saturday afternoon Paul Stewart rehearsed with sound effects but without Welles. He worked for a long time on the crowd scenes, the roar of cannon echoing in the Watchung Hills and the sound of New York Harbor as the ships with the last remaining survivors put out to sea.

Around six we left the studio. Orson, phoning from the theater a few minutes later to find out how things were going, was told by one of the CBS sound men, who had stayed behind to pack up his equipment, that it was not one of our better shows. Confidentially, the man opined, it just didn't come off. Twenty-seven hours later, quite a few of his employers would have found themselves a good deal happier if he had turned out to be right.

III

On Sunday, October 30, at 8:00 P.M., E.S.T., in a studio littered with coffee cartons and sandwich paper, Orson swallowed a second container of pineapple juice, put on his earphones, raised his long white fingers and threw the cue for the Mercury theme—the Tchaikovsky Piano Concerto in B Flat Minor #1. After the music dipped, there were routine introductions—then the announcement that a dramatization of H. G. Wells' famous novel, *The War of the Worlds,* was about to be performed. Around 8:01 Orson began to speak, as follows:

WELLES
We know now that in the early years of the twentieth century this world was being watched closely by intelligences greater than man's and yet as mortal as his own. We know now that as human beings

busied themselves about their various concerns they were scrutinized and studied, perhaps almost as narrowly as a man with a microscope might scrutinize the transient creatures that swarm and multiply in a drop of water. With infinite complacence people went to and fro over the earth about their little affairs, serene in the assurance of their dominion over this small spinning fragment of solar driftwood which by chance or design man has inherited out of the dark mystery of Time and Space. Yet across an immense ethereal gulf minds that are to our minds as ours are to the beasts in the jungle, intellects vast, cool, and unsympathetic regarded this earth with envious eyes and slowly and surely drew their plans against us. In the thirty-ninth year of the twentieth century came the great disillusionment.

It was near the end of October. Business was better. The war scare was over. More men were back at work. Sales were picking up. On this particular evening, October 30, the Crossley service estimated that thirty-two million people were listening in on their radios. . . .

Neatly, without perceptible transition, he was followed on the air by an anonymous announcer caught in a routine bulletin:

ANNOUNCER

. . . for the next twenty-four hours not much change in temperature. A slight atmospheric disturbance of undetermined origin is reported over Nova Scotia, causing a low pressure area to move down rather rapidly over the northeastern states, bringing a forecast of rain, accompanied by winds of light gale force. Maximum temperature 66; minimum 48. This weather report comes to you from the Government Weather Bureau. . . . We now take you to the Meridian Room in the Hotel Park Plaza in downtown New York, where you will be entertained by the music of Ramon Raquello and his orchestra.

At which cue, Bernard Herrmann led the massed men of the CBS house orchestra in a thunderous rendition of "La Cumparsita." The entire hoax might well have exploded there and then—but for the fact that hardly anyone was listening. They were being entertained by Charlie McCarthy—then at the height of his success.

The Crossley census, taken about a week before the broadcast, had given us 3.6 per cent of the listening audience to Edgar Bergen's 34.7 per cent. What the Crossley Institute (that hireling of the advertising agencies) deliberately ignored, was the healthy American habit of dial-twisting. On that particular evening, Edgar Bergen in the person of Charlie McCarthy temporarily left the air about 8:12 P.M., E.S.T., yielding place to a new and not very popular singer. At that point, and during the following minutes, a large number of listeners started twisting their dials in search of other entertainment. Many of them turned to us—and when they did, they stayed put! For by this time the mysterious meteorite had fallen at Grovers Mill in New Jersey, the Martians had begun to show their foul leathery heads above the ground, and the New Jersey State Police were racing to the spot. Within a few minutes people all over the United States were praying, crying, fleeing frantically to escape death from the Martians. Some remembered to rescue loved ones, others telephoned farewells or warnings, hurried to inform neighbors, sought information from newspapers or radio stations, summoned ambulances and police cars.

The reaction was strongest at points nearest the tragedy—in Newark, New Jersey, in a single block, more than twenty families rushed out of their houses with wet handkerchiefs and towels over their faces. Some began moving household furniture. Police switchboards were flooded with calls inquiring, "Shall I close my windows?" "Have the police any extra gas masks?" Police found one family waiting in the yard with wet cloths on faces contorted with hysteria. As one woman reported later:

> I was terribly frightened. I wanted to pack and take my child in my arms, gather up my friends and get in the car and just go north as far as we could. But what I did was just sit by one window, praying, listening, and scared stiff, and my husband by the other sniffling and looking out to see if people were running. . . .

In New York hundreds of people on Riverside Drive left their homes ready for flight. Bus terminals were crowded. A woman calling up the Dixie Bus Terminal for information said impatiently, "Hurry please, the world is coming to an end and I have a lot to do."

In the parlor churches of Harlem evening service became "end of the world" prayer meetings. Many turned to God in that moment:

> I held a crucifix in my hand and prayed while looking out of my open window for falling meteors. . . . When the monsters were wading across the Hudson River and coming into New York, I wanted to run up on my roof to see what they looked like, but I couldn't leave my radio while it was telling me of their whereabouts.

> Aunt Grace began to pray with Uncle Henry. Lily got sick to her stomach. I don't know what I did exactly but I know I prayed harder

and more earnestly than ever before. Just as soon as we were convinced that this thing was real, how petty all things on this earth seemed; how soon we put our trust in God!

The panic moved upstate. One man called up the Mt. Vernon Police Headquarters to find out "where the forty policemen were killed." Another took time out to philosophize:

I thought the whole human race was going to be wiped out—that seemed more important than the fact that we were going to die. It seemed awful that everything that had been worked on for years was going to be lost forever.

In Rhode Island weeping and hysterical women swamped the switchboard of the Providence *Journal* for details of the massacre, and officials of the electric light company received a score of calls urging them to turn off all lights so that the city would be safe from the enemy. The Boston *Globe* received a call from one woman "who could see the fire." A man in Pittsburgh hurried home in the midst of the broadcast and found his wife in the bathroom, a bottle of poison in her hand screaming, "I'd rather die this way than that." In Minneapolis a woman ran into church screaming, "New York destroyed this is the end of the world. You might as well go home to die I just heard it on the radio."

The Kansas City Bureau of the AP received inquiries about the "meteors" from Los Angeles; Salt Lake City; Beaumont, Texas; and St. Joseph, Missouri. In San Francisco the general impression of listeners seemed to be that an overwhelming force had invaded the United States from the air—was in process of destroying New York and threatening to move westward. "My God," roared an inquirer into a telephone, "where can I volunteer my services, we've got to stop this awful thing!"

As far south as Birmingham, Alabama, people gathered in churches and prayed. On the campus of a Southeastern college—

The girls in the sorority houses and dormitories huddled around their radios trembling and weeping in each other's arms. They separated themselves from their friends only to take their turn at the telephones to make long distance calls to their parents, saying goodbye for what they thought might be the last time. . . .

There are hundreds of such bits of testimony, gathered from coast to coast.

IV

At least one book* and quite a pile of sociological literature has appeared on the subject of "The Invasion from Mars." Many theories have been put forward to explain the "tidal wave" of panic that swept the nation. I know of two factors that largely contributed to the broadcast's extraordinarily violent effect. First, its historical timing. It came within thirty-five days of the Munich crisis. For weeks, the American people had been hanging on their radios, getting most of their news no longer from the press, but over the air. A new technique of "on-the-spot" reporting had been developed and eagerly accepted by an anxious and news-hungry world. The Mercury Theater on the Air by faithfully copying every detail of the new technique—including its imperfections—found an already enervated audience ready to accept its wildest fantasies. The second factor was the show's sheer technical brilliance. To this day it is impossible to sit in a room and hear the scratched, worn, off-the-air recording of the broadcast, without feeling in the back of your neck some slight draft left over from that great wind of terror that swept the nation. Even with the element of credibility totally removed it remains a surprisingly frightening show.

Radio drama was taken seriously in the thirties—before the Quiz and the Giveaway became the lords of the air. In the work of such directors as Reis, Corwin, Fickett, Welles, Robson, Spier, and Oboler there was an eager, excited drive to get the most out of this new, all too rapidly freezing medium. But what happened that Sunday, up on the twentieth floor of the CBS building, was something quite special. Beginning around two, when the show started to take shape under Orson's hands, a strange fever seemed to invade the studio—part childish mischief, part professional zeal.

First to feel it were the actors. I remember Frank Readick (who played the part of Carl Phillips, the network's special reporter) going down to the record library and digging up the Morrison recording of the explosion of the Hindenburg at Lakehurst. This is a classic reportage—one of those wonderful, unpredictable accidents of eyewitness description. The broadcaster is casually describing a routine landing of the giant gasbag. Suddenly he sees something. A flash of flame! An instant later the whole thing explodes. It takes him time—a

---

* *The Invasion from Mars* by Hadley Cantril, Princeton University Press, from which many of the above quotations were taken.

full second—to react at all. Then seconds more of sputtering ejaculations before he can make the adjustment between brain and tongue. He starts to describe the terrible things he sees—the writhing human figures twisting and squirming as they fall from the white burning wreckage. He stops, fumbles, vomits, then quickly continues. Readick played the record to himself, over and over. Then, recreating the emotion in his own terms, he described the Martian meteorite as he saw it lying inert and harmless in a field at Grovers Mill, lit up by the headlights of a hundred cars—the coppery cylinder suddenly opening, revealing the leathery tentacles and the terrible pale-eyed faces of the Martians within. As they begin to emerge he freezes, unable to translate his vision into words; he fumbles, retches—and then after a second continues.

A few moments later Carl Phillips lay dead, tumbling over the microphone in his fall—one of the first victims of the Martian Ray. There followed a moment of absolute silence—an eternity of waiting. Then, without warning, the network's emergency fill-in was heard— somewhere in a quiet studio, a piano, close on mike, playing "Clair de Lune," soft and sweet as honey, for many seconds, while the fate of the universe hung in the balance. Finally it was interrupted by the manly reassuring voice of Brigadier General Montgomery Smith, Commander of the New Jersey State Militia, speaking from Trenton, and placing "the counties of Mercer and Middlesex as far west as Princeton and east to Jamesburg" under Martial Law! Tension—release—then renewed tension. For soon after that came an eyewitness account of the fatal battle of the Watchung Hills; and then, once again, that lone piano was heard—now a symbol of terror, shattering the dead air with its ominous tinkle. As it played, on and on, its effect became increasingly sinister—a thin band of suspense stretched almost beyond endurance.

That piano was the neatest trick of the show—a fine specimen of the theatrical "retard," boldly conceived and exploited to the full. It was one of the many devices with which Welles succeeded in compelling, not merely the attention, but also the belief of his invisible audience. *The War of the Worlds* was a magic act, one of the world's greatest, and Orson was just the man to bring it off.

For Welles is at heart a magician whose particular talent lies not so much in his creative imagination (which is considerable) as in his proven ability to stretch the familiar elements of theatrical effect far beyond their normal point of tension. For this reason his productions require more elaborate preparation and more perfect execution than most. At that—like all complicated magic tricks—they remain, till the last moment, in a state of precarious balance. When they come off, they give—by virtue of their unusually high intensity—an impression of great brilliance and power; when they fail—when something in their balance goes wrong or the original structure proves to have been unsound—they provoke, among their audience, a particularly violent reaction of unease and revulsion. Welles' flops are louder than other men's. The Mars broadcast was one of his unqualified successes.

Among the columnists and public figures who discussed the affair during the next few days (some praising us for the public service we had rendered, some condemning us as sinister scoundrels) the most general reaction was one of amazement at the "incredible stupidity" and "gullibility" of the American public, who had accepted as real, in this single broadcast, incidents which in actual fact would have taken days or even weeks to occur. "Nothing about the broadcast," wrote Dorothy Thompson with her usual aplomb, "was in the least credible." She was wrong. The first few minutes of our broadcast were, in point of fact, strictly realistic in time and perfectly credible, though somewhat boring, in content. Herein lay the great tensile strength of the show; it was the structural device that made the whole illusion possible. And it could have been carried off in no other medium than radio.

Our actual broadcasting time, from the first mention of the meteorites to the fall of New York City, was less than forty minutes. During that time men traveled long distances, large bodies of troops were mobilized, cabinet meetings were held, savage battles fought on land and in the air. And millions of people accepted it—emotionally if not logically.

There is nothing so very strange about that. Most of us do the same thing, to some degree, most days of our lives—every time we look at a movie or listen to a broadcast. Not even the realistic theater observes the literal unities; motion pictures and, particularly, radio (where neither place nor time exists save in the imagination of the listener) have no difficulty in getting their audiences to accept the telescoped reality of dramatic time. Our special hazard lay in the fact that we purported to be, not a play, but reality. In order to take advantage of the accepted convention, we had to slide swiftly and imperceptibly out of the "real" time of a news report into the "dramatic" time of a fictional broadcast. Once that was achieved—without losing the audience's attention or arousing their skepticism, if they could be sufficiently absorbed and bewitched not to notice the transition—then, we felt, there was no extreme of fantasy through which they would not follow us. We were keenly aware of our problem; we found what we believed was the key to its solution. And if, that night, the American public proved "gullible," it was because enormous pains and a great deal of thought had been spent to make it so.

In the script, *The War of the Worlds* started extremely slowly— dull meteorological and astronomical bulletins alternating with musical interludes. These were followed by a colorless scientific interview and still another stretch of dance music. These first few minutes of routine broadcasting "within the existing standards of judgment of the listener" were intended to lull (or maybe bore) the audience into a false security and to furnish a solid base of realistic time from which to accelerate later. Orson, in making over the show, extended this slow movement far beyond our original conception. "La Cumparsita," rendered by "Ramon Raquello, from the Meridian Room of the Hotel Park Plaza in downtown New York," had been thought of as running only a few seconds; "Bobby Millette playing first 'Stardust' from the Hotel Martinet in Brooklyn," even less. At rehearsal Orson stretched both these numbers to what seemed to us, in the control room, an almost unbearable length. We objected. The interview in the Princeton Observatory—the clockwork ticking monotonously overhead, the woolly-minded professor mumbling vague replies to the reporters' uninformed questions—this, too, he dragged out to a point of tedium. Over our protests, lines were restored that had been cut at earlier rehearsals. We cried there would not be a listener left. Welles stretched them out even longer.

He was right. His sense of tempo, that night, was infallible. When the flashed news of the cylinder's landing finally came—almost fifteen minutes after the beginning of a fairly dull show—he was able suddenly to spiral his action to a speed as wild and reckless as its base was solid. The appearance of the Martians; their first treacherous act; the death of Carl Phillips; the arrival of the militia; the battle of the Watchung Hills; the destruction of New Jersey—all these were telescoped into a space of twelve minutes without overstretching the listeners' emotional credulity. The broadcast, by then, had its own reality, the reality of emotionally felt time and space.

V

At the height of the crisis, around 8:31, the Secretary of the Interior came on the air with an exhortation to the American people. His words, as you read them now, ten years later, have a Voltairean ring. (They were admirably spoken—in a voice just faintly reminiscent of the President's—by a young man named Kenneth Delmar, who has since grown rich and famous as Senator Claghorn.)

THE SECRETARY

Citizens of the nation: I shall not try to conceal the gravity of the situation that confronts the country, nor the concern of your Government in protecting the lives and property of its people. However, I wish to impress upon you—private citizens and public officials, all of you—the urgent need of calm and resourceful action. Fortunately, this formidable enemy is still confined to a comparatively small area, and we may place our faith in the military forces to keep them there. In the meantime placing our trust in God, we must continue the performance of our duties, each and every one of us, so that we may confront this destructive adversary with a nation united, courageous, and consecrated to the preservation of human supremacy on this earth. I thank you.

Toward the end of this speech (*circa* 8:32 E.S.T.), Davidson Taylor, supervisor of the broadcast for the Columbia Broadcasting System, received a phone call in the control room, creased his lips, and hurriedly left the studio. By the time he returned, a few moments later—pale as death—clouds of heavy smoke were rising from Newark, New Jersey, and the Martians, tall as skyscrapers, were astride the Pulaski Highway preparatory to wading the Hudson River. To us in the studio the show seemed to be progressing splendidly—how splendidly Davidson Taylor had just learned outside. For several minutes now, a kind of madness had seemed to be sweeping the continent—somehow connected with our show. The CBS switchboards had been swamped into uselessness but from outside sources vague rumors were coming in of deaths and suicides and panic injuries.

Taylor had requests to interrupt the show immediately with an explanatory station-announcement. By now the Martians were across the Hudson and gas was blanketing the city. The end was near. We were less than a minute from the Station Break. The organ was allowed to swirl out under the slackening fingers of its failing organist and Ray

Collins, superb as the "last announcer," choked heroically to death on the roof of Broadcasting Building. The boats were all whistling for a while as the last of the refugees perished in New York Harbor. Finally, as they died away, an amateur shortwave operator was heard, from heaven knows where, weakly reaching out for human companionship across the empty world:

> 2X2L Calling CQ
> 2X2L Calling CQ
> 2X2L Calling CQ
> Isn't there anyone on the air?
> Isn't there anyone?

Five seconds of absolute silence. Then, shattering the reality of World's End—the Announcer's voice was heard, suave and bright:

ANNOUNCER

You are listening to the CBS presentation of Orson Welles and the Mercury Theater on the Air in an original dramatization of *The War of the Worlds,* by H. G. Wells. The performance will continue after a brief intermission.

The second part of the show was extremely well written and most sensitively played—but nobody heard it. It recounted the adventures of a lone survivor, with interesting observations on the nature of human society; it described the eventual death of the Martian Invaders, slain—"after all man's defenses had failed by the humblest thing that God in his wisdom had put upon this earth"—by bacteriological action; it told of the rebuilding of a brave new world. After a stirring musical finale, Welles, in his own person, delivered a charming informal little speech about Halloween, which it happened to be.

I remember, during the playing of the final theme, the phone starting to ring in the control room and a shrill voice through the receiver announcing itself as belonging to the mayor of some Midwestern city, one of the big ones. He is screaming for Welles. Choking with fury, he reports mobs in the streets of his city, women and children huddled in the churches, violence and looting. If, as he now learns, the whole thing is nothing but a crummy joke—then he, personally, is coming up to New York to punch the author of it on the nose! Orson hangs up quickly. For we are off the air now and the studio door bursts open. The following hours are a nightmare. The building is suddenly full of people and dark blue uniforms. We are hurried out of the studio, downstairs, into a back office. Here we sit incommunicado while network employees are busily collecting, destroying, or locking up all scripts and records of the broadcast. Then the press is let loose upon us, ravening for horror. How many deaths have *we* heard of? (Implying they know of thousands.) What do *we* know of the fatal stampede in a Jersey hall? (Implying it is one of many.) What traffic deaths? (The ditches must be choked with corpses.) The suicides? (Haven't you heard about the one on Riverside Drive?) It is all quite vague in my memory and quite terrible.

Hours later, instead of arresting us, they let us out a back way. We scurry down to the theater like hunted animals to their hole. It is surprising to see life going on as usual in the midnight streets, cars stopping for traffic, people walking. At the Mercury the company is still stoically rehearsing—falling downstairs and singing the "Carmagnole." Welles goes up on stage, where photographers, lying in wait, catch him with his eyes raised up to heaven, his arms outstretched in an attitude of crucifixion. Thus he appeared in a tabloid that morning over the caption, "I Didn't Know What I Was Doing!" The *New York Times* quoted him as saying, "I don't think we will choose anything like this again."

We were on the front page for two days. Having had to bow to radio as a news source during the Munich crisis, the press was now only too eager to expose the perilous irresponsibilities of the new medium. Orson was their whipping boy. They quizzed and badgered him. Condemnatory editorials were delivered by our press-clipping bureau in bushel baskets. There was talk, for a while, of criminal action.

Then gradually, after about two weeks, the excitement subsided. By then it had been discovered that the casualties were not as numerous or as serious as had at first been supposed. One young woman had fallen and broken her arm running downstairs. Later the Federal Communications Commission held some hearings and passed some regulations. The Columbia Broadcasting System made a public apology. With that the official aspects of the incident were closed.

As to the Mercury—our new play, *Danton's Death,* finally opened after five postponements. Not even our fantastic publicity was able to offset its generally unfavorable notices. On the other hand, that same week the Mercury Theater on the Air was signed up by Campbell Soups at a most lavish figure.

Of the suits that were brought against us—amounting to over three-quarters of a million dollars for damages, injuries, miscarriages, and distresses of various kinds—none was substantiated or legally proved. We did settle one claim, however, against the advice of our lawyers. It was the particularly affecting case of a man in Massachusetts, who wrote:

"I thought the best thing to do was to go away. So I took three dollars twenty-five cents out of my savings and bought a ticket. After I had gone sixty miles I knew it was a play. Now I don't have money left for the shoes I was saving up for. Will you please have someone send me a pair of black shoes size 9B!"

We did.

Highbrow, Lowbrow, Middlebrow

by RUSSELL LYNES

FEBRUARY, 1949

The new American social structure—in the making since the old one collapsed with the stock market in 1929—got its first elite in the Roosevelt Brain Trust. But it wasn't until this famous article nearly twenty years later that we realized the full extent to which intellectualism had replaced money and family as the measure of one's prestige in society. Mr. Lynes is the son of an Episcopal minister and a graduate of Yale, class of 1932. He has been an editor of Harper's *since the war and is now managing editor. In addition to writing many upper-middlebrow articles for the magazine, he is also the author of several books, the most recent being* The Tastemakers *and a humorous "diversion,"* Cadwallader.

My wife's grandmother, the wife of a distinguished lawyer, once declined to dine with the Cartiers of jewelry fame because they were, as she put it, "in trade." Life for grandmother was relatively simple where social distinctions were concerned, but while there are still a few people who think and act much as she did, the passage of time has eliminated a great deal of that particular kind of snobbishness from American society. We are replacing it with another kind. The old structure of the upper class, the middle class, and the lower class is on the wane. It isn't wealth or family that makes prestige these days. It's high thinking.

Our heroes now are not the Carnegies or the Morgans but the intellectuals—the atomic scientists, the cultural historians, the writers, the commentators, the thinkers of global thoughts who, we assume for lack of another faith, know better than anyone else how we should cope with what we call with new resonance our national destiny. What we want are oracles, and the best substitutes we can find are the intellectuals. Einstein makes headlines as Milliken never did. Toynbee's popularity is to be reckoned with as Spengler's never was. Even Calvert whiskey has selected as Men of Distinction more artists, architects, writers, and commentators than it has industrialists or financiers. What we are headed for is a sort of social structure in which the highbrows are the elite, the middlebrows are the bourgeoisie, and the lowbrows are *hoi polloi.*

For the time being this is perhaps largely an urban phenomenon, and the true middlebrow may readily be mistaken in the small community for a genuine highbrow, but the pattern is emerging with increasing clarity, and the new distinctions do not seem to be based either on money or on breeding. Some lowbrows are as rich as Billy Rose, and as flamboyant, some as poor as Rosie O'Grady and as modest. Some middlebrows run industries; some run the women's auxiliary of the Second Baptist Church. Some highbrows eat caviar with their Proust; some eat hamburger when they can afford it. It is true that most highbrows are in the ill-paid professions, notably the academic, and that most middlebrows are at least reasonably well off. Only the lowbrows can be found in about equal percentages at all financial levels. There may be a time, of course, when the highbrows will be paid in accordance with their own estimate of their worth, but that is not likely to happen in any form of society in which creature comforts are in greater demand than intellectual uplift. Like poets they will have to be content mostly with prestige. The middlebrows are influential today, but neither the highbrows nor the lowbrows like them; and if we ever have intellectual totalitarianism, it may well be the lowbrows and the highbrows who will run things, and the middlebrows who will be exiled in boxcars to a collecting point probably in the vicinity of Independence, Missouri.

While this social shift is still in its early stages, and the dividing lines are still indistinct and the species not yet frozen, let us assume a rather lofty position, examine the principal categories, with their sub-divisions and splinter groups, and see where we ourselves are likely to fetch up in the new order.

II

The highbrows come first. Edgar Wallace, who was certainly not a highbrow himself, was asked by a newspaper reporter in Hollywood some years ago to define one. "What is a highbrow?" he said. "A highbrow is a man who has found something more interesting than women."

Presumably at some time in every man's life there are things he finds more interesting than women; alcohol, for example, or the World Series. Mr. Wallace has only partially defined the highbrow. Brander Matthews came closer when he said that "a highbrow is a person educated beyond his intelligence," and A. P. Herbert came closest of all when he wrote that "a highbrow is the kind of person who looks at a sausage and thinks of Picasso."

It is this association of culture with every aspect of daily life, from the design of his razor to the shape of the bottle that holds his sleeping pills, that distinguishes the highbrow from the middlebrow or the lowbrow. Spiritually and intellectually the highbrow inhabits a precinct well up the slopes of Parnassus, and his view of the cultural scene is from above. His vision pinpoints certain lakes and quarries upon which his special affections are concentrated—a perturbed lake called Rilke or a deserted quarry called Kierkegaard—but he believes that he sees them, as he sees the functional design of his razor, always in relation to the broader cultural scene. There is a certain air of omniscience about the highbrow, though that air is in many cases the thin variety encountered on the tops of high mountains from which the view is extensive but the details are lost.

You cannot tell a man that he is a lowbrow any more than you can tell a woman that her clothes are in bad taste, but a highbrow does not mind being called a highbrow. He has worked hard, read widely, traveled far, and listened attentively in order to satisfy his curiosity and establish his squatters' rights in this little corner of intellectualism, and he does not care who knows it. And this is true of both kinds of highbrow—the militant, or crusader, type and the passive, or dilettante, type. These types in general live happily together; the militant highbrow carries the torch of culture, the passive highbrow reads by its light.

The carrier of the torch makes a profession of being a highbrow and lives by his calling. He is most frequently found in university and college towns, a member of the liberal-arts faculty, teaching languages (ancient or modern), the fine arts, or literature. His spare time is often devoted to editing a magazine which is read mainly by other highbrows, ambitious undergraduates, and the editors of middlebrow publications in search of talent. When he writes for the magazine himself (or for another "little" magazine) it is usually criticism or criticism *of* criticism. He leaves the writing of fiction and poetry to others more bent on creation than on what has been created, for the highbrow is primarily a critic and not an artist—a taster, not a cook. He is often more interested in where the arts have been, and where they are going, than in the objects themselves. He is devoted to the proposition that the arts must be pigeonholed, and that their trends should be plotted, or as W. H. Auden puts it—

> Our intellectual marines,
> Landing in Little Magazines,
> Capture a trend.

This gravitation of the highbrows to the universities is fairly recent. In the twenties, when the little magazines were devoted to publishing experimental writing rather than criticism of exhumed experimental writing, the highbrows flocked to Paris, New York, and Chicago. The *transatlantic review, transition,* and the *Little Review,* of the lower-case era of literature, were all published in Paris; BROOM was published in New York; *Poetry* was (and still is) published in Chicago. The principal little magazines now, with the exception of *Partisan Review,* a New York product but written mostly by academics, are published in the colleges—the *Kenyon Review,* the *Sewanee Review,* the *Virginia Quarterly,* and so on—and their flavor reflects this. But this does not mean that highbrows do not prefer the centers in which cultural activities are the most varied and active, and these are still London, Paris, New York, and more recently Rome. Especially in the fine arts, the highbrow has a chance to make a living in the metropolis where museums are centered and where art is bought and sold as well as created. This is also true of commercial publishing, in which many highbrows find suitable, if not congenial, refuge.

But no matter where they may make their homes, all highbrows live in a world which they believe is inhabited almost entirely by Philistines—those who through viciousness or smugness or the worship of materialism gnaw away at the foundations of culture. And the highbrow sees as his real enemy the middlebrow, whom he regards as a pretentious and frivolous man or woman who uses culture to satisfy social or business ambitions; who, to quote Clement Greenberg in *Partisan Review,* is busy "devaluating the precious, infecting the healthy, corrupting the honest, and stultifying the wise."

It takes a man who feels strongly to use such harsh words, but the militant highbrow has no patience with his enemies. He is a serious man who will not tolerate frivolity where the arts are concerned. It is part of his function as a highbrow to protect the arts from the culture-mongers, and he spits venom at those he suspects of selling the Muses short.

The fact that nowadays everyone has access to culture through schools and colleges, through the press, radio, and museums, disturbs him deeply; for it tends to blur the distinctions between those who are serious and those who are frivolous. "Culturally what we have," writes William Phillips in *Horizon,* "is a democratic free-for-all in which every individual, being as good as every other one, has the right to question any form of intellectual authority." To this Mr. Greenberg adds, "It becomes increasingly difficult to tell who is serious and who not."

The highbrow does not like to be confused, nor does he like to have his authority questioned, except by other highbrows of whose seriousness he is certain. The result is precisely what you would expect: the highbrows believe in, and would establish, an intellectual elite, "a fluid body of intellectuals . . . whose accepted role in society is to perpetuate traditional ideas and values and to create new ones." Such an elite would like to see the middlebrow eliminated, for it regards him as the undesirable element in our, and anybody else's, culture.

"It must be obvious to anyone that the volume and social weight of middlebrow culture," Mr. Greenberg writes, "borne along as it has been by the great recent increase in the American middle class, have multiplied at least tenfold in the past three decades. This culture presents a more serious threat to the genuine article than the old-time pulp dime novel, Tin Pan Alley, *Schund* variety ever has or will. Unlike the latter, which has its social limits clearly marked out for it, middlebrow culture attacks distinctions as such and insinuates itself everywhere. . . . Insidiousness is of its essence, and in recent years its avenues of penetration have become infinitely more difficult to detect and block."

By no means all highbrows are so intolerant or so desperate as this, or so ambitious for authority. Many of them, the passive ones, are merely consumers totally indifferent to the middlebrows or supercilious about them. Others without a great deal of hope but in ardent good faith expend themselves in endeavor to widen the circle of those who can enjoy the arts in their purest forms. Many museums, colleges, and publishing houses are at least partly staffed by highbrows who exert a more than halfhearted effort to make the arts exciting and important to the public. But they are aware that most of their labors are wasted. In his heart of hearts nearly every highbrow believes with Ortega y Gasset that "the average citizen [is] a creature incapable of receiving the sacrament of art, blind and deaf to pure beauty." When, for example, the Metropolitan Museum planned to expand its facilities a few years ago, an art dealer who can clearly be classified as a highbrow remarked: "All this means is less art for more people."

There are also many highbrows who are not concerned in the least with the arts or with literature, and who do not fret themselves about the upstart state of middlebrow culture. These are the specialized highbrows who toil in the remote corners of science and history, of philology and mathematics. They are concerned with their investigations of fruit-flies or Elizabethan taxation or whatever it may be, and they do not talk about them, as the dilettante always talks of the arts, to the first person they can latch onto at a cocktail party. When not in their laboratories or the library, they are often as not thoroughly middlebrow in their attitudes and tastes.

The real highbrow's way of life is as intellectualized as his way of thinking, and as carefully plotted. He is likely to be either extremely self-conscious about his physical surroundings and creature comforts or else sublimely, and rather ostentatiously, indifferent to them. If he affects the former attitude, he will within the limits of his income surround himself with works of art. If he cannot afford paintings he buys drawings. Color reproductions, except as casual reminders tucked in the frame of a mirror or thrown down on a table, are beneath him. The facsimile is no substitute in his mind for the genuine, and he would rather have a slight sketch by a master, Braque or Picasso or even Jackson Pollack, than a fully realized canvas by an artist he considers not quite first-rate. Drawings by his friends he hangs in the bathroom. His furniture, if it is modern, consists of identifiable pieces by Aalto, or Breuer, or Mies van der Rohe, or Eames; it does not come from department stores. If he finds modern unsympathetic, he will tend to use Biedermaier or the more "entertaining" varieties of Victorian, which he collects piece by piece with an eye to the slightly eccentric. If he has antiques, you may be sure they are not maple; the cult of "early American" is offensive to him.

The food that he serves will be planned with the greatest care, either very simple (a perfect French omelette made with sweet butter) or elaborate recipes from *Wine and Food* magazine published in London and edited by André Simon. If he cannot afford a pound of butter with every guinea fowl, he will in all probability resort to the casserole, and peasant cookery with the sparer parts of animals and birds seasoned meticulously with herbs that he gets from a little importer in the wholesale district. His wine is more likely to be a "perfectly adequate little red wine" for eighty-nine cents a half-gallon than an imported French vintage. (Anybody with good advice can buy French wines, but the discovery of a good domestic bottle shows perception and educated taste.) He wouldn't dream of washing his salad bowl. His collection of phonograph records is likely to bulk large at the ends and sag in the middle—a predominance of Bach-and-before at one end and Stravinsky, Schönberg, Bartók, and New Orleans jazz at the other. The nineteenth century is represented, perhaps, by Beethoven quartets and late sonatas, and some French "art songs" recorded by Maggie Teyte. His radio, if he has one, is turned on rarely; he wouldn't have a television set in the house.

The highbrow who disregards his creature comforts does it with a will. He lives with whatever furniture happens to come his way in a disorganized conglomeration of Victorian, department store, and Mexican bits and pieces. He takes care of his books in that he knows where each one is no matter in what disorder they may appear. Every other detail of domestic life he leaves to his wife, of whose taste he is largely unaware, and he eats what she gives him without comment. If he is a bachelor, he eats in a cafeteria or drugstore or diner and sometimes spills soup on the open pages of his book. He is oblivious to the man who sits down opposite him, and if Edgar Wallace is right, to the woman who shares his table. He is not a man without passions, but they have their place. Dress is a matter of indifference to him.

The highbrows about whom I have been writing are mainly consumers and not creators—editors, critics, and dilettantes. The creative artists who are generally considered highbrows—such men as T. S. Eliot, E. M. Forster, Picasso, and Stravinsky—seem to me to fall in another category, that of the professional man who, while he may be concerned with communicating with a limited (and perhaps largely highbrow) audience, is primarily a doer and not a done-by. When Eliot or Forster or Picasso or Stravinsky sits down at his work-table, I do not know whether he says to himself, "I am going to create Art," but I very much doubt if that is what is in his mind. He is concerned rather with the communication of ideas within the frame of a poem, a novel, a painting, or a ballet suite, and if it turns out to be art (which many think it frequently does) that is to him a by-product of creation, an extra dividend of craftsmanship, intelligence, and sensibility. But when this happens he is taken up by the highbrow consumer and made much of. In fact he may become, whether he likes it or not, a vested interest, and his reputation will be every bit as carefully guarded by the highbrows as a hundred shares of Standard Oil of New Jersey by the middlebrows. He will be sold—at a par decided upon by the highbrows—to the middlebrows, who are natural gamblers in the commodities of culture.

In a sense it is this determination of par that is the particular contribution of the highbrow. Others may quarrel with his evaluations, but the fact remains that unless there were a relatively small group of self-appointed intellectuals who took it upon themselves to ransack the studios of artists, devour the manuscripts of promising writers, and listen at the keyholes of young composers, many talented men and women might pass unnoticed and our culture be the poorer. Their noncommercial attitude toward discovery of talent is useful, though they have an obsession with the evils of the monetary temptations with which America strews the artist's path. They stand as a wavering bulwark against the enticements of Hollywood and the advertising agencies, and they are saddened by the writers and painters who have set out to be serious men, as Hemingway did, and then become popular by being taken up by the middlebrows. They even go so far as to say that a story published in *Partisan Review* is a better story than if it were published in *The New Yorker* or *Harper's Bazaar*, for the reason that "what we have is at once a general raising and lowering of the level, for with the blurring of distinctions new writing tends to become more and more serious and intellectual and less and less bold and extreme. . . ."

This attitude, which is the attitude of the purist, is valuable. The ground in which the arts grow stays fertile only when it is fought over by both artists and consumers, and the phalanx of highbrows in the field, a somewhat impenetrable square of warriors, can be counted on to keep the fray alive.

III

The highbrow's friend is the lowbrow. The highbrow enjoys and respects the lowbrow's art—jazz for instance—which he is likely to call a spontaneous expression of folk culture. The lowbrow is not interested, as the middlebrow is, in pre-empting any of the highbrow's function or in any way threatening to blur the lines between the serious and the frivolous. In fact he is almost completely oblivious of the highbrow unless he happens to be taken up by him—as many jazz musicians, primitive painters, and ballad writers have been—and then he is likely to be flattered, a little suspicious, and somewhat amused. A creative lowbrow like the jazz musician is a prominent citizen in his own world, and the fact that he is taken up by the highbrows has very little effect on his social standing therein. He is tolerant of the highbrow, whom he regards as somewhat odd and out-of-place in a world in which people do things and enjoy them without analyzing why or worrying about their cultural implications.

The lowbrow doesn't give a hang about art *qua* art. He knows what he likes, and he doesn't care why he likes it—which implies that all children are lowbrows. The word "beautiful," which has long since ceased to mean anything to the highbrow, is a perfectly good word to the lowbrow. Beautiful blues, beautiful sunsets, beautiful women, all things that do something to a man inside without passing through the mind, associations without allusions, illusions without implications. The arts created by the lowbrow are made in the expression of immediate pleasure or grief, like most forms of jazz; or of usefulness, like the manufacturing of a tool or a piece of machinery or even a bridge across the Hudson. The form, to use a highbrow phrase, follows the function. When the lowbrow arts follow this formula (which they don't always do), then the highbrow finds much in them to admire, and he calls it the vernacular. When, however, the lowbrow arts get mixed up with middlebrow ideas of culture, then the highbrow turns away in disgust. Look, for example, at what happened to the circus, a traditional form of lowbrow art. They got in Norman Bel Geddes to fancy it up, and now its special flavor of authenticity is gone—all wrapped up in pink middlebrow sequins. This is not to say that the lowbrow doesn't like it just as much as he ever did. It is the highbrow who is pained.

Part of the highbrow's admiration for the lowbrow stems from the lowbrow's indifference to art. This makes it possible for the highbrow to blame whatever he doesn't like about lowbrow taste on the middlebrow. If the lowbrow reads the comics, the highbrow understands; he is frequently a connoisseur of the comics himself. But if he likes grade-B double features, the highbrow blames that on the corrupting influence of the middlebrow moneybags of Hollywood. If he participates in giveaway quiz programs, it is because the radio pollsters have decided that the average mental age of the listening audience is thirteen, and that radio is venal for taking advantage of the adolescent.

The lowbrow consumer, whether he is an engineer of bridges or a bus driver, wants to be comfortable and to enjoy himself without having to worry about whether he has good taste or not. It doesn't make any difference to him that a chair is a bad Grand Rapids copy of an eighteenth-century *fauteuil* as long as he's happy when he sits down in it. He doesn't care whether the movies are art, or the radio improving, so long as he has fun while he is giving them his attention and getting a fair return of pleasure from his investment. It wouldn't occur to him to tell a novelist what kind of book he should write, or a movie director what kind of movie to make. If he doesn't like a book he ignores it; if he doesn't like a movie he says so, whether it is a "Blondie" show or "Henry V." If he likes jive or square-dancing, he doesn't worry about whether they are fashionable or not. If other people like the ballet, that's all right with him, so long as he doesn't have to go himself. In general the lowbrow attitude toward the arts is live and let live. Lowbrows are not Philistines. One has to know enough about the arts to argue about them with highbrows to be a Philistine.

IV

The popular press, and also much of the unpopular press, is run by the middlebrows, and it is against them that the highbrow inveighs.

"The true battle," Virginia Woolf wrote in an unmailed letter to the *New Statesman,* ". . . lies not between highbrow and lowbrow, but between highbrows and lowbrows joined together in blood brotherhood against the bloodless and pernicious pest who comes between."

The pests divide themselves into two groups: the Upper Middlebrows and the Lower Middlebrows. It is the upper middlebrows who are the principal purveyors of highbrow ideas and the lower middlebrows who are the principal consumers of what the upper middlebrows pass along to them.

Many publishers, for example, are upper middlebrows—as are most educators, museum directors, movie producers, art dealers, lecturers, and the editors of most magazines which combine national circulation with an adult vocabulary. These are the men and women who devote themselves professionally to the dissemination of ideas and cultural artifacts and, not in the least incidentally, make a living along the way. They are the cultural do-gooders, and they see their mission clearly and pursue it with determination. Some of them are disappointed highbrows; some of them try to work both sides of the street; nearly all of them straddle the fence between highbrow and middlebrow and enjoy their equivocal position.

The conscientious publisher, for instance, believes in the importance of literature and the dignity of publishing as a profession. He spends a large part of his time on books that will not yield him a decent return on his investment. He searches out writers of promise; he pores over the "little" magazines (or pays other people to); he leafs through hundreds and hundreds of pages of manuscript. He advises writers, encourages them, coaxes them to do their best work; he even advances them money. But he is not able to be a publisher at all (unless he is willing to put his personal fortune at the disposal of financially naïve muses) if he does not publish to make money. In order to publish slender volumes of poetry he must also publish fat volumes of historical romance, and in order to encourage the first novel of a promising young writer he must sell tens of thousands of copies of a book by an old hand who grinds out one best seller a year. He must take the measure of popular taste and cater to it at the same time that he tries to create a taste for new talent. If he is a successful publisher he makes money, lives comfortably, patronizes the other arts, serves on museum boards and committees for the Prevention of This and the Preservation of That, contributes to the symphony, and occasionally buys pictures by contemporary painters.

The highbrow suspects that the publisher does not pace his book-lined office contriving ways to serve the Muses and that these same Muses have to wait their turn in line until the balance sheet has been served. He believes that the publisher is really happy only when he can sell a couple of hundred thousand copies of a novel about a hussy with a horsewhip or a book on how to look forty when forty-five. To the highbrow he is a tool to be cultivated and used, but not to be trusted.

The museum director is in much the same position, caught between the Muses and the masses. If he doesn't make a constant effort to swell the door-count, his middlebrow trustees want to know why he isn't serving the community; if he does, the highbrows want to know why he is pandering to popular taste and not minding his main business— the service of scholarship and the support of artists currently certified to be "serious." Educators are in the same position, bound to be concerned with mass education often at the expense of the potential scholar, and editors of all magazines except those supported by private angels or cultural institutions know that they must not only enlighten but entertain if they are to have enough readers to pay the bills. To the highbrow this can lead to nothing but compromise and mediocrity.

The upper-middlebrow consumer takes his culture seriously, as seriously as his job allows, for he is gainfully employed. In his leisure hours he reads Toynbee or Sartre or Osbert Sitwell's serialized memoirs. He goes to museum openings and to the theater and he keeps up on the foreign films. He buys pictures, sometimes old masters if he can afford them, sometimes contemporary works. He has a few etchings and lithographs, and he is not above an occasional color reproduction of a Van Gogh or a Cézanne. Writers and painters are his friends and dine at his house; if, however, his own son were to express an interest in being an artist, he would be dismayed ("so few artists ever really pull it off")—though he would keep a stiff upper lip and hope the boy would learn better before it was too late. His house is tastefully decorated, sometimes in the very latest mode, a model of the modern architect's dream of functionalism, in which case he can discourse on the theory of the open plan and the derivations of the international style with the zest and uncertain vocabulary of a convert. If his house is "traditional" in character, he will not put up with Grand Rapids copies of old pieces; he will have authentic ones, and will settle for Victorian if he cannot afford Empire. He, or his wife, will ransack secondhand shops for entertaining bibelots and lamps or a piece of Brussels carpet for the bedroom. He never refers to curtains as "drapes." He talks about television as potentially a new art form, and he listens to the Saturday afternoon opera broadcasts. His library contains a few of the more respectable current best sellers which he reads out of "curiosity" rather than interest. (Membership in any sort of book club he considers beneath him.) There are a few shelves of first editions, some of them autographed by friends who have dined at his house, some of them things (like a presentation copy of *Jurgen*) that he "just happened to pick up" and a sampling of American and British poets. There is also a shelf of paper-bound French novels—most of them by nineteenth-century writers. The magazines on his table span the areas from *Time* and *The New Yorker* to *Harper's* and the *Atlantic,* with an occasional copy of the *Yale* and *Partisan Reviews,* and the *Art News.*

From this it can be seen that he supports the highbrows—buys some of the books they recommend and an occasional picture they have looked upon with favor—and contributes to organized efforts to promote the arts both by serving on boards and shelling out money. In general he is modest about expressing his opinion on cultural matters in the presence of highbrows but takes a slightly lordly tone when he is talking to other middlebrows. If he discovers a "little" painter or poet the chances are excellent that the man has already been discovered and promoted by a highbrow or by an upper-middlebrow entrepreneur (art dealer or publisher). Once in a while he will take a flyer on an unknown artist, and hang his picture inconspicuously in the bedroom. He takes his function as a patron of the arts seriously, but he does it for the pleasure it gives him to be part of the cultural scene. If he does it for "money, fame, power, or prestige," as Virginia Woolf says he does, these motives are so obscured by a general sense of well-being and well-meaning that he would be shocked and surprised to be accused of venality.

V

If the upper middlebrow is unsure of his own tastes, but firm in his belief that taste is extremely important, the lower middlebrow is his counterpart. The lower middlebrow ardently believes that he knows what he likes, and yet his taste is constantly susceptible to the pressures that put him in knickerbockers one year and rust-colored slacks the next. Actually he is unsure about almost everything, especially about what he likes. This may explain his pronouncements on taste, which he considers an effete and questionable virtue, and his resentment of the arts; but it may also explain his strength.

When America and Americans are characterized by foreigners and highbrows, the middlebrows are likely to emerge as the dominant group in our society—a dreadful mass of insensible back-slappers, given to sentimentality as a prime virtue, the willing victims of slogans and the whims of the bosses, both political and economic. The picture painted by middlebrow exploiters of the middlebrow, such as the advertisers of nationally advertised brands, is strikingly similar to that painted by the highbrow; their attitudes and motives are quite different (the highbrow paints with a snarl, the advertiser with a gleam), but they both make the middlebrow out to be much the same kind of creature. The villain of the highbrow and the hero of the advertisers is envisaged as "the typical American family"—happy little women, happy little children, all spotless or sticky in the jam pot, framed against dimity curtains in the windows or decalcomania flowers on the cupboard doors. Lower-middlebrowism is a world pictured without tragedy, a world of new two-door sedans, and Bendix washers, and reproductions of hunting prints over the living-room mantel. It is a world in which the ingenuity and patience of the housewife are equaled only by the fidelity of her husband and his love of home, pipe, and radio. It is a world that smells of soap. But it is a world of ambition as well, the constant striving for a better way of life —better furniture, bigger refrigerators, more books in the bookcase, more evenings at the movies. To the advertisers this is Americanism; to the highbrows this is the dead weight around the neck of progress, the gag in the mouth of art.

The lower middlebrows are not like this, of course, and unlike the highbrows and the upper middlebrows, whose numbers are tiny by comparison, they are hard to pin down. They live everywhere, rubbing elbows with lowbrows in apartment houses like vast beehives, in row houses all alike from the outside except for the planting, in large houses at the ends of gravel driveways, in big cities, in medium cities and suburbs, and in small towns, from Boston to San Francisco, from Seattle to Jacksonville. They are the members of the book clubs who read difficult books along with racy and innocuous ones that are sent along by Messrs. Fadiman, Canby, Beecroft *et al.* They are the course-takers who swell the enrollments of adult education classes in everything from "The Technique of the Short Story" to "Child Care." They are the people who go to hear the lecturers that swarm out from New York lecture bureaus with tales of travel on the Dark Continent and panaceas for saving the world from a fate worse than capitalism. They eat in tea shoppes and hold barbecues in their back yards. They are hell-bent on improving their minds as well as their fortunes. They decorate their homes under the careful guidance of *Good Housekeeping* and the *Ladies' Home Journal,* or, if they are well off, of *House and Garden,* and are subject to fads in furniture so long as these don't depart too radically from the traditional and the safe, from the copy of Colonial and the reproduction of Sheraton. In matters of taste, the lower-middlebrow world is largely dominated by women. They select the furniture, buy the fabrics, pick out the wallpapers, the pictures, the books, the china. Except in the selection of his personal apparel and the car, it is almost *infra dig* for a man to have taste; it is not considered quite manly for the male to express opinions about things which come under the category of "artistic."

Nonetheless, as a member of the school board or the hospital board he decides which design shall be accepted when a new building goes up. The lower middlebrows are the organizers of the community fund, the members of the legislature, the park commissioners. They pay their taxes and they demand services in return. There are millions of them, conscientious stabilizers of society, slow to change, slow to panic. But they are not as predictable as either the highbrows or the bosses, political or economic, think they are. They can be led, they can be seduced, but they cannot be pushed around.

VI

Highbrow, lowbrow, upper middlebrow, and lower middlebrow—the lines between them are sometimes indistinct, as the lines between upper class, lower class, and middle class have always been in our traditionally fluid society. But gradually they are finding their own levels and confining themselves more and more to the company of their own kind. You will not find a highbrow willingly attending a Simon & Schuster cocktail party any more than you will find an upper middlebrow at a Rotary Club luncheon or an Elks' picnic.

The highbrows would like, of course, to eliminate the middlebrows and devise a society that would approximate an intellectual feudal system in which the lowbrows do the work and create folk arts, and the highbrows do the thinking and create fine arts. All middlebrows, presumably, would have their radios taken away, be suspended from society until they had agreed to give up their subscriptions to the Book-of-the-Month, turned their color reproductions over to a Commission for the Dissolution of Middlebrow Taste, and renounced their affiliation with all educational and other cultural institutions whatsoever. They would be taxed for the support of all writers, artists, musicians, critics, and critics-of-criticism whose production could be certified "serious"—said writers, artists, musicians, and critics to be selected by representatives of qualified magazines with circulations of not more than five thousand copies. Middlebrows, both upper and lower, who persisted in "devaluating the precious, infecting the healthy, corrupting the honest, and stultifying the wise" would be disposed of forthwith.

But the highbrows haven't a chance; things have gone too far. Everybody but the genuine lowbrow (who is more wooed than wedded by the highbrow) is jockeying for position in the new cultural class order. *Life* magazine, sensing the trend, has been catching us up on the past of Western Civilization in sixteen-page, four-color capsules. *Mademoiselle* walks off with the first prizes in the annual short-story contests. The Pepsi-Cola Company stages the most elaborate and highest-paying art competition in the country. Even *Partisan Review,* backed by a new angel, runs full-page ads in the *New York Times Book Review*. The Book-of-the-Month Club ships out a couple of hundred thousand copies of Toynbee's *A Study of History* as "dividends."

If life for grandmother, who wouldn't dine with the Cartiers, was simple in its social distinctions, life is becoming equally simple for us. The rungs of the ladder may be different, it may even be a different ladder, but it's onward and upward just the same. You may not be known by which fork you use for the fish these days, but you will be known by which key you use for your *Finnegans Wake*.

Whiskey Is for Patriots

by BERNARD DeVOTO

APRIL, 1951

Bernard DeVoto wrote 243 "Easy Chair" columns between 1935 and his unexpected death in 1955. In Number 241, he used the twentieth anniversary as an occasion to talk about the wide range of his comment, which he labeled "cultural criticism." He also wrote: "No one knows better than a journalist that his work is ephemeral. As I have said elsewhere, it is not important, it is only indispensable." Pulitzer Prize-winning historian, and a biographer of Mark Twain, DeVoto also was a vigorous champion of conservation policies. Here, he takes up the subject of whiskey and the Republic.

Whiskey has been the drink of patriots ever since freedom from her mountain-height unfurled her banner to the air. The American people achieved nationality and Old Monongahely in the same generation, which should surprise no one, since nations flower swiftly once their genius has budded. Take the Irish. They were a breed of half-naked cave dwellers sunk in ignorance and sin and somewhat given to contentiousness. Then the gentle St. Patrick appeared among them. He taught them to make usquebaugh and at once they became the most cultured people in the world.

Or take the Indians. They were a genial people on whom we inflicted repulsive cruelties. (For instance, after the French had educated them to brandy we corrupted their taste with rum.) Yet a philosopher may wonder whether they had it in them to rise to cultural distinction. They evoke both pity and dismay: north of Mexico they never learned to make a fermented beverage, still less a distilled one. That they had ingenuity is not to be denied and one of their achievements is a marvel: they took a couple of wild grasses and bred them up to corn. But what did they do with corn? Century succeeded century and, content to regard it as a mere food, they could not meet the challenge on which, as Mr. Toynbee recognizes, civilization hung.

Every damp spell rotted some of their stored corn. The historian watches, his breathing suspended, and sees the pointer settle toward decline. They threw the stuff out for the birds, rebuking their supernaturals, and never knew that the supernaturals had given them a mash.

The Americans got no help from heaven or the saints but they knew what to do with corn. In the heroic age our forefathers invented self-government, the Constitution, and bourbon, and on the way to them they invented rye. ("If I don't get rye whiskey I surely will die" expresses one of Mr. Toynbee's inexorable laws of history more succinctly than ever he did.) And that shows our proper place in the international order: no other nation ever gave mankind two whiskeys. Like our political institutions, which would be inconceivable without them, both express our national characteristics; both are distilled not only from our native grains but from our native vigor, suavity, generosity, peacefulness, and love of accord.

We have not fully lived up to them but, except for the small company of the best who keep idealism alight, have been content to live less purely than we might. We recognize the ideal: we have embodied it in a folk saying that constitutes our highest tribute to a first-class man, "He's a gentleman, a scholar, and a judge of good whiskey." Unhappily it is more often generous than deserved. Anyone who will work hard enough can become a scholar and nearly anyone can have or acquire gentility, but there are never many judges of good whiskey. Besides you and me there are only a few others. One reason is that there is little good whiskey to judge—we do not hold our fellows to the fullness of the nation's genius.

During our lapse into barbarism there was much scorn of Prohibition whiskey. But there was just about as much good whiskey during Prohibition as there had been before or is now. (It was then that a taste for Scotch, previously confined to a few rich men who drank an alien liquor as a symbol of conspicuous waste, spread among us—a blight which the true-born American regards as more destructive to the ancient virtues than communism. Regard it less as a repudiation of our heritage than as the will to believe. If we paid the bootlegger for Scotch, we thought, we might get the Real McCoy, but one whiskey is as easily made as another where they print the labels and compound the flavoring.) The good whiskey was hard to find then but when hadn't it been? Below the level of the truly good we went on drinking the same stuff we had drunk before. We are still drinking it now. The untutored are.

The bootlegger, that is, did just what the publican had done during our golden age, when the saloon business was organized on a basis of straightforward, standardized adulteration. Pick up any manual of trade practices published in that vanished time. You will find listed eleven grades of bourbon (or rye) that the proprietor is to compound on the premises, arranged in the order of their cost to him. The first five contain no whiskey at all; they are neutral spirits plus water and some sophisticating ingredients; the cheapest one has no flavoring but sugar. The next five are neutral spirits and whiskey mixed in varying proportions, eight to one in the cheapest, fifty-fifty in the most expensive, plus flavoring and coloring matter. The eleventh is two raw whiskeys in equal amounts, plus a dash of a somewhat better one, plus prune juice to supply body, and the manual says "this is considered the finest of all grades, as it contains no spirits." Getting past the eleventh, you reached unadulterated straight whiskey at its youngest and could then progress by regular steps to the best bonded stock. If you could trust the publican.

In our enlightened age we have shifted the burden of adulteration from the proprietor to a working partnership between the manufacturer and the Bureau of Internal Revenue. Everything (almost) is printed on the label for you to see and if you want less fusel oil, which is removed by the distilling process but restored in the flavoring extract, you can climb through the hierarchy as high as you choose to. If you trust the bar. Do not be cynical: there are some bars which you can trust and which will serve you no greater degree of adulteration than you may order by brand name. But of these, how many can you trust not to practice dilution? If you have found one, you have found a jewel and you are a judge of good whiskey.

This is for the best. Bars are for convenience and the fleeting hour, but the Americans are a home-loving people and the devotions proper to their indigenous water of life are best conducted in the home. And let us be fair: though there is never much good whiskey, there is always enough to supply those who reverence it. Resolution, obstinacy, and the spirit of our pioneers will take you to it in the end, though you had better provide yourself with thick-soled shoes, for the route may be long and is certain to be hard. (Having located a deposit, you will of course report to other members of the fellowship in good standing.)

Well, how good is it? Out in the bourbon country where the honor of the taste buds runs 180-proof, you can get an argument in ten seconds and a duel in five minutes by saying that it is as good as it used to be. Men weathered to wisdom by long experience will tell you that the glory departed when the big combine bought up the little local distillery. Contrariwise, the big distiller will tell you that the little stillhouse was steadily poisoning Kentucky—that he himself with his prime ingredients and methods controlled by modern science is making better bourbon than the melancholy gaffer ever tasted in the old time.

Devoted men, hewing a way through masses of legend, superstition, and vulgar error, have come out with one finding that leans a little toward the opinion of the elders. The old-time distillers, known locally as the priesthood, put their whiskey into bond below proof, that is with the percentage of alcohol under fifty. Four years of the aging process brought it to proof and they bottled it as it was, uncut.

The modern distiller, known everywhere as a servant of the people, impelled as much by government regulation as by the higher excise, bonds his stuff at a few per cent above proof. Aging in bond increases the percentage still more, so before bottling he cuts it back to proof with water.

There is instruction here: when you add water to whiskey, you change the taste. In the moment of devotion, therefore, the faithful will drink it straight. And, sirs, let your demeanor be worthy of that moment. Attentively but slowly, with the poise of a confidence that has never been betrayed since the Founding Fathers, with full consciousness that providence has bestowed a surpassing bounty on the Americans or that they have earned it for themselves. Our more self-conscious brethren, the oenophilists, are good men too and must not be dispraised but they vaingloriously claim more than we can allow. Their vintages do indeed have many subtleties but they are not superior to ours, only different. Like first-rate wines true rye and true bourbon wake delight with a rich and magical plenitude of overtones and rhymes and resolved dissonances and a contrapuntal succession of fleeting aftertastes. They dignify man as possessing a palate that responds to them and ennoble his soul as capable of shimmering in the response.

The modern distiller will tell you that whiskey comes to full maturity in its sixth year, that thereafter its quality declines. Do not believe him. He does not, obviously, believe himself. At mounting expense he keeps some of his product in bond for eight years and charges correspondingly, and the result is well worth the mark-up. Eight years is the longest period for which he can get bond but at still greater expense he keeps some in the wood for four years more—and with a twelve-year-old whiskey at hand Americans can hold their peace and let who will praise alien civilizations. The distiller will also tell you that nothing happens to the finest after it is bottled, and again he is wrong. He is especially wrong about rye. In the spacious time when taxes accounted for only four-fifths the price of whiskey, the wise bought it by the keg, in fact bought many kegs, and bottled it themselves and laid it away for their posterity. Better to inherit a rye so laid away in 1915 than great riches. I have known women past their youth and of no blatant charm to make happy marriages because Uncle John, always deplored as a wastrel by the family, had made them his residual legatee.

Such a marriage is always successful; a helpmeet so dowered will never lose her worth in a husband's heart. A rye thus kept becomes an evanescence, essential grace. It is not to be drunk but only tasted, and to be tasted only when one is conscious of having lived purely.

We drink whiskey straight not only for the palate's sake but in patriotic commemoration of the dead who made us a great nation. They walked up to the bar, stood on their own two feet or on one foot when the rail had been polished that morning, and called for whiskey straight in awareness of the national destiny, and we were a sound society, and without fear. . . . All those decades, all those bars. The St. Nicholas, toward which the Englishman on tour made by hackney coach direct from the boat, so that the magnificence of the New World could burst on him in his first hour. The Knickerbocker, which has been exactly reproduced in the most beautiful corner of paradise, admission by card only and saints to serve a probationary period before they can get cards. The Planters House, the Murray Hill, the Parker House, the Palmer House, the Mark Hopkins, Joe's Place, the Last Chance Saloon—Pittsburgh and Painted Post and Phoenix, New Orleans and Nashville and Nome—river boats and tents at trail's end and tables set up under the elms when the clergy met in convocation or the young gentlemen graduated from college—the last Americans in knee breeches, the first in trousers, deacons in black broadcloth, planters in white linen, cordwainers and hardrock men and conductors of the steam cars and drovers and principals of seminaries for young women and circuit riders and editors and sportsmen and peddlers—twenty-two hundred counties, forty-eight states, the outlying possessions. The roads ran out in dust or windswept grass and we went on, we came to a river no one had crossed and we forded it, the land angled upward and we climbed the peak and exulted, the desert stretched ahead and we plunged into it—and always the honeybee flew ahead of us and there was a hooker of the real stuff at day's end and one for the road tomorrow.

Nothing stopped us, nothing could stop us so long as the corncob plugged the mouth of the jug, and we built new commonwealths and constitutions and distilleries as we traveled, the world gaped, and destiny said here's how.

But there are times when neither the palate nor patriotism is to be consulted, and this is a versatile invention, ministering to many needs. That other supreme American gift to world culture, the martini cocktail, will do only at its own hour—when darkness begins to fall from the wings of night and the heart cries out for a swift healing. But man's lot is hard and distressful and he may want a drink at almost any hour, midafternoon, after dinner, at midnight, and some say in the morning. (These last were reared in error, learned to drink rum at their mother's knee, and are still bound by the silver cord.) At such times you may add water to the spirits of America. Charged water is permitted with rye, if you like it that way, and in the splendid city of St. Louis, which civilization made her abode long before the Yankees stopped honing their crabbedness on rum, you may call it "seltzer." But always plain water with the corn-spirit, "bourbon and branch water" our brethren say south of Mason's and Dixon's Line, "bourbon and ditch" west of the hundredth meridian. (You may detect the presence of the Adversary by a faint odor of brimstone and a request for ginger ale.) And no ice. Ice is for cocktails.

The water calls on our genius to show its gentleness, taking you by the hand and leading you as softly as the flowers breathe toward beneficence. Or as the homing bird soars on unmoving wings at eventide. On this firm foundation the Republic stands. In England they call for a division and the ministry falls, in Russia they shoot a thousand commissars, but in freedom's land they recess, speak the hallowed name of Daniel Webster, and send out for Dan'l's stand-by and some soda. Strife ceases, the middle way is found, the bill gets passed, and none shall break our union.

But first of all this touch softer than woman's is to restore you and me to humanity. I do not need the record, a priest, or a philosopher to remind me what I am, timorous, self-deceived, ground down by failure and betrayal of the dream, evidence that though mankind has evolved past the earthworm it has not got much farther. And you, you don't fool me, I know you, I need only look at you or hear you speak—if you were to quote the catechism, "God made me," you would be boastfully lying and on the edge of blasphemy, or over the edge.

The hell we are. This is merely the moroseness of tired and buffeted men and help is at hand to brush the illusion away. When weariness and discouragement come upon us there are many things we might put into our heads to steal away our brains—Marx, the Koran, *Mein Kampf,* addresses made at Commencement or on Mother's Day, the Chicago *Tribune.* But we were nourished in an honorable tradition and we don't, and I'll have mine with soda. The barb is blunted, the knife sheathed; a star appears above the treetop, the clatter of fools dies out, and all unseen there was a fire burning on the hearth. In a few minutes we see each other as we truly are, sound men, stout hearts, lovers of the true and upholders of the good. There's a good deal in what you're saying and you say it marvelously well. Dismay, annoyance, resentment—we should have remembered that they are traps the world sets for the unwary. The battle is to the brave, the game to the skillful, the day's job to who shall do it fortified. What a man needs is a moment of quickening, a reminder by wisdom laced with a little water that there are dignity and gallant deeds and dauntlessness and disregard of the odds, that evil yields and the shadows flee away. A moment of renewal and then get back in there and pitch, we're doing all right. Well, maybe a short one—and hey, there's Bill, get him over here for a minute, a man needs to be told it's all a lie.

The alchemists never found the philosopher's stone but they knew that when they did it would, by a process of fermentation and distillation, transmute base metals into gold. They were on the right track, they made a good start, and the genius of America finished the job. I give you confusion to the enemies of the Republic.

Subways Are for Sleeping

by EDMUND G. LOVE

MARCH, 1956

This word portrait of a New York City bum—a minor master-piece of authentic detail—was the result of the author's affinity for him. Mr. Love used to take a long walk in Manhattan during the evenings and, he says, bums would walk right past twenty people to get at him. He got interested in the species and met the subject of this portrait in Greenwich Village one evening. Henry Shelby is not the man's real name, of course. Mr. Love has done a good deal of free-lance writing and one movie script. During the war he was a combat historian in the Pacific. He holds a master's degree from the University of Michigan.

On March 4, 1953, at approximately 11:30 P.M., Henry Shelby walked into the New York City hotel where he had maintained an apartment for five months. Upon asking for his key at the desk, he was informed by the clerk that he had been locked out until such time as his bill was settled. The bill amounted to about one hundred and thirteen dollars. At the moment, Shelby had about fourteen dollars, no job, and no friends upon whom he felt free to call for help. Without any argument, he turned and walked back out the door.

In the time that has passed since that night, he has returned to the hotel only once, and then merely to see if he had any mail. He has not attempted to retrieve any of his belongings held by the management. With the exception of approximately three and one-half months, in the summer of 1953, he has been one of the thousands of men in various stages of vagrancy who wander the streets of New York City at all hours of the day and night.

Henry Shelby, today, is forty-one years old, but looks at least five years younger. He is five feet, eleven and one-half inches tall, weighs 162 pounds. His hair is black but thinning, and his eyes are a deep blue. He has no disfigurements, and his bearing is good. The key to his personality lies in his eyes which express the depth of his feeling, or a

58

quiet humor, depending upon his mood. When he is deep in thought, or troubled, he is apt to trace patterns on the floor, or in the dirt, with the toe of his shoe. At other times he moves briskly, and with some of the grace and sureness of an athlete.

He is a graduate of the University of Michigan with a master's degree in economics. He also holds a life teacher's certificate in the state of Michigan and was, at one time, a teacher in the public schools of Lansing. His master's degree studies were concentrated in the field of accounting procedure, and for four years after World War II, he was an accountant with the Post Office Department in Washington. His associates there consider him an excellent man in this field, and at least two of them say that he could probably qualify as a certified public accountant. In addition to these qualifications, he is experienced and capable in the field of public relations, where his approach has been described as "fresh" and "honest."

The city of New York has long been noted for the number and variety of its vagrants. Estimates as to the number of homeless and penniless men and women run from a conservative ten thousand to somewhere around half a million. Vagrants in other parts of the United States are a migratory lot, usually moving with the weather, but the New York variety stay put, occupying park benches, flophouses, gutters, and doorways in all seasons. There are many who possess qualifications as rich as Henry Shelby's. There are many who are literally human derelicts living out their days in a drunken stupor, waiting for an obscure death in the river or a ward at Bellevue. In between there are as many gradations as there are strata in normal society. Almost the only things all vagrants have in common are a hard luck story and an air of bewilderment. Not all of them have lost hope.

Henry Shelby is not a hopeless man, but he is certainly bewildered. He himself describes his present life as treading water, waiting to see how things come out. "In the meantime," he says, "I'm getting along all right. I'm perfectly happy."

In his months as a vagrant he has become an expert at management and has learned to put first things first. In his case this means food, cleanliness, and shelter, in that order. He prides himself on the fact that he has never panhandled, never visited a soup kitchen, or taken a night's lodging in one of the various hostels maintained by charitable agencies in the city. He has accepted handouts, but he can recall only one instance where anyone ever stepped up to him and gave him money: One night in the middle of winter he noticed advertisements for the première of a motion picture at a Broadway theater. He arrived early and took up a prominent position against the ropes under the marquee. As he stood there, watching the celebrities arrive in their limousines, a man came over to him and placed an unfolded ten-dollar bill in his hand.

Shelby has never been completely penniless except for one very brief period when he left New York. He has set fifteen cents, which represents subway fare, as the absolute minimum below which he will not allow his finances to sink. He has no maximum, but rarely possesses more than thirty dollars, which represents about one week's salary at present minimum levels. He acquires his money in a variety of ways. He is able to pick up a day's work here and there, carrying sandwich boards, working as a roustabout on the waterfront, washing dishes in cheap restaurants, shoveling snow for the city.

When he gets money, he nurses it carefully. He can tell, one minute after he gets it, exactly how long it will last, because he knows what he's going to eat, how many cigarettes he is going to smoke, and the amount it will cost him for lodging, or incidentals. There are no extras in his life.

Virtually all of Shelby's cash goes for food and cigarettes. His breakfasts, invariably, consist of a glass of fruit or vegetable juice; his lunches, of a sandwich, usually a frankfurter, and a glass of milk. His one substantial meal is supper, and into it he piles all the dietary necessities he has missed since he last ate such a meal. His plate is apt to be loaded with green vegetables, cooked vegetables, and meat. He will haggle back and forth with the counterman in order to get these items, usually trading off potatoes and dessert for them. He never looks at the contents of a meal until he looks at the prices and he always chooses the cheapest meal on the menu, unless it contains sea food, which he detests. He knows where all the best food bargains in town are to be found. A bargain means quantity, but once or twice a week he will seek out a place which serves something of which he is especially fond.

Between meals he drinks coffee, usually two cups during the morning and three cups during the afternoon and evening. When he is especially broke he cuts out regular meals and subsists entirely on coffee, loading all the sugar and cream he can into his cup. He explains that these are free calories, and that calories, no matter what form they take, will keep him going until he is able to eat regularly again.

Shelby says that the truest statement he has ever heard is that no one will ever starve to death in the United States, and his technique for getting food when he is low on money is a simple one. He walks the streets until he finds a restaurant with a sign in the window that reads "dishwasher wanted," or "counterman wanted." He goes in and works long enough to pay for a meal and earn a little extra money. Usually he completes whatever constitutes a full day's work, but if the restaurant is a pleasant place, if he is treated well and the food is good, he may stay a week, or even longer. He is a good worker, and is well liked by his bosses and fellow employees. Many of the latter are men like himself.

He has learned a lot of odd jobs around kitchens and has filled in as a chef at two cafeterias, and as a short-order cook at a counter restaurant. At one place where he worked for five weeks, the manager recommended him for the managership of another unit in the chain which had fallen vacant. In this particular restaurant Shelby can always be sure of a job of some kind when he is broke; the manager will put him to work washing windows if there is nothing else available. The same condition holds true at five or six other places in town, but Shelby never uses them unless he is really desperate. He refers to them humorously as his social security.

Shelby usually allots no more than fifteen cents a day for shelter. Occasionally he pays more than this, but only when he has gotten by for two or three days without spending anything extra. Shelter means a place to sleep to Shelby, nothing else. His great preference, month in and month out, is for the Sixth and Eighth Avenue subways. He very rarely sleeps on the IRT or BMT. The IRT, with its ramshackle, noisy cars and its seating arrangement, is uncomfortable. The BMT has suitable accommodations, but, as Shelby describes it, "an undesirable clientele."

Shelby usually boards the Eighth Avenue Subway at Pennsylvania Station between midnight and one in the morning and takes the first express that comes along. At that hour there is usually a seat, especially in the front car, and he immediately settles down and drops off to sleep. He has developed the happy faculty of being able to drop off, or awaken, almost at will. He sleeps lightly, not because he is afraid of being robbed—he never has enough money to worry about that—but because he is very cautious about oversleeping. The vagrant who is still sleeping soundly when the train reaches the end of the line is more than likely to be picked up and lodged in jail by the transportation police.

Upon reaching the end of the line, Shelby walks up the stairs from the train platform to the next level. The turnstiles are at this level, and rest rooms have been placed inside the turnstiles. He retires to one of these rest rooms, finds a booth, fastens the door, and smokes a leisurely cigarette. It is supposedly a misdemeanor to carry lighted tobacco within the turnstile area, but Shelby says he discovered quite early in his career that even the police use the privacy of the rest rooms to have a quiet cigarette. Of course, he takes no chances. If there is a policeman anywhere on the turnstile level he will forgo his smoke.

After his cigarette, he goes back to the train platform and boards the next train going in the opposite direction from the one he has just come. He quickly settles into a seat and goes to sleep again. He remains asleep until he reaches the other end of the line, then, as before, has his smoke and reboards a train. This time his nap is much shorter because he debarks at the Jay Street-Borough Hall station in Brooklyn and transfers to the Sixth Avenue Subway. On this he makes a full round trip, going all the way out to Queens, back to the Brooklyn end of the line, and then back to Jay Street. There he reboards the Eighth Avenue, which he rides back to Penn Station.

The whole trip consumes from four and a half to five and a half hours, during the course of which he has probably netted four hours of sleep. Over the months he has learned many of the habits and assignments of the transportation police, and he tries to keep himself from being too familiar a figure. For this reason he does not depend entirely upon the subway and does not dare ride it oftener than every other night.

On his off nights, in good weather, he sometimes uses the two great parks, Central and Prospect. By varying his hours of repose, carefully selecting secluded spots, and transferring his resting places often, he can spend one night a week in either one or the other of them. Also, in warm weather, there are fire escapes. Because he knows the city as well as he does, Shelby has been able to locate several covered, and therefore secluded, ones. Most of them are attached to theaters or warehouses and offer ideal accommodations. For some reason, the police never seem to bother vagrants who occupy these emergency exits. And on three or four occasions during the summer Shelby manages to get out to one of the beaches near the city. He can sleep unmolested there, especially on a hot night. There are always legitimate sleepers, as he calls them, who are trying to escape the heat.

Naturally, in the fall, winter, and early spring, Shelby has to find other places. The benches in the waiting rooms at Grand Central, Penn Station, and the Port Authority Bus Terminal are his favorite outside of the subway. As in every other place, however, there are strict rules of conduct which must be observed. Shelby learned early that the station police in each of the three establishments have set habits. They make two routine checks during the course of a night. At Grand Central, for example, these checks come at one-thirty and five-thirty. Between the checks there are both policemen and plain-clothes men on duty in the waiting room throughout the night, and they wander up and down, carefully checking trouble spots. Ordinarily, however, these roving guardians will not disturb people who are stretched out on the benches asleep. Between the checks, therefore, it is possible to get almost four hours of uninterrupted sleep in a prone position. Conditions at Penn Station are about the same, and at the bus terminal the checks are farther apart, but the lights are brighter and the crowds larger, giving less room to stretch out.

Shelby keeps, as part of his equipment for sleeping in one of the three terminals, three tickets: to Poughkeepsie, New York; Princeton, New Jersey; and Elizabeth, New Jersey, one for each of the three lines. Inspection of timetables has revealed that there are no busses or trains leaving New York for these points between one and six in the morning. In emergencies, should the station police question him too closely, Shelby flashes the appropriate ticket and claims that he missed the last train and is waiting for the first one in the morning. This has always worked, but on one occasion a station policeman escorted him to a six-thirty train and made certain he got on it. Shelby got off at 125th Street and walked back to Grand Central.

Shelby regards sleeping in hotel lobbies as an unsatisfactory experience, yet he feels bound to try it every now and then. No lobby can be occupied during the night, and daytime occupancy is limited to about two hours at most. While house officers will not ordinarily run a respectably dressed man out into the street, they will shake him awake every hour or so. In order to get four hours of sleep, Shelby estimates that he has to visit eight hotels during a day. He always apologizes profusely for having dozed off and never visits the same hotel oftener than every third month.

Shelby says that it is always advisable to carry something when sleeping in a lobby. House officers are apt to respect a man's privacy if he has an umbrella or brief case lying in his lap. When Shelby plans to use a hotel lobby, he will wander up and down the subway trains the day before until he finds what he is looking for. Subways are full of things that are suitable for hotel lobbies. He always turns in whatever he has found to the Board of Transportation's Lost and Found Department after he has used it, and he is always careful to check back later to find out whether there has been any reward. He collected twelve and a half dollars this way last year.

Shelby thinks that all-night theaters are the most overrated sleeping places for men like himself. He has used them, and still does occasionally, but compared to the subway, they are inordinately expensive and their seats, though much softer, are much less suited to sleeping. They tip back too much, and the head is apt to snap backward instead of forward. This always awakens Shelby. Furthermore, one cannot very well lean one's head on one's arm when elbow resting room has to be fought for with one's neighbor. The pictures are noisy in unexpected places, and the sounds that are thrown out from the screen are loud and unorthodox. On top of this, Shelby has found that no matter what picture is being shown, he cannot keep from watching it to see how it comes out. Thus, instead of getting some sleep, he gets entertained.

Most people do their personal grooming in the privacy of their own homes. Because Henry Shelby is homeless, he cannot. But for two reasons he places more importance on his personal appearance than he does on having a place to sleep. First, he is naturally a neat and tidy man to whom uncleanliness is distasteful. Second, good grooming is a safety factor in his existence. The police will always pick up an unkempt man and will generally walk right by a tidy man. A shower is not only a comfort, but a good investment.

From each five-dollar bill he gets, Shelby sets aside enough money to provide himself with a bath. If he goes six days without one, he will stop eating until he can pay for one. Most of Shelby's baths are taken in the public rooms of Grand Central Station and cost sixty-five cents. Shaving is also a problem. At Shelby's age, he cannot go for more than twenty-four hours without acquiring a heavily shaded face. After that his beard is apt to become a heavy stubble. Nevertheless, he tries to stretch the time between shaves to at least thirty-six hours for economic reasons: it costs twenty-five cents to use one of the booths at Grand Central set aside for this purpose. Like most New York City vagrants, Shelby always carries a safety razor in his pocket and will take any opportunity he can to get in a quick, free shave and a chance to brush his teeth. He uses ordinary soap for shaving cream.

Clothing is another important item of appearance. With the exception of his outer garments, Shelby owns two of everything: two white shirts, two suits of underwear, two pairs of socks, and two neckties. One set is always on his back and the other is usually in storage at some laundry in the Grand Central area. Whenever he takes his bath, Shelby drops by the laundry first and picks up his clean linen. After his shower he carefully wraps the soiled clothes in a bundle and leaves them in another laundry to be washed.

His outer garments are kept as neat as possible. Once or twice a week he drops in at one of the small tailor shops around town and sits in his shirt tails while his coat and trousers are being pressed. Unfortunately, he has never found a place where he can sit in a booth while the clothes are being cleaned. When his garments are quite dirty, and he gets enough money ahead, he picks up his clean laundry and retires to a cheap but good hotel. There he engages a room, paying for it in advance. Once the door is closed on the bellhop, he strips and calls valet service. For the next twenty-four hours, while the cleaners are at work on his coat and trousers, he spends his time in bed, or under the shower. He has slept for twenty-two hours on these occasions, and taken as many as fifteen showers. He never gets too much sleep or too many showers.

The whole twenty-four-hour period in the hotel, including cleaning, costs him about seven dollars. Shelby considers this gross extravagance, since his weekly average expenditure is about eight dollars, but for some time he never seemed to accumulate enough money to buy a second suit. Besides, he always comes out of his stay with a tremendous sense of pleasure and well-being.

One of the astounding things about Shelby's existence is that he has become a recluse, just as surely as though he lived on a desert island. For three or four days at a time he will speak to no one, nor will anyone speak to him. He is not solitary by nature, but his way of life and his desire to continue it without molestation impose this penalty upon him. While he might like to engage the policeman in the Grand Central waiting room in conversation, he realizes that if he did, he might be recognized easily the next time he visited there, and all subsequent visits would gradually peg him as a homeless person, making him liable to arrest and harassment.

This solitude has brought him one great problem which he senses but finds difficult to describe: the problem of passage of time. Shelby is waiting for something. He himself does not know what it is. When it comes he will either go back into the world from which he came, or sink out of sight in the morass of alcoholism or despair that has engulfed other vagrants. While he is waiting, he is plagued by a restlessness that keeps him on the move for seventeen or eighteen hours a day. He is likely to say that he moves about as much as he does because policemen will not stop a man who looks as though he is coming from some place or going to some place. What he does not say, because he does not realize it, is that he is working to keep his time occupied.

Shelby's search for entertainment has led him into every nook and cranny of the city and brought him knowledge which he might not otherwise have gained. One idiosyncrasy that he has discovered but cannot account for is the attitude of station policemen toward book readers. After seven-thirty in the evening, in order to read a book in Grand Central or Penn Station, a person either has to wear horn-rimmed glasses, or look exceptionally prosperous. Anyone else is apt to come under surveillance. On the other hand, newspaper readers never seem to attract attention and even the seediest vagrant can sit in Grand Central all night without being molested if he continues to read a paper. Shelby therefore spends one or two hours a night going over the daily papers. He regularly reads all seven final editions of New York journals, which he picks out of trash baskets.

Shelby is extraordinarily fond of museums and galleries and has become something of an art expert. Vagrants are rarely molested in New York museums and galleries. Shelby is apt to smile and say this is because the guards can never distinguish between a legitimate bum and an artistic one. They never disturb a person like him because they never know when they are trying to eject an artist who is holding a one-man show on the third floor.

Shelby began frequenting the big marble-coated buildings many months ago in search of shelter and warmth. He followed the guides around on their tours, often three or four times a day. In order to seem part of the group making the tour he would ask questions. And by this time he knows enough to stump most of the guides. He has developed a genuine love for the subject, knows where every show in town is being held and what it contains, and is thinking of trying to do a little painting himself. But when he goes to the shows, he is also still on the lookout for some obscure nook or cranny where he can stretch out and sleep for an hour or two. Even a corner behind a Grecian column where a man can sleep upright without interruption is valuable.

Another of Shelby's pastimes is to take the ferry ride from the Battery to Staten Island and back. He calls this the poor man's ocean voyage. Unfortunately, the round trip costs ten cents, which puts it in the luxury class. More often, he boards one of the numerous Central Railroad of New Jersey ferries and makes three or four round trips to the Jersey shore. If he gets on during the rush-hour periods he is not noticed and there is no expense.

Pursuing this pastime Shelby has picked up a surprising amount of information on navigation, and he is rapidly becoming an authority on the New York tidal flow. He seems to get a great deal of enjoyment out of criticizing the pilots of the ferries if they do not bring their vessels squarely into the slips, and almost the first thing he reads in the New York papers is the shipping news. Two or three times a week he journeys to the waterfront to watch the arrival or departure of one of the big liners. On other occasions he will go down to the Jersey ferry slips and board the little vessel that he estimates will come closest to the big ships as they move up the river or put out to sea.

The city offers other free sources of diversion too. Shelby always follows a fire engine; has a nose for street fights; and, if he stumbles upon an accident, never leaves the scene until the last policeman has closed his notebook. He stops to listen to every sidewalk preacher he comes across and likes to sing the hymns just for the pleasure of singing something. He knows every major construction project in town, but rarely watches such routine phases of the work as excavation or riveting. He looks the site over and then shows up at the exact moment some critical problem is about to be solved.

He is a steady visitor at the various courts around town, and is what he describes as a sucker for band music. For this reason he believes he is happier in New York than he would be in any other city in the world. New York is the only place where there is a parade of some kind every day in the year. On some days there are two or three. Last Armistice Day, Shelby visited five parades and took part in one.

The peculiar advantages of the microfilm room of the New York Public Library, which he came upon almost by accident, are probably Shelby's unique discovery. He had been advised by another vagrant that the library was a good place to keep warm on a cold day, and that it offered an opportunity for an hour or two of sleep. Several days later he made his first call there, provided with what he considered a plausible excuse for visiting the institution. He went to the main desk and asked for a copy of the *New York Times* for November 10, 1936. He was referred to the microfilm room, where the attendant produced a roll of film instead of the paper. He was then escorted to one of several viewing machines which were placed helter-skelter in a sort of alcove off to one side of a large room. Shelby put the film in the machine and looked at the image. Within half an hour, as he turned the crank, he dozed off. He was not disturbed and eventually woke up about five hours later.

He says, now, that at the time this seemed too good to be true, so a week later he went back again to see if it was an accident. He arrived about nine-fifteen in the morning and slept until almost four-thirty in the afternoon, again without being disturbed.

He since has become cognizant of several things. Most men in his condition who visit the Public Library go to the reading rooms. Either they have never heard of the microfilm room, or they underestimate its possibilities. Consequently, the attendants there have never met a real vagrant face to face. They assume that anyone who has heard of microfilm and wishes to use it is in search of learning. They check the film out to the applicant and never follow up. Moreover, the accommodations are very comfortable. The room is warm, and the upright film-display stands give a man an excellent place to rest his head.

For some time, Shelby put the microfilm room at the top of his list as a place of shelter, then suddenly he realized that it was a far more valuable place for pure entertainment. He never goes there to sleep now, but he often goes in early in the morning and spends the entire day reading. He has read all the old issues of the *New York Times* that are available on film, all his favorite comic strips from the date of their inception to the present, and every column Damon Runyon ever wrote.

A by-product of his many hours in the microfilm room is a system for playing the races which he developed by virtue of having been able to study every racing chart published in New York over the past twenty years. He has put this system to a test twice. At one time he worked quite steadily for almost a month and, with twenty-five dollars in his pocket, visited Aqueduct Race Track where he won eighty-seven dollars and forty cents, after expenses. Prudently, he took the money and bought himself a new suit of clothes, leaving the original twenty-five dollars untouched. A few days later he took the twenty-five and went to Belmont Park, where he lost it all. He hasn't visited the track since, but he remains an avid racing fan and plays the horses regularly in the microfilm room. Nowadays, however, he saves all the races until cold weather sets in and plays during the winter months. He never looks at the racing results beforehand. "I might just as well be honest about it," he says.

Shelby's favorite of all forms of recreation is walking. He usually walks the streets of Manhattan for four to ten hours a day, covering anywhere from five to twenty-five miles. He has walked the full length of every up-and-down avenue in the city and crossed the island on every crosstown street. He is a walking encyclopedia on plaques and knows every traffic bottleneck and short cut in town. He loves to window-shop and knows when most of the stores change their displays. At some time every day he manages to pass the window of the Christian Science Reading Room on Park Avenue and solemnly reads the Bible passage marked there.

At one time he estimated that he had about exhausted the possibilities of exploration in Manhattan and decided to concentrate on Brooklyn. He crossed the Brooklyn Bridge on foot one day, and on two other occasions took the subway. At the end of the third trip he gave the project up. "Walking in Brooklyn is like walking in Lansing, Michigan. I have the feeling I've seen everything before," he says. "Manhattan isn't like that."

At present, Henry Shelby seems content to take things as they come. "I don't know how long I'll live this life," he said not long ago, as he traced a design in the dirt with his foot. "I don't have much trouble. I've never gotten drunk and lain in a doorway all day. My name's never been on a police blotter for vagrancy. I haven't had to beg.

Maybe if things were like they were twenty years ago, when everybody was a bum, I might change. Maybe something will happen that will force me to change, one way or another. Yes, I guess that's about it, but it hasn't happened yet, and things seem so easy and natural this way they are now, that it's just as though it was supposed to be that way. I'm just not going to look at the future. All I can tell anybody, now, is that I intend to be up at a little delicatessen I know on Broadway. They serve a hell of a good boiled beef dinner up there for sixty-eight cents." He looked up at one of the big street clocks. "Which reminds me. If I'm going to get there by six o'clock, I'd better get going. Takes me almost an hour to walk it." His listener asked him why he didn't take the subway.

"Subways are for sleeping," Shelby said, smiled, and walked off.

Conversation at Midnight

by JOHN FISCHER

JANUARY, 1958

The Russian is the true realist in the world today, while we are "a bunch of dreamy poets." Such is the startling theme of this report by John Fischer, writing from Austria. Mr. Fischer started writing for the magazine in 1935, when a Rhodes Scholar at Oxford. He is a former editor-in-chief of Harper & Brothers trade book department, and since 1953 has been the seventh editor-in-chief of Harper's Magazine. *He is the author of* Master Plan, U. S. A. *and* Why They Behave Like Russians.

This castle is supposed to be haunted. A Nazi gauleiter shot his wife, his three children, and himself in the little lookout room on the top floor that morning when he saw the American tanks break into the valley; and other troubled spirits (I am told) have been mewling and clanking around the staircases for a good two hundred years. So it was only sensible to take precautions.

The best protection against ghosts, Father Florian said, was a bottle of the red wine put up by his fellow monks at the Peterskeller. It is not very good wine, but it is strong, and after a few glasses any apparition would hardly be noticeable. As my spiritual adviser (self-appointed) he had taken the liberty of bringing a liter with him.

"I detest being interrupted by spooks," he said as he pulled the cork. "Or, for that matter, by anyone else. Close the door. I have to reprove you, and I don't want those people wandering in with their silly questions."

This was unfair. "Those people" are fifty-eight young men and women who are, for the moment, living here; Father Florian is merely an occasional visitor, usually uninvited. They have come from sixteen European countries, because each of them has a professional interest in the United States, and because the Schloss is now occupied by a curious kind of school, known as The Seminar in American Studies. It is true that they often cross-examine the five Americans who serve as faculty until all hours of the night, but their questions are seldom silly. They are people of trained intelligence—diplomats, newspapermen, teachers, sociologists, civil servants—and their inquiries sometimes are uncomfortably sharp. Father Florian never asks questions; he gives answers, whether you want them or not. He is dogmatic, fat, and impertinent; and I am fond of him.

He filled two glasses and settled himself in the only comfortable chair in my study.

"The trouble with you Americans . . ." he said.

"Look," I interrupted, "let's get back to the ghosts. For the last month these people have been telling me what is wrong with Americans, and I am beginning to get the idea. We are a bunch of crude materialists. We've got no culture, no respect for tradition, no sense of history, no ideals, no palate. . . ."

"Nonsense," Father Florian said. "It is true that most Europeans believe those legends, but I am going to tell you what is *really* wrong with America. I traveled back and forth across your country for seven years, making a serious study of the American soul. And I don't think you understand yourselves any better than these youngsters who have been talking at you."

He loosened the rope he wore around the middle of his cassock and eased his throat with a little wine.

"The real trouble," he said, "is that you are a bunch of dreamy poets. You are besotted with culture. You spend more time and money on it than you can afford. Idealism is a fine thing, but you Americans have carried it too far—to the point where you can no longer bear to face a hard, material fact when you meet one. This is dangerous. You will have to learn to be practical, or you will perish.

"Now don't misunderstand me. We are grateful for your cultural leadership, though naturally we can't admit it. We have to snarl a little, to save our self-respect—but we are soaking up your culture like a parched field soaks up rain. We play your music, read your novels, and wear your clothes all over Europe. Look at all our girls in blue jeans and pony tails, and all our little boys in cowboy champs. Chaps? Ah, yes, thank you.

"Even alcoholic Paris, thank Heaven, is being infiltrated with milk bars, and half the boys in my parish are trying to play the trumpet like Satchmo. My city of Vienna invented musical comedy, but *Kiss Me, Kate* is the biggest hit there since the war. This is embarrassing, because we haven't produced a good musical of our own for thirty years. And Germany, which is temporarily out of playwrights, is making a national hero out of Thornton Wilder.

"At this very minute there isn't a housewife east of the Danube who isn't scheming to get a vacuum cleaner, a washing machine, and an icebox. Wonderful aids to the spiritual life. When a woman doesn't have to spend all her waking hours in drudgery, she can find time for literature and art and even, sometimes, for the Church. If we Europeans have a religious revival we should give part of the thanks to the United States. We won't do it, of course."

A strangulated moan began to reverberate through the west wall. Father Florian cocked an ear and suggested that perhaps we should send for another bottle. No need, I explained. That was the normal voice of the neo-baroque plumbing in the bathroom—the one with the three crystal chandeliers—which Max Reinhardt had installed when he lived here.

"Nevertheless I shall take another glass," the friar said, "for this castle and all its ghosts can bear testimony to the warning I am about to deliver. Schloss Leopoldskron is, in fact, a relic of a cultural spree, much like the one on which America is now embarking. And I must warn you that a nation can pay too high for such a flowering of the spirit.

"That is precisely the mistake we Austrians made a couple of centuries ago. Our Empire was then the first power on the Continent. We had recently won a terrible war. Our armies were invincible; our economy was thriving; our political system obviously was the soundest ever ordained by God. So we took all that for granted—indeed we affected a contempt for the material side of life—and for three generations we devoted our considerable energies to developing an extravagant and delightful civilization.

"Like yourselves, we were a religious people. We worshiped the Holy Trinity, instead of the automobile, but we lavished on it fully as much money, artistry, and sacrificial effort as you now devote to the products of Detroit's Big Three.

"Don't interrupt. I am not, at the moment, criticizing your faith. Other pagan countries have done worse. Your wheeled idol combines all the best features of Moloch, the Juggernaut, and the Golden Calf —and as a student of comparative religions I must admit that your consecration to it is impressive.

"How many lives do you offer up a year? Forty thousand? The Toltecs did no better for Quetzalcoatl, although their method of execution was less messy. How many priests in gray flannel habits sing its praises? How many farms and homes do you destroy to clear its path? What will you not sacrifice in toil, cash, and inconvenience in its service? I myself have watched your people at their Sunday afternoon devotions, standing bumper to bumper on the highway, their lips moving in silent prayer. And I have seen how your male children —acolytes, I presume—anoint their heads with oil and prostrate themselves for hours at a time beneath the sacred object. In its heathen way, such piety is admirable.

"But can you afford it? Austria couldn't—and I beg you to profit from our example while there is yet time.

"We, too, had no patience with anything old-fashioned. We tore down perfectly good Gothic churches and replaced them with bigger and fancier models. For our archbishops and their mistresses we built palaces by the dozen—like this one and Mirabell and Hellbrunn. Every inch we decorated with plaster curlicues and gold leaf, at immense expense, just as you encrust your rolling temples with chrome and fins and colored lights. Both you and we, it seems, have an insatiable taste for the rococo.

"Nor did we see anything wrong with combining our religious life with sensuality. Music and love and laughter were the *leitmotifs* of our eighteenth century. Our entertainment industry—like yours—grew enormous; our theaters and orchestras were the envy of the world. Mozart got as much homage as Dave Brubeck, and almost as much money. (Their work, as I am sure you have noticed, sounds oddly similar—two varieties, so to speak, of baroque chamber music.)

"And while we frivoled away our substance and brain-power in this joyous outburst of creativity, a glum little band of Frenchmen were incubating the revolution which—a few years later—was to destroy us. Nobody warned us, and perhaps we wouldn't have listened if they had. Who could believe that a ridiculous fat man named Bonaparte might one day stable his cavalry in our churches?

"He was a crude type, interested in cannon, not culture. Almost as crude as the Russians—who made the sputnik while you were making the Edsel. Now I don't doubt that the Edsel is an icon of surpassing loveliness. But is it practical? At this moment in history can you really afford to go on spending a billion dollars every year to make purely cosmetic changes in your automobiles? A less poetic nation, I should think, might use its money and its talent in less romantic ways.

"No, no, I am not talking about rockets. You will get those, all right, because your pride has been wounded. But the contest between you and the Russians will not be decided with rockets. You will have to keep them in reserve, of course, but neither side will dare to use them; you may be dreamy, but I don't think you are suicidal.

"Meanwhile the contest will be fought with far subtler weapons— weapons which you apparently can't build, and haven't the faintest idea how to use. Know-how—isn't that the phrase? Well, you Americans just haven't got it.

"Take diplomacy, for example. Since war 'is no longer feasible, diplomacy obviously has become a decisive instrument. The Communists have known this for a long time, and they have built a formidable diplomatic machine. All of its parts are tooled and polished to mesh together—a corps of highly trained diplomats, a superb intelligence apparatus, an even better propaganda setup, military pressure where needed, and all the economic levers from trade pacts to bribery. They have been using it to win one thumping victory after another.

"You Americans, on the other hand, apparently don't even know what diplomacy is. You still think of it in terms of striped pants and tea-sippers, and you treat its practitioners with contempt, as if they were male ballet dancers.

"Your policies—if I may use the word loosely—never seem to mesh. Your President, Vice President, and Secretary of State sometimes issue three contradictory statements on three successive days. Any blabber-mouthed Congressman, general, or Faubus can destroy months of patient diplomatic effort in a single hour, and often does.

"You do have a few competent diplomats—Charles Bohlen and George Kennan probably know as much about Russia as any men in the West—but for some reason (which no foreigner can possibly understand) you refuse to use them. One of them is rusting in Manila, the other is lecturing at Oxford.

"What you do use is a herd of amateurs. Your Whitneys and your Glucks are estimable gentlemen, no doubt, with a cultivated taste for race horses and convertible debentures—but in an Embassy they are strictly greenhorns. You wouldn't dream of asking them to play first base for the Yankees, or to fix your carburetor, or to fill your teeth. For these jobs you insist on professionals. Yet when your survival as a nation is at issue, you call in any stray millionaire who happened to contribute to the right campaign fund.

"You see why we foreigners cannot believe that you are a serious people?"

With considerable difficulty, I managed to interrupt. Only millionaires, I pointed out, could afford to accept appointment to a major Embassy. By ancient tradition the United States does not pay its Foreign Service professionals enough to cover the running costs of such a post.

"Thank you," he said, "for reminding me of another American habit which has always baffled me. Why are you always unwilling to pay for what you need most?

"In helping others you are incredibly generous. For luxuries—from deodorants to mink stoles—you spend your money with childlike abandon. But when it comes to the real necessities, you are stingier than a Styrian peasant.

"For the price of one ballistic missile, for one-tenth of what your women spend on lipstick, you could staff all your Embassies with well-trained professionals. And that is a comparatively petty example. Take a big one.

"All of you seem to be pretty well in agreement that you need schoolteachers. You have discovered, with alarm, that the Russians are way ahead of you in the kind of education that pays off. Their children get more hours of instruction in ten years than yours get in twelve—and better instruction, too, because they average seventeen pupils to a class, while you average twenty-seven. They turn out eighty thousand engineers a year; you turn out thirty thousand. *All* their high school graduates have a good, stiff training in mathematics, physics, and chemistry; less than a third of yours can match them in any one of these fields.

"What is more important still, Russian students learn foreign languages. In their higher institutions, 65 per cent of them study English alone. How many Americans learn Russian? One per cent?

"This fact ought to scare you more than the sputnik. Because skill in languages—not just for a few people, but for millions—is the place where a successful foreign policy begins. When a Russian goes abroad for any purpose, he can talk to the local people in their own tongue— whether they are Arab villagers or Burmese guerrillas or French scientists. When Colonel Rudolph Abel set up his spy center in Brooklyn he spoke Brooklynese like a Flatbush bartender. When Soviet technicians build a steel mill in India, their plans are drafted in Hindi.

"Yet of the half-million Americans who travel overseas every year, I don't think I have met a dozen who could manage even the simpler European languages with fluency. By the way, how well do you speak German?"

Father Florian had the tact not to wait for an answer. (I would have had to tell him that I can order a cup of coffee, and that—in a pinch—I can ask whether the train is on time. If the stationmaster speaks slowly enough, I can often understand his reply.)

"The Russians got ahead of you," he said, "because they are hardheaded businessmen who understand the law of supply and demand. When they wanted teachers they paid for them. Not just in cash— though I understand that their top professors do get the equivalent of about $50,000 a year. They also offered something more important: prestige. In any Soviet town a teacher is a Big Man. He enjoys as much standing in the community as a real estate speculator in New York or an oil-lease broker in Dallas. He lives in the best suburb, gets the best table in restaurants, and is invited to the best parties. So their bright youngsters head for the teaching profession just as naturally as yours head for Wall Street or Madison Avenue.

"But you Americans have never learned to meet a payroll—not in your schools, anyhow. You offer teachers less than truck drivers, and then you wonder why you have 135,000 classroom jobs unfilled. I have even heard—but this I can't believe, it must be Communist propaganda—that some of your universities will pay more for a football coach than for a physics professor.

"With my own eyes, however, I have seen how you go out of your way to make your scholars feel disreputable. You ridicule them in TV shows and comic strips. Your politicians harass them. Their own pupils treat them with disrespect. You call them names. Incidentally, would you be good enough to explain precisely what you mean by the term 'egghead'? . . . I see . . . Then tell me this: who but an egghead can make an intercontinental missile?

"Or, for that matter, a workable foreign policy. As I was saying a moment ago, this is where your impracticality shows up in its most embarrassing form. In other aspects of life you often behave with good sense; if a carpet sweeper or an adding machine breaks down, you get a new one. But when a foreign policy doesn't work, you cling to it all the tighter—out of sheer sentimentality, I suppose. Your China policy has been a farce for the last five years; your German policy is stalled on dead center; your Middle East policy has failed beyond the Kremlin's wildest hopes. Yet you cherish them like heirlooms.

"Much as our beloved Emperor Franz Josef did. He was a well-meaning old gentleman who devoted most of his time to shooting rabbits—golf had not reached Austria in his day. He was not an intellectual and he suffered from a sentimental attachment to old mistresses and old doctrines. He never would let go of his Balkan policy, for example, even when it plainly was dragging him to disaster. He was, you may remember, the last of our emperors. . . .

"It is this same softhearted streak, apparently, which keeps you from using what strength you have. You may be slipping militarily, but your economic strength is still unmatched. Here is your obvious instrument for a diplomatic offensive which might still save the Western world.

"The Russians already have showed you how, and with a fraction of your resources. They have used a few million rubles' worth of trade agreements—deployed along with their other diplomatic weapons—to rope in Egypt and Syria, and they are moving fast in India, Burma, and Ceylon.

"Why do you let them get away with it? Because—correct me if I am wrong—you insist on tying your hands with a protective tariff. To protect what? A couple of watchmakers, a bicycle manufacturer, and a few clothespin factories in Vermont. Because these gentlemen do not believe in the competitive free enterprise system, they have been weeping on the shoulders of Congress—to such good effect that your present Trade Agreements Act (modest as it is) may be gutted when it comes up for renewal in June.

"Only a nation of bleeding hearts would throw away its sharpest weapon, in the midst of dubious battle, for the sake of such a hard luck story. Can a country so impractical, so muddle-headed, be trusted in a harsh material world? Do you understand why we Europeans hesitate to tie our fate to yours—however charming your culture may be?"

The bottle was empty. The clock was striking two, and even the bathroom ghost had given up for the night. I was relieved when Father Florian at last heaved himself out of the chair and waddled to the door. He had not, I felt, been altogether considerate. He had known that I still had to prepare my notes for tomorrow morning's reassuring lecture about the United States.

II

Big Changes

The Little Laborers of New York City

by CHARLES LORING BRACE

AUGUST, 1873

Here is the shocking story of child labor in the factories of New York City as industrialism began to flourish after the Civil War. Working ten hours a day, six days a week, many children lost fingers in the dangerous machinery, and others had their health wrecked in dusty, unventilated sweatshops. Charles Loring Brace (1826–1890), one of the founders and the first head, in 1853, of the Children's Aid Society in New York, gained an international reputation for his work among the city's thousands of waifs, most of them children of poor, recently arrived immigrants.

One of the most touching facts to any one examining the lower strata of New York is the great number of young children toiling in factories and shops. With the children of the fortunate classes there are certain years of childhood which every parent feels ought to be freed from the burdens and responsibilities of life. The "struggle for existence," the labor of money-making, the toil for support, and all the cares and anxieties therewith, will come soon enough. And the parent is glad that the first years at least should be buoyant and free from care, with no shadow of after-life upon them. He knows how heavy the burden must be which the child will soon be forced to carry, and he is pleased that a few years can be left cheerful and happy and free from anxiety. But the father of the poor child can indulge in no such sentiments. He is compelled to harness the little one very early to the car of labor, or if he be not forced to this, he is indifferent to the child's natural growth and improvement, and believes that his boy ought to pass through the same hard experience which he had himself. He is struggling with poverty, and eager for every little addition which he can make to his income. The child's wages seem to him important, and, indeed, it requires a character of more disinterestedness and a mind of more scope of view than we usually find among the laboring class to be able to forgo present profit for the future benefit of the little one. The laborer sees the daily earnings, and does not think much of the future advantages which the child may win by being educated now. The father, accordingly, of a poor boy is found in all countries to be willing to neglect his education, if he can put him at profitable work. Neither his affection for his offspring nor his unselfishness can be relied upon as guarding his child's future. The law is forced to protect the minor. . . .

This terrible evil of the overwork of children was early felt in the State of Massachusetts. A great manufacturing population had concentrated there, and some of the economical conditions of the Old World were repeated. Children were found in various parts of the State enslaved to labor from their earliest years, without proper education, and weakened in bodily power. No thorough effort, however, was made to check the evil till 1866, when the Legislature passed an act "restraining the employing of children of tender years in manufacturing establishments." This was subsequently repealed, and a more thorough and stringent law passed in 1867. By this act no child under ten years of age could be employed in any manufacturing establishment in the State. Of children between the ages of ten and fifteen years no one was allowed to be thus employed unless he had attended a day school at least "three months of the year preceding," or a "half-time school" during the six months. And if this amount of education be not secured, the employer is obliged to at once dismiss the child. It is necessary also that the school should be a suitable one, and approved by the school committee of the town where the child resides. The "ten-hour provision" is also made applicable to children, and no child under fifteen can be thus employed more than sixty hours per week. If ever the "Eight-hour Act" was reasonable, it would be as applied to children, and forty-eight hours per week seems to us quite enough for any working boy or girl. The penalty for the violation of this act in Massachusetts is fifty dollars both to employer and parent.

The phraseology of the Massachusetts law does not seem as careful as would be desirable, and is not made sufficiently yielding in cases of hardship among the poor; neither is sufficient power given to the executive officer to enter manufacturing establishments, and no sufficient school certificates or forms of registration for the factory children are provided for.

It is evident, however, that, with all its defects, the law has brought about a great alleviation of the evil of children's overwork. The officer appointed for the execution of the act has been in correspondence with all the manufacturers of the State, and has visited their works. This has at once called the earnest attention of the employers of Massachusetts, who are a very intelligent and philanthropic class, to the extent of this great evil. They have immediately sought for themselves to remedy it. Some of them have established half-time schools, which they require all the children in their employ to attend; and their experience here is similar to that in England—that they secure thereby a much better class of workers. Others arrange double gangs of young operatives, so that one set may take the place of another in the factory while the latter are in school. Others, again, have founded night schools, and great numbers of the young factory laborers are trained in these. The law is considered throughout Massachusetts as having been the commencement of a great and much-needed reform.

The act passed in Rhode Island is very similar to that of Massachusetts, except that no child under twelve can be employed in any factory, and no child during the nine months of factory-work is allowed to be employed more than eleven hours per day. The penalty for the violation is only twenty dollars.

Connecticut is in advance in matters of educational reform. Her citizens early saw the terrible evil from children's overwork, and the Legislature passed acts against it as early as 1842. The final and most stringent law, however, passed on this subject in Connecticut was in 1869. This law includes agricultural as well as manufacturing labor, and it throws on the employer the responsibility of ascertaining whether the children employed have attended school the required time, or whether they are too young for labor. The rules, too, in regard to school attendance are exceedingly strict. The age at which three months' school-time is required is fourteen. The penalty for each offense is one hundred dollars.

The law, however, is defective in that it does not establish the lowest age under which a child may be employed in a factory, and does not limit the number of hours of labor per week for children in manufacturing establishments.

The manufacturers of Connecticut seem to have co-operated with the law with the utmost good sense and humanity. One of them writes to the State executive officer: "We do not dare to permit the children within and around our mills to grow up without some education. Better for us to pay the school expenses ourselves than have the children in ignorance." Others have followed the example of Massachusetts manufacturers, and have opened night schools and half-time schools for their little employees, while others have permitted the division of the children into alternate gangs, of whom one is in school while the other is in the factory.

It is difficult to obtain minute or accurate information in relation to children employed in factories in New York City, and more difficult still to gain access to the factories, owing to the reluctance of employers to admit strangers. The manufacturers naturally suspect some sinister motives on the part of the inquirers. They are jealous of one another, and desirous of keeping their various patents and modes of work secret from their competitors. There have been not infrequent instances of covert attempts by the members of one firm to get possession of the secrets of another, and they are consequently all somewhat suspicious of strangers making inquiries.

It is estimated on trustworthy grounds that over 100,000 children are at work in the factories of New York and the neighboring districts, while from fifteen to twenty thousand are "floaters," drifting from one factory to another. Of these the envelope factories employ about eight thousand children, one-quarter of whom are under fifteen years of age. The average earnings of the little workers are three dollars per week. The ventilation in these factories is generally good. The gold-leaf factories employ a large number of children, though the exact statistics of the number cannot be given. This occupation requires much skill and delicacy of touch; it is not severe, but demands constant attention. The outside air is carefully excluded from these factories, owing to the fragile nature of the material used. The girls employed are mostly over fifteen years of age. The burnishing of gold, silver, and chinaware is mostly done by girls, some of whom are under thirteen years of age. Singularly enough, it is said that men in this business require to wear breastplates, in order to prevent injury from the steel instruments employed, while the girls who labor at it sit at long tables, their undefended breasts pressing against the handles of the frame.

Paper-collar factories are a very important branch of children's labor. Fully eight thousand girls from twelve to sixteen years of age are employed in it. A girl can count and box eighteen thousand collars in a day of ten hours.

Paper-box factories, embracing all sorts and sizes, from a match to a work box, employ at least ten thousand children. These become very expert, and often invent new patterns. The material being cheap, the children are permitted to take home enough to do extra work, and are thus, in fact, excluded from night school.

In regard to factories for making artificial flowers it is extremely difficult to obtain trustworthy information, as access to the shops is rigidly refused. After considerable investigation, it seems to us that from ten to twelve thousand children are engaged in them, of whom nearly eight thousand are under twelve years of age. Many are only five and seven years old. The latter are employed preparing and cutting feathers for coloring. Employers claim this to be a healthy business, but, judging from the pale and sickly countenances of the girls, we doubt the assertion.

Another important industry employing children in the city is the manufacture of tobacco. The tobacco factories contain fully ten thousand children, of whom five thousand at least are under fifteen years. The youngest child we saw employed in them was four years of age. He was engaged in stripping tobacco, and his average earnings were about one dollar per week. Many laborers work all their lives in these factories. We saw persons as old as eighty years in them. A man seventy years of age told us he had spent thirty years in one factory. His two boys had entered the factory with him at the age of ten and twelve years, and were now at work as men in the same shop. Another, the foreman, and general workshop manager, had entered that factory thirty-five years ago, when a boy ten years of age. In some of these factories boys under fifteen years are employed in dusky cellars and basements, preparing, brining, and sweetening the weed preliminary to "stemming." The underground life in these damp, cavernous places tends to keep the little workers stunted in body and mind. Other boys from ten to twelve years were squatting on the floors, whetting the knives of the cutting machines with a mixture of rum and water applied with a sponge. The rapidity with which the girls work is wonderful. A girl of sixteen years can put up thirteen gross of packages of chewing tobacco in tin-foil, and twenty-two gross in paper, in one day. Girls and boys from twelve to fourteen years earn in this business from four to five dollars per week. Some little girls only eight years of age earn three dollars per week. The fact is that these children are often able to perform the same amount of this light labor as adults, while they only receive a portion of the pay given to older laborers. Thus the children who ought to be in school are made to deprive older laborers of their employment and remuneration.

Still another branch absorbs a great number of children—the twine factories. No accurate estimate can be obtained of the number of little laborers in these, but it is known to be very large. In one uptown factory alone, two hundred children, mostly girls, are employed. This work is dangerous. The "hackling machines" are generally tended by boys from ten to fifteen years of age. Their attention must be riveted on the machinery, and cannot relax for a moment, or the danger to life or limb is imminent. The "twisting machines," attended to by girls, are equally dangerous. Many have lost their fingers, or joints of them, that were caught in the twine. Only great presence of mind has saved many of these girls from losing the whole hand. We knew in one instance, in a single night school in New York, five factory girls who had each lost a finger or thumb. It is evident that strict legislation is needed here, as it has been in England, to protect these young workers from dangerous machinery. The air of these twine factories is filled with floating particles of cotton and flax, and must be exceedingly unhealthful.

It will be seen from these condensed statistics what an immense population of children in this city are the little slaves of capital. How intense and wearying is their daily toil, and how much of their health and education is sacrificed in these early years of premature labor! The evil in New York is evidently enormous, and most threatening to our future. These children, stunted in body and mind, are growing up to be our voters and legislators. There are already over sixty thousand persons in New York who cannot read or write. These little overworked operatives will swell this ignorant throng. Fortunately this great abuse has not escaped the attention of humane men.

There is one well-known benevolent organization in New York which has been especially the friend of working children—the Children's Aid Society. This has established in various parts of the city "industrial schools," where the children of the working classes are taught habits of industry, order, and cleanliness, together with common-school lessons and some industrial branch, and are then forwarded to places in the country. Besides these well-known institutions, which contain now during the year some nine thousand children, they have also founded night schools in destitute quarters, where boys and girls who labor all day can acquire a little education at night. The eagerness of these hard-working youths after a day of severe toil to obtain the rudiments of education is one of the most pathetic experiences in the field of the society's work. In one school, the Park School, near Sixty-eighth Street, young girls and lads, who have been working from seven o'clock till six, have been known to go without their supper in order not to miss the evening lessons. The stormiest weather and the worst walking do not keep them from these schools. . . .

Another ingenious effort for the benefit of the destitute children of the city is the "placing-out system," which has been carried out by the Children's Aid Society during the last twenty years with such remarkable success. The society early saw the immense benefit in taking advantage of the peculiar economical condition of this country in treating questions of pauperism. They at once recognized the fact, and resolved to make use in their plans, of the endless demand for children's labor in the Western country. The housekeeping life of a Western farmer is somewhat peculiar. The servants of the household must be members of the family, and be treated more or less as equals. It is not convenient nor agreeable for a Western matron to have a rude European peasant at the same table and in the same room with the family. She prefers a child whom she can train up in her own way. A child's labor is needed for a thousand things on a Western farm. Children, too, are valued and thought much of. The same opportunity is given to working children as to all other children. They share fully in the active and inspiring Western life. They are molded by the social tone around them, and they grow up under the very best circumstances which can surround a poor boy or girl. No treatment which man could devise could possibly be so beneficial to the laboring children of this city as that offered by Western farms. Moreover, a child's place at the table in our rural households is of small account. Of food there is enough and an abundance. Generosity, and especially toward children, is the rule in our Western districts. This benevolent association, taking advantage of these great facts, early made arrangements for scattering such little workers of the city as were friendless and homeless all through the Western country. Western agents are employed who travel through remote farming districts, and discover where there is an especial call for children's labor. An arrangement is then made with the leading citizens of the village to receive a little detachment of these homeless children of the great city.

On a given day in New York the ragged and dirty little ones are gathered to a central office from the streets and lanes, from the industrial schools and lodging-houses of the society, are cleaned and dressed, and sent away, under charge of an experienced agent, to seek "a new home in the West." When they arrive in the village a great public meeting is held, and a committee of citizens formed to decide on the applications. Farmers come in from twenty to twenty-five miles round, looking for the "model boy" who shall do the light work of the farm and aid the wife in her endless household labor; childless mothers seek for children that shall replace those that are lost; housekeepers look for girls to train up; mechanics seek for boys for their trades; and kindhearted men, with comfortable homes and plenty of children, think it is their duty to do something for the orphans who have no fair chance in the great city. Thus in a few hours the little colony is placed in comfortable homes. Subsequently, if changes should be necessary, the committee replace the children, or the agent revisits the village, while a steady correspondence is kept up by the central office with the employers. In this way something like 25,000 boys and girls have been placed in country homes during the past twenty years. Nearly three thousand a year are now sent forth by the society. Great numbers of these children have acquired property, or have grown up to positions of influence and respectability.

This association, not content with all these ingenious devices for the benefit of the working children, are now especially laboring to prevent the evil of overwork in factories. An act has been drawn up by their counsel, Charles E. Whitehead, Esq., and is now before the Legislature, designed for the protection of factory children. By this law no child under the age of ten years is allowed to be employed at all in a manufactory, and no child under the age of twelve, unless he can intelligibly read.

No child under the age of sixteen years is allowed to be employed more than sixty hours in one week, while four public holidays are secured to him. We think a humane amendment to this provision would have been the limiting of the day's work of children to eight hours. Other sections of a very stringent character secure to every factory child between the ages of ten and sixteen a certain proportion of education, either in night schools, half-time day schools, or by three months' annual schooling. Judicious exceptions are made in cases where a poor family is dependent on the labor of its children, in permitting such children to attend the night school instead of the usual day school.

Careful registers are required to be kept by the manufacturers or employers, showing the amount of schooling enjoyed by each child, the time of his labor in the factory, and other facts important for the execution of the law.

Humane provisions are also included in the act for the promotion of the good sanitary condition of the factories, and to protect the children from dangerous machinery. Under the proposed law a new official has to be appointed by the Governor, to be called the "Inspector of Factory Children." Such an officer, acting under so wise and humane a law, cannot but accomplish immense good throughout the State.

It is a matter deeply to be regretted that certain manufacturers in the State Legislature in Albany have not imitated their more enlightened and humane contemporaries in Massachusetts, and given their hearty support to so beneficent a measure. Instead of this, we are sorry to be informed that they are offering a factious opposition which may entirely defeat this act, and put New York in a very unfavorable position, as compared with the New England States, in her legislation to protect factory children.

Lord Macaulay on American Institutions

FEBRUARY, 1877

The arch-conservative Macaulay predicts here that majority rule in the United States—"rule by the poorest and most ignorant part of society"—will either bring anarchy in the twentieth century, or the government will be seized by some "Caesar or Napoleon." The two letters were addressed to Henry S. Randall, who had written a biography of Thomas Jefferson. A leading English statesman and the most widely read historian and essayist of his time, Lord Macaulay had no faith that the multitude could be educated sufficiently to govern themselves wisely. He was born in 1800 and died in 1859.

HOLLY LODGE, KENSINGTON,
LONDON, *May* 23, 1857.

DEAR SIR,—The four volumes of the *Colonial History of New York* reached me safely. I assure you that I shall value them highly. They contain much to interest an English as well as an American reader. Pray accept my thanks, and convey them to the Regents of the University.

You are surprised to learn that I have not a high opinion of Mr. Jefferson, and I am surprised at your surprise. I am certain that I never wrote a line, and that I never, in Parliament, in conversation, or even on the hustings—a place where it is the fashion to court the populace—uttered a word indicating an opinion that the supreme authority in a state ought to be intrusted to the majority of citizens told by the head; in other words, to the poorest and most ignorant part of society. I have long been convinced that institutions purely democratic must, sooner or later, destroy liberty or civilization, or both.

In Europe, where the population is dense, the effect of such institutions would be almost instantaneous. What happened lately in France is an example. In 1848 a pure democracy was established there. During a short time there was reason to expect a general spoliation, a national bankruptcy, a new partition of the soil, a maximum of prices, a ruinous load of taxation laid on the rich for the purpose of supporting the poor in idleness. Such a system would, in twenty years, have made France as poor and barbarous as the France of the Carlo-vingians. Happily the danger was averted; and now there is a despot-ism, a silent tribune, an enslaved press. Liberty is gone, but civiliza-tion has been saved. I have not the smallest doubt that, if we had a purely democratic government here, the effect would be the same. Either the poor would plunder the rich, and civilization would perish, or order and prosperity would be saved by a strong military govern-ment, and liberty would perish.

You may think that your country enjoys an exemption from these evils. I will frankly own to you that I am of a very different opinion. Your fate I believe to be certain, though it is deferred by a physical cause. As long as you have a boundless extent of fertile and unoccu-pied land, your laboring population will be far more at ease than the laboring population of the Old World, and, while that is the case, the Jefferson politics may continue to exist without causing any fatal calamity. But the time will come when New England will be as thickly peopled as old England. Wages will be as low, and will fluctuate as much with you as with us. You will have your Manchesters and Bir-minghams, and in those Manchesters and Birminghams hundreds of thousands of artisans will assuredly be sometimes out of work. Then your institutions will be fairly brought to the test.

Distress everywhere makes the laborer mutinous and discontented, and inclines him to listen with eagerness to agitators who tell him that it is a monstrous iniquity that one man should have a million while another cannot get a full meal. In bad years there is plenty of grum-bling here, and sometimes a little rioting. But it matters little. For here the sufferers are not the rulers. The supreme power is in the hands of a class, numerous indeed, but select; of an educated class; of a class which is, and knows itself to be, deeply interested in the secu-rity of property and the maintenance of order. Accordingly, the mal-contents are firmly yet gently restrained. The bad time is got over without robbing the wealthy to relieve the indigent. The springs of national prosperity soon begin to flow again: work is plentiful, wages rise, and all is tranquillity and cheerfulness. I have seen England pass three or four times through such critical seasons as I have described.

Through such seasons the United States will have to pass in the course of the next century, if not of this. How will you pass through them? I heartily wish you a good deliverance. But my reason and my wishes are at war, and I cannot help foreboding the worst. It is quite plain that your government will never be able to restrain a distressed and discontented majority. For with you the majority is the government, and has the rich, who are always a minority, absolutely at its mercy.

The day will come when in the State of New York a multitude of people, none of whom has had more than half a breakfast, or expects to have more than half a dinner, will choose a Legislature. Is it possible to doubt what sort of a Legislature will be chosen? On one side is a statesman preaching patience, respect for vested rights, strict observance of public faith. On the other is a demagogue ranting about the tyranny of capitalists and usurers, and asking why any body should be permitted to drink Champagne and to ride in a carriage while thousands of honest folks are in want of necessaries. Which of the two candidates is likely to be preferred by a working-man who hears his children cry for more bread? I seriously apprehend that you will, in some such season of adversity as I have described, do things which will prevent prosperity from returning; that you will act like people who should in a year of scarcity devour all the seed-corn, and thus make the next a year not of scarcity, but of absolute famine.

There will be, I fear, spoliation. The spoliation will increase the distress. The distress will produce fresh spoliation. There is nothing to stop you. Your Constitution is all sail and no anchor. As I said before, when a society has entered on this downward progress, either civilization or liberty must perish. Either some Caesar or Napoleon will seize the reins of government with a strong hand, or your republic will be as fearfully plundered and laid waste by barbarians in the twentieth century as the Roman Empire was in the fifth, with this difference, that the Huns and Vandals who ravaged the Roman Empire came from without, and that your Huns and Vandals will have been engendered within your own country by your own institutions.

Thinking thus, of course, I cannot reckon Jefferson among the benefactors of mankind. I readily admit that his intentions were good and his abilities considerable. Odious stories have been circulated about his private life; but I do not know on what evidence those stories rest, and I think it probable that they are false or monstrously exaggerated.

I have no doubt that I shall derive both pleasure and information from your account of him.

I have the honor to be, dear Sir, your faithful servant,

T. B. MACAULAY.

H. S. RANDALL, Esq., etc., etc., etc.

HOLLY LODGE, KENSINGTON,
October 9, 1858.

SIR, I beg you to accept my thanks for your volumes, which have just reached me, and which, as far as I can judge from the first hasty inspection, will prove both interesting and instructive.

Your book was preceded by a letter, for which I have also to thank you. In that letter you expressed, without the smallest discourtesy, a very decided dissent from some opinions which I have long held firmly, but which I should never have obtruded on you except at your own earnest request, and which I have no wish to defend against your objections. If you can derive any comfort as to the future destinies of your country from your conviction that a benevolent Creator will never suffer more human beings to be born than can live in plenty, it is a comfort of which I should be sorry to deprive you. By the same process of reasoning one may arrive at many very agreeable conclusions, such as that there is no cholera, no malaria, no yellow fever, no negro slavery, in the world. Unfortunately for me, perhaps, I learned from Lord Bacon a method of investigating truth diametrically opposite to that which you appear to follow.

I am perfectly aware of the immense progress which your country has made and is making in population and wealth. I know that the laborer with you has large wages, abundant food, and the means of giving some education to his children. But I see no reason for attributing these things to the policy of Jefferson. I see no reason to believe that your progress would have been less rapid, that your laboring people would have been worse fed or clothed or taught, if your government had been conducted on the principles of Washington and Hamilton. Nay, you will, I am sure, acknowledge that the progress which you are now making is only a continuation of the progress which you have been making ever since the middle of the seventeenth century, and that the blessings which you now enjoy were enjoyed by your forefathers who were loyal subjects of the kings of England.

The contrast between the laborer of New York and the laborer of

Europe is not stronger now than it was when New York was governed by noblemen and gentlemen commissioned under the English great seal. And there are at this moment dependencies of the English crown in which all the phenomena which you attribute to purely democratical institutions may be seen in the highest perfection. The colony of Victoria, in Australia, was planted only twenty years ago. The population is now, I suppose, near a million. The revenue is enormous, near five millions sterling, and raised without any murmuring. The wages of labor are higher than they are even with you. Immense sums are expended on education. And this is a province governed by the delegate of a hereditary sovereign.

It therefore seems to me quite clear that the fact which you cite to prove the excellence of purely democratic institutions ought to be ascribed not to those institutions, but to causes which operated in America long before your Declaration of Independence, and which are still operating in many parts of the British Empire. You will perceive, therefore, that I do not propose, as you thought, to sacrifice the interests of the present generation to those of remote generations. It would, indeed, be absurd in a nation to part with institutions to which it is indebted for immense present prosperity from an apprehension that, after the lapse of a century, those institutions may be found to produce mischief. But I do not admit that the prosperity which your country enjoys arises from those parts of your polity which may be called, in an especial manner, Jeffersonian. Those parts of your polity already produce bad effects, and will, unless I am greatly mistaken, produce fatal effects if they shall last till North America has two hundred inhabitants to the square mile.

With repeated thanks for your present, I have the honor to be, Sir, your faithful servant,   MACAULAY.

Who Is Loyal to America?

by HENRY STEELE COMMAGER

SEPTEMBER, 1947

*This was one of the first counterattacks on the ignorance and
hysteria which reached their apogee in McCarthyism a few years
back. Henry Steele Commager, professor of history and American studies at Amherst, is a distinguished student of the development and heritage of America. He has written and edited many
American history books, and also is the author of many magazine
articles on current problems seen in historical perspective. Born
in Pittsburgh in 1902, he was educated at the University of Chicago and the University of Copenhagen.*

On May 6 a Russian-born girl, Mrs. Shura Lewis, gave a talk to the
students of the Western High School of Washington, D. C. She talked
about Russia—its school system, its public health program, the position
of women, of the aged, of the workers, the farmers, and the professional classes—and compared, superficially and uncritically, some
American and Russian social institutions. The most careful examination of the speech—happily reprinted for us in the *Congressional
Record*—does not disclose a single disparagement of anything American unless it is a quasi-humorous reference to the cost of having a
baby and of dental treatment in this country. Mrs. Lewis said nothing
that had not been said a thousand times, in speeches, in newspapers,
magazines, and books. She said nothing that any normal person could
find objectionable.

Her speech, however, created a sensation. A few students walked
out on it. Others improvised placards proclaiming their devotion to
Americanism. Indignant mothers telephoned their protests. Newspapers took a strong stand against the outrage. Congress, rarely concerned for the political or economic welfare of the citizens of the
capital city, reacted sharply when its intellectual welfare was at stake.
Congressmen Rankin and Dirksen thundered and lightened; the District of Columbia Committee went into a huddle; there were demands

95

for housecleaning in the whole school system, which was obviously shot through and through with Communism.

All this might be ignored, for we have learned not to expect either intelligence or understanding of Americanism from this element in our Congress. More ominous was the reaction of the educators entrusted with the high responsibility of guiding and guarding the intellectual welfare of our boys and girls. Did they stand up for intellectual freedom? Did they insist that high-school children had the right and the duty to learn about other countries? Did they protest that students were to be trusted to use intelligence and common sense? Did they affirm that the Americanism of their students was staunch enough to resist propaganda? Did they perform even the elementary task, expected of educators above all, of analyzing the much-criticized speech?

Not at all. The District Superintendent of Schools, Dr. Hobart Corning, hastened to agree with the animadversions of Representatives Rankin and Dirksen. The whole thing was, he confessed, "a very unfortunate occurrence," and had "shocked the whole school system." What Mrs. Lewis said, he added gratuitously, was "repugnant to all who are working with youth in the Washington schools," and "the entire affair contrary to the philosophy of education under which we operate." Mr. Danowsky, the hapless principal of the Western High School, was "the most shocked and regretful of all." The District of Columbia Committee would be happy to know that though he was innocent in the matter, he had been properly reprimanded!

It is the reaction of the educators that makes this episode more than a tempest in a teapot. We expect hysteria from Mr. Rankin and some newspapers; we are shocked when we see educators, timid before criticism and confused about first principles, betray their trust. And we wonder what can be that "philosophy of education" which believes that young people can be trained to the duties of citizenship by wrapping their minds in cotton-wool.

Merely by talking about Russia Mrs. Lewis was thought to be attacking Americanism. It is indicative of the seriousness of the situation that during the same week the House found it necessary to take time out from the discussion of the labor bill, the tax bill, the International Trade Organization, and the world famine, to meet assaults upon Americanism from a new quarter. This time it was the artists who were undermining the American system, and members of the House spent some hours passing around reproductions of the paintings which the State Department had sent abroad as part of its program for advertising American culture. We need not pause over the exquisite humor which congressmen displayed in their comments on modern art: weary statesmen must have their fun. But we may profitably remark the major criticism which was directed against this unfortunate collection of paintings. What was wrong with these paintings, it shortly appeared, was that they were un-American. "No American drew those crazy pictures," said Mr. Rankin. Perhaps he was right. The copious files of the Committee on Un-American Activities were levied upon to prove that of the forty-five artists represented "no less than twenty were definitely New Deal in various shades of Communism." The damning facts are specified for each of the pernicious twenty; we can content ourselves with the first of them, Ben-Zion. What is the evidence here? "Ben-Zion was one of the signers of a letter sent to President Roosevelt by the United American Artists which urged help to the USSR and Britain after Hitler attacked Russia." He was, in short, fellow-traveler of Churchill and Roosevelt.

The same day that Mr. Dirksen was denouncing the Washington school authorities for allowing students to hear about Russia ("In Russia equal right is granted to each nationality. There is no discrimination. Nobody says, you are a Negro, you are a Jew") Representative Williams of Mississippi rose to denounce the *Survey-Graphic* magazine and to add further to our understanding of Americanism. The *Survey-Graphic,* he said, "contained 129 pages of outrageously vile and nauseating anti-Southern, anti-Christian, un-American, and pro-Communist tripe, ostensibly directed toward the elimination of the custom of racial segregation in the South." It was written by "meddling un-American purveyors of hate and indecency."

All in all, a busy week for the House. Yet those who make a practice of reading their *Record* will agree that it was a typical week. For increasingly Congress is concerned with the eradication of disloyalty and the defense of Americanism, and scarcely a day passes that some Congressman does not treat us to exhortations and admonitions, impassioned appeals and eloquent declamations, similar to those inspired by Mrs. Lewis, Mr. Ben-Zion, and the editors of the *Survey-Graphic*. And scarcely a day passes that the outlines of the new loyalty and the new Americanism are not etched more sharply in public policy.

And this is what is significant—the emergence of new patterns of Americanism and of loyalty, patterns radically different from those which have long been traditional. It is not only the Congress that is busy designing the new patterns. They are outlined in President Truman's recent disloyalty order; in similar orders formulated by the New York City Council and by state and local authorities throughout the country; in the programs of the D.A.R., the American Legion, and similar patriotic organizations; in the editorials of the Hearst and the McCormick-Patterson papers; and in an elaborate series of advertisements sponsored by large corporations and business organizations. In the making is a revival of the red hysteria of the early 1920's, one of the shabbiest chapters in the history of American democracy; and more than a revival, for the new crusade is designed not merely to frustrate Communism but to formulate a positive definition of Americanism, and a positive concept of loyalty.

What is the new loyalty? It is, above all, conformity. It is the uncritical and unquestioning acceptance of America as it is—the political institutions, the social relationships, the economic practices. It rejects inquiry into the race question or socialized medicine, or public housing, or into the wisdom or validity of our foreign policy. It regards as particularly heinous any challenge to what is called "the system of private enterprise," identifying that system with Americanism. It abandons evolution, repudiates the once popular concept of progress, and regards America as a finished product, perfect and complete.

It is, it must be added, easily satisfied. For it wants not intellectual conviction nor spiritual conquest, but mere outward conformity. In matters of loyalty it takes the word for the deed, the gesture for the principle. It is content with the flag salute, and does not pause to consider the warning of our Supreme Court that "a person gets from a symbol the meaning he puts into it, and what is one man's comfort and inspiration is another's jest and scorn." It is satisfied with membership in respectable organizations and, as it assumes that every member of a liberal organization is a Communist, concludes that every member of a conservative one is a true American. It has not yet learned that not everyone who saith Lord, Lord, shall enter into the kingdom of Heaven. It is designed neither to discover real disloyalty nor to foster true loyalty.

II

What is wrong with this new concept of loyalty? What, fundamentally, is wrong with the pusillanimous retreat of the Washington educators, the barbarous antics of Washington legislators, the hysterical outbursts of the D.A.R., the gross and vulgar appeals of business corporations? It is not merely that these things are offensive. It is rather that they are wrong—morally, socially, and politically.

The concept of loyalty as conformity is a false one. It is narrow and restrictive, denies freedom of thought and of conscience, and is irremediably stained by private and selfish considerations. "Enlightened loyalty," wrote Josiah Royce, who made loyalty the very core of his philosophy,

> means harm to no man's loyalty. It is at war only with disloyalty, and its warfare, unless necessity constrains, is only a spiritual warfare. It does not foster class hatreds; it knows of nothing reasonable about race prejudices; and it regards all races of men as one in their need of loyalty. It ignores mutual misunderstandings. It loves its own wherever upon earth its own, namely loyalty itself, is to be found.

Justice, charity, wisdom, spirituality, he added, were all definable in terms of loyalty, and we may properly ask which of these qualities our contemporary champions of loyalty display.

Above all, loyalty must be to something larger than oneself, untainted by private purposes or selfish ends. But what are we to say of the attempts by the NAM and by individual corporations to identify loyalty with the system of private enterprise? Is it not as if officeholders should attempt to identify loyalty with their own party, their own political careers? Do not those corporations which pay for full-page advertisements associating Americanism with the competitive system expect, ultimately, to profit from that association? Do not those organizations that deplore, in the name of patriotism, the extension of government operation of hydroelectric power expect to profit from their campaign?

Certainly it is a gross perversion not only of the concept of loyalty but of the concept of Americanism to identify it with a particular economic system. This precise question, interestingly enough, came before the Supreme Court in the Schneiderman case not so long ago—and it was Wendell Willkie who was counsel for Schneiderman. Said the Court:

> Throughout our history many sincere people whose attachment to the general Constitutional scheme cannot be doubted have, for vari-

ous and even divergent reasons, urged differing degrees of governmental ownership and control of natural resources, basic means of production, and banks and the media of exchange, either with or without compensation. And something once regarded as a species of private property was abolished without compensating the owners when the institution of slavery was forbidden. Can it be said that the author of the Emancipation Proclamation and the supporters of the Thirteenth Amendment were not attached to the Constitution?

There is, it should be added, a further danger in the willful identification of Americanism with a particular body of economic practices. Many learned economists predict for the near future an economic crash similar to that of 1929. If Americanism is equated with competitive capitalism, what happens to it if competitive capitalism comes a cropper? If loyalty and private enterprise are inextricably associated, what is to preserve loyalty if private enterprise fails? Those who associate Americanism with a particular program of economic practices have a grave responsibility, for if their program should fail, they expose Americanism itself to disrepute.

The effort to equate loyalty with conformity is misguided because it assumes that there is a fixed content to loyalty and that this can be determined and defined. But loyalty is a principle, and eludes definition except in its own terms. It is devotion to the best interests of the commonwealth, and may require hostility to the particular policies which the government pursues, the particular practices which the economy undertakes, the particular institutions which society maintains. "If there is any fixed star in our Constitutional constellation," said the Supreme Court in the Barnette case, "it is that no official, high or petty, can prescribe what shall be orthodox in politics, nationalism, religion, or other matters of opinion, or force citizens to confess by word or act their faith therein. If there are any circumstances which permit an exception they do not now occur to us."

True loyalty may require, in fact, what appears to the naïve to be disloyalty. It may require hostility to certain provisions of the Constitution itself, and historians have not concluded that those who subscribed to the "Higher Law" were lacking in patriotism. We should not forget that our tradition is one of protest and revolt, and it is stultifying to celebrate the rebels of the past—Jefferson and Paine, Emerson and Thoreau—while we silence the rebels of the present.

"We are a rebellious nation," said Theodore Parker, known in his day as the Great American Preacher, and went on:

> Our whole history is treason; our blood was attainted before we were born; our creeds are infidelity to the mother church; our constitution, treason to our fatherland. What of that? Though all the governors in the world bid us commit treason against man, and set the example, let us never submit.

Those who would impose upon us a new concept of loyalty not only assume that this is possible, but have the presumption to believe that they are competent to write the definition. We are reminded of Whitman's defiance of the "never-ending audacity of elected persons." Who are those who would set the standards of loyalty? They are Rankins and Bilbos, officials of the D.A.R. and the Legion and the NAM, Hearsts and McCormicks. May we not say of Rankin's harangues on loyalty what Emerson said of Webster at the time of the Seventh of March speech: "The word honor in the mouth of Mr. Webster is like the word love in the mouth of a whore."

What do men know of loyalty who make a mockery of the Declaration of Independence and the Bill of Rights, whose energies are dedicated to stirring up race and class hatreds, who would straitjacket the American spirit? What indeed do they know of America—the America of Sam Adams and Tom Paine, of Jackson's defiance of the Court and Lincoln's celebration of labor, of Thoreau's essay on Civil Disobedience and Emerson's championship of John Brown, of the America of the Fourierists and the Come-Outers, of cranks and fanatics, of socialists and anarchists? Who among American heroes could meet their tests, who would be cleared by their committees? Not Washington, who was a rebel. Not Jefferson, who wrote that all men are created equal and whose motto was "rebellion to tyrants is obedience to God." Not Garrison, who publicly burned the Constitution; or Wendell Phillips, who spoke for the underprivileged everywhere and counted himself a philosophical anarchist; not Seward of the Higher Law or Sumner of racial equality. Not Lincoln, who admonished us to have malice toward none, charity for all; or Wilson, who warned that our flag was "a flag of liberty of opinion as well as of political liberty"; or Justice Holmes, who said that our Constitution is an experiment and that while that experiment is being made "we should be eternally vigilant against attempts to check the expression of opinions that we loathe and believe to be fraught with death."

III

There are further and more practical objections against the imposition of fixed concepts of loyalty or tests of disloyalty. The effort is itself a confession of fear, a declaration of insolvency. Those who are sure of themselves do not need reassurance, and those who have confidence in the strength and the virtue of America do not need to fear either criticism or competition. The effort is bound to miscarry. It will not apprehend those who are really disloyal, it will not even frighten them; it will affect only those who can be labeled "radical." It is sobering to recall that though the Japanese relocation program, carried through at such incalculable cost in misery and tragedy, was justified to us on the ground that the Japanese were potentially disloyal, the record does not disclose a single case of Japanese disloyalty or sabotage during the whole war. The warning sounded by the Supreme Court in the Barnette flag-salute case is a timely one:

> Ultimate futility of such attempts to compel obedience is the lesson of every such effort from the Roman drive to stamp out Christianity as a disturber of pagan unity, the Inquisition as a means to religious and dynastic unity, the Siberian exiles as a means to Russian unity, down to the fast-failing efforts of our present totalitarian enemies. Those who begin coercive elimination of dissent soon find themselves exterminating dissenters. Compulsory unification of opinion achieves only the unanimity of the graveyard.

Nor are we left to idle conjecture in this matter; we have had experience enough. Let us limit ourselves to a single example, one that is wonderfully relevant. Back in 1943 the House Un-American Activities Committee, deeply disturbed by alleged disloyalty among government employees, wrote a definition of subversive activities and proceeded to apply it. The definition was admirable, and no one could challenge its logic or its symmetry:

> Subversive activity derives from conduct intentionally destructive of or inimical to the Government of the United States—that which seeks to undermine its institutions, or to distort its functions, or to impede its projects, or to lessen its efforts, the ultimate end being to overturn it all.

Surely anyone guilty of activities so defined deserved not only dismissal but punishment. But how was the test applied? It was applied to two distinguished scholars, Robert Morss Lovett and Goodwin Watson, and to one able young historian, William E. Dodd, Jr., son of our former Ambassador to Germany. Of almost three million persons employed by the government, these were the three whose subversive activities were deemed the most pernicious, and the House cut them off the payroll. The sequel is familiar. The Senate concurred only to save a wartime appropriation; the President signed the bill under protest for the same reason. The Supreme Court declared the whole business a "bill of attainder" and therefore unconstitutional. Who was it, in the end, who engaged in "subversive activities"—Lovett, Dodd, and Watson, or the Congress which flagrantly violated Article One of the Constitution?

Finally, disloyalty tests are not only futile in application, they are pernicious in their consequences. They distract attention from activities that are really disloyal, and silence criticism inspired by true loyalty. That there are disloyal elements in America will not be denied, but there is no reason to suppose that any of the tests now formulated will ever be applied to them. It is relevant to remember that when Rankin was asked why his Committee did not investigate the Ku Klux Klan he replied that the Klan was not un-American, it was American!

Who are those who are really disloyal? Those who inflame racial hatreds, who sow religious and class dissensions. Those who subvert the Constitution by violating the freedom of the ballot box. Those who make a mockery of majority rule by the use of the filibuster. Those who impair democracy by denying equal educational facilities. Those who frustrate justice by lynch law or by making a farce of jury trials. Those who deny freedom of speech and of the press and of assembly. Those who press the special favors against the interest of the commonwealth. Those who regard public office as a source of private gain. Those who would exalt the military over the civil. Those who for selfish and private purposes stir up national antagonisms and expose the world to the ruin of war.

Will the House Committee on Un-American Activities interfere with the activities of these? Will Mr. Truman's disloyalty proclamation reach these? Will the current campaigns for Americanism convert these? If past experience is any guide, they will not. What they will do, if they are successful, is to silence criticism, stamp out dissent

—or drive it underground. But if our democracy is to flourish it must have criticism, if our government is to function it must have dissent. Only totalitarian governments insist upon conformity and they—as we know—do so at their peril. Without criticism abuses will go unrebuked; without dissent our dynamic system will become static. The American people have a stake in the maintenance of the most thorough-going inquisition into American institutions. They have a stake in nonconformity, for they know that the American genius is nonconformist. They have a stake in experimentation of the most radical character, for they know that only those who prove all things can hold fast that which is good.

IV

It is easier to say what loyalty is not than to say what it is. It is not conformity. It is not passive acquiescence in the status quo. It is not preference for everything American over everything foreign. It is not an ostrich-like ignorance of other countries and other institutions. It is not the indulgence in ceremony—a flag salute, an oath of allegiance, a fervid verbal declaration. It is not a particular creed, a particular version of history, a particular body of economic practices, a particular philosophy.

It is a tradition, an ideal, and a principle. It is a willingness to subordinate every private advantage for the larger good. It is an appreciation of the rich and diverse contributions that can come from the most varied sources. It is allegiance to the traditions that have guided our greatest statesmen and inspired our most eloquent poets— the traditions of freedom, equality, democracy, tolerance, the tradition of the higher law, of experimentation, co-operation, and pluralism. It is a realization that America was born of revolt, flourished on dissent, became great through experimentation.

Independence was an act of revolution; republicanism was something new under the sun; the federal system was a vast experimental laboratory. Physically Americans were pioneers; in the realm of social and economic institutions, too, their tradition has been one of pioneering. From the beginning, intellectual and spiritual diversity has been as characteristic of America as racial and linguistic. The most distinctively American philosophies have been transcendentalism—which is the philosophy of the Higher Law—and pragmatism—which is the philosophy of experimentation and pluralism. These two principles are the very core of Americanism: the principle of the Higher Law, or of obedience to the dictates of conscience rather than of statutes, and the principle of pragmatism, or the rejection of a single good and of the notion of a finished universe. From the beginning Americans have known that there were new worlds to conquer, new truths to be discovered. Every effort to confine Americanism to a single pattern, to constrain it to a single formula, is disloyalty to everything that is valid in Americanism.

The Coming—and Disciplining—of Industrialism, 1850-1950

by FREDERICK LEWIS ALLEN

OCTOBER, 1950

Marxism has been confounded, not by dogma, but by advanced industrialism, says Frederick Lewis Allen in this penetrating study of the democratization of American capitalism. Born in Boston in 1890, Mr. Allen was educated at Groton and Harvard, and joined the Harper's *staff in 1923. He became editor-in-chief in 1941 and retired from that post in 1953 to devote himself mainly to writing, but he remained on the staff as a consulting editor. He died unexpectedly in 1954. Among his books is the classic* Only Yesterday, *an informal social history of the 1920's and a pioneering work of its kind.*

In an upper hallway of the New York Public Library there have been hanging, this year, a series of prints of American cities dating from about 1850. To the eye of today these pictures show what look like overgrown villages and small towns—clusters of red brick and white wooden houses, here and there crowded closely along narrow streets, elsewhere set comfortably apart from one another, with clumps of trees about them and green gardens sloping down to the inevitable river. In a few of these towns one will see a factory chimney or two rising above the roof-tops; but the striking thing, to the eye of 1950, is that in most of the pictures—whether they are of Davenport, Iowa, or Hartford, Connecticut, or even New York City—the skyline is broken only by church spires. Hence the village effect; for today it is only a village which is dominated by its steeples.

If we should wish to see where we have come from in a hundred years—how the everyday life of American men and women and children has changed since 1850, what people lacked then that we take for granted now, what people possessed then that is only a memory now, and whether the gap between rich and poor has narrowed or widened since industrialism began to transform American life—I suggest that we begin by trying to look through those pictures to the reality that lay behind them, a full century ago.

To begin with, are those engravings fair portraits of the America of 1850? Well, we must remember that American life was vastly more varied geographically then than now. At that moment in the mid-nineteenth century when the United States had only just reached out to its present continental boundaries (as a result of the Mexican War), and when California had only just become, abruptly, a land of bright American opportunity (as a result of the discovery of gold at Sutter's Mill), America was still a land of violent contrasts. A silk-waistcoated merchant prince of Boston or New York or Philadelphia lived in a wholly different world from a family of homespun pioneers setting out by covered wagon from the bleak and muddy streets of Independence to cross the "Great American Desert." The high-thinking Transcendentalists of Concord, strolling about Walden Pond to note the blooming of the arbutus and to discuss natural aristocracy, were continents apart, in their way of life, from Brigham Young's Mormons building their new city beside the Great Salt Lake, or from the black slaves of a Georgia plantation, or from the gold-hungry prospectors in the town of tents and shacks that was San Francisco, or from the farmer trying out a new McCormick reaper on a quarter-section of scraggly Illinois prairie.

If America was so varied geographically, this was largely because it took so much time and effort for either people or goods to get about. When young Joseph Jefferson, the actor, traveled from New Orleans to New York in 1846, what he had to do was to take a Mississippi River steamboat to Wheeling, in what is now West Virginia (being delayed for days by ice, for it was winter); then bump for twenty-four hours in a chilly stagecoach over rutted roads to Cumberland, Maryland, stopping every few hours for a meal while the horses were changed; then proceed by primitive train to his destination. Early in the eighteen-fifties Ralph Waldo Emerson, taking a lecture trip in Michigan, had to make a forty-eight-mile journey through the woods from town to town by horse and buggy. And the fastest time anybody could make from New York to San Francisco was eighty-nine days by swift clipper ship around the Horn.

We must remember, too, when we look at those engravings of American cities in 1850, that the men who made them did not show us the grimier streets, or the citizens eating with their knives or blowing their noses with their fingers. They could not show us the smell of household privies. Yet those pictures of red and white and green towns clinging to banks of sailboat-studded rivers do reflect the central fact of the United States of 1850; that as a whole it was still a land of farmers, shopkeepers, merchants, and artisans—above all, farmers. Today, among "gainfully employed" Americans, only about one in five works on a farm; at that time, over half of them did. And the cities were small. New York, then as now the biggest of them, had about one-tenth of its present population.

To be sure, industrialism had long since begun its smoky invasion of the land. Along the banks of the Merrimac and other New England rivers, big textile mills were turning out cotton and woolen cloth, and there were a few scattered factories even west of the Alleghenies. But the basic units of American life were still the village and the farm; and the great majority of the American people—the lively, sociable, irritable, dyspeptic, boastful, uncouth, energetic, disorderly, wasteful, and hospitable American people—were villagers at heart.

How well did they live? It is easy today to forget that many comforts and conveniences which we now take for granted were then available to nobody, or almost nobody. For one thing, cities were just beginning to install water-supply and drainage systems. Philadelphia had been an early innovator with its Fairmount Water Works, which long had been pumping water from the Schuylkill River, but New York did not have Croton water till 1842, and Boston did not introduce Cochituate water till 1848. Before public water supplies became general, you either subscribed for water provided by a private company such as the Jamaica Pond Corporation in Boston, or, if you were not within reach of its piping system or could not pay the price, you relied on a well of your own. In Boston, for instance, a census taken in 1845 showed that the 10,370 houses in the city got their water from no less than 5,287 separate wells, and supplemented this supply with rain water collected (for washing purposes) in 4,445 cisterns. (As the city gradually became smokier, cistern water naturally became sootier.)

Even after public reservoirs and aqueducts had been built, it took a long time to lay the water mains to take this new blessing to people's houses. All through the late eighteen-forties, for example, New York was busily constructing mains along the streets of the city, and the authorities were discovering to their dismay how much water people used when all they needed to do to get it was to turn a tap. In 1853 the head of the Croton Aqueduct Department, in his annual report, remarking that a modern hotel on Broadway had installed "more than four hundred openings through which water is delivered, and discharged into public sewers," said in tones of despair, "With such arrangements for the consumption of water, under the control of a little army of careless servants, and irresponsible guests, how is any reasonable economy in its use to be expected?"

The sewers that this official mentioned were brand-new; for as late as 1845 even the biggest city in the country had had no public sewerage system at all. And although the modern hotel which he described had had a number of suites equipped with bath and water closet, and had installed in the basement six water closets for domestics, and had provided, adjacent to the barroom, nine public water closets and three washbasins with hot and cold water, these were innovations connoting extreme luxury. In all or almost all private houses there was still no such thing as a water closet; people relied upon chamber pots or upon a drafty expedition to the privy; or—in the case of the prosperous—upon commodes which the servants would periodically empty. And except along the chief streets of the chief cities, they relied too upon cesspits and culverts and the gutters of the streets to dispose of their sewage.

No wonder their well water was widely contaminated; and no wonder the term of life was so short, particularly in the cities. Today the average expectation of life in the United States is over 67, and rising; in 1850 it was under 40. A health report published in Boston in 1850 disclosed that the average age of all who died in the city was 21.43 years, and that among the Catholic population—who were, of course, mostly poor immigrants from Ireland—it was less than 14 years. Those grim figures reflect not only a general ignorance of antisepsis and sanitation, but also the result of living, in fast-growing cities, under conditions which were still those of primitive village life.

Nor were private houses centrally heated. Even the wealthy depended on kitchen stoves, Franklin stoves, and open fireplaces for warmth in winter. Mark Twain describing in *Life on the Mississippi* the typical big house of any town along the river in about 1850—"a big, square, two-story frame house painted white and porticoed like a Grecian temple behind a white paling fence," noted that there was no bathroom and added that there might be, but wouldn't certainly be, a pitcher and washbowl in each of the square bedrooms upstairs. The first duty of the average American householder, in the morning, was to light the fires and empty the slops; until the fires really took hold, the chill of the house made any but the most cursory washing an ordeal. And the German writer, Ole Munch Raeder, describing a trip which he took in 1847 through what we now call the Middle West, remarked on the lamentable but general custom of spitting at the stove, not always accurately, adding with evident relief that there were cuspidors in some of the better homes in Madison, Elkhorn, and Janesville. All in all, it is likely that if we of 1950 were to visit the United States of 1850, we should find it a dirty place inhabited by dirty people.

Ready-made clothing was limited in amount and kind, ill-fitting, and hand-sewn. Accordingly, shirts and underwear were generally stitched at home by the housewife, from materials spun by the textile mills and bought by the yard at the store; shoes were made by shoemakers, suits by tailors (or sometimes by the housewife), dresses by the housewife or by seamstresses and dressmakers. The well-to-do imported their suits from London, their dresses from Paris, or else employed tailors and dressmakers versed in the foreign modes to fashion them out of fine imported materials. Naturally a new article of clothing represented a considerable expense, in either money or toil; the people in any gathering were far more varied in costume than today; and the women of the family were perpetually sewing.

Against these and other lacks and inconveniences must be set certain advantages. First of all, space and air. The shopkeeper or blacksmith in an Ohio town was likely to have a house with more room in it than can be found today in the New York or Chicago apartment of a $30,000-a-year executive. In Philadelphia, my grandfather as a young man could take his wife skating in winter, or sailing in summer, on a Schuylkill River as yet undarkened by commerce or industry. Not yet was there any need for week-end escape from the cities, or for summer places, or for elaborately organized sports; the vast majority of the people found chances to walk, ride, drive, skate, swim, fish, or shoot, within ready reach on almost any day when the weather suited —if their long labors left them time enough. Although the American public school system was only partly established, although great numbers of children could not get even elementary schooling, and few went on to high school, and far fewer yet to college, at least the average American boy and girl had a countryside close at hand to run wild in when the chores that were their share in the work of family life were done. And one final advantage was possessed by nine families out of ten: when the crops failed, when the family store went broke, when their jobs folded up, they could tighten their belts and go on working —if not in their home communities, then at least in the beckoning West. In a land still dominated by small-scale and individual enterprise, a self-reliant man could be far more independent than could his son or grandson in later years.

The gulf between rich and poor was great, both in income and in the nature of their clothing, equipment, and pattern of life. At a time when the dollar was so big that $5,000 a year was an inviting salary to offer to the head of an insurance company, there were merchants in the seaboard cities who were making hundreds of thousands a year; one Boston merchant is said to have cleared $100,000 from one voyage of one of his ships. Not only was such a man rich—with of course no income tax to pay—and not only did he have fine carriages, and a splendid house with satin-covered furniture and a paneled library and a cellar full of Madeira and other imported wines, and a staff of dutiful servants, but his wealth was instantly apparent to anybody who saw him and his lady on the street. You could tell at a distance of fifty paces that their clothes were quite different in material and cut from those of ordinary folk.

By contrast, not only the slaves of the South (who were looked after well or ill according to the whim of their slaveholder) but also the poorer people of the Northern cities and towns, were in miserable plight. For the floor of wages had been dropping. Years of famine in Ireland had brought into the country a horde of newcomers willing to work for next to nothing. In earlier years the rising textile mills of

Lawrence and Lowell and Fall River had largely employed farmers' daughters; but as Irish labor became available a change was taking place. Wages fell—even when profits were booming—until whole families labored at the machines for three or four dollars a week per worker; a twelve-hour day was average, and a fourteen-hour day was not unusual. Stop for a moment and reflect upon what it would be like to work a fourteen-hour day—say from five o'clock in the morning till eight at night, with half an hour off for breakfast and half an hour for dinner—six days a week, in an ill-lighted, ill-ventilated factory; and ask yourself how much recreation, how much sunshine, how much education for children of fourteen or less, such an appalling routine permitted.

Meanwhile the wages of seamen, which in the early years of the century had been as high as eighteen dollars a month, had fallen to eight dollars or ten dollars or twelve dollars a month, and the adventurous farmer boys who had formerly yearned for two years before the mast had been supplanted by foreign deck-hands, until the slim and beautiful clipper ships of the eighteen-fifties were manned by the drifting scum of many continents. When, for example, the *Reindeer* sailed from Canton to Boston in 1851 she had as her crew 2 French, 1 Portuguese, 1 Cape Verde Islander, 1 Azores man, 1 Italian, 1 Dutchman, 1 Mulatto, 2 Kanakas, 1 Welshman, 1 Swede, 2 Chinese, and 2 Americans.

One catches a glimpse of the labor market in the mid-century in an article in *Harper's* for October 1866, outlining a reasonable budget for a young couple living in the outskirts of New York on $2,000 a year—roughly equivalent to perhaps $6,000 or $7,000 now—with one servant. At a time when roast beef cost 35 cents a pound, corned beef 23½ cents a pound, fish 12 cents a pound, bread 10 cents a loaf, milk 10 cents a quart, and sugar 15 cents a pound— prices which were mostly, though not all, a fraction of what they are today—this family was allowed $114.75 a year for coal (for the kitchen range and a "portable furnace" in the cellar), and a mere $96 a year for the servant's wages—*at the rate of $8 a month!*

What did people think of these contrasts? Most people apparently regarded them as part of the order of nature. That men and women of the favored class approved of them is of course not surprising; the striking fact is that the tailor, the farmer, and the mill-hand on the whole agreed. For the reigning idea in America was that every individual should have a fair chance in the contest of life, and that he should be on his own, beholden to no man; to work for somebody else was spineless unless one were a young apprentice, or a girl waiting for marriage, or an immigrant who didn't know any better; and if such people chose to work for very little, this was their own affair. Couldn't they break away and get better jobs if they had the ability and the will? Meanwhile employers had a virtually unquestioned right to make all the money they could lay their hands on. For America was a young country with a future, in which it was considered every man's duty to play a constructive part; and if he made money—a lot of it—this was a good sign that he was contributing to the common weal. If he made a million while paying his workers a pittance, that was mighty smart. If he outwitted his neighbor in a slick trade, that was mighty smart. Disapprove of him? People admired him, and hoped to be as fortunate themselves one day.

For the tide of industrialism was only beginning to run strong, and opportunity still seemed to be within the reach of all. Americans felt this in their bones, and held their heads high. Said Oliver Wendell Holmes to Edward Dicey, an English visitor, "We should find it hard to match five thousand American gentlemen with five thousand English, but we could match five million ordinary Americans against the same number of your countrymen, without fear of the result." If there were almost 25,000 paupers in Massachusetts, were not 91 per cent of them foreigners, and were they not therefore simply people who had not yet got off to a start in the free-for-all race? Even the ill-clad immigrants felt the breezes of hope in the air. Said a poor Irishwoman to Dicey, "This is a blessed country, sir; I think God made it for the poor."

II

As the second half of the nineteenth century began, industrialism took a new lease on life. Samuel Colt, making revolvers at Hartford, had pushed to a new perfection Eli Whitney's principle of the use of interchangeable parts; Colt had completely mechanized his factory, so that presently, with the aid of some 400 machines, his men were turning out over 24,000 revolvers a year. Such a performance was an eye-opener to inventors, manufacturers, investors: couldn't you make almost anything cheaply and swiftly, provided you had the right machines to do it with? And now the most essential tools for the making of such machines were ready; for the stocking lathe, the universal miller, and the turret lathe had all been invented. Elias Howe, Jr., had conceived the sewing machine, and now Isaac Singer was producing this new contrivance in quantity. Telegraph lines were being extended from town to town. In 1858 the first cable was laid across the Atlantic Ocean. The next year oil was discovered in Pennsylvania —an event destined to end the era of the whale-oil lamp. Meanwhile thousands of miles of railroad track were being laid; and as the fat-funneled locomotives wound their way through the wooded Alleghenies and chugged across the vast flatlands of the central basin, they brought town after town into new and exciting contact with the news and ideas of the outside world.

Each new miracle of invention seized the public imagination. When Joseph Jefferson received the first telegram of his life in Cumberland, Maryland, he could hardly believe that he was actually hearing from the partner in Baltimore to whom he had written only the day before. "I called at the office to inquire if it were really so; yes, there could be no doubt of it. A small group of people had collected about the operator . . . all wearing a look of surprise and incredulity. We began showing one another our dispatches. . . . People were rushing to and fro with little messages in their hands, and stopping one another in the street to talk and wonder over the new event." Just so, in scores of American towns, the new instruments and gadgets set boys and men to dreaming fantastic dreams—of getting a scientific training, devising some new wonder which would simplify the long labor of manufacturing, setting up a company to produce it, selling it by the thousands, and making a fabulous fortune. The future seemed full of wild promise.

The Civil War, though it left the South prostrate, did not halt the march of industrialism in the North, but rather accelerated it, bringing as it did outsize demands for weapons and equipment and quicker communication, and especially for uniforms in quantity. By the war's end industrialism was in full flood, irresistible and tremendous.

It brought with it both wonders and abominations. The wonders have become so familiar to us that it is hard for us to imagine a world in which they did not exist. Yet even a short list of the changes that came between 1850 and 1900 is staggering. Here are some of them:

A vast growth of steel production, resulting from the Bessemer process, the multiplication of steel mills, and the coming of the open-hearth furnace. (This meant more and better steel for rails, wires, bridges, ships, steel-skeleton buildings, and a host of other uses; steel became the basic material out of which the new industrial era was built.)

An equally vast boom in railroad-building, till the rails not only crossed the Rockies to unite East with West, but made a network tying the whole country together into one economic unit.

The installation of improved water and sewerage systems for cities and towns, making possible—for those who could afford it—the immense convenience of modern plumbing.

The lighting of homes, as well as city streets, by gaslight and then by the magic of electric light.

Electrical transportation: the coming of the cable car, the trolley car, the elevated railroad (powered at first by steam, then by electricity), and the subway.

The development of electric motors and dynamos to do more and more of the work of the country; the introduction of the electric-power plant and of modern hydroelectric systems, so that the virtue of electricity could be on tap miles—or hundreds of miles—away from its source.

That incredible annihilator of distance, both between friends and between business offices, the telephone.

The revolutionizing of business life by the invention of the typewriter—which incidentally began to bring women into business life—and by the electric elevator, which, along with the development of steel-skeleton construction, made possible the skyscraper.

And, finally, the beginnings of that prime revolutionizer, the automobile, which had been introduced abroad as early as 1884 but did not begin to take its American forms until the early nineties.

To these wonders one might add the introduction of seaworthy ocean-going steamships; the opening of the Great Plains to settlement with the aid of the invention of barbed wire; the simplification and improvement of photography, and the coming of the half-tone process which accommodated it to publication; the invention of the linotype, to the great benefit of printing; and the contriving of all the machines which supplemented Elias Howe's sewing machine to facilitate the growth of the clothing and shoe industries. Yet even if we extended this list of new marvels indefinitely, we could hardly begin to convey a sense of the magnitude of the change which was wrought between

1850 and 1900. A land of formerly separate communities had been linked together. A land mostly of farmers and villagers had become a land mostly of cities and roaring industrial towns. Comforts, conveniences, and wealth had so piled up as to make possible a great extension of education on every level and a general widening of horizons. It was almost as if a whole new world had been invented for people to work and play in.

But industrialism in those days of its raw growth brought abominations too. To begin with, wherever it advanced, ugliness came with it —smoke, soot, grime, the darkening of skies once clear, the withering of foliage once green, the pollution of rivers once clean. Indeed, so completely did men assume that money-making and beauty lived in separate compartments—beauty being something which you could buy after you made the money, or must run away to, from the city or the factory where the money was produced—that even the profitable building of houses, except for the rich, was undertaken as if by blind men. It should come as no surprise that the grimmest sections of most of our cities today date from between 1850 and 1900.

Not only did industrialism uglify the land wherever it moved; it also, while subduing it, despoiled it. Forests were hacked to pieces, farmland misused and overused, natural resources plundered right and left as if the bounties of America would be forever inexhaustible.

Morally, too, industrialism proved at first to be a destroyer of standards. So thoroughly had the idea sunk into men's minds that it was smart to make money in any way, straight or crooked, that the third quarter of the nineteenth century brought a contagion of fraudulence. It brought, too, a trend toward monopoly that if unchecked would have drawn all the economic power of the country into the hands of a few men. But the most disturbing thing about industrialism, in those days of its spring blooming, was the way in which it distributed the wealth it produced.

In the early days of the factory system in England, David Ricardo had enunciated the grim principle which he called the Iron Law of Wages: the principle that all wages tend to fall to the level which the most unskillful or most desperate man will accept. In preindustrial times this Iron Law had not often operated unchecked. The prince, or the baron, or the squire, or the neighbors had tended to look after those who by reason of incompetence or illness or adversity were in want. And in the preindustrial United States, as we have seen, men and women who were in want could at least go on working, for whatever pittance they could command, or could move on elsewhere to try again. But the new industrial community brought a change. For when a man built a mill or factory surrounded by a mill village or factory town, those who came to work for him were in great degree imprisoned by their choice. They did not own the tools with which they worked, and therefore were dependent on what employment the mill offered; and anyhow there was not enough other work in such a community for all who would be looking for it if the mill shut down. And if their wages were low they could not afford to look elsewhere for jobs. So they ceased to be free agents. They were at their employer's mercy. And the Iron Law really went into action.

One great advantage the American workingman had—if he could raise the cash. He could still go West. But as the discards of industrialism, along with the men of most adventurous ambition, became Western pioneers, their places were taken by an imported proletariat— the incoming immigrants. First it was the Irish, who in the eighteen-fifties were the diggers of ditches, the builders of levees, the new class of mill-workers; then, as the Irish bettered themselves, it was the Italians, and then the Slavs of Eastern Europe. Each group tended to form a proletarian layer under the previous one. (At the bottom, in the most menial and ill-paid jobs of all, remained our own Negro population, slaves no longer, but remaining largely in a servitude of ignorance and exclusion from opportunity.) Thus the very hope that was symbolized by the Goddess of Liberty brought immigrants in such vast numbers as to glut the labor markets and delay the modification of the Iron Law.

As time went on there were to be other mitigating factors. One was the slow and uneven growth of labor unions. Another was the belated recognition, by a gradually aroused public conscience, of the horrors of American poverty; little by little the law began to prescribe more decent conditions of work. And another, of course, was the fact that the abounding flow of wealth from hugely increased productivity *did* tend to percolate down through the ranks of society and lift the living standard for the great majority. By 1891 wages in twenty-two industries had increased since 1860 on the average over 68 per cent, while wholesale prices had declined over 5 per cent. Yes, the *average* well-being, even in industry, was rising fast.

But there were subaverage areas where the terms of life were miserable. As late as 1887 a writer for *Harper's* found a coal-yard laborer in an Eastern mill town who earned seven dollars a week, while his wife earned five dollars, their elder daughter four dollars, and their fourteen-year-old daughter three dollars and a quarter, working from 6:30 in the morning till 6:30 at night in the mill. Total per year for *four* money-earners—$924. Not much improvement there over the conditions of the mid-century. The status of the anthracite workers in the Pennsylvania coal fields was sharply worse: there the workers who slaved grimly and dangerously underground were kept in a state of perpetual debt to the company on which they were dependent for their meager housing, their food, everything. And worse still were the conditions on New York's Lower East Side, where 290,000 people were packed into one square mile of tenements; where, in the filth and stench of Mulberry Bend, Jacob Riis found twelve men and women sleeping for "five cents a spot" in one room not thirteen feet square; where the wife of an incapacitated invalid earned an income of $1.20 a week making shirts, while her oldest daughter cut out Hamburg edging for the noble wage of 2½ cents per hour for ten hours of steady labor. Here, at the very bottom of the pit of poverty, the Iron Law was iron indeed.

Meanwhile at the other end of the scale there was magnificence unstinted. Consider, for example, the mansion which Samuel Colt had built near Hartford out of the profits of his industrial pioneering. In 1876, reported a rapt chronicler in the *Art Journal,* the Colt lawn was daily rolled, cut, and trimmed to perfection by thirty men; while the greenhouses, 2,634 feet in length, produced yearly at least a ton of grapes, to say nothing of eight thousand figs, peaches, and other fruits, and four hundred quarts of strawberries. By the early eighteen-eighties American millionaires, led by the Vanderbilts, had become possessed with the idea that a successful man should build himself a mansion suitable for a European prince. They hired accomplished architects to produce for them Renaissance palaces, monumental Italian villas, or turreted French châteaux, with authentically princely bronze doors, grilled iron gates, ancient fireplaces, tapestries, and paintings imported from abroad; and in these feudal edifices, staffed in many cases by thirty or more servants, they lived in marble grandeur. Nor was the luxury of the rich limited to their palaces. Pierpont Morgan, whose house in New York was comparatively unassuming, as were his house in London, his country estate outside London, his American country

estate on the Hudson, his Adirondack estate, his fishing box at Newport, and his suite at Jekyll Island, satisfied his desire for big things
by building in 1898 a steam yacht 302 feet long, and by amassing an
art collection worth at least fifty million dollars. Those were the days
when private yachts, private art galleries, and racing stables were multi-
plying; when dinner parties included up to twenty courses; and when
one young blood would be heard remarking to another, "Never ask
the old man for less than fifty thousand."

It was on contrasts like these, at an early stage of European industrialism, that Karl Marx had predicated his theory of revolution.
But one did not have to have a radical bias to be dismayed at the gulf
one saw widening between rich and poor. In the year 1882—just a
few months before the Vanderbilt fancy-dress ball on which was spent
an estimated quarter of a million dollars (equivalent to much more
than half a million today)—Junius Henry Browne wrote in *Harper's:*
"Year after year New York seems to justify the painful, dispiriting
averment that it is a city of paupers and millionaires. Are not the rich
growing richer and the poor poorer as time moves on? Will there
ever be a period when the distance between them will be less? Hope
answers, 'Yes'; Reason answers, 'No.' "

The answer was still "No" at the turn of the century. At about that
time—a period of relative prosperity—the mass of unskilled workers
were receiving less than $460 a year in wages in the North, less than
$300 in the South; while Andrew Carnegie's *personal* share of the
profits of his steel company was a little over six and a half million
dollars for the year 1898, a little over twelve million dollars for 1899,
and more than twenty-three million dollars for 1900. With no income
taxes whatever to pay.

III

It could not go on without making a mockery of democracy. It did
not go on. The story of American progress during the first half of the
twentieth century has been the story of the repeal of the Iron Law, and
of the slow disciplining of an industrialism still expandingly and
excitingly productive.

A vehement rebellion against the way things were going had begun
during the latter decades of the nineteenth century, chiefly among the
farmers and small business men of the Midwest and the Great Plains,
where the old Jeffersonian idea of a nation of self-reliant free men

had been reinforced, within living memory, by frontier experience. It was the indignation of these people against the greedy and arbitrary power of the big railroad and manufacturing companies that was chiefly responsible for the passage of the Interstate Commerce Act of 1887 and the Sherman Anti-Trust Act of 1890, and for the fervor of the Populist movement of the early nineties. This grass-roots rebellion was reinforced by the anger of industrial workers, who were making grim and often bloody attempts to unionize. And as time went on it was still further reinforced by what might be called the revolt of the American conscience: a widespread and rising disapproval, among citizens by the millions, of what looked to them like the coming of a new feudalism. When they read the eye-opening reports of men like Jacob Riis on slum life, when the muckraking journalists uncovered for them the sordid business deals and political corruption of the day, their dismay had a moral basis: the way things had been going was not right.

And so the center of gravity of American opinion began to shift. In all walks of life, during the first fifteen years or so of the twentieth century, people began to think of society at large as an entity for which they were partly responsible. This feeling lent strength to political progressives and liberals like Theodore Roosevelt, the elder LaFollette, and Woodrow Wilson. In the churches there was a new emphasis on the "social gospel"; social service began to be recognized as a profession; economists for the first time produced the concept of the "national income"; the two richest Americans, Carnegie and Rockefeller, converted great parts of their fortunes into foundations for the public weal; and Henry Ford, by voluntarily raising wages and cutting prices, dramatized a concept of industrialism as different from that of the nineteenth-century mill-owners as his assembly line was different from their crude mechanization. The Iron Law was on its way out.

Meanwhile invention continued at a breathless pace. We are all familiar with what it has brought us in the half-century since 1900: such marvels as the airplane, the movies, the radio, television, a bewildering array of plastics and synthetics, and electronics. If we broaden the term "invention" to include a wider range of research, it has brought us a greatly increased knowledge of nutrition, a new battery of useful drugs, and—along with innumerable other wonders —the certainty of the future boon of atomic power, a certainty which only the misuse of atomic knowledge for purposes of mutual human destruction can long forestall. Likewise our increase in technological efficiency has been steady and formidable; during World War II our rate of production astonished the world. But along with this furious advance of industrialism has gone the disciplining of industrialism: its transformation from a force which made the rich richer and the poor poorer into a force which has narrowed the gulf between rich and poor.

For this great change there has been a surprising variety of causes. We need not detail here the long series of events through which they have manifested themselves—World War I, with its demand for high production at high wages; the confident competition of the nineteen-twenties; the crisis of the Great Depression, which dramatized the helplessness of the unemployed; the resulting spate of New Deal laws; World War II, with its unprecedented need for goods in quantity and its unprecedented government controls; and the post-1945 boom. Let us forget chronology and look at the tamers of industrialism group by group, in all their wild variety. We can lump them into five general classes:

(1) *Legislation*—including not only all manner of laws to protect the health and safety of the worker, to grant him a minimum wage, to permit him to organize, and to protect him as tenant and consumer, but also laws for the regulation of business practices, and—immensely important—the graduated income tax, first adopted in 1913, which has increasingly redistributed the national prosperity.

(2) *Public Services*—including the vast expansion of public school systems, state universities, highway systems, park systems, and government aids and benefits of innumerable kinds. Municipal, state, and federal governments have all grown colossally; for instance, the federal government now spends *eighty* times as much money annually as in 1900. Most of the expansion of the public services has been attributable, not to any conscious trend toward socialism, but to recognition of the simple fact that in a complex urbanized society, people cannot live decently unless the organized community provides them with services and opportunities which in earlier days the self-reliant man could get for himself.

(3) *Union action*—which, especially during the past fifteen years,

has helped to lift wage-rates and standards of employment far above the level they would have remained at under the Iron Law.

(4) *A change in the attitude of business managements*—a growing realization that good working conditions, handsome factories, acceptable housing for workers, and an intelligent concern with worker relations, and also with public relations, can be business assets. This change has been gradual and in some degree forced by public hostility, as well as by government regulations which have placed big business in the bright glare of publicity: a goldfish has got to be good. But the change has been pervasive and salutary.

And (5) *the logic of mass production*—which is that the more goods you can produce, the less it costs to produce them; and that the more people are well off, the more they can buy, thus making this lavish and economical production possible. The continuing discovery and demonstration of this logic has been, in some ways, the most powerful force for change of the lot. For it has had its corollaries: that a nation of men and women secure against exploitation and acute poverty is a nation of delighted buyers of goods, to everybody's profit; that it pays better to produce the same sort of food, clothing, and equipment for everybody, of all income levels, than to produce luxury goods for a few, and second- and third-rate goods for the rest; and that therefore one can make money by lowering class barriers. Thus is Marxism confounded—not by dogma, but by the logic of advanced industrialism itself; or, to put it another way, by capitalism turned to democratic ends.

So much for generalization. Now let us glance at a few of the specific things that this modernized and disciplined industrial order has brought us during the past half century.

In fifty years, the amount of goods consumed per person in America has gone up two and a half times, while the average work week has dropped from about fifty-eight hours to about forty.

The telephone dates from 1876, but in 1900 there were only a little over a million and a third telephones in America. At the end of 1949 there were over forty and a half million—just about thirty times as many.

The automobile, too, dates from the late nineteenth century, but in 1900 there were still only a few thousand of them in the country.

They were a rich man's luxury (and a mechanic's despair). Now there are over forty million—with paved roads everywhere to drive on.

And not only has the radio, which as a distributor of entertainment dates only from 1920, become a possession of almost every family in the country, but its new-come rival, television, has not even begun its career in the old-time way, as a plaything of the rich: from the beginning of the television boom in 1947, sales of sets have been distributed fairly evenly among all income groups. The logic of mass production has dictated for them a falling price and a mass appeal; and the purchase of a set has been, accordingly, an index less of wealth than of gadget-mindedness.

Or, to move into another field, take a look at education. In 1900 less than one American boy or girl out of ten of high school age was actually at high school; now over four out of five are. Meanwhile the number of students in American universities, colleges, and teacher-training institutions has increased eightfold. If we have a crisis in education today, this is because our training and paying of teachers have not yet caught up with the spread of American opportunity.

What has been taking place has been both a narrowing of the gap *in income* between rich and poor—though there are still islands of deep poverty in America, and there are also families and individuals by the millions who, through illness or adversity, live on the ragged edge of want—and, even more impressively, *a narrowing of the difference between rich and poor in their ways of living.*

For instance, consider the matter of personal appearance, remembering that in 1850 the merchant prince and his wife, or in 1900 the frock-coated, silk-hatted banker and his Paris-gowned wife were recognizable at a distance, if they ventured among the common herd, as beings apart. Forty or fifty years ago the countryman in a metropolis was visibly a "hayseed"; the purchaser of inexpensive men's clothing was betrayed by his tight-waisted jackets and bulbous-toed shoes. Today the difference in appearance between a steel-worker (or a clerk) and a high executive is noticeable only to the attentive eye. And as for women, the difference in appearance between the one who spends $5,000 a year on clothes and the one who spends $250 is by no means as conspicuous as the difference between the woman who has good taste and the woman who lacks it. The fact that the wealthy woman has thirty dresses to the poor woman's three is not visible on the street, and the fact that her dresses are made of better materials and are better cut is observable only by the expert eye at close range. Fashion used to be decreed by Paris, imported by the most expensive dress shops, then modified by the more expensive American dress manufacturers, and finally—after an interval of six months to a year—modified still further, almost beyond recognition, by the manufacturers of cheap dresses. The process is now quicker and the differences much less sharp. Women of every income group wear nylon stockings (which offer the perfect illustration of the democratic logic of mass production). Unless the poor woman is exceptionally poor—or indifferent—she like the rich woman has had her hair recently shampooed and set. It could almost be said that the only easily visible mark of wealth which a woman can put on is a mink coat. A generation ago the great mail-order houses produced different clothes for the Western farmer's wife and for the city woman in the East; today there is no such distinction, and a friend of mine whose train stopped recently at a small Oklahoma town remarked that the girls on the railroad platform there were virtually indistinguishable in appearance from girls on Madison Avenue or Michigan Boulevard.

Let us proceed from clothes to the equipment of daily living. As Professor H. Gordon Hayes pointed out in *Harper's* in 1947, the rich man smokes the same sort of cigarettes as the poor man, shaves with the same sort of razor, uses the same sort of telephone, vacuum cleaner, and radio, has the same sort of lighting and heating equipment in his house, and so on indefinitely. The differences between his automobile and the poor man's are minor. Essentially they have similar engines, similar fittings. In the early years of the century there was a hierarchy of automobiles. At the top, as marks of dashing wealth, were such imported cars as the Rolls-Royce, Mercedes-Benz, and Isotta Fraschini. There was also an American aristocracy of the Pierce Arrow, Peerless, and Packard. Then came group after group, in descending scale, till you reached the homely Model-T Ford. Today, except for a few survivals such as the obstinately rectangular Rolls-Royces of the old school, and a few oddities such as the new British sports cars, there is a comparative uniformity; and although the owner of a big, brand-new car probably has a large income, he may merely, like the purchaser of a television set, be someone who adjusts a slender budget to cover the machines that entrance him.

In the matter of running water and plumbing, uniformity has approached much more slowly but nevertheless steadily. Throughout the latter part of the nineteenth century the rich and the middle-income group in the cities and towns were progressively installing running water, bathrooms, and water closets in their houses; but at the turn of the century not only did factory workers and farmers (except for a few owners of big farms) hardly dream of enjoying such luxuries, but even in the houses of well-to-do people beyond the reach of city water and sewerage lines, there was likely to be no bathroom. Not until 1908 did Ellsworth M. Statler build in Buffalo the first hotel which offered every guest a room and private bath at a moderate price. Not until 1916 did the double-shell enameled bathtub go into mass production, replacing the painted cast-iron tub with roll-rim and claw feet. Today only the older and poorer tenements and dwellings in American cities and towns lack bathtubs or showers and water closets, and these conveniences are fast being installed in farmhouses.

Meanwhile the electrification of American farms has reached a point which would have been unimaginable in 1900, when even the prosperous city-dweller had only just begun to install electricity in his new house without adding gas, too, lest the current fail suddenly. The coming of the electric refrigerator and also, increasing, the deep-freeze unit has not only made for domestic convenience but also—along with our expanding knowledge of nutrition—has improved the year-round diet of millions. (Where, today, is the once-famous American dyspepsia?) Meanwhile the servant class has almost vanished, although servants' wages have a purchasing power today from five to ten times bigger than in 1900; its virtual disappearance—which has imposed upon all but a tiny percentage of American families the chores of cooking and cleaning and washing (with, increasingly, the aid of a dishwasher and a washing machine)—marks the virtual absorption of the immigrant proletariat of yore into general American society, in which domestic service has always been regarded as humiliating.

One of the most striking effects of the logic of mass production has been the way in which the mass circulation magazines, the movies, and the radio have tended to impose upon Americans of all income levels the same patterns of emulation: in other words, to make them all want to be the same sort of people. This has been a purely twentieth-century phenomenon, for the big magazines were just beginning to push their circulations over the million mark in 1900, while the first nickelodeon theaters did not begin to show movies till about 1905, and radio broadcasting dates only from 1920.

In the movies, popular stars like Clark Gable, Cary Grant, Gary Cooper, Humphrey Bogart, and Gregory Peck may play the parts of people who are supposed to be rich and stylish, or of people who are at the end of their economic rope; but whatever role any one of them assumes, his popularity depends upon his representing a kind of charm that any young American male can appreciate and at least approach; in other words, upon his conforming to what old-fashioned people would call middle-class standards of speech and behavior—standards which might more properly be called classless or all-American. Whether he is cast as a millionaire's son or as a truck driver, he remains essentially the same. In radio Jack Benny, for all his big income, plays the part of a Jack Benny who lives in a modest house, owns a wheezy old car, watches the pennies, and has for his sole servant a jack-of-all-trades helper with whom he is on the breeziest of terms. Thus the logic of mass production pushes the idols of Hollywood into roles which represent general American behavior.

And what is the result? Both the rich man's fourteen-year-old son, who dismays his conservative parents by trying to talk like Humphrey Bogart, and the truck-driver's son, who longs to be as funny as Bob Hope, will grow up to behave more like their idols—and thus, more like one another—than they would have otherwise. And something else happens too. Half a century ago a coal-miner who found himself at a fashionable restaurant would not have had the faintest notion of how to behave; nowadays he has only to ask himself, "How would Gregory Peck do it?" In short, the social distance between the extremes of American society is shrinking.

Whenever I think of this change, I think of something I saw the other day in New York City. A street was being torn up for repairs, and while the workmen were standing waiting for the arrival of new equipment, one of them, who had in his hands an iron rod presumably used for prying off manhole covers, was enjoying a little relaxation. I looked twice to see what he was doing with that rod. He was practicing a graceful golf stroke.

IV

So much for the change since 1850. And where are we headed now—during the next half-century, or century, if you will?

I believe that we have hardly started; that the expansion of industrialism is still in its early stages, and its civilizing is in a still earlier stage. Professor Sumner H. Slichter says that by such an early date as 1980 the annual output of goods and services in the United States should rise from about $4,065 per worker to at least $5,744 per worker (at present prices), and probably more, while the labor week is being reduced from an average of forty hours today to an average of thirty hours. That seems to me a modest estimate—if we can surmount certain dangers which threaten us.

The first danger is, of course, that total war may smash the whole system. But in this particular context, even this danger can be exaggerated. It is quite true that the existence of atom bombs, and the possibility of hydrogen bombs, threaten millions of us with annihilation. But it is useful to recall that in the twenties and thirties many people predicted that another world war would "end civilization"; but that when the war came, on a lethal scale, it was accompanied and followed by an unexpected *increase* in population, not only in the United States but in other warring nations; and that although international trade has since then been hobbled, production has more or less recovered in Europe and has been given a new boost in the United States. The danger of extinction for whole communities is real; the danger to the progress of industrialism is not necessarily final.

The second danger is that we may defeat our great experiment in the negating of the Iron Law by applying the lessons of that defeat on too rapid a scale. We may get the fatal notion that benefits to various sections of the population can be brought about by government handouts and guarantees larger than the increase in our national productivity can support. This is not primarily a danger of socialism, which in its doctrinaire form is almost as outdated a concept as communism; among the guarantees and handouts that could most endanger our national solvency are the kind that even the most conservative citizens (such as potato-growers) delight in—when they are the beneficiaries. The balance between economic liberty and political intervention offers a delicate problem in adjustment.

There is a third danger: that the trend toward American uniformity may reach the point where we are standardized into universal acceptance of the second-rate—or, even worse, into complete susceptibility to mass emotion, which in turn could be manipulated to turn the United States into a police state. Well, possibly. Every wave of hysteria which crosses the country—like that which today fills many people with a preposterous terror of American communism—reminds us once more that eternal vigilance is the price of liberty. But if American flexibility, horse sense, and humor carried us through the dark days of 1933, they ought to be able to do it again.

If these dangers can be surmounted, the prospects are exciting. The remaining islands of real poverty in America are a challenge; so are our congested and debt-laden cities, which become more expensive to run, and offer their inhabitants a more unnatural and nerve-racking life, as they lure more and more people to enjoy their glitter; so is the failure, thus far, of most Americans to get any chance to savor the joy of work done under agreeable conditions for a satisfying purpose. The best of our factories, today, are things of a new and lively beauty; the worst—which include most of the older ones—are still in essence "dark, Satanic mills." More satisfaction and enjoyment on the job might prove even more desirable for the general well-being than more pay for less work. But in all these directions progress can be made, with luck, if we can keep wide open the roads along which scientific research and technology are taking us—and can steer around those other dangers that I have mentioned. The technicians were never more active than today; science, like industrialism, is still in its youth; a single new discovery, like that of atomic power, if harnessed for peaceable use, could by the year 2000 help to make 1950 seem as primitive a time as 1900, to say nothing of 1850, seems to us today.

Those villages of 1850 were mighty pretty, with their lawns reaching to the river. I see no reason why—if we keep our wits about us—American communities of 2000 and 2050 should not be just as satisfying to the eye; far cleaner, more convenient, more comfortable; far prouder as residences for even the least fortunate man, woman, and child who live in them; and more favorable as seed-beds of the human spirit.

The Great Wall Street Crash

by JOHN KENNETH GALBRAITH

OCTOBER, 1954

Greed and folly, unreasoning hope, fear bordering on hysteria—
these were elements in the stock-market catastrophe of 1929.
Here a well-known Harvard economics professor reviews the
record in the light of history, and poses the question: Can it
happen again? Mr. Galbraith is the author of the 1958 best-
seller, The Affluent Society, *and another of his books,* American
Capitalism, *also was widely read and discussed. He is a former*
government official and a former editor of Fortune.

Senator Couzens: Did Goldman, Sachs, & Co. organize the Goldman
Sachs Trading Corporation?
Mr. Sachs: Yes, sir.
Senator Couzens: And it sold its stock to the public?
Mr. Sachs: A portion of it. The firm invested originally in 10 per cent
of the . . . issue.
Senator Couzens: And the other 90 per cent was sold to the public?
Mr. Sachs: Yes, sir.
Senator Couzens: At what price?
Mr. Sachs: At 104 . . . the stock was [later] split two for one.
Senator Couzens: And what is the price of the stock now?
Mr. Sachs: Approximately 1¾.

> *—Hearings before Senate Committee*
> *on Banking and Currency on Stock*
> *Exchange Practices. May 20, 1932.*

A case can readily be made that, with the single exception of the
Civil War, no event of the past hundred years so deeply impressed
itself upon the thoughts, attitudes, and voting behavior of the American people as the Great Depression. This importance is hardly reflected in the dignity with which history treats of the tragedy. The
climactic stock-market crash which launched the depression—and

which was considerably more important in relation to what followed than the shots at Sumter—occurred only twenty-five years ago this month, but it has already receded far into the mists of memory. One measure of this neglect is the widespread and quite erroneous assumption that there was one day in October 1929 when the great crash occurred. Another indication is the total absence of agreement as to what day it was. Thus Thursday, October 24, the first day on which panic seized the market, has regularly been cited as the Black Thursday of the crash. But the professionals have always leaned to the following Monday or Tuesday, when the losses were far greater and when the volume of trading reached its all-time incredible high. Others have picked still other days. In a book explaining the œbacle, Professor Irving Fisher of Yale—Professor Fisher as the acknowledged prophet of the boom was left with much explaining to do—singled out October 21 as the day of catastrophe. (On that day trading was very heavy but the declines relatively modest.) The authorized biographers of Herbert Hoover, in 1935, refused to settle on any one day but—along with the twenty-ninth—picked October 23 and October 26. (The twenty-third was the day preceding Black Thursday; the twenty-sixth was a Saturday when things were tolerably quiet.) Not, certainly, since the siege of Troy has the chronology of a great event been so uncertain.

As a matter of fact, economic history, even at its most violent, has a much less exciting tempo than military or even political history. Days are rarely important. All of the autumn of 1929 was a terrible time, and all of that year was one of climax. With the invaluable aid of hindsight it is possible to see that throughout all of the early months the stage was being set for the final disaster.

On the first of January 1929, the Coolidge Bull Market was at least four years old. The *New York Times* average of the prices of twenty-five representative industrial stocks which had stood at 110 at the beginning of 1924 had eased up to 135 at the beginning of 1925. At the close of trading on January 2, 1929, it was at 338.35. Apart from mild setbacks notably in early 1926 and early 1928, this climb had been almost uninterrupted. There were very few months when the averages did not show an improvement on the month preceding. There had been, in short, a speculative upsurge of unparalleled magnitude and duration.

There were some reasons for thinking that 1929 might be different.

For one thing, Mr. Hoover would replace President Coolidge in the White House in March and, in the narrow political spectrum of the day, that meant a marked shift to the left. Mr. Coolidge, as Mr. Hoover himself has testified, knew nothing and cared less about the speculative orgy in which the country was indulging itself. (A few days before leaving office he assured the country that things were "absolutely sound" and that stocks were a good buy at current prices.) Moreover, the instrument through which Mr. Coolidge would have had to act was the Federal Reserve Board, and in his time the possibility of this body's initiating any drastic measures was remarkably slight. Its authority, constitutional and moral, was shared with the powerful Federal Reserve Bank of New York. The Chairman of the Board, one Daniel R. Crissinger, had become a central banker by grace of the doctrine, which had held sway a few years before, that what was good enough for Marion, Ohio, was good enough for the country. His colleagues, with one exception, have been described by Mr. Hoover, with his characteristic conservatism, as mediocrities.

In his memoirs, Mr. Hoover suggests that, by the beginning of 1929, the halting of the stock-market boom had become practically an obsession with him. This was a fairly well-kept secret, for the market hailed his election in November with the wildest advance to date, and a day or two before he took office in March there was a fine upsurge which was dubbed the "inaugural market." However, Mr. Hoover did know what was going on, and late in 1927 Crissinger had been replaced by Roy A. Young, a more substantial figure. There was now at least a chance that an effort might be made to restrain the speculation.

There remained, however, the problem of what could be done— and at what cost. Stocks, overwhelmingly, were being bought on margin. That meant that someone had to put up as a loan the part of the price which the purchaser wasn't paying. The task of the Federal Reserve was to get control of the funds that were being thus used to finance the speculative purchase of securities. But the rates on these broker's loans were high—through January 1929, for example, they averaged a shade under 7 per cent. Seven per cent with near-perfect safety and your money available on demand is a very decent return. Individuals and especially corporations were finding this an increasingly attractive outlet for surplus cash, and the Federal Reserve had no obvious way of checking this source of money for the market.

However, in many respects this was a detail. There was the much more inconvenient question of whether any control could be exercised which, if effective, wouldn't bring an awful smash. It is easy enough to burst a bubble. To incise it with a needle so that it subsides gradually is an operation of undoubted delicacy. Collapse and an ensuing depression would be unpleasant for, among others, those who were blamed for bringing them about. This was sensed if not seen.

Yet, there was the danger that if the bull market were allowed to go roaring along there would eventually be an even more violent crack-up. So early in 1929 the monetary authorities began debating the relative merits of sudden death and a slightly more horrible demise a little later on. Secretary Mellon was passionately for inaction; Governor Young and a part of his Board were for action although there was dispute on the particular controls to be invoked.

The issue was never decided, but the knowledge that the debate was going on began to be a source of uneasiness in Wall Street.

Meanwhile, there were more serious sources of uneasiness from within the market itself. In a market like that of 1929 there are three possible reasons why people buy stocks. One is for the old-fashioned purpose of sharing in the current income of an enterprise. Some eccentrics were undoubtedly so motivated in those days, although in the case of such a speculative favorite as Radio, which, adjusted for split-ups, reached 505 on September 3, 1929, up from 94½ in the preceding eighteen months, the desire for immediate income must have been fairly slight. The stock had never paid a dividend. Elsewhere the showing was better. A hundred dollars' worth of shares which provided an average return of $5.90 in 1921 paid $3.50 in 1929. Yields did not keep pace with market values, but neither, as some have suggested, did they vanish.

A second and far larger group of people were buying stocks because they had heard that the stock market was a place where people could get rich and they were righteously persuaded that their right to be rich was as good as the next person's. These were the innocent, although it was also their misfortune to believe—perhaps with some assistance from a customer's man—that they were really very wise. These buyers talked of the prospects for Steel, GM, United Corporation, and Blue Ridge with the familiarity of a friend and the unique certainty, not of one who knows, but of one who doesn't know that he doesn't know.

Finally, stocks were being bought by those who knew that a boom was on but who intended to get out—or even, at a high level of professionalism, to go short—before the crash came. As 1929 wore along, it was this group that became increasingly nervous. The market was making phenomenal advances; one couldn't get out while there were still such gains to be made. But whenever there was upsetting news the market dropped sharply on large volume. Some *were* getting out.

Thus, in February, when the Federal Reserve finally decided to issue a warning—"a member bank is not within its reasonable claims for rediscount facilities at the Federal Reserve Bank when it borrows for the purpose of making speculative loans"—prices broke sharply. There was a prompt recovery, but in the following month it became known that the Federal Reserve Board was meeting daily on its problem of suicide *versus* eventual disaster. The market broke again, and on March 26, 8,239,000 shares changed hands on the New York Stock Exchange. (Once in the early days of the bull market it had been said that men might live to see a five-million-share day.) Prices fell precipitately, and call money rates that day went to 20 per cent, which meant that anyone who bought General Electric on margin paid at the rate of 20 per cent per annum for that day to carry a security which was yielding around 1.25 per cent.

There is a chance—no one will ever know—that the bubble might have been pricked then and there, but, in an act of historic arrogance, Charles E. Mitchell, Chairman of the Board of the National City Bank, put his bank behind the boom. "We feel that we have an obligation which is paramount to any Federal Reserve warning, or anything else, to avert . . . any dangerous crisis in the money market." The National City let it be known that it was loaning freely in the call market and had more to come if rates got unduly high, *i.e.*, much above 15 per cent. The market steadied and by the end of March 26 most of that day's losses had been recovered.

There were further breaks and more nervousness during the next two months. However, the Federal Reserve remained quiet and presumably undecided. In any case, it had met Mr. Mitchell on the field, Mr. Mitchell had spoken, and the field was Mitchell's. So there was a brief recovery of confidence, and prices started on their last great zoom. There was no summer lull in Wall Street that year. Each day the market went on to new highs. Not everyone was playing it as legend holds—the great majority of Americans were then as innocent of knowledge of how to buy a stock as they are today—but subsequent estimates of undoubted unreliability have suggested that as many as a million people were involved in the speculation. During that summer, practically all of them made money. Never, before or since, have so many people so suddenly got so wonderfully rich.

On the first of June the *Times* industrial average—industrial stocks were the locus of the heavy speculation—stood at 342; by the first of July it was 394; on the first of August it was 418; when the market reopened on September 3 after the Labor Day holiday it reached 452. This was a gain of 110 points—25 per cent—in ninety days. The *New York Times* financial section on September 3 ran to fifteen full pages. Call money rates were 9 per cent; the rediscount rate at the Federal Reserve Bank, increased in August, was 6 per cent. Later in the week it was announced that brokers' loans had reached the remarkable total of $6,354,000,000. (In the preceding three months they had been increasing at a rate in excess of $400,000,000 a month.) However, the end was near, although never so far from being in sight.

On September 5 there was a new break and the industrial averages fell about ten points. The nervousness of those who wanted both to stay to the last and get out in time was admirably indicated by the cause of this setback. It followed a statement by Mr. Roger Babson on September 4 that "Sooner or later a crash is coming and it may be terrific." (The drop was promptly labeled the Babson Break.) All honor must go to Mr. Babson for his historic omniscience, although it deserves to be added that he had been making similar predictions at frequent intervals for some four years.

The market was ragged the rest of September and into October. There were days of strength, but there were also days of weakness and generally speaking the direction was down. In the arresting terminology of the time—as used in this instance by the *Wall Street Journal*— "Price movements in the main body of stocks continued to display the characteristics of a major advance temporarily halted for technical readjustments." Others even spoke of the possibility of a further drop, although mostly to explain why it couldn't happen. And no one should suppose that the old enthusiasm was gone.

On September 20 the *New York Times* reported that "Investors and speculators alike appear keen for 'new names.' . . . An example of this is in the Lehman Corporation which was offered at $104 and yesterday sold at $136. . . . Another is in the new Midland Marine, whose offering at $60.00 or thereabouts a share has not yet been made but which yesterday commanded $85.00 in the over-the-counter market." On October 8, from Germany, Charles E. Mitchell announced that "nothing can arrest the upward movement in the United States," and a week later, on taking the boat for home, he helpfully added that the market was now "in a healthy condition" and that "values have a sound basis in the general prosperity of our country." During the same week, Irving Fisher announced his historic conclusion that stocks had reached a "new high plateau," and *Time* Magazine, young and not yet omniscient, got ready its issue of October 28 with a cover story on Ivar Kreuger. (The following week it featured Samuel Insull.)

On Saturday, October 19, Washington dispatches reported that Secretary of Commerce Lamont was having trouble finding the $100,000 in government funds which would be required to pay the upkeep of the yacht *Corsair* which J. P. Morgan had just given to the government. (Morgan's deprivation was not unbearable; a new $3,-000,000 *Corsair* was being readied at Bath, Maine.) There were other and more compelling indications of an unaccustomed stringency. The papers told of a very weak market the day before—there were heavy declines on late trading and the *Times* industrial average had dropped about seven points. Meanwhile, that day's market was behaving very badly. In the second heaviest Saturday's trading in history, 3,488,100 shares were changing hands. At the close the *Times* industrial index was down twelve points.

On Sunday the break was front-page news—the *Times* headline read, "Stocks driven down as wave of selling engulfs market." The *Times* financial editor, who along with the editor of the *Commercial and Financial Chronicle* had never wavered in his conviction that the market had gone insane, suggested that, for the moment at least, "Wall Street seemed to see the reality of things." The news stories featured two other observations which were to become wonderfully familiar in the next fortnight. It was said, at the end of Saturday's trading, an exceptionally large number of margin calls went out. It was predicted that, come the following week, "organized support" could definitely be expected for the market.

Monday, October 21, was another poor day. Sales totaled 6,091,870, the third greatest volume in history, and hundreds of thousands who were watching the market throughout the country made a disturbing discovery. There was no way of telling what was happening. Previously on big days of the bull market the ticker had often fallen behind, and one didn't discover until well after the market closed how much richer he had become. But with a falling market things were very different. Now one might be ruined, totally and forever, and not know it. And even if one were not ruined, there was a strong tendency to imagine it. From the opening on the twenty-first the ticker lagged and by noon it was an hour late. Not until an hour and forty minutes after the close of the market did it record the last transaction. Every ten minutes prices of selected stocks were printed on the bond ticker, but the wide divergence between these and the prices on the tape only added to the uneasiness—and to the growing conviction that it might be best to sell.

This conviction notwithstanding, the market closed well above its low for the day—the net loss on the *Times* industrial averages was only about six points—and on Tuesday there was a further though rather shaky gain. Possibly some credit for this improvement should go to Wall Street's two cheeriest seers. On Monday in New York Professor Fisher said that the declines had represented only a "shaking out of the lunatic fringe." He went on to explain why he felt that the prices of stocks during the boom had not caught up with their real value. Among other things, the market had not yet reflected the beneficent effects of Prohibition, which had made the American worker "more productive and dependable."

On Tuesday, Charles E. Mitchell dropped anchor with the observation that "the decline had gone too far." (Time and sundry Congressional and court proceedings were to show that Mr. Mitchell had strong personal reasons for feeling that way.) He added that conditions were "fundamentally sound," that too much attention had been paid to the large volume of brokers' loans, and that the "situation is one which will correct itself if left alone." There was, however, another jarring suggestion from Babson. He recommended selling stocks and buying gold.

By Wednesday, October 23, the effect of this cheer had been dissipated. Instead of further gains there were heavy losses. The opening was quiet enough, but toward mid-morning motor accessory stocks were sold heavily, and volume began to increase throughout the list. The last hour was quite phenomenal—2,600,000 shares changed hands at rapidly declining prices. The *Times* industrial average for the day dropped from 415 to 384, giving up all of its gains since the end of the previous June. Again the ticker was far behind, and to add to the uncertainty an ice storm in the Middle West caused widespread disruption of communications. That afternoon and evening thousands of speculators decided to get out while—as they mistakenly supposed —the getting was good. Other thousands were told they would have no choice but to get out unless they posted more collateral for, as the day's business came to an end, an unprecedented volume of margin calls went out.

Speaking in Washington, even Professor Fisher was fractionally less optimistic. He told a meeting of bankers that "security values *in most instances* were not inflated." However, he did not weaken on the unrealized efficiencies of Prohibition. The papers that day contained one souvenir of a fast-departing era. Formidable advertisements announced subscription rights in a new offering of certificates in Aktiebolaget, Kreuger & Toll at $23.00. There was also one bit of cheer. It was everywhere predicted that, on the morrow, the market would begin to receive "organized support."

Thursday, October 24, is the first of the days which history—such as it is on the subject—identifies with the panic of 1929. Measured by disorder, fright, and confusion, it deserves to be so regarded. 12,894,-650 shares changed hands that day, most of them at prices which shattered the dreams and the hopes of those who had owned them. Of all the mysteries of the stock exchange there is none so impenetrable as why there should be a buyer for everyone who seeks to sell. October 24, 1929 showed that what is mysterious is not inevitable. Often there were no buyers, and only after wide vertical declines could anyone be induced to bid.

The morning was the terrible time. The opening was unspectacular, and for a little prices were firm. Volume, however, was large and soon prices began to sag. Once again the ticker dropped behind the market. Prices fell farther and faster, and the ticker lagged more and more. By eleven o'clock what had been a market was only a wild scramble to sell. In the crowded board rooms across the country the ticker told of a frightful collapse. But the selected quotations coming in over the bond ticker also showed that current values were far below the ancient history of the tape. The uncertainty led more and more people to try to sell. Others, no longer able to respond to margin calls, were sold. By 11:30, panic, pure and unqualified, was in control.

Outside on Broad Street a weird roar could be heard. A crowd gathered and Police Commissioner Grover Whalen dispatched a special police detail to Wall Street to insure the peace. A workman appeared to accomplish some routine repairs atop one of the high buildings. The multitude, assuming he was a would-be suicide, waited impatiently for him to jump. At 12:30 the visitors' gallery of the Exchange was closed on the wild scenes below. One of the visitors who had just departed was displaying his customary genius for being on hand with history. He was the former Chancellor of the Exchequer, Mr. Winston Churchill. It was he in 1925 who returned Britain to a gold standard that substantially over-valued the pound. To help relieve the subsequent strain the Federal Reserve eased money rates and, in the conventional though by no means unimpeachable view, it thereby launched the bull market. However, there is no record of anyone's that day having reproached Winston for the trouble he was causing. It is most unlikely that he reproached himself. Economics was never his strong point.

At noon, however, things took a turn for the better. At last came the long-awaited organized support. The heads of the National City Bank, Chase, Guaranty Trust, and Bankers Trust met with Thomas W. Lamont, the senior Morgan partner, at 23 Wall Street. All quickly agreed to come to the support of the market and to pool substantial resources for this purpose. Lamont then met with reporters and, in what Frederick Lewis Allen in his superb account of the day's events in *Only Yesterday* described as "one of the most remarkable understatements of all time," said: "There has been a little distress selling on the Stock Exchange." He added that this passing inconvenience was "due to a technical situation rather than any fundamental cause," and he told the newsmen the situation was "susceptible to betterment."

Meanwhile, word had reached the Exchange floor that the bankers were meeting and succor was on the way. These were the nation's most potent financiers; they had not yet been pilloried and maligned by the New Dealers. Prices promptly firmed and rose. Then at 1:30 Richard Whitney, widely known as a floor broker for Morgan's, walked jauntily to the post where Steel was traded and left with the specialist an order for 10,000 shares at several points above the current bids. He continued the rounds with this largesse. Confidence was wonderfully revived, and the market actually boomed upward. In the last hour the selling orders which were still flooding in turned it soft again, but the net loss for the day—about twelve points on the *Times* industrial averages—was far less than the day before. Some issues, Steel among them, were actually higher on the day's trading.

However, this recovery was of distant interest to the tens of thousands who had sold or been sold out during the decline and whose dreams of opulence had gone glimmering along with most of their merchantable possessions. It was eight and a half minutes past seven that night before the ticker finished recording the day's misfortunes. In the board rooms speculators who had been sold out since early morning sat silently watching the tape. The habit of months or years, however idle it had now become, could not be broken at once. Then, as the final trades were registered, they made their way out into the gathering night.

In Wall Street itself lights blazed from every office as clerks struggled to come abreast of the day's business. Messengers and boardroom boys, caught up in the excitement and untroubled by losses, went skylarking through the streets until the police arrived to quell them. Representatives of thirty-five of the largest wire houses assembled at the offices of Hornblower and Weeks and told the press on departing that the market was "fundamentally sound" and "technically in better condition than it has been in months." The host firm dispatched a market letter which stated that "commencing with today's trading the market should start laying the foundation for the constructive advance which we believe will characterize 1930." Charles E. Mitchell announced that the trouble was "purely technical" and that "fundamentals remained unimpaired." Senator Carter Glass said the trouble was due to Charles E. Mitchell. Senator Wilson of Indiana attributed the crash to Democratic resistance to a higher tariff.

On Friday and Saturday trading continued heavy—just under six million on Friday and over two million at the short session on Saturday. Prices, on the whole, were steady—the averages were a trifle up on Friday but slid off on Saturday. It was thought that the bankers were able to dispose of most of the securities they had acquired while shoring up the market. Not only were things better, but everyone was clear that it was the banking leaders who had made them so. They had shown both their courage and their power, and the people applauded warmly and generously. Commenting on Friday's market the *Times* said: "Secure in the knowledge that the most powerful banks in the country stood ready to prevent a recurrence [of panic] the financial community relaxed its anxiety yesterday."

From other sources came statements of reassurance and even of self-congratulation. Colonel Leonard Ayres of Cleveland thought no other country could have survived such a crash so well. Eugene M. Stevens, the President of the Continental Illinois Bank, said, "There is nothing in the business situation to justify any nervousness"; Walter Teagle said there had been no "fundamental change" in the oil business to justify concern; Charles M. Schwab said that the steel business had been making "fundamental progress" toward stability and added that this "fundamentally sound condition" was responsible for the prosperity of the industry; Samuel Vauclain, Chairman of the Baldwin Locomotive Works, declared that "fundamentals are sound"; President Hoover said that "The fundamental business of the country, that is production and distribution of commodities, is on a sound and prosperous basis." H. C. Hopson, the head of Associated Gas & Electric, omitted the standard reference to fundamentals and said it was "undoubtedly beneficial to the business interests of the country to have the gambling type of speculator eliminated." (Mr. Hopson, himself a speculator, although perhaps more of the sure-thing type, was also eliminated in due course.) A Boston investment trust took space in the *Wall Street Journal* to say, "S-T-E-A-D-Y Everybody! Calm thinking is in order. Heed the words of America's greatest bankers." A single dissonant note, though great in portent, went completely unnoticed. Speaking in Poughkeepsie, Governor Franklin D. Roosevelt criticized the "fever of speculation."

On Sunday there were sermons suggesting that a certain measure of divine retribution had been visited on the Republic and that it had not been entirely unmerited. It was evident, however, that almost everyone believed that this heavenly knuckle-rapping was over and that speculation could be now resumed in earnest. The papers were full of the prospects for next week's market. Stocks, it was agreed, were again cheap and accordingly there would be a heavy rush to buy. Numerous stories from the brokerage houses, some of them possibly inspired, told of a fabulous volume of buying orders which was piling up in anticipation of the opening of the market. In a concerted advertising campaign in Monday's papers, stock-market firms urged the wisdom of buying stocks promptly. On Monday the real disaster began.

Trading on Monday, though in great volume, was smaller than on the previous Thursday—9,212,800 as compared with the nearly thirteen million. But the sustained drop in prices was far more severe. The *Times* industrial average was down 49 points for the day. General Electric was off 47½; Westinghouse, 34½; Tel. & Tel., 34. Indeed, the decline on this one day was greater than that of all the preceding week of panic. Once again a late ticker left everyone in ignorance of what was happening save that it was bad.

At 1:10 there was a momentary respite—Charles E. Mitchell was detected going into Morgan's and the news ticker carried the magic word. Steel rallied and went from 193½ to 198. But this time Richard Whitney did not appear; "organized support" was not forthcoming. Support, organized or otherwise, could no longer contend with the wild desire to sell. The market weakened again and in the last hour three million shares changed hands at rapidly declining prices.

The bankers assembled once again at Morgan's and remained in session from 4:30 to 6:30. They were described as having a "philosophical attitude," and they told the press that the situation "retained hopeful features." But there was a more important clue to what was discussed for the two hours. It was explained at the conclusion that it was no part of the bankers' purpose to maintain any particular level of prices on the market. Their operations were confined to seeing that the market was orderly—that offers would be met by bids at some price, and that "air holes," as Mr. Lamont dubbed them, would not be allowed to appear in the market. Like many lesser men, Mr. Lamont and his colleagues had obviously found themselves overcommitted. The time had come to go short on promises. It was also chilling news. To the man who held stock on margin, disaster wore only one face and that was falling prices. He wanted to be saved from disaster. Now he must comfort himself with the knowledge that his ruin would be accomplished in an orderly and becoming manner.

Tuesday, October 29, was the most devastating day in the history of the New York stock market, and it may have been the most devastating in the history of markets. Selling began at once and in huge volume. The air holes, which the bankers were to close, opened wide. Repeatedly and in many issues there was a plethora of selling orders and no buyers at all. Once again, of course, the ticker lagged—at the close it was two and a half hours behind. By then 16,410,030 shares had been known to have been traded—more than three times the number that had once been considered a fabulously big day. (On an average good day last summer sales were running about three million shares.) Despite a closing rally on dividend news, the losses were again appalling. The *Times* industrial averages were down forty-three points, canceling all of the huge gains of the preceding twelve months. Losses on individual issues were far greater. By the end of trading, members were near collapse from strain and fatigue. Office staffs, already near the breaking point, now had to tackle the greatest volume of transactions yet. By now, also, there was no longer quite the same certainty that things would get better. Perhaps they would go on getting worse.

During the preceding week, the slaughter had been of the innocents. Now it was the well-to-do and the wealthy—the men of affairs and the professionals—who were experiencing the egalitarianism long supposed to be the first fruit of avarice. Where the board rooms were crowded the week before, now they were nearly empty. The new victims had facilities for suffering in private. The bankers met at noon and again in the evening of the twenty-ninth, but there was no suggestion that they were philosophical. In truth, their prestige had been falling even more disconcertingly than the market. During the day the rumor had swept the Exchange that, of all things, the "organized support" was busy selling stocks, and Mr. Lamont met the press after the evening session with the trying assignment of denying that this was so. It remained for Mayor James J. Walker to come up with the only constructive proposal of the day. Addressing an audience of motion picture exhibitors, he asked them to "show pictures that will reinstate courage and hope in the hearts of the people."

On the Exchange itself a strong feeling was developing that courage and hope might best be reinstated if the market were closed and everyone were given a breathing spell. This simple and forthright thought derived impressive further support from the fact that everyone was badly in need of sleep. The difficulty was that the announcement of the closing of the Exchange might simply worsen the panic. At noon on the twenty-ninth the issue came to a head. So as not to attract attention, the members of the Governing Committee left the floor in twos and threes to attend a meeting; the meeting itself was held not in the regular room but in the office of the Stock Clearing Corporation below the trading floor. As the unfortunate Richard Whitney later described the session, the air quickly became blue with tobacco smoke as the tired and nervous brokers lit cigarettes, stubbed them out, and lit fresh ones. Everyone wanted a respite from the agony. Quite a few firms needed a few hours to ascertain whether they were still solvent.

But caution was on the side of keeping the market open at least until it could be closed on a note of strength and optimism. The decision was to carry on till things improved. Again the lights blazed all night. In one brokerage house an employee fainted from exhaustion, was revived, and promptly put back to work again.

Next day those imponderable forces were at work which bring salvation just at the moment when salvation seems impossible. Volume was still enormous, but prices were much better—the *Times* industrial average rose thirty-one points, and individual issues made excellent gains. Possibly it was the reassurances that accomplished the miracle —in any case these were forthcoming in volume. On the evening of the twenty-ninth, Julius Klein took to the radio to remind the country that President Hoover had said that the "fundamental business of the country" was sound and prosperous. He added, "The main point I want to make is the fundamental soundness of [the] great mass of economic activities." On Wednesday, Wadill Catchings, the head of Goldman, Sachs, announced on returning from a Western trip that general business conditions were "unquestionably fundamentally sound." (The same, it subsequently developed, could not unquestionably be said for all of Goldman, Sachs.) R. R. Reynolds, President of Selected Industries, Inc., another investment trust, said that "The fundamentally strong position of the nation's industries justified confidence." Of more importance, perhaps, from Pocantico Hills came the first public statement from John D. Rockefeller in some decades: "Believing that fundamental conditions of the country are sound . . . my son and I have for some days been purchasing sound common stock."

Just before the Rockefeller statement arrived things looked good enough on the Exchange so that Richard Whitney felt safe in announcing that the market would not open until noon the following day (Thursday) and that on Friday and Saturday it would stay shut. The announcement was greeted by cheers. Nerves were clearly past the breaking point. On La Salle Street in Chicago a boy exploded a firecracker. Like wildfire the rumor spread that gangsters whose margin accounts had been closed out were shooting up the street. Several squads of police arrived to make them take their losses like honest men. In New York the body of a commission merchant was fished out of the Hudson. The pocket contained $9.40 in change and some margin calls.

No feature of the Great Crash was more remarkable than the way it passed from climax to anticlimax to destroy again and again the hope that the worst had passed. Even on the thirtieth the worst was still to come, although henceforth it came more slowly. Day after day during the next two weeks prices fell with monotonous regularity. At the close of trading on October 29 the *Times* industrial average stood at 275. In the rally of the next two days it gained more than fifty points, but by November 13 it was down to 224 for a further net loss of fifty points.

And these levels were wonderful compared with what were to follow. On July 8, 1932, the average of the closing levels of the *Times* industrials was 58.46. This was not much more than the amount by which the average dropped on the next single day of October 28, and considerably less than a quarter of the closing values on October 29. By then, of course, business conditions were no longer sound, fundamentally or otherwise.

What might be called the everyday or utility-style history book tells of the Great Depression of the thirties which began with the great stock-market crash of 1929. Among sophisticates—professional students of the business cycle in particular—there has long been a tendency to decry the importance that this attributes to the stock-market crash as a cause of the depression. The crash was part of the froth, rather than the substance of the situation. A depression, it was pointed out, had been in the making since midsummer of 1929, when numerous of the indexes began to turn down.

In this matter the history books are almost certainly right. The market crash (and, of course, the speculation that set the stage) was of profound importance for what followed. It shrank the supply of investment funds and, at the same time, it shocked the confidence on which investment expenditure depends. The crash also reduced personal expenditures and deeply disrupted international capital flows and international trade. The effect of all this on economic activity was prompt and very real. Nothing else is a fraction so important for explaining the severity of the depression that followed.

Since it was important, the question inevitably arises whether a similar cycle of speculation and collapse could again occur. The simple answer is of course! Laws have been passed to outlaw some of the more egregious behavior which contributed to the big bull market of the twenties. Nothing has been done about the seminal lunacy which possesses people who see a chance of becoming rich. On the assumption that history does not repeat itself precisely, we may never again see the particular lunacy of the late twenties. But if we survive to suffer such things, we can undoubtedly count on some variation. The time to worry will be when important people begin to explain that it cannot happen because conditions are fundamentally sound.

The Southern Case Against Desegregation

by T. R. WARING

JANUARY, 1956

In an editorial note, the magazine said it was publishing this article for four reasons: (1) the rest of the country needed to understand the "state of mind" this Southern writer represented; (2) there had been "almost no rational discussion between the men of good will on each side of the issue" and until such a dialogue could be started, "the angry men will dominate the field"; (3) other points of view on the issue have been presented in the magazine; and (4) "one of the duties of an independent magazine, allied to no party or interest group, is to give a hearing to significant bodies of opinion which cannot find expression elsewhere—even when the editors disagree." T. R. Waring is editor of the News and Courier *in Charleston, S. C., perhaps the most Southern of all cities and where his family has lived for nine generations. Following this article is one by William Faulkner of Mississippi, who favors integration.*

Although the Supreme Court has declared that separation of the races in public schools is unconstitutional, few white Southerners are able to accept the prospect of mingling white and Negro pupils. Resistance to the court decree is stiffening throughout the region.

Many white Northerners are unable to understand the depth of feeling in the Southern states, whose area is about a sixth of the nation and whose population is roughly a fourth of the total. The purpose of this article is to try to put before the open-minded readers of this magazine the point of view of the Southerner—whom the rest of the United States apparently cannot believe to be open-minded at all on the subject of race.

At the outset it is only fair to warn the Northern reader that he may be infuriated long before he reaches the end. This, I suspect, is just as inevitable as the outraged feelings of the Southerner when he reads the Northern press with its own interpretation of the American dilemma. Both sides have been shouting at each other so loudly that it is difficult any longer to hear facts through the din of name-calling. If, in the course of speaking for the South, I should raise blood pressure among some Northerners, I apologize for causing pain—with the hope that I may be able to reach Northern minds that are truly open so that some good may come along with the discomfort.

The reader outside the South may, unfortunately, react in still another way. He may find it difficult, if not impossible, to believe much of what I say. To this I can only reply that as editor of a South Carolina newspaper with a circulation of 56,000, with twenty-eight years of journalistic experience in both the North and the South, I have had to be in possession of accurate information on this as on any other subject covered in my work. Across an editor's desk pass, day by day and year after year, reports, letters, statistics—in other words, facts. By means of these facts, plus personal conversations with people from all over the world, an editor manages to keep in touch with public opinion.

It is the public opinion of the South that I am about to report. That opinion is a fact. It exists, and can be demonstrated. What I am saying is documented by facts and statistics. If these should seem to the reader to add up merely to bias, bigotry, and even untruth, I shall regret it. Facts, however, remain facts.

One of the reasons these facts may be unfamiliar—and therefore incredible—is the almost unanimous attitude of the national press—daily and weekly—toward the subject of race. I read many newspapers and news magazines, and people send me clippings from others that I do not see regularly. From my observation, the testimony these publications print is almost entirely one-sided. While less violent than the Negro press—which understandably presents only the militant anti-segregation case—the metropolitan press almost without exception has abandoned fair and objective reporting of the race story. For facts it frequently substitutes propaganda.

Furthermore, with the exception of a small coterie of Southern writers whom Northern editors regard as "enlightened," spokesmen for the Southern view cannot gain access to Northern ears. This article will be one of the few of its kind published in a magazine of national circulation. The South, alas, lacks a magazine or other organ with nationwide distribution.

Perhaps my first assertion of a seldom realized truth will be the most difficult to believe. This statement is that white Southerners of good will—and the percentage of decency runs about the same in the South as anywhere else—favor uplift of the Negro, and that these white Southerners are in the vast majority. If it is impossible to prove the percentage of decency among Southerners, it is equally impossible to show that people in the North—or any other region—have a monopoly of it. But the South fears, and with reason, that the uplift is being forced at too fast a pace. The vagaries of custom and race taboos have many inconsistencies. The rules of segregation, both written and unwritten, change with conditions. And the sudden rewriting by the Supreme Court of regional laws and state constitutions has stirred as much resentment in Southern breasts as would be aroused among Northerners if suddenly their own freedom from race restrictions were denied by federal fiat. (Do I hear a muffled cheer from one or two Northerners who may take a dim view of mingling the races?)

Interference with sovereignty usually produces rage. In matters of education, the states long have been sovereign—until suddenly nine men have held otherwise.

Is it any wonder that the Southerner is bitter over what he believes to be a flouting of the Constitution for political reasons?

Aside from legal questions—and they are deep and broad—the Southerner believes that as a practical matter, he is better equipped by experience to cope with race problems than people from other regions, no matter what their intellectual or political attainments. One of the proofs that this belief is founded not merely on pride or emotional prejudice lies in the fact that Northerners who spend some time in the South—not tourists or weekend visitors, but people who make their homes here—come rather sooner than later to agree that this is so. These transplanted Northerners come to see that there are far more bonds of friendship and active, productive good will between the white Southerner and his Negro neighbor than they had believed—or could believe until they became eye-witnesses and partakers of this relationship.

Although the South is both willing and eager to have the Negro earn greater acceptance on many levels—especially economic—it does not consider, for reasons that I shall submit, that mixed education is the way to achieve this acceptance—certainly not at this stage of affairs.

What may lie in the distant future is more than any of us can predict with accuracy. Southerners know that race problems are as old as history. While views and philosophies may change through the ages, some basic truths stand out like the Ten Commandments. Southerners are not yet ready to accept an eleventh, "Thou shalt not protect the purity of thy race."

Before going into the actual reasons for the Southerner's objections to mixed education—before asking the burning question, how can the races best live together—let us examine for a moment the pattern of separation. It is a pattern that Thomas Jefferson, Abraham Lincoln, and at one time Dwight D. Eisenhower have favored as best for both races. In 1888, Henry W. Grady, Atlanta editor—described by Don Shoemaker of the Southern Education Reporting Service as a Southern "liberal" of his time—summed up the situation as follows:

> Neither "provincialism" nor "sectionalism" holds the South together but something deeper than these and essential to our system. The problem is how to carry within her body politic two separate races, and nearly equal in numbers. [Since Grady spoke, the whites in the South have come to outnumber the Negroes four to one, but the proportions vary greatly by neighborhoods.] She must carry these races in peace—for discord means ruin. She must carry them separately—for assimilation means debasement. She must carry them in equal justice—for to this she is pledged in honor and gratitude. She must carry them to the end, for in human probability she will never be quit of either.

While Grady's statements were made nearly seventy years ago and therefore are subject to the criticism that they do not reflect "modern conditions," to many Southerners they are truth both now and for the future.

The presence of large numbers of Negroes—especially in the tide-water regions of Virginia, the Carolinas, and Georgia, and the plantation country of Alabama and Louisiana, Mississippi and East Texas—means that the races necessarily live in intimate daily association. Why, then, should not the children of people who live in the same community—sometimes as close neighbors—attend the same schools?

Southerners believe they have valid reasons, aside from "prejudice" about the color of skin, for their insistence on sending white children to exclusively white schools. Without debating superiority of either race, they are keenly aware of cultural differences. In some ways the standards of white people are none too high. The same economic conditions that have held back Negroes have worked against the whites. The increasing prosperity of the South is removing some of these disadvantages for both races, though not necessarily in precisely the same way.

Whether all the differences will eventually be removed, or enough of them to make mixed education acceptable to a substantial number of white people, the differences are too great *at present* to encourage white parents to permit their children to mingle freely in school. This has nothing to do with the frequent practice of children of both races of playing together when young, or with cordial relationships in many other contacts of ordinary life.

Volumes could be written on racial differences from many angles, including anthropology and sociology. I shall merely try to summarize five of the differences that most immediately come to the minds of white parents in the South. These are health; home environment; marital standards; crime; and a wide disparity in average intellectual development.

(1) *Health*. Negro parents as a whole—for reasons that white people may sympathetically deplore but which nevertheless exist—are not so careful on the average as their white neighbors in looking after the health and cleanliness of their children. The incidence of venereal disease for instance is much greater among Negroes than among whites.

Statistics to document this statement are difficult to come by, though the statement itself would be generally accepted in the South. The U. S. Public Health Service some years ago quietly stopped identifying statistics by races. South Carolina figures, available for 1952–53, give a clue to the situation in that state; it probably is much the same elsewhere in the South. Out of a population 60 per cent white and 40 per cent Negro, 6,315 cases of syphilis were reported, of which 89 per cent were among Negroes. Infection with gonorrhea was found in six Negroes to one white person, but some physicians report that many cases of gonorrhea among Negroes go unrecorded.

During the same period—1952–53—a campaign against venereal disease was carried on, county by county. A spot check of four representative counties in different parts of South Carolina showed that cases of syphilis were found among 1.3 per cent of the white persons examined. This was a fairly constant percentage. The percentage of infection among Negroes ranged in the same counties from 8.5 to 10.8 per cent, averaging more than 9 per cent.

Fastidious parents do not favor joint use of school washrooms when they would not permit it at home—and there's no use to tell them that it is unlikely that anyone will catch venereal disease from a toilet seat. They just don't want to take risks of any kind with their children.

(2) *Home environment.* For most colored children in the South the cultural background is different in many ways from that of their white neighbors—and while these differences may have various explanations, they add up in the public's mind as racial. Slavery is so long in the past that nobody thinks about it any more, but the master and servant, or boss and laborer, relationship between whites and Negroes is still the rule rather than the exception. The emergence of a middle class among the Negroes has been extremely slow—again, the reasons count for less in the minds of white parents than the fact itself. Indeed, the professional and commercial class among Negroes is so small that its members are in perhaps the most unenviable position of all. They have progressed beyond the cultural level of the vast bulk of their own people, but are not accepted among the whites, who fear to let down any dikes lest they be engulfed in a black flood.

Someone may suggest that here is an opening wedge for integration in the schools, by admitting a few well scrubbed and polished colored children of cultivated parents. In reply, let me say that this would be no more acceptable to the colored people than to the whites. The solution, perhaps—as it is among upper-bracket white people who do not send their children to public schools—might be private schools for prosperous Negroes as for prosperous whites. In any case, white people feel that cultural gaps on other levels should be filled in before discussing integrated schools.

(3) *Marital habits.* Among many Southern Negroes they are, to state it mildly, casual—even more so, in fact, than among the often-divorced personalities of Northern café society. Many Negro couples —the statistics are not readily available, for obvious reasons—do not bother with divorce because there was no actual marriage in the first place. Statistics on the results of such casual unions, however, are available. On the average one Southern Negro child in five is illegitimate. It is possible the figure may be even higher, since illegitimate births are more likely to go unrecorded. Even among Negroes who observe marriage conventions, illegitimacy has little if any stigma.

Many white persons believe that morals among their own race are lax enough as it is, without exposing their children to an even more primitive view of sex habits. Moreover, while these parents do not believe there is any surge of desire among their offspring to mate with colored people, they abhor any steps that might encourage inter-marriage. They believe that lifting the racial school barriers would be such a step. Miscegenation has been on the wane of recent years. Whatever mixing of blood may have occurred—and admittedly that was due largely to lustful white men seeking out acquiescent Negro women—has been without benefit of either law or custom. On some levels of society, breaking the racial barriers might lead to mixed marriages. The mixture of races which white Southerners have observed in Latin American countries gives them a dim view of legalizing cohabitation with Negroes.

(4) *Crime.* For many years, crime in the South has been more prevalent among Negroes than among white people. Though the Northern press no longer identifies criminals by race, white Southerners have reason to believe that much of the outbreak of crime and juvenile delinquency in Northern cities is due to the influx of Negro population. They believe the North now is getting a taste of the same race troubles that the South fears would grow out of mixed schooling, on a much bigger scale. They want no "Blackboard Jungles" in the South.

Maintaining order is a first concern of Southerners. What they have heard about the fruits of integration in the North does not encourage them to adopt the Northern race pattern. In Chicago, three hundred policemen have been assigned for a year or more to guard a non-segregated housing project, with no bigger population than a Southern village where a single constable keeps the peace. In the County of Charleston, South Carolina—with 190,000 population, nearly half

Negro—the total law enforcement manpower of combined city and county forces is 175.

While the homicide rate in the South is high, it is due in large measure to knifings and shootings among the colored people. Interracial homicide is relatively rare. (One of the reasons why the ghastly killing of Emmett Till in Mississippi made hot news—and some of that news was superheated and garnished with prejudice for the Northern press—was the very fact that it *was* unusual. No lynching, as even most Northerners now realize, has occurred in years.)

With racial bars down and rowdies of both races daring one another to make something of the vast increase in daily contacts, opportunities for interracial strife are frightening. Conservative, law-abiding people —and believe it or not, they constitute the bulk of Southern whites— are deeply fearful that hatred and bloodshed would increase without separation of the races.

And they know that, in the long run, if there is riotous bloodshed it will be for the most part Negroes' blood. The thin tolerance of the ruffian and lower elements of the white people could erupt into animosity and brutality if race pressure became unbearable. Schools would be a focal point for such disturbance, first among pupils themselves and later by enraged parents. Instead of learning out of books, the younger generation would be schooled in survival—as several Northern sources have told me already is happening in some areas of New York, Philadelphia, and Washington, D. C.

(5) *Intellectual development*. Again for whatever the reasons may be, Southern Negroes usually are below the intellectual level of their white counterparts. *U. S. News and World Report*—the fairest nationally circulated publication I am acquainted with in its treatment of the race issue—has reported that in Washington, colored children are about two grades behind the whites in attainment. This discrepancy, I believe, is about par for other communities. In Washington it was found that there were even language difficulties to surmount. The children used different terms for some things.

Some advocates of integration say the way to cure these differences is to let the children mingle so that the Negroes will learn from the whites. The trouble with this theory is that even if it works, a single generation of white children will bear the brunt of the load. While they are rubbing off white civilization onto the colored children, Negro culture will also rub off onto the whites.

Few Southern parents are willing to sacrifice their own offspring in order to level off intellectual differences in this fashion. They reason that their children will get along better in later life if they have, as youngsters, the best available cultural contacts. Such an attitude is not, I understand, altogether unknown in the North. Many parents in New York City, for example, make considerable financial sacrifices to send their children to private schools, to spare them the undesirable associations and the low-geared teaching standards of most public schools.

If this sounds snobbish to a Northern reader, let me ask you to examine your own conscience. Can you honestly say that you are eager to send your own child to a classroom where the majority of other pupils will be considerably more backward in their studies, and extremely different in social background and cultural attainment? Which would you *really* put first: your theory of racial justice, or justice to your own child?

In reply to objections to integration by white Southerners, someone may ask: What about the Negroes? What do they think?

At the outset, let me say that as a person who has spent most of his life in the South, has known Negroes from earliest childhood, and as a newspaperman has been dealing with race matters every day for many years, I cannot say just what goes on in the minds of the Negroes. Nor do I believe that a white man can put himself in the place of a colored man any more than he can, by taking thought, add a cubit to his stature. Until the school question became agitated in recent years, however, race relations on the whole were good. Since the agitation, relations are not yet bad in a broad sense—but they are not improving by reason of the crusade for integration.

The leadership in that crusade comes from outside the South. It is sparked by the National Association for the Advancement of Colored People. Southerners have reason to believe that this organization has a very large measure of white influence among its leaders. They recognize that both major political parties are courting the Negro vote, which holds the balance of power in key cities of populous Northern states. They are bewildered by the array of power aligned on the side of the NAACP in press, pulpit, and politics. The NAACP and its allies seem well supplied with money. They have won legal victories and they are not disposed to compromise on any front. In fact, the NAACP seems—to white Southerners—more interested in forcing the Negro into the white man's company than in equipping the Negro to qualify fully for such association.

A small but pointed illustration occurred in Charleston when a white community theater group tried to produce *Porgy* (the original play, not the opera) with a Negro cast in the city where the story is laid. There was a grave question about how the community, in a time when racial agitation was so bitter, would accept a play performed almost exclusively by Negroes. Many difficulties had to be surmounted in casting and production. But the sponsoring group, in consultation with NAACP and other Negro spokesmen, decided to proceed, and spent a sizable amount of money getting the production under way.

One of the key questions was the seating of the audience. Under South Carolina law separate seating for the races is required. The chairman of the local NAACP chapter agreed in writing, I have been informed, to an arrangement for separate seating by means of a vertical line down the center aisle, whites on one side and Negroes on the other. At the last moment, with the play already in rehearsal, the NAACP repudiated the agreement.

The Negro cast pleaded with the white sponsors to go through with the production in spite of the NAACP. By this time, however, it became obvious that the delicate circumstances had become too explosive and the production was canceled. A possible good-will gesture, opening a new line of communication, thus was halted because the NAACP would accept nothing less than complete integration—regardless of both state law and local custom.

Whether the NAACP really speaks for the rank and file of Negroes is debatable. Public expressions of opinion from Negroes in the South, other than the NAACP, are relatively few. Some white people feel that a Negro is so accustomed to telling a white man what he thinks the white man wants to hear, that they put little stock in whatever the Negro says on race. It would not be hard to believe that, given a choice, a Negro naturally would prefer all restrictions to be removed. That does not mean, however, that all Negroes want to associate with white people. Far from it; many Negroes prefer their own churches and, it stands to reason, should be equally satisfied with their own schools, so long as an equal allotment of public money is given them.

While the allotment has not always been equal—Negroes pay only a small fraction of taxes—the sums of money spent on Negro schooling have increased by leaps and bounds. On the average the South spends a greater percentage of its per capita income on schools than other regions, and nowadays the Negroes are getting their share in most areas. One thing is certain: if the schools were integrated, many a Negro school teacher would lose his or ᴊer job. Even if the white people would accept mixed pupils—and few apparently would do so —they would insist on white teachers.

Whenever a Southern Negro does object to the drive for integration, he is subject to pressure from his own people. Two Negro clergymen —what are known as "local preachers"—recently wrote letters to newspapers in lower South Carolina opposing the mixing of schools. Both were disciplined by their church superiors. Many white people on friendly terms with Negroes are convinced that as a rule, the Negroes are not eager for mixed schools so long as the schools for Negroes are adequate.

This conviction leads them to hope that a voluntary approach eventually may help to solve the problem within the Supreme Court ruling. Judge John J. Parker of Charlotte, North Carolina, senior judge of the Fourth Circuit Court of Appeals, has said:

> It is important that we point out exactly what the Supreme Court has decided and what it has not decided in this [the Clarendon County] case. . . . It has not decided that the states must mix persons of different races in the schools. . . . Nothing in the Constitution or in the decision of the Supreme Court takes away from the people freedom to choose the schools they attend. The Constitution, in other words, does not require integration. It does not forbid such segregation as occurs as the result of voluntary action. It merely forbids the use of governmental power to enforce segregation. The Fourteenth Amendment is a limitation upon the exercise of power by the state or state agencies, not a limitation upon the freedom of individuals.

The Alabama state legislature has set up a new basis for assignment of pupils which does not mention race, though its provisions might tend to keep white and Negro pupils apart. In South Carolina, a committee of fifty-two representative citizens is circulating a resolution— already signed by many thousands—asking the State Legislature to interpose its authority between the federal government and local school boards to maintain segregation. Such a move would be based on the Tenth Amendment to the U. S. Constitution, reserving to the states and the people all powers not specifically granted to the federal government.

These are only two of many tentative plans to get around the Supreme Court's decision by methods of law. Another proposal is revival of the principle of nullification, which states both in the North and South have used in years gone by. A recent example was the public disregard of Prohibition. Segregation, perhaps, may be bootlegged in some regions. How that can be done is not immediately apparent—but the resourcefulness of the rum-runners and speakeasies was not foreseen by sponsors of the Volstead Act.

As in Prohibition, there is danger that white hoodlums may enter the picture. Sporadic outbreaks of the Ku Klux Klan have been reported. To combat the lawless element, law-abiding white men—who are determined not to yield to pressures they still regard as contrary to the guarantees of the Constitution—have been forming protective organizations. These go under many names. In Mississippi, South Carolina, and some of the other states they are called Citizens' Councils.

Much has been said about the adoption of "economic pressure" as a weapon by these white groups. In some instances Negroes have reported that their sharecropper contracts have not been renewed because they signed petitions to integrate schools. Other forms of pressure have been reported, and in some localities Negroes have retaliated with boycotts against white merchants who were active in the Councils. White leaders of the resistance movements repeatedly have said they were not organizing boycotts and pressures against the Negroes and that they are determined there shall be no reign of terror as predicted by some of the Negro spokesmen.

Hodding Carter—one of a handful of Southern writers granted access to the national magazines—has predicted that attempts to enforce integration in the public schools of Mississippi would be likely to create violence. White leaders are exploring many other avenues in hopes of preventing strong-arm methods from being tried. They fear also that the very existence of the public schools is in peril. Rather than accept mixed public schools, some white Southerners may seek other means of educating their children.

Even if the schools are not abandoned, it seems unlikely that the white people will submit to heavy taxation to operate schools that many of them refuse to patronize. If they are not throttled outright, the public school systems in some areas may be starved to death. The spread of resistance organizations, far from being the product of demagogues, is at the local level among ordinary people, without "big-name" leadership. School trustees and other officials are getting the message from the grass roots.

Acceptance of the Supreme Court's order in border states and lip service in some other quarters have encouraged some advocates to believe that many Southern communities soon will yield to integration. While the borders of the old Confederacy may narrow, the determination of white people in areas with heavy Negro population is not relaxing. Not only regions where Negroes predominate by ten to one are rejecting the prospect of mixed schools. Pickens County in Piedmont South Carolina has the smallest number of Negroes (about one in ten) of any county in the state; its grand jury—most fundamental of all bodies safeguarding the people's liberty—has gone on record against mixed schools. On Edisto Island, at the opposite side of the state, where a white face looks out of place, insistence on mingling would be almost academic. If any attempt were made to force white children into Negro schools, the white people would move off the island, or find other means of educating their children.

Talk about segregation may promote migration of Negroes from the South. Already thousands have left the cotton fields and villages to seek jobs in Northern cities. On the farms, machines have replaced them. With the minimum wage advancing to one dollar an hour, Southern employers will demand production from their laborers that not all Negroes will be able or willing to supply. These employers also may seek ways to mechanize or to employ white labor. As industries move South, more attractive opportunities for white people are opening.

If the North continues to appeal to Negroes as a land of integration and the South continues to attract white settlers, the racial proportions may grow more nearly equal. Then the North may become more tolerant of the Southerners' view of race problems, and the South better able to handle its dwindling Negro problem. Southerners will gladly share the load.

Meanwhile, stripped of emotions, the race problem for both Southern whites and Negroes is a practical matter of daily living. The problem has been recognized by thoughtful Americans from the early days of the Republic. It would be foolish to deny that any Negro pupils ever will enter Southern white schools. (Some already have.) But it would be equally foolhardy to predict that their numbers will be significant at an early date.

On Fear—The South in Labor

by WILLIAM FAULKNER

JUNE, 1956

There is no "solid South" on the segregation question. Missis-
sippi's Nobel and Pulitzer Prize-winning author supports the
United States Supreme Court decision outlawing racially segre-
gated schools. "To live anywhere in the world today and be
against equality because of race or color, is like living in Alaska
and being against snow," he says. The preceding article by
Thomas R. Waring, a South Carolinian, presents a different
viewpoint.

Immediately after the Supreme Court decision abolishing segregation in schools, the talk began in Mississippi of ways and means to
increase taxes to raise the standard of the Negro schools to match the
white ones. I wrote the following letter to the open forum page of our
most widely read Memphis paper:

We Mississippians already know that our present schools are not
good enough. Our young men and women themselves prove that to us
every year by the fact that, when the best of them want the best of education which they are entitled to and competent for, not only in the
humanities but in the professions and crafts—law and medicine and
engineering—too, they must go out of the state to get it. And quite
often, too often, they don't come back.

So our present schools are not even good enough for white people;
our present state reservoir of education is not of high enough quality
to assuage the thirst of even our white young men and women. In
which case, how can it possibly assuage the thirst and need of the
Negro, who obviously is thirstier, needs it worse, else the federal
government would not have had to pass a law compelling Mississippi
(among others of course) to make the best of our education available to him.

That is, our present schools are not even good enough for white
people. So what do we do? Make them good enough, improve them

to the best possible? No. We beat the bushes, rake and scrape to raise additional taxes to establish another system at best only equal to that one which is already not good enough, which therefore won't be good enough for Negroes either; we will have two identical systems neither of which are good enough for anybody.

A few days after my letter was printed in the paper, I received by post the carbon copy of a letter addressed to the same forum page of the Memphis paper. It read as follows:

> When Weeping Willie Faulkner splashes his tears about the inadequacy of Mississippi schools . . . we question his gumption in these respects, etc.

From there it went on to cite certain facts of which all Southerners are justly proud: that the seed-stock of education in our land was preserved through the evil times following the Civil War when our land was a defeated and occupied country, by dedicated teachers who got little in return for their dedication. Then, after a brief sneer at the quality of my writing and the profit motive which was the obvious reason why I was a writer, he closed by saying: "I suggest that Weeping Willie dry his tears and work up a little thirst for knowledge about the basic economy of this state."

Later, after this letter was printed in the Memphis paper in its turn, I received from the writer of it a letter addressed to him by a correspondent in another small Mississippi town, consisting in general of a sneer at the Nobel Prize which was awarded me, and commending the Weeping Willie writer for his promptness in taking to task anyone traitorous enough to hold education more important than the color of the educatee's skin. Attached to it was the Weeping Willie writer's reply. It said in effect:

> In my opinion Faulkner is the most capable commentator on Southern facts of life to date. . . . If we could insult him into acquiring an insight into the basic economy of our region, he could [sic] do us a hell of a lot of good in our fight against integration.

My answer was that I didn't believe that insult is a very sound method of teaching anybody anything, of persuading anyone to think or act as the insulter believes they should. I repeated that what we needed in Mississippi was the best possible schools, to make the best possible use of the men and women we produced, regardless of what color they were. And even if we could not have a school system which would do that, at least let us have one which would make no distinction among pupils except that of simple ability, since our principal and perhaps desperate need in America today was that all Americans at least should be on the side of America; that if all Americans were on the same side, we would not need to fear that other nations and ideologies would doubt us when we talked of human freedom.

But this is beside the point. The point is, what is behind this. The tragedy is not the impasse, but what is behind the impasse—the impasse of the two apparently irreconcilable facts which we are faced with in the South: the one being the decree of our national government that there be absolute equality in education among all citizens, the other being the white people in the South who say that white and Negro pupils shall never sit in the same classroom. Only apparently irreconcilable, because they must be reconciled since the only alternative to change is death. In fact, there are people in the South, Southerners born, who not only believe they can be reconciled but who love our land—not love white people specifically nor love Negroes specifically, but our land, our country: our climate and geography, the qualities in our people, white and Negro too, for honesty and fairness, the splendors in our traditions, the glories in our past—enough to try to reconcile them, even at the cost of displeasing both sides. These people are willing to face the contempt of the Northern radicals who believe we don't do enough, and the contumely and threats of our own Southern reactionaries who are convinced that anything we do is already too much.

The tragedy is the reason behind the fact, the fear behind the fact that some of the white people in the South—people who otherwise are rational, cultured, gentle, generous, and kindly—will—must—fight against every inch which the Negro gains in social betterment. It is the fear behind the desperation which could drive rational and successful men (my correspondent, the Weeping Willie one, is a banker, perhaps president of a—perhaps the—bank in another small Mississippi town like my own) to grasp at such straws for weapons as contumely and threat and insult, to change the views or anyway the voice which dares to suggest that betterment of the Negro's condition does not necessarily presage the doom of the white race.

Nor is the tragedy the fear so much as the tawdry quality of the fear—fear not of the Negro as an individual Negro nor even as a race, but as an economic class or stratum or factor, since what the Negro threatens is not the Southern white man's social system but the Southern white man's economic system—that economic system which the white man knows and dares not admit to himself is established on an obsolescence—the artificial inequality of man—and so is itself already obsolete and hence doomed. He knows that only three hundred years ago the Negro's naked grandfather was eating rotten elephant or hippo meat in an African rain-forest, yet in only three hundred years the Negro produced Dr. Ralph Bunche and George Washington Carver and Booker T. Washington. The white man knows that only ninety years ago not one per cent of the Negro race could own a deed to land, let alone read that deed; yet in only ninety years, although his only contact with a county courthouse is the window through which he pays the taxes for which he has no representation, he can own his land and farm it with inferior stock and worn-out tools and gear—equipment which any white man would starve with—and raise children and feed and clothe them and send them North where they can have equal scholastic opportunity, and end his life holding his head up because he owes no man, with even enough over to pay for his coffin and funeral.

That's what the white man in the South is afraid of: that the Negro, who has done so much with no chance, might do so much more with an equal one that he might take the white man's economy away from him, the Negro now the banker or the merchant or the planter and the white man the sharecropper or the tenant. That's why the Negro can gain our country's highest decoration for valor beyond all call of duty for saving or defending or preserving white lives on foreign battlefields, yet the Southern white man dares not let that Negro's children learn their ABC's in the same classroom with the children of the white lives he saved or defended.

Now the Supreme Court has defined exactly what it meant by what it said: that by "equality" it meant, simply, equality, without qualifying or conditional adjectives: not "separate but equal" nor "equally separate," but simply, equal; and now the Mississippi voices are talking of something which does not even exist any more.

In the first half of the nineteenth century, before slavery was abolished by law in the United States, Thomas Jefferson and Abraham Lincoln both held that the Negro was not yet competent for equality.

That was more than ninety years ago, and nobody can say whether their opinions would be different now or not.

But assume that they would not have changed their belief, and that that opinion is right. Assume that the Negro is still not competent for equality, which is something which neither he nor the white man knows until we try it.

But we do know that, with the support of the federal government, the Negro is going to gain the right to try and see if he is fit or not for equality. And if the Southern white man cannot trust him with something as mild as equality, what is the Southern white man going to do when he has power—the power of his own fifteen millions of unanimity backed by the federal government—when the only check on that power will be that federal government which is already the Negro's ally?

In 1849, Senator John C. Calhoun made his address in favor of secession if the Wilmot Proviso was ever adopted. On October 12 of that year, Senator Jefferson Davis wrote a public letter to the South, saying:

> The generation which avoids its responsibility on this subject sows the wind and leaves the whirlwind as a harvest to its children. Let us get together and build manufactories, enter upon industrial pursuits, and prepare for our own self-sustenance.

At that time the Constitution guaranteed the Negro as property along with all other property, and Senator Calhoun and Senator Davis had the then undisputed validity of States' Rights to back their position. Now the Constitution guarantees the Negro equal right to equality, and the States' Rights which the Mississippi voices are talking about do not exist anymore. We—Mississippi—sold our state's rights back to the federal government when we accepted the first cotton price-support subsidy twenty years ago. Our economy is not agricultural any longer. Our economy is the federal government. We no longer farm in Mississippi cotton fields. We farm now in Washington corridors and Congressional committee rooms.

We—the South—didn't heed Senator Davis' words then. But we had better do it now. If we are to watch our native land wrecked and ruined twice in less than a hundred years over the Negro question, let us be sure this time that we know where we are going afterward.

There are many voices in Mississippi. There is that of one of our United States Senators, who, although he is not speaking for the United States Senate and what he advocates does not quite match the oath he took when he entered into his high office several years ago, at least has made no attempt to hide his identity and his condition. And there is the voice of one of our circuit judges, who, although he is not now speaking from the Bench and what he advocates also stands a little awry to his oath that before the law all men are equal and the weak shall be succored and defended, makes no attempt either to conceal his identity and condition. And there are the voices of the ordinary citizens who, although they do not claim to speak specifically for the white Citizens' Councils and the NAACP, do not try to hide their sentiments and their convictions; not to mention those of the schoolmen—teachers and professors and pupils—though, since most Mississippi schools are state-owned or supported, they don't always dare to sign their names to the open letters.

There are all the voices in fact, except one. That one voice which would adumbrate them all to silence, being the superior of all since it is the living articulation of the glory and the sovereignty of God and the hope and aspiration of man. The Church, which is the strongest unified force in our Southern life since all Southerners are not white and are not democrats, but all Southerners are religious and all religions serve the same single God, no matter by what name He is called. Where is that voice now? The only reference to it which I have seen was in an open forum letter to our Memphis paper which said that to his (the writer's) knowledge, none of the people who begged leave to doubt that one segment of the human race was forever doomed to be inferior to all the other segments, just because the Old Testament five thousand years ago said it was, were communicants of any church.

Where is that voice now, which should have propounded perhaps two but certainly one of these still-unanswered questions?

(1) The Constitution of the U. S. says: Before the Law, there shall be no artificial inequality—race, creed or money—among citizens of the United States.

(2) Morality says: Do unto others as you would have others do unto you.

(3) Christianity says: I am the only distinction among men since whosoever believeth in Me shall never die.

Where is this voice now, in our time of trouble and indecision? Is it trying by its silence to tell us that it has no validity and wants none outside the sanctuary behind its symbolical spire?

If the facts as stated in the *Look* magazine account of the Till affair are correct, this is what ineradicably remains: two adults, armed, in the dark, kidnap a fourteen-year-old boy and take him away to frighten him. Instead of which, the fourteen-year-old boy not only refuses to be frightened, but, unarmed, alone, in the dark so frightens the two armed adults that they must destroy him.

What are we Mississippians afraid of? Why do we have so low an opinion of ourselves that we are afraid of people who by all our standards are our inferiors?—economically: *i.e.,* they have so much less than we have that they must work for us not on their terms but on ours; educationally: *i.e.,* their schools are so much worse than ours that the federal government has to threaten to intervene to give them equal conditions; politically: *i.e.,* they have no recourse in law for protection from nor restitution for injustice and violence.

Why do we have so low an opinion of our blood and traditions as to fear that, as soon as the Negro enters our house by the front door, he will propose marriage to our daughter and she will immediately accept him?

Our ancestors were not afraid like this—our grandfathers who fought at First and Second Manassas and Sharpsburg and Shiloh and Franklin and Chickamauga and Chancellorsville and the Wilderness; let alone those who survived that and had the additional and even greater courage and endurance to resist and survive Reconstruction, and so preserved to us something of our present heritage. Why are we, descendants of that blood and inheritors of that courage, afraid? What are we afraid of? What has happened to us in only a hundred years?

For the sake of argument, let us agree that all white Southerners (all white Americans maybe) curse the day when the first Briton or Yankee sailed the first shipload of manacled Negroes across the Middle Passage and auctioned them into American slavery. Because that doesn't matter now. To live anywhere in the world today and be against equality because of race or color, is like living in Alaska and being against snow. We have already got snow. And as with the Alaskan, merely to live in armistice with it is not enough. Like the Alaskan, we had better use it.

Suddenly about five years ago and with no warning to myself, I adopted the habit of travel. Since then I have seen (a little of some, a little more of others) the Far and Middle East, North Africa, Europe, and Scandinavia. The countries I saw were not Communist (then) of course, but they were more: they were not even Communist-inclined, where it seemed to me they should have been. And I wondered why. Then suddenly I said to myself with a kind of amazement: It's because of America. These people still believe in the American dream; they do not know yet that something happened to it. They believe in us and are willing to trust and follow us not because of our material power: Russia has that: but because of the idea of individual human freedom and liberty and equality on which our nation was founded, which our founding fathers postulated the word "America" to mean.

And, five years later, the countries which are still free of Communism are still free simply because of that: that belief in individual liberty and equality and freedom which is the one idea powerful enough to stalemate the idea of Communism. And we can thank our gods for that, since we have no other weapon to fight Communism with; in diplomacy we are children to Communist diplomats, and production in a free country can always suffer because under monolithic government all production can go to the aggrandizement of the state. But then, we don't need anything more since that simple belief of man that he can be free is the strongest force on earth and all we need to do is use it.

Because it makes a glib and simple picture, we like to think of the world situation today as a precarious and explosive balance of two irreconcilable ideologies confronting each other: which precarious balance, once it totters, will drag the whole universe into the abyss along with it. That's not so. Only one of the opposed forces is an ideology. The other one is that simple fact of Man: that simple belief of individual man that he can and should and will be free. And if we who are still free want to continue so, all of us who are still free had better confederate, and confederate fast, with all others who still have a choice to be free—confederate not as black people nor white people nor blue or pink or green people, but as people who still are free, with all other people who are still free; confederate together and stick together too, if we want a world or even a part of a world in which individual man can be free, to continue to endure.

And we had better take in with us as many as we can get of the nonwhite peoples of the earth who are not completely free yet but who want and intend to be, before that other force which is opposed to individual freedom, befools and gets them. Time was when the nonwhite man was content to—anyway, did—accept his instinct for free-

dom as an unrealizable dream. But not any more; the white man himself taught him different with that phase of his—the white man's—own
culture which took the form of colonial expansion and exploitation
based and morally condoned on the premise of inequality, not because
of individual incompetence but of mass race or color. As a result of
which, in only ten years we have watched the nonwhite peoples expel
by bloody violence when necessary, the white man from all the portions of the Middle East and Asia which he once dominated, into
which vacuum has already begun to move that other and inimical
power which people who believe in freedom are at war with—that
power which says to nonwhite man:

"We don't offer you freedom because there is no such thing as
freedom; your white overlords whom you have just thrown out have
already proved that to you. But we offer you equality, at least
equality in slavedom; if you are to be slaves, at least you can be slaves
to your own color and race and religion."

We, the Western white man who does believe that there exists an
individual freedom above and beyond this mere equality of slavedom,
must teach the nonwhite peoples this while there is yet a little time
left. We, America, who are the strongest national force opposing
Communism and monolithicism, must teach all other peoples, white
and nonwhite, slave or (for a little while yet) still free. We, America,
have the best opportunity to do this because we can begin here, at
home; we will not need to send costly freedom task forces into alien
and inimical nonwhite places which are already convinced that there
is no such thing as freedom and liberty and equality and peace for
nonwhite people too, or we would practice it at home. Because our
nonwhite minority is already on our side; we don't need to sell the
Negro on America and freedom because he is already sold; even when
ignorant from inferior or no education, even despite the record of his
history of inequality, he still believes in our concepts of freedom and
democracy.

That is what America has done for the Negro in only three hundred years. Not done *to* them: done *for* them, because to our shame
we have made little effort so far to teach them to be Americans, let
alone to use their capacities and capabilities to make us a stronger
and more unified America. These are the people who only three hundred years ago lived beside one of the largest bodies of inland water
on earth and never thought of sail, who yearly had to move by whole

villages and tribes from famine and pestilence and enemies without once thinking of the wheel; yet in three hundred years they have become skilled artisans and craftsmen capable of holding their own in a culture of technocracy. The people who only three hundred years ago were eating the carrion in the tropical jungles have produced the Phi Beta Kappas and the Doctor Bunches and the Carvers and the Booker Washingtons and the poets and musicians. They have yet to produce a Fuchs or Rosenberg or Gold or Burgess or Maclean or Hiss, and for every Negro Communist or fellow-traveler there are a thousand white ones.

The Bunches and Washingtons and Carvers and the musicians and the poets, who were not just good men and women but good teachers too, taught him—the Negro—by precept and example what a lot of our white people have not learned yet: that to gain equality, one must deserve it, and to deserve equality, one must understand what it is: that there is no such thing as equality *per se,* but only equality *to:* equal right and opportunity to make the best one can of one's life within one's capacity and capability, without fear of injustice or oppression or violence. If we had given him this equality ninety or fifty or even ten years ago, there would have been no Supreme Court ruling about segregation in 1954.

But we didn't. We dared not; it is our Southern white man's shame that in our present economy the Negro must not have economic equality; our double shame that we fear that giving him more social equality will jeopardize his present economic status; our triple shame that even then, to justify our stand, we must becloud the issue with the bugaboo of miscegenation. What a commentary that the one remaining place on earth where the white man can flee and have his uncorrupted blood protected and defended by law, is in Africa— Africa: the source and origin of the threat whose present presence in America will have driven the white man to flee it.

Soon now all of us—not just Southerners nor even just Americans, but all people who are still free and want to remain so—are going to have to make a choice, lest the next (and last) confrontation we face will be, not Communists against anti-Communists, but simply the remaining handful of white people against the massed myriads of all the people on earth who are not white. We will have to choose not between color nor race nor religion nor between East and West either, but simply between being slaves and being free. And we will have to choose completely and for good; the time is already past now when we can choose a little of each, a little of both. We can choose a state of slavedom, and if we are powerful enough to be among the top two or three or ten, we can have a certain amount of license—until someone more powerful rises and has us machine-gunned against a cellar wall.

But we cannot choose freedom established on a hierarchy of degrees of freedom, on a caste system of equality like military rank. We must be free not because we claim freedom, but because we practice it; our freedom must be buttressed by a homogeny equally and unchallengeably free, no matter what color they are, so that all the other inimical forces everywhere—systems political or religious or racial or national—will not just respect us because we practice freedom, they will fear us because we do.

III

Our Perennial Flirtation

The Sex Taboo at Puka-Puka

by ROBERT DEAN FRISBIE

DECEMBER, 1930

A rare and delightful report on the uninhibited sex life of the Polynesians on Puka-Puka, chief island of the Danger group. Robert Dean Frisbie, born in Cleveland in 1896, was a writer, trader, and navigator living in the South Seas. He married a native girl and they had five children. She died in 1939 and he nine years later, at Rarotonga, Cook Islands.

Sitting on the veranda of the Puka-Puka trading station, I can see the panorama of atoll life moving drowsily beneath me. It is true that the main portion of the village is behind me, but there are a half-dozen huts scattered along the beach fifty yards away; and it is here that the fishermen paddle in from the lagoon, the children splash about the shallow water, old women sit in the shade and breeze to plait their pandanus hats, and the wild youth of the three villages meet to wrestle, play marbles, make intricate cats' cradles, or discuss the coming love fests on the outer beach.

Some evenings the canoes of Leeward Village come from Frigate Bird Islet. I can see them from afar, their sails bellying to a beam wind; twenty or thirty of them moving so rapidly that it seems no more than a moment before the spray from their torpedo-shaped bows is visible; then they have dodged among the coral heads of the bay and beached in full view from my veranda. They are loaded high above the gunwales with fern and *pukatea* leaves—green manure for the main islet's taro beds. And there are husked drinking nuts, long strings of brown ripe ones, and a hundred or more young boobies, tied by their feet like a bunch of onions, squawking raucously.

A procession of laughing, shouting Puka-Pukans passes on either side of the trading station, carrying the bundles of leaves and nuts on their heads; the children run before them with the birds, swinging them over their heads with the unconcerned cruelty of young savages, to me appalling. I turn my head, half-sick at the sight. I have tried to stop them, even asked Sea Foam to preach a sermon against cruelty to dumb animals; but he could not find a text, nor could I. And when I have mentioned diffidently to my neighbors that animals feel pain the same as men they have laughed at me for a sentimental fool.

Before long the leaves and nuts are stacked in the outhouses, and now all the men help, turn and turn about, carrying one another's canoes to the shoring logs. They bail them out, dry them with masses of coconut fiber, and pile plaited fronds on top of them. It requires a year or more for a Puka-Pukan to build a canoe, so he appreciates its value and takes great care of it, making it last a lifetime.

The men stroll back to their houses. The sun has set, and the tropical night is deepening by perceptible degrees; in a half-hour it will be dark. A flash of light falls from the sky as a cloud, still aglow with the sun, passes over the lagoon, diffusing its radiance on the rippling water in kaleidoscopic colors. But in a moment it has gone, the coral heads have vanished, the distant reef has dissolved into the sea. A cricket sounds his strident love call from under the veranda; a rooster crows from his perch in a coconut palm. It is evening, the hour of reverie and of melancholy.

Newly married Mrs. Wail-of-Woe leaves her house and walks to the beach, followed by her younger sister. Both are as naked as the day they were born. A few moments later the sandy stretch between the houses and the beach is dotted with the figures of my neighbors, all quite nude, old and young alike, on their way to the lagoon for their evening bath. Men and women intermingle, naked urchins jump whooping about, young Mr. Chair puts his arm around his sweetheart's waist and they run to the lagoon and jump in. No one is self-conscious, for they have done this since they were babies, and to them there is no mystery in sex and no consciousness of its exposure. Visually, their sexes interest them no more than the sexes of animals; psychically, it is otherwise, for they are an ardent race.

And now I, who have traded on this atoll for years, am becoming indifferent to nakedness, though at first it was quite disturbing. But still I have not attained the healthy incuriousness of my neighbors, for when pretty Miss Tern runs from Sea Foam's house, a hundred yards from the station, and trips gracefully down the beach, the innocent and lovely creation of a fairy wand, I am not nearly enough of a Saint Anthony not to feel a warm tremor pass over me.

At such times I rise from my steamer chair and, leaving the veranda, open the station for the evening trade. I am piqued with myself because I cannot show the impassivity of my neighbors. One evening it was especially disturbing. I had opened the store, and though it was still quite light, was touching a match to the lamp when Miss Tern came running in, dripping wet and still unclothed, her hair clinging to her tawny skin.

"Sea Foam wants some perfume quickly, for baby is sick!" she cried, out of breath, her panting agitating her breasts.

When I gave her a bottle of the favorite Puka-Puka remedy, she clutched it and ran out of the store, unaware of her nudity and unable to understand that she had left me very much shaken and greatly aggravated with myself. Why could not I look upon a live nude figure in the same way the natives do? The answer was easily found: it was because I was brought up to consider sex both shameful and desirable—a vice to be indulged in clandestinely, while the Puka-Pukans look upon it as a religious ritual, and certainly anything but shameful. With them it is spoken of casually in the family circle, and no child of five is puzzled as to how the race is propagated.

Night has come before the people leave their bath, for they are playful, and the old grandpas and grandmas enjoy splashing and ducking, turning somersaults and playing porpoise in the water as much as do the youngsters. When at last they return to their homes, the older people clothe themselves in *pareus,* dungaree pants, and grass skirts; but the young fry seldom worry about such things. Then tiny coconut-shell fires flash through the villages, revealing groups of squatting natives cooking their evening meals. The fires subside, the villages are obscured in soft shadows, the old folk and the married attend to their own affairs; but the young unmarried slip unhindered through the gloom of the coconut groves to the moon-gleaming outer beach, in the eternal quest of love.

II

I had not been long on Puka-Puka before I wondered why, if the natives are not ashamed of their bodies, they wear clothes at any time.

I knew why they wore European clothes, and why they attended church dressed in the heterogeneous costumes of many nations, professions, and sports. It was the self-same silly vanity which makes a woman paint her face and a man spend hours over his selection of neckties. But the natives wore clothes before the coming of the whites; they were a part of the ritual of the primitive Puka-Pukan life. They were given to him when he reached maturity, but were forbidden before that time. The age of maturity was decided by a council of the village fathers. The youth or maiden was taken before this council, and if it was thought that he or she was old enough to look upon the opposite sex, clothes were decreed and nakedness forbidden except at stated times, such as when bathing in the lagoon or turtle hunting at sea. These garments consisted of a loin cloth of pandanus matting bound around the waist with sennit for the men, and a grass skirt or girdle of fern leaves for the women.

But why any clothes at all?

My retainer, the old heathen William, answered this question one day while we were strolling through the islet, deciphering the tombstone symbolism in the little graveyards among the groves. As I stood in one such clearing I caught sight of Miss Tern passing on her way to the taro beds. She was dressed in a girdle of frond leaves and was quite as conscious of it as a boy with his first long pants. She tripped along with a pretty movement of her hips that was accentuated by the girdle, and as her eyes dropped to the garment a smile of gratification played on her lips. She gave me the impression that, now her sex was hidden, she was conscious of it for the first time.

Only yesterday the council had decided that Miss Tern was mature —or to be more accurate, had reached puberty—so they had "made her into a woman," or "*akawawine*," as the ceremony of bestowing the first clothes is called. Unless Sea Foam's Christian notions had kept her indoors last night, which is improbable, she had gone to the outer beach where some wild youth of another village had initiated her into the meaning of sex.

"William," I asked the lone heathen of Puka-Puka, "why do the natives start wearing clothes when they reach maturity?"

The old retainer has always looked upon me as an inordinately ignorant young man and, though I feed both him and his garrulous old wife, Mama, he shows me little respect. Now he clutched my arm and led me off into the groves to stop before a heavily laden coconut tree.

"You see," he cried, pretending to be exasperated, "this is a coconut tree."

"Yes," I replied readily.

"Hm," grunted the old man, as though to acknowledge that I had some intelligence after all.

"Well, you see that she has been tabooed?"

"Yes," said I. "The village fathers have set this tree aside for one man's use; and to warn anyone from accidentally taking its nuts, they have wrapped a coconut frond around its bole."

"They have wrapped a coconut frond around its bole!" William repeated my sentence with irony. Then he shouted, leaning over until his sparsely bearded chin nearly touched my face, "Hell and damnation! What a way to say that they have put a grass skirt on her!"

I glanced up at the tree. The frond wrapped around its bole did look like a grass skirt tied about the slim body of a girl. I began to see light.

"Oh, so that's how it is!" I cried. "The grass skirt around the girl means that she is taboo, or the property of one man, just the same as the frond around this tree means that it is a single man's property."

"My son," William said in a gentler tone, "that is it exactly."

"But," I went on, "how did it all start? Is the grass skirt on the tree copied after the old method of tabooing a woman?"

The irascible old heathen flew off the handle again. "God damn," he cried. "What ignorance! Of course not; the coconut tree came first, and the tabooing of the woman was a copy of it. What does a woman amount to in comparison to a coconut tree?"

I wanted to ask William why a woman wore the taboo garment before marriage, for certainly she was anything but the property of one man; but I saved my question for a later date, for the old man was in a fiery humor. When I did ask him, over a bottle of home-brewed ale, he replied vaguely that she was the property of only one man at a time, and that is as much as I was able to learn concerning this slightly contradictory detail.

III

With the exception of old Bones, the local voluptuary, there is no sex morbidity at Puka-Puka; but if these happy-go-lucky, half-god, half-animal people come in closer contact with the civilized world the result will be disastrous. Already the missionaries have made havoc with their morals. Narrow-minded and self-seeking, in their myopic way they have insisted on the maidens clothing themselves at twelve and the youths at thirteen. The Puka-Pukans have taken this as a permit to sexual relations at these ages, for, as has been explained, clothes are considered a tacit permission to enter the love fests. A coconut tree reaches the age of fructification; it is claimed by a man; tabooed by being "clothed," and the fruit is used by that man. The parallel is the same with a woman; but though one must wait until a coconut tree comes to maturity before he can harvest its fruit, it is otherwise with a girl—much to her detriment—and this the missionaries have blindly brought into existence. Rather than see a naked adolescent body, they have made child mistresses and lovers of the youngsters of this atoll. Perhaps the missionaries are not as clean-minded as the natives who look upon a naked body with indifference.

It must be said that the missionaries are unaware of the harm they are doing. They come to such islands as Puka-Puka only for a day at a time; they turn topsy-turvy the traditions, customs, and religion of the islanders, and then rush off to write articles about their uplifting work; but they do not remain to witness its disastrous results. It is my conviction that they have, more than any others, contributed to the injury of the Polynesians.

But here the injury has been slight, for the people are too natural a race to feel sexual inclinations before the bodies have matured. The meetings on the outer beach are not an orgy of lust; probably much less actual intercourse exists than would among our civilized youth under similar conditions.

I recall two illustrations in a volume about John Williams and his torchbearing voyage through the South Seas. One was of Puka-Puka before, and the other of the same island after Williams' visit. The first picture depicted a night scene on the beach, with savages dancing by torchlight. They were clothed in grass skirts and fantastic headdresses, their faces were tattooed, they had strings of shark teeth around their necks and war clubs in their hands. In the background idols of extraordinary ugliness stared from the shadow of gnarled atoll trees. The scene was alive with the abandon of savage islands and, though the artist had done his best to make it repellent, one felt that here was a virile race with a tradition of its own, full of the love of life, independent, flourishing.

The other picture showed a potential Puka-Puka under missionary rule—far from what it actually is, thank God! There was the same stretch of beach, but across it walked an upright, god-fearing Puka-Pukan dressed in clothes suitable for Sunday services. In one hand he held a leash attached to a fat pig; in the other a Bible. Behind him, the gnarled atoll trees and the idols had given way to straight rows of coconut palms, where other natives, also properly dressed, split and dried coconuts to help supply the world's margarine. What bathos! A civilization had been destroyed to make Christians and margarine! Happily, the artist was a false prophet; but such conditions have come to pass elsewhere in the Pacific.

IV

A Puka-Pukan seldom marries his first love—or his second, third, or twentieth, for that matter; but when he does marry it is almost invariably successful. Unfaithful husbands and wives are such a rarity here that one may as well say that they do not exist. The reason is evident: there is no grab-bag luck. Before marriage they know one another intimately, know dozens of others intimately; there is no mystery to be disillusioned away; they settle down in married life satisfied, through actual experience, that they have the mate who is best suited to them.

Several reasons would forbid such a practice in civilized countries. We have a heritage of jealousy which makes the thought of marrying a woman who has been loved by another objectionable. This heritage has been developed through ages of ego assertion, when the attainment of food, shelter, safety, and a mate has been consummated by our proving ourselves superior to others. It has been a strife in which the lineage of the weakling has been exterminated. We have idolized personal property; "this is mine" has become a religion to us, and our pride has been injured when others have conquered our property.

The Puka-Pukans have little personal property, for all the land is communally owned. They have no fear of losing their wives to another, for the precedent has not been set—the fear has not been created. All the wives of this island are faithful to their husbands, so there has been no call for jealousy. As to jealousy among the young unmarried, it exists only in the mildest form. Probably they avoid it unconsciously, for it would disorganize their premarriage promiscuous intercourse, and this would be a great evil indeed.

A second reason for chastity in civilized countries is because an illegitimate child is given an opprobrious name, incurs disgrace from the accident of his birth, and in some cases even loses his right to inherit. The mother is designated by a still more opprobrious name and has little chance of living in respectable society. Her future is hopeless and her child an outcast.

But on such a primitive island as I write about an unmarried mother is honored; and what is more, she has a better chance than a maiden to find a good husband. The sane-minded Puka-Pukan desires a child to carry his name and tradition beyond his grave. When he finds a woman who is both congenial and of proven fecundity he marries her at once, happy in the prospect of an offspring.

Whether they be illegitimate children or gray-haired deacons of the church, each Puka-Pukan has an equal interest in the land and all it produces, and in all the fish, turtles, and birds taken in the community catches. Hence, the mother's premarriage child is no problem at all: he belongs to the village, a taro bed is set aside for him, ten coconut trees are tabooed, and he receives his share of the village copra before, figuratively, he is out of his swaddling clothes. And finally, the Puka-Pukans are a child-loving race, so if the mother does not wish to take her baby to her husband's home there will be a score of families fighting for him. After all, he brings no expense or disgrace upon the adopting family.

In most countries the economic status of a woman makes her dependent upon a man, especially when she has reached middle age and borne children. This is the rule; there are many exceptions, but it will never be changed until women cease to bear children, or the government takes them and their children under its care—as do the Puka-Puka village councils. But all this and all it implies are too much of an everyday experience to be expatiated upon; yet, when I told some of my native friends about the situation of an unmarried mother in America, they could not believe that a country so superior to their atoll should allow any member of its community to suffer from want.

The Puka-Pukan mother is actually better off than when she was a maid, for she has her own share of the island's wealth as well as her baby's and a native baby requires little more than its mother's milk. Thus it can be said that a premium is given to motherhood.

V

William and I discussed the relative merits of the sex taboo in civilized and primitive societies one night while we were fishing on the reef. There is a coral boulder on the north reef, high and dry during southeasterly trades, when very little sea washes over the coral barrier.

To one side a deep crevice leads to the sea, an excellent place to catch *malau,* a red, big-eyed fish, fat and unsurpassed for flavor. They bite a white fly on the fourteenth to the seventeenth nights of the moon; and on these nights, when the sea and weather permit, William and I fish until well into the morning hours.

One evening we crossed the main islet, waded through two hundred yards of shallows, and took our customary places on the boulder. The moon had risen with the setting sun, and the trade wind died to the memory of a breeze. Along the shore the coconut trees stood stately and mute, gleaming faintly above the white glare of the beach. We could see the coral patches in the shallows outlined like shadows on the water. The reef lay ahead of us, a dark-red highway dotted with glittering pools of water where spotted sea eels lay coiled, and crabs and lobsters stared into the night with eyes like coals. The outer side of the reef was aglow with a fringe of surf, phosphorescent and un-earthly, washing sibilantly across the coral and sobbing deep down in the caverns. At our feet was the crevice with its black water surging back and forth slowly; but at times, when a heavy sea poured over the reef, the break in the coral would whiten with foam. Then we would set our poles aside waiting for the water to clear and the red *malau* to dart about the surface again, dissolve into the deep black, magically reappear and leap at our flies, or more likely smell them and fin wisely away.

Presently two figures appeared on the beach; others followed until a score or more were sitting on the sand in pairs and fours, strolling along the water's edge or into the obscurity of the *ngangei* bushes beneath the palms.

A girl's voice rose in the still night air, wild and piercing, chanting one of the old song-legends in tones of savage abandon. Soon other voices joined, girls carrying the leading refrain, while boys sang a counter melody or chanted deep rhythmical monotones like the beat of kettle drums:

> Aye, aye, aye, aye, aye, aye, aye!
> Aye! Ah! Aye! Ah!

Sometimes they sang in a minor key, a melody of two or three bars, weird and beautiful. Then I felt a quickening of my pulse and a gust of emotion sweep over me—an emotion I could not define; but at the moment of its being I found myself trying to recall some place I had never seen, or some experience which had never taken place. A lone voice rose above the others to sing a hymn to the stars—a refrain of but a score of notes which told of the past glory of the Polynesians, the loneliness of remote islands, the joy of living, the tragedy of death, the passion of sex. A girl voice broke in, shrilling her call like an old crone wailing over the body of a stillborn baby; the others joined with a clamor of voices, soon to languish to a chanted Lydian measure, soft and sensuous, then end abruptly, as though a surge of emotion had swept over them, choking their voices.

A cloud rolled before the moon. When it had passed, the beach was deserted.

William and I fished vigorously, for now the *malau* were biting well. As I pulled out one fish after another and dropped it into my basket, my mind was far from the sport. I was wondering what would happen if the Puka-Puka love fests were permitted among the youth at home.

"William," I said presently, "I've been thinking about these wild youth on the outer beach at night, and it has occurred to me that it is a pity that such natural love-making cannot be practiced in civilized countries. But it is impossible. We have diseases which make chastity a health measure. You have sailed in whaling ships so you know what I mean. Have any such afflictions ever reached this island?"

"Once," William replied as he jerked his fly through the water; "but the Puka-Pukans were too smart for him. A ship came here when I was a boy. The captain was a big man with a black beard, so we called him 'Huru-Huru.' You've heard the chant about him:

> Akatu 'u tet'i waka pei Huru-Huru,
> Akatere 'u e anere maire ki Rapanui.

> I shall build a canoe like Big-Beard's
> And sail a hundred miles to Easter Island.

"Well, one of the girls of Yato was sent out to him to show that we were friendly. A few days later she was ill, and then one of the Roto boys found he had the sickness. They told their fathers about it and a general council was called. Oh! the old men of Puka-Puka were a wise set. Believe it or not, they put the girl and the boy in a canoe, gave them some food and water, and pushed them across the reef, warning them never to return. From then on the Puka-Puka girls had good reason to keep away from sailors. When I came back from whaling I couldn't get a wife for two days; then I went out and took one whether she liked it or not, and that ended the trouble."

"That was a hard fate for the boy and girl."

"Damnation!" cried the old heathen, expressing a sentiment he did not feel. "There were plenty of youngsters on the island, so what did those two amount to?"

"Is that the only case?"

The old man nodded his head in affirmation.

I knew that nowadays the danger is slight, for the captains of the trading schooners see to it that no harm of this kind will reach such outposts as Puka-Puka. Few sailors are allowed ashore, and strangers are not carried as passengers. For a European to reach Puka-Puka, he would have to sail in his own ship, and even then it is unlikely that the port officials at Rarotonga would give him permission to land on the outlying islands.

"It would never work on the outer beach of San Francisco or New York," I said. "The whites are a highly strung race of extremists, and they would react differently; they would become voluptuaries, as have some of the European people to whom greater sexual license has been allowed. These people have developed to a state where perversion is the rule; where prostitution is commoner than marriage and seldom leads to marriage. There is no parallel between the sex life of the civilized and the primitive man. It resolves into no more than an interesting contrast."

I had been talking to myself more than to the old retainer. Now I turned to him, and asked, "William, you have seen something of the world. Who do you think meets this sex problem most effectively and logically, the white men or the people of this island?"

"Hell and damnation!" William roared. "What do the white people know about such things?"

"You mean," I said, paraphrasing Laurence Sterne, "that they handle matters much better at Puka-Puka?"

The old man agreed with a grunt, and as the smoky light of morning was rising above the eastern skyline we rose from our boulder and waded back to the main islet.

"Listen to This, Dear"

by JAMES THURBER

JANUARY, 1932

One of the most engaging humorists this country has ever had traces the origin of woman's primeval urge to interrupt her husband while he's reading. The author also has some suggestions on combating this female behavior. James Thurber's wit has delighted The New Yorker's *audience since the mid-1920's.*

It is a commonplace that the small annoyances of the marriage relationship slowly build up its insupportabilities, as particles of sediment build up great deltas. And yet I have never seen, even among the profundities of our keenest researchers into divorce, a competent consideration of the problem that is created by the female's habit of interrupting the male when he is reading. It is, indeed, more than a habit; I believe it is a law of woman's behaviorism as deeply rooted as her instinct to attract the male. And it causes almost as much trouble.

In the early ages of mankind, woman's security, and hence her contentment, were assured by the activity of the male and jeopardized by his inactivity. The male rampant—killing animals for food and for clothing, digging out caves, and putting up huts, driving off enemies—early came to be associated in the mind of the elemental female with warmth, well-being, safety, and the kindred creature comforts. Lying down, or even sitting down, the male was a symbol of possible imminent disaster: famine, exposure, capture and servitude, even death. Any masculine posture of relaxation or repose, therefore, became a menace which must be removed.

The reasonable dismay of the primeval female at the sight of her mate doing nothing was so powerful that it remains ineradicable in the mind and the heart of the female of today, although logical motivation for her original dread has largely disappeared with the shaping up of our civilization. The softer centuries, it is true, have reduced her primal terror to a kind of hazy uneasiness, just as they have tempered

182

the violence of her protest, but the instinct to prod the inert male into action nevertheless persists. Where once woman shook man, or struck him with a rock, or at least screamed imprecations at him, when he sat down to draw pictures on the walls of the cave, she now contents herself with talking to him when he is reading. The male's ability to lose himself in the printed page brings back to the female, from vanished wildernesses, the old, dim fear of masculine inertia.

"I must tell you what happened to the base of the Spencers' child's brain," a wife will begin when her husband has just reached the most exciting point in the sports extra's account of a baseball game or a prize-fight, and she will proceed to go into details which, although interesting, or even horrific, lack the peculiar excitement of competitive competition to which the husband has adjusted his consciousness. Or she will say, "I want you to listen to this, dear," and she will read him a story from *her* section of the evening paper about a New Jersey dentist who tried to burn up his wife and collect her insurance. Telling the plots of plays, and speculating as to why a certain couple were drawn together, or drifted apart—as the case may have been—are other methods a wife frequently uses to interrupt her husband's reading.

Of the various ways of combating this behavior of the female, open resentment, manifested by snarling or swearing or throwing one's book or newspaper on the floor in a rage, is the worst, since nine times out of ten it will lead to quarrels, tears, slamming of doors, and even packing of suitcases, and the disruption of family life. The husband may gain, by this method, the privacy of his club, but he will no longer be in the proper frame of mind for quiet reading. He will find himself wondering where his wife is, whether she has gone home to her mother, whether she has taken veronal (I am dealing, of course, with those high-strung, sensitive couples who make up such a large percentage of present-day families). He will then fall to recalling miserably the years of their happiness, and end up by purchasing a dozen roses for his wife, and five or six rye highballs for himself, after which he must still face the ordeal of patching things up, a business made somewhat easier perhaps by the fact of the roses, but correspondingly harder by the fact of the highballs. This whole method of protest, in a word, takes a great deal out of a man and is not to be recommended.

The best way of dealing with a wife who tells long stories of the day's happenings, or reads accounts of murders aloud when her husband has settled down to his book or journal, is to pretend to listen but not really to listen at all. To the uninitiated this may seem simple, but the husband who has perfected the method knows that it calls for a unique bifurcation of the faculty of attention, and a remarkable development of the power of concentration. In order to go right on with his own reading while his wife is talking, the husband must deaden his mind to the meaning of her words and at the same time remain conscious of the implications of her inflections. Thus he will be able, at the proper places in her recitation, to murmur an interested "Yes?" or an incredulous "No!", although not following her narrative at all and still getting the sense of what he is reading. "Um," "Hm," and "Um hm" should also be freely used, but never "Hm?" for it denotes a lapse of attention. Exclamations of astonishment or high interest, such as "You don't say!" are extremely dangerous and should be interjected only by the oblivious husband who is so sensitive to the tempo and pitch of his wife's voice that he can be positive when she has reached some (to her) important climax in whatever she is relating.

This form of deception is, of course, fairly easy to practice when the female is reading aloud, for her eyes must naturally be upon the printed page before her. It is not so easy when she is relating an occurrence, or a chain of occurrences, for her eyes are then likely to be upon the male. In this case he should contrive, as soon as she begins, to drop his magazine or newspaper on his knee, as if he had abandoned it—all the time, however, keeping the type within range. I know of one husband who drops his newspaper on the floor before him and then bends over it with his hand to his brow, shielding his eyes, his elbow on his knee, as if he were intent upon his wife's words. He continues to read right along, however.

A defense against forward passes, as they say in football, must also be carefully built up by the inattentive husband. By forward passes, I mean sudden and unexpected questions which the wife is likely to fling at any minute, such as, for example, "Would you think Hilda Greeb capable of a thing like that?" In building up a defense against this trick play, the husband must keep a little corner of his consciousness alert, like the safety man on a defensive football team, for all sentences beginning with "would," "should," "are," "have," "can," and the like. In this way he can spot a question coming in time to have some sort of response ready. In the case of the question we have already cited, "Would you think Hilda Greeb capable of a thing like that?" it is probable that either a "Yes" or a "No" would see the husband safely by the crisis. If he says "Yes," the wife will probably say, "Well, so would I of course," and if he says "No," she will probably say, "Well, of course *I* would, knowing her as well as I do." However, each particular husband, knowing the twists and turns of his particular wife's mind, must work out his own system of defense against forward passes. The greatest care should be taken by every husband, however, to answer only those questions which are directed to him. He must, I mean, be on guard against "inner-quote queries." For example, if a wife should say, in the course of whatever she is telling, "So I asked her, 'what time is it?'" the husband is lost if he is caught off guard and replies, "About a quarter after eight, I think." This is bound to lead to accusations, imprecations, quarrels, tears, slamming of doors, etc.

I know a few husbands who simply evade the whole problem by giving up reading. They just don't read anything any more. It seems to me that this is cowardly.

The Only Woman in the Lifeboat—The Story of Mary Cornish of the City of Benares

by ELSPETH HUXLEY

JANUARY, 1942

Here is a story of a woman's high courage and devotion in a wartime ordeal that won the admiration of the whole Free World. Her cheerfulness giving heart to the boys in her charge, and her petticoat on the masthead as a distress signal, Mary Cornish was in a lifeboat in the North Atlantic with forty-five other people, all males. The author, Mrs. Elspeth Huxley, is an English novelist and writer of travel books and detective stories. She has also written much about Kenya Colony in East Africa, where she was born in 1907, the daughter of a British major. She is the wife of Gervas Huxley, a grandson of Thomas Henry Huxley and a first cousin to Aldous Huxley.

The *City of Benares* was four days out of Liverpool when the torpedo struck. For those four days ninety British children, bound for the safety of Canada, had kept their ten escorts busy—nursing those who were seasick, keeping the others entertained and out of mischief.

The escorts—men and women who had volunteered to accompany the children on the voyage—had no peace by day, and Mary Cornish, for one, had little sleep by night. Even if sick children did not need attention she lay awake, half-dressed, alert to catch the first intimations of danger. It was hard work, but rewarding, for in a very short time a real affection sprang up between escorts and escorted. From the first day there was a cheerful, friendly atmosphere aboard the *City of Benares*.

As for the children, they were free of worries and in the highest of spirits. Never had they encountered such entrancing places to play as on this ship. Never had they (or those who were not seasick) eaten such resplendent meals, served by white-coated, brown-faced stewards. The *City of Benares* had been built for the India run; so while her officers were British, brown-skinned Lascars made up her crew.

But an undercurrent of tension ran through the ship, at least among the grown-up passengers. Mines to begin with, and later raiders; powerful Focke-Wulf aircraft, and the ever-prowling U-boats; all these threatened their safety at every hour of the night and day. Yet everything had been done to guard against the danger and to prepare for it, and few passengers feared anything worse than a ducking and the loss of their kit. Whatever happened—and the ship's officers shared and encouraged this belief—the *City of Benares,* with her precious cargo of children, would be well looked after. Two other ships of the convoy flanked her on either side, at times almost within shouting distance. Should she be torpedoed, both these vessels were confidently expected to stand by and pick up survivors. An hour or two in the lifeboats at the most, it was thought, was all they had to fear.

Boat drills were held every day. Passengers carried their life jackets about with them and few undressed at night. The children slept in warm pajamas and life jackets; coats and shoes were stacked in readiness at the bottom of their bunks.

Then on the evening of September 17, 1940, tension was relaxed. The passengers for the first time looked forward to undressing completely when they went to bed. Not until they reached the St. Lawrence could all danger be at an end, but now it was only a shadow. People congratulated one another on having reached virtual safety; passengers stood one another drinks. The sea, which had been rough, had gone down a little, and all but the most seasick of the children were up. With every day that passed they became more excited; already they looked healthier and slept better, and the salt wind had whipped color into their cheeks.

That evening the escorts toasted the children and their future in the New World. They were in high spirits, with more than half the weight of responsibility lifted from their shoulders. After the children had said prayers the escorts, as usual, tucked them into bed and said good night. Tomorrow, they hoped, might be calm and fine.

II

At about nine o'clock, after coffee, Mary Cornish went on deck to get a breath of fresh air. There was a strong breeze and the sea was choppy. The moon was nearly full, but cloud-wrack drifted across it and only now and again did it shine out clearly over the sea. On either beam two black shapes showed plainly—the two vessels keeping steadily abreast of the *City of Benares*.

Mary Cornish had never before been on an ocean voyage. For twenty years she had been studying and teaching music. At the age of forty-one, wanting to do what she could in the war emergency, she had volunteered to act as a children's escort for the government's Children's Overseas Reception Board. Down in cabins astern were her fifteen charges—girls ranging in age from six to fifteen.

After about an hour on deck, Mary Cornish decided to go below. She had reached the end of the alleyway on C Deck, leading off to the children's quarters, when the torpedo struck. The ship shuddered; the lights went out. The explosion sounded like a heavy muffled thud, followed by a noise of crashing glass and splintering woodwork. Mary Cornish started along the alleyway toward the children's cabins, found her progress blocked part way along by a mass of debris, and saw that she was gazing down into a black abyss where the bathrooms had been. She realized that she was looking into a vast hole blown in the center of the ship, a hole that was quickly filling with the sea. The torpedo had struck the afterpart of the ship, passed just below the children's cabins, and exploded beneath the central row of bathrooms, blowing them to smithereens.

Her job now was to reach her batch of children and get them into a boat. She started, with her bare hands, to tear a hole in the debris blocking the alleyway, wrenching aside splintered partitions, lacerating her hands, until the gap was just large enough to crawl through. Mrs. Towns, one of the other escorts, was with the children on the far side. She had been asleep and the explosion had thrown her out of bed. Rallying the children, she and an engineer officer who had arrived on the scene managed to extract them from the shattered cabins. Mary Cornish pulled them through the gap in the debris and got them up on deck.

The children were frightened but not panicky. The force of the explosion—almost directly beneath them—had hurled most of them out of their beds, and in the darkness and confusion there was no chance to recover the coats, shoes, and spare blankets neatly folded at each bunk's foot for such an emergency. To calm them Mary Cornish found herself repeating in soothing tones: "It's all right, it's only a torpedo"

—until it occurred to her that this was perhaps rather an odd form of reassurance.

There was no chance of reaching the boat station allotted to her group. On deck people were starting to climb into the boats under the supervision of the ship's officers. By this time the emergency lighting had come on. Leaving her charges with Mrs. Towns, Mary Cornish returned below to make quite certain that none of her girls had been trapped in their cabins. In the blocked alleyway she bumped into an officer coming forward from the children's quarters.

"I've just been through there," he told her. "There's nobody left. Go on deck." She obeyed, returning with him to the upper deck; but by that time Mrs. Towns and the children had disappeared. She started aft to find them, but the ship's officer ordered her into the nearest boat. She hesitated, wondering whether to obey or whether to search for her own charges. Looking into the lifeboat, she could see that it was full of Lascars from the ship's crew, and that among them were huddled several small boys.

Her own children, she reflected, were well looked after by Mrs. Towns and by one of the stewardesses, a trained nurse. Here were several small boys in a boat full of Lascars; and the officer had ordered her into the boat. There was no time to think it over. She climbed in.

They crouched in the boat for what seemed a long time, swinging from the davits. In the changing moonlight, now strong, now clouded, she could see other lifeboats, but dimly, as they were in the ship's shadow. Below them was a black, heaving ocean. During this interlude Miss Day came by and shouted to Mary Cornish that the girls of her group were safe in other boats. At intervals people slid down a rope from the deck above and landed in the boat, causing a mild commotion while others squeezed away to make room for them. They could hear creakings and shouts as other boats were lowered into the rough sea. One capsized as it reached the water, spilling out its occupants; Mary Cornish heard the screams of children and the shouts of people on deck who threw down rafts and life belts. Her boat was one of the last to be lowered and the last to pull away. From the crests of the waves, in fitful moonlight, she could see other lifeboats dotted about, and brief signals flashed from torches, and sometimes the speck of a head or a tossing raft whirling by. Now and again a shout would rise above the wind's screaming, to be quickly drowned again. During the night four or five dripping, half-conscious figures were hauled over the side of her boat, rescued from an ice-cold sea.

It seemed a long time later that the *City of Benares* went down. All the lights were ablaze, and it looked to the passengers as if she were on fire. At the last moment her bow dipped, her stern reared, and she sank slowly into the ocean. Although hours seemed to have elapsed since the torpedo struck, in fact the interval, as later established, was only forty minutes.

There was no sign of the other ships in the convoy. Indeed, both the ships that had flanked them went down that night. The rest of the convoy scattered and sailed on, for that is the rule, leaving lifeboats and rafts and swimming figures alone with the storm and the sea.

The night seemed endless. It was bitterly cold. No one was dressed to meet a storm in the North Atlantic in an open boat. The boys wore pajamas and the kapok life jackets in which, luckily, they had slept; but only one had a coat and two wore shoes. Mary Cornish had on a thin silk blouse, a thin skirt, a short-sleeved jacket, and silk stockings with sandals. She soon became numb with cold as well as seasick, and the cuts and bruises sustained while pulling her children through the debris on board the *City of Benares* grew sore. She was wedged among the Lascars too tightly to move. In face of great difficulties the crew, with the fourth officer in command, managed to keep the bows head-on to the waves, and thus to prevent their boat from shipping water and becoming swamped.

Dawn broke at last, gray, sullen, and cold. There was no rescuing vessel steaming toward them; no fellow lifeboats; not even a raft; only now and again a sodden piece of wreckage bobbing quickly past. They were alone, with the wind rising and the seas high.

III

After this cheerless dawn those in the lifeboat took stock of the situation and sorted themselves out. The boat was thirty feet long— four feet longer than a London bus. Into it forty-six people were crammed. The fourth officer was at the tiller in the stern. With him were four other British members of the crew: a signalman, a steward, a naval gunner, and a young cadet. There were thirty-two Lascars in all, huddled together on the thwarts and on the floor of the boat. Among them were the boys, six in number; Mr. Nagorski, a Polish passenger, and Mary Cornish herself. Only when daylight came did she discover that the boys had after all an escort, Father O'Sullivan, a Roman Catholic priest. For two days before the disaster he had been ill, running a temperature and suffering from acute seasickness and a severe chill. He had carried one small boy and shepherded others to the lifeboat, clad only in pajamas and a coat, without shoes; during the night he had lain in the bottom of the boat, incapacitated by sickness.

The spirits of the passengers rose with daylight in spite of the cold and the cramp from which everyone was suffering. The steward busied himself by issuing blankets and rigging a canvas awning over the bows to make a shelter. When this was done the six boys, their escort, and Mary Cornish were separated from the Lascars and moved into the bows, where they arranged themselves as best they could along the thwarts and in, and on top of, a locker which occupied most of the space.

The boat was equipped not with oars, but with a propelling apparatus. Two handles, like those used in bars for drawing beer, only much larger, stood up from the floor between each pair of seats. By pulling these backward and forward with a regular motion, a crew of ten turned a shaft which revolved a screw under the rudder; this propelled the boat. The handles had been used during the night to keep the boat head-on to the waves. In the morning the two handles in the bows were taken out of their sockets to make more room, and the fourth officer called for volunteers to take regular turns at working the remaining four pairs. He turned the bows eastward, and set a course for the nearest land—the coast of Ireland.

IV

Of the boys, the youngest was eight, the eldest thirteen. When daylight came they were lively and cheerful in spite of the loneliness of the sea; at this stage the whole thing was a great adventure. No one seriously doubted that a destroyer would pick them up that day. But two of the boys had younger brothers in the *City of Benares;* they had seen a lifeboat capsize and heard the cries of frightened people. They had to be reassured that it would be all right, they would see their brothers in a day or two—perhaps in the destroyer that would pick them up that afternoon at the latest.

The steward served the first meal at noon—one sardine each on a ship's biscuit and a dipperful of water. The dipper was a small cylinder, of about the diameter of an English penny; it held something less than a quarter of a pint. Even by noon on the first day—Wednesday—they were all thirsty and wanted more than this. The steward had full charge of the provisions. He started from the first day to ration water on the assumption that water would be the problem.

As time went on it became clear to Mary Cornish that her greatest problem was to keep the boys occupied. They were cramped and uncomfortable and had nothing to do. The awning was so low that the escorts could not sit upright beneath it, except on the floor of the boat. Mary Cornish had to crouch on the foresheets with bent back and shoulders; after a few hours it was a form of torture.

The boat rolled and pitched ceaselessly with a short, buckling, ill-tempered motion. Mary Cornish, seated on the foresheets, had to grip hold of a stanchion to keep her position. There was no relaxation, no rest. To move about you had to pick your way among human heads, limbs, and bodies so closely packed that you were hard put to it not to stamp on somebody's feet or fingers. At night, if you wished to move, others had to guide your feet into place with their hands. For this reason progress from one end of the boat to the other was ruled out except when it was essential; as, for instance, when the steward brought food and water from his locker in the stern (though even that was passed from hand to hand after the first day or so), or when one of the sailors went up to the bows to snatch a few hours' sleep in the shelter of the awning. Although the fourth officer was only about thirty feet away, Mary Cornish could not speak to him—even shouts would not carry over the noises of a storm. A phalanx of Lascars was wedged between the escorts and boys and the English sailors in the stern.

In these conditions the problem of keeping the boys' attention occupied was a tough one. How could their minds be distracted from their physical discomforts?

At first they sang popular songs: "Roll Out the Barrel," "There'll Always Be an England," and "Run, Rabbit, Run." Then there was talk: a repetition, over and over again, of all that they could remember of the shipwreck.

"Which would you rather be," the boys asked Miss Cornish, presenting that strange choice confronting their generation, "bombed at home or torpedoed in the Atlantic?" For the first few days the boys agreed that it was more exciting to be torpedoed. Other prevailing topics were the loss of their clothes and pocket money, and the prospects of food. The first was a major disaster.

"Four-and-eight, I had," a boy would reflect, as one still unable to grasp the extent of his loss. "Four-and-eight. Saved up, it was, ever since Mum said I was to go to Canada. Dad give me two shillings. I'll never be able to get that much again."

On the first day everyone kept watch. By perching on the gunwale the watcher could lean out from beneath the awning to feel the full strength of the wind on his face, to see far and wide across a wilderness of waters. Gulls soared by, and the wind tore the sound of their screams from their beaks, dispersing it; land could not be so very far, the escorts said, since gulls were about. Later on the boys took turns as lookout beside the creaking mast, standing up and hanging on while the boat pitched and shook, watching the horizon for a finger of smoke, and the sky for a speck of Sunderland. But the days wore on without sight of a vessel.

The boys' worst enemy was cold. The blankets, of which they had only two, could barely be stretched to cover them completely; or if, with some difficulty, this were managed, a few moments later a twitching arm or leg would jerk the blanket, and some part of a boy would become exposed.

Mary Cornish had only a thin, short-sleeved jacket to break a half-gale in the north Atlantic. The boys slept fitfully; she was forever having to tuck in their blankets, rearrange their limbs, or soothe them with a word of reassurance. But at least they slept. There was no sleep for her. There was no room to move her legs; a Lascar pressed against them. The boat rolled continuously; there was not even a blanket to soften the sharp edges of the boards. The noise alone would have prevented sleep: the slapping of waves, the wind's shriek, the mast's groaning; but in any case the bitter cold, the endless motion, above all, the misery of not being able to move made it seem as if the nights would never end.

Volunteers took turns working the handles. There were plenty of Lascars to do it, but their energies flagged as the voyage went on.

It was a strange experience to travel at such close quarters with men so alien and apart. They spoke few words of English but talked endlessly in their own tongue. All night long they kept up a noisy and incessant debate. What were they talking about so intently, crouched in the middle of the boat? The Englishmen in the stern sat in silence, watching the stars when the clouds broke to reveal them and the waning moon, gaging the strength of the wind, trying to hold their eastward course.

Sometimes the Lascars sheltered under the sail after dark. They made a sort of tent out of it and retired there to smoke the queer-smelling cigarettes they had somehow managed to bring with them, secreted in their loose, thin cotton garments. The smell of these cigarettes was sweet and yet acrid—perhaps drugged. They passed a cigarette from mouth to mouth, and as each one drew on it the brief glow lighted up a lean, coppery face—to a white man's eye so like its fellows, so baffling in its lack of expression.

Their religion too was strange. At dawn, at noon, and in the evening they rinsed their mouths and washed their faces with sea water, and then, cleansed, chanted their prayers to an alien god. At night they lay huddled in blankets, an indistinguishable mass. They slithered about on the floor of the boat and under the thwarts. Sometimes, under cover of darkness, they crept into the bows, under the awning; but there was no room for them and the escorts had to push them back. They made no protest. When the English seamen gave orders they obeyed, but for the most part without briskness, as if they did not really believe that the order would serve a useful purpose. Allah was compassionate and would save them if he wished; Allah was wise and would send storms if he deemed it best. It was the will of Allah, which no foreign infidel could mitigate or alter. They were very clean, and washed their turbans and their shirts continually, hanging them out to dry over the awning.

As the days went by, the Lascars' presence put an extra strain on the Europeans, outnumbered (not counting the children) by four to one. A gulf, intangible as light but wide as the universe, stood between them and their closest companions. They must put a guard on their tongues, a governor on their actions. No trace of despondency, however momentary, must be allowed to show in their manner or expression, lest it infect the Lascars with the virus of alarm.

v

On the second morning the wind abated somewhat, and the sea went down; hopes of rescue were high. The sail was hoisted and the boat drove forward at a fine speed, while the passengers forgot their discomfort in the exhilaration of sailing before a strong wind across the open sea. The boys were cheerful, still enjoying the adventure; but they missed their breakfast. The first meal of the day was issued at noon. It consisted of bully beef on a ship's biscuit. The boys wolfed the bully beef but found the biscuit very dry, with only a dipper of water to wash it down. After the second or third day they could not eat the biscuit, yet they did not like to throw it away.

"Auntie, will you mind my biscuit, please?" they would ask. So Mary Cornish found herself the repository of scraps of dry biscuit, which soon filled her pockets and overflowed into odd crannies of the boat. One of the Lascars asked her to mind his biscuit too. No one ever asked for his piece back but they all liked to know that the biscuits were there, safely minded.

Conversation turned on the first meal they would eat on landing. They talked a great deal about their homes and of the surprise of Mum and Dad when they returned. They wanted to take Mum a present; then the loss of their pocket money returned to them with poignancy. But Mr. Nagorski found a way out.

"Don't worry," he said, "when we get back I will make up to each of you the pocket money you have lost." This was greeted with delight. The boys' gravest anxiety was now allayed.

Mary Cornish started games. They played "Animal, Vegetable, or Mineral," and when that palled, "I Spy." But there were not so many things to be spied from a small boat in mid Atlantic. Their companions, the boat's essentials—sail, mast, tiller, handles, a barrico of water and tins of bully; at sea the waves, spray, clouds, and a few sea birds.

When games ran out Mary Cornish started to tell them stories. Dim recollections of *The Thirty-Nine Steps* and *Bulldog Drummond* lingered in her mind. Now she tried to drag from her memory tattered shreds of these and other stories and to hang them on a new framework. It was a desperate task for she was not by nature a storyteller, although fortunately a nephew had provided her with some experience of small boys' tastes. Captain Drummond was the hero: square-jawed, strong, lean, tough, and fearless. In the first installment he became deeply embroiled with a gang of Nazi spies. Airplanes, submarines, parachutists, secret wireless installations, masterminds, and ciphers were soon involved. The story reached a point where she could think of no way out for Captain Drummond, and the first installment ended.

"Go on, Auntie, *please* go on!" they implored. They were promised more next day. Thereafter there was no escape. The installment of the day, eagerly awaited, was given after supper (a few swigs of condensed milk sucked out of a hole punched in the tin) before settling down for the night.

To invent new episodes for Captain Drummond every day became almost a nightmare. Only the most thrilling adventures, the most hair-raising escapes, the most breathless fights, would satisfy her audience.

It was hard to keep clean and to preserve something of the decencies. Escorts and boys washed their faces every morning and evening, using for sponge a handkerchief tied to a piece of string and dangled over the side. But they had no soap. For handkerchiefs they used scraps of a Polish newspaper discovered in Mr. Nagorski's coat pocket. On the third day out Mr. Critchley, the cadet, was seen to be using a comb; this was seized upon with shouts of delight and made public property, being passed morning and evening from hand to hand.

Sanitary arrangements were more difficult. Privacy was out of the question in a boat where you could not flex an elbow without hitting a neighbor. There was a bucket and a bailer on board. The bucket was heavy and clumsy and the bailer was used until it was lost overboard on the fifth day out. Then only the bucket remained, and empty sardine tins. An order was given to reserve the bucket for Miss Cornish, but it was needed also as a bailer and it was kept in the stern. If she needed it word was passed along. "Who wants it?" the query would come back. A helpful shout would go up from the Lascars: "The memsahib!" and the bucket would come from hand to hand down the line. Nobody could move from his place, nor could his neighbors do more to ease the situation than to look the other way. But the body has little to eliminate on half a pint of water or less and a sardine and a mouthful of bully beef a day, so that such embarrassments became fewer as the voyage went on.

A little before dark Purvis, the steward, passed round tins of condensed milk to suck from and a dipperful of water for each person. There was no food. The boys said their prayers (this they did every evening without needing to be told) and disposed themselves for the night as best they could on the hard boards and the locker-top. All day long eyes had raked the sea in vain; ears, strained to catch the drone of aircraft engines, had heard only the pounding of waves on the boat's timbers and the cry of gulls. Now another night had fallen and long, weary hours of cold discomfort lay ahead. It was at such moments only that the boys' spirits fell. Sometimes a half-stifled whimper would come from under the blankets.

After the first three or four days the boys' feet and legs began to give trouble. Blood grown sluggish failed to nourish them, and this laid a strain on the heart: the earliest stages of death from exposure threatened them all.

Sometimes, in the past, when one of her music pupils had been playing in public Mary Cornish had massaged the pianist's hands at the last moment, coaxing blood into the fingertips. Now she tried this technique on the boys' feet and ankles before they went to sleep and when they woke in the night, stirred by cold. This kept their feet from going numb and enabled them to sleep. Her own feet she could not massage, and by the end of the fourth or fifth day they had become as nerveless as blocks of wood. The only way to stretch the aching limbs and to generate a little warmth in the body was to work the handles. Mary Cornish volunteered to take her turn. It raised blisters on her hands, but the exertion helped to keep her circulation going, and the handles drove the boat steadily closer to the Irish shore.

The gunner sometimes made his way to the children's end of the boat. He was a small, wiry sailor, tough as leather and colorful in his language, to whom a shipwreck was all part of the day's work. He believed in good discipline, getting on with the job in hand, and no nonsense. Probably the most experienced seaman in the boat, perhaps twenty years older than the man in command, he had no part in the navigation, and did not trouble to conceal his doubts as to whether it was being efficiently conducted. "Ought to be in Ireland by now," he would mutter. He had a poor opinion of the Lascars and their ways, and sometimes said so in terms which caused a little uneasiness among the rest of the party, since there were thirty-two Lascars and only six English members of the crew.

The gunner took an active interest in the welfare of the boys. But he seemed to develop a knack of coming up to the bows at the wrong moment from the escorts' point of view—when a boy had kicked his legs clear of his bit of blanket, or another had just waked up to complain of the cold.

"Here, what's all this?" he would demand. "This boy's got no blanket on. No wonder he's cold, poor little bastard. Come on, son, let's tuck the blanket under—that's the way—ought to be someone keeping an eye on these kids."

The escorts took these strokes of intervention in the kindly spirit in which they were meant, although sometimes the gunner's visits—always undertaken for helpful purposes—did not make their task any easier. At night, believing the boys to be asleep, he would speak freely of the difficulties facing the crew: of dwindling water, ignorance of their true position, the unlikelihood of reaching Ireland alive. His raucous whisper, raised to overtop the noises of the sea and swinging handles, would sometimes wake the boys, and his words, though true enough, were hardly calculated to reassure them.

So Friday and Saturday passed, the third and fourth day on the same pattern. By Saturday no one could even attempt to eat the daily ration of ship's biscuit. With difficulty the passengers swallowed a little bully beef or tinned salmon at noon, but at night their throats were so dry that they could barely suck the condensed milk out of the tins. Thirst was the thing. Throats became painfully swollen, tongues harsh and dry.

Sometimes gray walls of rain swept over the water, driving in at them under the awning. Once a hailstorm tattooed the sea with countless pinpricks, and all the empty tins on board were held up to catch the stones. But it was surprising how little could be trapped in a tin. Next time it rained they rigged up the sail to catch a puddle, but the salt with which the canvas was impregnated made the rainwater no sweeter than the sea, and the crew decided that it was not fit for drinking. The Lascars protested at this, claiming that in the part of India they came from all the water was brackish, so that they were used to salt. Disobeying orders, they drank the sail water, but it did not seem to slake their thirst.

The Lascars were beginning to grow surly, and when the fourth officer appealed for volunteers to work the handles they sometimes sat quite still, refusing to co-operate. Luckily the cadet knew a little of their language and was able to give them orders in it, while the man who appeared to be their leader did his best to make them obey. They were disheartened and sick rather than mutinous. Many of them had cuts and bruises, and these men would make their way to Mary Cornish, who had charge of the first-aid box, and ask her to dress their wounds. On one such occasion the head Lascar warned her against one of his fellows: a bad man, he said, who was watching her when he should have been looking away. "Don't speak to him," he advised.

Sense of time grew blurred. It became harder to remember what had happened yesterday and what the day before; each day was a repetition of the last; they seemed to have been a lifetime in the boat. One night there was a cruel storm, and they could make no progress either with the handles or the sail. The sea-anchor was thrown out, and all night long the boat pitched and heaved throwing the passengers about without respite, till their limbs were freshly bruised and battered.

A dozen times that night it seemed that they were done for, as a wave came at them from above like a falling tower. The men bailed without respite. The boys were frightened, chilled, and seasick, and slept only in snatches. But dawn found them still afloat, and when morning came the storm went down. It was hard to believe that they had lived through such a night, and impossible to imagine that they could survive another.

VI

The fifth day was Sunday. The steward promised them a special Sunday dinner. It came down at noon: a small segment of canned peach. Soft and cool, it slid easily down their thirst-contracted throats. But a dipperful of water poured carefully into an empty condensed-milk tin and eked out, on this occasion by a little peach juice, was still their ration, and by now their lips were cracked and dry.

They sighted a steamer on Sunday afternoon. A shout went up, and hope bounded like a porpoise. No false hope either. A speck on the horizon slowly expanded before their eyes. It grew into a dot, and then a fine feather of smoke, and then the plain outline of a steamer. The boys jumped up, waving, long before there was any chance of being spotted through the strongest telescope. Mary Cornish's petticoat, requisitioned on the first day as a signal of distress, was run up to the masthead. Father O'Sullivan called on the boys to pray that they would be sighted from the approaching steamer.

The steamer headed directly toward them. She had altered course; there could be no doubt that she had seen them. A cargo vessel of medium tonnage, she appeared. Everyone was in high spirits. The signalman was busy with his flags in the stern and the children were shouting and singing in the bows. The lifeboat was under sails and a good breeze was carrying them rapidly toward the rescue ship.

The steamer stopped and turned slowly until she was broadside on. Those in the lifeboat guessed that her crew were preparing to throw down a line and to lower a rope ladder.

One of the sailors had taken down the awning. Now he came round pulling out of their sockets the heavy iron stanchions that supported it, for fear lest the boys' legs should be crushed between the stanchions and the steamer's side. There was nowhere to stow them so he threw two of them (out of three) overboard. They would not be needed any more. It was a great moment. In a few minutes they would be safe, their ordeal over, free to stretch their limbs and straighten their backs, above all to slake their thirst. Their approaching security seemed all the sweeter because another savage storm was getting up. Already the dark seas were rising, and beyond the steamer black, angry clouds were massing on the horizon.

Then the unbelievable happened. The steamer had seen the lifeboat —there could be no doubt about that. Now they saw her turning slowly around and the water churning behind her screw. Then slowly, inexorably, incredibly she steamed away.

In the lifeboat they gazed after her in horror, silent with incredulity and dismay. No signal showed from the steamer. She grew smaller and smaller until only a streak on the horizon remained. Then the storm that had been threatening gathered force and swept toward them, and the smoke too disappeared.

Darkness fell soon after the unknown steamer left them. In the life-boat they discussed the matter, but not for long, because they had to shout above the sound of the rising storm, and their throats pained them. German U-boats, it was said, had been known to disguise themselves as lifeboats, and then to fire on ships that approached to the rescue. The only explanation that could be suggested of the steamer's strange and terrible behavior was that her crew had suspected the lifeboat of being an enemy submarine so concealed, and had made off without waiting for proof. Now that two of the three stanchions supporting the awning had gone, the canvas was forced down lower than ever on the boys' and the escorts' heads. This added a great deal to their discomfort. The gunner made his way for'ard. In such moments of distress his confident outlook was a tonic. The episode of the steamer he dismissed as a good omen, nothing more.

"That ship shows we've reached the sea lanes," he said briskly. "What's the matter now? Down'earted 'cos she didn't pick us up?

That's nothing to worry about. We'll see plenty more ships tomorrow now we've reached the sea lanes."

They rode out the storm that night with the aid of their sea-anchor. The boys slept at times in spite of the buffeting, but the escorts could not rest at all. Once more they lived through a night that no small boat, it would seem, could have survived except by a kind of miracle.

By the next morning they were beginning to feel symptoms of exhaustion. Feet and legs were numb, their limbs black and blue from bruises. Water was running low. Several of the Lascars were too weak to move. They lay in the bottom of the boat, red-eyed and silent. It was part of their religion to rinse out their mouths before prayer, and this all the Lascars did, using of course sea water. The English feared that they were swallowing surreptitious mouthfuls of brine. They seemed to be sinking into a sort of coma, with the will to live dying down in them. Only a few now responded to the calls made to man the handles. When rations were doled out at noon and sunset they followed with their eyes every movement of the steward as he measured out the water.

Dawn was gray and stormy. They strained their eyes to find the land and saw nothing. Progress was slow in such heavy seas, but they did not give up hope. In the afternoon a shout went up that the land had been sighted. And there it lay, a long, low band of indigo smudged across the horizon.

They gazed at it until their eyes ached. The edge was surely too hard and sharp for cloud, the whole thing too solid. Low hills were outlined against the sky, and in front a foreshore. They could doubt no longer. It *was* land.

Once again excitement rose. A strong wind carried them forward under sail. Was it Ireland? Scotland? The Shetlands? And would they make landfall before night? Behind them the sun was sinking, silvering the ragged edges of a cloud deflated by the passing of the storm. Night was coming; it was a race with time.

The land did not get any closer, but they did not despair. Twilight overtook them, and the land's outline faded. Night came. The fourth officer had a flare hoisted on the masthead, a signal to the coast guards or to coastwise shipping. All night long it made a pool of light in the encircling blackness.

That night one of the boys became delirious. He was suffering acute pains in his feet. Mary Cornish took off her jacket and wrapped it round them after massaging them in an effort to restore the circulation. After a long while he fell into a fitful sleep.

They passed through a belt of phosphorescence and leaned over the side of the boat to watch it, fascinated and forgetful of their thirst and bruises. It flashed in the water like molten silver, and fishes, silver-scaled and fiery, leapt by. At dawn all eyes were strained toward the eastern horizon. The sky paled flat and empty. When light came they could see only the familiar gray desert of waves. The land had vanished, with the cloud that mocked them.

VII

This was on Tuesday. They had been a week at sea. The strength of the boys was ebbing fast. They had barely eaten for five days and their thirst was becoming acute. Almost as bad was the constant pressure against other bodies, the aching of bruised muscles, and the pain of sleepless, bloodshot eyes. Several of the Lascars were lying semiconscious in the bottom of the boat. Still the lifeboat kept her course, under sail now, for the sea was a little calmer.

At noon the steward brought round the usual water ration, which each person poured into his empty condensed-milk tin. This was the last time—although the steward did not tell them then—that they would get water at noon. Next day the ration was to be halved, and issued only in the evening. They were nearing the bottom of the cask.

The delirious boy recovered with the coming of daylight although he was weak and his feet were sore. Thirsty or not, that evening the boys still wanted their bedtime installment of Captain Drummond, and Mary Cornish gave it to them. She found the effort considerable, for not only was it difficult to speak with a parched, dry throat and a swollen tongue, but a week with little food and water, and with constant anxiety over the boys had begun to affect her mind. She had to force her thoughts with conscious effort, like squeezing hardened paint out of a tube. But she managed to think of the day's plot somehow, although her voice sounded thick and barely intelligible in her own ears.

That evening messages came down from the stern that the Lascars were restive and needed to be watched. On board was a hatchet used to split open cases of canned provisions. This was kept in the bows, and the escorts by way of precaution put it down within easy reach. After nightfall another of the boys became delirious. His feet were so painful that he could not bear to have them touched. As the night wore on he became obsessed with the fear of going mad. Sometimes he screamed horribly and shouted: "I'm mad, I'm going mad, I *know* I'm going mad."

A message came down from the stern: could the escorts for God's sake keep that boy quiet; his screams might drive the Lascars over the edge. Mary Cornish tried to calm him, but if anyone touched him he shouted all the more. Father O'Sullivan said in French:

"This boy is dying of thirst."

"The others aren't. He must hang on somehow."

A message went back to the steward: could he spare an extra dipperful of water? A few drops were smuggled past the Lascars by one of the seamen. But after this no more could be done. Only one torch with a live battery was left on board and the Lascars had it. They were keeping its beam on the sick boy in the bows. They were not taking any chances; no one was going to cheat them of their share of water by giving an extra ration to the sick boy.

There was one service that the priest alone could perform. He knelt beside the boy and offered prayers for his soul. The others could not understand the rapid Latin phrases, but the low-voiced words had a soothing effect.

There was a disturbance among the Lascars, and then the gunner appeared. He took in the situation at a glance: the boy's exposed legs and feet—he had kicked off the blanket—the kneeling priest, and the solemn atmosphere.

"What's going on here *now?*" he demanded. "What's wrong with the poor little blighter?"

The boy, croaking like a frog, cried out for water.

"Water?" the gunner said. "Is *that* all? Of course you want water; we all do. You'll get some in the morning."

The boy only cried out again for water.

"Now you forget about it," the gunner commanded. "You'll have plenty of water when we're picked up, and that won't be long now. Is *that* all that's wrong with you?"

"My feet are cold," the boy answered weakly.

The gunner snorted triumphantly and glared at the escorts. "Huh! So your feet are cold. That's a nice way to look after a kid. . . ."

The cadet took his coat off to give to the boy, and the gunner wrapped it round the sick boy's feet and tucked it in.

"There. Any better?" he demanded.

"My feet are still cold."

"No, they're not," the gunner said firmly. "They're wrapped up properly now and they'll be warm as toast in half a jiffy. Now, are your feet warm?"

"My feet——" the boy began.

"Don't let me hear another sound out of you till morning," the gunner said fiercely. "No more of this yelling out. Now—*are your feet warm?*"

"Yes," the boy whispered feebly.

"Then you'll be all right till the morning."

He went off, muttering under his breath about boys with cold feet, women who didn't know how to look after kids, and the respective merits of saying prayers and keeping children warm. His methods were effective; the boy did not scream any more and he gradually quieted down.

The sun rose into a clear sky, over a blue and sparkling ocean. Now at last the sea was calm, for the first time since the sinking of the *City of Benares*. There was little wind, and the boat idled along under a white sail toward a misty horizon. Even those in the lifeboat, weary and thirsty as they were, felt life quickening in their thickened blood. A sense of exhilaration came as the sun warmed their stiff limbs.

For the first time since their long voyage started they could move about without risk of being hurled off their feet and into the laps of their neighbors. Mary Cornish took down the canvas awning so the boys could sit in the sun, and allowed them (all save the sick one) to dangle their cramped feet over the side. The gunner made the most of his first smooth day and swam alongside the boat for some time before climbing back, apparently in the best of health and spirits.

At noon, the steward sent round portions of tinned salmon on the usual ship's biscuit that nobody ate. There was no water.

VIII

It was a boy who first saw the flying boat. With a cry of "Sunderland!" he pointed to the west. A speck in the sky was growing larger. Nobody believed it at first. A dozen Sunderlands had already been sighted, only to resolve themselves into gulls. But this time it was real. By freak of chance the path of a flying boat patrolling far out into the Atlantic had crossed their own.

Once more the white petticoat was run up to the masthead. Even the Lascars came to life. Beyond doubt the Sunderland had seen the lifeboat. It came straight for them, and swooped low in a wide circle. A helmeted pilot leaned out and waved. They waved wildly back. Their arms were heavy, but the excitement made them forget their thirst and fatigue.

The flying boat circled round several times and then made off eastward. The people in the boat knew they were saved.

Sometime later—they were not sure how long—another Sunderland came. Her crew dropped a note and a parcel done up in a Mae West jacket. The note said that a destroyer was coming and that she was only forty miles away. The parcel contained food—beans in tomato sauce, cans of salmon and peaches. They cheered and laughed as the steward went to work with a tin-opener. Someone in the stern produced a mouth-organ, and a sing-song followed. Then they feasted: the best meal they had eaten since the voyage began. They drained every drop of peach juice and tomato sauce out of the tins. But the steward refused to issue the last of the water. They were not rescued yet, he said. Never count your chickens. The Lascars protested, but to no purpose. They were still eating when, a few hours later, the destroyer came in sight. There was no mistake this time. She raced toward them at an astonishing speed, came round, and hove to within a few yards of their lifeboat—a beautiful piece of seamanship. Sailors on deck threw down the lines and in a moment they were made fast.

Even then Mary Cornish could scarcely believe it. She had the feeling that all this was happening to someone else and that she was looking on. This gave way to an irrational fear that the destroyer was German. She knew the fear was stupid but could not banish it. She distinctly heard one of the crew say something about "herren"—and then realized that the voice was Scottish, and was referring to the stern. The lifeboat passengers looked up at the grinning faces of the sailors who lined the rails, and smiled thankfully back. Two ratings jumped down into the lifeboat to help the boys out. The Navy was there.

When the survivors reached Gourock in Scotland they learned that of the ninety children who had sailed on the *City of Benares* only thirteen were saved. Seven, including only one of the girls in Mary Cornish's group, had been picked up by a destroyer. Only two of the ten escorts besides herself and Father O'Sullivan (who had to go to a hospital on his arrival) had got back alive.

For weeks thereafter Mary Cornish suffered acutely from the effects of her ordeal. Sores in her mouth, neuralgia, fiery pain in her feet, nightmares, sleeplessness. This was part of the price exacted for eight days in an open boat.

In March, 1941, Mary Cornish and Fourth Officer Cooper of the *City of Benares* were invested by the King with the medal of the British Empire. Some months later Purvis, the steward, received the same honor. Mary Cornish did not feel that her part in the episode merited a decoration; she was only carrying out to the best of her ability the responsibilities of an escort's job. She thought of herself in her own words as an adjunct to the children; and this is perhaps the best summary that can be given of her part in the affair.

The Little Woman

by I. A. R. WYLIE

NOVEMBER, 1945

Woman must get "down into the dusty arena with her sleeves rolled up," says one who has done just that, or Man is going to blow up the world. Ida Alexa Ross Wylie has been swinging verbal (and real, she reveals here) haymakers all her life—and writing novels and stories for many magazines. She was born in Australia in 1885, and enjoyed a self-regulated childhood in England, becoming an experienced traveler, alone, over her own country and the Continent before she was in her teens. Miss Wylie is unmarried and lives on a farm at Belle Mead, New Jersey.

The famous jester, Joe Miller, probably under the influence of a Restoration banquet, once boasted that, at a moment's notice, he could make a joke on any subject. He was immediately challenged to make a joke about the King. As in those days jests about the monarchy were an unhealthy amusement, Mr. Miller had to think fast.

"The King, gentlemen," he said, "is no subject."

And thereby won his bet and withdrew his neck into safety.

Contrariwise, Woman is always a subject. Whenever lecturers, essayists, psychoanalysts, or women themselves have nothing else to talk, write, or worry about, they can always propound such questions as, "Do Women—?", "Why Don't Women—?", or "Are Women—?" and find an audience, if no answer. It would seem that Woman, who by accepted tradition is always a woman before she is anything else, in counterdistinction to a man who may be first and foremost a poet or a plumber, is a sort of chronic interrogation mark, the unsolved riddle of the ages, a poor bewildered and bewildering creature who in spite of her long sojourn on earth has never properly adjusted herself to herself or to her environment, let alone to her fellow-wayfarer, Man. In vain she takes up determined attitudes in various niches. Sooner or later she falls out of them, sometimes by accident, sometimes, in a fit of neurotic self-dissatisfaction, deliberately, but always to sounds of disapprobation or rude mirth from the spectators.

At some periods, as in the Victorian era, she assumes the pose of Wife and Mother and develops—as apparently inevitable by-products —megrims, vapors, and the ability to faint at the sight of a mouse. Or going into reverse she may become a Career Woman who tends to strut, snort, shoot her cuffs, blow smoke through her nose, and generally behave like some strange and wondrous beast that has never been before and will never be again—in other words the Exceptional Woman who has, incidentally, no use for other women of any ilk. (It is typical that Lady Astor, the first woman member of Parliament, was, and probably still is, a violent antisuffragist. What is sauce for the goose, obviously, is not sauce for geese.) Or, consumed with managerial energies and debarred from the council chambers of her country, she may become a *Femme Fatale* and run it by remote control from the councilor's bedroom. Or, as a desperate compromise, she may assay to be everything at once, Wife, Mother, Career Woman, and *Femme Fatale,* at which point the psychoanalyst steps into the picture and at umpty dollars an hour, at least once a week over a period of years, endeavors to discover what is the matter with her, and to bring her back to whatever he happens, at the moment, to consider normality.

As a one-time suffragette who knocked off policemen's helmets and sandbagged Cabinet Ministers in the cause of Woman's emancipation,

I have to admit, as indeed I had to admit at the height of my crusading fervor, that next to the dinosaurus, Woman is probably nature's most outstanding failure. For the life of me, I cannot think of any sphere of activity in which she is even passably successful, except in the matter of surviving, where obviously she has the dinosaurus licked. Her most determined admirer would be hard put to it to produce one first-class genius in any of the creative arts, and more than a very few top-ranking talents in the interpretive arts. In science, Madame Curie has to be produced over and over again like a succession of rabbits out of a conjuror's hat. The Brontës and Jane Austen confront an endless chain of masculine storytellers and writers from Homer to Steinbeck. A fragmentary and dubious Sappho, a wispy Emily Dickinson, a somewhat overlyrical Elizabeth Browning, are about all the sex has to show for itself in poetry. There have been no great women painters or composers. Even in fields marked off as peculiarly their own, women, judged by masculine standards, are lamentably second rate. The best couturiers, hairdressers, home-designers, and cooks are men. I suspect that, were it biologically possible, men would make better mothers.

Worst of all, women are conscious failures and consequently in a chronic state of discontent which may be divine but is certainly uncomfortable. They suffer in a way in which men—who, whatever mess they make of themselves and their environment, are always self-satisfied—never suffer. In spite of energetic and heavily sponsored drives on behalf of wifehood and motherhood and her own overemphasis on the importance of those roles, the Wife and Mother when challenged will invariably describe herself as "just a Wife and Mother." The Exceptional Woman, who reminded Dr. Johnson of a dog walking on its hind legs, in spite of struts and snorts, feels in her deepest consciousness that she is, in fact, a freak. Now to be either "just" anything or freakish is not a happy state. And it is a fact that as one-half of a hapless species, women are the more unhappy.

Yet, demonstrably, they are not stupider than men. They couldn't be. Let us consider for a moment our world, governed as it is by masculine genius of every sort, from the point of view of a visiting and impartial Martian. He would see that it was, at best, a difficult setting for a very brief career. Four-fifths of it is under water. Vast tracts are uninhabitable. The climate—except, I will admit without argument, in California—has to be endured and combated. It is subject to typhoons, hurricanes, quakes, droughts, and floods. It is foredoomed to extinction. We ourselves, physically speaking, appear to have been dreamed up by a plumber of the Heath Robinson variety, and that the plumbing works at all for any length of time is its most astounding feature. Thanks to an increasing number of spells and counterspells evolved by our witch-doctors, we survive an increasing number and variety of diseases but only long enough to make the dour discovery that we have been pitch-jerked without so much as a will-you-won't-you into a dance whose steps and rhythm have never been explained to us. The Martian would naturally suppose that Man, with these horrific handicaps, would bend all his energies and capacities to prolonging his life and making it, if not reasonable, at least endurable. He observes, on the contrary, that no sooner has Man discovered one cure for his disabilities than he works out a new and better way for making himself miserable.

The rocket-bomb follows penicillin as the night the day. A new technique for dealing with dreadful wounds is followed by new ways of inflicting them. Having found means to prolong his pitiable span of life Man proceeds to cut himself down in the high noon of his youth. He creates the ideals of justice and mercy only to treat his fellow-man with an inhumanity that would puzzle a normal tiger. In his domestic life he builds Better Homes, equipped with every sort of labor-saving device (though in reality labor is the only occupation that gives him any real satisfaction, and his so-called pleasures more often than not goad him to drink), and promptly lays them flat with high explosives, driving himself into the wilderness to perish with quite unnecessary discomfort. New methods of communication are followed up by customs, censorships, tariffs, frontiers, travel restrictions, and, if necessary, wars so that countries now literally within speaking distance of each other, are more isolated than in the days of sail and coach. Generalizing roughly, the Martian, on his return, would have to report that Man, having found ways to make his life longer and better, at once, as though goaded by invisible Furies, sets about making it shorter and worse. And this, the Martian would decide, is just plain stupid.

It is so stupid that it is unbeatable. I maintain, in all fairness, that Woman, in Man's place, couldn't make a worse mess of things. Conceivably she might do better. At least she would not delude herself that she was making a howling success of them, which is the method by which Man keeps himself smug and relatively satisfied in the midst of his own self-invoked and insane chaos.

Yet Woman, herself a victim, makes only sporadic and feeble efforts to take the reins. And no gentleman has so much as offered her a place on the saddle with him.

II

Now Man has brains. To the Martian they may seem rudimentary, but they are at any rate good enough to enable him to find out some interesting and even useful facts about himself and his minute universe. That he uses them to his own undoing surely denotes, therefore, some emotional maladjustment, a lack of ballast and balance which we have learned to describe as a neurosis. Somewhere, at any rate, under his erratic leadership, humanity has gone wrong and figuratively taken to drink to drown its awareness of sin and failure. Since one-half of it, from the dawn of its disastrous history, has been intellectually inert and physically inadequate, the tragedy is understandable and inevitable. Any four-cylindered engine, bearing a heavy load, and firing on only two cylinders, is doomed eventually to fall apart. But why and when did the other two cylinders stop firing? And can they be put into action again before the whole machine reels onto the scrap-heap?

We know, in spite of our erudite pretensions, very little of our origins. Peering back through the mists of history we can only dimly discern the First Man and the First Woman fighting, for no very obvious reason, to survive. In that struggle one thing is biologically certain. Though there were undoubtedly differences in point of view and temperament, there was little to choose between them in muscle and brain power. (If anything the woman may have been the more agile and enduring and almost certainly, as are all female animals, she was more dangerous as an antagonist.) There wasn't much talk of any sort and none at all about Woman's Sphere. Whatever the man was, stoop-shouldered, bow-legged, low-browed, and squint-eyed, the woman was. Whatever he had to be, cunning, ferocious, and tenacious, she had to be. True, she was in addition a mother, but incidentally, casually, and with no more fuss and feathers than the man gave to the business of his no less incidental and casual fatherhood. If George Jr. survived that was all right. If he didn't that was all right too. There were, apparently, plenty more where he came from. Mother love, if such it could be called, was a very brief emotional episode, liable under prolonged pressure to turn into violent antipathy. (It was not until much later that it began to exert a stranglehold upon the species.) Men and women hunted and fought side by side, and when they quarreled it was a matter of chance whose skull got cracked first. They were neither lovely, loving, nor lovable. Their advance on their uncharted course toward the stars or wherever they were going, was slow and clumsy. But at any rate they were on their way together.

Then something disastrous happened and they parted company. The man went on and the woman sat down and waited for him to come back from time to time and tell her, more or less accurately, what he had been up to. Like so many convulsions in our history I imagine that the change was brought about by some trivial incident. (One is reminded of Priestley's play, *Dangerous Corner,* where the course of half a dozen lives hangs on the decision of one character— if I remember correctly—to pick up a cigarette box.) Perhaps on some dismal winter's day some prehistoric woman, armed *cap à pie* for the hunt or a raid on a neighboring larder, took the unprecedented notion to stay home and let George do it. Perhaps she had a headache, perhaps George Jr. was imminent and to be caught with him in a hand-to-hand scuffle would be to put her at an obvious disadvantage. At any rate, for whatever reason, she laid her flint aside, built herself a nice fire, warmed up the equivalent of a pot of coffee, figuratively turned on the radio, and gave herself a day. She found she liked it. (We always like the line of least resistance and it is always fatal. That woman happened to find it first was, no doubt, pure accident.)

She tried it again. By grapevine communication other women learned of the experiment and gave it a satisfactory trial. Then, of course, some sort of alibi had to be concocted. The habit of staying home had to be explained in noble and resounding terms. Or as we would say nowadays, it had to be rationalized and proved to everyone's satisfaction that Woman, far from turning sybarite and parasite, was sacrificing herself on the altar of her Duty. Whereupon her mind, always a shade more agile than George's (Sr. or Jr.), lit on Mother Love and the Woman's Sphere. Henceforward it was her business in life to keep the home fires burning (not for herself, of course, but against the return of her warrior-hunter), his slippers by the embers, and the stew simmering. She herself became The Little Woman, or as Fleta Campbell Springer once sardonically described her, The Blue Birdie in the Blue Nesty. And George Sr. for the first time cast lascivious glances at the *Femme Fatale* of his period and thought up divorce as a social out from acute domestic boredom. George Jr., overwhelmed and overburdened by Mother Love, took to the woods.

But though bored, puzzled, and slightly resentful, George Sr. began to realize that Woman's new and self-ordained role in the scheme of things had its advantages even for him. Without his knowing she had, it seemed, cramped his style. There was a tiresome, restraining reasonableness about her. She killed only what she needed. She fought only when she had to. Without her plucking at his coat-tails with her everlasting "Enough's enough" he was now free to fight and kill without rhyme or reason. He in his turn had to produce an alibi—an equally lofty explanation for the scalps and carcasses with which the family cave was now embarrassingly cluttered. They became therefore not merely testimonies of his unbridled skill in destruction but tributes to the Little Woman who by this time had become one of his possessions and therefore an object of pride and responsibility. (In due course she ranked with his ox and his ass and anything else that was his.) His shield covered her. Without it, he liked to think and said so interminably, she must surely perish. The Little Woman, in her turn, was at first surprised and annoyed. But once she grasped the idea that the scalps and carcasses were tributes and that on their superior number depended her prestige among other women, she accepted them graciously and presently demanded them. In due course she began to nag for them.

Thus chivalry was established as an institution. War became Man's main preoccupation. And civilization, still in the making, bore with it in the womb of time the seeds of its own dissolution.

III

Somewhere in that massive masterpiece *Black Lamb and Grey Falcon,* Rebecca West observes that the main difference between men and women is that men are lunatics and women idiots. By which she means, obviously, that men are actively and women passively insane. Certainly from the moment that women began confining themselves to the home and centering their happiness and *raison d'être* on its inhabitants who were never intended or able to carry such an abnormal burden, they became intellectually inert and physically they deteriorated. Whereas men grew straight of limb, keen-sighted and fleet-footed, women developed knock-knees and when they ran, which was seldom, for running had become unwomanly, it was with a wobbly, teetering gait reminiscent of an alarmed duck. Their marksmanship, even in the home, became deplorable and an unfailing source of masculine humor.

Henceforward, whenever a woman suffered an urge to create something over and above such contributions to the home and family as crocheted antimacassars, hand-painted vases, or woolen scarves, whenever she had "immortal longings," she knew that she was becoming "freakish" and either suppressed or hid them, shamefacedly, as did the Brontës and a certain Mlle. Dupin, under a stalwart masculine alias. Thus the capacity to create, like her muscles, withered in her. Even in the home she became uninventive, conservative, and amateurishly second-rate. It was George who thought up the new sauce, the better stuffings, the back-saving washtubs. Since it pleased him, and it was her business in life, not to mention her livelihood, to please him (and she still retained a tough urge to survive) she stood by in respectful admiration.

"He for God only, she for God in him," Milton sang with forthright masculine modesty. He did not add, for he certainly did not realize it, that George had already begun to suffer from his own excess of divinity and the Little Woman's overpowering appreciation of it. He and George Jr. were, as they might have said, homesick, by which they meant sick of home. If they were spineless they finally yielded to its enticements and became that product of excess Mother Love and bane of the world, chronic adolescents. If they had guts they fled it, with one lofty excuse after another, to the far corners of the earth. As scientists and explorers they discovered poles and desert wastes where they couldn't live. They intruded on continents where they did not belong, and as the original inhabitants raised objections, started the glorious business of converting, or in other words, exterminating them—unless, as sometimes happened, they were exterminated first. They invented new and faster ways of getting further and further. When the Little Woman and the nest grew altogether too domestic they invented wars, deciding that some foul foreigner—and this on a little two-by-four earth, small as an antheap in a ridiculous little universe—had insulted them, or, what was worse, the Little Woman; and nothing less than blood, floods of it and even their own, could wash out the dishonoring stain. The Little Woman stayed home, wept, and knitted socks and pull-overs for her hero and defender. She was still

faintly puzzled by him but also proud and happy to think that he was
prepared to kill and even be killed for her sake. Did he not sing to her:

> I could not love thee, dear, so much
> Loved I not honor more?

And wasn't that beautiful?

The notion that she ought to step into the fracas and bat him and
George Jr. over the head on the off-chance of knocking some sense
into them, as her dynamic ancestresses would have done, flickered
faintly in her from time to time, but it was not until the first decade of
the twentieth century that, again thanks to a trivial incident, the
smoldering spark burst into a small, hot flame.

The Right Honorable Herbert Asquith, Prime Minister of Great
Britain, provided the incident. Amiably amused at the mild protests
of a group of women who besides being wives, mothers, and taxpayers
had an unreasonable urge to become voters, he pointed out to them
in a public speech that men, when they had demanded the suffrage,
had cared enough to fight for it. They had torn up paving-stones,
destroyed property, and broken heads. They had even died for it. The
Little Woman, of course, would not and indeed could not do such
things. Ergo, she didn't care enough. Ergo, since she could not fight
for her rights, she hadn't any. Ergo, she must depend on masculine
chivalry, exercising that well-known sway in her own peculiar sphere,
the nest. And so forth and so on.

Having uttered which pious and paternal platitudes Mr. Asquith
went his placid way. Soon afterward, when he was again on a public
platform, a flour barrel, cunningly concealed in the flies of the auditorium, and to the shrill screams of "Votes for Women!" emptied itself
over his astonished head. The fat was in the fire. Or, more poetically
speaking, Mr. Asquith had involuntarily ushered in the dawn. With
what can only be described as a hell of a yell thousands of wives and
mothers burst out of their nests, and, according to prescription, tore
up paving-stones, destroyed property, and broke heads; and though
they rigidly adhered to their old feminine characteristic of avoiding
the kill, save in dire necessity, many of them died.

The results were startling. It was discovered that a relative handful
of human beings, unarmed save with a resolute fighting temper and a
conviction of justice, could set the forces of society—armed to the
teeth but with a bad conscience—right back on their heels. It was in

vain that the police force reorganized itself to cope with an unprecedented situation. They didn't cope. The Houses of Parliament, in a state of panic, passed the famous (or infamous) Cat-and-Mouse Act. It didn't work. The First World War mercifully came to the men's aid and enabled them to present the Little Women with their vote without obvious loss of face. But what was really important news was the effect on the Little Women themselves of their own outrageous conduct. To that, as one of them, I can bear witness.

I am not very clear how or why I had become one of them. My adolescence had been spent in Germany, where I had acquired a lofty contempt for women in general and a slinking distrust of myself. But besides being a vigorous creature, spoiling for a fight—though I did not know it and as a woman would certainly never have acknowledged it—I had, I like to believe, a rudimentary sense of justice. Since women, whether they were idiots or not, paid taxes, they had a right to vote. For which ostensible reason, at any rate, I plunged into the fray. To my astonishment I found that women, in spite of knock-knees and the fact that for centuries a respectable woman's leg had not even been mentionable, could at a pinch outrun the average London bobby. Their aim with a little practice became good enough to land ripe vegetables in ministerial eyes, their wits sharp enough to keep Scotland Yard running round in circles and looking very silly. Their capacity for impromptu organization, for secrecy and loyalty, their iconoclastic disregard for class and established order were a revelation to all concerned but especially themselves.

Best of all was discovery that when it came down to a real slugging match they were not at such a hopeless disadvantage as tradition would have had them suppose. The day that, with a straight left to the jaw, I sent a fair-sized CID officer, who was attempting to arrest an escaped "mouse," into the orchestra pit of the Pavillion Theatre where we were holding one of our belligerent meetings, was the day of my own coming-of-age. (Incidentally, I met my victim at Southampton during the war. I was on my way to France and my late antagonist passed me through the Secret Service controls ahead of all the brass hats. He explained that he knew from experience I was a good citizen, and we shook hands warmly.) Since I was no genius the episode could not make me one, but it set me free to be whatever I was to the top of my bent. Had Emily Brontë had my chance to deliver that straight left, assuredly she would have written a masterpiece thereafter that would have made her actual accomplishment look like the cramped, tormented struggles of a winged and caged eagle.

For two years of wild and sometimes dangerous adventure I worked and fought alongside vigorous, happy, well-adjusted women who laughed instead of tittering, who walked freely instead of teetering, who could outfast Gandhi and come out with a grin and a jest. I slept on hard floors between elderly duchesses, stout cooks, and young shopgirls. We were often tired, hurt, and frightened. But we were content as we had never been. We shared a joy of life that we had never known. Most of my fellow-fighters were Wives and Mothers. And strange things happened to their domestic life. Husbands came home at night with a new eagerness, at first perhaps because they knew that the Little Woman was safe in Holloway Jail, but later because it was good to find her home, fun to hear how she had thumb-nosed that old fuddy-duddy at Bow Street or outsmarted the CID boys again. Sometimes, since she was often tired and battered, he got supper for her. He gave her the high sign when the plain-clothes police, on the watch across the way, had gone off to supper or for other causes, and gave her a leg up over the garden wall. When he was very brave he marched with banners in her processions. Little as they may have realized it they were recapturing the old comradeship that their ancestors had lost for them.

As for the children, their attitude changed rapidly from one of affectionate toleration for poor darling mother to one of wide-eyed wonder. Released from the smother of mother love—for she was too busy to be more than casually concerned with them—they discovered that they liked her. She was a great sport. She had guts. For the first time they began to boast about her, not on the strength of her domestic virtues but on the length of her prison sentences. The home, which had been showing marked signs of disintegration, was in the fire of battle being welded into a new unity. Those women who stood outside the fight—I regret to say the vast majority—and who were being more than usually Little Women, hated the fighters with the venomous rage of envy.

In the war, at the height of the struggle, the fighters put their cause aside to merge themselves in the national effort. But some of their gains remained. Shorts at Wimbledon and women in uniform testified to a revolution. It was not yet a total war and total effort was not demanded of them. They were not yet to fight and die, except by accident, in their own right. That right came to them in the Second World War. Then their capacities *had* to be acknowledged and accepted. They proved what many of them had already suspected, that they were physically as brave as men and often more enduring. They were born warriors who in a cause which their reason declared vital could and would fight effectively to the last ditch. After untold centuries some of them were themselves again.

Will they remain themselves? Are they too few to save so many? Will the Blue Birdie in the Blue Nesty prove too strong for them? On the answer to these questions hangs our human survival.

IV

Recently we witnessed the United Nations draw up blueprints for a world organization supposedly on a democratic basis, with a full half of its inhabitants almost entirely unrepresented. Dean Gildersleeve, as a sop tossed to the American women voters, was allowed to trot along with other minor minorities. Great Britain, who literally owed her existence to her women, sent Ellen Wilkinson and two or three others, not to speak for them, for as far as the general public was concerned they never opened their mouths in council, but to come along and watch George do it again.

The spectacle would have been ludicrous if it had not been, in its implications, tragic. It foreshadowed fresh disaster. For sooner or later, without the checks and balances of a healthy two-party system, Man's passion for power for its own sake, his unbridled creativeness, will overwhelm his platitudes and we shall have another explosion that may literally rock our physical world to its axis.

Women cannot justly blame men for this state of affairs. If they want to go back to First Causes they can blame the first woman who exchanged her birthright for what she mistakenly imagined was a sheltered life. Then they can blame themselves for treading supinely in her footsteps. If men still pat them on the head and allow them to write their speeches for them in the back office, it is for good and sufficient reason. Men, whatever else they are not, are at least professionals who treat their talents or their genius with respect. No love of home or wife or child ever stopped a man who was worth his salt from doing his duty—which is, in the first place, to whatever gifts the chance meeting of sperm and ovum have given him. If men bar the doors of their council-chambers, their universities, and their professions to women, it is because they know from experience that, at the first love-call, women however talented will toss their careers over the windmill and retire into the nest where a long, expensive training and perhaps their genius will be of no further use to them or to their world. They are the eternal amateurs and no professional, except as an off-day amusement, wants to work with amateurs. Their very attitude toward themselves and the job damns them to second-rateness.

Heaven knows, the Little Woman is not inactive in the world's affairs. She is the very heart and soul of those well-meaning, and, as things are, necessary organizations which, among their good deeds, convince Man-on-the-Rampage that, lost in wonder at his prowess, the Little Woman is waiting at home for him with bands and bandages. She tosses committees from hand to hand, like a juggler, with a brisk complacency and floods of talk that may be an endeavor to silence the still, small grunts of a disgusted ancestress. For the times demand much more of her, and perhaps in the depths of her conscience she knows it. That they are as they are is largely her responsibility. She has stood by and applauded while the other half of her species dealt her civilization blows from which it may never recover. The sands are running out fast.

If anything is to be saved, the Little Woman will have to move faster, out of the nest (which will then become, for her too, a place to return to but not to live in) and down into the dusty arena with her sleeves rolled up. Human relations, relieved at last from the crushing burden of her dependence on them, may then become what they should be, the adornment of life but not its foundations. And her children, now clinging to childhood till they find another and more permanent womb, may escape her stifling claims on them to become full-grown. Most important of all, she may recover her own fighting temper. (For pacifism is the symptom of a weak spine and a weak head or both, and leads, as we know to our bitter cost, to bigger and worse wars.) What she will fight for, if and when she takes the chance, is anybody's guess. But whatever she wants enough to fight for she can have. Actually and potentially she is very strong. Without resorting to violence—though she must be capable of violence—by merely refusing to play an idiot Martha to a lunatic Mars, she can gain her point. I believe it would be a sane one.

Will she or even can she? Habits of mind and body, centuries old, are not reversed in a decade and the experience women have had of themselves—as in Great Britain where they alone fought for their own emancipation and where, as citizens of the only country which challenged the enemy and remained undefeated, they have acquired a new pride in citizenship—may be too limited. Neither the vote, too easily won, nor the war, fought at too great a distance, has affected American women to any encouraging extent. Other progressive countries lie under the paralyzing blight of defeat. Russia, where a more vigorous conception of women's responsibilities seemed in the making, is reverting to the Woman's Sphere and significantly and sinisterly at the same time to a passionate nationalism.

But we have to hope. If we want to survive—and it seems we do— we can do no other. We have seen what the unbalanced masculine element has made of Germany and Japan and what, in extension, it has done to us. One more heave, as Churchill would say, and the unknown star beating its way toward us through uncharted space, need not bother to bump us into eternal nothingness. Our world will already be an empty, howling waste.

Lines to a Daughter—Any Daughter

by AGNES ALLEN

FEBRUARY, 1947

Author and editor, Agnes Allen has written many lively books and magazine pieces on such widely diverse subjects as social history, women, and Abraham Lincoln. She produced several books with her husband, Frederick Lewis Allen, Harper's *editor until his death in 1954. A Vassar graduate, Mrs. Allen has been an editor with* The Reader's Digest *since 1947.*

One of the things that you really should know
Is when to say "yes," and when to say "no."
It's terribly, terribly risky to guess
At when to say "no" and when to say "yes."
Girls who are slaving for Woolworth and Kress

Lament for the day when they might have said "yes,"
Others are crying at night apropos
Of moments when clearly they should have said "no."

There aren't any textbooks, there aren't many rules,
The subject's neglected in orthodox schools.
Experience helps, but you seldom remember
Your April mistakes by the first of November.
You can't be consistent; there's often a reason
For changing your mind with a change in the season.
You may be quite right in accepting at seven
Suggestions you'd better refuse at eleven.

Perhaps you'll consider these tentative hints:
"No" to a dirndl of highly glazed chintz,
"Yes" to the bashful young man at the dance,
"No" to the man who's been living in France,
"Yes" to a walk in the park in the rain,
"Yes" if he asks for a chance to explain,
"No" to all slacks unless you're too thin,
"No" to that impulse to telephone him,

"Yes" to a baby, and "no" to a bore,
"No" if you're asked if you've heard it before,
"Yes" to the friend when she says, "Don't you think
Rabbit is just as becoming as mink?"
"Yes" to a Saturday, "no" to a Monday,
"Yes" to a salad and "no" to a sundae,
"No" to a wastrel and "yes" to a ranger,
"No" to a toady, and "yes" to a stranger

(That is, providing you use some discretion),
"No" to three cocktails in rapid succession,
"No" to magenta and chocolate brown,
"Yes" to a whisper and "no" to a frown,
"No" if he's misunderstood by his wife,
"Yes" if you want it the rest of your life.
Remember, my darling, careers and caresses
Depend on our choices of "noes" and of "yesses."

Good-by to Oedipus

by HELEN EUSTIS

JUNE, 1953

As a message for parents of boys, this delightful essay is worth more than many a weighty tome by learned child psychologists. The author is a Smith College graduate, the mother of one son, and the ex-den mother of seven Cub Scouts. Her first novel, The Horizontal Man, *won the Mystery Writers of America award for 1946; she also is the author of short stories and a boy's book,* The Fool Killer.

At something before three o'clock, we would park the cars on the gravel apron and sit in them smoking, looking through a newspaper, filling out a marketing list, or chatting with the mother in the next car. Through the school windows we could see the heads industriously inclined; outside against the brick wall, a few bicycles leaned like patient steeds tied to a hitching rail.

From where we were, we could not hear the final bell, but we could see the response to it: the sudden rising, bustling, emptying of rooms; the back door opening to the stragglers who preceded the rush —a first-grader with only one sleeve of his jacket on; two sixth-grade girls convulsed with arcane giggles—and after them, the mob.

Out they would pour, not two by two as from Noah's Ark, but male with male, female with female, aged six to fourteen, more or less. With a practiced eye, I would sort out the males for size (too big—fifth or sixth grade; too small—first or second), so as to corral my carload before it disappeared over the hill for a last informal scrimmage. . . . And the same thought came always to my mind: *The running of the bulls.*

The girls were otherwise—the girls were something else again— but mine was a boy, as were my other passengers; it was the boys I watched. They came leaping, yelling, hitting, falling, laughing, occasionally weeping; looking uncouth, angelic, bedraggled, hangdog, or business-like, descending on the more or less subdued creatures who had given birth to them like a troop of satyrs racing down the slope of Olympus. Male—my God, they were male!—with a strangely absolute phallic beauty emerging from their childhood bloom and incompleteness. There was about them the suspense and excitement of the breathless moment of *just before*—just before the wave breaks, just before the rain falls, just before the lips meet to kiss. It comes later to girls, in the freshness and perfection which are soon after puberty and just before womanhood, but for boys, it is in their preadolescent years. Already a few of the twelve-, thirteen-, and fourteen-year-olds had began to molt their bright feathers, to look sheepish and dimmed.

Somewhere between seven and nine it erupts, this cataclysm of male assertion—I date it for myself as third grade. Once I heard a teacher say she had rather teach any other than third grade, and I knew why. When I had finally collected my crew into the car, by means of stentorian threats and yells, I would drive slowly away from school with the lot of them hopping like jumping beans, howling like banshees, throwing things out the windows, blowing gum bubbles—(why, oh Lord, must bubble gum *smell* so pink?)—and swearing. Third grade is the great period of the discovery of the drama of the four-letter word. Out of the innocent era of

> Inka bink,
> A bottle of ink;
> The cork fell out
> And you stink!

burgeons that fine salacious glee which may find its fruition in the aesthetic efforts of a Norman Mailer, a James Jones, or simply in the vocabulary of the United States armed services.

Frequently I would consider stopping the car to give a short biological lecture on the actual meaning of *That Word*. But meaning was not the issue. To them, the significance was kinetic, not semantic, like a firecracker, a stink bomb, or itching powder. So I would wait for the linguistic excitement which had been suppressed all day in the classroom to subside; if in due time it did not, I would threaten to make the next one who said *It* get out and walk. Sometimes one did.

"You can talk any way you like when you're by yourselves," I would tell them. "You can say philoprogenitive or antidisestablishmentarianism for all I care. But I'm a Lady, and I DON'T WANT TO HEAR IT!"

Naturally they had not been unaware of my prejudice in this matter. Otherwise what would have been the fun in saying It? They would giggle. Once they seemed safely subdued, I may have giggled myself.

Then I would deposit them at their various stopping points (praying God and exhorting them that the door not be opened before the car stopped), and all afternoon they would go charging around the neighborhood on their various businesses.

"Hey, Gordie, ya coming over?"

"Listen, you *had* your turn—give it to me!"

"Mom, can I charge a candy bar at the store?"

Loud bang of cap pistol. "You're dead!"

"I am not—you never even nicked me!"

"Ah gee, how can we play if you won't be *fair?*"

Toward sundown, the atmosphere would grow either more quarrelsome or quieter as appetites waxed and energies waned. Then, as the light faded and the automobiles began to show headlights, back doors would open; beings with cheeks as red as Christmas tree ornaments, with a fine crystal trickle descending the upper lip, with muddy jeans and muddier shoes, would enter another world. A warm bright world with a smell of things cooking in it. A world of

"How many times do I have to tell you to wipe your feet?"

"Hang your coat and cap in the closet, please."

"I want you to wash those hands *right now,* with your sleeves rolled up, and *not just to the wrist!*"

Also, a world in which one sat next to a comfortable creature and was read aloud to until Daddy came home, a world of cookies, chocolate milk, and Mercurochrome, being kissed and tucked in bed. . . . A woman's world. . . .

In fourth grade, it was Cub Scouts, and I found myself a Den Mother (a title which never failed to remind me of Romulus' and Remus' wolf). My Den consisted of a Den Chief, a Den Dad, and seven Cubs. The books said not to worry—that the Den Chief would manage practically everything while I went on about household business, but more often he phoned to say he regretted his inability to attend, but was called to a high-school basketball game. The Den Dad was a miracle of discipline, know-how, and support, but was available even less frequently than the Chief. That left me alone with the Cubs who were, respectively, a Bad Boy, a Bright Boy, two Cut-Ups, a Disorganized Boy, a Sensitive Boy, and my own.

It was the Bad Boy who turned out to be my mainstay. When the Den Chief didn't show up, he knew how to do all the things I couldn't figure out from the manuals. He fetched and carried and hit other people over the head if they interrupted. He really was a Bad Boy in other places and at other times; I believe that my patent inefficiency and equally unconcealable weakness for Bad Boys roused him to unexpected heights of chivalry and compassion. The two Cut-Ups had one simple aim, which was to break up any situation which evidenced elements of harmony. When there was general disorder, they were in the first rank of virtue, shushing the others ostentatiously. The Bright Boy always knew a better and more complicated way of doing whatever was being done and insisted on telling it. As for the Disorganized Boy, my feeling for him began in exasperation and ended in affection when it dawned on me that he was not, like the Cut-Ups, an *agent provocateur,* but simply a child who never got anything right the first time, and who had hit upon the camouflage of pretending he had done it wrong on purpose. The Sensitive Boy was an old friend; my own and I wordlessly evolved an agreement to act as if we didn't belong to each other during Cub meetings, which worked, on the whole, remarkably well.

Together, the lot of us accomplished very little. The Den Chief directed some backyard ball games in the grand old tradition of the unjust umpire. When the Den Dad could come, he put them to doing gymnastics—handstands, cartwheels, tip-ups, pyramids. (The Disorganized Boy always managed to be at the bottom of these last, so that they collapsed.) We made some kites which wouldn't fly. Various individuals passed various achievement tests, thereby reaching the rank of Wolf or Bearcat. We made trips to local points of interest—a trap rock company, a state police station, an animal farm. . . . The boys were sometimes interested, sometimes bored, sometimes on the brink of revolution, mostly resigned. To them, as nearly as I could make out, the whole business was simply another of those cages grownups were always putting them into for indecipherable reasons. To me, it was a wild combination of nightmare and delight: the nightmare of *Can I Manage Them?* the delight, simply the boys—Bad, Bright, Cut-Ups, Sensitive, and my own alike.

Because (if my experience and that of some of my contemporaries is not so isolated as to have no statistical value) the famous Oedipus Complex is by no means a one-way affair. If, as they emerge from babyhood, sons fall in love with their mothers for a while, so do mothers fall in love with their sons. And when I say "in love," I do mean something which comprises sexual feeling—not sexual desire, but rather what is almost a sense of worship for the emergence of this other sort of being which is so necessary and dear to one's own kind. Sandwiched between babyhood and adolescence, boys exhibit a startling masculinity which is unsurpassed at any other time in their lives. The toughest Marine cannot seem as male as a ten-year-old boy sometimes does—because the boy is free to make all the promises of manhood without being called upon to keep them until that distant future day when his physical and psychological growth will have enabled him to do so. During this heady time, fantasy intermittently overpowers reality; there are moments when the preadolescent boy not only pretends to be but *is* King Arthur, Robin Hood, Hercules— and moments when his mother (herself not immune to the stimulus of dreams) believes he is too.

Yet it is just when his masculinity is making its appearance in this glamorous and untarnished form that the boy is caught in what is mostly a woman's world. He returns from a school where women teachers are likely to outnumber men to a home from which his father is absent most of the day. Had he lived in a period when part of education was apprenticeship to a trade, should he live on a farm, were he to attend a boys' school, this would be less true. Today, he is more likely to be growing up in a situation in which things are otherwise. Like it or not, we live in the world in which the Industrial Revolution happened; for the moment, at least, its results include a pattern of life which places fathers mostly in offices and factories, mothers mostly in homes. So it is Mom who rules the roost for the boy—has to —and the negative aspects of her regime have been stressed until mothers are subject to moments of fear with their growing sons which equal that awful first moment of being alone with the first-born. As terrified of doing wrong as they are confused as to what is right, they listen to muddled echoes of the redoubtable Dr. Freud, the fractious Mr. Wylie, the misogynistic Mr. Faulkner, and anticipation of failure can freeze them to pure paralysis.

And a major factor in their fear is that adoring love for their man-children of which I speak. A mother, feeling delighted affection for her daughter who is going into womanhood, can confidently draw her into an orbit of feminine thinking and activity. Confronted with that first overwhelming evidence that her son is growing into a man, the mother who has any awareness, sensitivity, or honest wish for his healthy maturity finds her desire to draw him close instinctively countered by the stabbing prayer, "Oh God, teach me when to leave him alone!"

When to leave him alone is indeed the question—far simpler, even if more painful, to leave him entirely alone—but she cannot and must not. First, he needs her love as much as ever, in spite of needing it with a difference; second, he is still an unformed and incomplete human being for whose inadequacies of judgment it is her responsibility to compensate so long as he is in her care. Literally, he has not yet sense enough to come in out of the rain; he cannot be turned loose with a .22; he must be prevented from smoking clandestine cigarettes in the tinderbox of a barn; he must occasionally wear galoshes and underwear, take medicine, and wash; all of which acts he will respectively commit or evade if allowed to get away with it.

Long before this preadolescent time, of course, a mother must have learned the use of the words *No* and *Don't,* at least for the simple necessities of keeping her son from being run over by automobiles, from turning the handles of the gas stove, from venturing into water over his head before he has learned to swim. What is new to her is the recognition that now there are many things to which she must *not* say No in order to keep this wild but wonderful individual whole and growing. Which are these things? She is not at all sure. Her own childhood may have included baseball, tree-climbing, pants, and an abhorrence of dolls; she may have been the biggest tomboy on the block—but she was never a boy. Though she can guess something of what it is like, the rest is silence. How can she find out? She reads books on child psychology, she consults her husband—and still feels baffled. Too often she resolves her indecision by jumping to the conclusion that, except for the more obvious prohibitions and exhortations about rubbers, tooth-brushing, and roof-climbing, she will now treat her son like a grownup.

What happens to the child who is treated as an adult is that he gets fresh—becomes impertinent, disobedient, whiny, and a pest. Nobody enjoys him much any more, beginning with himself. Even to his loving mother he sometimes gives a stiff pain in the neck. But if she has read a book—oh, almost any book about children's behavior written after World War I—she knows that this is because he feels anxious and insecure. Therefore she controls her impulse to warm his tail and send him to bed without supper; she treats him, instead, with monumental patience and slightly forced demonstrations of affection. Daddy, who comes home from the office pretty tired, in need of a drink and some peaceful home life, is likely to be less long-suffering. He may even raise the possibility of cracking down. This causes the hair of Mother (who has read about the effects of authoritarian behavior) to stand right up on end. She now begins to compensate to her son for his father's hard heart—she not only treats him like an adult, but lets him treat her like a child. When the mood strikes him, he may without hindrance say, "Shut up!" or, "Give me that!" or, "Oh, you don't know anything!" to his mother, and often to other adults as well. In the neighborhood, he becomes not only disliked, but well disliked.

The vicious cycle in which children are turned into grownups and grownups into children can end with all concerned in the hands of a psychiatrist unless common sense, nature, and/or the grace of God intervene—which (thanks to good luck rather than good judgment) was what happened to me and mine.

We were well into the gambit: I was treating my son like a college professor of fifty-five (he was seven); he was treating me like an unwanted orphan of three (I was older); my husband was grumbling; I was waking and tossing in the night, wondering what the unconscious sources of our son's anxiety and insecurity and his parents' resultant misery could be when things simply got so bad that self-preservation set in.

After one of our long disagreeable days, we came out of a grocery store, my son and I, and I observed a puddle, a good three feet ahead.

"Don't step in the water, please, dear," said I.

There was a considerable pause for the announcement of intention; then in went his foot with a splash.

There was no pause at all before I whacked him on the ear as hard as I could.

Ensued a series of bellows of rage and pain, preceding me to the car like a fanfare of trumpets. I followed them unmoved, the thought rotating fiercely if ungrammatically in my mind, "It was him or me—him or me!"

Before this, of course, I had lost my temper and behaved in a manner which I hasten to recommend to no one. The difference was that now I did not apologize, soften, or make it up. That day and the next

I was curt, cool, aloof, and What I Said Went. And once started, I didn't dare stop, because suddenly the house was heaven! Like a miracle, I had a terribly nice child, who said *please* and *thank you,* did as he was told, and acted as if he liked both me and himself.

Why? I kept asking myself. *Why? Do you have to be horrible to them? That can't be the answer!*

But the answer came to me in a day or two, by indirection, from my son himself. I had put him on the kitchen stool with a towel around his neck, and was cutting his hair. Sometimes the scissors would tweak, and I could see him grimace. Then he would announce, "I'm not crying, Mom! You notice I'm not crying?"

I noticed, all right. Previously, haircuts had been such signals for hysteria that I had thought, *Better myself who gave birth to this monster than some poor overworked barber!* But the New Mom only replied, "I wouldn't brag about it if I were you. I'd be ashamed of having been such a crybaby before."

He was not satisfied. "You know *why* I'm not crying?" he demanded.

"No," I said, breaking down a little, "why not?"

"Because I know that if I cry you'll get mad, and *boy! when you get mad, you really get mad!*"

And he turned his head to give me a look—not of apprehension, fear, or abjectness, but of such relief and love that my heart turned absolutely molten and I had to kiss him then and there.

Because it was apparent from his eyes, his face, and everything that had happened in the last two days that what had been troubling him, what had made him anxious, insecure, miserable, and obnoxious was the fact that he *was* a little boy, not an adult; I *was* an adult, not a child, and the way I had been turning things around would have been enough to drive anyone crazy!

In this year of our Lord, children who are treated like adults we have always with us, filling us with pity, terror, or righteous indignation as the case may be—for I have never seen a child treated as an adult who filled anyone with joy, any more than I have seen a child who seemed to thrive on being treated like a baby, or being told untruths of other kinds. It is simply *not true* that children are adults (or adults children) and anyone who behaves toward a child as if he were grownup is acting a lie—as well as laying upon the child a burden of responsibility which he is not yet ready to bear.

Yet the mother who treats her boy too much as a man does not have the conscious goal of confusing or overtaxing him, whatever the results may be; the mother whose behavior toward her child is what is known in the trade (educational and psychiatric, that is) as "permissive" does not set out to turn him into an offensive brat who rouses antagonism in the breasts of all whom he encounters. Instead, she has had two perfectly valid aims in mind. In treating him as an adult, she means to express toward her son that respect for individuality which she rightly believes to be due him as a human being. In permitting him impertinence and disobedience, she confuses the license for these with the freedom to experience and sometimes express the normal and necessary emotion of anger. . . . Only, just as surely as the tyrannical Victorian parent is said to have done in an opposite way, she has forgotten that respect and justice must be two-way streets.

Honor thy father and thy mother sounds like a one-sided commandment until one considers how difficult it is for the child who does not do so to honor himself. Like adults, children want to be proud of the government under which they live and can stand anything better than indecision and anarchy. A boy in particular will feel honored by a degree of just severity—he takes his parents' demands on him as a mark of belief in his growing power to meet those demands. Indeed, the Scylla which drive many mothers to the Charybdis of overpermissiveness and overestimation of their sons' maturity is the fact that boys will accept even injustice if it sound authoritative enough, simply because they so deeply fear the appearance in adults of those weaknesses and uncertainties which they feel in their own unfinished selves.

As early as preadolescence, boys have begun to sense that society is going to make demands on them as men which it will not make on their sisters as women. Without being able to articulate what those demands are to be, boys still feel the evidence of them; out of that sense comes their surging need for whatever will help them to grow strong enough to meet their futures. They seek the company of men, without which they can never learn to become men themselves; then, because the pattern of their culture forces them to live more than ever before in the company of women, even more than before they need to find a strength and firmness in their mothers which will support their own need to grow strong.

For all these reasons, mothers of boys have the trickiest of channels to sail. They must be strong—but not overpowering. They must be loving—but not overprotective. They must be grown-up with a recollection of what it means to be a child; female with a sense of what it might feel like to be male. And they can only be some of the right things some of the time; they can't avoid the major boners and minor falls from grace which are the occasional lot of all parent-kind.

On the other hand, mothers of boys have a lot of fun which they could never otherwise have had. Through the magical sympathy and empathy which extend the identity of the mother into their child, there are moments when they can actually know the experience of what it is to be a boy. If they keep their ears open and their mouths shut, they are treated to delectably voyeuristic glimpses of a secret all-male world. If they are themselves sufficiently mentally arrested, they are afforded some of the best laughs of their lives by the terrible jokes they may hear—for there is nothing so convulsively contagious as the laughter of little boys. And (with intermissions for normal behavior) they live in the company of gods and heroes, by whom they are worshiped, whom they, in turn, adore. . . .

For me and mine, the end of the idyll is very much in view. He is on the turn, now, like milk just ready to curdle. His feet get longer and his shoulders broader every time I look at him; one day I will turn round to find that he has crossed the threshold of the mysterious cavern of adolescence, where, if I know what is good for both of us, I had better not try to follow him. Without half trying, I could get as sentimental about the impending transition as the mother of a bride, divided between feeling, "But I don't *want* to lose him!" and, "Oh, Lord, have I done everything all right?" But in reasonable moments I know that all there really is left to say (with as stiff an upper lip as I can muster) is:

Ave atque vale, King Arthur, Tom Sawyer, Robin Hood, my particular Oedipus Rex!

The Loving Care of Determined Women

by JOHN FISCHER

AUGUST, 1955

This short little essay caused a national outcry whose echoes are still heard, but the author, Harper's *editor-in-chief, still had a wife as this book went to press.*

Like all brides, she looked heartbreakingly sweet and tremulous. As they turned to march up the aisle, she lifted a radiant face to the man beside her and whispered:

"Stand a little straighter, dear."

These tender words were, of course, spoken in the splendid pioneer tradition of American womanhood. She was merely starting early to civilize the wilderness she had just married.

To her—as most brides in this country—her husband represented 175 pounds of raw material. So raw, indeed, that a less courageous race of females might shrink from the task of trying to refine anything from such earthy and intractable ore. No such doubts, however, bother a true American girl. She knows it is her duty to make something out of the sorry clod, if she has to wear her tongue down to the roots.

This undaunted approach may, perhaps, have something to do with the divorce rate, ax murders, and the number of morose characters nursing a shot glass late at night in men's bars. Nevertheless, it has made American civilization the envy of the world; or, anyhow, the feminine half of it. Never before in history has any nation devoted so large a share of its brains and resources to the sole purpose of keeping its women greased, deodorized, corseted, enshrined in chrome convertibles, curled, slenderized, rejuvenated, and relieved of all physical labor.

In benighted lands, from England to Indonesia, women are still deluded into thinking that they ought to make life a little pleasanter and easier for their breadwinners; only here is the Ideal Male one who dedicates his life to the pampering of women. In India, for example, as recently as 1953, a woman was observed in the act of fixing a quiet room and a cool drink for a husband on his way home from work. In Dallas and Des Moines, as we all know, the ladies make a different kind of preparation.

That precious moment when the male stumbles back to his lair, numb and exhausted, is what they have been waiting for all day. By striking hard while his resistance is low, they know they can pressure him into almost anything. This, then, is the Conversation Hour: the time to touch lightly on the need for a new vacuum cleaner, his gaucheries at last night's bridge party, the prospects for remedying his cultural poverty by a course of lectures at the Women's Club, and his duties at the PTA meeting—which, by happy coincidence, will start in just twenty minutes.

For, in return for their emancipation, American women have undertaken to reform their menfolks. This goal they inherited from Grandmother, who had to tame the frontier. She did it by boiling lye soap out of skillet grease and wood ashes, scrubbing puncheon floors, busting up saloons, shooting Indians, building log churches, and shearing both the mane and the six-guns off the Wild Bill Hickok types who infested what would be, someday, a nice residential neighborhood. Since these robust chores are now pretty well finished, her granddaughters have to focus their civilizing zeal on the one thing in sight which still needs to be tamed and curried.

The measure of their success is the number of Walter Mittys in our society. Again, never in history has any country contained such a high proportion of cowed and eunuchoid males, drilled with Prussian thoroughness to shun all household sins. Never, but never, do they drop cigar ashes in the icebox, prop their feet on a coffee table, leave an unwashed dish in the sink, kick a baby, or stuff a sofa cushion into the mouth of a babbling guest. They endure their married lives in mute docility, and die mercifully early in life from ulcers and high blood pressure.

Occasionally, however, the domestic reform program proves unsatisfying. Perhaps the subject escapes, or proves impossibly obdurate; more frequently he yields so promptly to The Treatment that after a few years he no longer offers a challenge to his wife's talent. Then she is almost certain to turn her energies either to good works or to politics. They both offer much the same thing: a new field ripe for reform.

IV

Our Love Affair with Culture

The Literary Twenties—The Younger Generation

by CARL VAN DOREN

AUGUST, 1936

Many of the first stirrings of today's America began in the avant-garde atmosphere of New York literary circles in the early twenties. As one of the leading critics of the day, Carl Van Doren knew intimately many of the young writers of that period. Dr. Van Doren's life of Benjamin Franklin won a Pulitzer Prize in 1938, and his biography of Swift also is a standard work. He was a brother of Mark Van Doren and taught at Columbia for many years. He died in 1950.

When we say we know that the world is changing we mean we have noticed that it has changed. We learn piecemeal through the senses and reflect only when perceptions force themselves on our minds. Then we shape some kind of image and compare it with the image already in our memory. If they are not alike we talk of change.

Even this friendly spring which came so soon after the harsh winter of Illinois (where I write) had several intermediate days in which flesh had been relieved and nerves relaxed before the thought of spring was a thought. So with what was to be the postwar spring, though it was marked off by the Armistice from the long winter of the War. It was a chaos of sensations before it took any form that we were conscious of. The first sensation was a wild joy that the killing had ended. But the second sensation was conflict. Now we could go back to the good days before the War: now we could run ahead to better days. Every man was divided between the two sentiments. So were men in general. The conservative majority in the United States made Harding President, and Coolidge. The minority had for its most articulate spokesmen the Younger Generation.

A few weeks ago I heard a young woman say that, though she had been twenty in 1920 and had then lived gaily in New York, she had never moved in the heart of the Younger Generation but only near to it. She was the third person I had heard say the same thing in three years. They were right in thinking they had never quite belonged to the Younger Generation, wrong in thinking there had ever been one to belong to unmistakably. For the Younger Generation was nothing more than a generalization.

If it can now best be studied in the literature it produced, so could it then. Randolph Bourne was its philosopher, the earliest young thinker with a program, the soonest dead. He was an undergraduate in Columbia when I came back from Europe, his body misshapen, his mind straight and clear. I remember his reading his poem "Sabotage" before a literary society. Only a few of the undergraduates who heard it (this must have been 1912) thought the subject proper for a poem. Another of them read a blank-verse monologue in which a troubadour lamented times lamentably past. When Bourne declared in an article that nobody ever got a new idea after twenty-five, his elders at Columbia pointed out that he was twenty-five. When later he published, in the *New Republic,* satirical portraits which might have been of President Butler and John Erskine, most of the professors, who all read them, thought them in bad taste. Bourne, it was told, had said he could write only when he hated. One of the professors mentioned Pope, another crooked poet. John Dewey had been Bourne's teacher, the *New Republic* was his chief outlet. After they had found pragmatic reasons why the United States should go to war, Bourne, who had meant peace when he talked about it, was lost. The War killed him early, and he survives only as a pitiful small legend. But his *History of a Literary Radical* is the whole history of the thoughtful young men of his decade, and his scheme for a league of youth which was to rejuvenate the fallen age had in it all the Younger Generation's purposive if naïve faith.

If Bourne was its philosopher, John Reed was its hero, Edna St. Vincent Millay its lyric poet, Eugene O'Neill its dramatist, Sinclair Lewis its satirist, Van Wyck Brooks its critic. The Younger Generation respected Bourne but hardly knew him: he died too soon. Reed's league of youth was the Soviet government: this narrowed his influence with a generation which had few Communists. But Edna Millay was a song and a flame, more daring and lighthearted about love than any woman had ever been in English verse. O'Neill was the Younger Generation's challenge to the American cult of the happy ending:

strong meat for young nerves. Lewis laughed at sacred cows. Brooks argued that the older America had destroyed its artists, even the great Mark Twain, who had not dared to be himself.

All these had been heard by 1920. In that year the Younger Generation put on new colors. Scott Fitzgerald was younger still. He had gone off to war from college, like E. E. Cummings and John Dos Passos and Ernest Hemingway and Laurence Stallings and Edmund Wilson. But Fitzgerald was precocious, found his voice before any of his contemporaries, and was heard along with writers ten years older. The public did not distinguish the two ages. The name Younger Generation was fitted to whatever in the early twenties was rebellious, aspiring, experimental: to whatever was restless. Name-calling was not enough. The Younger Generation was personified in Fitzgerald's heroes and heroines. "Few things more significantly illustrate the moving tide of which the revolt from the village is a symptom than the presence of such unrest as this among these bright barbarians. The traditions which once might have governed them no longer hold. They break the patterns one by one and follow their wild desires. And as they play among the ruins of the old, they reason randomly about the new, laughing."

So it appeared in 1921. But even then it was plain that Fitzgerald was a romancer. Where in actual life are the young men and women all beautiful and witty, and all poets? They were not in the early twenties. Fitzgerald had created—had invented—his light and lively characters. He set a fashion. Not that there were many boys and girls who could be like those in his stories; that would have called for too much talent. Though nature may want to follow art, it seldom can. When observers tried to imagine or describe the Younger Generation, and found themselves limited in experience of it and faced by its contradictions, they took Fitzgerald's version for the truth and did not look beyond it. The moralists did not need to know more or the sensationalists. They talked of the Younger Generation in one breath. Beautiful but Damned. All the Sad Young Men. Baby Byrons.

Stuart Sherman, visiting in New York and Cornwall, studied my household with puzzled eyes.

"You and Carl see a great deal of your children, don't you?" he said to Irita.

"Why, yes, of course."

"You like being with them."

"Absurdly. But why shouldn't we? What are you driving at?"

"Well, I had supposed . . . you with a job . . . not much interested in such matters . . . The Younger Generation."

He had been reading in Urbana, and had generalized, trying to put incompatibles together and wondering why they did not match.

II

There were two Younger Generations, one rebelling against old ideas, one against old manners.

Whoever tries to compare succeeding generations starts with the hopeless disadvantage that he belongs to one of them and cannot really know the other. I have heard parents boast that they knew all their children did or thought, and have seen the children look guilty or embarrassed or sly. I have had children tell me what they said was all about their parents, and have never believed them. Before parents can be parents they must have lived a good part of their lives. They remember their experience less as itself than as its consequences. But the children's experience is still itself, with its consequences to come. The two experiences are not the same and there is no common language for them. I loved danger, says the father, and it hurt me. The son says, I love danger. On both sides there is special pleading. The parents give advice which either justifies what they have done or else urges the children to do the same thing better, that the parents through them may have another chance at living. Do as I did. Avoid what I should have avoided. But the children do not want to justify or repeat or vary what has been done. With the pride of strength goes the sense of originality, or the illusion of it. Times have changed, father, and I must do what I do as I do it. The wisdom of neither is communicable to the other. All wisdom is incommunicable. When we say a man is wise we are saying only that what he says agrees with our own experience. So parents and children, with no common experience and no common language, must be largely strangers. Not till they both are old, if the parents live so long, can they draw close together. Then it is too late to matter.

I am not sure that I know more about what goes on in the minds of my children, when I see them every day, than about what went on in the minds of my parents before I was born. I must guess in either case. But I have the impression that when my father and mother were young they accepted the authority of their elders not only because they were obliged to but because they did not challenge their elders' right to rule. I knew I grew up, though dissatisfied with individuals, taking such a right in general for granted. It gave life a logical pattern. Human beings had to live to maturity to find out how to live. Then they knew and could go on without further mishaps. If their children, still immature, went off in wrong directions, the parents called them back—if necessary, compelled them back. The line of life was a straight line drawn through the adults of the generations.

Suddenly, about 1920, this pattern no longer served. It had been fading for half a century and the War seemed to have rubbed it out. Down with authority. Up with instinct. Youth was as likely to be right as age. Youth, the Younger Generation held, was always right.

That youth was precious instinct, not raw trial and error—this was the basic doctrine of the early twenties. Randolph Bourne thought much about schools and about how youth, being educated, might not lose its natural creative force. The inquiring minds of the Younger Generation looked at the world from the side of revolutionary youth. Let generous instinct guide it rather than weary craft. What blunders had not fear and prudence made! Fear led to war between nations and classes. Prudence put and kept the management of affairs in hands that were already half-dead. Under the rule of fear and prudence life went on stiffening into rigidity. Life must be flexible and free or it would be unjust and dull. Life in America had been standardized till it was mere habit, the dry routine of middle age. Give youth and genius the reins. Or at least tolerate youth and genius, the saving ferment.

These were the simple tenets of the rebels against old ideas. The more dramatic rebels against old manners were what the public took to be the Younger Generation.

III

For their critic they had Mencken, who on most points was conservative. In a superficial time he believed in learning. He believed in civil order if men had to go back to aristocracy to get it. He believed in monogamy and industry and economy in private life. The expatriates only tickled him: he stayed at home and worked like any good citizen. But the rebels did not examine his ideas closely. They liked the strong beat of his satirical prose, hitting away at foolish heads.

What he had in common with the young rebels was not his special ideas but his general love of liberty. "The stupidity against which he wages his hilarious war," I wrote in 1923, "is the stupidity which, unaware of its defects, has first sought to shackle the children of light. It is chiefly at sight of such attempts that his indignation rises and that he rushes forth armed with a bagpipe, a slapstick, a shillelagh, a pitchfork, a butcher's cleaver, a Browning rifle, a lusty arm, and an undaunted heart. What fun, then! Seeing that the feast of fools still has its uses, he elects himself boy-bishop, gathers a horde of revelers about him, and burlesques the universe."

Beware of metaphor, which abridges the truth while it dramatizes it. The image of Mencken and the rebels as the boy-bishop and his revelers is only a composite picture, true at large but true of nothing in particular. The rebellion against old manners was merely a widespread unrest, with no focus but in literature. It was like the unrest of any young generation except that it was now easier than it would once have been for the restless young to learn how numerous they were, and so conspire. They read *Main Street,* in which restlessness was heroic, and *This Side of Paradise,* in which it was romantic. At home the old-fashioned family had broken up. The young could get into automobiles and almost at once be miles away. They could go to the movies and at once be worlds away. Dress and speech had become informal in the emergency of the War. The chaperon had disappeared. Boys leaving to be killed, it might be, had claimed the right to see their girls alone, and the sexes had drawn together in a common need and daring. After the War they were still not divided. The sexes would be comrades, they thought.

In the same year with *Main Street* and *This Side of Paradise* Edna Millay in *Aria da Capo* distilled in exquisite allegory the War and the mood which followed it. The early poems of Edna Millay are the essence of the Younger Generation. Ask the romantic Younger Generation what it demanded and it answered, to be free. Ask it free for what, and it did not answer, but drove faster, drank more, made love oftener. When it came to the sterner time after 1929 it had to give up its habits or else seem like an elderly beau, amusing to the youngsters. The youngsters now condescend to the early twenties as to an age of amateurs.

IV

The Younger Generation believed that with it love in America had for the first time discovered it had a body.

It must be a long time since any human being has discovered anything about love which, however new to him, was not old to someone else. Whatever rapture of the mind, ecstasy of the flesh, quirk of the nerves the lover may cherish as his own, he can probably find it in an ancient Chinese poet or, if he is willing to talk about it, in a candid neighbor. The young, first feeling love, half-think they have invented it and are sure their elders cannot understand. They see their elders as parents not as lovers, and find it incredible or repugnant to think of them in love, ardent and agitated. Between two generations there is no topic so charily, so clumsily discussed as this. Neither speaker dares to cite his own experience and is afraid what he says may be taken as that. They speak in terms so general that they mean nothing. As no one knows both generations, no one can unerringly compare them.

Certainly in this account of the Younger Generation's discovery, or belief in a discovery, I surmise as often as I know. I had grown up in a rustic, had lived in an academic, community. That prewar world of mine had been greatly unlike my postwar world of Greenwich Village, and no doubt went on being. Time was not what made the difference. I had not merely gone ahead in time but had stepped aside in space, from one parallel world to another. I must not mistake the differences between New York and Hope or Urbana for differences between the Younger Generation and that preceding it. And yet I am convinced that love in America about the time of the War began to seem—which means to be—something different from what it had been before.

In all American history there has been no hero, real or imaginary, who was known particularly as a lover. No Nelson, no Parnell, of course no Louis XIV or Catherine the Great, no Dante and Beatrice, no Tristan and Isolde, no Manon. The heroes and heroines of the nation had lived vigorously apart except when they were joined in reasonable wedlock, like George and Martha Washington. If there had been talk about the loves of conspicuous men, it had been scandal, as about Thomas Jefferson or Henry Ward Beecher or Warren Gamaliel Harding. Indeed most Americans would have been startled to hear that Daniel Boone had a wife. The American poets had not made their loves into legends, though there were sentimental stories about Poe and the child he married, about Emily Dickinson and the man she did not marry. Whitman seemed a rowdy old bachelor, the other poets gray professors. American fiction had created no memorable lover besides Hester Prynne, expiating the sin of love. Rip Van Winkle was the runaway husband of a shrew; Leatherstocking was wedded to the forest and eluded women. The dark, sultry lovers of Herman Melville were almost unknown in 1914. Mark Twain had written about love as if his hands were tied behind him. The characters of William Dean Howells and Henry James were sufficiently occupied with love, but their love was not passionate enough to be contagious. Frank Norris and Theodore Dreiser and Upton Sinclair had written with a more realistic warmth; Norris had died young; Dreiser had been long suppressed, and Sinclair had turned to other subjects. As to the run of novels in 1914, which must have been some kind of mirror to the time, a reader could never guess that their heroes felt desire or that their heroines ever would.

About 1924 I was talking with a pleasant, worried man of sixty who did his best to keep up with new books and plays. "I don't understand these novels," he said, "when they deal with love. The people seem to have such strange feelings and sensations. I don't believe it used to be like that. A young fellow would fall in love with a girl and want to marry her. There might be difficulties, but he would wait and generally things would come out all right. That was all there was to it. But now the whole business is a fever. It doesn't seem natural to me."

He was a serious and intelligent man, though conventional, and I could not doubt that he was saying what he thought was true. Still it could not be true of his whole generation. Desire was as old as love, and older, and had not come to America in 1917. A nation did not declare a state of desire as of war. I reflected that in the older novels the word lover meant suitor, not, as it had come to mean in the language of my day, possessor. An age of innocence, when there were only two orders of men, husbands and lovers, and no need to distinguish between the lovers who simply wooed and those who had already won? Human life was always more headstrong than that. But if enough people had thought as this man of sixty did, desire might have been less active in his youth than in the twenties of this century. There is usually a kind of wild reason in desire, limiting it to what seems not too impossible. It was easy enough to imagine lovers who, assuming that desire could and must not have its object yet, would put off thinking of it and so not let it get its insatiable hold. It was easy to remember them—me, as a youth, among them. Desire in such circumstances was not so much repressed, and dangerous, as postponed, and stimulating.

The War changed the face of postponement. It might be forever. Young soldiers do not think often about death, but they think about it oftener than young civilians. Mark and Paul both noticed in the army that it was common for the younger men to feel horror at the prospect of being killed before they had known women. Their instincts demanded to be used while there was time. Love before death. To the instincts of men the instincts of women naturally responded. There were hurried marriages. There was love-making that the moon would never have seen but for the War. If a boy was ready to give his life, what could a girl refuse to give? This was the feverish logic of the feverish time. And when the short war was over, the older, simpler form of love, with its dualisms of mind and body, love and lust, romance and desire, could not soon come back. Spirit and flesh had discovered each other and would not be divided.

I suppose the same thing happened in the Civil War, but that was not followed by a brilliant critical generation to rationalize the instinctive process. The twenties had a new philosophy of love—new to America—to support its impulses. Love need not be thought of as having two natures, one higher and one lower. It might be one, spirit informing flesh, flesh enriching spirit. If both were fused the mind might draw strength from the body and the body hold up its head in self-respect and joy. In any case love was instinct, love was nature. Nothing unnatural had come in. The Younger Generation had found all this in itself, and would not cover it over and keep it down. It did not think that love was like pigs, to be penned. Love was life at its best. Release it.

Here, I think, is an epitome of all moral changes. New customs are not imported for new times but are brought up with the rise of instincts which the old times kept dormant. Men remake themselves from within themselves, whatever outer forces suggest and drive.

This renascence of the flesh in love was what most disturbed the elders in the twenties. They objected to the increase of drinking after Prohibition had made liquor harder to get in public than at home. They objected to the noise and irresponsibility and hit-or-miss manners of the young. But they especially objected to what they thought the shameless ways of young women, exposing and adorning their persons like the trollops of an earlier day, drinking and smoking with young men at all hours, and saying what they thought. A shocked elder who had sat beside one of them at dinner told about her in words that were a classic for a season: "Why, she would talk about anything, and she wouldn't talk about anything else." His words showed as much about him as about her. He assumed that his anything could be only one thing: the last-mentionable theme of sex. It had become so notorious that even women knew about it.

At one point the two generations actually went to law over the new philosophy of love: in the proceedings against Dreiser's *Genius* and Cabell's *Jurgen* and various European books, all of which are now as freely circulated as readers choose. Lewd, lascivious, and obscene the guardians of the old philosophy called them. There was no prosecution of books for blasphemy or heresy, any more than for cruelty or stupidity, and none for sedition. The one thing that roused the older generation was candor about love and desire. If a book had that it was a dirty book: a nuisance and a menace. There could be no agreement between the two philosophies. Krutch said it was simple: such books should be permitted because some people liked to read them. The law is not as simple as good sense. The cases had to be taken up one by one, and judge or jury had to decide. The Younger Generation defended them all, the better with the worse, and went on writing freely about sex until the subject became tiresome. By that time the guardians of the old philosophy had temporarily lost hope. For the present at least American literature might be like any other good literature and deal with any matter it could find in life.

The release of love seemed to be rather a release of women than of men. Men had a tradition of desire. In the English-speaking countries for something like a hundred years reputable women had been supposed not to feel it. Whether they did or not, most of them had accepted the fashion which identified chastity with coldness. The earlier feminists, demanding equality with men, had almost never demanded equality of desire. The feminists of the Younger Generation did. The period of the War had done more than the feminist argument. The absence of young men and the chance that they would not come back seemed to wake in women an instinctive agitation. No men, no mates, and sterile lives. Women need not be conscious of their instinct to be stirred by it. If after the War there had been a quick return to an old stability, the agitation might have passed. But the turmoil lasted, speech and manners became bolder, and more and more women, feeling free to feel desire, felt it.

They had a poet. "What sets Miss Millay's love poems apart from almost all those written in English by women," it seemed to me in 1923, "is the full pulse which, in spite of their gay impudence, beats through them. She does not speak in the name of forlorn maidens or of wives bereft, but in the name of women who dare to take love at the flood, if it offers, and who later, if it has passed, remember with exultation that they had what no coward could have had. Conscience does not trouble them, nor any serious division in their natures. . . . Miss Millay has given body and vesture to a sense of equality in love: to the demand of women that they be allowed to enter the world of adventure and experiment in love which men have long inhabited. But Miss Millay does not, like any feminist, argue for that equality. She takes it for granted, exhibits it in action, and turns it into beauty."

If the guardians of the old philosophy were alert they must have seen that here was implicit doctrine as dangerous as any they tried to suppress. There cannot have been too many women like the hero-ines of Edna Millay's poems. A woman has to be in part a poet to be like a poet's heroine. But early in the twenties it was plain that women, feeling and acknowledging desire as a natural part of love, had become lovers of what seemed a new kind. The change was so rapid that many men even of the Younger Generation stared. Young husbands and lovers wondered what had become of the traditional modesty they had heard about. Young women, cheerfully dressing before unshaded windows, laughed at men as the modest sex. When men and women swam together without clothes, as here and there they began to do, the women were less self-conscious than the men, and sooner naked. One girl, so timid before that she had made others hesitant, unex-pectedly emerged one day from her shapeless feminist uniform on a remote beach with a dozen friends, so beautiful that they all applauded, though it was the convention, elaborately kept up, that no one should notice anyone in particular. As chaste as ever, she became another person, pleased with herself because she had given pleasure.

Modesty in women, it appeared, was part instinct and part conven-tion. The convention went like an old fashion. Discovering their own flesh, they seemed to have discovered it in general. It had been conven-tional for women, lagging in desire, to blame husbands or lovers for their impatience, and to resent it. Now they began to take it as tribute: a carnal compliment I heard one girl call it. Tributes are easy to tolerate and pleasant to respond to. Companions in work and play, men and women were companions in love—believing that this was new in the world's history, and excited by the sense of adventure. Since it was actually newer to the women, I think they outran the men, trying to catch up with them. I am sure I observed as much courting begun by women as by men, and I think more. It may be this had been always true in sly ways, but now the ways were as frank and direct as the women knew how to make them. Power came up in women as if America had tapped a new natural resource.

Music in Aspic

by OSCAR LEVANT

OCTOBER, 1939

A symphonic conductor should reconcile himself to the realization that, regardless of his approach or temperament, the eventual result is the same—the orchestra will hate him. So says Oscar Levant, who knows from experience as a conductor and soloist with orchestra, in this lively article on the relationship between the two. The piece is sprinkled with many revealing anecdotes about those greats, Arturo Toscanini and Leopold Stokowski. Mr. Levant, who is also a composer, is widely known for his range of musical knowledge.

It has been frequently remarked, and with truth, that a conductor embarking on a debut in New York is confronted with the most critical audience in the world; save that this should be amended to read—at his first rehearsal. Long before a symphonic conductor appears before an audience to impress his qualities on the listeners, critical and otherwise, he has already made the impression that eventually determines the extent of his success or failure—on the members of the orchestra, whose attitude toward any new conductor may be epitomized as "a hundred men and a louse."

Contrary to the general opinion, a good ambitious orchestra can do more to ruin a conductor than it can to make him. One of the smuggest, most cohesive groups in American music, with the greatest threat of power, is the New York Philharmonic-Symphony Orchestra; and it is followed closely by the Philadelphia Orchestra.

It is perhaps a corollary that the opinion of an orchestral musician about a conductor or a piece of new music is quite invalid. So many factors of self-interest are concerned that the purely musical values involved in the judgment of each are beyond the player's objective appraisal.

So far as it concerns a conductor, it may be remarked that an orchestra of the de luxe type mentioned above develops in time a collective identity derived from its strongest personalities. This remains constant except in the presence of the most strong-willed conductors. The strings of the Philharmonic, for example, amount to some thirty-two Piastros, deriving their style and mannerisms from their concertmaster. There is no trace in their playing of what might be called a "Barbirolli style." Nevertheless, when this same string section was conducted by Toscanini it did not possess this thick, rich Russian overwash—it had a leanness and strength directly induced by him.

Essentially the question is one of domination—whether the conductor dominates the orchestra or the orchestra dominates the conductor. Utter control of a performance, to the point at which ninety or a hundred players become not merely a cohesive group but the single-minded extension of one personality, is a rare talent among musicians —possessed, among conductors now active in America, only by Koussevitzky, Stokowski, and Toscanini.

I have found in my varied experience as a conductor, soloist with orchestra, and ordinary listener, that there is a general misuse of power all round, depending upon in whose hands it happens to repose in any given instance. The orchestra which finds that it has at its mercy a conductor—whom it may dislike for any reason from lack of musicianship to mere unsociability—is frequently as ruthless in its use of power as the conductor who exercises authority merely because he does not fancy a violinist's complexion or the way he sits while playing.

Pundits may talk of a conductor's "authority," his "beat," and his "knowledge of scores," but actual control of an orchestra is most frequently founded on the less gaudy basis of economics. When an orchestra is aware that the conductor has in his inside pocket a contract for next season and the one after that, carrying with it the power to rearrange the personnel "for the best interests of the orchestra"—

in other words, to hire and to fire—its attitude is apt to be somewhat more respectful than if he is merely an interloper to be tolerated for a brief guest engagement.

When Stokowski spent his memorable, and brief, guest engagement with the Philharmonic some years ago (as part of the famous exchange in which Toscanini conducted the Philadelphia Orchestra) he certainly did not leave his "authority," "beat," and "knowledge of scores" in the green room with his topcoat. But no one who recalls the occurrence will forget the playing of the Philharmonic, which led Stokowski to describe the two weeks as "one of the unhappiest experiences of my life."

To be sure, he made the initial mistake of asking the orchestra to learn, for the first time in its history, Stravinsky's "Le Sacre du Printemps," a work not previously in its repertory. This exertion, coupled with the orchestra's desire—at that time—for Toscanini to emerge as victor in the competition, induced a state of extreme resentment and internal opposition. This attitude was encouraged, to no small extent, by Stokowski's request, on beginning the rehearsal, for "hundred per cent co-operation." As one member of the orchestra says: "Well, you know, after all—a hundred per cent co-operation . . ." as though to say, who does he think he is anyway?

He also indicated his preference for absolute silence from the men when he was giving instructions to a particular choir or soloist. This was in effect an open invitation for whispers and privately exchanged jokes. When one of the bass players had the effrontery to smile during a Stokowskian monologue he was summarily banished from the rehearsal. Expecting contriteness, Stokowski was astounded to hear him say: "Thank you—I haven't had a Thursday evening off all winter." This witticism evoked a giggle from a rear desk 'cellist, who was promptly directed to join his colleague in exile.

Plainly, neither of these occurrences would have happened in Philadelphia, where Stokowski exacts his "hundred per cent co-operation" not merely by will power, his beautiful hands, and exquisite gestures, but, more pertinently, through the players' knowledge that dismissal from a rehearsal is not for a day or a week, but for all time.

It is hardly surprising, therefore, that present-day orchestral players in the more prominent ensembles have become almost as great prima donnas as the glamour boys of music whom they derisively decorate with that epithet. There is the charming and somewhat pathos-tinged happening that involved Bruno Walter during one of his first guest appearances with the Philharmonic. Innocent and unwarned, he had endured for several rehearsals and the first pair of concerts the mannerisms of Alfred Wallenstein, the orchestra's brilliant first 'cellist, whose gaze was everywhere—on the music, in the hall, up at the ceiling—but not on Walter. Since the first 'cellist sits almost within baton-length of the conductor, his idiosyncrasy could hardly be overlooked.

At last Walter invited him to a conference and said: "Tell me, Mr. Wallenstein, what is your ambition?"

The 'cellist replied that he someday hoped to be a conductor.

"Well," said the conductor, with his sweet and patient smile, "I only hope you don't have Wallenstein in front of you."

II

In the relationship of conductor and orchestra much depends of course on the first meeting. As a human equation, it has much the same atmosphere as the meeting of the principals in a prearranged Hungarian wedding, with the bride and groom thoroughly aware that they are fated to make common cause whether they are enamored of each other or not. These are not marriages made in heaven; they are made mostly in the office of Mr. Arthur Judson.

The methods of approach by the conductor vary as widely as the literary tempers of Dale Carnegie's *How to Win Friends and Influence People* and Adolf Hitler's *Mein Kampf*. To this mating, the orchestra brings suspicion, skepticism, and mistrust in equal proportions. Unconsciously every conductor feels this and has developed a personal technique for breasting this psychological Maginot Line. With the less secure, the approach is invariably based on talk—a tribute to the magnificent musicianship of the band, a small disquisition on its splendid traditions (in whose future the conductor implies he hopes to play a part), a sigh of anticipation for the pleasure the conductor expects to derive from playing on "this superb instrument." An appeal is made to the co-operative spirit of the men, together with an apostrophe to "What beautiful music we can make together." This is further known as the Clifford Odets or Gary Cooper-Madeleine Carroll approach, with the orchestra inclined to regard the conductor's part in the making of the beautiful music as perhaps an act of supererogation.

Violently opposed to this is approach II, the martinet or "knock this off if you dare" type, in which the baton is, symbolically, a chip on the shoulder. Such conductors invariably enter unexpectedly (thus immediately placing the orchestra at a disadvantage), clothed in a black half-smock buttoned to the chin, a perfect stage setting for the indispensable Il Duce frown. No word of greeting is exchanged; a curt rap of the stick and a brisk command: "Beethoven." This the orchestra is expected to interpret to mean the symphony of the program. Further communication by word is withheld until the first mistake, no matter how slight. This provides the opportunity for which the conductor has been waiting to address a negative greeting to his co-workers, in which are mingled supercilious endearment and patronizing contempt.

Falling somewhere between these two is approach III—the good-fellow or Uriah Heep type. The conductor walks in calmly, clothed in a smile, shakes hands with the concertmaster, taps gently for attention, and addresses the orchestra as "Gentlemen." A harmless, well-prepared joke follows, leading up to the suggestion that since they are going to be together for weeks and months it would be best to develop a "Just call me Al" *entente cordiale*. Sometimes this flowers into a "mingling-with-the-help" manner: the conductor cultivates a program of socio-musical escapades with members of the orchestra, invites them to his home for chamber-music evenings, and sponsors Christmas parties for the children of the musicians. His purpose is to efface the social (and monetary) disparities between conductor and players, to give them an illusion of fraternal equality, to cultivate the impression that he is "just one of the boys." This usually endures only for the first season, after which the chrysalis is discarded, and he emerges from the cocoon to try his wings as a martinet.

More to be pitied than censured is the nervous-irritable type, generally hired for only two weeks in the middle of the season, and secretly convinced that the orchestra is out to get him. His problem is to make a lightning impression on an audience for which the permanent conductor has just directed every sure-fire work in the standard repertory. He is much in the position of a batter who steps to the plate after the previous man has hit a home run with the bases full. Entering with hasty, energetic steps, he mounts the podium in a leap, snaps his fingers with brittle impatience and says: "Three measures before letter C." Before the musicians have a chance to open their scores or raise their instruments, his right arm is describing arcs and angles. Naturally confusion ensues, and he is apt to smite his forehead in despair and expostulate: "I won't have it I won't *have* it I *won't* have it."

In such circumstances the musicians are likely to reply, "Take your time, buddy."

A recent development, in the post-Toscanini period, is the fabulous-memory type. He is shrewd enough to realize that an orchestra is no longer impressed with a musician who uses a score for rehearsals and conducts only his concerts from memory, so he scorns the use of a score in his rehearsals also. He has memorized not only the notes and tempo indications, but also the numbers of the pages, the lettered subdivisions of the movements, and the very accent marks in the bassoon part.

It is a part of orchestral folk-legend that one such virtuoso, intent upon impressing the orchestra with his memory, planted several errors in obscure places. In the midst of a furious *tutti* he stopped the orchestra, singled out the third horn player, and said: "Third horn—I heard you play a C. It should be a C sharp."

The horn player responded, with proper contempt: "Some jackass wrote in a C natural, but I know the piece backward, so I played it C sharp as it should be."

Unquestionably the most pathetic of all conductorial types is the man-who-has-risen-from-the-ranks, who frequently combines in his indeterminate manner some elements of all these approaches. As a former member of the orchestra which he is now conducting, he is subconsciously aware that the musicians are only waiting for the end of the rehearsal to get off together and discuss his failings, as they have discussed, innumerable times in the past, those of the conductors he has played under himself. His method of generating authority cannot adhere to any of the stereotyped categories, since his case is a special one, in which he first has to convince himself of his authority before he can transmit it to the players. Another accessible pitfall is eclecticism, the risk of reproducing the effects or mannerisms of some distinguished predecessor, thereupon permitting the members of the orchestra to say that he got this bar from so-and-so, that bar from another so-and-so.

III

A conductor should reconcile himself to the realization that, regardless of his approach or temperament, the eventual result is the same—the orchestra will hate him. This is true—hold your breath—even of Toscanini.

When Willem Mengelberg first exercised his virile vocabulary and exciting personality on the men of the Philharmonic, early in the 1920's, their enthusiasm for the new conductor mounted quickly from eager acceptance to blind idolatry. Perhaps there was an influence in the fact that his predecessor had been Josef Stransky.

This devotion endured for several seasons until a dark cloud, in the form of Arturo Toscanini, appeared on the horizon. For some time the loyalty of the Mengelberg faction in the orchestra resisted the defection of the Toscanini cohorts, until it became apparent, from the actions of the board and the public, that the Mengelberg tenure was approaching its end. In the words of one of the players: "The boys knew there was a new boss coming in"—and Mengelberg was gleefully sabotaged. There was perhaps no organized plan, but, somehow, an orchestra which had played the first symphony of Beethoven times without number disagreed on the necessity for a repeat after the trio of the minuet. With the woodwinds espousing one opinion and the strings another, the helpless conductor found himself engulfed in dissonance.

In his turn, Toscanini passed through much the same cycle of endearment, questioning, and resentment. There was rarely a cavil with his sincerity or extraordinary equipment, but his insistence on quality eventually won him the characterization which orchestral musicians apply to any intense and insatiable workman—"slave-driver." This reached open rebellion during his last season, in the preparation of "Iberia" for an all-Debussy program at one of his final concerts. Contrary to the legend that Toscanini is unswervingly faithful to the smallest detail of a composer's conception, he felt that a horn passage in the coda required reinforcement by a trumpet, and directed the incomparable Harry Glantz, first-chair man of that section, to play with the horns. Moreover, he specified that the addition be played *forte*. [Subsequently Glantz has given me many versions, one of which was that Reiner had introduced these changes in the parts previously.]

There was an unconscious reluctance on Glantz's part, to play the note aggressively, and his *forte* was hardly more than a *mezzo piano*. Toscanini interrupted the rehearsal and launched into a diatribe against Glantz, whose playing he had on many occasions praised. Angrily Glantz replied: "The trouble with you is you don't know how to handle men."

Such forthright opposition was unknown to Toscanini, and he stormily demanded an apology, whereupon Glantz walked out.

Unpredictably, the reaction in the orchestra was not sympathetic to Glantz. They felt he was right, but they condemned the action on the eve of Toscanini's farewell to the orchestra. Shortly before, in the preparation of an all-Wagner program, the strings had resented Toscanini's demands for individual playing of a complex passage, impossible to play accurately, man by man, at any time, and sheer absurdity in their season-end state of nervous fatigue. They had discussed the possibilities of a strike, but agreed, as in the case of Glantz, that the time to take action was the year before—when Toscanini still had a power of dismissal over his men.

The difficulty between the two men was resolved by their mutual admiration—the fine musician for the peerless conductor, the demanding conductor for the irreplaceable musician. Through the mediation of van Praag, manager of the orchestra personnel, an armistice was effected—without apology—for the duration of the concert. At its conclusion Glantz's magnificent performance won him a forgiving kiss on the cheek from the maestro.

Though it is commonly believed that a Toscanini performance is the highest reward a composer may expect for creating a work, it is an experience that sometimes has its embarrassing consequences. There was the happening several years ago at a Philharmonic rehearsal at which Ernest Schelling was present as soloist in the preparation of his "Impressions from an Artist's Life" for piano and orchestra. According to his custom, Toscanini was conducting without score while Schelling, the composer, had the music propped up on the stand before him.

The rehearsal progressed without incident for some minutes, when Toscanini, listening to Schelling expound a solo passage against a light orchestral background, suddenly rapped his stick imperiously on the stand beside him and called to Schelling: "What are you playing there?"

Schelling looked up in surprise, and repeated the measures he had just played.

"No, no," said Toscanini. "Let me see the score."

He raised the score close to his eyes, in the legendary way, peering intently at the page. Suddenly he looked up. "Just as I thought," he said. "You were playing wrong."

Schelling confirmed this astounding dictum by returning to the piano and playing a minutely different form of the passage he had just delivered. As he said afterward, he had always played it that way, never bothering to check it against the notes he had originally written.

Another example of Toscanini's remarkable musical faculties was the remark he made to Bernard Wagenaar, Dutch-American composer, after studying his first symphony for a performance of several years ago. Toscanini brought it back with him on a return trip from Europe, studying the score on the boat wholly by sight. When Wagenaar went to greet him at his hotel the day he arrived, Toscanini congratulated him on the work, but added: "There are several places which don't 'sound' "—a revelation that his memorization of the score included the ability to hear the actual *timbres* of the orchestra. The rehearsals revealed precisely the flaws in the texture of the scoring that he had predicted. This incident is in strong contrast to the opinion of Stokowski, who contends that only an actual playing will show the weaknesses of an orchestration. As a footnote to this, it might be added that the dissonant conclusion of the first movement left Toscanini unsatisfied, and he insisted on adding a pure C major chord to the composer's final page.

It is history, however, that one eminent contemporary felt otherwise than flattered by Toscanini's treatment of his music. This was the late Maurice Ravel, who was honored by a performance of his "Bolero" in Paris during the Philharmonic's European trip. It was an initial irritation for Ravel that no tickets had been sent to him and he made his way into the crowded hall with great difficulty, to discover that Toscanini's tempo for "Bolero" was unforgivably fast. He added audible, unscored verbal comments from his box as the work progressed, in a mounting crescendo that paralleled the surge of the music. This monotone of invective brought a storm of shushing from the intent Parisians, to whom Ravel was not a world-famous composer but merely an ill-mannered listener.

The performance completed, Ravel descended angrily upon the green room to deliver his annoyance with the performance in person to the maestro. With voluble gestures and insistent pounding of his

feet, he delineated the impossibility of dancing a "bolero," his or anyone else's, at such a pace. There was the charm of novelty in this
experience for Toscanini, since only a composer of Ravel's stature
could be thus indifferent to his reaction.

Despite this unprecedented happening, Toscanini continued to
conduct "Bolero," content perhaps to regard its unparalleled opportunity for orchestral virtuosity as compensation for the bad manners
of the composer. After several brilliant performances with the Philharmonic, in which he had been delighted by the meticulous playing of
the orchestra's percussion section, he summoned its members to his
room and expressed his particular pleasure with the snare drummer,
Schmehl, whose superb *pianissimo* and imperceptible crescendo
excelled anything in his experience.

A large florid man with the muscularity of a heavyweight wrestler
and a speech compounded equally of Brooklynese and Hemingway,
Schmehl replied casually: "Tanks, boss—glad you feel that way about
me."

The praise apparently aroused Schmehl to the difficulty of his task,
and a consciousness of how well he had accomplished it, for at the
next repetition of "Bolero" he was swept by panic, beginning his
opening solo at a rapidly increasing *forte*. A contortion of rage suf-
fused Toscanini's face, and he muttered imprecations. Schmehl's partner sought to retrieve the sticks and play the solo himself, but the
drummer was too nervous to understand the request. The fury of
Toscanini with Schmehl transmitted itself to the rest of the orchestra,
a trombone exploded a blast instead of a tone at the climax of his solo,
and the performance moved swiftly into confusion.

When the final chord had been reached, Toscanini stalked from the
stage without a glance at the audience, and rushed to his room, crying: "Where is Schmehl? I want Schmehl! *Send me Schmehl!*"

The culprit finally appeared, to be greeted by a torrent of "*Stupido.*"
. . . "Shame." . . . "You play no more for me." All this to the
man he had recently decorated with garlands of praise.

Truculently Schmehl accepted the abuse with the patience born of
forty years' experience in orchestral playing and, waiting his opportunity, finally said: "You don't like my work? Get yourself another
boy."

Nevertheless, the happening cost him his post in the orchestra,
for one misgauged *pianissimo*.

There might have been a similar outcome for another impasse at a Philharmonic rehearsal had not the player shrewdly adapted himself to one of Toscanini's few limitations. The problem arose in the rehearsing of Berlioz's "Queen Mab" scherzo (in the "Romeo and Juliet" music). This contains an effect scored for antique cymbals, the tiny equivalents of the familiar large cymbals. Toscanini demanded that the rapid tinkling of the instruments be mathematically precise and metronomically exact, the rhythm sharply articulated.

One after another the percussion players took their turns at attempting to meet Toscanini's requirements, only to find that the task of rustling the two tiny dials together at the proper speed and with the desired clarity defied any technique with which they were acquainted. They were all waved impatiently aside until Sam Borodkin, virtuoso of the gong, tam-tam, bass drum, and glockenspiel, pushed his way to the stand and said he'd like to try.

The orchestra began, and Borodkin stood poised with the small cymbals (each no larger than a silver dollar) in his hands. When his entrance approached, Borodkin bent over the stand, in an attitude of extreme attentiveness, meanwhile substituting a metal triangle stick for the cymbal in his right hand. Then, with his hands barely visible over the top of the stand, he beat out the rhythm perfectly.

Toscanini dropped his baton and called out: "Bravo, Borodkin. Bravo"—being unable to penetrate the deception with his weak vision. No doubt if he could have seen that far he would have found some reason to be displeased with the results.

It is such arbitrary and unpredictable attitudes that exhaust the patience of men who feel that their status, tried and approved, entitles them to better treatment.

In this genre there is the classic experience of the violinist Mischel ("Mike") Gussikoff, who was engaged as concertmaster of the Philadelphia Orchestra after Stokowski personally scouted his playing of the solo violin part of Strauss's "Ein Heldenleben" with the St. Louis Symphony. When the orchestra assembled to begin its season, Gussikoff took his place at the first desk, but noticed that Stokowski did not shake hands with him, greet him by name, or even nod.

This situation endured not only for the first rehearsal, but through the week's concerts and for all of the next month. Eventually Gussikoff began to worry about this silent relationship with Stokowski, and sought to identify it with possible flaws in his playing. He could not find any that justified such mute indictment, and in final desperation he sought out Stokowski during a train trip from a New York concert, and said:

"Please, Dr. Stokowski, I have done something to displease you?"

"No," said the conductor.

"You don't like the way I play my solos?"

"I have no complaint," said Stokowski.

"Then why," questioned Gussikoff, "Why don't you *say* something to me?"

"When I say something," answered Stokowski, "that will be the time to worry."

Baffled by this negative endorsement, Gussikoff withdrew and shortly afterward found himself a position with another orchestra.

IV

It is possible that Gussikoff reacted with particular sensitivity because he had been reared in the prewar Russian Symphony Orchestra, under the genial guidance of Modest Altschuler. This was the orchestra that was a veritable training school for concertmasters, producing among others, Frederic Fradkin (of the Boston Symphony), Maximillian Pilzer (of the Philharmonic), Ilya Skolnik (of the Detroit Symphony), Louis Edlin (of the National Orchestral Association), and the conductors Nikolai Sokoloff and Nat Finston (of the movies). It was this orchestra that introduced many of the finest scores by Scriabin, Rachmaninoff, and Stravinsky (his first Symphony and "L'Oiseau de Feu" particularly outraging the Krehbiels and Fincks) to New York, long before the established orchestras were aware of their existence.

An ardent propagandist for such works, Altschuler also delighted in expounding his conceptions of the scores with illustrated lectures. Attempting to elicit a more soulful solo from his oboist in a rehearsal of "Scheherazade" he stopped and said: "Here is the princess [pointing to the concertmaster, who plays the overfamous violin cadenza] and you are making love to her." Then, studying the pimpled complexion of the violinist, he added: "I'm sorry I can't do better."

Life in this orchestra was much like attendance at a private university. Such men as Harry Glantz, the admired first trumpet of the Philharmonic, had their early training in the German school of playing almost wholly revised under Altschuler's guidance. When the orchestra toured—as it frequently did—the travels resembled a mass picnic, with baskets of native delicacies ranging from salamis to cheeses carted along as sustenance against the barbaric foods to be found inland.

It was in this orchestra, its scattered survivers of today claim, that there originated the fable that has since been attributed to every musical organization that gives outdoor concerts, from the Philharmonic Orchestra to the Goldman Band. They were playing the "Leonore No. 3" overture of Beethoven during a summer engagement, and the first trumpeter had stolen from his place to give the off-stage fanfare heralding the approach of the Minister of Justice.

Retreating an appropriate distance from the orchestra stand, he raised his instrument, waited for the cue, and was just about to blow when a park policeman rushed up and bellowed: "You can't do that here! Don't you know there's a concert going on?"

Regardless of their respect for a conductor's musicianship an orchestra is frequently made uncomfortably aware of his feet of clay as they are of his head in the clouds. Several seasons ago, I am told, the men of the Philadelphia Orchestra were baffled by Stokowski's desire to conduct, at one of his final rehearsals of the regular season, Strauss' "The Blue Danube" waltz. It was not scheduled for any remaining concert of the year, and the conductor's meticulous preparation of the score, his insistence on this effect and that phrasing, could only be interpreted as a whim.

The incident had passed from their minds by the time they reassembled to play their summer series of concerts at Robin Hood Dell, of which the first was conducted by a guest. Following the intermission, the chairman appeared before the audience, thanked the listeners for their attendance, and added: "Perhaps you have not noticed that we have among us tonight a distinguished guest—our beloved Dr. Stokowski. I know you would be delighted to have him conduct something for us this evening."

Stokowski resisted the flattery with gestures of unassuming modesty, listened to the applause, and finally indicated that he was powerless to deny the audience its wish. He mounted the stage, and suggested that the librarian distribute the parts of—"The Blue Danube."

Not one paper the following day failed to mention how brilliantly he had made his wishes apparent, how forcefully he had imposed his will on the orchestra—all without a single rehearsal!

Occasionally, and at widely separated intervals, a musician will give forth an opinion based not only on his reaction to a given situation, but summing up in sparse phrases his reaction to a conductor's whole personality. When such an incident occurs it is preserved not merely for its succinctness but also for its assertiveness, enduring as part of the folk-legend of orchestral players.

A famous incident of that nature involved, by coincidence, two musicians almost miraculously opposed in size, type, and temperament—the six-foot-four Otto Klemperer, probably the tallest conductor extant, and the barely five-foot Bruno Labate, diminutive oboe virtuoso of the Philharmonic-Symphony Orchestra.

It is traditional that orchestral conductors follow one of two practices in their rehearsals of standard works. Generically, conductors of the German school will begin a work, say Beethoven's "Eroica," and play it methodically from beginning to end, indicating as they progress their preferences in dynamics, accents, and phrasings. Others, particularly English and French conductors, in order to expedite rehearsals during a brief guest engagement, will assume that an experienced orchestra is competent to deal with the large aspects of such a work without measure-by-measure supervision, and merely rehearse those sections in which their ideas are personal—perhaps in the development or at the beginning of the recapitulation.

It was a trait of the thoroughgoing Klemperer to espouse *both* methods, beginning with the scattered-intensive, and progressing thereafter to the over-all-extensive. This treatment he frequently interrupted in the preparation of a Beethoven work with discourses on the metronome of Beethoven's time and the state of the composer's relations with his nephew Karl when the work was written, with perhaps even a monologue on the alterations of pitch in the hundred years since.

Having completed such a discourse on one occasion, he turned to Ravel's "Le Tombeau de Couperin" and proceeded to dissect it, page by page, with particular attention to a rather difficult oboe phrase which recurs frequently in the Prelude. Four times, five times, he asked to hear it, and even at the sixth playing he was not satisfied. Disregarding the difficulty an oboist has in controlling his breath for long stretches, and the inevitable tiring of the player's lips, he asked for it again, pausing for a brief footnote on Ravel's use of the oboe before he raised his baton.

Labate peered over his stand at the mountainous conductor and pronounced the undying words: "Mr. Klemps', you talka too much."

The Reviewing Business

by CLIFTON FADIMAN

OCTOBER, 1941

Clifton Fadiman is an admired critic and essayist; in radio and television he is known as the Master of Ceremonies of highly successful informative programs. He has been chief editor for a large publishing house, book reviewer for The New Yorker *for many years, and the editor of several volumes of good reading. He is currently a regular columnist for* Holiday. *In this article he gives readers a behind-the-scenes look at a little-understood occupation.*

The word "business" in the title of this article is used as a wedge to separate book-reviewing from literary criticism. Literary criticism is an art, like the writing of tragedies or the making of love, and, similarly, does not pay. Book-reviewing is a device for earning a living, one of the many weird results of Gutenberg's invention. Movable type made books too easy to publish. Some sort of sieve had to be interposed between printer and public. The reviewer is that sieve, a generally honest, usually uninspired, and mildly useful sieve.

To use an example conveniently near at hand, the writer of this article is a book-reviewer. To the best of his knowledge and belief he has never written a sentence of literary criticism in his life. Unless he becomes a vastly different person from what he now is, he never will. He and his colleagues are often called critics, a consequence of the amiable national trait that turns Kentuckians into colonels and the corner druggist into Doc.

True literary criticism is a subtle and venerable art. You can number the top-notchers on your fingers and toes: Aristotle, Horace, Coleridge, Lessing, Sainte-Beuve, Taine, Goethe, Arnold, Shaw (one of the greatest), and a few others. In our own time and nation literary criticism is almost a lost art, partly because no one except a few other literary critics cares to read it.

What follows, then, is not a discussion of literary criticism but merely shop talk about my trade. A literary critic (just this once and then we're through with him) is a whole man exercising his wholeness through the accidental medium of books and authors. A reviewer is not a whole man; he is that partial man, an expert. Many of his human qualities are vestigial, others hypertrophied. All experts are monsters. I shall now briefly demonstrate the reviewer's monstrosity.

We must first of all remember that reading maketh not a full man. Any reviewer who has been in harness for twenty years or so will be eager to tell you that Bacon was just dreaming up sentences. I suppose I have read five or ten thousand books—it doesn't matter which—in the past couple of decades. Every so often I catch myself wondering whether I shouldn't be a sight wiser if I had read only fifteen, and they the right ones. You see, a reviewer does not read to instruct himself. If he remembered even a moderate quantum of what he read he would soon be unfit for his job. Forced to comment on book Z, he would at once recollect everything that books A to Y, previously reviewed, contained that might throw light on Z. This is not the mental attitude that makes for useful book-reviewing. As a matter of fact, what the reviewer should have above all things is a kind of mental virginity, a continual capacity to react freshly. I said that he was an expert. He is—he is an expert in surprisability. The poor fool is always looking forward to the next book.

This does not mean that the reviewer has the memory of a moron. He doubtless remembers something of what he has read, but not enough to handicap him. His mind is not so much well stocked as well indexed. If challenged, I think I could tell you the authors and titles of the three or four best books of the past ten years dealing with the ancient Maya civilization. I can even make a fair fist at grading the books in the order of their completeness, authority, and readability. But what I don't know about the Mayans in the way of real information would fill several volumes and, no doubt, has done so.

The reviewer, then, granting him any mind at all, has a fresh one. Frank Moore Colby, whom I greatly admire, held a different point of view. In 1921 he wrote a little piece entitled "Beans Again," from which I quote:

If a man had for one day a purée of beans, and the next day *haricots verts,* and then in daily succession bean soup, bean salad, butter beans, lima, black, navy, Boston baked, and kidney beans, and then back to purée and all over again, he would not be in the relation of the general eater to food. Nor would he be in the relation of a general reader to books. But he would be in the relation of a reviewer toward novels. He would soon perceive that the relation was neither normal nor desirable, and he would take measures, violent if need be, to change it. He would not say on his navy-bean day that they were as brisk and stirring little beans of the sea as he could recall in his recent eating. He would say grimly, "Beans again," and he would take prompt steps to intermit this abominable procession of bean dishes.

If change for any reason were impossible he would either conceive a personal hatred toward all beans that would make him unjust to any bean however meritorious, or he would acquire a mad indiscriminateness of acquiescence and any bean might please. And his judgment would be in either case an unsafe guide for general eaters.

This, I believe, is what happens to almost all reviewers of fiction after a certain time, and it accounts satisfactorily for various phenomena that are often attributed to a baser cause. It is the custom at certain intervals to denounce reviewers for their motives. They are called venal and they are called cowardly by turns. They are blamed for having low standards or no standards at all. I think their defects are due chiefly to the nature of their calling; that they suffer from an occupational disease.

Now I can understand why Colby felt this way. He could afford to be superior; he was an encyclopedia editor, which is several cuts above a reviewer. But his beans-again notion, through plausible, is not cogent. The truth is that a competent reviewer's stomach does not summon up remembrance of beans past. Though there are exceptions (I shall mention some of my own weaknesses in a moment), he does not hail or damn novels out of a kind of hysteria of surfeit. If he makes a stupid judgment it is simply because his judgment is stupid. It may be stupid for a variety of reasons, no one of which may have anything to do with the fact that he reads half a dozen novels a week. In other words, a jaded reviewer sooner or later realizes that he is not a good reviewer, and tries to get another job. A good reviewer is a perennially fresh hack.

But, as I say, this doesn't work out one hundred per cent of the time. For example, I confess that I no longer look forward to next week's American historical novel with any bridegroom eagerness. I have read too many such. I am positive that they (not I, you see) have slipped into a groove, are standardized products, and therefore there is nothing helpful I can say about them. (Yet my fatuousness is such that I do not honestly believe I should muff another *Red Badge of Courage* if by some miracle one were published tomorrow.)

Never to be bored is merely an active form of imbecility. Do not trust the man who is "interested in everything." He is covering up some fearful abyss of spiritual vacancy. Ennui, felt on the proper occasions, is a sign of intelligence. All this is by way of saying that, of course, no reviewer is interested in every book he reads. He should have the ability to be bored, even if this ability is much feebler than his ability not to be bored. A competent reviewer knows his blind spots, tries to counteract them, and, if he can't, never drives himself into phony enthusiasm. Indiscriminate love of books is a disease, like satyriasis, and stern measures should be applied to it.

I, to take that familiar example once more, do not react eagerly to books on the delights of gardening; to novels about very young men lengthily and discursively in love; to amateur anthropologists who hide a pogrom-mania under learned demonstrations of the superiority of Nordic man; to books by bright children Who Don't Know How Funny They're Being; to diplomatic reminiscences by splendid gaffers with long memories and brief understandings; to autobiographies by writers who feel that to have reached the age of thirty-five is an achievement of pivotal significance; to thorough jobs on Chester A. Arthur; to all tomes that aim to make me a better or a more successful man than I should be comfortable being; to young virile novelists who would rather be found dead than grammatical; to most anthologies of humor; to books about Buchmanism, astrology, Yogi, and internal baths; to the prospect of further "country" books, such as *Country Mortician, Country Dog-Catcher,* and *Country Old Ladies' Home Attendant.*

It is such books as these that make a successful appeal to my apathy. Every reviewer has his own list. He does his best to keep it a small one, for he knows that his responsibility is to his public, not himself. He knows that he cannot afford to any great extent the luxury of indulging his own prejudices. A reviewer is not in the self-expression business. If he were he would run the risk of becoming an artist. He is, by the nature of his trade, uncreative, or, if his creative impulses are too strong, he sooner or later finds himself a dud at his job and turns into a writer. But if he is a good reviewer and keeps in the groove fifteen or twenty years he has no more chance of becoming a writer than a pig has of flying. There is nothing tragic about this, and no reviewer who has any respect for his trade wastes any sentimentality over it. One decent hack, to my mind, is worth a stable of would-be Pegasuses.

II

Reviewers interest the public. I cannot fathom the reason, for we are among the mildest and most conventional of citizens, pure Gluyas Williams types. A life spent among ephemeral best-sellers and publishers' announcements is not apt to produce characters of unusual contour. But the fact remains that people are curious about us, and are likely to ask more questions of a reviewer than they would of a successful truss-manufacturer, though probably the trussman leads the more abundant life. To satisfy this curiosity I list herewith a few of the queries most commonly directed at my tribe, together with one man's answers.

Do you really read all those books? This question is generally put with an odd inflection, combining cynical disbelief with man-of-the-world willingness to overlook any slight dishonesty. But there is no need for this hard-boiled attitude. Reviewers read the books they review, exactly as an accountant examines his cost sheets, with the same routine conscientiousness. It's his job, that's all.

Back of this question, however, lies a peculiar condition, which baffles me and I think many others who are forced to read a great deal. The reason people think we bluff is that they themselves read so slowly they cannot believe we read as "fast" as we actually do. Now I do not believe dogmatically either in fast or slow reading. I believe tripe should be read practically with the speed of light and, let us say, Toynbee's *A Study of History* with tortoise deliberation. And most books are nearer to tripe than to Toynbee. But the trouble with most of us is that we suffer from chronic reverence. We make the unwarranted assumption that because a man is in print, he has something to say, and, acting on this assumption, we read his every word with scrupulous care. This may be good manners but it's a confounded waste of time.

I am simply unable to understand, for example, those—and there must be millions of them—who spend hours over the daily paper. Why, if you add up those hours you will find that some people spend more time with the *Herald Tribune* than they do with their wives or husbands. I do not draw from this any conclusions about the state of either American journalism or American matrimony; I merely infer that such papermaniacs simply do not know how to skip, to take in a paragraph at a time, to use the headlines, one of mankind's most blessed inventions. In a little book by Walter Pitkin called *The Art of Rapid Reading,* written by a master of the art of rapid writing, slow readers will find some excellent advice on this head.

No, reviewers do their job—but they know how to read quickly, in large units, to seize a point and be off to the next one while the author is still worrying the first one to death. Anybody can learn to do this; the reviewer simply is forced to learn it. I happen to be an exceptionally rapid reader, which is no more to my credit than would be the possession of exceptionally bushy eyebrows. Of the average novel (a description that covers virtually all novels) I can read one hundred pages an hour. Of the average historical novel I can read two hundred pages an hour, but that is because I am so familiar with the plot and characters. It took me two weeks, about five hours a day, to read Thomas Mann's *Joseph in Egypt.* I submit that in all three cases I did my reading with the proper speed and with conscientious attention to the value of what was being said.

How do you select books for review? Well, each reviewer has his own system. Here's mine. I try to juggle five factors, whose relative importance varies with each book. First, I ask myself whether the book is apt to interest *me.* This is only fair: I am apt to write better, more usefully about something that naturally engages my attention. I don't have to like the book necessarily. It may interest me because its author happens to represent a great many things I dislike, as is the case with Gertrude Stein, Mabel Dodge Luhan, Charles Morgan, and William Faulkner.

Second, does the book have news value? A book-reviewer is partly a purveyor of news. Any book by Ernest Hemingway would have to be reviewed whether it be a good one, like *For Whom the Bell Tolls* or a poor one, like *Green Hills of Africa,* for Hemingway is news. This does not make him a better or a worse writer of course. It has nothing to do with his literary value, but it has a great deal to do with whether or not the public expects information about his new book. Let me give you another example. A few years ago everybody was all worked up over the Edward-Simpson affair (remember?): I said then and I say now (nobody listened then and nobody's listening now) that the whole mess was of very little political importance and that the persons involved were not sufficiently interesting even for the thing to have much scandal value. I was in a chilly minority of one. But one week, with public interest at fever-heat, three or four books bearing on the case appeared. Not one of them would have been worth a line of comment had it not possessed at the moment an inflated news value. To my mind they weren't worth a line of comment anyway, but I should have been an incompetent reviewer had I not given them considerable space. A reviewer is a journalist.

The third factor is allied to the second: Is the book apt to be of interest to the reviewer's particular audience? At the present time I have a job with *The New Yorker,* a humorous and satirical family magazine. There is no such animal as a typical *New Yorker* reader, but we know that most of this magazine's readers do not enjoy Temple Bailey, and no doubt *vice versa.* Miss Bailey has her virtues (indeed she is *all* virtue), but they are not the virtues that happen to interest the people who read my small screeds. Hence Miss Bailey does not get a look-in in my column. I cannot notice that her sales suffer in consequence.

The fourth factor is the only one that might not be apt to occur to a nonprofessional. A reviewer in selecting books takes into careful account the opinion of the *publisher* with respect to his own publications. If a publisher writes me that Hyacinthe Doakes' novel is terrific, that it is his fall leader, that he is going to lay ten thousand dollars' worth of advertising money on the line—why I make a note to read Hyacinthe's book with care. I may not like it, and in that case will say so. (I have not once, in almost twenty years in the trade, received a letter of protest from any publisher whose offering I had panned, except in a few cases when I had made misstatements of fact.) But the truth is that I am more apt to like it than I am to like some little yarn that this same publisher is so ashamed of he hides it away in the back of his catalogue. Publishers have their faults (a profound remark that I have often heard them apply to reviewers), but they do know a good deal about books and their judgment of the relative values of their productions is hearkened to by any sensible reviewer.

Finally, a book may not be of great personal interest, it may possess no news value, my audience may not care deeply about it, and the publisher will not be in a position to give it any special publicizing. Nevertheless, I shall review it in some detail. Why? Because I feel it to be important. That is to say, it is a book of literary or instructive value by a criterion (a cloudy one, I admit) that has nothing to do with the four factors already mentioned. A short time ago there appeared a long, scholarly, rather solemn work of literary criticism, *American Renaissance,* by F. O. Matthiessen. Factor 1 applied moderately; factors 2, 3, 4 hardly applied. But I gave it a column and a half. I did so because the book is clearly an important work of creative scholarship and in years to come is bound to take a considerable place in its restricted field. It is my duty (to whom I don't know; I suppose to Literature itself) to comment on such a book to the best of my ability. Every reviewer feels the same way and does the same thing.

How reliable are reviewers' estimates? There's no exact answer to that one. If his estimates weren't appreciably more reliable than those of your dinner-table companion he wouldn't hold his job long. But he is several light-years distant from infallibility. He works under pressure, he's human, he's been out too late the night before, his eyes bother him—for one reason or another the result may be a stupid verdict. I have rendered many. At the end of each year I give myself something life itself, less generous than I am, doesn't allow us: a second chance. I go over the books I've reviewed and correct my first estimates. I try to be honest, but it's not easy.

As to this question of reliability I would say that on the whole, we reviewers err in the direction of overamiability, though not so noticeably as was the case fifteen years ago when the Great American Novel was being hailed about as regularly as a Fifth Avenue bus.

What has happened, roughly, is that the old type of book-reviewer, to whom the job was a game, has gradually been replaced by a new type, to whom the job is a job. In the days of Laurence Stallings and Heywood Broun you would on occasion get superb pieces of enthusiastic journalism, but more frequently sickening examples of hullabalunacy. Today book-reviewing is staider, duller, but unquestionably juster and more serious. It has a professional touch; it is growing up.

Nevertheless, I should hazard that its standards of judgment are still too relaxed. Just what my tribe has to be mellow about I can't figure out, but we *are* mellow, and the result is a certain lack of acerbity. There's too much good-nature-faking among us, a continuous observance of Be-Kind-To-Dumb-Novelists Week. Literature does not grow only on praise. It needs the savage and tartarly note, even the astringence of insult.

In order to keep his sword sharp the reviewer should see to it that he does not make too many close friends among writers. A decade or so ago during the heyday of the literary tea and the publisher's cocktail party, this was a difficult assignment. Today, now that book publishers have finally put on long pants, the problem is easier. A reviewer may go from one end of the year to the other without flushing a single novelist, and I have known some reviewers, now quite grown men, who have never met a literary agent in the flesh. This alienation from what used to be known laughingly as the Literary Life is a good thing for us. It makes possible a cool inhumanity toward authors, which in turn results in more detached comment. The road to a reviewer's disintegration is marked by many milestones, each one a statue erected to commemorate a beautiful friendship. I am sure of this even though I would not go so far as to agree with the man who thought the proper relationship between reviewer and author should be that between a knife and a throat.

What, then, is a reviewer to do when unavoidably confronted with a book by a close friend? I have had to face this situation perhaps a dozen times in the course of my daily work, and it is not an easy one to handle if one wishes to be scrupulously honest. In my case the difficulty was never disastrous for it is my policy, when choosing friends who write, to choose of course only those who write well, thus making it a matter of inexorable duty for me to praise their work. So far this policy has worked pretty successfully. I do not know what would happen in the event that I should get to conceive a warm personal affection for, let us say, Miss Gertrude Stein. However, careful planning should enable me to head off this possibility.

The fact is that no reviewer is really objective when dealing with a friend's book, for if the book has anything to it at all he is really dealing with the friend himself. He does the best he can, trying not to crack his spine in an attempt to lean over backward, but I doubt the final accuracy of his judgment. For example, I have praised rather heatedly two books by close friends of mine: Mortimer Adler's *How to Read a Book* and Oscar Levant's *A Smattering of Ignorance*. I still do not know whether these books are as good as I made them out to be. On rereading my admittedly amiable pieces I detect no conscious dishonesty. Of course, as one of my most sympathetic readers, I may be giving myself the benefit of the doubt. There are some Alexanders among us who cut the Gordian knot, such as the famous literary commentator who is reported to have said with dulcet candor, "Any reviewer who won't praise a friend's book is a louse."

III

How influential are reviewers? This is a hard one to answer. All the publishers' questionnaires, scientifically designed to discover just why a given book is bought, throw but a dim light on the subject, though they provide any desired quantity of statistics. Reader A buys a book because his friend B has mentioned it; that is apparently the strongest single definable factor. But this means nothing until you know why B happened to mention it. You ask B. B replies, let us suppose, that he himself bought, read, and recommended the book as the result of reading an advertisement. Now you have to find out what in that particular advertisement caused the positive reaction to the book. Was it the publisher's statement of the book's merits? Was it a quotation from a reviewer? If the latter, B bought the book because the reviewer liked it—and therefore A indirectly did the same. The whole matter is very complex.

With a great best-seller, a large number of factors operate simultaneously or follow rapidly on one another, causing an irresistible, constantly mounting wave of popularity. If we take the case of *For Whom the Bell Tolls* we might list these factors somewhat as follows, in the order of their conceivable importance:

(1) Author's reputation (but that didn't make a best-seller of his previous book).
(2) Timeliness and importance of the subject matter.
(3) Literary excellence.
(4) It was a Book-of-the-Month Club selection, which automatically set in motion a wave of bookish conversation, for the club members form a mighty army of talkers.
(5) Almost unanimously favorable reviews.
(6) Erotic and "shocking" passages.
(7) Bookstore recommendation (a factor very difficult to judge—perhaps it should be placed much higher in the list).

(8) Publisher's advertising and general promotion—in this case, I
    should say, a minor factor.
Talkability. I don't give this a number because any of the factors
    1 to 8 might have contributed to the book's talkability, and
    no one can determine the relative importance of any of them.

Now this casual analysis (whose arrangement would probably be
sharply questioned by my colleagues, the publisher, and Mr. Hemingway) would not apply identically to any other best-seller. In some
cases (8) might be very near the head of the list. *Anthony Adverse,*
for example, benefited by one of the most skillful advertising campaigns
in recent publishing history; *Jurgen* was made mainly by (6), or rather
by a vice society's alert appreciation of (6); and so it goes. Mrs.
Lindbergh's sublime example of the prophetic fallacy, *The Wave of the
Future,* succeeded through a combination of (1) and (2) plus certain
other less savory factors.

The reviewer alone cannot make a book popular. A superb novel
such as Elizabeth Bowen's *The Death of the Heart* may be praised by
every reviewer who knows his job, and still sell but a few thousand
copies. Only factors (3) and (5) applied to this particular book; other
factors would have been necessary to push it over into solid popularity.

Occasionally a book may be "made" or set in motion by one man's
recommendation. William Lyon Phelps did a great deal for *The Bridge
of San Luis Rey.* Will Rogers' admiration for *The Good Earth* helped
that book. A book of some years back called *Recovery,* by Sir Arthur
Salter, owed its success almost entirely to Walter Lippmann. More
recently Alexander Woollcott tickled the lachrymatory glands of all
America to the considerable advantage of Mr. James Hilton. It is
interesting to observe that none of these four commentators is or was
a regular day-in-day-out book-reviewer. They're Gentlemen rather
than Players. We professionals do not in the nature of things wield
any such power. I have never heard of Lewis Gannett or Harry Han-
sen or Malcolm Cowley or Sterling North or Joseph Henry Jackson
or Donald Adams or Clifton Fadiman "making" a book single-
handed.

A minor trait in the American character makes us pay less attention
to the literary judgments of professionals than to those of distinguished
nonprofessionals. A striking instance, to go back almost a generation,
is the instant popularity into which J. S. Fletcher, the English detec-
tive-story writer, sprang when Woodrow Wilson, then President, hap-

pened to praise his work, which was no better nor worse than that of fifty other thriller manufacturers. A parallel instance in England was Stanley Baldwin's endorsement, some years ago, of the novels of Mary Webb. They were at once gobbled up by the thousand, unfortunately a little too late to do the author any good; for she had died some time before in utter poverty.

If Franklin D. Roosevelt should happen to go all out for some novel tomorrow it would at once become a best-seller, irrespective of its real merits. But if he should issue a weekly verdict on new books, his opinion within a few months would cease to have any great influence.

Columnists, radio commentators, editorial writers, lecturers, even big businessmen will on occasion influence the sale of books more sharply than reviewers can. On the other hand, preachers whose literary influence a generation or so ago was marked, have now sunk to a minor role as book recommenders.

One of the paradoxes of book selling, observable only during the past few years, is that a book may be helped by one or more of the so-called competitive media. A book's sale will be *increased* by its translation into a moving picture. Alice Duer Miller's *The White Cliffs* became a best-seller largely because it was so successfully broadcast. And, to take a more striking example, the condensations of popular books to be found in the *Reader's Digest* frequently tend to accelerate the sale of these publications in their original form. There is no such thing as bad publicity for books.

One thing that does *not* sell them is the publisher's jacket blurb. This is generally written after much brow-furrowing and is almost completely ineffective. Sometimes blurbs help the reviewer, but not much; more often they aid the harried bookseller. Yet I have never seen a potential book-buyer influenced by them. My own practice is to be wary of them. Their extravagance is often so absurd that the reviewer loses his detachment and is unduly severe with the innocent book. "One of the outstanding biographers of our time," said the blurbist a year or two ago—about whom? About a journalist named Hector Bolitho, who has devoted himself to the extremely dull task of composing official slop about the English royal family. "The greatest of living historians" is the blurb characterization of Philip Guedalla, a writer of considerable quality, but no more the greatest of living historians than I am. A tedious Scandinavian was tagged by his publishers as "One of the great writers of the day," which may have been literally true, the day being unspecified. This jacket racket alienates reviewers.

And I guess that's enough about us.

Barker's Wild Oats

by GEORGE BERNARD SHAW

JANUARY, 1947

He died in 1950 at the age of ninety-four, regarded by many as the greatest literary figure of modern times. A spry wit and a remarkable person in every way right up to the end, Shaw reminisces here about his early struggle for recognition in London as a dramatist, and about his role as go-between in arranging a divorce for a pair of his associates.

In the year 1904, when I was forty-eight years old, I was an unacted playwright in London, though certain big box office successes abroad, notably those of Agnes Sorma as Candida in Germany and Richard Mansfield in New York as The Devil's Disciple, had proved that my plays were both actable, and possibly highly lucrative. But the commercial theaters in London (and there were no others) would have nothing to do with them, regarding them as untheatrical and financially impossible. There were no murders, no adulteries, no sexual intrigues in them. The heroines were not like heroines: they were like women. Although the rule of the stage was that any speech longer than twenty words was too long, and that politics and religion must never be mentioned and their places taken by romance and fictitious police and divorce cases, my characters had to declaim long speeches on religion and politics in the Shakespearean or "ham" technique.

Besides, I could not offer my plays to the established managers because I was a noted professional critic, and, as such, would have been understood as inviting bribery.

I had, therefore, not only to publish my plays, but to make plays readable. A leading friendly publisher whom I approached had published the plays of a fashionable playwright, and had shown me the ledger account of the transaction, recording absolutely no sales except in the little batches indicating amateur performances for which copies of the play had to be bought for rehearsal.

I substituted readable descriptions for technical stage directions, and showed how to make the volumes as attractive in appearance as novels. A young publisher, Grant Richards, rose to the occasion with pioneer pluck. His venture succeeded; and plays broke into the publishing market as Literature. And I, though unacted, made my mark as a playwright. My plays formed a unique reserve stock available for any management with sufficient flair to try the experiment of a Shavian theater.

Meanwhile, in looking about for an actor suitable for the part of the poet in *Candida* at a Stage Society performance, I had found my man in a very remarkable person named Harley Granville-Barker. He was at that time twenty-three years of age, and had been on the stage since he was fourteen. He had a strong strain of Italian blood in him, and looked as if he had stepped out of a picture by Benozzo Gozzoli. He had a wide literary culture and a fastidiously delicate taste in every branch of art. He could write in a difficult and too precious but exquisitely fine style. He was self-willed, restlessly industrious, sober, and quite sane. He had Shakespeare and Dickens at his finger ends. Altogether the most distinguished and incomparably the most cultivated person whom circumstances had driven into the theater at that time.

I saw him play Hauptmann's *Friedensfest*, and immediately jumped at him for the poet in *Candida*. His performance of this part —a very difficult one to cast—was, humanly speaking, perfect.

Presently a gentleman with a fancy for playing Shakespearean parts, and money enough to gratify it without much regard to public support, took the Court Theater in Sloan Square, made famous by the acting of John Hare, Clayton, Cecil, Ellen Terry, and by the early comedy-farces of Pinero. He installed therein as his business manager the late J. E. Vedrenne, who, when his principal was not indulging in Shakespearean matinées, kept the theater going by letting it by night to amateurs. Granville-Barker was engaged for one of these revivals in the ordinary course of his professional routine. I have said that he was a self-willed Italianate young man with qualifications far beyond those which the theater could ordinarily attract. I need not describe the steps by which the Court Theater presently became virtually his theater, with Vedrenne in the manager's office. They began with matinées of *Candida,* the expenses of which were guaranteed by a few friends; but the guarantee was not needed: the matinées paid their way. More matinées of my plays followed with Barker as the leading actor; and before long Vedrenne and Barker were in a position to take the theater over from the Shakespearean enthusiast as a full-blown management; and I ceased to write plays for anybody who asked me, and became playwright in ordinary to this new enterprise.

But it is not enough to have a fascinating actor for your heroes: you must also have an interesting actress for your heroine. She dropped from Heaven on us in the person of Lillah McCarthy, who, having learned her business in the course of a tour round the world as the beautiful Mercia in *The Sign of the Cross* after playing Lady Macbeth at the age of sixteen like an immature Mrs. Siddons, burst in on me and demanded a Siddonian part. After one glance at her I handed her *Man and Superman,* and told her she was to create Ann Whitefield in it.

We were now complete. The Court experiment went through with flying colors. Barker, aiming at a National Repertory Theater, with a change of program every night, was determined to test our enterprise to destruction as motor tires are tested, to find out its utmost possibilities. I was equally reckless. Vedrenne, made prudent by a wife and family, was like a man trying to ride two runaway horses simultaneously. Barker worked furiously: he had not only to act, but to produce all the plays except mine, and to find and inspire all the artists whom he drew into the theater to carry out his idea. In the end he had to give up acting and devote himself entirely to producing, or, under all the pressure I could put on him, to writing plays. The Court was abandoned for larger and more central theaters, not always one at a time. The pace grew hotter and hotter; the prestige was immense; but the receipts barely kept us going and left no reserves with which to nurse new authors into new reputations.

At last we were in debt and had to put up the shutters. Having ruined Vedrenne in spite of his remonstrances we could not ask him to pay the debts; and we were bound to clear him without a stain on his character. Barker paid all he possessed; I paid the rest; and so the firm went down with its colors flying, leaving us with a proved certainty that no National Theater in London devoted to the art of the theater at its best can bear the burden of London rents and London rates. Freed from them it might pay its way under a director content to work hard for a modest salary. For the evidence read the book Barker wrote in collaboration with William Archer.

The combination, Lillah-Barker-Shaw, still remained, and was reinforced by Shakespeare. Barker reached the summit of his fame as a producer by restoring Shakespeare to the London stage, where he lingered only in the infamous mutilations of his works by the actor-managers and refreshment bar renters.

But this was done at the cost of an extravagance which could not be sustained. Without Vedrenne to plead for economy Barker was reckless. Lord Howard de Walden came nobly to the rescue financially; and Barker gave him full value artistically, but made ducks and drakes of his heavily taxed spare money.

II

Quite early in this history, however, Lillah and Barker got married. I knew that this was all wrong; that there were no two people on earth less suited to one another; that in the long run their escapade could not stay put. But there was nothing to be done but make the best of it. Certainly, for the moment, it worked very well, and had every air of being a brilliant success. She was an admirable hostess; and her enjoyment of the open air and of traveling made her a most healthy companion for him. He, in spite of the vagabondage of his profession, was not in the least a Bohemian; and the dignity of marriage was quite right for him and good for him. The admirations and adorations the pair excited in the cultured sections of London society could be indulged and gratified in country houses where interesting and brilliant young married couples were welcome. And professionally they were necessary to one another just as I was necessary to them. It actually made for the stability of the combination that they were never really in love with one another, though they had a very good time together. The appalling levity with which actors and actresses marry is a phenomenon much older than Hollywood; and I had no excuse for being surprised and every reason for finding the arrangement a convenient one. Still, I was instinctively dismayed.

My misgivings were finally justified by a domestic catastrophe. When we had tested the possibility of a highbrow repertory theater in London

to the insolvency and winding-up of the Vedrenne-Barker management, Barker, cleaned out financially, went to New York to consider
an offer of the directorship of the new Millionaires' Theater there.
Finding the building unsuitable he turned down the offer, and was
presently overtaken by the 1914–1918 Armageddon and came back
to present himself to me in the guise of a cadet gunner, and later on
(he being obviously wasted as a gunner), as an intelligence officer in a
Sam Browne belt. He looked the part to perfection.

In New York, however, the Italian volcano in him had erupted
unexpectedly and amazingly. He fell madly in love—really madly
in the Italian manner—and my first effective intimation was a demand
that I should, before the end of the week, procure him a divorce, or a
promise of one, from Lillah.

Not yet realizing that I was dealing with a lunatic, I naturally
thought that Lillah was prepared for this, and that they had talked
it out and agreed to it before she left America. As I had never believed in the permanence of their marriage, and thought that a divorce would restore the order of nature in their case and be a very
good thing for both of them, I approached Lillah to arrange the
divorce. I was at once violently undeceived. Lillah was as proud as
ten thousand empresses. The unprepared proposal for a divorce struck
her simply as an insult: a monstrous, incredible, unbearable, un-
pardonable, vulgar insult: something that might happen to common
women but could never happen to her.

I had a difficult time of it; for I at once lost the confidence of both
parties: of Lillah because instead of indignantly repudiating the proposed outrage and renouncing Barker as the infamous author of an
unheard-of act of *lèse majesté,* I was acting as his go-between and
treating the divorce as inevitable and desirable; of Barker, because my
failure to obtain a decree nisi within twenty-four hours showed that
I was Lillah's accomplice in the worst of crimes, that of delaying his
instant remarriage. There were no broken hearts in the business; for
this wonderful pair, who had careered together so picturesquely, and
made such excellent and quite kindly use of the coincidence of their
ages and gifts, had never really cared a rap for one another in the way
of what Shakespeare called the marriage of true minds; so that now,
in the storm raised by the insensate impatience of the one and the
outraged pride of the other, there was no element of remorse or
tenderness, and no point of contact at which they could be brought

to reason. They had literally nothing to say to each other; but they had a good deal to say to me, mostly to the effect that I was betraying them both.

And now it may be asked what business all this was of mine. Well, I had thrown them literally into one another's arms as John Tanner and Ann Whitefield; and I suppose it followed that I must extricate them. I succeeded at last; but I could have done it easily six months sooner if they had been able to escape for a moment from their condition of passionate unreasonableness; and I came out of the conflict much battered from both sides, Barker blaming me for the unnecessary delay, and Lillah for having extorted her consent by arguments that almost amounted to blackmail.

III

Happily the very unreality in their marriage that made the tempest over its dissolution so merciless also cleared the sky very suddenly and completely when it was over. The ending was quite happy. In a prophetic moment in the struggle I had told Lillah that I foresaw her, not as Barker's leading lady to all eternity, but as a handsome chatelaine with a title and a distinguished "honest to God" husband, welcoming a crowd of the best people on the terrace of a beautiful country house. She took this as being in the worst possible taste, her imagination being just then full of a tragic and slaughterous Götter-dämmerung of some kind as the end of Lillah. But it is exactly what has happened to her.

When these twain who worked with me in the glory of their youth settled down handsomely in the dignity of their maturity, I rejoiced in their happiness and leisure.

My part in the divorce had been complicated by the attitude of the lady who had enchanted Barker. This lady was not a private nobody. She was a personage of distinguished talent as a novelist and poetess. Unfortunately for me, she was an American, which meant then that the latest great authors for her were Henry James and Meredith; the final politicians Jefferson and Washington. Socialism was to her simple sedition, and Shaw a most undesirable acquaintance for her beloved. Nothing I could do could conciliate her to maintain our alliance. After their retirement to Devon and then to Paris he became a highly respectable professor. Besides his *Prefaces to Shakespeare*, he wrote two more plays, and collaborated with his wife in translations from the Spanish. Virtually we never met again. Our old sympathy remained unaltered and unalterable; but he never dared to show it; and I could not intrude where I was not welcome. He had well earned a prosperous and happy retirement after his long service and leadership in the vanguard. I hope his widow has come to see that the wild oats he sowed with me have produced a better harvest than she foresaw, and that his original contributions to our dramatic literature are treasures to be preserved, not compromising documents to be destroyed.

In what has been written lately, too much has been said of him as a producer, too little as an actor, and much too little as an author. Producing kills acting: an actor's part dies if he is watching the others critically. You cannot conduct an orchestra and play the drums at the same concert. As long as I was producing and Barker acting all was well: he acted beautifully; and I took care to make the most of him. But I kept pressing for the enlistment of other authors, and urging Barker to write, which he did slowly, repeatedly protesting that as it was not his profession, and was mine, it was easy for me and very hard for him. Galsworthy, Masefield, Laurence Housman, and St. John Hankin (for the moment forgotten or neglected, but a master of serious comedy) came into our repertory, financed at first by revivals of my potboiler, Barker's *You Never Can Tell*. His production of his own plays and Galsworthy's was exquisite: their styles were perfectly sympathetic, whereas his style and taste were as different from mine as Debussy's from Verdi's. With Shakespeare and with me he was not always at his happiest and best; but he was absolutely faithful to the plays and would not cut a line to please himself; and the plays pulled him through with the bits that suited him enchanting and the scenery and dressing perfect.

He adopted my technique of production, but was utterly inconsiderate in its practice. I warned him again and again that the end of it would be a drastic Factory Act regulating the hours of rehearsals as strictly as the hours of weaving in a cotton mill. But he would not leave off until the unfortunate company had lost their last trains and busses and he had tired himself beyond human powers of maintaining the intense vigilance and freshness which first-rate production, or indeed any production, demands. I myself put a limit of such attention at three hours or less between breakfast and lunch, and absolutely refused to spend more time than that in the theater.

His only other fault was to suppress his actors when they pulled out all their stops and declaimed as Shakespeare should be declaimed. They either underacted, or were afraid to act at all lest they should be accused of ranting or being "hams." I once asked a violinist of great experience as an orchestral leader, William Reed (Elgar's Billy Reed), whether he agreed with Wagner that the first duty of a conductor is to give the right time to the band. "No," said he; "the first duty of a conductor is to let the band play." I still want the Factory Act, and hold with Billy that the perfect producer lets his actors act, and is their helper at need and not their dictator. The hint is meant specially for producers who have begun as actors. They are the first instead of the last to forget it.

Gertrude Stein: A Self-Portrait

by KATHERINE ANNE PORTER

DECEMBER, 1947

In a letter to the Editor about this article, Katherine Anne Porter said of Miss Stein: "She has had, I realize, a horrid fascination for me, really horrid, for I have a horror of her kind of mind and being; she was one of the blights and symptoms of her very sick times." Probably Miss Porter's best-known books are Pale Horse, Pale Rider, Flowering Judas, *and* The Leaning Tower. *Besides being a distinguished writer of fiction, she has been a free-lance journalist, a newspaper reporter, and, of course, a critic. She was born in Indian Creek, Texas, in 1894.*

. . . I want to say that just today I met Miss Hennessy and she was carrying, she did not have it with her, but she usually carried a wooden umbrella. This wooden umbrella is carved out of wood and looks like a real one even to the little button and the rubber string that holds it together. It is all right except when it rains. When it rains it does not open and Miss Hennessy looks a little foolish but she does not mind because it is after all the only wooden umbrella in Paris. And even if there were lots of others it would not make any difference.

Gertrude Stein: *Everybody's Autobiography*

When Kahnweiler the picture dealer told Miss Stein that Picasso had stopped painting and had taken to writing poetry, she confessed that she had "a funny feeling" because "things belonged to you and writing belonged to me. I know writing belongs to me, I am quite certain," but still it was a blow. ". . . No matter how certain you are about anything belonging to you if you hear that somebody says it belongs to them it gives you a funny feeling."

Later she buttonholed Picasso at Kahnweiler's gallery, shook him, kissed him, lectured him, told him that his poetry was worse than bad, it was offensive as a Cocteau drawing and in much the same way, it was unbecoming. He defended himself by reminding her that she had said he was an extraordinary person, and he believed an extraordinary person should be able to do anything. She said that to her it was a repellent sight when a person who could do one thing well dropped it for something else he could not do at all. Convinced, or defeated, he promised to give back writing to its natural owner.

Writing was no doubt the dearest of Miss Stein's possessions, but it was not the only one. The pavilion atelier in rue de Fleurus was a catch-all of beings and created objects, and everything she looked upon was hers in more than the usual sense. Her weighty numerous divans and armchairs covered with dark, new-looking horsehair; her dogs, Basket and Pépé, conspicuous, special, afflicted as neurotic children; her clutter of small tables each with its own clutter of perhaps valuable but certainly treasured objects; her Alice B. Toklas; her visitors; and finally, ranging the walls from floor to ceiling, giving the impression that they were hung three deep, elbowing each other, canceling each other's best effects in the jealous way of pictures, was her celebrated collection of paintings by her collection of celebrated painters. These were everybody of her time whom Miss Stein elected for her own, from her idol Picasso (kidnaped bodily from brother Leo, who saw him first) to miniscule Sir Francis Rose, who seems to have appealed to the pixy in her.

Yet the vaguely lighted room where things accumulated, where they appeared to have moved in under a compulsion to be possessed once for all by someone who knew how to take hold firmly, gave no impression of disorder. On the contrary, an air of solid comfort, of inordinate sobriety and permanence, of unadventurous middle-class domesticity—respectability is the word, at last—settled around the shoulders of the guest like a Paisley shawl, a borrowed shawl of course, something to be worn and admired for a moment and handed back to the owner. Miss Stein herself sat there in full possession of herself, the scene, the spectators, wearing thick no-colored shapeless woolen clothes and honest woolen stockings knitted for her by Miss Toklas, looking extremely like a handsome old Jewish patriarch who had backslid and shaved off his beard.

Surrounded by her listeners, she talked in a slow circle in her deep voice, the word "perception" occurring again and again and yet again like the brass ring the children snatch for as their hobby horses whirl by. She was in fact at one period surrounded by snatching children, the literary young, a good many of them American, between two wars in a falling world. Roughly they were divided into two parties: those who were full of an active, pragmatic unbelief, and those who searched their own vitals and fished up strange horrors in the style of *transition*. The first had discovered that honor is only a word, and an embarrassing one, because it was supposed to mean something wonderful and was now exposed as meaning nothing at all. For them, nothing worked except sex and alcohol and pulling apart their lamentable Midwestern upbringings and scattering the pieces. Some of these announced that they wished their writings to be as free from literature as if they had never read a book, as indeed too many of them had not up to the time. The *transition* tone was even more sinister, for though it was supposed to be the vanguard of international experimental thought, its real voice was hoarse, anxious, corrupted mysticism speaking in a thick German accent. The editor, Eugene Jolas, had been born in the eternally disputed land of Alsace, bilingual in irreconcilable tongues, French and German, and he spoke both and English besides with a foreign accent. He had no mother tongue, nor even a country, and so he fought the idea of both, but his deepest self was German: he issued frantic manifestoes demanding that language be reduced to something he could master, crying aloud in "defense of the hallucinative forces," the exploding of the verb, the "occult hypnosis of language," "chthonian grammar"; reason he hated, and defended the voice of the blood, the disintegration of syntax—with a special grudge against English—preaching like an American Methodist evangelist in the wilderness for "the use of a language which is a mantic instrument, and which does not hesitate to adopt a revolutionary attitude toward word syntax, going even so far as to invent a hermetic language, if necessary." The final aim was "the illumination of a collective reality and a totalistic universe." Meanwhile Joyce, a man with a mother-tongue if ever there was one, and a master of languages, was mixing them in strange new forms to the delight and enrichment of language for good and all.

Miss Stein had no problems: she simply exploded a verb as if it were a soap bubble, used chthonian grammar long before she heard it named (and she would have scorned to name it), was a born adept in occult hypnosis of language without even trying. Serious young men who were having a hard time learning to write realized with relief that there was nothing at all to it if you just relaxed and put down the first thing that came into your head. She gave them a romantic name, the Lost Generation, and a remarkable number of them tried earnestly if unsuccessfully to live up to it. A few of them were really lost, and disappeared, but others had just painted themselves into a very crowded corner. She laid a cooling hand upon her agitated brows and asked with variations, What did it matter? There were only a few geniuses, after all, among which she was one, only the things a genius said made any difference, the rest was "just there," and so she disposed of all the dark questions of life, art, human relations, and death, even eternity, even God, with perfect Stein logic, bringing the scene again into its proper focus, upon herself.

Some of the young men went away, read a book, began thinking things over, and became the best writers of their time. Humanly, shamefacedly, they then jeered at their former admiration, and a few even made the tactical error of quarreling with her. She enjoyed their discipleship while it lasted, and dismissed them from existence when it ended. It is easy to see what tremendous vitality and direction there were in the arts all over the world; for not everything was happening only in France, for life was generated in many a noisy seething confusion in many countries. Little by little the legitimate line of succession appeared, the survivors emerged each with his own shape and meaning, the young vanguard became the Old Masters and even old hat.

In the meantime our heroine went on talking, vocally or on paper, and in that slow swarm of words, out of the long drone and mutter and stammer of her lifetime monologue, often there emerged a phrase of ancient native independent wisdom, for she had a shrewd deep knowledge of the commoner human motives. Her judgments were neither moral nor intellectual, and least of all aesthetic, indeed they were not even judgments, but simply her description from observation of acts, words, appearances giving her view; limited, personal in the extreme, prejudiced without qualification, based on assumptions founded in the void of pure unreason. For example, French notaries' sons have always something strange about them—look at Jean Cocteau. The Spaniard has a natural center of ignorance, all except Juan Gris. On the other hand, Dali had not only the natural Spanish center of ignorance, but still another variety, quite malignant, of his own. Preachers' sons do not turn out like other people—E. E. Cummings, just for one. Painters are always little short round men— Picasso and a crowd of them. And then she puts her finger lightly on an American peculiarity of our time: ". . . so perhaps they are right the Americans in being more interested in you than in the work you have done, although they would not be interested in you if you had not done the work you had done." And she remarked once to her publisher that she was famous in America not for her work that people understood but for that which they did not understand. That was the kind of thing she could see through at a glance.

It was not that she was opposed to ideas, but that she was not interested in anybody's ideas but her own, except as material to put down on her endless flood of pages. Like writing, opinion also belonged to Miss Stein, and nothing annoyed her more—she was easily angered about all sorts of things—than for anyone not a genius or who had no reputation that she respected, to appear to be thinking in her presence. Of all those GI's who swarmed about her in her last days, if anyone showed any fight at all, any tendency to question her pronouncements, she smacked him down like a careful grandmother, for his own good. Her GI heroes Brewsie and Willie are surely as near to talking zombies as anything ever seen in a book, and she loved, not them, but their essential zombiness.

Like all talkers, she thought other people talked too much, and there is recorded only one instance of someone getting the drop on her—who else but Alfred Stieglitz? She sat through a whole session at their first meeting without uttering one word, a feat which he mentioned with surprised approval. If we knew nothing more of Stieglitz than this we would know he was a great talker. She thought that the most distressing sound was that of the human voice, other people's voices, "as the hoot owl is almost the best sound," but in spite of this she listened quite a lot. When she was out walking the dogs, if workmen were tearing up the streets she would ask them what they were doing and what they would be doing next. She only stopped to break the monotony of walking, but she remembered their answers. When a man passed making up a bitter little song against her dog and his conduct vis-à-vis lamp posts and house walls, she put it all down, and it is wonderfully good reporting. Wise or silly or nothing at all, down everything goes on the page with the air of everything being equal, unimportant in itself, important because it happened to her and she was writing about it.

II

She had not always been exactly there, exactly that. There had been many phases, all in consistent character, each giving way in turn for the next, of her portentous being. Ford Madox Ford described her, in earlier Paris days, as trundling through the streets in her high-wheeled American car, being a spectacle and being herself at the same time. And this may have been near the time of Man Ray's photograph of her, wearing a kind of monk's robe, her poll clipped, her granite front and fine eyes displayed at their best period.

Before that, she was a youngish stout woman, not ever really young, with a heavy shrewd face between a hard round pompadour and a round lace collar, looking more or less like Picasso's earliest portrait of her. What saved her then from a good honest husband, probably a stockbroker, and a houseful of children? The answer must be that her envelope was a tricky disguise of Nature, that she was of the company of Amazons which nineteenth-century America produced among its many prodigies: not-men, not-women, answerable to no function in either sex, whose careers were carried on, and how successfully, in whatever field they chose: they were educators, writers, editors, politicians, artists, world travelers, and international hostesses, who lived in public and by the public and played out their self-assumed, self-created roles in such masterly freedom as only a few earlier medieval queens had equaled. Freedom to them meant precisely freedom from men and their stuffy rules for women. They usurped with a high hand the traditional masculine privileges of movement, choice, and the use of direct, personal power. They were few in number and they were not only to be found in America, and Miss Stein belonged with them, no doubt of it, in spite of a certain temperamental passivity which was Oriental, not feminine. With the top of her brain she was a modern girl, a New Woman, interested in scientific experiment, historical research, the rational view; for a time she was even a medical student, but she could not deceive herself for long. Even during her four years at Radcliffe, where the crisp theories of higher education battled with the womb-shaped female mind (and they always afterward seemed foolish to her at Radcliffe) she worried and worried, for worrying and thinking were synonyms to her, about the meaning of the universe, the riddle of human life, about time and its terrible habit of passing, God, death, eternity, and she felt very lonely in the awful singularity of her confusions. Added to this, history taught her that whole civilizations die and disappear utterly, "and now it happens again," and it gave her a great fright. She was sometimes frightened afterward, "but now well being frightened is something less frightening than it was," but her ambiguous mind faced away from speculation. Having discovered with relief that all knowledge was not her province, she accepted rightly, she said, every superstition. To be in the hands of fate, of magic, of the daemonic forces, what freedom it gave her not to decide, not to act, not to accept any responsibility for anything—one held the pen and let the mind wander. One sat down and somebody did everything for one.

Still earlier she was a plump solemn little girl abundantly upholstered in good clothes, who spent her allowance on the work of Shelley, Thackeray, and George Eliot in fancy bindings, for she loved reading and *Clarissa Harlowe* was once her favorite novel. These early passions exhausted her; in later life she swam in the relaxing bath of detective and murder mysteries, because she liked somebody being dead in a story, and of them all Dashiell Hammett killed them off most to her taste. Her first experience of the real death of somebody had taught her that it could be pleasant for her too. "One morning we could not wake our father." This was in East Oakland, California. "Leo climbed in by the window and called out that he was dead in his bed and he was." It seems to have been the first thing he ever did of which his children, all five of them, approved. Miss Stein declared plainly they none of them liked him at all: "As I say, fathers are depressing but our family had one," she confessed, and conveys the notion that he was a bore of the nagging, petty sort, the kind that worries himself and others into the grave.

Considering her tepid, sluggish nature, really sluggish like something eating its way through a leaf, Miss Stein could grow quite ani-

mated on the subject of her early family life, and some of her stories are
as pretty and innocent as lizards running over tombstones on a hot
day in Maryland. It was a solid, getting-on sort of middle-class Jewish
family of Austrian origin, Keyser on one side, Stein on the other: and
the Keysers came to Baltimore about 1820. All branches of the family
produced their individual eccentrics—there was even an uncle who
believed in the Single Tax—but they were united in their solid understanding of the value of money as the basis of a firm stance in this
world. There were incomes, governesses, spending money, guardians
appointed when parents died, and Miss Stein was fascinated from
childhood with stories about how people earned their first dollar. When,
rather late, she actually earned some dollars herself by writing, it
changed her entire viewpoint about the value of her work and of her
own personality. It came to her as revelation that the only difference
between men and four-footed animals is that men can count, and
when they count, they like best to count money. In her first satisfaction at finding she had a commercial value, she went on a brief binge
of spending money just for the fun of it. But she really knew better.
Among the five or six of the seven deadly sins which she practiced
with increasing facility and advocated as virtues, avarice became her
favorite. Americans in general she found to be rather childish about
money: they spent it or gave it away and enjoyed it wastefully with no
sense of its fierce latent power. "It is hard to be a miser, a real miser,
they are as rare as geniuses it takes the same kind of thing to make one,
that is time must not exist for them. . . . There must be a reality
that has nothing to do with the passing of time. I have it and so had
Hetty Green . . ." and she found only one of the younger generation
in America, a young man named Jay Laughlin, who had, she wrote,
praising him, avarice to that point of genius which makes the true
miser. She made a very true distinction between avarice, the love of
getting and keeping, and love of money, the love of making and
spending. There is a third love, the love of turning a penny by ruse,
and this was illustrated by brother Michael, who once grew a beard to
make himself look old enough to pass for a G.A.R. veteran, and so
disguised he got a cut-rate railway fare for a visit home during a
G.A.R. rally, though all the men of his family fought on the Confederate side.

The question of money and of genius rose simultaneously with the
cheerful state of complete orphanhood. Her mother disappeared early

after a long illness, leaving her little nest of vipers probably without regret, for vipers Miss Stein shows them to have been in the most Biblical sense. They missed their mother chiefly because she had acted as a buffer between them and their father, and also served to keep them out of each other's hair. Sister Bertha and Brother Simon were simple-minded by family standards, whatever they were, Brother Leo had already started being a genius without any regard for the true situation, and after the death of their father, Brother Michael was quite simply elected to be the Goat. He had inherited the family hatred of responsibility—from their mother, Miss Stein believed, but not quite enough to save him. He became guardian, caretaker, business manager, handy-man, who finally wangled incomes for all of them, and set them free from money and from each other. It is pleasant to know he was a very thorny martyr who did a great deal of resentful lecturing about economy, stamping and shouting around the house with threats to throw the whole business over and let them fend for themselves if they could not treat him with more consideration. With flattery and persuasion they would cluster around and get him back on the rails, for his destiny was to be useful to genius, that is, to Miss Stein.

She had been much attached to her brother Leo, in childhood they were twin souls. He was two years older and a boy, and she had learned from Clarissa Harlowe's uncle's letter that older brothers are superior to younger sisters, or any boy to any girl in fact. Though she bowed to this doctrine as long as it was convenient, she never allowed it to get in her way. She followed her brother's advice more or less, and in turn he waited on her and humored and defended her when she was a selfish lazy little girl. Later he made a charming traveling companion who naturally, being older and a man, looked after all the boring details of life and smoothed his sister's path everywhere. Still, she could not remember his face when he was absent, and once was very nervous when she went to meet him on a journey, for fear she might not recognize him. The one thing wrong all this time was their recurring quarrel about who was the genius of the two, for each had assumed the title and neither believed for a moment there was room for more than one in the family. By way of proving himself, brother Leo took the pavilion and atelier in the rue de Fleurus, installed himself well, and began trying hard to paint. Miss Stein, seeing all so cozy, moved in on him and sat down and began to write—no question of trying. "To try is to die," became one of her several hundred rhyming aphorisms designed to settle all conceivable arguments; after a time, no doubt overwhelmed by the solid negative force of that massive will and presence, her brother moved out and took the atelier next door, and went on being useful to his sister, and trying to paint.

But he also went on insisting tactlessly that he, and not she, was the born genius; and this was one of the real differences between them, that he attacked on the subject and was uneasy, and could not rest, while his sister reasoned with him patiently at first defending her title, regretting she could not share it. Insist, argue, upset himself and her as much as he liked, she simply, quietly knew with a Messianic revelation that she was not only a genius, but *the* genius, and sometimes, she was certain, one of not more than half a dozen real ones in the world. During all her life, whenever Miss Stein got low in her mind about anything, she could always find consolation in this beautiful knowledge of being a born genius, and her brother's contentiousness finally began to look like treason to her. She could not forgive him for disputing her indivisible right to her natural property, genius, on which all her other rights of possession were founded. It shook her—she worried about her work. She had begun her long career of describing "how every one who ever lived eats and drinks and loves and sleeps and talks and walks and wakes and forgets and quarrels and likes and dislikes and works and sits,"—everybody's autobiography, in fact, for she had taken upon herself the immense task of explaining everybody to himself, of telling him all he needed to know about life, and she simply could not have brother Leo hanging around the edges of this grandiose scheme pinching off bits and holding them up to the light. By and by, too, she had Alice B. Toklas to do everything for her. So she and her brother drifted apart, but gradually, like one of Miss Stein's paragraphs. The separation became so complete that once, on meeting her brother unexpectedly, she was so taken by surprise she bowed to him, and afterward wrote a long poem about it in which her total confusion of mind and feeling was expressed with total incoherence: for once, form, matter and style stuttering and stammering and wallowing along together with the agitated harmony of roiling entrails.

III

There are the tones of sloth, of that boredom which is a low-pressure despair, of monotony, of obsession, in this portrait; she went walking out of boredom, she could drive a car, talk, write, but anything else made her nervous. People who were doing anything annoyed her: to be doing nothing, she thought, was more interesting than to be doing something. The air of deathly solitude surrounded her; yet the parade of names in her book would easily fill several printed pages, all with faces attached which she could see were quite different from each other, all talking, each taking his own name and person for granted—a thing she could never understand. Yet she could see what they were doing and could remember what they said. She only listened attentively to Picasso—for whose sake she would crack almost any head in sight—so she half-agreed when he said Picabia was the worst painter of all; but still, found herself drawn to Picabia because his name was Francis. She had discovered that men named Francis were always elegant, and though they might not know anything else, they always knew about themselves. This would remind her that she had never found out who she was. Again and again she would doubt her own identity, and that of everyone else. When she worried about this aloud to Alice B. Toklas, saying she believed it impossible for anyone ever to be certain who he was, Alice B. Toklas made, in context, the most inspired remark in the whole book. "It depends on who you are," she said, and you might think that would have ended the business. Not at all.

These deep-set, chronic fears led her to a good deal of quarreling, for when she quarreled she seems to have felt more real. She mentions quarrels with Max Jacobs, Francis Rose, with Dali, with Picabia, with Picasso, with Virgil Thomson, with Braque, with Breton, and how many others, though she rarely says just why they quarreled or how they made it up. Almost nobody went away and stayed, and the awful inertia of habit in friendships oppressed her. She was sometimes discouraged at the prospect of having to go on seeing certain persons to the end, merely because she had once seen them. The world seemed smaller every day, swarming with people perpetually in movement, full of restless notions which, once examined by her, were inevitably proved to be fallacious, or at least entirely useless. She found that she could best get rid of them by putting them in a book. "That is very funny if you write about any one they do not exist any more, for you, so why see them again. Anyway, that is the way I am."

But as she wrote a book and disposed of one horde, another came on, and worried her afresh, discussing their ludicrous solemn topics, trying to understand things, and being unhappy about it. When Picasso was fretful because she argued with Dali and not with him, she explained that "one discusses things with stupid people but not with sensible ones." Her true grudge against intelligent people was that they talked "as if they were getting ready to change something." Change belonged to Miss Stein, and the duty of the world was to stand still so that she could move about in it comfortably. Her top flight of reasoning on the subject of intelligence ran as follows: "The most actively war-like nations could always convince the pacifists to become pro-German. That is because pacifists were such intelligent beings they could follow what any one is saying. If you follow what any one is saying then you are a pacifist you are a pro-German . . . therefore understanding is a very dull occupation."

Intellectuals, she said, always wanted to change things because they had an unhappy childhood. "Well, I never had an unhappy childhood, what is the use of having an unhappy anything?" Léon Blum, then Premier of France, had had an unhappy childhood, and she inclined to the theory that the political uneasiness of France could be traced to this fact.

There was not, of course, going to be another war (this was in 1937!), but if there was, there *would* be, naturally; and she never tired of repeating that dancing and war are the same thing "because both are forward and back," while revolution, on the contrary, is up and down, which is why it gets nowhere. Sovietism was even then going rapidly out of fashion in her circles, because they had discovered that it is very conservative, even if the Communists do not think so. Anarchists, being rarities, did not go out of fashion so easily. The most interesting thing that ever happened to America was the Civil War; but General Lee was severely to be blamed for leading his country into that war, just the same, because he must have known they could not win; and to her, it was absurd that anyone should join battle in defense of a principle in face of certain defeat. For practical purposes, honor was not even a word. Still it was an exciting war and gave an interest to America which that country would never have had without it. "If you win you do not lose and if you lose you do not win." Even as she was writing these winged words, the Spanish Civil War, the Republicans against the Franco-Fascists, kept obtruding itself. And why? "Not because it is a revolution, but because I know so well the places they are mentioning and the things there they are destroying." When she was little in Oakland, California, she loved the big, nice American fires that had "so many horses and firemen to attend them," and when she was older, she found that floods, for one thing, always read worse in the papers than they really are; besides how can you care much about what is going on if you don't see it or know the people? For this reason she had Santa Teresa being indifferent to faraway Chinese while she was founding convents in Spain. William Seabrook came to see her to find out if she was as interesting as her books. She told him she was, and he discovered black magic in the paintings of Sir Francis Rose. And when she asked Dashiell Hammett why so many young men authors were writing novels about tender young male heroines instead of the traditional female ones, he explained that it was because as women grew more and more self-confident, men lost confidence in themselves, and turned to each other, or became their own subjects for fiction. This, or something else, reminded her several times that she could not write a novel, therefore no one could any more, and no one should waste time trying.

Somehow by such roundabouts we arrive at the important, the critical event in all this eventful history. Success. Success in this world, here and now, was what Miss Stein wanted. She knew just what it was, how it should look and feel, how much it should weigh and what it was worth over the counter. It was not enough to be a genius if you had to go on supporting your art on a private income. To be the center of a recondite literary cult, to be surrounded by listeners and imitators and seekers, to be mentioned in the same breath with James Joyce, and to have turned out bales of titles by merely writing a half-hour each day: she had all that, and what did it amount to? There was a great deal more and she must have it. As to her history of the human race, she confessed: "I have always been bothered . . . but mostly . . . because after all I do as simply as it can, as commonplacely as it can say, what everybody can and does do; I never know what they can do, I really do not know what they are, I do not think that any one can think because if they do, then who is who?"

It was high time for a change, and yet it occurred at hazard. If there had not been a beautiful season in October and part of November 1932, permitting Miss Stein to spend that season quietly in her country house, the *Autobiography of Alice B. Toklas* might never have been written. But it was written, and Miss Stein became a best-seller in America; she made real money. With Miss Toklas, she had a thrilling tour of the United States and found crowds of people eager to see her and listen to her. And at last she got what she had really wanted all along: to be published in the *Atlantic Monthly* and the *Saturday Evening Post*.

Now she had everything, or nearly. For a while she was afraid to write any more, for fear her latest efforts would not please her public. She had never learned who she was, and yet suddenly she had become somebody else. "You are you because your little dog knows you, but when your public knows you and does not want to pay you, and when your public knows you and does want to pay you, you are not the same you."

This would be of course the proper moment to take leave, as our heroine adds at last a golden flick of light to her self-portrait. "Anyway, I was a celebrity." The practical result was that she could no longer live on her income. But she and Alice B. Toklas moved into an apartment once occupied by Queen Christina of Sweden, and they began going out more, and seeing even more people, and talking, and Miss Stein settled every question as it came up, more and more. But who wants to read about success? It is the early struggle which makes a good story.

IV

She and Alice B. Toklas enjoyed both the wars. The first one especially being a lark with almost no one getting killed where you could see, and it ended so nicely too, without changing anything. The second was rather more serious. She lived safely enough in Bilignin throughout the German occupation, and there is a pretty story that the whole village conspired to keep her presence secret. She had been a citizen of the world in the best European tradition; for though America was her native land, she had to live in Europe because she felt at home there. In the old days people paid little attention to wars, fought as they were out of sight by professional soldiers. She had always liked the notion, too, of the gradual Orientalization of the West, the peaceful penetration of the East into European culture. It had been going on a great while, and all Western geniuses worth mentioning were Orientals: look at Picasso, look at Einstein. Russians are Tartars, Spaniards are Saracens—had not all great twentieth-century painting been Spanish? And her cheerful conclusion was, that "Einstein was the creative philosophic mind of the century, and I have been the creative literary mind of the century also, with the Oriental mixing with the European." She added, as a casual afterthought, "Perhaps Europe is finished."

That was in 1938, and she could not be expected to know that war was near. They had only been sounding practice *alertes* in Paris against expected German bombers since 1935. She spoke out of her natural frivolity and did not mean it. She liked to prophesy, but warned her hearers that her prophecies never came out right, usually the very opposite, and no matter what happened, she was always surprised. She was surprised again: as the nations of Europe fell, and the Germans came again over the frontiers of France for the third time in three generations, the earth shook under her own feet, and not somebody else's. It made an astonishing difference. Something mysterious touched her in her old age. She got a fright, and this time not for ancient vanished civilizations, but for this civilization, this moment; and she was quite thrilled with relief and gay when the American Army finally came in, and the Germans were gone. She did not in the least know why the Germans had come, but they were gone, and so far as she could see, the American Army had chased them out. She remembered with positive spread-eagle patriotism that America was her native land. At last America itself belonged to Miss Stein, and she claimed it, in a formal published address to other Americans. Anxiously she urged them to stay rich, to be powerful and learn how to use power, not to waste themselves; for the first time she used the word "spiritual." Ours was a spiritual as well as a material fight; Lincoln's great lucid words about government of the people by the people for the people suddenly sounded like a trumpet through her stammering confession of faith, she wanted nothing now to stand between her and her newly discovered country. By great good luck she was born on the winning side and she was going to stay there. And we were not to forget about money as the source of power; "Remember the depression, don't be afraid to look it in the face and find out the reason why, if you don't find out the reason why you'll go poor and my God, how I would hate to have my native land go poor."

The mind so long shapeless and undisciplined could not now express any knowledge out of its long willful ignorance. But the heart spoke its crude urgent language. She had liked the doughboys in the other war well enough, but this time she fell in love with the whole American Army below the rank of lieutenant. She "breathed, ate, drank, lived GI's," she told them, and inscribed numberless photographs for them, and asked them all to come back again. After her flight over Germany in an American bomber, she wrote about how, so often, she would stand staring into the sky watching American war planes going over, longing to be up there again with her new loves, in the safe, solid air. She murmured, "Bless them, bless them." She had been impatient with many of them who had still been naïve enough to believe they were fighting against an evil idea that threatened everybody; some of them actually were simple enough to say they had been—or believed they had been—fighting for democratic government. "What difference does it make what kind of government you have?" she would ask. "All governments are alike. Just remember you won the war." But still, at the end, she warned them to have courage and not be just yes or no men. And she said, "Bless them, bless them."

It was the strangest thing, as if the wooden umbrella feeling the rain had tried to forsake its substance and take on the nature of its form; and was struggling slowly, slowly, much too late, to unfold.

Art for Art's Sake

by E. M. FORSTER

AUGUST, 1949

This brilliant short statement by the author of A Passage to India *is far more than just another argument in the long debate on Art for Art's Sake. It also takes up the question of order in the world—which society and political institutions have never achieved—and it tells how the artist will always be an outsider in the society to which he has been born. Novelist, essayist, and critic, Mr. Forster, a Briton, was born in 1879 and educated at Tonbridge and at King's College, Cambridge.*

I believe in art for art's sake. It is, as you know, an unfashionable belief, and some of my statements must be of the nature of an apology. Fifty years ago I should have faced you with more confidence. A writer or a speaker who chose "Art for Art's Sake" for his theme fifty years ago could be sure of being in the swim, and could feel so confident of success that he sometimes dressed himself in aesthetic costumes suitable to the occasion—in an embroidered dressing gown, perhaps, or a blue velvet suit with a Lord Fauntleroy collar; or a toga, or a kimono, and carried a poppy or a lily or a long peacock's feather in his medieval hand. Times have changed. Not thus can I present either myself or my theme today. My aim rather is to ask you quietly to reconsider for a few minutes a phrase which has been much misused and much abused, but which has, I believe, great importance for us—has, indeed, eternal importance.

Now we can easily dismiss those peacock's feathers and other affectations—they are but trifles—but I want also to dismiss a more dangerous heresy, namely the silly idea that only art matters, an idea which has somehow got mixed up with the idea of art for art's sake, and has helped to discredit it. Many things, besides art, matter. It is merely one of the things that matter, and high though the claims are that I make for it, I want to keep them in proportion. No one can spend his or her life entirely in the creation or the appreciation of masterpieces. Man lives, and ought to live, in a complex world, full of conflicting claims, and if we simplified them down into the aesthetic he would be sterilized. Art for art's sake does not mean that only art matters, and I would also like to order out such phrases as "The Life of Art," "Living for Art," and even, "Art's High Mission." They confuse and mislead.

What does the phrase mean? Instead of generalizing, let us take a specific instance—Shakespeare's *Macbeth*, for example, and pronounce the words, *"Macbeth* for *Macbeth's* sake." What does that mean? Well, the play has several aspects—it is educational, it teaches us something about legendary Scotland, something about Jacobean England, and a good deal about human nature and its perils. We can study its origins, and study and enjoy its dramatic technique and the music of its diction, as Edith Sitwell has. All that is true. But *Macbeth* is furthermore a world of its own, created by Shakespeare and existing in virtue of its own poetry. It is in this aspect *Macbeth* for *Macbeth's* sake, and that is what I intend by the phrase "art for art's sake." A work of art—whatever else it may be—is a self-contained entity, with a life of its own imposed on it by its creator. It has internal order. It may have external form. That is how we recognize it.

Take for another example that picture of Seurat's which I saw two years ago in Chicago—*"La Grande Jatte."* Here again there is much to study and to enjoy: the pointillism, the charming face of the seated girl, the nineteenth-century Parisian Sunday sunlight, the sense of motion in immobility. But here again there is something more; *"La Grande Jatte"* forms a world of its own, created by Seurat and existing by virtue of its own poetry: *"La Grande Jatte" pour "La Grande Jatte"*: *l'art pour l'art*. Like *Macbeth* it has internal order and internal life.

It is to the conception of order that I would now turn. This is important to my argument, and I want to make a digression, and glance at order in daily life, before I come to order in art.

In the world of daily life, the world which we perforce inhabit, there is much talk about order, particularly from statesmen and politicians. They tend, however, to confuse order with orders, just as they confuse creation with regulations. Order, I suggest, is something evolved from within, not something imposed from without; it is an internal stability, a vital harmony, and, in the social and political category, it has never existed except for the convenience of historians. Viewed realistically, the past is really a series of *dis*orders, succeeding one another by discoverable laws, no doubt, and certainly marked by an increasing growth of human interference, but disorders all the same. So that, speaking as a writer, what I hope for today is for disorder which will be more favorable to artists than is the present one, and which will provide them with fuller inspirations and better material conditions. It will not last—nothing lasts—but there have been some advantageous disorders in the past—for instance, in ancient Athens, in Renaissance Italy, eighteenth-century France, periods in China and Persia—and we may do something to accelerate the next one. But let us not again fix our hearts where true joys are not to be found. We were promised a new order after the First World War through the League of Nations. It did not come, nor have I faith in present promises, by whomsoever endorsed. The implacable offensive of Science forbids. We cannot reach social and political stability for the reason that we continue to make scientific discoveries and to apply them, and thus to destroy the arrangements which were based on more elementary discoveries. If Science would discover rather than apply—if, in other words, men were more interested in knowledge than in power—mankind would be in a far safer position, the stability statesmen talk about would be a possibility, there could be a new order based on vital harmony, and the earthly millennium might approach. But Science shows no sign of doing this: she gave us the internal combustion engine, and before we had digested and assimilated it with terrible pains into our social system, she harnessed the atom, and destroyed any new order that seemed to be evolving. How can man get into harmony with his surroundings when he is constantly altering them? The future of our race is, in this direction, more unpleasant than we care to admit, and it has sometimes seemed to me that its best chance lies through apathy, uninventiveness, and inertia. Universal exhaustion might promote that Change of Heart which is at present so briskly recommended from a thousand pulpits. Universal exhaustion would certainly be a new experience. The human race has never undergone it, and is still too perky to admit that it may be coming and might result in a sprouting of new growth through the decay.

I must not pursue these speculations any further—they lead me too far from my terms of reference and maybe from yours. But I do want to emphasize that order in daily life and in history, order in the social and political category, is unattainable under our present psychology.

Where is it attainable? Not in the astronomical category, where it was for many years enthroned. The heavens and the earth have become terribly alike since Einstein. No longer can we find a reassuring contrast to chaos in the night sky and look up with George Meredith to the stars, the army of unalterable law, or listen for the music of the spheres. Order is not there. In the entire universe there seem to be only two possibilities for it. The first of them—which again lies outside my terms of reference—is the divine order, the mystic harmony, which according to all religions is available for those who can contemplate it. We must admit its possibility, on the evidence of the adepts, and we must believe them when they say that it is attained, if attainable, by prayer. "O thou who changest not, abide with me," said one of its poets. *"Ordina questo amor, o tu che m'ami,"* said another: "Set love in order thou who lovest me." The existence of a divine order, though it cannot be tested, has never been disproved.

The second possibility for order lies in the aesthetic category, which is my subject here: the order which an artist can create in his own work, and to that we must now return. A work of art, we are all agreed, is a unique product. But why? It is unique not because it is clever or noble or beautiful or enlightened or original or sincere or idealistic or useful or educational—it may embody any of those qualities—but because it is the only material object in the universe which may possess internal harmony. All the others have been pressed into shape from outside, and when their mold is removed they collapse. The work of art stands up by itself, and nothing else does. It achieves something which has often been promised by society, but always delusively. Ancient Athens made a mess—but the *Antigone* stands up. Renaissance Rome made a mess—but the ceiling of the Sistine got painted. James I made a mess—but there was *Macbeth*. Louis XIV—but there was *Phèdre*. Art for art's sake? I should just think so, and more so than ever at the present time. It is the one orderly product which our muddling race has produced. It is the cry of a thousand sentinels, the echo from a thousand labyrinths; it is the lighthouse which cannot be hidden: *c'est le meilleur témoignage que nous puissions donner de notre dignité. Antigone* for *Antigone's* sake, *Macbeth* for *Macbeth's*, "La Grande Jatte" pour "La Grande Jatte."

If this line of argument is correct, it follows that the artist will tend to be an outsider in the society to which he has been born, and that the nineteenth-century conception of him as a Bohemian was not inaccurate. The conception erred in three particulars: it postulated an economic system where art could be a full-time job, it introduced the fallacy that only art matters, and it overstressed idiosyncrasy and waywardness—the peacock-feather aspect—rather than order. But it is a truer conception than the one which prevails in official circles on my side of the Atlantic—I don't know about yours: the conception which treats the artist as if he were a particularly bright government advertiser and encourages him to be friendly and matey with his fellow citizens, and not to give himself airs.

Estimable is mateyness, and the man who achieves it gives many a pleasant little drink to himself and to others. But it has no traceable connection with the creative impulse, and probably acts as an inhibition on it. The artist who is seduced by mateyness may stop himself from doing the one thing which he, and he alone, can do—the making of something out of words or sounds or paint or clay or marble or steel or film which has internal harmony and presents order to a permanently disarranged planet. This seems worth doing, even at the risk of being called uppish by journalists. I have in mind an article which was published some years ago in the London *Times,* an article called "The Eclipse of the Highbrow," in which the "Average Man" was exalted, and all contemporary literature was censured if it did not toe the line, the precise position of the line being naturally known to the writer of the article. Sir Kenneth Clark, who was at that time director of our National Gallery, commented on this pernicious doctrine in a letter which cannot be too often quoted. "The poet and the artist," wrote Clark, "are important precisely because they are not average men; because in sensibility, intelligence, and power of invention they far exceed the average." These memorable words, and particularly the words "power of invention," are the Bohemian's passport. Finished with it, he slinks about society, saluted now by a brickbat and now by a penny, and accepting either of them with equanimity. He does not consider too anxiously what his relations with society may be, for he is aware of something more important than that—namely the invitation to invent, to create order, and he believes he will be better placed for doing this if he attempts detachment. So round and round he slouches, with his hat pulled over his eyes, and maybe with a louse in his beard, and—if he really wants one—with a peacock's feather in his hand.

If our present society should disintegrate—and who dare prophesy that it won't?—this old-fashioned and démodé figure will become clearer: the Bohemian, the outsider, the parasite, the rat—one of those figures which have at present no function either in a warring or a peaceful world. It may not be dignified to be a rat, but many of the ships are sinking, which is not dignified either—the officials did not build them properly. Myself, I would sooner be a swimming rat than a sinking ship—at all events I can look around me for a little longer—and I remember how one of us, a rat with particularly bright eyes called Shelley, squeaked out, "Poets are the unacknowledged legislators of the world," before he vanished into the waters of the Mediterranean.

What laws did Shelley propose to pass? None. The legislation of the artist is never formulated at the time, though it is sometimes discerned by future generations. He legislates through creating. And he creates through his sensitiveness and his power to impose form. Without form the sensitiveness vanishes. And form is as important today, when the human race is trying to ride the whirlwind, as it ever was in those less agitating days of the past, when the earth seemed solid and the stars fixed, and the discoveries of science were made slowly, slowly. Form is not tradition. It alters from generation to generation. Artists always seek a new technique, and will continue to do so as long as their work excites them. But form of some kind is imperative. It is the surface crust of the internal harmony, it is the outward evidence of order.

My remarks about society may have seemed too pessimistic, but I believe that society can only represent a fragment of the human spirit, and that another fragment can only get expressed through art. And I wanted to take this opportunity, this vantage ground, to assert not only the existence of art but its pertinacity. Looking back into the past, it seems to me that that is all there has ever been: vantage grounds for discussion and creation, little vantage grounds in the changing chaos, where bubbles have been blown and webs spun, and the desire to create order has found temporary gratification, and the sentinels have managed to utter their challenges, and the huntsmen, though lost individually, have heard each other's calls through the impenetrable wood, and the lighthouses have never ceased sweeping the thankless seas. In this pertinacity there seems to me, as I grow older, something more and more profound, something which does in fact concern people who do not care about art at all.

In conclusion, let me summarize the various categories that have laid claim to the possession of Order.

(1) The social and political category. Claim disallowed on the evidence of history and of our own experience. If man altered psychologically, order here might be attainable; not otherwise.

(2) The astronomical category. Claim allowed up to the present century, but now disallowed on the evidence of the physicists.

(3) The religious category. Claim allowed on the evidence of the mystics.

(4) The aesthetic category—the subject of this article. Claim allowed on the evidence of various works of art, and on the evidence of our own creative impulses, however weak these may be, or however imperfectly they may function. Works of art, in my opinion, are the only objects in the material universe to possess internal order, and that is why, though I don't believe that only art matters, I do believe in Art for Art's Sake.

"A Platform and a Passion or Two"

by THORNTON WILDER

OCTOBER, 1957

One of America's most revered—and revolutionary—playwrights tells how he is trying to shake up the theater, and why. Mr. Wilder has won three Pulitzer Prizes—the first for his novel, The Bridge of San Luis Rey, *in 1928, and the others for the plays,* Our Town *in 1938, and* The Skin of Our Teeth, *1942. He is acclaimed by theatergoers abroad and has traveled widely as a cultural ambassador. He was born in Madison, Wisconsin, in 1897, and earned degrees at Yale and Princeton.*

Toward the end of the twenties I began to lose pleasure in going to the theater. I ceased to believe in the stories I saw presented there. When I did go it was to admire some secondary aspect of the play, the work of a great actor or director or designer. Yet at the same time the conviction was growing in me that the theater was the greatest of all the arts. I felt that something had gone wrong with it in my time and that it was fulfilling only a small part of its potentialities. I was filled with admiration for presentations of classical works by Max Reinhardt and Louis Jouvet and the Old Vic, as I was by the best plays of my time, like *Desire Under the Elms* and *The Front Page;* but it was with a grudging admiration, for at heart *I didn't believe a word of them*. I was like a schoolmaster grading a paper; to each of these offerings I gave an A+, but the condition of mind of one grading a paper is not that of one being overwhelmed by an artistic creation. The response we make when we "believe" a work of the imagination is that of saying: "This is the way things are. I have always known it without being fully aware that I knew it. Now in the presence of this play or novel or poem (or picture or piece of music) I know that I know it." It is this form of knowledge which Plato called "recollection." We have all murdered, in thought; and been murdered. We have all seen the ridiculous in estimable persons and in ourselves. We have all known terror as well as enchantment. Imaginative literature has nothing to say to those who do not recognize—who cannot be *reminded*—of such conditions. Of all the arts the theater is best endowed to awaken this recollection within us—to believe is to say "yes"; but in the theaters of my time I did not feel myself prompted to any such grateful and self-forgetting acquiescence.

This dissatisfaction worried me. I was not ready to condemn myself as blasé and overfastidious, for I knew that I was still capable of belief. I believed every word of *Ulysses* and of Proust and of *The Magic Mountain,* as I did of hundreds of plays when I read them. It was on the stage that imaginative narration became false. Finally, my dissatisfaction passed into resentment. I began to feel that the theater was not only inadequate, it was evasive; it did not wish to draw upon its deeper potentialities. I found the word for it: it aimed to be *soothing*. The tragic had no heat; the comic had no bite; the social criticism failed to indict us with responsibility.

I began to search for the point where the theater had run off the track, where it had chosen—and been permitted—to become a minor art and an inconsequential diversion.

The trouble began in the nineteenth century and was connected with the rise of the middle classes—they wanted their theater soothing.

There's nothing wrong with the middle classes in themselves. We know that now. The United States and Scandinavia and Germany are middle-class countries, so completely so that they have lost the very memory of their once despised and ludicrous inferiority (they had been inferior not only to the aristocracy but, in human dignity, to the peasantry). When a middle class is new, however, there is much that is wrong with it. When it is emerging under the shadow of an aristocracy, from the myth and prestige of those well-born Higher-ups, it is alternately insecure and aggressively complacent. It must find its justification and reassurance in making money and displaying it. To this day, members of the middle classes in England, France, and Italy feel themselves to be a little ridiculous and humiliated.

The prestige of aristocracies is based upon a dreary untruth: that moral superiority and the qualifications for leadership are transmittable through the chromosomes, and the secondary lie, that the environment afforded by privilege and leisure tends to nurture the flowers of the spirit. An aristocracy, defending and fostering its lie, extracts from the arts only such elements as can further its interests, the aroma and not the sap, the grace and not the trenchancy.

Equally harmful to culture is the newly arrived middle class. In the English-speaking world the middle classes came into power early in the nineteenth century and gained control over the theater. They were pious, law-abiding, and industrious. They were assured of eternal life in the next world and, in this, they were squarely seated on Property and the privileges that accompany it. They were attended by devoted servants who knew their place. They were benevolent within certain limits, but chose to ignore wide tracts of injustice and stupidity in the world about them; and they shrank from contemplating those elements within themselves that were ridiculous, shallow, and harmful. They distrusted the passions and tried to deny them. Their questions about the nature of life seemed to be sufficiently answered by the demonstration of financial status and by conformity to some clearly established rules of decorum. These were precarious positions; abysses yawned on either side. The air was loud with questions that must not be asked.

These middle-class audiences fashioned a theater which could not disturb them. They thronged to melodrama (which deals with tragic possibilities in such a way that you know from the beginning that all will end happily) and to sentimental drama (which accords a total license to the supposition that the wish is father to the thought) and to comedies in which the characters were so represented that they always resembled someone else and not oneself. Between the plays that Sheridan wrote in his twenties and the first works of Wilde and Shaw there was no play of even moderate interest written in the English language. (Unless you happen to admire and except Shelley's *The Cenci.*) These audiences, however, also thronged to Shakespeare. How did they shield themselves against his probing? How did they smother the theater—and with such effect that it smothers us still? The box-set was already there, the curtain, the proscenium, but not taken "seriously"—it was a convenience in view of the weather in northern countries. They took it seriously and emphasized and enhanced everything that thus removed, cut off, and boxed the action; they increasingly shut the play up into a museum showcase.

Let us examine why the box-set stage stifles the life in drama and why and how it militates against belief.

Every action which has ever taken place—every thought, every emotion—has taken place only once, at one moment in time and place. "I love you," "I rejoice," "I suffer," have been said and felt many billions of times, and never twice the same. Every person who has ever lived has lived an unbroken succession of unique occasions. Yet the more one is aware of this individuality in experience (innumerable! innumerable!) the more one becomes attentive to what these disparate moments have in common, to repetitive patterns. As an artist (or listener or beholder) which "truth" do you prefer—that of the isolated occasion, or that which includes and resumes the innumerable? Which truth is more worth telling? Every age differs in this. Is the Venus de Milo "one woman"? Is the play *Macbeth* the story of "one destiny"? The theater is admirably fitted to tell both truths. It has one foot planted firmly in the particular, since each actor before us (even when he wears a mask!) is indubitably a living breathing "one"; yet it tends and strains to exhibit a general truth since its relation to a specific "realistic" truth is confused and undermined by the fact that it is an accumulation of untruths, pretenses, and fiction.

All the arts depend on preposterous fictions, but the theater is the most preposterous of all. Imagine asking us to believe that we are in Venice in the sixteenth century, and that Mr. Billington is a Moor, and that he is about to stifle the much-admired Miss Huckaby with a pillow; and imagine trying to make us believe that people ever talked in blank verse—more than that: that people were ever so marvelously articulate. The theater is a lily that inexplicably arises from a jungle of weedy falsities. Yet it is precisely from the tension produced by all this absurdity, "contrary to fact," that it is able to create such poetry, power, enchantment, and truth.

The novel is pre-eminently the vehicle of the unique occasion, the theater of the generalized one. It is through the theater's power to raise the exhibited individual action into the realm of idea and type and universal that it is able to evoke our belief. But power is precisely what those nineteenth-century audiences did not—dared not—confront. They tamed it and drew its teeth; squeezed it into that removed showcase. They loaded the stage with specific objects, because every concrete object on the stage fixes and narrows the action to one moment in time and place. (Have you ever noticed that in the plays of Shakespeare no one—except occasionally a ruler—ever sits down? There were not even chairs on the English or Spanish stages in the time of Elizabeth I.) So it was by a jugglery with time that the middle classes devitalized the theater. When you emphasize *place* in the theater, you drag down and limit and harness time to it. You thrust the action back into past time, whereas it is precisely the glory of the stage that it is always "now" there. Under such production methods the characters are all dead before the action starts. You don't have to pay deeply from your heart's participation. No great age in the theater ever attempted to capture the audience's belief through this kind of specification and localization. I became dissatisfied with the theater because I was unable to lend credence to such childish attempts to be "real."

I began writing one-act plays that tried to capture not verisimilitude but reality. In *The Happy Journey to Trenton and Camden* four kitchen chairs represent an automobile and a family travels seventy miles in twenty minutes. Ninety years go by in *The Long Christmas Dinner*. In *Pullman Car Hiawatha* some more plain chairs serve as berths and we hear the very vital statistics of the towns and fields that passengers are traversing; we hear their thoughts; we even hear the planets over their heads. In Chinese drama a character, by straddling a stick, conveys to us that he is on horseback. In almost every No play of the Japanese an actor makes a tour of the stage and we know that he is making a long journey. Think of the ubiquity that Shakespeare's stage afforded for the battle scenes at the close of *Julius*

Caesar and *Antony and Cleopatra*. As we see them today what a cutting and hacking of the text takes place—what condescension, what contempt for his dramaturgy.

Our Town is not offered as a picture of life in a New Hampshire village; or as a speculation about the conditions of life after death (that element I merely took from Dante's *Purgatory*). It is an attempt to find a value above all price for the smallest events in our daily life. I have made the claim as preposterous as possible, for I have set the village against the largest dimensions of time and place. The recurrent words in this play (few have noticed it) are "hundreds," "thousands," and "millions." Emily's joys and griefs, her algebra lessons and her birthday presents—what are they when we consider all the billions of girls who have lived, who are living, and who will live? Each individual's assertion to an absolute reality can only be inner, very inner. And here the method of staging finds its justification —in the first two acts there are at least a few chairs and tables; but when she revisits the earth and the kitchen to which she descended on her twelfth birthday, the very chairs and table are gone. Our claim, our hope, our despair are in the mind—not in things, not in "scenery." Molière said that for the theater all he needed was a platform and a passion or two. The climax of this play needs only five square feet of boarding and the passion to know what life means to us.

The Matchmaker is an only slightly modified version of *The Merchant of Yonkers*, which I wrote in the year after I had written *Our Town*. One way to shake off the nonsense of the nineteenth-century staging is to make fun of it. This play parodies the stock company plays that I used to see at Ye Liberty Theatre, Oakland, California, when I was a boy. I have already read small theses in German comparing it with the great Austrian original on which it is based. The scholars are very bewildered. There's most of the plot (except that our friend Dolly Levi is not in Nestroy's play); there are some of the tags; but it's all "about" quite different matters. Nestroy's wonderful and sardonic plays are—like most of Molière's and Goldoni's—"about" the havoc that people create in their own lives and in those about them through the wrong-headed illusions they cherish. My plan is about the aspirations of the young (and not only of the young) for a fuller, freer participation in life. Imagine an Austrian pharmacist going to the shelf to draw from a bottle which he knows to contain a stinging corrosive liquid, guaranteed to remove warts and wens; and imagine his surprise when he discovers that it has been filled with very American birch-bark beer.

The Skin of Our Teeth begins, also, by making fun of old-fashioned playwriting; but the audience soon perceives that he is seeing "two times at once." The Antrobus family is living both in prehistoric times and in a New Jersey commuter's suburb today. Again the events of our homely daily life—this time the family life—are depicted against the vast dimensions of time and place. It was written on the eve of our entrance into the war and under strong emotion, and I think it mostly comes alive under conditions of crisis. It has been often charged with being a bookish fantasia about history, full of rather bloodless schoolmasterish jokes. But to have seen it in Germany soon after the war, in the shattered churches and beer halls that were serving as theaters, with audiences whose price of admission meant the loss of a meal and for whom it was of absorbing interest that there was a "recipe for grass soup that did not cause the diarrhea," was an experience that was not so cool. I am very proud that this year it has received a first and overwhelming reception in Warsaw.

The play is deeply indebted to James Joyce's *Finnegans Wake*. I should be very happy if, in the future, some author should feel similarly indebted to any work of mine. Literature has always more resembled a torch race than a furious dispute among heirs.

The theater has lagged behind the other arts in finding the "new ways" to express how men and women think and feel in our time. I am not one of the dramatists we are looking for. I wish I were. I hope I have played a part in preparing the way for them. I am not an innovator but a rediscoverer of forgotten goods and I hope a remover of obtrusive bric-a-brac. And as I view the work of my contemporaries I seem to feel that I am exceptional in one thing—I give (don't I?) the impression of having enormously enjoyed it?

Mark Twain Speaks Out

by MARK TWAIN

DECEMBER, 1958

Mark Twain had many stories, essays, and sketches in the maga-
zine, including "The Man That Corrupted Hadleyburg" and
"Tom Sawyer, Detective." But nearly all have been reprinted in
many other anthologies. Fortunately, some fresh material, never
before published, appeared in the December, 1958 issue—parts
of his autobiography which he had directed not to be published
for various periods after his death. Samuel Langhorne Clemens
was born in Florida, Missouri, in 1835, and spent his boyhood,
as everybody knows, in Hannibal. He died in 1910, the most
celebrated humorist America has produced.

I. No Terrors for Me

The very reason that I speak from the grave is that I want the satisfaction of sometimes saying everything that is in me instead of bottling
the pleasantest of it up for home consumption. I can speak more
frankly from the grave than most historians would be able to do, for
the reason that whereas they would not be able to *feel* dead, howso-
ever hard they might try, I myself am able to do that. They would be
making believe to be dead. With me, it is not make-believe. They
would all the time be feeling, in a tolerably definite way, that that
thing in the grave which represents them is a conscious entity; conscious of what it was saying about people; an entity capable of feeling shame; an entity capable of shrinking from full and frank expression, for they believe in immortality. They believe that death is
only a sleep, followed by an immediate waking, and that their spirits
are conscious of what is going on here below and take a deep and
continuous interest in the joys and sorrows of the survivors whom
they love and don't.

But I have long ago lost my belief in immortality—also my interest
in it. I can say now what I could not say while alive—things which it
would shock people to hear; things which I could not say when alive

because I should be aware of that shock and would certainly spare myself the personal pain of inflicting it.

When we believe in immortality we have a reason for it. Not a reason founded upon information, or even plausibilities, for we haven't any. Our reason for choosing to believe in this dream is that we desire immortality, for some reason or other, I don't know what. But I have no such desire. I have sampled this life and it is sufficient. Another one would be another experiment. It would proceed from the same source as this one. I should have no large expectations concerning it, and if I may be excused from assisting in the experiment I shall be properly grateful. Annihilation has no terrors for me, because I have already tried it before I was born—a hundred million years—and I have suffered more in an hour, in this life, than I remember to have suffered in the whole hundred million years put together. There was a peace, a serenity, an absence of all sense of responsibility, an absence of worry, an absence of care, grief, perplexity; and the presence of a deep content and unbroken satisfaction in that hundred million years of holiday which I look back upon with a tender longing and with a grateful desire to resume, when the opportunity comes.

It is undesirable that when I speak from the grave it is not a spirit that is speaking; it is a nothing; it is an emptiness; it is a vacancy; it is a something that has neither feeling nor consciousness. It does not know what it is saying. It is not aware that it is saying anything at all, therefore it can speak frankly and freely, since it cannot know that it is inflicting pain, discomfort, or offense of any kind.

II. Honorary Degrees

A cablegram arrived from England three weeks ago inviting me to come to Oxford and receive an honorary degree on the 26th of next month [June, 1907]. I accepted, and without any waste of time. During the past two years I have been saying with great decision that my traveling days were permanently over and that nothing would ever induce me to cross the ocean again, yet I was not surprised at the alacrity with which I put that resolution behind me when this flattering invitation came. I could have declined an invitation to come over and accept a London town lot and I could have done it without any difficulty, but a university degree is a quite different matter; that is a prize which I would go far to get at any time.

I take the same childlike delight in a new degree that an Indian takes in a fresh scalp and I take no more pains to conceal my joy than the Indian does. I remember the time that I found a battered old-time picayune in the road, when I was a boy, and realized that its value was vastly enhanced to me because I had not earned it. I remember the time, ten years later, in Keokuk, that I found a fifty-dollar bill in the street, and that the value of that bill also was vastly enhanced to me by the reflection that I had not earned it. I remember the time in San Francisco, after a further interval of eight years, when I had been out of work and out of money for three months, that I found a ten-cent piece in the crossing at the junction of Commercial and Montgomery Streets, and realized that that dime gave me more joy, because unearned, than a hundred earned dimes could have given me. In my time I have acquired several hundred thousand dollars, but inasmuch as I earned them they have possessed nothing more than their face value to me and so the details and dates of their capture are dim in my memory and in many cases have passed from my memory altogether. On the contrary, how eternally and blazingly vivid in my recollection are those three unearned finds!

Now then, to me university degrees are unearned finds, and they bring the joy that belongs with property acquired in that way; and the money-finds and the degree-finds are just the same in number up to date—three: two from Yale and one from Missouri University. It pleased me beyond measure when Yale made me a Master of Arts, because I didn't know anything about art; I had another convulsion of pleasure when Yale made me a Doctor of Literature, because I was not competent to doctor anybody's literature but my own, and couldn't even keep my own in a healthy condition without my wife's help. I rejoiced again when Missouri University made me a Doctor of Laws, because it was all clear profit, I not knowing anything about laws except how to evade them and not get caught. And now at Oxford I am to be made a Doctor of Letters—all clear profit, because what I don't know about letters would make me a multimillionaire if I could turn it into cash.

Oxford is healing a secret old sore of mine which has been causing me sharp anguish once a year for many, many years. Privately I am quite well aware that for a generation I have been as widely celebrated a literary person as America has ever produced, and I am also privately aware that in my own peculiar line I have stood at the head of my guild during all that time, with none to dispute the place with me; and so it has been an annual pain to me to see our universities confer an aggregate of two hundred and fifty honorary degrees upon persons of small and temporary consequence—persons of local and evanescent notoriety, persons who drift into obscurity and are forgotten inside of ten years—and never a degree offered to me! In these past thirty-five or forty years I have seen our universities distribute nine or ten thousand honorary degrees and overlook me every time. Of all those thousands, not fifty were known outside of America, and not a hundred are still famous in it. This neglect would have killed a less robust person than I am, but it has not killed me; it has only shortened my life and weakened my constitution; but I shall get my strength back now. Out of those decorated and forgotten thousands not more than ten have been decorated by Oxford, and I am quite well aware—and so is America, and so is the rest of Christendom—that an Oxford decoration is a loftier distinction than is conferrable by any other university on either side of the ocean, and is worth twenty-five of any other, whether foreign or domestic.

Now then, having purged myself of this thirty-five years' accumulation of bile and injured pride, I will drop the matter and smooth my feathers down and talk about something else.

III. Amateur Writings

From old experience I know that amateur productions, offered ostensibly for one's honest cold judgment, to be followed by an uncompromisingly sincere verdict, are not really offered in that spirit at all. The thing really wanted and expected is compliment and encouragement. Also, my experience has taught me that in almost all amateur cases compliment and encouragement are impossible—if they are to be backed by sincerity.

I have this moment finished reading this morning's pair of offerings and am a little troubled. If they had come from strangers I should not have given myself the pain of reading them, but should have returned them unread, according to my custom, upon the plea that I lack an editor's training and therefore am not qualified to sit in judgment upon anyone's literature but my own. But this morning's harvest came from friends and that alters the case. I have read them and the result is as usual: they are not literature. They do contain meat but the meat is only half-cooked. . . . One of this morning's samples does really come near to being literature, but the amateur hand is exposed with a fatal frequency and the exposure spoils it. The author's idea is, in case I shall render a favorable verdict, to offer the manuscript to a magazine.

There is something about this naïve intrepidity that compels admiration. It is a lofty and reckless daring which I suppose is exhibited in no field but one—the field of literature. We see something approaching it in war, but approaching it only distantly. The untrained common soldier has often offered himself as one of a forlorn hope and stood cheerfully ready to encounter all its perils—but we draw the line there. Not even the most confident untrained soldier offers himself as a candidate for a brigadier-generalship, yet this is what the amateur author does. With his untrained pen he puts together his crudities and offers them to all the magazines, one after the other—that is to say, he proposes them for posts restricted to literary generals who have earned their rank and place by years and even decades of hard and honest training in the lower grades of the service.

I am sure that this affront is offered to no trade but ours. A person untrained to shoemaking does not offer his services as a shoemaker to the foreman of a shop—not even the crudest literary aspirant would be so unintelligent as to do that. He would see the humor of it; he would see the impertinence of it; he would recognize as the most commonplace of facts that an apprenticeship is necessary in order to qualify a person to be tinner, bricklayer, stone-mason, printer, horse-doctor, butcher, brakeman, car conductor, midwife—and any and every other occupation whereby a human being acquires bread and fame. But when it comes to doing literature, his wisdoms vanish all of a sudden and he thinks he finds himself now in the presence of a profession which requires no apprenticeship, no experience, no training —nothing whatever but conscious talent and a lion's courage. . . .

We must imagine a kindred case—the aspirant to operatic distinction and cash, for instance. The aspirant applies to the management for a billet as second tenor. The management accepts him, arranges the terms and puts him on the pay-roll.

After the first act the manager calls the second tenor to account and wants to know. He says:

"Have you ever studied music?"

"A little—yes, by myself, at odd times, for amusement."

"You have never gone into regular and laborious training, then, for the opera, under the masters of the art?"

"No."

"Then what made you think you could do second tenor in *Lohengrin?*"

"I thought I could. I wanted to try. I seemed to have a voice."

"Yes, you have a voice, and with five years of diligent training under competent masters you could be successful, perhaps, but I assure you you are not ready for second tenor yet. You have a voice; you have presence; you have a noble and childlike confidence; you have a courage that is stupendous and even superhuman. These are all essentials and they are in your favor but there are other essentials in this great trade which you still lack. If you can't afford the time and labor necessary to acquire them leave opera alone and try something which does not require training and experience. Go away now and try for a job in surgery."

IV. Humor

Repetition is a mighty power in the domain of humor. If frequently used, nearly any precisely worded and unchanging formula will eventually compel laughter if it be gravely and earnestly repeated, at intervals, five or six times.

I undertook to prove the truth of this forty years ago in San Francisco on the occasion of my second attempt at lecturing. My first lecture had succeeded to my satisfaction. Then I prepared another one but was afraid of it because the first fifteen minutes of it was not humorous. I felt the necessity of preceding it with something which would break up the house with a laugh and get me on pleasant and friendly terms with it at the start, instead of allowing it leisure to congeal into a critical mood, since that could be disastrous.

With this idea in mind I prepared a scheme of so daring a nature that I wonder now that I ever had the courage to carry it through. San Francisco had been persecuted for five or six years with a silly and pointless and unkillable anecdote which everybody had long ago grown weary of—weary unto death. It was as much as a man's life was worth to tell that moldy anecdote to a citizen. I resolved to begin my lecture with it, and keep on repeating it until the mere repetition should conquer the house and make it laugh.

There were fifteen hundred people present, and as I had been a reporter on one of the papers for a good while I knew several hundred of them. They loved me, they couldn't help it; they admired me; and I knew it would grieve them, disappoint them and make them sick at heart to hear me fetch out that odious anecdote with the air of a person who thought it new and good. I began with a description of my first day in the overland coach; then I said,

"At a little 'dobie station out on the plains, next day, a man got in and after chatting along pleasantly for a while he said 'I can tell you a most laughable thing indeed, if you would like to listen to it. Horace Greeley went over this road once. When he was leaving Carson City he told the driver, Hank Monk, that he had an engagement to lecture at Placerville and was very anxious to go through quick. Hank Monk cracked his whip and started off at an awful pace. The coach bounced up and down in such a terrific way that it jolted the buttons all off of Horace's coat and finally shot his head clean through the roof of the stage, and then he yelled at Hank Monk and begged him to go easier —said he warn't in as much of a hurry as he was a while ago. But Hank Monk said, "Keep your seat, Horace, I'll get you there on time!" —and you bet he did, too, what was left of him!' "

I told it in a level voice, in a colorless and monotonous way, without emphasizing any word in it, and succeeded in making it dreary and stupid to the limit. Then I paused and looked very much pleased with myself and as if I expected a burst of laughter. Of course there was no laughter, nor anything resembling it. There was a dead silence. As far as the eye could reach that sea of faces was a sorrow to look upon; some bore an insulted look; some exhibited resentment; my friends and acquaintances looked ashamed, and the house, as a body, looked as if it had taken an emetic.

I tried to look embarrassed and did it very well. For a while I said nothing, but stood fumbling with my hands in a sort of mute appeal to the audience for compassion. Many did pity me—I could see it. But I could also see that the rest were thirsting for blood. I presently began again and stammered awkwardly along with some more details of the overland trip. Then I began to work up toward my anecdote again with the air of a person who thinks he did not tell it well the first time and who feels that the house will like it the next time, if told with a better art. The house perceived that I was working up toward the anecdote again and its indignation was very apparent. Then I said,

"Just after we left Julesburg, on the Platte, I was sitting with the driver and he said, 'I can tell you a most laughable thing indeed if you would like to listen to it. Horace Greeley went over this road once. When he was leaving Carson City he told the driver, Hank Monk, that he had an engagement to lecture at Placerville and was very anxious to go through quick. Hank Monk cracked his whip and started off at an awful pace. The coach bounced up and down in such a terrific way that it jolted the buttons all off of Horace's coat and finally shot his head clean through the roof of the stage, and then he yelled at Hank Monk and begged him to go easier—said he warn't in as much of a hurry as he was a while ago. But Hank Monk said, "Keep your seat, Horace, I'll get you there on time!"—and you bet he did, too, what was left of him!' "

I stopped again and looked gratified and expectant, but there wasn't a sound. The house was as still as the tomb. I looked embarrassed again. I fumbled again. I tried to seem ready to cry, and once more, after a considerable silence, I took up the overland trip again, and once more I stumbled and hesitated along—then presently began again to work up toward the anecdote. The house exhibited distinct impatience, but I worked along up, trying all the while to look like a person who was sure that there was some mysterious reason why these people didn't see how funny the anecdote was, and that they must see it if I could ever manage to tell it right, therefore I must make another effort. I said,

"A day or two after that we picked up a Denver man at the cross-roads and he chatted along very pleasantly for a while. . . . [And then I told the whole story once more, winding up with . . .] 'Keep your seat, Horace, I'll get you there on time!'—and you bet he did, too, what was left of him!"

All of a sudden the front ranks recognized the sell and broke into a laugh. It spread back, and back, and back, to the furthest verge of the place; then swept forward again, and then back again, and at the end of a minute the laughter was as universal and as thunderously noisy as a tempest.

It was a heavenly sound to me, for I was nearly exhausted with weakness and apprehension, and was becoming almost convinced that I should have to stand there and keep on telling that anecdote all night, before I could make those people understand that I was working a delicate piece of satire. I am sure I should have stood my ground and gone on favoring them with that tale until I broke them down, under the unconquerable conviction that the monotonous repetition of it would infallibly fetch them some time or other.

A good many years afterward there was to be an Authors' Reading at Chickering Hall, in New York, and I thought I would try that anecdote again and see if the repetition would be effective with an audience wholly unacquainted with it and who would be obliged to find the fun solely in the repetition, if they found it at all, since there would be not a shred of anything in the tale itself that could stir anybody's sense of humor but an idiot's. I sat by James Russell Lowell on the platform and he asked me what I was going to read. I said I was going to tell a brief and wholly pointless anecdote in a dreary and monotonous voice and that therein would consist my whole performance. He said,

"That is a strange idea. What do you expect to accomplish by it?"
I said,
"Only a laugh. I want the audience to laugh."

He said, "Of course you do—that is your trade. They will require it of you. But do you think they are going to laugh at a silly and pointless anecdote drearily and monotonously told?"

"Yes," I said, "they'll laugh."

Lowell said, "I think you are dangerous company. I am going to move to the other end of this platform and get out of the way of the bricks."

When my turn came I got up and exactly repeated—and most gravely and drearily—that San Francisco performance of so many years before. It was as deadly an ordeal as ever I have been through in the course of my checkered life. I never got a response of any kind until I had told that juiceless anecdote in the same unvarying words *five times;* then the house saw the point and annihilated the heartbreaking silence with a most welcome crash. It revived me, and I needed it, for if I had to tell it four more times I should have died— but I would have done it, if I had had to get somebody to hold me up. The house kept up that crash for a minute or two, and it was a soothing and blessed thing to hear.

Mr. Lowell shook me cordially by the hand and said,

"Mark, it was a triumph of art! It was a triumph of grit, too. I would rather lead a forlorn hope and take my chances of a soldier's bloody death than try to duplicate that performance."

He said that during the first four repetitions, with that mute and solemn and wondering house before him, he thought he was going to perish with anxiety for me. He said he had never been so sorry for a human being before and that he was cold all down his spine until the fifth repetition broke up the house and brought the blessed relief.

V

Scalawags and Hard Cases

Wild Bill

by GEORGE WARD NICHOLS

FEBRUARY, 1867

*This is a collector's item among students of the early West.
George Ward Nichols, who had been an aide to General Sherman
in the March to the Sea, arrived in the frontier town of Springfield, Missouri, a few days after James Butler Hickok had killed
a man in a gun duel in the town square. Nichols got a firsthand
account from Wild Bill of some of his most famous exploits.
Hickok later repudiated the part about killing ten members of the
McCanles Gang single-handed, claiming he didn't tell Nichols
that. (The author erroneously refers to Wild Bill as "William
Hitchcock" and spells McCanles "M'Kandlas.") Hickok is buried
in Deadwood, South Dakota, where he was murdered in 1876.
Nichols became a leading citizen of Cincinnati, Ohio. He died
in 1885.*

Several months after the ending of the civil war I visited the city of
Springfield in Southwest Missouri. Springfield is not a burgh of extensive dimensions, yet it is the largest in that part of the State, and all
roads lead to it—which is one reason why it was the *point d'appui,* as
well as the base of operations for all military movements during the
war.

On a warm summer day I sat watching from the shadow of a broad
awning the coming and going of the strange, half-civilized people who,
from all the country round, make this a place for barter and trade.
Men and women dressed in queer costumes; men with coats and
trowsers made of skin, but so thickly covered with dirt and grease as
to have defied the identity of the animal when walking in the flesh.
Others wore homespun gear, which oftentimes appeared to have seen
lengthy service. Many of those people were mounted on horseback or
muleback, while others urged forward the unwilling cattle attached to
creaking, heavily-laden wagons, their drivers snapping their long whips
with a report like that of a pistol-shot.

319

In front of the shops which lined both sides of the main business street, and about the public square, were groups of men lolling against posts, lying upon the wooden sidewalks, or sitting in chairs. These men were temporary or permanent denizens of the city, and were lazily occupied in doing nothing. The most marked characteristic of the inhabitants seemed to be an indisposition to move, and their highest ambition to let their hair and beards grow.

Here and there upon the street the appearance of the army blue betokened the presence of a returned Union soldier, and the jaunty, confident air with which they carried themselves was all the more striking in its contrast with the indolence which appeared to belong to the place. The only indication of action was the inevitable revolver which everybody, excepting, perhaps, the women, wore about their persons. When people moved in this lazy city they did so slowly and without method. No one seemed in haste. A huge hog wallowed in luxurious ease in a nice bed of mud on the other side of the way, giving vent to gentle grunts of satisfaction. On the platform at my feet lay a large wolf-dog literally asleep with one eye open. He, too, seemed contented to let the world wag idly on.

The loose, lazy spirit of the occasion finally took possession of me, and I sat and gazed and smoked, and it is possible that I might have fallen into a Rip Van Winkle sleep to have been aroused ten years hence by the cry, "Passengers for the flying machine to New York, all aboard!" when I and the drowsing city were roused into life by the clatter and crash of the hoofs of a horse which dashed furiously across the square and down the street. The rider sat perfectly erect, yet following with a grace of motion, seen only in the horsemen of the plains, the rise and fall of the galloping steed. There was only a moment to observe this, for they halted suddenly, while the rider springing to the ground approached the party which the noise had gathered near me.

"This yere is Wild Bill, Colonel," said Captain Honesty, an army officer, addressing me. He continued:

"How are yer, Bill? This yere is Colonel N———, who wants ter know yer."

Let me at once describe the personal appearance of the famous Scout of the Plains, William Hitchcock, called "Wild Bill," who now advanced toward me, fixing his clear gray eyes on mine in a quick, interrogative way, as if to take "my measure."

The result seemed favorable, for he held forth a small, muscular hand in a frank, open manner. As I looked at him I thought his the handsomest *physique* I had ever seen. In its exquisite manly proportions it recalled the antique. It was a figure Ward would delight to model as a companion to his "Indian."

Bill stood six feet and an inch in his bright yellow moccasins. A deer-skin shirt, or frock it might be called, hung jauntily over his shoulders, and revealed a chest whose breadth and depth were remarkable. These lungs had had growth in some twenty years of the free air of the Rocky Mountains. His small, round waist was girthed by a belt which held two of Colt's navy revolvers. His legs sloped gradually from the compact thigh to the feet, which were small, and turned inward as he walked. There was a singular grace and dignity of carriage about that figure which would have called your attention meet it where you would. The head which crowned it was now covered by a large sombrero, underneath which there shone out a quiet, manly face; so gentle is its expression as he greets you as utterly to belie the history of its owner, yet it is not a face to be trifled with. The lips thin and sensitive, the jaw not too square, the cheek bones slightly prominent, a mass of fine dark hair falls below the neck to the shoulders. The eyes, now that you are in friendly intercourse, are as gentle as a woman's. In truth, the woman nature seems prominent throughout, and you would not believe that you were looking into eyes that have pointed the way to death to hundreds of men. Yes, Wild Bill with his own hands has killed hundreds of men. Of that I have not a doubt. "He shoots to kill," as they say on the border.

In vain did I examine the scout's face for some evidence of murderous propensity. It was a gentle face, and singular only in the sharp angle of the eye, and without any physiognomical reason for the opinion, I have thought his wonderful accuracy of aim was indicated by this peculiarity. He told me, however, to use his own words:

"I allers shot well; but I come ter be perfeck in the mountains by shootin at a dime for a mark, at bets of half a dollar a shot. And then until the war I never drank liquor nor smoked," he continued, with a melancholy expression; "war is demoralizing, it is."

Captain Honesty was right. I was very curious to see "Wild Bill, the Scout," who, a few days before my arrival in Springfield, in a duel at noonday in the public square, at fifty paces, had sent one of Colt's pistol-balls through the heart of a returned Confederate soldier.

Whenever I had met an officer or soldier who had served in the Southwest I heard of Wild Bill and his exploits, until these stories became so frequent and of such an extraordinary character as quite to outstrip personal knowledge of adventure by camp and field; and the hero of these strange tales took shape in my mind as did Jack the Giant Killer or Sinbad the Sailor in childhood's days. . . .

In order to give the reader a clearer understanding of the condition of this neighborhood, which could have permitted the duel mentioned above, and whose history will be given hereafter in detail, I will describe the situation at the time of which I am writing, which was late in the summer of 1865, premising that this section of country would not today be selected as a model example of modern civilization.

At that time peace and comparative quiet had succeeded the perils and tumult of war in all the more Southern States. The people of Georgia and the Carolinas were glad to enforce order in their midst; and it would have been safe for a Union officer to have ridden unattended through the land.

In Southwest Missouri there were old scores to be settled up. During the three days occupied by General Smith—who commanded the Department and was on a tour of inspection—in crossing the country between Rolla and Springfield, a distance of 120 miles, five men were killed or wounded on the public road. Two were murdered a short distance from Rolla—by whom we could not ascertain. Another was instantly killed and two were wounded at a meeting of a band of "Regulators," who were in the service of the State, but were paid by the United States Government. It should be said here that their method of "regulation" was slightly informal, their war-cry was, "A swift bullet and a short rope for returned rebels!"

I was informed by General Smith that during the six months preceding not less than 4,000 returned Confederates had been summarily disposed of by shooting or hanging. This statement seems incredible; but there is the record, and I have no doubt of its truth. History shows few parallels to this relentless destruction of human life in time of peace. It can be explained only upon the ground that, before the war, this region was inhabited by lawless people. In the outset of the rebellion the merest suspicion of loyalty to the Union cost the patriot his life; and thus large numbers fled the land, giving up home and every material interest. As soon as the Federal armies occupied the country these refugees returned. Once securely fixed in their old homes they resolved that their former persecutors should not live in their midst. Revenge for the past and security for the future knotted many a nerve and sped many a deadly bullet.

Wild Bill did not belong to the Regulators. Indeed, he was one of the law and order party. He said:

"When the war closed I buried the hatchet, and I won't fight now unless I'm put upon."

Bill was born of Northern parents in the State of Illinois. He ran away from home when a boy, and wandered out upon the plains and into the mountains. For fifteen years he lived with the trappers, hunting and fishing. When the war broke out he returned to the States and entered the Union service. No man probably was ever better fitted for scouting than he. Joined to his tremendous strength he was an unequaled horseman; he was a perfect marksman; he had a keen sight, and a constitution which had no limit of endurance. He was cool to audacity, brave to rashness, always possessed of himself under the most critical circumstances; and, above all, was such a master in the knowledge of woodcraft that it might have been termed a science with him—a knowledge which, with the soldier, is priceless beyond description. Some of Bill's adventures during the war will be related hereafter.

The main features of the story of the duel was told me by Captain Honesty, who was unprejudiced, if it is possible to find an unbiased mind in a town of 3,000 people after a fight has taken place. I will give the story in his words:

"They say Bill's wild. Now he isn't any sich thing. I've known him goin on ter ten year, and he's as civil a disposed person as you'll find he-e-arabouts. But he won't be put upon.

"I'll tell yer how it happened. But come inter the office; thar's a good many round hy'ar as sides with Tutt—the man that's shot. But I tell yer 'twas a far fight. Take some whiskey? No! Well, I will, if yer'l excuse me.

"You see," continued the Captain, setting the empty glass on the table in an emphatic way, "Bill was up in his room a-playin seven-up, or four-hand, or some of them pesky games. Bill refused ter play with Tutt, who was a professional gambler. Yer see, Bill was a scout on our side durin the war, and Tutt was a reb scout. Bill had killed Dave Tutt's mate, and, atween one thing and another, there war an onusual hard feelin atwixt 'em.

"Ever sin Dave come back he had tried to pick a row with Bill; so Bill wouldn't play cards with him any more. But Dave stood over the man who was gambling with Bill and lent the feller money. Bill won bout two hundred dollars, which made Tutt spiteful mad. Bime-by, he says to Bill:

" 'Bill, you've got plenty of money—pay me that forty dollars yer owe me in that horse trade.'

"And Bill paid him. Then he said:

" 'Yer owe me thirty-five dollars more; yer lost it playing with me t'other night.'

"Dave's style was right provoking; but Bill answered him perfectly gentlemanly:

" 'I think yer wrong, Dave. It's only twenty-five dollars. I have a memorandum of it in my pocket down stairs. Ef it's thirty-five dollars I'll give it yer.'

"Now Bill's watch was lying on the table. Dave took up the watch, put it in his pocket, and said: 'I'll keep this yere watch till yer pay me that thirty-five dollars.'

"This made Bill shooting mad; fur, don't yer see, Colonel, it was a-doubting his honor like, so he got up and looked Dave in the eyes, and said to him: 'I don't want ter make a row in this house. It's a decent house, and I don't want ter injure the keeper. You'd better put that watch back on the table.'

"But Dave grinned at Bill mighty ugly, and walked off with the watch, and kept it several days. All this time Dave's friends were spurring Bill on ter fight; there was no end ter the talk. They blackguarded him in an underhand sort of a way, and tried ter get up a scrimmage, and then they thought they could lay him out. Yer see Bill has enemies all about. He's settled the accounts of a heap of men who lived round here. This is about the only place in Missouri whar a reb can come back and live, and ter tell yer the truth, Colonel—" and the Captain, with an involuntary movement, hitched up his revolver-belt, as he said, with expressive significance, "they don't stay long round here!

"Well, as I was saying, these rebs don't like ter see a man walking round town who they knew in the reb army as one of their men, who they now know was on our side, all the time he was sending us information, sometimes from Pap Price's own headquarters. But they couldn't provoke Bill inter a row, for he's afeard of hisself when he gits *awful* mad; and he allers left his shootin irons in his room when he went out. One day these cusses drew their pistols on him and dared him to fight, and then they told him that Tutt was a-going ter pack that watch across the squar next day at noon.

"I heard of this, for everybody was talking about it on the street, and so I went after Bill, and found him in his room cleaning and greasing and loading his revolvers.

" 'Now, Bill,' says I, 'you're going ter git inter a fight.'

" 'Don't you bother yerself, Captain,' says he. 'It's not the first time I have been in a fight; and these d——d hounds have put on me long enough. You don't want me ter give up my honor, do yer?'

" 'No, Bill,' says I, 'yer must keep yer honor.'

"Next day, about noon, Bill went down on the squar. He had said that Dave Tutt shouldn't pack that watch across the squar unless dead men could walk.

"When Bill got onter the squar he found a crowd stanin in the corner of the street by which he entered the squar, which is from the south, yer know. In this crowd he saw a lot of Tutt's friends; some were cousins of his'n, just back from the reb army; and they jeered him, and boasted that Dave was a-goin to pack that watch across the squar as he promised.

"Then Bill saw Tutt stanin near the courthouse, which yer remember is on the west side, so that the crowd war behind Bill.

"Just then Tutt, who war alone, started from the courthouse and walked out into the squar, and Bill moved away from the crowd toward the west side of the squar. Bout fifteen paces brought them opposite to each other, and bout fifty yards apart. Tutt then showed his pistol. Bill had kept a sharp eye on him, and before Tutt could pint it Bill had his'n out.

"At that moment you could have heard a pin drop in that squar. Both Tutt and Bill fired, but one discharge followed the other so quick that it's hard to say which went off first. Tutt was a famous shot, but he missed this time; the ball from his pistol went over Bill's head. The instant Bill fired, without waitin ter see ef he had hit Tutt, he wheeled on his heels and pointed his pistol at Tutt's friends, who had already drawn their weapons.

" 'Aren't yer satisfied, gentlemen?' cried Bill, as cool as an alligator. 'Put up your shootin-irons, or there'll be more dead men here.' And they put 'em up, and said it war a far fight."

"What became of Tutt?" I asked of the Captain, who had stopped at this point of his story, and was very deliberately engaged in refilling his empty glass.

"Oh! Dave? He was as plucky a feller as ever drew trigger; but, Lord bless yer! it was no use. Bill never shoots twice at the same man, and his ball went through Dave's heart. He stood stock-still for a second or two, then raised his arm as if ter fire again, then he swayed a little, staggered three or four steps, and then fell dead.

"Bill and his friends wanted ter have the thing done regular, so we went up ter the Justice, and Bill delivered himself up. A jury was drawn; Bill was tried and cleared the next day. It was proved that it was a case of self-defense. Don't yer see, Colonel?"

I answered that I was afraid that I did not see that point very clearly.

"Well, well!" he replied, with an air of compassion, "you haven't drunk any whiskey, that's what's the matter with yer." And then, putting his hand on my shoulder with a half-mysterious half-conscious look in his face, he muttered, in a whisper:

"The fact is, thar was an undercurrent of a woman in that fight!"

The story of the duel was yet fresh from the lips of the Captain when its hero appeared in the manner already described. After a few moments' conversation Bill excused himself, saying:

"I am going out on the prarer a piece to see the sick wife of my mate. I should be glad to meet yer at the hotel this afternoon, Kernel."

"I will go there to meet you," I replied.

"Good-day, gentlemen," said the scout, as he saluted the party; and mounting the black horse who had been standing quiet, unhitched, he waved his hand over the animal's head. Responsive to the signal, she shot forward as the arrow leaves the bow, and they both disappeared up the road in a cloud of dust. . . .

I went to the hotel during the afternoon to keep the scout's appointment. The large room of the hotel in Springfield is perhaps the central point of attraction in the city. It fronted on the street, and served in several capacities. It was a sort of exchange for those who had nothing better to do than to go there. It was reception-room, parlor, and office; but its distinguished and most fascinating characteristic was the bar, which occupied one entire end of the apartment. Technically, the "bar" is the counter upon which the polite official places his viands. Practically, the bar is represented in the long rows of bottles, and cut-glass decanters, and the glasses and goblets of all shapes and sizes suited to the various liquors to be imbibed. What a charming and artistic display it was of elongated transparent vessels containing every known drinkable fluid, from native Bourbon to imported Lacryma Christi!

The room, in its way, was a temple of art. All sorts of pictures budded and blossomed and blushed from the walls. Sixpenny portraits of the Presidents encoffined in pine-wood frames; Mazeppa appeared in the four phases of his celebrated one-horse act; while a lithograph of "Mary Ann" smiled and simpered in spite of the stains of tobacco-juice which had been unsparingly bestowed upon her originally encarmined countenance. But the hanging committee of this undesigned academy seemed to have been prejudiced—as all hanging committees of good taste might well be—in favor of *Harper's Weekly;* for the walls of the room were well covered with wood-cuts cut from that journal. Portraits of noted generals and statesmen, knaves and politicians, with bounteous illustrations of battles and skirmishes, from Bull Run number one to Dinwiddie Court House. And the simple-hearted comers and goers of Springfield looked upon, wondered, and admired these pictorial descriptions fully as much as if they had been the masterpieces of a Yvon or Vernet.

A billiard-table, old and out of use, where caroms seemed to have been made quite as often with lead as ivory balls, stood in the center of the room. A dozen chairs filled up the complement of the furniture. The appearance of the party of men assembled there, who sat with their slovenly shod feet dangling over the arms of the chairs or hung about the porch outside, was in perfect harmony with the time and place. All of them religiously obeyed the two before-mentioned characteristics of the people of the city—their hair was long and tangled, and each man fulfilled the most exalted requirement of laziness.

I was taking a mental inventory of all this when a cry and murmur drew my attention to the outside of the house, when I saw Wild Bill riding up the street at a swift gallop. Arrived opposite to the hotel, he swung his right arm around with a circular motion. Black Nell instantly stopped and dropped to the ground as if a cannon-ball had knocked the life out of her. Bill left her there, stretched upon the ground, and joined the group of observers on the porch.

"Black Nell hasn't forgot her old tricks," said one of them.

"No," answered the scout. "God bless her! she is wiser and truer than most men I know on. That mare will do anything for me. Won't you, Nelly?"

The mare winked affirmatively the only eye we could see.

"Wise!" continued her master; "why, she knows more than a judge. I'll bet the drinks for the party that she'll walk up these steps and into the room and climb up on the billiard-table and lie down."

The bet was taken at once, not because any one doubted the capabilities of the mare, but there was excitement in the thing without exercise.

Bill whistled in a low tone. Nell instantly scrambled to her feet, walked toward him, put her nose affectionately under his arm, followed him into the room, and to my extreme wonderment climbed upon the billiard-table, to the extreme astonishment of the table no doubt, for it groaned under the weight of the four-legged animal and several of those who were simply bifurcated, and whom Nell permitted to sit upon her. When she got down from the table, which was as graceful a performance as might be expected under the circumstances, Bill sprang upon her back, dashed through the high wide doorway, and at a single bound cleared the flight of steps and landed in the middle of the street. The scout then dismounted, snapped his riding-whip, and the noble beast bounded off down the street, rearing and plunging to her own intense satisfaction. A kindly-disposed individual, who must have been a stranger, supposing the mare was running away, tried to catch her, when she stopped, and as if she resented his impertinence, let fly her heels at him and then quietly trotted to her stable.

"Black Nell has carried me along through many a tight place," said the scout, as we walked toward my quarters. "She trains easier than any animal I ever saw. That trick of dropping quick which you saw has saved my life time and again. When I have been out scouting on the prarer or in the woods I have come across parties of rebels, and have dropped out of sight in the tall grass before they saw us. One day a gang of rebs who had been hunting for me, and thought they had my track, halted for half an hour within fifty yards of us. Nell laid as close as a rabbit, and didn't even whisk her tail to keep the flies off, until the rebs moved off, supposing they were on the wrong scent. The mare will come at my whistle and foller me about just like a dog. She won't mind any one else, nor allow them to mount her, and will kick a harness and wagon all ter pieces ef you try to hitch her in one. And she's right, Kernel," added Bill, with the enthusiasm of a true lover of a horse sparkling in his eyes. "A hoss is too noble a beast to be degraded by such toggery. Harness mules and oxen, but give a hoss a chance ter run."

I had a curiosity, which was not an idle one, to hear what this man had to say about his duel with Tutt, and I asked him:

"Do you not regret killing Tutt? You surely do not like to kill men?"

"As ter killing men," he replied, "I never thought much about it. The most of the men I have killed it was one or t'other of us, and at sich times you don't stop to think; and what's the use after it's all over? As for Tutt, I had rather not have killed him, for I want ter settle down quiet here now. But thar's been hard feeling between us a long while. I wanted ter keep out of that fight; but he tried to degrade me, and I couldn't stand that, you know, for I am a fighting man, you know."

A cloud passed over the speaker's face for a moment as he continued:

"And there was a cause of quarrel between us which people round here don't know about. One of us had to die; and the secret died with him."

"Why did you not wait to see if your ball had hit him? Why did you turn round so quickly?"

The scout fixed his gray eyes on mine, striking his leg with his riding-whip, as he answered,

"I *knew* he was a dead man. I never miss a shot. I turned on the crowd because I was sure they would shoot me if they saw him fall."

"The people about here tell me you are a quiet, civil man. How is it you get into these fights?"

"D—d if I can tell," he replied, with a puzzled look which at once gave place to a proud, defiant expression as he continued—"but you know a man must defend his honor."

"Yes," I admitted, with some hesitation, remembering that I was not in Boston but on the border, and that the code of honor and mode of redress differ slightly in the one place from those of the other.

One of the reasons for my desire to make the acquaintance of Wild Bill was to obtain from his own lips a true account of some of the adventures related of him. It was not an easy matter. It was hard to overcome reticence which marks men who have lived the wild mountain life, and which was one of his valuation qualifications as a scout. Finally he said:

"I hardly know where to begin. Pretty near all these stories are true. I was at it all the war. That affair of my swimming the river took place on that long scout of mine when I was with the rebels five months, when I was sent by General Curtis to Price's army. Things had come pretty close at that time, and it wasn't safe to go straight inter their lines. Everybody was suspected who came from these parts. So I started off and went way up to Kansas City. I bought a horse there and struck out onto the plains, and then went down through Southern Kansas into Arkansas. I knew a rebel named Barnes, who was killed at Pea Ridge. He was from near Austin in Texas. So I called myself his brother and enlisted in a regiment of mounted rangers.

"General Price was just then getting ready for a raid into Missouri. It was sometime before we got into the campaign, and it was mighty hard work for me. The men of our regiment were awful. They didn't mind killing a man no more than a hog. The officers had no command over them. They were afraid of their own men, and let them do what they liked; so they would rob and sometimes murder their own people. It was right hard for me to keep up with them, and not do as they did. I never let on that I was a good shot. I kept that back for big occasions; but ef you'd heard me swear and cuss the blue-bellies, you'd a-thought me one of the wickedest of the whole crew. So it went on until we came near Curtis's army. Bime-by they were on one side Sandy River and we were on t'other. All the time I had been getting information until I knew every regiment and its strength; how much cavalry there was, and how many guns the artillery had.

"You see 'twas time for me to go, but it wasn't easy to git out, for the river was close picketed on both sides. One day when I was on picket our men and the rebels got talking and cussin each other, as you know they used to do. After a while one of the Union men offered to exchange some coffee for tobacco. So we went out onto a little island which was neutral ground like. The minute I saw the other party, who belonged to the Missouri cavalry, we recognized each other. I was awful afraid they'd let on. So I blurted out:

" 'Now, Yanks, let's see yer coffee—no burnt beans, mind yer—but the genuine stuff. We know the real article if we is Texans.'

"The boys kept mum, and we separated. Half an hour afterward General Curtis knew I was with the rebs. But how to git across the river was what stumped me. After that, when I was on picket, I didn't trouble myself about being shot. I used to fire at our boys, and they'd bang away at me, each of us taking good care to shoot wide. But how to git over the river was the bother. At last, after thinking a heap about it, I came to the conclusion that I always did, that the boldest plan is the best and safest.

"We had a big sargent in our company who was allus a-braggin that he could stump any man in the regiment. He swore he had killed more Yanks than any man in the army, and that he could do more daring things than any others. So one day when he was talking loud I took him up, and offered to bet horse for horse that I would ride out into the open, and nearer to the Yankees than he. He tried to back out of this, but the men raised a row, calling him a funk, and a bragger, and all that; so he had to go. Well, we mounted our horses, but before we came within shooting distance of the Union soldiers I made my horse kick and rear so that they could see who I was. Then we rode slowly to the river bank, side by side.

"There must have been ten thousand men watching us; for, besides the rebs who wouldn't have cried about it if we had both been killed, our boys saw something was up, and without being seen thousands of them came down to the river. Their pickets kept firing at the sargent; but whether or not they were afraid of putting a ball through me I don't know, but nary a shot hit him. He was a plucky feller all the same, for the bullets zitted about in every direction.

"Bime-by we got right close ter the river, when one of the Yankee soldiers yelled out, 'Bully for Wild Bill!'

"Then the sargent suspicioned me, for he turned on me and growled out, 'By God, I believe yer a Yank!' And he at onst drew his revolver; but he was too late, for the minute he drew his pistol I put a ball through him. I mightn't have killed him if he hadn't suspicioned me. I had to do it then.

"As he rolled out of the saddle I took his horse by the bit, and dashed into the water as quick as I could. The minute I shot the sargent our boys set up a tremendous shout, and opened a smashing fire on the rebs who had commenced popping at me. But I had got into deep water, and had slipped off my horse over his back, and steered him for the opposite bank by holding onto his tail with one hand, while I held the bridle rein of the sargent's horse in the other hand. It was the hottest bath I ever took. Whew! For about two minutes how the bullets zitted and skipped on the water. I thought I was hit again and again, but the reb sharpshooters were bothered by the splash we made, and in a little while our boys drove them to cover, and after some tumbling at the bank got into the brush with my two horses without a scratch.

"It is a fact," said the scout, while he caressed his long hair, "I felt sort of proud when the boys took me into camp, and General Curtis thanked me before a heap of generals.

"But I never tried that thing over again; nor I didn't go a scouting openly in Price's army after that. They all knew me too well, and you see 'twouldn't a been healthy to have been caught."

The scout's story of swimming the river ought, perhaps, to have satisfied my curiosity; but I was especially desirous to hear him relate the history of a sanguinary fight which he had with a party of ruffians in the early part of the war, when, single-handed, he fought and killed ten men. I had heard the story as it came from an officer of the regular army who, an hour after the affair, saw Bill and the ten dead men —some killed with bullets, others hacked and slashed to death with a knife.

As I write out the details of this terrible tale from notes which I took as the words fell from the scout's lips, I am conscious of its extreme improbability; but while I listened to him I remembered the story in the Bible, where we are told that Samson "with the jawbone of an ass slew a thousand men," and as I looked upon this magnificent example of human strength and daring, he appeared to me to realize the powers of a Samson and Hercules combined, and I should not have been inclined to place any limit upon his achievements. Besides this, one who has lived for four years in the presence of such grand heroism and deeds of prowess as was seen during the war is in what might be called a "receptive" mood. Be the story true or not, in part, or in whole, I believed then every word Wild Bill uttered, and I believe it today.

"I don't like to talk about that M'Kandlas affair," said Bill, in answer to my question. "It gives me a queer shiver whenever I think of it, and sometimes I dream about it, and wake up in a cold sweat.

"You see this M'Kandlas was the Captain of a gang of desperadoes, horse-thieves, murderers, regular cut-throats, who were the terror of everybody on the border, and who kept us in the mountains in hot water whenever they were around. I knew them all in the mountains, where they pretended to be trapping, but they were there hiding from the hangman. M'Kandlas was the biggest scoundrel and bully of them all, and was allers a-braggin of what he could do. One day I beat him shootin at a mark, and then threw him at the back-holt. And I didn't drop him as soft as you would a baby, you may be sure. Well, he got savage mad about it, and swore he would have his revenge on me some time.

"This was just before the war broke out, and we were already takin sides in the mountains either for the South or the Union. M'Kandlas and his gang were border-ruffians in the Kansas row, and of course they went with the rebs. Bime-by he clar'd out, and I shouldn't have thought of the feller agin ef he hadn't crossed my path. It 'pears he didn't forget me.

"It was in '61, when I guided a detachment of cavalry who were comin in from Camp Floyd. We had nearly reached the Kansas line, and were in South Nebraska, when one afternoon I went out of camp to go to the cabin of an old friend of mine, a Mrs. Waltman. I took only one of my revolvers with me, for although the war had broke out I didn't think it necessary to carry both my pistols, and, in all or'nary scrimmages, one is better than a dozen, ef you shoot straight. I saw some wild turkeys on the road as I was goin down, and popped one of 'em over, thinking he'd be just the thing for supper.

"Well, I rode up to Mrs. Waltman's, jumped off my horse, and went into the cabin, which is like most of the cabins on the prarer, with only one room, and that had two doors, one opening in front and t'other on a yard, like.

" 'How are you, Mrs. Waltman?' I said, feeling as jolly as you please.

"The minute she saw me she turned as white as a sheet and screamed: 'Is that you, Bill? Oh, my God! they will kill you! Run! run! They will kill you!'

" 'Who's a-goin to kill me?' said I. 'There's two can play at that game.'

" 'M'Kandlas and his gang. There's ten of them, and you've no chance. They've jes gone down the road to the corn-rack. They came up here only five minutes ago. M'Kandlas was dragging poor Parson Shipley on the ground with a lariat round his neck. The preacher was most dead with choking and the horses stamping on him. M'Kandlas knows yer bringin in that party of Yankee cavalry, and he swears he'll cut yer heart out. Run, Bill, run!—But it's too late; they're comin up the lane.'

"While she was a-talkin I remembered I had but one revolver, and a load gone out of that. On the table there was a horn of powder and some little bars of lead. I poured some powder into the empty chamber and rammed the lead after it by hammering the barrel on the table, and had just capped the pistol when I heard M'Kandlas shout:

" 'There's that d——d Yank Wild Bill's horse; he's here; and we'll skin him alive!'

"If I had thought of runnin before it war too late now, and the house was my best holt—a sort of fortress, like. I never thought I should leave that room alive."

The scout stopped in his story, rose from his seat, and strode back and forward in a state of great excitement.

"I tell you what it is, Kernel," he resumed, after a while, "I don't mind a scrimmage with these fellers round here. Shoot one or two of them and the rest run away. But all of M'Kandlas's gang were reckless, bloodthirsty devils, who would fight as long as they had strength to pull a trigger. I have been in tight places, but that's one of the few times I said my prayers.

" 'Surround the house and give him no quarter!' yelled M'Kandlas. When I heard that I felt as quiet and cool as if I was a-goin to church. I looked round the room and saw a Hawkins rifle hangin over the bed.

" 'Is that loaded?' said I to Mrs. Waltman.

" 'Yes,' the poor thing whispered. She was so frightened she couldn't speak out loud.

" 'Are you sure?' said I, as I jumped to the bed and caught it from its hooks. Although my eye did not leave the door, yet I could see she nodded 'Yes' again. I put the revolver on the bed, and just then M'Kandlas poked his head inside the doorway, but jumped back when he saw me with the rifle in my hand.

" 'Come in here, you cowardly dog!' I shouted. 'Come in here, and fight me!'

"M'Kandlas was no coward, if he was a bully. He jumped inside the room with his gun leveled to shoot; but he was not quick enough. My rifle-ball went through his heart. He fell back outside the house, where he was found afterward holding tight to his rifle, which had fallen over his head.

"His disappearance was followed by a yell from his gang, and then there was a dead silence. I put down the rifle and took the revolver, and I said to myself: 'Only six shots and nine men to kill. Save your powder, Bill, for the death-hug's a-comin!' I don't know why it was, Kernel," continued Bill, looking at me inquiringly, "but at that moment things seemed clear and sharp. I could think strong.

"There was a few seconds of that awful stillness, and then the ruffians came rushing in at both doors. How wild they looked with their red, drunken faces and inflamed eyes, shouting and cussing! But I never aimed more deliberately in my life.

"One—two—three—four; and four men fell dead.

"That didn't stop the rest. Two of them fired their bird-guns at me. And then I felt a sting run all over me. The room was full of smoke. Two got in close to me, their eyes glaring out of the clouds. One I knocked down with my fist. 'You are out of the way for a while,' I thought. The second I shot dead. The other three clutched me and crowded me onto the bed. I fought hard. I broke with my hand one man's arm. He had his fingers round my throat. Before I could get to my feet I was struck across the breast with the stock of a rifle, and I felt the blood rushing out of my nose and mouth. Then I got ugly, and I remembered that I got hold of a knife, and then it was all cloudy like, and I was wild, and I struck savage blows, following the devils up from one side to the other of the room and into the corners, striking and slashing until I knew that everyone was dead.

"All of a sudden it seemed as if my heart was on fire. I was bleeding everywhere. I rushed out to the well and drank from the bucket, and then tumbled down in a faint."

Breathless with the intense interest with which I had followed this strange story, all the more thrilling and weird when its hero, seeming to live over again the bloody events of that day, gave way to its terrible spirit with wild, savage gestures. I saw then—what my scrutiny of the morning had failed to discover—the tiger which lay concealed beneath that gentle exterior.

"You must have been hurt almost to death," I said.

"There were eleven buck-shot in me. I carry some of them now. I was cut in thirteen places. All of them bad enough to have let out the life of a man. But that blessed old Dr. Mills pulled me safe through it, after a bed siege of many a long week."

"That prayer of yours, Bill, may have been more potent for your safety than you think. You should thank God for your deliverance."

"To tell you the truth, Kernel," responded the scout with a certain solemnity in his grave face, "I don't talk about sich things ter the people round here, but I allers feel sort of thankful when I get out of a bad scrape." . . .

"I would like to see you shoot."

"Would yer?" replied the scout, drawing his revolver; and approaching the window, he pointed to a letter O in a signboard which was fixed to the stone-wall of a building on the other side of the way.

"That sign is more than fifty yards away. I will put these six balls into the inside of the circle, which isn't bigger than a man's heart."

In an off-hand way, and without sighting the pistol with his eye, he discharged the six shots of his revolver. I afterward saw that all the bullets had entered the circle.

As Bill proceeded to reload his pistol, he said to me with a naïveté of manner which was meant to be assuring:

"Whenever you get into a row be sure and not shoot too quick. Take time. I've known many a feller slip up for shootin' in a hurry."

It would be easy to fill a volume with the adventures of that remarkable man. My object here has been to make a slight record of one who is one of the best—perhaps the very best—example of a class who more than any other encountered perils and privations in defense of our nationality.

One afternoon as General Smith and I mounted our horses to start upon our journey toward the East, Wild Bill came to shake hands good-by, and I said to him:

"If you have no objection I will write out for publication an account of a few of your adventures."

"Certainly you may," he replied. "I'm sort of public property. But, Kernel," he continued, leaning upon my saddle-bow, while there was a tremulous softness in his voice and a strange moisture in his averted eyes, "I have a mother back there in Illinois who is old and feeble. I haven't seen her this many a year, and haven't been a good son to her, yet I love her better than any thing in this life. It don't matter much what they say about me here. But I'm not a cut-throat and vagabond, and I'd like the old woman to know what'll make her proud. I'd like her to hear that her runaway boy has fought through the war for the Union like a true man."

[William Hitchcock—called *Wild Bill, the Scout of the Plains*—shall have his wish. I have told his story precisely as it was told to me, confirmed in all important points by many witnesses; and I have no doubt of its truth.—G. W. N.]

The Evolution of the Cow-Puncher

by OWEN WISTER

SEPTEMBER, 1895

Every fictional cowboy-hero who ever drew a gun was born right here. For it was in this article that Owen Wister first took the nineteenth century's romantic conception of the chivalrous Knight in Shining Armor and draped it over the shoulders of the American cow-puncher. The creation made possible The Virginian, *the granddaddy of all Westerns. That novel grew out of a series of stories in* Harper's, *written at the request of editor Henry Mills Alden. Earlier, Alden had published Wister's first Western story, "Hank's Woman." He also assigned Frederic Remington to illustrate Wister's work. Wister was born in Philadelphia in 1860, was educated in music and law at Harvard, and first went West for his health in 1885. He died in 1938.*

Throughout his career it has been an Englishman's love to push further into the wilderness, and his fate thereby to serve larger causes than his own. In following his native bent he furthers unwittingly a design outside himself; he cuts the way for the common law and self-government, and new creeds, polities, and nations arise in his wake; in his own immense commonwealth this planless rover is obliterated. Roving took him (the Viking portion of him) from his Norse crags across to Albion. From that hearth of Albion the footprints of his sons led to the corners of the earth; beside that hearth how inveterate remains his flavor! At Hastings he tasted defeat, but was not vanquished; to the Invincible Armada he proved a grievous surprise; one way or another he came through Waterloo—possibly because he is inveterately dull at perceiving himself beaten; when not otherwise busy at Balaklava or by the Alma, he was getting up horse-races, ready for sport or killing, and all with that silver and cut-glass finish which so offends our whistling, vacant-minded democracy. Greatest triumph and glory of all, because spiritual, his shoulders bore the Reformation when its own originators had tottered. Away from the hearth the cut-glass stage will not generally have been attained by him, and in Maine or Kentucky you can recognize at sight the chip of the old rough block. But if you meet him upon his island, in the shape of a peer, and find him particular to dress for dinner seven days of the week, do not on that account imagine that his white tie has throttled the man in him. That is a whistling Fourth-of-July misconception. It's no symptom of patriotism to be unable to see a man through cut glass, and if it comes to an appraisement of the stranger and the peer, I should say, put each in the other's place, and let us see if the stranger could play the peer as completely as the nobleman played the cowboy. Sir Francis Drake was such a one; and Raleigh, the fine essence of Anglo-Saxon, with his fashionable gallant cloak, his adventure upon new seas, and his immediate appreciation of tobacco. The rover may return with looted treasure or incidentally stolen corners of territory to clap in his strong-box (this Angle is no angel), but it is not the dollars that played first fiddle with him, else our Hebrew friends would pioneer the whole of us. Adventure, to be out-of-doors, to find some new place far away from the postman, to enjoy independence of spirit or mind or body (according to his high or low standards)—this is the cardinal surviving fittest instinct that makes the Saxon through the centuries conqueror, invader, navigator, buccaneer, explorer, colonist, tiger-shooter; lifts him a pilgrim among the immortals at Plymouth Rock, dangles him a pirate from the gallows on the docks of Bristol. At all times when historic conditions or private stress have burst his domestic crust and let him fly out naturally, there he is, on Darien's peak, or through Magellan, or across the Missouri, or up the Columbia, a Hawkins, a Boone, a Grey, or a nameless vagrant, the same Saxon, ploughing the seas and carving the forests in every shape of man, from preacher to thief, and in each shape changelessly untamed. And as he has ruled the waves with his ship from that Viking time until yesterday at Samoa, when approaching death could extract no sound from him save American cheers and music, so upon land has the horse been his foster-brother, his ally, his playfellow, from the tournament at Camelot to the round-up at Abilene. The blood and the sweat of his jousting, and all the dirt and stains, have faded in the long sunlight of tradition, and in the chronicles of romance we hear none of his curses or obscenity; the clash of his armor rings mellow and heroic down the ages into our modern ears. But his direct lineal offspring among our Western mountains has had no poet to connect him with the eternal, no distance to lend him enchantment; though he has fought single-handed with savages, and through skill and daring prevailed, though he has made his nightly bed in a thousand miles of snow and loneliness, he has not, and never will have, the "consecration of memory." No doubt Sir Launcelot bore himself with a grace and breeding of which our unpolished fellow of the cattle trail has only the latent possibility; but in personal daring and in skill as to the horse, the knight and the cowboy are nothing but the same Saxon of different environments, the nobleman in London and the nobleman in Texas; and no hoof in Sir Thomas Mallory shakes the crumbling plains with quadruped sound more valiant than the galloping that has echoed from the Rio Grande to the Big Horn Mountains. But .we have no Sir Thomas Mallory! Since Hawthorne, Longfellow, and Cooper were taken from us, our flippant and impoverished imagination has ceased to be national, and the rider among Indians and cattle, the frontiersman, the American who replaces Miles Standish and the Pathfinder, is now beneath the notice of polite writers.

From the tournament to the round-up! Deprive the Saxon of his horse, and put him to forest-clearing or in a countinghouse for a couple of generations, and you may pass him by without ever seeing that his legs are designed for the gripping of saddles. Our first hundred years afforded his horsemanship but little opportunity. Though his out-of-door spirit, most at home when at large, sported free in the elbow-room granted by the surrender of Cornwallis, it was on foot and with an ax that he chiefly enjoyed himself. He moved his log cabin slowly inward from the Atlantic, slowly over the wooded knolls of Cumberland and Allegheny, down and across the valley beyond, until the infrequent news of him ceased, and his kinsfolk who had stayed by the sea, and were merchanting themselves upwards to the level of family portraits and the cut-glass finish, forgot that the prodigal in the backwoods belonged to them, and was part of their United States, bone of their bone. And thus did our wide country become as a man whose East hand knoweth not what his West hand doeth.

Mr. Herndon, in telling of Lincoln's early days in Illinois, gives us a complete picture of the roving Saxon upon our continent in 1830. "The boys . . . were a terror to the entire region—seemingly a necessary product of frontier civilization. They were friendly and good-natured. . . . They would do almost anything for sport or fun, love or necessity. Though rude and rough, though life's forces ran over the edge of their bowl, foaming and sparkling in pure deviltry for deviltry's sake, . . . yet place before them a poor man who needed their aid, . . . a defenceless woman, . . . they melted into sympathy and charity at once. They gave all they had, and willingly toiled or played cards for more. . . . A stranger's introduction was likely to be the most unpleasant part of his acquaintance. . . . They were in the habit of 'cleaning out' New Salem." Friendly and good-natured, and in the habit of cleaning out New Salem! Quite so. There you have him. Here is the American variety of the Saxon set down for you as accurately as if Audubon himself had done it. A colored plate of Robin Hood and the Sheriff of Nottingham should go on the opposite page. Nothing but the horse is left out of the description, and that is because the Saxon and his horse seldom met during the rail-splitting era of our growth. But the man of 1830 would give away all that he had and play cards for more. Decidedly nothing was missing except the horse—and the horse was waiting in another part of our large map until the man should arrive and jump on his back again.

A few words about this horse—the horse of the plains. Whether or no his forefathers looked on when Montezuma fell, they certainly hailed from Spain. And whether it was missionaries or thieves who carried them northward from Mexico, until the Sioux heard of the new animal, certain it also is that this pony ran wild for a century or two, either alone or with various red-skinned owners; and as he gathered the sundry experiences of war and peace, of being stolen, and of being abandoned in the snow at inconvenient distances from home, of being ridden by two women and a baby at once, and of being eaten by a bear, his wide range of contretemps brought him a wit sharper than the street Arab's, and an attitude towards life more blasé than in the united capitals of Europe. I have frequently caught him watching me with an eye of such sardonic depreciation that I felt it quite vain to attempt any hiding from him of my incompetence; and as for surprising him, a locomotive cannot do it, for I have tried this. He relishes putting a man in absurd positions, and will wait many days in patience to compass this uncharitable thing; and when he cannot bring a man to derision, he contents himself with a steer or a buffalo, helping the man to rope and throw these animals with an ingenuity surpassing any circus, to my thinking. A number of delighted passengers on the Kansas Pacific Railway passed by a Mexican vaquero, who had been sent out from Kansas City to rope a buffalo as an advertisement for the stock-yards. The train stopped to take a look at the solitary horseman fast to a buffalo in the midst of the plains. José, who had his bull safely roped, shouted to ask if they had water on the train. "We'll bring you some," said they. "Oh, I come get," said he; and jumping off, he left his accomplished pony in sole charge of the buffalo. Whenever the huge beast struggled for freedom, the clever pony stiffened his legs and leaned back as in a tug of war, by jumps and dodges so anticipating each move of the enemy that escape was entirely hopeless. The boy got his drink, and his employer sent out a car for the buffalo, which was taken in triumph into Kansas City behind the passenger train. The Mexican narrated the exploit to his employer thus: "Oh, Shirley, when the train start they all give three greata big cheers for me, and then they give three mucha bigger cheers for the little gray hoss!"

Ah, progress is truly a wonder! and admirable beyond all doubt it is to behold the rapid new square miles of brick, and the stream rich with the contributions of an increased population, and tall factories that have stopped dividends just for the present, and long empty railroads in the hands of the receiver; but I prefer that unenlightened day when we had plenty of money and cheered for the little gray hoss. Such was the animal that awaited the coming of the railsplitter. The meeting was a long way off in 1830. Not the Mexican war, not the gold on the Pacific in '49 (though this, except for the horse, revealed the whole Saxon at his best and worst, and for a brief and beautiful moment waked once more the American muse), not any national event until the war of the rebellion was over and we had a railroad from coast to coast, brought the man and his horse together. It was in the late sixties that this happened in Texas. The adventurous sons of Kentucky and Tennessee, forever following the native bent to roam, and having no longer a war to give them the life they preferred, came into a new country full of grass and cattle. Here they found Mexicans by the hundred, all on horses and at large over the flat of the world. This sight must have stirred memories in the rail-splitter's blood, for he joined the sport upon the instant. I do not think he rode with bolder skill than the Mexican's, but he brought other and grittier qualities to bear upon that wild life, and also the Saxon contempt for the foreigner. Soon he had taken what was good from this small, deceitful alien, including his name, *Vaquero*, which he translated into Cowboy. He took his saddle, his bridle, his spurs, his rope, his methods of branding and herding—indeed, most of his customs and accouterments—and with them he went rioting over the hills. His play-ground was two thousand miles long and a thousand wide. The hoofs of his horse were tough as iron, and the pony waged the joyous battle of self-preservation as stoutly as did his rider. When the man lay rolled in his blankets sleeping, warm and unconcerned beneath a driving storm of snow, the beast pawed through to the sage-brush and subsisted; so that it came to be said of such an animal, "A meal a day is enough for a man who gets to ride that horse."

The cow-puncher's play-ground in those first glorious days of his prosperity included battle and murder and sudden death as every-day matters. From 1865 to 1878 in Texas he fought his way with knife and gun, and any hour of the twenty-four might see him flattened behind the rocks among the whiz of bullets and the flight of arrows, or dragged bloody and folded together from some adobe hovel. Seventy-five dollars a month and absolute health and strength were his wages; and when the news of all this excellence drifted from Texas eastward, they came in shoals—Saxon boys of picked courage (none but plucky ones could survive) from South and North, from town and country. Every sort and degree of home tradition came with them from their far birthplaces. Some had known the evening hymn at one time, others could remember no parent or teacher earlier than the street; some spoke with the gentle accent of Virginia, others in the dialect of baked beans and codfish; here and there was the baccalaureate, already beginning to forget his Greek alphabet, but still able to repeat the two notable words with which Xenophon always marches upon the next stage of his journey. Hither to the cattle country they flocked from forty kinds of home, each bringing a deadly weapon.

What motlier tribe, what heap of cards shuffled from more various unmatched packs, could be found? Yet this tribe did not remain motley, but soon grew into a unit. To begin with, the old spirit burned alike in all, the unextinguished fire of adventure and independence. And then, the same stress of shifting for self, the same vigorous and peculiar habits of life, were forced upon each one: watching for Indians, guarding huge herds at night, chasing cattle, wild as deer, over rocks and counties, sleeping in the dust and waking in the snow, cooking in the open, swimming the swollen rivers. Such gymnasium for mind and body develops a like pattern in the unlike. Thus, late in the nineteenth century, was the race once again subjected to battles and darkness, rain and shine, to the fierceness and generosity of the desert. Destiny tried her latest experiment upon the Saxon, and plucking him from the library, the haystack, and the gutter, set him upon his horse; then it was that, face to face with the eternal simplicity of death, his modern guise fell away and showed once again the medieval man. It was no new type, no product of the frontier, but just the original kernel of the nut with the shell broken.

This bottom bond of race unified the divers young men, who came riding from various points of the compass, speaking university and gutter English simultaneously; and as the knights of Camelot prized their armor and were particular about their swords, so these dusty successors had an extreme pride of equipment, and put aside their jeans and New York suits for the tribal dress. Though each particle of gearing for man and horse was evoked from daily necessity, gold and silver instantly stepped in to play their customary ornamental part, as with all primitive races. The cow-puncher's legs must be fended from the thorny miles of the Rio Grande, the thousand mongrel shrubs that lace their bristles together stiff over the country—the mesquite, the shin-oak, the cat's-claw, the Spanish-dagger; wide-spreading, from six inches to ten feet high, every vegetable vicious with an embroidery of teeth and nails; a continent of peevish thicket called *chaparral,* as we indiscriminately call a dog with too many sorts of grandfathers a cur. Into this saw-mill dives the wild steer through paths and passages known to himself, and after him the pursuing man must also dive at a rate that would tear his flesh to ribbons if the blades and points could get hold of him. But he cases his leg against the hostile *chaparral* from thigh to ankle in chaps—leathern breeches, next door to armor: his daily bread is scarcely more needful to him. Soon his barbaric pleasure in finery sews tough leather fringe along their sides, and the leather flap of the pocket becomes stamped with a heavy rose. Sagging in a slant upon his hips leans his leather belt of cartridges buckled with jaunty arrogance, and though he uses his pistol with murderous skill, it is pretty, with ivory or mother-of pearl for a handle. His arm must be loose to swing his looped rope free and drop its noose over the neck of the animal that bounds in front of his rushing pony. Therefore he rides in a loose flannel shirt that will not cramp him as he whirls the coils; but the handkerchief knotted at his throat, though it is there to prevent sunburn, will in time of prosperity be chosen for its color and soft texture, a scarf to draw the eye of woman. His heavy splendid saddle is, in its shape and luxury of straps and leather thongs, the completest instrument for night and day travel, and the freighting along with you of board and lodging, that any nomad has so far devised. With its trappings and stamped leather, its horn and high cantle, we are well acquainted. It must stand the strain of eight hundred sudden pounds of live beef tearing at it for freedom; it must be the anchor that shall not drag during the furious rushes of such a typhoon. For the cattle of the wilderness have often run wild for three, four, and five years, through rocks and forests, never seeing the face of man from the day when as little calves they were branded. And some were never branded at all. They have grown up in company with the deer, and like the deer they fly at the approach of the horseman. Then, if he has ridden out to gather these waifs from their remote untenanted pastures and bring them to be counted and driven to sale, he must abandon himself to the headlong pursuit. The open easy plain with its harmless footing lies behind, the steep valley narrows up to an entering wedge among the rocks, and into these untoward regions rush the beeves. The shale and detritus of shelving landslides, the slippery knobs in the beds of brooks, the uncertain edges of the jumping-off place, all lie in the road of the day's necessity, and where the steer goes, goes the cow-puncher too—balancing, swaying, doubling upon his shrewd pony. The noose uncoiling flies swinging through the air and closes round the throat—or perhaps only the hind leg—of the quarry. In the shock of stopping short or of leaning to circle, the rider's stirrups must be long, and his seat a forked pliant poise on the horse's back; no grip of the knee will answer in these conditions; his leg must have its straight length, a lever of muscle and sinew to yield or close viselike on the pony's ribs; and when the steer feels that he is taken and the rope tightens from the saddle horn, then must the gearing be solid, else, like a fisherman floundering with snapped rod and tangled line, the cow-puncher will have misfortunes to repair and nothing to repair them with. Such a thing as this has happened in New Mexico: The steer, pursued and frantic at feeling the throttle of flung rope, ran blindly over a cliff, one end of the line fast to him, the other to the rider's saddle horn, and no time to think once, much less twice, about anything in this or the next world. The pony braced his legs at the edge, but his gait swept him onward, as with the fast skater whose skate has stuck upon a frozen chip. The horse fell over the mountain, and with him his rider: but the sixty-foot rope was new, and it hooked over a stump. Steer and horse swung like scales gently above the man, who lay at the bottom, hurt nearly to death, but not enough to dull his appreciation of the unusual arrangement.

It is well, then, to wear leathern armor and sit in a stout saddle if you would thrive among the thorns and rocks; and without any such casualty as falling over a mountain the day's common events call for uncommon strength of gear. Not otherwise can the steer be hooked and landed safely, and not otherwise is the man to hoist resisting beeves up a hill somewhat as safes are conducted to the sixth story, nor could the rider plunge galloping from the sixth story to the ground, or swerve and heavily lean to keep from flying into space, were his stirrup leathers not laced, and every other crucial spot of strain independent of so weak a thing as a buckle. To go up where you have come down is another and easier process for man and straps and everything except the horse. His breath and legs are not immortal. And in order that each day the man may be hardily borne over rough and smooth he must own several mounts—a "string"; sometimes six and more, either his own property, or allotted to him by the foreman of the outfit for which he rides. The unused animals run in a herd—the *ramuda;* and to get a fresh mount from the ramuda means not seldom the ceremony of catching your hare. The ponies walk sedately together in the pasture, good as gold, and eying you without concern until they perceive that you are come with an object. They then put forth against you all the circus knowledge you have bestowed upon them so painfully. They comprehend ropes and loops and the law of gravity; they have observed the errors of steers in similar cases, and the unattractive result of running inside any enclosure, such as a corral,

they strategize to keep at large, and altogether chasing a steer is
tortoise play to the game they can set up for you. They relish the sight
of you whirling impotent among them, rejoice in the smoking pace
and the doublings they perpetrate; and with one eye attentive to you
and your poised rope, and the other dexterously commanding the
universe, they will intertangle as in cross-tag, pushing between your
design and its victim, mingling confusedly like a driven mist, and all
this with nostrils leaning level to the wind and bellies close to the
speeding ground. But when the desired one is at last taken and your
successful rope is on his neck, you would not dream he had ever
wished for anything else. He stands, submitting absent-mindedly to bit
and blanket, mild as any unconscious lamb, while placidity descends
once more upon the herd; again they pasture good as gold, and butter
would not melt in the mouth of one of these conscientious creatures.
I have known a number of dogs, one crow, and two monkeys, but
these combined have seemed to me less fertile in expedient than the
cow-pony, the sardonic cayuse. The bit his master gave him, and the
bridle and spurs, have the same origin from necessity and the same
history as to ornament. If stopping and starting and turning must be
like flashes of light, the apparatus is accordingly severe; and as for the
spurs, those wheels with long spikes cease to seem grotesque when you
learn that with shorter and sharper rowels they would catch in the
corded meshes of the girth, and bring the rider to ruin. Silver and gold,
when he could pay for them, went into the make and decoration of
this smaller machinery; and his hat would cost him fifteen dollars, and
he wore fringed gloves. His boots often cost twenty-five dollars in his
brief hour of opulence. Come to town for his holiday, he wore his
careful finery, and from his wide hat-brim to his jingling heels made
something of a figure—as self-conscious and deliberate a show as any
painted buck in council or bull-elk among his aspiring cows; and
out of town in the mountains, as wild and lean and dangerous as buck
or bull knows how to be.

As with his get-up, so it went with his vocabulary; for any manner
of life with a rule and flavor of its own strong enough to put a new
kind of dress on a man's body will put new speech in his mouth, and
an idiom derived from the exigencies of his days and nights was soon
spoken by the cow-puncher. Like all creators, he not only built, but
borrowed his own wherever he found it. *Chaps,* from *chapparajos,* is
only one of many transfers from the Mexican, one out of (I should

suppose) several hundred; and in *lover-wolf* is a singular instance of half-baked translation. *Lobo,* pronounced *lovo,* being the Spanish for wolf, and the coyote being a sort of wolf, the dialect of the southern border has slid into this name for a wolf that is larger, and a worse enemy to steers than the small coward coyote. Lover-wolf is a word anchored to its district. In the Northwest, though the same animal roams there as dangerously, his Texas name would be as unknown as the Northwest's word for Indian, *siwash,* from *sauvage,* would be along the Rio Grande. Thus at the top and bottom of our map do French and Spanish trickle across the frontier, and with English melt into two separate amalgams which are wholly distinct, and which remain near the spot where they were molded; while other compounds, having the same Northern and Southern starting-point, drift far and wide, and become established in the cow-puncher's dialect over his whole country. No better French specimen can be instanced than *cache,* verb and noun, from the verb *cacher,* to conceal. In our Eastern life words such as these are of no pertinent avail; and as it is only universal pertinence which can lift a fragment of dialect into the dictionary's good society, most of them must pass with the transient generation that spoke them. Certain ones there are deserving to survive; *cinch,* for instance, from *cincha,* the Mexican girth. From its narrow office under the horse's belly it has come to perform in metaphor a hundred services. In cinching somebody or something you may mean that you hold four aces, or the key of a political crisis; and when a man is very much indeed upper-dog, then he is said to have an air-tight cinch; and this phrase is to me so pleasantly eloquent that I am withheld from using it in polite gatherings only by that prudery which we carry as a burden along with the benefits of academic training. Besides the foreign importations, such as *arroyo* and *riata,* that stand unchanged, and those others which under the action of our own speech have sloughed their native shape and come out something new, like quirt—once *cuerta,* Mexican for rawhide—is the third large class of words which the cowboy has taken from our sober old dictionary stock and made over for himself. Pie-biter refers not to those hailing from our pie belt, but to a cow-pony who secretly forages in a camp kitchen to indulge his acquired tastes. Western whiskey, besides being known as tonsil varnish and a hundred different things, goes as benzine, not unjustly. The same knack of imagery that upon our Eastern slope gave visitors from the country the brief, sure name of hayseed, calls their Western equivalents junipers. Hay grows scant upon the Rocky Mountains, but those seclusions are filled with evergreens. No one has accounted to me for *hobo*. A hobo is a wandering unemployed person, a stealer of rides on freight-trains, a diner at the back door, eternally seeking honest work, and when brought face to face with it eternally retreating. The hobo is he against whom we have all sinned by earning our living. Perhaps some cowboy saw an Italian playing a pipe to the accompaniment of the harp, and made the generalization: oboe may have given us hobo. Hobo-ken has been suggested by an ingenious friend; but the word seems of purely Western origin, and I heard it in the West several years before it became used in the East. The cow-puncher's talent for making a useful verb out of anything shows his individuality. Any young strong race will always lay firm hands on language and squeeze juice from it; and you instantly comprehend the man who tells you of his acquaintances, whom you know to be drunk at the moment, that they are *helling* around town. Unsleeping need for quick thinking and doing gave these nomads the pith of utterance. They say, for instance, that they intend *camping on a man's trail,* meaning, concisely, "So-and-so has injured us, and we are going to follow him day and night until we are quits." Thus do these ordinary words and phrases, freshened to novelty by the cow-puncher's wits, show his unpremeditated art of brevity, varying in aptness, but in imagination constant; and with one last example of his fancy I shall leave his craft of word-making.

It is to be noted in all peoples that for whatever particular thing in life is of frequent and familiar practice among them they will devise many gradations of epithet. *To go* is in the cattle country a common act, and a man may go for different reasons, in several manners, at various speeds. For example:

"Do I understand you went up the tree with the bear just behind you?"

"The bear was not in front of me."

Here the cowboy made ordinary words suffice for showing the way he went, but his goings can be of many sorts besides in front of and behind something, and his rich choice of synonyms embodies a latent chapter of life and habits. To the several phases of going known to the pioneer as vamose, skip, light out, dust, and git, the cowboy adds, burn the earth, hit, hit the breeze, pull your freight, jog, amble, move, pack, rattle your hocks, brindle, and more, very likely, if I knew or

could recall them; I think that the observer who caught the shifting
flicker of a race or a pursuit, and said brindle first, had a mind of live-
liness and art.

It may be that some of these words I have named as home-bred
natives of our wilderness are really of long standing and archaic repute,
and that the scholar can point to them in the sonnets of Shakespeare,
but I, at least, first learned them west of the Missouri.

With a speech and dress of his own, then, the cow-puncher drove
his herds to Abilene or Westport Landing in the Texas times, and the
easy abundant dollars came, and left him for spurs and bridles of
barbaric decoration. Let it be remembered that the Mexican was the
original cowboy, and that the American improved on him. Those were
the days in which he was long in advance of settlers, and when he
literally fought his right of way. Along the waste hundreds of miles
that he had to journey, three sorts of inveterate enemies infested the
road—the thief (the cattle-thief, I mean), who was as daring as himself; the supplanted Mexican, who hated the new encroaching Northern race; and the Indian, whose hand was against all races but his own
immediate tribe, and who flayed the feet of his captives, and made them
walk so through the mountain passes to the fires in which he slowly
burned them. Among these perils the cow-puncher took wild pleasure
in existing. No soldier of fortune ever adventured with bolder care-
lessness, no fiercer blood ever stained a border. If his raids, his triumphs, and his reverses have inspired no minstrel to sing of him who
rode by the Pecos River and the hills of San Andreas, it is not so much
the Rob Roy as the Walter Scott who is lacking. And the Flora
McIvor! Alas! the stability of the clan, the blessing of the home background, was not there. These wild men sprang from the loins of no
similar father, and begot no sons to continue their hardihood. War
they made in plenty, but not love; for the woman they saw was not the
woman a man can take into his heart. That their fighting Saxon ancestors awoke in them for a moment and made them figures for poetry
and romance is due to the strange accidents of a young country, where,
while cities flourish by the coast and in the direct paths of trade, the
herd-trading interior remains medieval in its simplicity and violence.
And yet this transient generation deserves more chronicling than it
will ever have. Deeds in plenty were done that are all and more than
imagination should require. One high noon upon the plains by the Rio
Grande the long irons lay hot in the fire. The young cattle were being

branded, and the gathered herd covered the plain. Two owners claimed one animal. They talked at first quietly round the fire, then the dispute quickened. One roped the animal, throwing it to the ground to burn his mark upon it. A third came, saying the steer was his. The friends of each drew close to hear, and a claimant thrust his red-hot iron against the hide of the animal tied on the ground. Another seized it from him, and as they fell struggling, their adherents flung themselves upon their horses, and massing into clans, volleyed with their guns across the fire. In a few minutes fourteen riders lay dead on the plain, and the tied animal over which they had quarreled bawled and bleated in the silence. Here is skirmishing enough for a ballad. And there was a certain tireless man in northern New Mexico whose war upon cattle-thieves made his life so shining a mark that he had in bank five thousand dollars to go to the man who killed the man who killed him. A neighborhood where one looks so far beyond his own assassination as to provide a competence for his avenger is discouraging to family life, but a promising field for literature.

Such existence soon makes a strange man of any one, and the early cow-punchers rapidly grew unlike all people but each other and the wild superstitious ancestors whose blood was in their veins. Their hair became long, and their glance rested with serene penetration upon the stranger; they laughed seldom, and their spirit was in the permanent attitude of war. Grim lean men of few topics, and not many words concerning these; comprehending no middle between the poles of brutality and tenderness; indifferent to death, but disconcerted by a good woman; some with violent Old Testament religion, some avowing none, and all of them uneasy about corpses and the dark. These hermited horsemen would dismount in camp at nightfall and lie looking at the stars, or else squat about the fire conversing with crude somberness of brands and horses and cows, speaking of *humans* when they referred to men.

Today they are still to be found in New Mexico, their last domain. The extreme barrenness of those mountains has held tamer people at a distance. That next stage of Western progress—that unparalleled compound of new hotels, electric lights, and invincible ignorance which has given us the Populist—has been retarded, and the civilization of Colorado and silver does not yet redeem New Mexico. But in these shrunk days the cow-puncher no longer can earn money to spend on ornament; he dresses poorly and wears his chaps very wide and ungainly. But he still has three mounts, with seven horses to each mount, and his life is in the saddle among vast solitudes. In the North he was a later comer, and never quite so formidable a person. By the time he had ridden up into Wyoming and Montana the Indian was mostly gone, the locomotive upon the scene, and going West far less an exploration than in the Texas days. Into these new pastures drifted youths from town and country whose grit would scarcely have lasted them to Abilene, and who were not the grim long-haired type, but a sort of glorified farm hand. They too wore their pistols, and rode gallantly, and out of them nature and simplicity did undoubtedly forge manlier, cleaner men than what our streets breed of no worse material. They galloped by the side of the older hands, and caught something of the swing and tradition of the first years. They developed heartiness and honesty in virtue and in vice alike. Their evil deeds were not of the sneaking kind, but had always the saving grace of courage. Their code had no place for the man who steals a pocket-book or stabs in the back.

And what has become of them? Where is this latest outcropping of the Saxon gone? Except where he lingers in the mountains of New Mexico he has been dispersed, as the elk, as the buffalo, as all wild animals must inevitably be dispersed. Three things swept him away— the exhausting of the virgin pastures, the coming of the wire fence, and Mr. Armour of Chicago, who set the price of beef to suit himself. But all this may be summed up in the word Progress. When the bankrupt cow-puncher felt Progress dispersing him, he seized whatever plank floated nearest him in the wreck. He went to town for a job; he got a position on the railroad; he set up a saloon; he married, and fenced in a little farm; and he turned "rustler," and stole the cattle from the men for whom he had once worked. In these capacities will you find him today. The ex-cowboy who set himself to some new way of wage-earning is all over the West, and his old courage and frankness still stick to him, but his peculiar independence is of necessity dimmed. The only man who has retained that wholly is the outlaw, the horse and cattle thief, on whose grim face hostility to Progress forever sits. He has had a checkered career. He has been often hanged, often shot; he is generally "wanted" in several widely scattered districts. I know one who used to play the banjo to me on Powder River as he swung his long boots over the side of his bunk. I have never listened to any man's talk with more interest and diversion. Once he has been to Paris on the proceeds of a lengthy well-conducted theft; once he has been in prison for murder. He has the bluest eye, the longest nose, and the coldest face I ever saw. This stripe of gentleman still lives and thrives through the cattle country, occasionally goes out into the waste of land in the most delicate way, and presently cows and steers are missed. But he has driven them many miles to avoid livestock inspectors, and it may be that if you know him by sight and happen to be in a town where cattle are bought, such as Kansas City, you will meet him at the best hotel there, full of geniality and affluence.

Such is the story of the cow-puncher, the American descendant of Saxon ancestors, who for thirty years flourished upon our part of the earth, and, because he was not compatible with Progress, is now departed, never to return. But because Progress has just now given us the Populist and silver in exchange for him, is no ground for lament. He has never made a good citizen, but only a good soldier, from his tournament days down. And if our nation in its growth have no worse distemper than the Populist to weather through, there is hope for us, even though present signs disincline us to make much noise upon the Fourth of July.

The Heist—The Theory and Practice of Armed Robbery

by EVERETT DeBAUN

FEBRUARY, 1950

Here is the fascinating, inside story of how the most highly skilled robbers in the world—the professional "heist-men"—plan and execute the holdups of banks and payrolls. Everett De-Baun was a leading practitioner in this elite group of the underworld. (But even pros make mistakes sometimes, and he wrote this article in prison.) DeBaun also is a skillful writer who received encouragement from H. L. Mencken, Kathleen Hoagland, and John Fischer. Lately he has been in Hollywood as a technical adviser to the makers of crime movies.

The holdup was a relatively rare form of crime forty or fifty years ago, though well publicized even then. Nowadays it is the most common form of serious crime. It would be interesting to know the reasons for this sudden rise in popularity. No doubt the ever-increasing complexity of our way of life has had something to do with it. Psychologists declare that excessive discipline is likely to result in impulses of cruelty and destruction, and it seems probable that the innumerable social pressures to which the individual is subjected in our society give rise to aggressive feelings ultimately requiring outlets—certainly our preoccupation with bloodthirsty comics, movies, radio programs, and mystery and detective fiction is not accidental. And certainly the stickup is an aggressive action of classic directness and simplicity.

Such an explanation may account in part for the innumerable holdups of drug stores and filling stations, the frequent heists pulled with glass pistols, cap pistols, water pistols, air guns; the haberdasheries and cigar stores stuck up as Jesse James might have stuck up banks; the sadistic little jobs whose main purpose seems to be maltreatment of the victims: the Lovers Lane holdups, the cab-drivers robbed of fares and tips. Such holdups undoubtedly have a large emotional, or neurotic, component. Obviously, the motivation is not a rational weighing of risks against possible gain, for banks might be robbed almost as cheaply—not that bank robbery is lightly punished, but that we punish robbery of any type more severely than several varieties of murder (in some states by death), a lesson in applied Christianity as pointed, in this way, as our custom of requisitioning lives though not money in time of war, or the size of the vote polled by Norman Thomas.

There are more tangible reasons for the emergence of the holdup as a *professional* technique, though here too emotional and social factors of course are present. Technological change occurs in the underworld, as elsewhere. During the past few generations several ancient and dishonorable professions have given way to others better suited to the times. In comparison with the burgeoning of the holdup, the decline of the box-busting racket is a case in point. Forty or fifty years ago, the safe-cracker was considered the prince of thieves. Though the best of the modern boxmen can open modern safes as efficiently as the peter-men of half a century ago could open those of that day, the profession is fast on the down-grade. Cash simply is not kept in safes as it was. For the most part, business is carried on by check, and checks are worthless as loot. Similarly, securities are now seldom readily negotiable, stamps are giving way to postage meters, jewelry is a drug on the market—"slum," as it is familiarly called, brings but from 15 to 20 per cent of the replacement value at fence, while silver is hardly worth carrying off, and watches can be disposed of for no more than a portion of the value of the metal in the cases. Furthermore, that infallible source of cash in large amounts, the bank, is no longer vulnerable to the safe-cracker, thanks chiefly to the time lock, a device which may be set to jam the bolt mechanism for a period during which a vault may not be opened even by someone possessing the combination. Consequently, the Max Shinburnes, Leonidas Leslies, Chauncy Johnsons, Adam Worths, Bob Scotts, and Jimmy Hopes who during the last quarter of the past century burglarized banks of sums said to total close to a hundred million dollars—a number of the individual "scores" were for more than a million—have gone the way of the horse and buggy. Their present-day counterparts are top-grade holdupmen—"heist-men" in the underworld argot.

For technical reasons, chief among them the relative scarcity of readily convertible securities, holdups the size of the old-time bank burglaries are few and far between. Scores running into the hundreds of thousands are no rarity, but so far as I know there has been only one million-dollar holdup—that of a bank in Lincoln, Nebraska, in the early thirties. These big jobs are the work of what are probably the most highly skilled professional thieves in the world, but even on its lower levels the holdup in the hands of the professional has little but the name in common with the amateur, or neurotic, article. The almost invariable mark of the latter—called "cowboy-job" by the professional in derisive reference to the stagecoach holdups in Western movies—is recklessness. Planning is often nonexistent; the simplest precautions may be ignored; victims may be unnecessarily maltreated; the robber is not infrequently caught in the act. A psychiatrist once said to me that the frequency with which holdup-men of this stamp manage to be caught on the job indicated to him a desire to *be* caught and punished—the social conscience at work. The idea is not as wild as it may sound. However, under our system punishments are so ferocious that the guilt-ridden culprit speedily becomes the aggrieved, free to work off his cholers without troublesome pangs of conscience. This state of mind, which may of course arise more often from causes other than imprisonment, is characteristic of the professional thief. Not very surprisingly, the earmarks of the professional holdup are careful planning and efficient execution.

A seventeenth-century cookbook advises those who would prepare jugged hare first to catch their hare. To pull a heist, first find your "mark." A mark may be any considerable sum of money or the equivalent in readily convertible swag. Professional heist-men judge marks in terms of the probable cash return relative to the risks involved.

Marks are either dug up or tipped off. When a heist-man says that he has dug one up, he means that he has found it himself. He may have sought it out, tailing ladies who appear in public festooned like Christmas trees with jewels, or armored cars making deliveries of payrolls, for instance. Or he may just have stumbled upon it, like one who was introduced by a casual resort acquaintance into a private poker game in which some $12,000 was in play, or another who noticed that the proprietor of a saloon where he occasionally stopped for a beer made a practice of cashing pay-checks for employees of a nearby refinery. Marks that have been tipped off are those that have been pointed out by others. One who tips off marks is called a fingerman or tipster; he may or may not be of the underworld. Sometimes pickpockets, gamblers, and other footloose grifters tip marks off to heist-men as a side-line. The standard remuneration for this service is 10 per cent of the gross score. A surprisingly large number of marks are tipped off by legit, or ostensibly honest, people, and no few are put up (whence, incidentally, the colloquial expression "put-up job") or prearranged: a truck driver would like a share of the value of the load of cigarettes or whiskey he will be carrying; a jeweler wants to beat his insurance company; a bank manager wishes to cover his embezzlements. As the police are well aware of this, many heist-men fight shy of such tips, for the legit citizen, having odd notions of honor by the thief's standards, is likely to break down under close questioning, and promises of immunity for himself, and finger his partners as thoroughly as he formerly fingered the mark.

Other things being equal, the cash mark is always preferable. There is nothing like a bank for cold cash in large amounts, and until recently the "jug" was beyond argument the best type of mark by professional criteria. It is true that for many years banks of any size have had what looks to be formidable protection, but in robbery as in warfare of other types the aggressor has a heavy advantage. Armed guards, vaults with walls of steel and concrete several feet in thickness, and elaborate alarm systems did not prevent heist-mobs from knocking over an average of about two banks a day during the early thirties. In 1934, however, Congress passed an act making bank robbery a federal offense and bringing it under the jurisdiction of the FBI, a police organization having almost unlimited funds and unique facilities, the most important of these being a corps of stool-pigeons probably as extensive as any outside Russia. Simultaneously, the flat twenty-five-year sentence for bank robbery became mandatory, and the government established a special prison for "jug-heists" (the species populates Alcatraz almost 100 per cent), operated on principles that would turn the stomach of a Turk. These additional risks require that others be at a minimum if a bank is to be marked nowadays, and the same is true of the mails.

There are numerous types of cash mark which do not involve federal heat, however. Of these, the payroll is probably the most popular. Although payrolls do not compare in size with banks as marks, they are far more numerous and, since their physical protection is usually comparatively light, are vulnerable to smaller mobs. Anyone working as a member of a three-handed mob scoring three $10,000 payrolls fares as well financially as if he had taken part in a five-handed bank robbery worth $50,000, at about one-tenth the risk.

Marks for swag, or loot readily convertible into cash, are still more numerous and usually even less well protected, but they have the considerable disadvantage that the take must be fenced, or sold. Since this involves a suicidal risk if undertaken through legitimate channels, swag is usually sold to a professional buyer of stolen goods. The fence not only helps himself to a whopping profit—he seldom pays more than 20 per cent even for gilt-edge swag—but often he is not reliable in the face of police pressure, and not uncommonly does business with police and politicians, or pays in money and information for tacit permission to operate. Sometimes, particularly when jewelry or securities are involved, it is possible to by-pass the fence in favor of the company which has insured the loss. Settlement in such cases runs about 20 per cent of the insured amount, no questions asked. Several private detective agencies are widely known as specialists in negotiating such transactions, which also are often handled through attorneys. If the robbery was the doing of Americans, it is a safe bet that the $785,000 in jewelry heisted from the Aga Khan last fall will be recovered on this basis.

Given a mark, the next step is mobbing up, or getting together the men who will work the job. A working unit of underworld professionals of any type is called a mob. There are "single-o" heist-men, such as the one known in the papers as Slick Willie, who has robbed large and well-protected banks single-handed, but the vast majority of the brotherhood work in mobs. A heist-mob may comprise from two to six or eight members—the type of mark is usually the determining factor. Thus, the "same" mob—*i.e.*, several of a group of stickup-men who sometimes work together—may be five-handed for a jug-heist and three-handed for a payroll job. There are excellent reasons why the mob is generally of the minimum size compatible with efficient operation. One is selfish: "The smaller the mob, the bigger the cut." The other is protective: each additional member adds to the risk of a fall, paradoxical as this may seem. The answer is that the professional runs little danger of falling either *en flagrante* or, despite the highly imaginative information ladled out for popular consumption along this line, as a result of acute detective work. Almost always he is caught because of information given to police.

Eddie suddenly squares his debts and springs with a new car, for instance, or begins shooting high craps and buying drinks for the house, or buys a fur coat for Marge, who cannot resist throwing the needles to that catty Doris, who puts two and two together and confides the result to Nettie, whose husband Louie peddles dope or does a bit of pimping or wants to get City Hall's okay to book numbers or horses in his cigar store. In every city, police permit numerous Louies to operate in consideration for periodical cash donations, plus just such favors as the one Louie is now in a position to confer. If Eddie cannot stand up under the beatings he will now undergo as a matter of police routine, or if Marge knows who his partners are and can be talked or frightened into trading the information for a lighter sentence for him, the whole mob may fall.

Popular notions notwithstanding, the basic units of a heist-mob are not a "mastermind" and some servile morons who carry out his orders. As a matter of fact, among "heavy" * thieves no one gives orders for the good reason that no one takes them—the heavy is as independent a character as walks the earth. Within the mob, equality reigns. All share equally in risk and gain. All have equal authority. This is not to imply that the members of a mob simply behave as they please on the job. There a rather rigid discipline prevails, but all have had a voice in the plan being carried out and authority has been delegated willingly.

The true essentials of a heist-mob are a wheel-man and a rod-man. The former is a skilled driver, often a specialist who takes no other part (this is preferred practice). Yet if the mob is short-handed or somewhat slipshod in operation he may work the inside with the others. The rod-man's title is self-explanatory. A rod is a gun. Since most holdups involve the close control of a number of people during the course of the actual robbery, most mobs have two or more gun-wielding members. In special cases, a mob may use a man on the outside in addition to the man on the wheel. For example, the getaway route for a job located in the business section of a city may begin with a run down a narrow alley or a one-way street, in which case a tail, a car or truck which cuts in behind the getaway car and blocks

---

* Professional thieves fall into two categories. The "heavy" is primarily the rebel-without-a-cause; his attitudes are inflexibly antiauthoritarian; his techniques are based upon the use or threat of force. The "grifter" is essentially the businessman whose line happens to be illegal; his attitudes are closer to the conventional; his techniques feature superior dexterity or chicane.

the way long enough for the former to get a sufficient jump, may be used. But the great majority of heist-mobs work with a single man on the wheel and either two or three on the inside.

A mob forms rather casually. Eddie, let us say, has a promising mark. He decides that it can "go" three-handed. Thinking over the experienced men of his acquaintance who are out for action he fixes on Big Pete. His choice is based upon several considerations. Pete has a rep as a good man, which means that he is known to be trustworthy, dependable, and resourceful. When he makes a meet, or engagement, he keeps it. He has plenty of belly, or courage. He has shown that he is a sticker who will not panic and leave the others to shift for themselves in the event of trouble, and he has repeatedly stood up, or kept his mouth shut, under police questioning—American police question prisoners; only foreigners torture them. Furthermore, he will not burn, or cheat, his partners; he does not flash, or make a show of his money; and he has an air of calm authority which is valuable on the job: he can control a whole roomful of people without frightening them so that someone may do something foolish.

Eddie and Pete talk the job over—"cut it up," they say. If a tip is involved, Eddie lets Pete know that there will be a tipster's end (10 per cent) to come off the top, or before any deductions have been made, but without telling him who the tipster is, just as he will not tell the latter who will work the job, for by his code anyone who deals with him is entitled to full protection, and he considers them bound by the same standard. Other details are discussed. Yes, between them, the two can handle the inside without trouble. Probably they could handle the whole thing, but to be on the safe side they had better have a man on the wheel.

Since the mark is Eddie's, he is boss in this respect. He "owns" the job; it is therefore his right to select those who are to participate. Anyone who does not wish to work with any of the others may pull out, or withdraw. If one who pulls out should thereupon get his own mob together and take the job, Eddie would feel morally justified in shooting him, though if another mob working independently happened to beat Eddie to the job he would not consider himself wronged. If something happened to prevent him from taking part in the touch and Pete filled in another man and took it, Eddie would be entitled to half an end, or share, even though he was in prison when the job came off.

In this case, there is no trouble in filling the mob. Both Eddie and

Pete are friendly with Bangs, so called from his habit of causing his car to backfire during chases to the end of instilling a proper caution in amateur pursuers, who seldom require much encouragement to imagine they are being shot at. One of them looks him up and inquires casually if he wants "a little action on the wheel." Bangs asks questions: what kind of action? what's in it? who is working? If the answers, which are given in general terms, are to his liking, he says, "Okay, I'm in," and the mob is complete. Only then is he given specific details.

The detailed planning and preparation which constitute the next stage are the most important part of the heist. If this layout is done well, the mark is in the bag. The robbery itself becomes a simple trans-action lasting but a few moments—sometimes less than thirty seconds.

Professionals agree that casing is far and away the most important part of laying out a heist. This word, which like many others of under-world origin is coming into popular use, is from the argot of faro, once as popular a betting game as craps is today. It originally referred to a record of the cards played as kept on an abacus-like contraption called a "case." As used in the underworld, the word means gathering infor-mation from observation.

Even when the tip includes detailed information, a good mob cases its marks with care. Tipsters often err. One mob, whose tipster worked in the place to be taken, was furnished with a layout-chart so complete that they did not bother casing the inside, to their subsequent sorrow, for the tipster had neglected to indicate that the partitions setting off the office they were to rob did not extend to the ceiling, and police were waiting for them when they came out.

Several matters are cased with particular care. The size of the score is checked in advance whenever possible—tipsters are likely to be very optimistic about the size of a prospective touch. If the mark is a bank, checking may involve little more than a glance at the quar-terly statement, available at the local library or Chamber of Com-merce, and the size of payrolls may be estimated satisfactorily from the number of employees, but most other kinds of mark are difficult to case accurately for size. A knowledge of the floor plan, arrangement of furniture, placement of doors and windows, and so forth, is essential to a fast, smooth piece of work.

On the theory that it helps to know where trouble is likely to come from, some heist-men like to get an advance look at the people on the inside as well. Impressionable young squirts who attend the movies too often and an occasional old towser who has had his job for thirty years—"heroes," the heist-man calls them sardonically—may, if not closely watched, rise in defense of the insurance company's stockholders, especially if women or big bosses are present. It is always well to know how many women must be dealt with, since they are an occupational hazard of the first order which I will describe later on. Armed guards are of course cased with care, though unless ensconced in a protective cage or turret they represent a threat more apparent than real, since they cannot go about with cocked pistols. A well-executed job takes so little time that alarm systems call for little or no attention, unless the mark is a bank. Bank heists usually take several minutes.

Sometimes ingenuity is required to case a job without attracting attention. Unless there is heavy pedestrian traffic, outside casing is usually done from a car or the window of a nearby building. Various ruses are resorted to in casing the inside, the commonest being the pose of having business to transact. This can be excellent vocational training—at least, it proved to be in the case of Keister (Suitcase) John, an old-timer who came by his moniker in honor of a battered salesman's case full of janitor supplies which he used as a prop, religiously charging off the full original cost of the outfit, some forty dollars, against the nut, or expense, of every job he worked. A time came when jokes about his "ten grand" suitcase circulating in the hangouts came to the ears of police, and John went to stir. There he came to the conclusion that he was becoming too old and too well known to continue in his wicked ways, so upon release he set up in the building maintenance business, in which he prospered.

Generally speaking, casing is the job of the inside-men. The wheel-man has work of his own. The procurement of the getaway car is one of his responsibilities. There are many car-thieves who will deliver to specifications of year and make for a moderate fee, but heist-men seldom patronize them for reasons of security. The simple job of stealing a car may be considerably complicated by the wheel-man's personal predilections. Most of them have strong convictions concerning various makes of car for this particular kind of service. Certain makes, widely known as "dogs on the get-out," which is to say that they accelerate slowly from a standing start, automatically are ruled out. In general, a small, fast car of common make is preferred for work in city traffic, but a heavy one where the getaway entails a long run over country roads. Having procured a suitable car, the wheel-man provides it with license plates which are not hot and plants it, or places it somewhere out of harm's way, until it is needed.

The wheel-man's other major responsibility is the layout of the get, or getaway route, a simple matter if the job is in a city and the mob intends to piece up there, but complicated if a run to another locality is in prospect, as is usually the case if the mark is located in a small community. In the latter event, he must cruise back roads and country lanes until he has pieced together a route which bypasses towns, main highways, and, so far as is possible, roads followed by telephone lines. He runs this route until thoroughly familiar with it, and may even chart it in detail:

> L over bridge
> 40 for S-bend mi. 4
> R fork Bull sign mi. 6½
> weaves over 55 gravel. . . .

Such a chart is called a "running get." The back-country getaway—the idea of a specific route, which was once a close professional secret—is said to have been tipped off to the FBI by Brown Derby Bentz, a bank robber until recently in Alcatraz, and there for this reason shunned by many of his professional brethren. Whether or not the rap is a right one for Bentz, the principle of the get is now so well known that a movie glorifying the G-men has been based upon it.

There will be other details requiring attention. Perhaps the job is located in a town whose approaches may quickly be blocked off. If so, the mob may want to hide out in town until the heat has somewhat subsided, in which case a suitable plant, or hideout, will be required. There will have to be bags for the money—the paper shopping bags used by housewives are as good as any. And there is the matter of guns.

Mobs composed of men who often work together may have a small armory of weapons belonging to the mob as a whole, but as a general thing each man furnishes his own weapon, usually a pistol. Revolvers are preferred to automatics, for many of the Colt .45's circulating in the underworld came originally from army or other federal sources, and if one is used on a job the G-heat may assume it has been stolen and enter the case on that basis. Moreover, if the magazine clip of an automatic is kept loaded for a protracted time its spring may become "tired" and the gun may jam when used. The submachine guns so common in the movies are rarely used in real-life holdups. They are cumbersome, difficult to acquire, and at once bring the crime under federal jurisdiction. Sprayers, which are automatic pistols of a foreign make provided with a detachable stock and custom-made magazines holding fifty or more bullets, are sometimes used on jobs where there are a large number of people to be controlled, but sawed-off shotguns are cheaper, far easier to obtain, less lethal (except at point-blank range), and more effective in terms of shock effect upon the victims.

The job is ready to go when it has been cased and the other details have been attended to. The mob will have met several times to cut up, or talk things over, and to lay the job out, or make a detailed plan of action. The preparations in their entirety will have taken anywhere from a few hours to several weeks, depending upon the mark and the class, or quality, of the mob—the better the mob, the more thorough the layout.

As has been intimated, there is not much to the holdup itself if the layout has been well done. Each man knows just what to do on the job, when to do it, and what to expect of the others. Unforeseeable complications aside, the actual robbery is largely a matter of going through the motions on schedule. The term "schedule" is used advisedly, for the time element is important—so important that the time taken to "get in, get it, and get out" is a good measure of professional competence. It is not unusual for a class mob to carry out a run-of-the-mill holdup in half a minute.

The emphasis placed upon speed on the job probably owes less to fear of interference than to the hard-earned knowledge that surprise renders the average person incapable of comprehending what goes on about him with any accuracy, so that he is likely unconsciously to fill in from his imagination. This phenomenon has been verified by psychologists by means of experiments in which several people suddenly burst in upon a group engaged in some routine activity and act out a scene which those present are asked to describe. Witnesses are found prone to take urgent cries of "Onions!" or some other incongruous word, for "Help!" to take bananas for revolvers and the explosions of blown-up paper bags for shots, and to fail to recognize participants known to them from everyday association. Holdups executed without waste of time or motion have a similar effect upon witnesses.

Thus, one man who is six feet three, skinny, and more or less blond, has been declared to be a redhead weighing over two hundred, a double for George Raft, and, following an occasion when he was masked and worked with a man who spoke with a Southern accent, a Negro.

This tendency to fill in from imagination gaps in perception occurring under sudden stress also has its bad side from the viewpoint of the heist-man. While it is by no means the rule, it is not a rarity for these gentry to be convicted for robberies committed by others, for it is police practice to give witnesses information ranging from hints to detailed descriptions of suspects as an aid to identification, and witnesses often convince themselves that the pictures thus built up are in fact retained from their own experience.

In working a heist, the mob usually goes out from a meet, or appointment held a short time before the job is to go. Here the layout is gone over again, clothes are changed—if the mark is in a factory district the mob may work in coveralls, if in a business district in business suits; the idea is to remain as inconspicuous as possible—and other last-minute details are attended to. The members of the mob leave singly and go to the mark by separate routes in order to avoid the possibility of being seen together by coppers to whom they may be known. Possibly they do not rod up, or arm themselves, until they reach the job, just in case one of them might be stopped and searched. The wheel-man brings the guns in the car.

The mob meet the car a block or so from the mark and rod themselves up. They walk to the job; the wheel-man pulls ahead and parks near the entrance in such a way that he can swing out from the curb in a hurry. If possible, the inside-men work covered, or masked. This usually can be managed without difficulty unless the place must be entered directly from the street, and even then if scarves fastened with pins so that they may quickly be twitched up over the month and chin are used—the lower part of the face is the most easily identifiable.

Covered or bald, the mob enters as casually as any other visitors. Melodramatics are for the movies. One man does the talking: "All right, folks, stay where you're at! Keep quiet! Keep your hands where I can see them! Nobody but the insurance company is gonna get hurt, so take it easy." Generally this fellow stands near the door where he can keep the whole room under observation as well as intercept anyone who may come in while the robbery is in progress. He is an authoritative figure, the center of attention. Most witnesses hardly notice the other inside-men, who go about their job of collecting the score as quickly and with as little fuss as possible.

So far as may be, the mob are calm and polite on the job. "Cowboying," or the wild brandishing of pistols and shouting of orders in all directions is frowned upon—fear has made more heroes than courage ever has. People will not be gratuitously abused. The professional does not become so tensed up by fear and excitement that he strikes out blindly upon insignificant provocation. As one puts it: "When you're out on a heist you're out to get the dough and keep out of trouble. Halloween's the night for scaring people." However, courtesy on the job does not include softness or indecision. A holdup may easily become a shambles if the people under the gun think they detect nervousness or hesitation on the part of the man behind it.

The boys are particularly careful if women are present. Nobody can tell how women will react—at least, such is the considered opinion of the heist-men with whom I have cut up this situation. Looks tell nothing. One who has all the earmarks of a lady pipefitter may just roll up her eyes and swoon, while the little mouse who looks so scared a man itches to pat her on the head and say something soothing is really coolly examining the mob for warts or moles or counting the hairs on their knuckles as a means of future identification. Guns or no guns, some women will give out large pieces of their minds, and the less of this commodity they have to spare the more generous they appear to be with it. There are old ladies—one heist mob had a harrowing experience at the hands of a motherly soul who got into the middle of a loan-office heist before she realized what was going on. Then she was horrified and spoke severely to the mob. They should be ashamed, for she could tell that they were good boys at heart who had got off on the wrong foot. Since this was precisely what the boys secretly thought of themselves, they were moved; they ordered one of the clerks to destroy the record of the old lady's loan at once. This intended kindness only shocked her more, and she began to pray for them. The boys sweated copiously and might even have left if the manager, who had the combination to the safe, had not been due at that moment.

Let us not overlook the screamers, who are legion. The automatic yelper, who lets go involuntarily, from surprise, is not much of a problem. Her scream is little more than a species of exclamation. The aboriginal, or ritual, screamer is a little more troublesome. Her scream is a notice to all males that a poor defenseless female is in distress, and what are they going to do about it? Still, heist-men find that this one need only be ordered sharply to shut up and she will subside. Then there is the smarty who puts the primitive, or come-and-get-poor-little-me, scream to more sophisticated uses. She lets out a shriek that can be heard over traffic for two blocks and then claps hand to mouth and gives with the big eyes as if to say: "Her didn't mean to, but her couldn't help it; gweat big you *fwightened* her so!" Actually a brontosaurus wouldn't scare her. She has been feeding that great-big-you line to voracious males so long and so successfully that she would spring it with confidence on the first lion she met walking down the street. What is on her mind at the moment are newspaper headlines: HEROINE OUTWITS DESPERATE BANDITS; PRETENDS HYSTERICS AND SUMMONS HELP, and she is just the cookie who will identify great big you with such dramatics that every man on the jury will yearn to see you hung and quartered, whether or not you happen to have been on that particular job. The consensus is that a good kick in the pants is what this number is asking for.

Worst of all screamers is the hysterical screamer. This one takes a kind of fit—clenches her eyes shut and lets loose at the top of her voice, and anything done to calm her is only likely to make her worse, if possible. Heist-men know of no formula for dealing with this kind of screamer, though isolated successes are spoken of. One says he stopped her cold by asking in the ordinary disgusted tone one might use to a bothersome child why she didn't quit that damn howling. Another claims to have done it with paper clips. He had to pass the woman's desk on the way to the score; she apparently had the idea that he was coming to cut her throat, rose screaming, to retreat, stumbled over her chair, and hit the floor in a sitting position. There she sat, eyes tight shut and mouth wide open, screeching like a calliope gone wild. In passing, he picked up some paper clips from a desk and tossed a couple into her mouth. Presto!

Sometimes screamers can be a real hazard on the job, as when the mob must be inside for several minutes, but on the ordinary job they are more bothersome than dangerous and the mob ignores them. In some circumstances, as when there is a safe which must be opened, it may take the mob several minutes to get the score, but usually it is merely a matter of picking it up and carrying it out. The man on the door remains a few seconds to give the others time to get to the car, for despite his warning someone will probably throw up a window and begin yelling as soon as he leaves. As he comes out, the car already is inching ahead.

It is off the instant his foot touches the running board. Unless a policeman is where he cannot avoid responding to the cries coming from the window—policemen on a beat are seldom eager to careen along in chase of someone who may shoot back; they are not paid or very well trained for that kind of work and are likely to shoot their revolvers on double action, to the peril of spectators in upstairs windows—or unless some civilian in search of excitement gives chase, reckless driving is not indulged in. The car whisks around the first corner, takes several others in quick succession, then straightens out for a run of two or three blocks down a street having little traffic.

If no chase car shows up behind, the getaway car heads for wherever the front car—one legitimately owned by one of the mob—is parked. Meanwhile, the inside-men may have gotten into or out of coveralls and transferred the money into the receptacle provided: where there is no pedestrian traffic outside, the mob may not take time on the job to put the loot into bags but carry it out in a wastepaper basket or any other handy container. One of the mob takes the score and pistols in the front car to the place prearranged for the meet. The other inside-men may accompany him, or, if they want to play it safe all the way, go separately. The wheel-man continues in the getaway car to another part of the city, where, having wiped down the interior to remove fingerprints, he ditches it.

By the time he arrives at the meet, the money probably already has been pieced up into as many piles as there are members of the mob. "There she is," one of the others says. "Latch onto one."

VI

Poetry–
Imagination All Compact

Carol for the New Year

by ALFRED TENNYSON
FEBRUARY, 1851

Ring out, wild bells, to the wild sky,
    The flying cloud, the frosty light.
    The year is dying in the night;
Ring out, wild bells, and let him die.

Ring out the old, ring in the new,
    Ring, happy bells, across the snow;
    The year is going, let him go;
Ring out the false, ring in the true.

Ring out the grief that saps the mind,
    For those that here we see no more;
    Ring out the feud of rich and poor,
Ring in redress to all mankind.

Ring out a slowly dying cause,
    And ancient forms of party strife;
    Ring in the nobler modes of life,
With sweeter manners, purer laws.

Ring out the want, the care, the sin,
    The faithless coldness of the times;
    Ring out, ring out my mournful rhymes,
But ring the fuller minstrel in.

Ring out false pride in place and blood,
    The civic slander and the spite;
    Ring in the love of truth and right,
Ring in the common love of God.

Ring out the shapes of foul disease,
    Ring out the narrowing lust of gold;
    Ring out the thousand wars of old,
Ring in the thousand years of peace.

Little Mattie

by ELIZABETH BARRETT BROWNING

JULY, 1861

Dead! Thirteen a month ago!
   Short and narrow her life's walk.
Lover's love she could not know
   Even by a dream or talk:
Too young to be glad of youth;
   Missing honor, labor, rest,
And the warmth of a babe's mouth
   At the blossom of her breast.
Must you pity her for this,
And for all the loss it is—
You, her mother with wet face,
Having had all in your case?

Just so young but yesternight,
   Now she is as old as death.
Meek, obedient in your sight,
   Gentle to a beck or breath
Only on last Monday! yours,
   Answering you like silver bells
Lightly touched! an hour matures:
   You can teach her nothing else.
She has seen the mystery hid
Under Egypt's pyramid.
By those eyelids pale and close
Now she knows what Rhamses knows.

Cross her quiet hands, and smooth
   Down her patient locks of silk,
Cold and passive as in truth
   You your fingers in spilt milk
Drew along a marble floor;
   But her lips you can not wring
Into saying a word more,
   "Yes" or "no," or such a thing.
Though you call and beg and wreak

Half your soul out in a shriek,
She will lie there in default
And most innocent revolt.

The Waving of the Corn

by SIDNEY LANIER
AUGUST, 1877

Ploughman, whose gnarly hand yet kindly wheeled
Thy plough to ring this solitary tree
 With clover, whose round plat, reserved afield,
In cool green radius twice my length may be—
 Scanting the corn thy furrows else might yield,
To pleasure August, bees, fair thoughts, and me,
 That here come oft together—daily I,
 Stretched prone in summer's mortal ecstasy,
Do stir with thanks to thee, as stirs this morn
  With waving of the corn.

Unseen, the farmer's boy from round the hill
Whistles a snatch that seeks his soul unsought,
 And fills some time with tune, howbeit shrill;
The cricket tells straight on his simple thought—
 Nay, 'tis the cricket's way of being still;
The peddler bee drones in, and gossips naught;
 Far down the wood, a one-desiring dove
 Times me the beating of the heart of love:
And these be all the sounds that mix, each morn,
  With waving of the corn.

From here to where the louder passions dwell,
Green leagues of hilly separation roll:
 Trade ends where yon far clover ridges swell.
Ye terrible Towns, ne'er claim the trembling soul
 That, craftless all to buy or hoard or sell,
From out your deadly complex quarrel stole
 To company with large amiable trees,
 Suck honey summer with unjealous bees,
And take Time's strokes as softly as this morn
  Takes waving of the corn.

Robert Burns

by HENRY WADSWORTH LONGFELLOW
AUGUST, 1880

I see amid the fields of Ayr
A ploughman, who, in foul or fair,
    Sings at his task,
So clear we know not if it is
The laverock's song we hear or his,
    Nor care to ask.

For him the ploughing of those fields
A more ethereal harvest yields
    Than sheaves of grain:
Songs flush with purple bloom the rye;
The plover's call, the curlew's cry,
    Sing in his brain.

Touched by his hand, the way-side weed
Becomes a flower; the lowliest reed
    Beside the stream
Is clothed with beauty; gorse and grass
And heather, where his footsteps pass,
    The brighter seem.

He sings of love, whose flame illumes
The darkness of lone cottage rooms;
    He feels the force,
The treacherous under-tow and stress,
Of wayward passions, and no less
    The keen remorse.

At moments, wrestling with his fate,
His voice is harsh, but not with hate;
    The brush-wood hung
Above the tavern door lets fall
Its bitter leaf, its drop of gall,
    Upon his tongue.

But still the burden of his song
Is love of right, disdain of wrong;
    Its master-chords
Are Manhood, Freedom, Brotherhood;
Its discords but an interlude
    Between the words.

And then to die so young, and leave
Unfinished what he might achieve!
    Yet better sure
Is this than wandering up and down,
An old man, in a country town,
    Infirm and poor.

For now he haunts his native land
As an immortal youth; his hand
    Guides every plough;
He sits beside each ingle-nook;
His voice is in each rushing brook,
    Each rustling bough.

His presence haunts this room to-night,
A form of mingled mist and light,
    From that far coast.
Welcome beneath this roof of mine!
Welcome! this vacant chair is thine,
    Dear guest and ghost!

Death's Valley

(*To accompany a picture; by request*)

by WALT WHITMAN

APRIL, 1892

Nay, do not dream, designer dark,
Thou hast portray'd or hit thy theme entire:
I, hoverer of late by this dark valley, by its confines, having glimpses of it,
Here enter lists with thee, claiming my right to make a symbol too.

For I have seen many wounded soldiers die,
After dread suffering—have seen their lives pass off with smiles;

And I have watch'd the death-hours of the old; and seen the infant die;
The rich, with all his nurses and his doctors;
And then the poor, in meagreness and poverty;
And I myself for long, O Death, have breathed my every breath
Amid the nearness and the silent thought of thee.

And out of these and thee,
I make a scene, a song, brief (not fear of thee,
Nor gloom's ravines, nor bleak, nor dark—for I do not fear thee,
Nor celebrate the struggle, or contortion, or hard-tied knot),
Of the broad blessed light and perfect air, with meadows, rippling tides,
    and trees and flowers and grass,
And the low hum of living breeze—and in the midst God's beautiful eter-
    nal right hand,
Thee, holiest minister of Heaven—thee, envoy, usherer, guide and last of all,
Rich, florid, loosener of the stricture-knot call'd life,
Sweet, peaceful, welcome Death.

The Look

by SARA TEASDALE
JANUARY, 1914

Strephon kissed me in the spring,
    Robin in the fall,
But Colin only looked at me
    And never kissed at all.

Strephon's kiss was lost in jest,
    Robin's lost in play,
But the kiss in Colin's eyes
    Haunts me night and day.

Ships

by JOHN MASEFIELD
DECEMBER, 1914

The Ore
Before Man's laboring wisdom gave me birth
   I had not even seen the light of day;
Down in the central darkness of the earth,
   Crushed by the weight of continents I lay,
Ground by the weight to heat, not knowing then
The air, the light, the noise, the world of men.

The Trees
We grew on mountains where the glaciers cry,
   Infinite somber armies of us stood
Below the snow-peaks which defy the sky;
   A song like the gods moaning filled our wood;
We knew no men—our life was to stand stanch,
Singing our song, against the avalanche.

The Hemp and Flax
We were a million grasses on the hill,
   A million herbs which bowed as the wind blew,
Trembling in every fiber, never still;
   Out of the summer earth sweet life we drew.
Little blue-flowered grasses up the glen,
Glad of the sun, what did we know of men?

The Workers
We tore the iron from the mountain's hold,
   By blasting fires we smithied it to steel;
Out of the shapeless stone we learned to mold
   The sweeping bow, the rectilinear keel;
We hewed the pine to plank, we split the fir,
We pulled the myriad flax to fashion her.

Out of a million lives our knowledge came,
   A million subtle craftsmen forged the means;
Steam was our handmaid and our servant flame,
   Water our strength—all bowed to our machines.

Out of the rock, the tree, the springing herb
We built this wandering beauty so superb.

The Sailors
We, who were born on earth and live by air,
   Make this thing pass across the fatal floor,
The speechless sea; alone we commune there
   Jesting with death, that ever open door.
Sun, moon, and stars are signs by which we drive
This wind-blown iron like a thing alive.

The Ship
I march across great waters like a queen,
   I whom so many wisdoms helped to make;
Over the uncruddled billows of seas green
   I blanch the bubbled highway of my wake.
By me my wandering tenants clasp the hands
And know the thoughts of men in other lands.

The Heretic

by WILLIAM ROSE BENÉT
NOVEMBER, 1915

"Then," said my Angel, "I leave you!"
   "So!" whispered my Devil, "I come!"
But my lips framed no regretting;
   I stood struck dumb.

With pathos the angels would grieve you;
   With threats the devils would fright.
Man travails within, begetting
   A god of light.

Now though all Heaven bereft me
   Of flowers and music's sound,
Now though all Hell, to win me,
   Flamed red around,

Only one thing was left me,
   One only since time began:
To speak the truth that was in me
   And play the man.

A Bather

by AMY LOWELL
AUGUST, 1917

Thick dappled by circles of sunshine and fluttering shade,
Your bright, naked body advances, blown over by leaves,
Half-quenched in their various green, just a point of you showing,
A knee or a thigh, sudden glimpsed, then at once blotted into
The filmy and flickering forest, to start out again
Triumphant in smooth, supple roundness, edged sharp as white ivory,
Cool, perfect, with rose rarely tinting your lips and your breasts,
Swelling out from the green in the opulent curves of ripe fruit,
And hidden, like fruit, by the swift intermittence of leaves.
So, clinging to branches and moss, you advance on the ledges
Of rock which hang over the stream, with the wood-smells about you,
The pungence of strawberry plants and of gum-oozing spruces,
While below runs the water impatient, impatient—to take you,
To splash you, to run down your sides, to sing you of deepness,
Of pools brown and golden, with brown-and-gold flags on their borders,
Of blue, lingering skies floating solemnly over your beauty,
Of undulant waters a-sway in the effort to hold you,
To keep you submerged and quiescent while over you glories
The summer.
                    Oread, Dryad, or Naiad, or just
Woman, clad only in youth and in gallant perfection,
Standing up in a great burst of sunshine, you dazzle my eyes
Like a snow-star, a moon, your effulgence burns up in a halo,
For you are the chalice which holds all the races of men.

You slip into the pool and the water folds over your shoulder,
And over the tree-tops the clouds slowly follow your swimming,
And the scent of the woods is sweet on this hot summer morning.

Fire and Ice

by ROBERT FROST
DECEMBER, 1920

Some say the world will end in fire,
  Some say in ice.
From what I've tasted of desire
I hold with those who favor fire.
  But if it had to perish twice,
I think I know enough of hate
  To know that for destruction ice
Is also great,
  And would suffice.

Washington Monument by Night

by CARL SANDBURG
APRIL, 1922

The stone goes straight.
A lean swimmer dives into night sky,
Into half-moon mist.

Two trees are coal black.
This is a great white ghost between.
It is cool to look at.
Strong men, strong women, come here.

Eight years is a long time
To be fighting all the time.

The republic is a dream.
Nothing happens unless first a dream.

The wind bit hard at Valley Forge one Christmas.
Soldiers tied rags on their feet.
Red footprints wrote on the snow—
And stone shoots into stars here,
Into half-moon mist to-night.

Tongues wrangled dark at a man.
He buttoned his overcoat and stood alone.
In a snowstorm, red holly berries, thoughts,
He stood alone.

Women said: He is lonely,
Fighting, fighting, eight years.

The name of an iron man goes over the world.
It takes a long time to forget an iron man.

The Philosophers

by ROBERT GRAVES

MAY, 1922

Thought has a bias,
  Direction a bend,
Space its inhibitions,
  Time a dead end.

Is whiteness white?
  Oh, then, call it black:
Farthest from the truth
  Is yet halfway back.

Effect ordains Cause,
  Head swallowing its tail;
Does whale engulf sprat,
  Or sprat assume whale?

Contentions weary,
  It giddies us to think,
Then kiss, girl, kiss!
  Or drink, fellow, drink!

To a Foreigner

by CHRISTOPHER MORLEY

JUNE, 1923

[Children, leprechauns, women beutifulle and yonge, these be forrainers alle.
—Sir Eustace Peachtree]

Aye, for I knew you foreign! Plain to me
    The anxiety that trembled in your gaze—
Your brave but heavy-burning secrecy
    Compelled by our more coarse and clumsy ways.

O lovely, lovely! Terror in the eyes,
    Poor eagerness to do what men expect:
Willing to stifle your own gay surprise
    And pass unquestionable, trim, correct—

Shall you, who have untellable things to say,
    Who hear inaudibles, guess the unknown,
"Assimilate," bewildered *émigré,*
    In our suspicious and mechanic zone?

Be ever foreign, beautiful and strange!
    Nor naturalize (wild word!) that rebel blood:
Docility and use must never change
    Your sweet enchanting reckless alienhood.

How did I know you foreign? Your most droll
    Blithe candor, so unlike our timid style;
Courteous to our queer modes, yet you console
    Your humor with a small comparative smile.

How did I know you stranger, troubled, lonely,
    Thrilled and yet puzzled in a foreign land,
Dear excommunicate?—Ah perhaps only
    Since I am outlandish too. You understand.

The Birds

by JOHN JAY CHAPMAN

JUNE, 1923

Month of triumph, month of mirth,
May doth repossess the earth.
Hillsides of a dazzling green
Against the clearest heavens are seen.
Naked forests don a pale
Empurpled palpitating veil.
The very dandelions hold
A fresh, intense, celestial gold;
While the cloudlets as they rise
Blush like blossoms in the skies.
May is brightness, May is splendor,
Fire ethereal, fierce and tender,
Living in the liquid blue,
With every color in its hue;
Touching everything we see
Into immortality.

What wonder if the birds give throat
To see the silvery vapors float,
Loiter, drift, and pass along?
The wren cannot contain his song—
Rippling into ecstasy
That the world so bright should be.
Robins revel as they roam
Drunk with new elysium;
While the songster-sparrow sits
Seized with sudden music fits.
Uncontrollably they sing,
Mad with joy at everything.
Round about, above and under.
May's a great white-thoughted wonder,
All creation's holiday,
Liquid, tender, brilliant May.

Sneezles

by A. A. MILNE
FEBRUARY, 1926

Christopher Robin
Had wheezles
And sneezles,
They bundled him
Into
His bed.
They gave him what goes
With a cold in the nose,
And some more for a cold
In the head.
They wondered
If wheezles
Could turn
Into measles,
If sneezles
Would turn
Into mumps;
They examined his chest
For a rash,
And the rest
Of his body for swellings and lumps.
They sent for some doctors
In sneezles
And wheezles:
To tell them what ought to be done.
All sorts and conditions
Of famous physicians
Came hurrying round
At a run.
They all made a note
Of the state of his throat,
They asked if he suffered from thirst;
They asked if the sneezles
Came *after* the wheezles,

Or if the first sneezle
Came first.
They said, "If you teazle
A sneezle
Or wheezle,
A measle
May easily grow.
But humor or pleazle
The wheezle
Or sneezle,
The measle
Will certainly go."
They expounded the reazles
For sneezles
And wheezles,
The appearance of measles
When new.
They said "If he freezles
In draughts and in breezles,
Then *Phtheezles*
May even ensue."

.   .   .   .   .

Christopher Robin
Got up in the morning,
The sneezles had vanished away.
And the look in his eye
Seemed to say to the sky,
"Now, how to amuse them to-day?"

Epitaph Upon a Young Soldier

by S. FOSTER DAMON
MAY, 1926

He gave us all he never had
Wife, children, comrades myriad;
And all we have we cannot give
To make those unborn pleasures live.

Salome

by MARY CAROLYN DAVIES
JANUARY, 1928

She stamped her foot, "I want his head!"
　　And her brow was black as she looked at John:
"I want his head in my hands," she said,
　　"And I don't care whether it's off or on."

John would not kiss, so he had to die;
　　She was willful as she was proud,
And she bore the head on a salver, high,
　　And kissed its lips and triumphed loud.

For what woman cares if his soul she kill,
　　When a man to her whim she has chanced to find,
If she only can fondle his hair at will,
　　And kiss his lips when she has a mind?

To Praisers of Women

by ARCHIBALD MacLEISH
SEPTEMBER, 1929

The praisers of women in their proud and beautiful poems,
Naming the grave mouth and the hair and the eyes,
Boasted those they loved should be forever remembered.
These were lies.

The words sound, but the face in the Istrian sun is forgotten.
The poet speaks, but to her dead ears no more.
The sleek throat is gone and the breast that was troubled to listen:
Shadow from door.

Therefore, I will not praise your knees and your fine walking,
Telling you men shall remember your name as long
As lips move or breath is spent or the iron of English
Rings from a tongue.

I shall say you were young and your arms straight and your mouth scarlet.
I shall say you will die, and none will remember you;
Your arms change and none remember the swish of your garments
Nor the click of your shoe.

Not with my hands' strength, not with difficult labor
Springing the obstinate words to the bones of your breast
And the stubborn line to your young stride and the breath to your breathing
And the beat to your haste,
Shall I prevail on the hearts of unborn men to remember.

What is a dead girl but a shadowy ghost,
Or a dead man's voice but a distant and vain affirmation
Like dream words most?

Therefore, I will not speak of the undying glory of women.
I shall say you were young and straight and your skin fair—
And you stood in the door, and the sun was a shadow of leaves on your
    shoulders,
And a leaf on your hair.

I will not speak of the famous beauty of dead women.
I shall say the shape of a blown leaf lay on your hair.
Till the world ends and the sun is out and the sky broken
Look! It is there!

Crystal Moment

by ROBERT P. TRISTRAM COFFIN
DECEMBER, 1931

Once or twice this side of death
Things can make one hold his breath.

From my boyhood I remember
A crystal moment of September.

A wooded island rang with sounds
Of church bells in the throats of hounds.

A buck leaped out and took the tide
With jewels flowing past each side.

With his high head like a tree,
He swam within a yard of me.

I saw the golden drop of light
In his eyes turned dark with fright.

I saw the forest's holiness
On him like a fierce caress.

Fear made him lovely past belief,
My heart was trembling like a leaf.

He leaned towards the land and life
With need above him like a knife.

In his wake the hot hounds churned,
They stretched their muzzles out and yearned.

They cried no more, but swam and throbbed,
Hunger drove them till they sobbed.

Pursued, pursuers reached the shore
And vanished. I saw nothing more.

So they passed, a pageant such
As only gods could witness much,

Life and death upon one tether·
And running beautiful together.

Consecrated Ground

by MARGARET EMERSON BAILEY
AUGUST, 1932

Here's one place I'll not draw near;
Puritans were buried here.
Not a one of them shall stir,
Saying, "Who converted her?
Who has taught her mullein's wool
Is, in texture, beautiful?
Where the fox grapes go to waste,
Who has given her the taste
For a goblet tilted up

Like a little stirrup cup?
Who has culled for her from dusk,
Rarer fragrances than musk;
And in woods where thrushes flute,
Offered her a substitute
For the flageolet and lute?
We once shattered saints in glass—
Who has brought her to a pass
Where a pool's inverted trees
Are as sacred images.
All we loved, but put away,
She rejoices in to-day."

I shall take the long way round
From this consecrated ground,
Out of courtesy, not fear.
Puritans were buried here,
Who begot a Cavalier.

I Will Leave This House

by JOSEPH AUSLANDER
NOVEMBER, 1934

I will leave this house, being tired of this house
And too much talk;
I will walk down to the sea where the wind blows
The waves to chalk,
And the sand scratches like a silver mouse . . .
I will leave everything here and walk.

I do not know why grass like golden leather
Whipped into strings
Should quiet the heart, or why this autumn weather,
This salt that stings
My eyes and eyelids should heal me altogether—
I do not know the reason for such things.

I only know that here are walls that harden
The eyes and brain;

I only know words hiss and hurt and pardon—
Only to hurt again;
And that the sea is like Death's emerald garden
Dripping with silver wind and silver rain.

Man

by ROSS EDWARD PIERCE
OCTOBER, 1935

                                    Confected
Of a tissue so capricious yet so magical—
Pockets the lightning, computes infinities,
Has at the dark and misty realms of thunder
And plays the prophet to a host of suns,
Yet
Cools at a bird song, wavers at a kiss,
And at a hint of crimson in a flower
Grows silent.

Will the Class Please . . .

by MILDRED BOIE
MAY, 1936

You do not know how loved you are
Who bow above your books, hasty
With pen, and sprawling careless of
Your shape. Minds centered in your ears,
You see no room of you as whole,
Taut breasts in sweaters bright like fruit,
Heads dark and sorrel, sunshine-streaked,
Legs compassed slim in riding breeches,
In silk or skin brown still with summer.
You cannot watch the light that flares
Across your faces in response

To sounds from one who talks of books
And thinks behind her casual voice
How beautiful in youth you are,
How loved in your young-woman beauty!

To a Calvinist in Bali

by EDNA ST. VINCENT MILLAY
OCTOBER, 1938

You that are sprung of northern stock,
And nothing lavish—born and bred
With tablets at your foot and head,
And CULPA carven in the rock,

Sense with delight but not with ease
The fragrance of the quinine trees,
The *kembang-spatu's* lolling flame
With solemn envy kin to shame.

Ah, be content!—the scorpion's tail
Atones for much; without avail
Under the sizzling solar pan
Our sleeping servant pulls the fan.

Even in this island richly blest,
Where Beauty walks with naked breast,
Earth is too harsh for Heaven to be
One little hour in jeopardy.

Sonnet

by EDNA ST. VINCENT MILLAY
APRIL, 1947

Tranquillity at length, when autumn comes,
Will lie upon the spirit like that haze
Touching far islands on fine autumn days
With tenderest blue, like bloom on purple plums;

Harvest will ring, but not as summer hums,
With noisy enterprise—to broaden, raise,
Proceed, proclaim, establish: autumn stays
The marching year one moment; stills the drums.

Then sits the insistent cricket in the grass;
But on the gravel crawls the chilly bee;
And all is over that could come to pass
Last year; excepting this: the mind is free
One moment, to compute, refute, amass,
Catalogue, question, contemplate, and see.

Box-Car Kid

by MARY N. S. WHITELEY
DECEMBER, 1939

The hobo waits to jump with practiced eye
On the screaming wheels, knowing that every freight
Contains some box car where his fellows lie.
Also he knows that if he jump too late
Or earlier than the strict-timed forward fling
There will be no obituary tales
To trim his deed, and no high voice will sing
Of one kid less who smeared the guilty rails
And tramped the road. And as he stands to go
On his death-fed spring, counting the passing cars,
His mind sees rails turn into iron bars
More cold than death and twenty times as slow.
And so his muscles flex for the crucial leap
To a friendly box car or a final sleep.

Is Now

by MARK VAN DOREN
FEBRUARY, 1943

Eternity is not to be pursued.
Run, and it shortens; arrive, and it is shut:
Forward or backward, nothing but the folds
Of time, that you will tighten, fumbling them.

Eternity is only to be entered
Standing. It is everywhere and still.
Slow, and it opens; stop, and it is whole
As love about your head, that rests and sees.

Eternity is now or not at all:
Waited for, a wisp; remembered, shadows.
Eternity is solid as the sun:
As present, as familiar, as immense.

Primitive

by SYLVIA STALLINGS
MARCH, 1946

They're shocked, but I know what I live for
And what will you give for
My afternoon among crickets
Where creeper and honeysuckle thickets
Tangle the eye?
I'll lie
Like a raisin at the bottom of a bowl
The whole
Day meadow-morphosed like a blown
Oat that was never sown
By a Massachusetts man, but O!
What he missed he'll never know!

Nothing's worthwhile, though they won't admit it,
Except the exquisite
Etching of leaf on sky
And afternoons where cowbells cry.
Farewell, ladies and gentlemen;
I doubt if you see me here again,
But knock my door down Piedmont way
Any day, any day
I'm at home, with creek-bottom mud in my toes
And God knows
What you'll get for dinner
From such a sinner.

Well Said, Old Mole

by PETER VIERECK
JULY, 1947

How frail our fists are when they bash or bless
The deadpan idiot emptiness of sky!
In this immortal hoax of Time and Space
(Our creeds and wisecracks equally awry)
We have no solace—no, nor soul—but by
The mortal gesture of a doomed caress:
Man's first and last and honorable reply.
Against the outside Infinite, man weighs
The inwardness within one finite face
And finds all Space less heavy than a sigh
And finds all Time less lingering than *tendresse.*
We are alone and small, and heaven is high;
Quintillion worlds have burst and left no trace;
A murderous star aims straight at where we lie.
And we, all vulnerable and all distress,
Have no brief shield but love and loveliness.
Quick—let me touch your body as we die.

For G. B. S., Old

by WILLIAM CARLOS WILLIAMS

AUGUST, 1948

When the mind burns
the external is swallowed
nor can cold
censor it when it launches
its attack

Sever man
into his parts of bird and fish
Wake him
to the plausibilities
of those changes
he contemplates but does not **dare**

Until by acceptance
he forfeits
the green perspectives
which frightened him off
to his own destruction—

the mirage
the shape of a shape
become the shape he feared
his Tempest frozen
into a pattern
of ice.

Sacred and Profane Love, or There's Nothing New Under the Moon Either

by PETER DeVRIES

APRIL, 1951

When bored by the drone of the wedlocked pair,
When bromides of marriage have started to wear,
Contemplate those of the crimson affair:
    "I *had* to see you," and, "Tonight belongs to us."

Skewered on bliss of a dubious sort
Are all individuals moved to consort
With creatures inspiring *this* hackneyed retort:
    "I can't fight you any longer."

Some with such wheezes have gone to the dead,
Unwitting that *Liebestod* lurked up ahead,
That pistols would perforate them as they said:
    "This thing is bigger than both of us."

Experimentation in matters of sin
Pales on the instant it's destined to win;
Paramours end as conformers begin:
    "I don't want just this—I want *you*."

Explorers are highly unlikely to hear
Novelties murmured into their ear;
Checkered with such is the checkered career:
    "It's not you I'm afraid of, it's myself."

Such liturgies standardize lovers in league
That someone will cry in the midst of intrigue
(And someone will hear in the midst of fatigue):
    "You don't want *me*—you just want sex!"

Strait is the gate and narrow the way
Closing at last on the ranging roué;
Who plucks a primrose plants a cliché:
    "We're married in the eyes of Heaven."

The dangerous life is so swiftly prosaic
You might as well marry and live in Passaic;
It ends and begins in established mosaic:
  "I'm all mixed up."

The lexicon's written for groom and for rake.
Liaisons are always a give-and-take.
Disillusionment's certain to follow a break.
  "For God's sake be careful, or someone will hear you!"

The Wren

by RAYMOND HENRI
MARCH, 1952

If a wren
With three, four thimblesful of fledglings,
Who must carve her luncheon inch worm and
Puree the supper pea . . .

If a wren,
Not from need, nor threat, nor fear,
Will spring into a fury, fly
At any other wrens that dare contest
The title to her green and gravel acre
That lies between the latitudes of angleworms and heaven . . .

If a wren
Will fling herself against trespassing feathers
As against a horde of mailed invaders;
Comparatively chattering, decibel to inch,
Enough to sound the trumpets of an army . . .

If a wren
That, mothering her nest,
Or skating on the morning ponds of cold Spring air,
Or momentarily perched upon a brushstroke of a twig,
Looking something shaped of sugar
Lying in an angel's hand,
Can yet be suddenly impelled

Into such buzzsaw of behavior . . .
Why do you say some men and nations are enigmas?

Preach peace? First preach it to the wren,
The bloody, raucous little wren;
And preach goodwill to shrikes;
And codify the rights of grasshoppers,
Especially *that* grasshopper
The shrike impaled upon a hawthorn tine.

And preach it to the owl
Whose wisdom chooses mice and all things small
But never full-grown rabbits.

All you with faith in men,
Come watch the wren.

Godiva

by ANNE GOODWIN WINSLOW
AUGUST, 1954

Where he fell there Thomas lies,
Eternal darkness on his eyes;

No bolt from heaven struck him down,
But Beauty riding through the town.

Down from the castle high and grim
The message came to all, to him—

Stir not abroad lest you should meet
The morning star upon the street;

Let every house be closed and still,
The crescent moon slips down the hill;

Let time on every steeple wait
Till she re-enter at the gate!

—Should he not risk one mortal eye
To see the lights of heaven go by?

Now doors are open, clocks tick on,
And moon and star for him are gone.

Troubled, Frustrated—

by LEONARD BACON
SEPTEMBER, 1954

Troubled, frustrated, ill-behaved,
And by fantasy enslaved,
He has not braved what should be braved.

He has not dared what should be dared,
But cared—Who cares for what he cared?—
And later, like a fool despaired,

Though even in that dark he knew,
However false, he must grow true,
Still trusting what he trusted to.

He has more often than he ought
Trafficked in what he thought was thought,
Until by sharp experience taught

That it was but a hurricane,
Small, but enough to break a brain
Not well designed for stress and strain.

Try courage. From exposed conceit,
From bitterness at length complete,
Men learn the measure of the Sweet,

And from their deep excogitate
Height which they cannot estimate,
Remote, superb, inviolate.

Emerson

by ERNEST KROLL

SEPTEMBER, 1955

Melville had Emerson's number:
He saw within the man the "gaping flaw,"
Rectitude without compassion,
Which would draw
The knotted cord of life
Reluctant through the needle's eye;
And heard, within the voice that sang
The "beautiful necessity,"
The crack that all too clearly sprang,
Not from any lack of art,
But from a defect in the region of the heart.

"Mr. E. is horribly narrow here,
And has his Dardanelles,"
Said Melville, "for his every Marmora."
"Like all artesian wells,"
Said Meredith, "he has a narrow bore,
But the water that he lifts is sweet."

Narrow, sweet; sweet and narrow—
He reasoned though his heart was sore;
Sore-hearted, yet serene and bland,
He took the Devil by the hand,
Acknowledged him a gentleman,
And smiled that evil was no more.

Horace to Tibullus

(*Carmina* 1.33, in the original meter)

by GILBERT HIGHET

APRIL, 1956

Now don't overindulge grief for your lost coquette,
my poor comrade, and don't publish lugubrious
dark-blue dirges for love, endlessly asking why
     she broke faith, took a younger man.
See how Audrey—a rare beauty with clustered curls—
burns for David; and he yearns for the arrogant
Eileen; yet we shall see slavering mountain wolves
     mate with delicate fallow deer
far, far sooner than Eileen will indulge his lust.
Cruel Love always conjoins two inappropriate
hearts, minds, bodies in one pair of unbroken chains:
     Love does relish a savage joke.
I too, though a liaison with a kinder girl
was quite possible, still clung to my cruel Sue—
slum-bred woman, and wild: stormier than the waves
     wind-whipped, lashing Atlantic rocks!

VII

Daguerreotype of America

A Bit of Life in Oregon

ANONYMOUS

DECEMBER, 1853

*The loveliest two weeks we ever heard of were spent by the
unknown author of this short piece on a tiny island at Port Orford, Oregon. He was not alone.*

My jaunt to Oregon was indirectly owing to the fertilizing powers
of guano; although the action of that renovator of worn-out lands was
not exerted in its usual manner. It happened thus: A fine clipper ship,
which had agreed to carry us around the world, on arriving at San
Francisco, consented to prostitute its noble powers to an ignoble office;
and instead of visiting the Celestial Regions for teas, sailed to the
Chincha Islands for guano, whither I declined going—not being
tempted even by the bright eyes and sunny skies of Lima. In consequence I became that most unfortunate of beings, an idler in San
Francisco; until one lucky day, when a friend requested me to transact
some business for him in Oregon.

A bag, a pair of blankets, a red woolen hunting-shirt, and a revolver,
completed my baggage; and we were soon sailing through the beautiful bay and along the Golden Horn, whose waters and shores require
only associations and a pen to make them rank with many spots, less
beautiful, but more praised. We entered the broad Pacific, then very
boisterous, and coasting along past Punta de los Reyes, Cape Mendo-
cino, Trinidad, Crescent City, etc., arrived on the fifth day at Port
Orford, our destination. Spirits of the Pilgrims of the Mayflower! how
little could you imagine, as you landed on that desolate rock, amid
all that could depress the energies of man, that, in less than two centuries and a half, your descendants would be building towns upon the
western borders of *their* country—a country broader than the Atlantic
you had passed!

Camp-life was soon commenced in good earnest, as there was no
hotel in Port Orford. Provisions were unpacked and ranged in the cup-

board (an old box), sundry cooking utensils were neatly hung on the pantry-shelf (the projecting limb of an old tree); and the fireplace was constructed after the most approved Indian mode; that is to say, a few stones for the hearth, with two upright posts and a cross-stick for pot-hanger. As night came on we began to prepare supper; but were much chagrined to find that our frying-pan had been stolen—a sad accident, as the fresh sea-breezes and plenty of out-door exercise had given us keen appetites. We were beginning to discuss the propriety of eating our bacon raw, when necessity seized the shovel, and we broiled what we needed in a style that would have delighted the great Soyer himself. Never was a supper of bacon, potatoes, and coffee eaten with better relish. . . .

While waiting here, let me sandwich a small amount of useful information respecting Oregon, more especially for the benefit of invalids. The climate is delightful, and although in the same latitude with New York, the summer is cooler and the winter warmer than those of the Empire State. Upon the coast above Cape Blanco, the prevalent winds are from the northwest, but even these are less unpleasant than the easterly winds at New York. At Port Orford, which is sheltered from these winds by a projecting bluff, the climate may challenge comparison with the most favored portions of Italy. The atmosphere is wonderfully clear and transparent. There were but two or three foggy days during the month, and these were far more pleasant than similar days in Florence, when the cold winds come down from the Apennines.

It was a common saying at Port Orford, among the sixty or seventy residents, that it was impossible to be sick there. The equability of the climate renders this perhaps the most healthful portion of the Union; and it cannot be long before our Eastern physicians, instead of sending their consumptive patients to Italy or Cuba, will recommend them to take the Pacific Railway to Oregon, to recruit their health.

Just in front of Port Orford there is a small island, just large enough for a snug little house and garden. Eighteen months since it was the scene of a bloody fight. The Indians, seven hundred in number, drove Kirkpatrick, with the whole population of the town (eight men only), upon this natural castle, where, after attempting to slaughter them and failing, they determined to starve them. Kirkpatrick had one large gun, besides rifles, and shot down over seventy of the savages as they attempted to climb the steep side of the island, or showed themselves upon the beach. After waiting a month, however, and finding the whites superior to both arrows and want, the patience of the Indians became exhausted, and they made a treaty, which they have kept to this day.

It was upon this hill that, having accomplished the business which I had undertaken, I spent the afternoons of two weeks awaiting the steamer. My companions were too lazy to climb it, and I was left alone to my book and meditations.

I said *alone*, but I was not quite so. Half the charm of that spot consisted in the company of a young Indian girl, who could not have seen more than sixteen summers, and who was almost the only handsome Indian woman I had seen. She had seen me mounting the hill frequently, and thought it no harm to follow, owing perhaps to my having paid her more deference than she was accustomed to receive, and perhaps also on account of some trifling presents I had given her.

It was a beautiful spot where we used to sit, this wild Indian girl and myself, and watch the sun setting every evening in the Pacific. The trees and shrubbery completely sheltered us from the wind, as well as from observation, behind; while in front of our grassy little nook, the view was open to the endless blue waves of the ocean. The atmosphere was of that pleasant nature which makes the mere sensation of existence happiness. I was reading "My Novel"; and here were sketches of the most polished style of life on earth placed beside the most uncivilized: "Violante" and sweet "Nora Avenel" beside this child of the forest; and was I blind or smitten, that I say the latter did not suffer by the contrast? Then you also would have been blind had you sat and seen those large Oriental eyes beaming on you. You would have been smitten too by those delicate features, and that fair form, just rounded to womanhood! I named her "Graziella," and appointed her my teacher of the Indian language. She laughed immoderately when I wrote down the names which she translated into her tongue, being as much puzzled by my hieroglyphics as I was by her barbarous speech; and I must confess that whatever of the savage was wanting in her appearance, was fully made up by the harsh sounds issuing from her mouth. Her language seemed to abound more in consonants than the Spanish does in vowels. For instance, she called boots *khrehr* (a word to test one's guttural powers); pantaloons were *tlsoos;* hand was *shlah*, and so on.

The dress of my young teacher was very unique, and would have attracted attention in Broadway or Regent-street. Her head-covering was nothing more than an inverted basket, of various colors, tightly woven, and fitting her head closely, like a jockey cap, having withal a very coquettish air; her dark locks flowed down from underneath, and hung closely over her shoulders and neck; her waist was encircled by a skirt, which, in size and shape, appeared to have been cut after a pattern sent out by some of our theatrical *danseuses,* only it was of very different texture, being made of strings of bark, instead of lace, which hung down to her knees, displaying a limb of which the Venus de Medici might have been proud. A skin, thrown loosely over her shoulders, completed her attire, excepting the usual ornaments of beads in the nose and about the neck. And truly, however ridiculous nose-ornaments may appear to our civilized ladies of the East, I certainly thought they were an advantage in the present instance. Rings belong as naturally to the nose as to the ears, for this practice of boring the body for ornament is at best but a barbarism, whether the nose or the ears be the sufferer. Pardon me, ladies!

Apropos of Indian dress; at Crescent City I saw a most laughable specimen of taste in two young squaws. One of them had on a skirt similar to the one described, and above it a dragoon jacket, which completed her costume; the other marched up with great dignity, with nothing on but a black frock coat, tightly buttoned.

Graziella was beginning to make rapid improvement in English, while I was making a corresponding advancement in her language—not to say in another too, which is common to all nations. She was good-natured, playful, and of great natural intelligence, as could be easily discovered by the readiness with which she acquired the English. Why not educate and marry her? She was the daughter of a chief, and her father offered to sell her for a gun and a pair of blankets! To an Indian the word *gun* involves all the happiness attached by us to houses, lands, furniture, books, etc.; therefore the price was not depreciatory of the *article* offered for sale; and considering the scarcity of wives in California and Oregon, and the romance attaching to the act, my lady readers will not be in the least surprised that I should have been tempted to accept the offer. But, on the other hand, a salutary doubt as to the reception my uncivilized bride, although of noble blood, would meet with from the female portion of my family of ignoble blood, decided me to let the forest retain its own, and I declined alliance with the blood of the Tagonishas!

But the steamer comes in sight. Would you like to see my parting with Graziella? Of course it was touching in the extreme, and my last act was to present her with my red hunting shirt, in virtue of which she now undoubtedly reigns as the belle of Oregon.

Chivalrous and Semi-Chivalrous Southrons

by J. W. DeFOREST

JANUARY–FEBRUARY, 1869

As a subject for interesting study, the Southerner is unsurpassed. One of the first writers to appreciate his unique character was John William DeForest (1826–1906), a son of Connecticut who was a Union Army officer. Later he was commander of a district of the Freedman's Bureau with headquarters in Greenville, S.C. DeForest was a short story writer, novelist, and author of battle sketches for Harper's *during the war. Southerners sometimes identified themselves as "Southrons," as in the title of the article.*

They certainly are, these "Southrons," a different people from us Northerners; they are, perhaps, as unlike to us as the Spartans to the Athenians, or the Poles to the Germans; they are more simple than we, more provincial, more antique, more picturesque; they have fewer of the virtues of modern society, and more of the primitive, the natural virtues; they care less for wealth, art, learning, and the other delicacies of an urban civilization; they care more for individual character and reputation of honor.

Cowed as we are by the Mrs. Grundy of democracy; molded into tame similarity by a general education, remarkably uniform in degree and nature, we shall do well to study this peculiar people, which will soon lose its peculiarities; we shall do better to engraft upon ourselves its nobler qualities. . . .

Pugnacities

Self-respect, as the Southerners understood it, has always demanded much fighting. A pugnacity which is not merely war-paint, but which is, so to speak, tattooed into the character, has resulted from this high sentiment of personal value, and from the circumstances which produced the sentiment. It permeates all society; it has infected all individualities. The meekest man by nature, the man who at the North would no more fight than he would jump out of a second-story window, will at the South resent an insult by a blow, or perhaps a stab or pistol-shot.

I knew a middle-aged South Carolinian, at one time a representative of our country to one of the minor courts of Europe, who temporarily withdrew his connection from the church of which he was a member in order to give himself elbow-room for a duel. . . .

Courage in the Field

The pugnacious customs of Southern society explain in part the extraordinary courage which the Confederate troops displayed during the rebellion. A man might as well be shot doing soldierly service at Bull Run or The Wilderness as go back to Abbeville and be shot there in the duel or street rencontre which awaited him. The bullet-hole was a mere question of time, and why not open one's arms to it on the field of glory? . . .

Unquestionably a strong military tone is perceptible in the character of the "chivalrous Southron." Notably brave, punctilious as to honor, pugnacious to quarrelsomeness, authoritative to imperiousness, generous to extravagance, somewhat formal in his courtesy, somewhat grandiose in his self-respect, there is hardly an agreeable or disagreeable trait in him which you cannot find in the officers of most armies. This is doubtless one reason why, at the opening of the war, many of our old regulars leaned to the rebel side; there was a relationship of sentiment between the professional militaire and the feudal head of a plantation; moreover, the latter had always treated the former with distinguished hospitality. . . .

Virility

It seems to me that the central trait of the "chivalrous Southron" is an intense respect for virility. He will forgive almost any vice in a man who is manly; he will admire vices which are but exaggerations of the masculine. If you will fight, if you are strong and skillful enough to kill your antagonist, if you can govern or influence the common herd, if you can ride a dangerous horse over a rough country, if you are a good shot or an expert swordsman, if you stand by your own opinions unflinchingly, if you do your level best on whiskey, if you are a devil of a fellow with women, if, in short, you show vigorous masculine attributes, he will grant you his respect. I doubt whether a man who leaves behind him numerous irregular claimants to his name is regarded with disfavor at the South. He will be condemned theoretically; it may be considered proper to shoot him if he disturbs the peace of respectable families; but he will be looked upon as a nobler representative of his sex than Cœlebs. The good young man, as pure as a young girl, whom one finds in the Abrahamic bosom of Northern Puritanism, would not be made a Grand Lama of in Dixie. The chivalrous Southron would unite with the aristocracy of Europe in regarding him as a sort of monster of neutral insipidity. I doubt whether even the women of our meridional regions admire that sort of youth. "I shouldn't fancy a hen-husband," said a lively Southern girl, alluding to a man without vices.

It may be taken for granted that a people which so highly prizes virility looks upon man as a lord of creation, and has the old-fashioned ideas as to what is the proper sphere of woman. If the high-toned gentleman continues to be influential at the South, it will be a long time before the "strong-minded" obtain much of a following there, a very long time before they will establish female suffrage. Next to our supposed passion for putting the negro on an equality with the white, there is nothing in Northern life so abhorrent to the Southerners, of both sexes, as the movement in favor of woman's rights.

"I do think," said an emphatic old planter to me, "that your free-love business, and women's voting, and all that, is just the miserablest mess that ever was invented. I don't see what ails you to go for such vile nonsense. But then you always were as full of whimsies as the devil." . . .

Before the war things were growing worse, instead of better. Bullied and reproached by abolitionism, scared at the prospect of losing two thousand millions of dollars invested in negroes, the chivalry concentrated its intellect into a defense of slavery, and actually thought of little else. The subject was dwarfing the Southern mind; it had infolded and partially stifled that fine genius which produced so many of our early statesmen, and wrote no small part of the *Federalist;* it was like a theological dogma which insists on being taken for granted, and,

being so taken, destroys the freedom and power of logic. The Southerners, trammeled by admitting slavery, could no more reason on politics than the Jews, trammeled by the Mosaic dispensation, could reason on Christianity. . . .

The Southerners are equally wrong-headed, at least according to
our view of the matter and "the sword of Brennus," in pointing out the
causes of the war. Over and over have they assured me that the contest arose not from the necessity of slavery to rule or ruin, but from
the aggressive spirit of the Northerners, and particularly of the New
Englanders.

"They always were, you know, the most quarrelsome people that
God ever created," remarked a Greenville planter. "They quarreled
in England, and cut off the king's head. They have been quarreling
here ever since they came over in the *Mayflower*. They got after the
Indians and killed them by thousands. They drove out the Baptists
and whipped the Quakers and hung the witches. Then they were the
first to pick a fight with the old country. It's my opinion, Sir, and I
think you must agree with me, that God never made such another
quarrelsome set. What in h–ll he made them for passes my comprehen-
sion." . . .

Political opinions had necessarily been somewhat muddled by the
results of the war. The logic of events had been so different from
the logic of *De Bow's Review* and the *Charleston Mercury* that men
scarcely knew what to think. A soul which had been educated in the
belief that slavery is a divine and reverend institution could not help
falling more or less dumb with amazement when it found that there
was no slavery to revere. On this point, however, the Southern mind
presently accepted the situation, and I found a surprisingly general
satisfaction over the accomplished fact of abolition, mixed with much
natural wrath at the manner of the accomplishment. "I am glad the
thing is done away with," was a frequent remark; "it was more plague
than pleasure, more loss than profit." Then would perhaps follow the
Southern *Delenda est Carthago*—that is to say, "D—n the Yankees!"
—always appropriate. . . .

Political Feeling

We of the North can but faintly imagine the alarm and hate which
have trembled through millions of hearts at the South at the phrase,
"The Yankees are coming!" The words meant war, the fall of loved

ones, the burning of homes, the wasting of property, flight, poverty, subjugation, humiliation, a thousand evils, and a thousand sorrows. The Southern people had never before suffered anything a tenth part so horrible as what befell them in consequence of this awful formula, this summons to the Afrites and Furies of desolation, this declaration of ruin. Where the conquering army sought to be gentlest it still devoured the land like locusts; where it came not at all it nevertheless brought social revolution, bankruptcy of investments, and consequently indigence. A population of bereaved parents, of widows, and of orphans, steeped in sudden poverty, can hardly love the cause of its woes. The great majority of the Southerners, denying that they provoked the war, looking upon us not as the saviors of a common country, but as the subjugators of their sovereign States, regard us with detestation.

I speak of the "chivalrous Southrons," the gentry, the educated, the socially influential, the class which before the war governed the South, the class which may soon govern it again. Even if these people knew that they had been in the wrong they would still be apt to feel that their punishment has exceeded their crime, because it has been truly tremendous and has reached many who could not be guilty. I remember a widowed grandmother of eighty and an orphan granddaughter of seven from each of whom a large estate on the Sea Islands had passed beyond redemption, and who were in dire poverty. When the elder read aloud from a newspaper a description of some hundreds of acres which had been divided among negroes, and said, "Chattie, that is your plantation," the child burst into tears. I believe that it is unnatural not to sympathize with this little plundered princess, weeping for her lost domains in fairy-land.

Imagine the wrath of a fine gentleman, once the representative of his country abroad, who finds himself driven to open a beer saloon. Imagine the indignation of a fine lady who must keep boarders; of another who must go out to service little less than menial; of another who must beg rations with low-downers and negroes. During the war I saw women of good families at the South who had no stockings; and here I beg leave to stop and ask the reader to conceive fully, if he can, the sense of degradation which must accompany such poverty; a degradation of dirt and nakedness, and slatternly uncomeliness, be it observed; a degradation which seemed to place them beside the negro. Let us imagine the prosperous ladies of our civilization prevented only from wearing the latest fashions; what manliest man of us all would like to assume the responsibility of such a piece of tyranny? . . .

Southern Individuality

Whether chivalrous or semi-chivalrous, the Southerner has more individuality of character than the Northerner, and is one of the most interesting, or, at all events, one of the most amusing, personages on this continent, if not in the world. He has salient virtues, vices, and oddities; he has the right, practical humor which is totally unconscious of being humoristic; he in the gravest manner decorates his life with ludicrous and romantic adventures; in short, he is a prize for the anecdotist and novelist. Dixie has thousands of high-toned gentlemen who suppose themselves to be patterns of solemn and staid propriety, but who would be fit to associate with the Caxtons and Doctor Ricca-bocca. In that land of romance you will find Uncle Toby and Squire Western and Sir Pitt Crawley and Colonel Newcome and Mr. Pickwick and Le Chourineur, all moving in the best society and quite sure that they are Admirable Crichtons.

In what other part of the civilized earth would a leading statesman write a ponderous political work in dialogue, after the fashion of the essays of Plato and Cicero? Such a gusto of classical imitation might possibly be found in a Harvard Sophomore; but at the South we dis-cover it in an ex-United States Congressman and ex-Vice-President of the Confederacy. Alexander H. Stephens is as redolent of Greeks and Romans, as verdant with lore, as Keitt or Pryor.

Where else could you meet such a curious incarnation of the apos-tolic character as —— ——, a planter by profession and habitude, but a preacher by mission? He was a passionate religionist; if he met you in the street he buttonholed you and vented upon you his dogmas; chance passers-by were beckoned to until he had a circle; you listened because you dared not run away. One Sunday, exhorting in a little cross-roads church, and having been annoyed by two negroes stealing out of the house, he came to a solemn pause in his service, and then spoke as follows: "Next Lord's day I shall hold worship in this same place. I shall bring my double-barreled gun; I shall stand that gun, brethren, in the pulpit, alongside of me; and, if any man gets up and goes out while I am preaching, by ——! I'll shoot him."

A half-fuddled planter called on me one evening and invited me out to a treat of stewed oysters. The restaurant was the back-room of a bakery; we sat on broken chairs, among sticky pans, spilled flour, and loaves of dough; the oyster-cans were opened with an old bowie-knife. When the stews were before us my friend observed: "Come, don't let's eat this like savages. Major, can't you ask a blessing?" As I declined, he pulled his broad-brimmed felt from his muddled cranium and said grace himself.

I knew a worthy old South Carolinian, bearing a name of Revolutionary notoriety, who would not invest his money at high profits, holding that "six per cent., my dear Sir, is the interest of a gentleman."

I knew another worthy old person who raised a set of white and a set of black children, treated both with generosity and affection, maintained an excellent character in his church, and died in the odor of public esteem.

I knew a planter who, having said in a drunken spree that he would sell his plantation for twenty thousand dollars, would not revoke his words when sober, although it was worth thirty thousand.

I knew of another planter who beat his beautiful wife as long as he lived, and at his death willed her a considerable property, on condition that she should never quit the State, he knowing that her chiefest desire was to remove to the North.

I knew Southerners who taught their slaves to read in spite of severe prohibitory laws, and who labored for their growth in morality and piety as missionaries labor for the conversion of the heathen.

I knew of a Louisiana lady who flogged a negro woman with her own hands until the sufferer's back was a vast sore of bruised and bloody flesh.

Audacity, vehemence, recklessness, passion, sentiment, prejudice, vanity, whimwhams, absurdities, culture, ignorance, courtliness, barbarism! The individual has plenty of elbow-room at the South; he kicks out of the traces with a freedom unknown to our steady-pulling society; he is a bull in Mrs. Grundy's china-shop. Strangest of all, he believes that he is like the rest of the world, or, more accurately, that the rest of the world should be like him.

This remarkable personage, more striking in character and habits than the strange people whom the Brontë girls brought out of the depths of Yorkshire, has hitherto found no worthy painter. Even Mrs. Stowe has but faintly sketched two or three Southern portraits: a Louisianian—the type of languid gentility, without a vice, without a shadow; a Virginian—the type of well-bred jollity and good-nature, also without a shadow; a field-preacher—shrewd, coarse, humorous, and well enough. Her Eva is no more distinctively Southern than her Uncle Tom is honestly African. Her Mrs. St. Clair I consider a libel on the hard-working, careful, Southern housewife and mistress of a plantation.

The chivalrous Southron has been too positively and authoritatively a political power to get fair treatment in literature. People have not described him; they have felt driven to declaim about him; they have preached for him or preached against him. Northern pens have not done justice to his virtues, nor Southern pens to his vices.

The romances of Dixie, produced under a mixed inspiration of namby-pambyism and provincial vanity, strong in polysyllables and feeble in perception of character, deserve better than any other results of human labor that I am aware of the native epithet of "powerful weak." The novelist evidently has but two objects in view: First, to present the Southron as the flower of gentility; second, to do some fine writing for his own glory. Two or three works by Kennedy and by the authoress of "Marion Harland" are the only exceptions to this rule. Not until the Southerners get rid of some of their local vanity, not until they cease talking of themselves only in a spirit of self-adulation, not until they drop the idea that they are Romans and must write in the style of Cicero, will they be able to so paint their life as that the world shall crowd to see the picture. Meantime let us pray that a true Southern novelist may soon arise, for he will be able to furnish us vast amusement and some instruction. His day is passing; in another generation his material will be gone; the "chivalrous Southron" will be as dead as the slavery that created him.

How shall we manage this eccentric creature? We have been ruled by him; we have fought him, beaten him, made him captive; now what treatment shall we allot him? My opinion is, that it would be good both for him and for us if we should perseveringly attempt to put up with his oddities and handle him as a pet. He resembles the ideal white bears described in the "Pearl of Orr's Island"; "there ain't no kinder creetur in the whole world if you'll only get the right side of him." It is true that he has wanted to eat us, which is exasperating; it is true that he still talks of eating us at some convenient season, which is ridiculous; but I believe that he suffered too much in our late struggle to seriously think of renewing it; I hold that his war snorts are mere election buncombe.

A little letting alone, a little conciliation, a little flattery even, would soothe him amazingly; and if united with good government would in the end be sure to reconstruct him as a quiet citizen and sound patriot. The Republican party, while firmly maintaining the integrity of the country and the great results of the war in the advancement of human freedom, ought to labor zealously for the prosperity of the South, treat tenderly its wounded pride, forget the angry past, be patient with the perturbed present, and so create a true, heart-felt national unity.

The Plains as I Crossed Them

by HORACE GREELEY

MAY, 1869

In the summer of 1859, the editor of the New York Tribune *journeyed from New York to San Francisco. He toured California and returned by way of Panama, bringing back a conviction which he summed up in the advice, "Go West, young man!" He wrote this article in 1869, when interest in the new Western lands was at its height. A great editor and moral leader, Greeley made the* Tribune *one of the nation's most influential papers during the Civil War period. His political ambition brought about his downfall. As the Democratic presidential nominee in 1872, he was crushingly defeated by President U. S. Grant, and died insane a few weeks later.*

The Mississippi is the King of Rivers. Taking rise almost on the northern limit of the temperate zone, it pursues its majestic course nearly due south to the verge of the tropic, with its tributaries washing the Alleghanies on the one hand and the Rocky Mountains on the other, throughout the entire length of those great mountain chains. . . .

Its valley includes more than one million square miles of the richest soil on earth, and is capable of sustaining in plenty half the population of the globe; its head-springs are frozen half the year, while cane ripens and frost is rarely seen at its mouth; and a larger and richer area of its surface is well adapted at once to Indian corn, to wheat, and to grass —to the apple, the peach, and the grape—than of any other commensurate region of earth. Its immense prairies are gigantic natural gardens, which need but the plow to adapt them to the growth of the most exacting and exhausting plants. It is the congenial and loved home of the choicest animals: I judge that more game is now roving at will over its immeasurable wilds and pastures than is found on an equal area all the world besides. It is the geographic heart of North America, and probably contains fully half the arable land in the New World north of the Isthmus of Darien.

Its recent progress in industry and civilization has been rapid beyond parallel. At the birth of this century, its only city was a village; its total white population was less than one million. Today, it has five cities, averaging two hundred thousand inhabitants each, and its civilized population exceeds fifteen millions.

And to its luxuriant and still unpeopled expanse all nations, all races, are yet eagerly flocking. The keen-eyed sons of cold and hard New England there meet the thrifty Dutchmen of Pennsylvania, the disinherited children of Scandinavia, of Northern Germany, and of the British Isles. From every quarter, every civilized land, the hungry, the portionless, the daring, hie to the Great Valley, there to forget the past buffets of niggard fortune and hew out for their offspring the homes of plenty and comfort denied to their own rugged youth. Each year, as it flits, sees the cultivated portion of the Great Valley expand; sees the dominion of the brute and the savage contracted and driven back; sees the aggregate product of its waving fields and fertile glades dilate and increase. Another century, if signalized by no unforeseen calamity, will witness the Great Valley the home of one hundred millions of energetic, efficient, intelligent farmers and artisans, and its chief marts the largest inland cities of the globe.

The Mississippi and its eastern tributaries are among the most placid, facile, tractable of rivers. A single fall wholly arrests navigation on the former; the Ohio rolls its bright volume a thousand miles unbroken by one formidable cataract. If half the steam-vessels on earth are not found on these waters, the proportion is not much less than that. It may almost be said that steam navigation and the development of Great Valley have hitherto gone hand in hand, and that the former is the vital impulse, the indispensable main-spring, of the latter. . . .

But, the moment the Great River is crossed, all this is changed. The turbid, resistless Missouri waters a far larger area than the other "inland sea" of Mr. Calhoun, wherewith it blends at St. Louis; yet its tonnage is but a fraction when compared with that of the latter; and, while boats of liberal size are overshadowed by the Alleghanies at almost each day's journey along their western base, the rays of no setting sun were ever yet intercepted on their way to a steamboat deck by the peaks of the Rocky Mountains.

Time will doubtless multiply the keels plying on the Missouri and its affluents; but human genius can never wholly overcome the obstacles to secure and speedy navigation presented by the nature of that resistless current, or rather of the country it traverses. The eager thousands pressing westward overland each summer to the shores of the Pacific find no relief from the length, the weariness, of their tedious journey in the shrill but welcome whistle of the fire-propelled, floating caravanserai. For weeks, they stalk in dusty, somber array, beside the broad, impetuous Platte: finding obstruction, not furtherance, in its rippling, treacherous current; this moment scarcely knee-deep, and the next far over head; only their thirst, with that of their fainting beasts, is assuaged thereby. For all other uses, its bed might as well—perhaps better—be a stretch of uniformly thirsty, torrid sand.

For the wide PLAINS, which slope imperceptibly, regularly upward from the bluffs of the Missouri to the bases of the Rocky Mountains, are unlike any other region of earth. They labor under what, with no reference to our current politics, may be fitly characterized as a chronic deficiency of *back-bone*. Rock, to be sure, is sometimes seen here in place; but very rarely, save in the *buttes,* or perpendicular faces of hills, which are mainly confined to the vicinity of mountains, and are obviously a sort of natural *adobe*—a modern product of sun and rain and wind, out of the mingled clay and sand which form the subsoil of all this region. . . .

The prevalent impression made on the stranger's mind by the Plains is one of loneliness—of isolation. You press on, day after day, without seeing a house, a fence, a cultivated field, or even a forest—nought but a few shy wild beasts at intervals, or undelightful birds, and rarely a scanty, niggard stream, with a few mean, low, scrubby trees thinly strewn along its banks—often one of them only; and, as you go farther west, even these disappear, or are only seen in thin patches, miles apart.

If you are traveling along a river, you are amazed at the sparseness, the feebleness, of its tributaries, the dryness of their beds, the bareness of their banks. At length, the river itself disappears, or is only seen in pools and in hollows along its bed, where a deep excavation has been gullied under one of its banks; at last, the necessary, but not particularly inviting, fluid has wholly vanished, and you are compelled to make your way hurriedly over the long "divide" that separates this stream from one, often less considerable, but which heads in or near a range of mountains, and, therefore, maintains its current nearly or quite through the summer. This "divide" may be thirty, fifty miles across—it may be a hundred—wood and grass upon it, and, in summer, water also, are out of the question; only a few straggling weeds, with the worthless shrubs here known as grease-wood and sage-bush, relieve the monotony of the sterile, dreary waste.

What wonder if the patient ox, weary, famished, foot-sore, should here lie down to his long rest, leaving his master and more pitiable mate to get on without him as they may?

It would be rather Hibernian to pronounce dead oxen the only signs of life to be encountered during many days' journey on the Plains; but I have no doubt that the carcasses of fifty thousand cattle are now slowly decomposing above-ground on the arid, treeless, dewless stretches which separate Kansas and Nebraska from California and Oregon.

Verily, the carrion-crow is lord of the Plains—the only ample feeder in those famished regions—quick-sighted, impudent, and, though gorged to heaviness, abundantly able to take care of himself. I cannot guess where he finds nest-accommodation; probably in the face of some high, perpendicular creek-bank, the brow of some *butte,* not too remote from the emigrant trail to enable him to gorge his young ones as he gorges himself. He is as decorously jolly as an undertaker in cholera-time, and sports a grave demeanor and a black coat professionally, and with no thought of evincing sorrow, or exciting sympathy, still less of mortifying the flesh. On the Plains, the crow is general executor and universal heir.

On the hither side of this broad, bleak domain—say a little below the forks of the Platte—two great lines of emigration in early summer intersect each other. One is that of the adventurous thousands who push westward from the yet unmade garden of the world to find still ruder homes by the shores of the great Pacific. Its vanguard appears at this point early in May, is composed of cavaliers well-mounted on steeds just beginning to be the worse for wear, followed by light wagons, drawn respectively by two mules or horses each, carrying but two emigrants or speculators, with their provisions and scanty baggage, eagerly pushing on to cross the Sierra Nevada at farthest by the first of August. Following these, come straggling slowly along heavy wagons and carts, drawn by horses, mules, or oxen, five to twenty teams in a company for mutual assistance and protection, with sober matrons, ruddy damsels, and tow-headed children looking wistfully out from beneath the white cotton cover of most wagons, or trudging slowly, dustily along, from ten to sixty rods in front. Droves of loose cattle, the frolic all worked out of them, move behind, before, and on either flank of the wagons, already tired of the scanty fare and hard usage of the Plains, but without a suspicion that they have not yet begun to conceive what hardship really is—a point on which their experience will be decidedly enlarged within the next three months. But the whip cracks, the oxen strain at the yoke, the well-mounted herdsmen gallop hither and thither along the rear of the straggling throng; and, through sand and dust, the whole caravan moves slowly westward, with many similar caravans pressing on before and behind it. Of the cattle thus impelled toward the setting sun, perhaps three-fourths will live to cross the Sierra Nevada—famine, fatigue, the diseases engendered by bad, alkaline water, and the crows taking the rest; but of the tens of thousands thus urged through the South Pass, not even hundreds will ever return. They have cropped their last of the ample herbage of Kansas and Missouri, and must make up their mouths to the dryer, seeded grasses of Utah or California for the residue of their lives. Of their human companions on this long, rugged exodus, probably one-fourth—hardly more—will live to see water running toward the Atlantic again.

The transverse line of migration which intersects the great trail near the forks of the Platte is that of the American bison or buffalo. Having wintered, as they best might, amidst the timber and grass of Northern Texas, of Eastern New Mexico, of the Indian Territory, of Western Arkansas—by the sources of the Red River of Louisiana, the Cimarone, the Ouchita—the buffalo, half-famished and thoroughly miserable, start with the springing grass, and, in April or early May, turns his face northward in quest of "fresh fields and pastures new." Traveling in countless legions, sufficient to cover at once whole townships, the bison avoids, so far as possible, the timbered valleys of streams, and, driven outward by hunger and the speedy disappearance of the coarse, short, sturdy buffalo-grass beneath the feet of his all-devouring myriads, crosses successively the Arkansas, the Smoky Hill, the Solomon, the Republican, and begins to show a dark front of over a hundred miles along the south bank of the Platte from its forks eastward, as the later half of the emigration is toiling up both sides of that broad, shallow, rapid river. Collisions naturally ensue, and thousands of the noblest natives of the Plains bite the dust—most of them shot in sheer wantonness by hunters already gorged and overladen with buffalo-meat, whose only poor excuse for this wanton butchery is a passion for slaughter. Where food is the object—and the hides are good for nothing in Spring and early Summer—cows or calves are marked out for destruction; thus increasing the proportion, already far too great, of surviving males, and dooming the race to earlier extinction. Sometimes, advantage is taken of the blind, bisonic instinct of following, and a whole herd driven pell-mell down a precipitous brook bank, to the certain destruction of scores, whose carcasses are left to rot where they fell. Nowhere is the blind, senseless human appetite for carnage, for destruction, more strikingly, more lamentably evinced than in the rapidly-proceeding extermination of the buffalo.

For the white man, though his greatest, is by no means his only destroyer. The Indian watches for him in every thicket, by every wooded brook-side, and the calf that unwittingly goes down to quench his thirst is saluted by an arrow through his loin. The gray wolf lurks in every hollow, and sneaks through every ravine, in the rear and on the flanks of each mammoth herd, watching ravenously for some heedless cow, some foolish calf, some wounded or aged bull, to straggle to one side or fall limpingly behind, where a spring from his hiding-place, a snap at the predestined victim's ham-strings, will leave nothing to chance but the appearance of some hungry compatriot to claim a dividend of the spoil.

But the wolf and the Indian, though persistent in their warfare, are not wantonly destructive—*they* kill to eat, and stop when their appetites are glutted, their wants fully supplied. Civilized man alone kills for the mere pleasure of destroying, the pride of having killed. For thousands of years, the wolf and the Indian fed and feasted on the buffalo; yet the race multiplied and diffused itself from the Hudson and the Delaware to the Columbia and the Sacramento—from the

Ottawa and the Saskatchewan to the Alabama and the Brazos. But civilized man, with his insatiate rapacity and his devilish enginery of fire-arms, has been on his track for a bare century, and already the range of the buffalo is shrunk to one-tenth of its former dimensions, and the noble brute is palpably doomed to speedy extinction. Press on, then, hunters! to your exciting, cruel sport! but make a speedy end of your victims, and do not merely wound and leave them to drag their broken limbs, their maimed bodies, after the frightened, flying herds, fighting off the greedy wolves through weeks of fruitless agony!

The roads over the Plains, and farther west, have one striking peculiarity—yes, two—a dearth of laterals, and an almost total absence of houses along their sides.

You are traveling a broad, well-marked, well-beaten highway, whereon you pass and meet teams, trains, droves, almost hourly; but no cross-roads present themselves, no hospitable tavern-sign salutes you, for hundreds of miles. There may be half a dozen "trading-posts," so called, between Fort Kearney and Salt Lake—a distance of nearly a thousand miles—each trading-post being usually a very poor and empty country store, blent with a most detestable low grog-shop or canal grocery. The total stock in trade of the eight or ten of these concerns which flourish outside of Salt Lake City, between Fort Kearney and Carson Valley—a distance, by way of the South Pass and Salt Lake, of nearly two thousand miles—may have cost $20,000; whereof the alcoholic potables—if you please to consider such execrable concoctions potable—must have absorbed the larger share.

Every man who ventures upon the Plains is presumed to carry the blankets that form his bed, and the pork, flour, and coffee, that constitute his food; leaving whiskey the only necessary of Western life that you may exhaust without incurring the imputation of foolhardiness.

Marvelous is it to see so much active, moving, vigorous Caucasian humanity so scantily provided—for the most part, so utterly *un*provided with house-room—living in such utter independence of protecting roofs and floors. Wherever night overtakes you, you unroll your faithful blankets, spread them on the dry ground, crawl into them, and sleep soundly in the cool breeze, under the over-arching sky; if the rattlesnake or the centipede creep to your couch for shelter and warmth, he has usually the politeness to crawl under your blankets, not into them; if the clouds that rolled angrily at dark discharge hail and rain as well as thunder and wind before dawn, you know that their liquid efflux in summer is rarely or never copious; and, even if you are wet through and chilled as you sleep, it will be the easier to rise early in the morning. If a path leads away from the main trail, you know that it runs to no settlement or village, but to some spring or creek where water or grass may be, at least has been, obtained; no thirsty soul need follow it under the fond illusion that it leads to any fluid more exhilarating than Adam's ale. Thousands traverse the Plains, but few civilized men live on them; those who stay here draw their subsistence mainly from the Federal Treasury, in connection with the Army, the Mail Service, Indian Agencies, or something of the sort.

For hundreds of miles, there is no fenced field, no growing grain, no tolerable house, and only the merest spot of garden by some military post or mail station, some Indian agent's lodge, many a weary day's journey from any other. Nature's ruggedness and man's indolence, or impatience of meagerly rewarded labor, combine to render this pre-eminently the region of rude living, discomfort, and a prevalent despair of disdain of anything better. Yet, even here, this shall not always be.

I have said that the predominant impression made on the stranger's mind by the Plains is one of loneliness—of isolation. For days, if with the mail, for weeks by any other conveyance, you travel westward, still westward, with never a mountain, and scarcely a hill, with never a forest, with seldom a tree, with rarely a brook or spring, to break the monotony of the barren, mainly grassless, dewless landscape, out of which the sun rises at morning, into which it settles at night. God's works are around you; but those of man, save the trail beneath your feet, the wagon which conveys you, are absent.

And yet a nearer, steadier, more familiar gaze reveals symptoms of life which you had at first overlooked. At intervals, the fleet antelope looks shyly down on you a moment from the crest of a "divide," then is off on the wings of the wind. The gray wolf more rarely surveys you deliberately from a respectful distance, and, seeing no opening for a speculation, slinks off in quest of more available game. The paltry cuyota, to which the name of prairie-wolf has unwisely been given, since it has in its nature nothing of the wolf but his ravenous appetite, and would hardly be a match for a stout fox or raccoon, lingers near you, safe in his own worthlessness and your contempt. The funny, frisky little prairie-dog—a condensed or foreshortened gray squirrel— barks with amusing alarm at your approach, then drops into his hole.

which, for mutual defense and advantage, he shares with an owl and a rattlesnake, and is silent as the grave till you pass out of hearing. Ten or twenty thousand of these little imps, with their odd partners, cover a square rood or two together with their holes, dug irregularly at distances of ten or twelve feet apart, but, I think, rarely communicating underground, as one may be drowned out by pouring in upon him twenty or thirty pails of water. . . .

The mail (which was but weekly when I crossed) is one of the redeeming features of the Plains, calling into existence perhaps eighty of the hundred huts or station-tents that sparsely dot the fifteen hundred miles of else uninhabited, uncivilized country, which, on either side of the Salt Lake settlements, divide Kansas from California. As the emigrant toils slowly, wearily, up and over a long "divide," anxiously, wistfully looking around and ahead for grass and water for his fainting beasts, a dim speck near the horizon arrests his regard; it soon develops into a wagon and six mules, which rapidly approach; as they meet, its conductor and charioteer exchange a pleasant or spicy word with him ere it whirls by in a cloud of its own dust, and is lost to his vision. Yet that transient apparition, that hurried greeting, have had a value for him which you, sitting cozily at home, cannot fully realize; the teamster's weary, listless step has become once more elastic; his sunken eye, veiled and goggled to shield it from the blinding glare of the mid-day sun on the naked clay, is fired once more with hope, and no longer expressive merely of dogged resolution; that flitting wagon, those jaded, panting mules, bear tidings, perhaps but twelve days old, from the region of telegraphs and newspapers, to which he bade adieu so many weary weeks ago; its news, now threadbare in the States, is fresh and deeply interesting to him; possibly, some passenger may drop or throw him a newspaper, or part of one, not yet a month printed, nor yet worn out, save at the folds, containing the bulletins of some far-off battle, the reports of some great trial— some marvelous achievement, heroic exploit, or noble effort—some fearful marine disaster by explosion, wreck, or fire—over which his wife and children will tonight spell themselves into unconsciousness by the flickering light of their fire of burning grease-wood, and sleep to dream of scenes and loved ones far away, yet consciously less distant than they seemed a few hours ago. For that mail-wagon represents Civilization, Intelligence, Government, Protection, and gives assurance to the pilgrim family that they are not absolutely at the mercy of daring outlaws and prowling savages—that, beneath the unsleeping Eye, there is a terrestrial Providence also that watches over their safety, and would seek to avenge their wrongs.

And thus the emigrant, no longer heart-sick, walks firmly, proudly on, beside the team that is conveying all he loves best to that far Western home by the Pacific which none among them ever saw—for Bunker Hill, Saratoga, Yorktown, Plattsburgh, New Orleans, the starry flag, and the American Union, are all vividly, confusedly mirrored to his mind's eye in that canvas-covered mule-wagon which, bearing the United States mail, swept past him an hour ago.

The New Sequoia Forests of California

by JOHN MUIR

NOVEMBER, 1878

This is Muir's beautiful account of his discovery of the full range of the sequoia, 90 per cent of which had been unknown before he made this journey alone. Educated at the University of Wisconsin, the pioneer conservationist was largely responsible for the establishment of Yosemite National Park and Sequoia National Park. At his urging, President Theodore Roosevelt supported legislation setting aside 148,000,000 acres of forest reserves. Muir died in 1914.

The main forest belt of the Sierra Nevada is restricted to the western flank, and extends unbrokenly from one extremity of the range to the other, waving compliantly over countless ridges and cañons at an elevation of from three to eight thousand feet above the level of the sea.

Here grow the noblest conifers in the world, averaging about two hundred feet in height, and from five to twenty feet in diameter—the majestic Douglass spruce; the libocedrus, with warm yellow-green, plumelike foliage; the two silver-firs (*Picea amabilis* and *P. grandis*), towering to a height of more than two hundred feet, with branches pinnated like ferns, and whorled around the trunk in regular collars, like the leaves of lilies; the yellow pine, forming arrowy spires of verdure; and the priestly sugar-pine, with feathery arms outspread as if addressing the forest. But the great master-existence of these unrivaled woods is *Sequoia gigantea,* or "big tree"—a monarch of monarchs.

The sequoia belt extends from the well-known Calaveras groves on the north to the head of Deer Creek on the south—a distance of nearly two hundred miles; the northern limit being a little above the thirty-eighth parallel, the southern a little below the thirty-sixth, and the elevation above sea-level varies from about five to eight thousand feet.

From the Calaveras to the south fork of King's River the sequoia occurs only in small isolated groves and patches, so sparsely distributed along the belt that two gaps occur nearly forty miles in width, one between the Calaveras and Tuolumne groves, the other between those of the Fresno and King's River. But from here southward nearly to Deer Creek the trees are nowhere gathered together into small sequestered groups, but stretch majestically across the broad rugged basins of the Kaweah and Tule in noble forests a distance of nearly seventy miles, the continuity of this magnificent belt being broken only by deep sheer-walled cañons. . . .

The average stature attained by the Big Tree under favorable conditions is perhaps about 275 feet, with a diameter of twenty feet. Few full-grown specimens fall much short of this, while many are twenty-five feet in diameter and nearly 300 feet high. Fortunate trees, so situated as to have escaped the destructive action of fire, are occasionally found measuring thirty feet in diameter, and very rarely one that is much larger.

Yet so exquisitely harmonious are even the very mightiest of these monarchs in all their proportions and circumstances, there never is any thing overgrown or huge-looking about them, not to say monstrous; and the first exclamation on coming upon a group for the first time is usually, "See what *beautiful* trees!" Their real godlike grandeur in the meantime is invisible, but to the loving eye it will be manifested sooner or later, stealing slowly on the senses like the grandeur of Niagara, or of some lofty Yosemite dome. Even the mere arithmetical greatness is never guessed by the inexperienced as long as the tree is comprehended from a little distance in one harmonious view. When, however, we approach so near that only the lower portion of the trunk is seen, and walk round and round the wide bulging base, then we begin to wonder at their vastness, and seek a measuring rod.

Sequoias bulge considerably at the base, yet not more than is required for beauty and safety; and the only reason that this bulging is so often remarked as excessive is because so small a section of the shaft is seen at once. The real taper of the trunk, beheld as a unit, is perfectly charming in its exquisite fineness, and the appreciative eye ranges the massive columns, from the swelling muscular instep to the lofty summit dissolving in a crown of verdure, rejoicing in the unrivaled display of giant grandeur and giant loveliness.

About a hundred feet or more of the trunk is usually branchless, but its massive simplicity is relieved by the fluting bark furrows, and loose tufts of rosettes of slender sprays that wave lightly on the breeze and cast flecks of shade, seeming to have been pinned on here and there for the sake of beauty alone.

The young trees wear slender, simple branches all the way down to the ground, put on with strict regularity, sharply aspiring at top, horizontal about half-way down, and drooping in handsome curves at the base. By the time the sapling is five or six hundred years old, this spiry, feathery, juvenile habit merges into the firm rounded dome form of middle age, which in turn takes on the eccentric picturesqueness of old age. No other tree in the Sierra forests has foliage so densely massed, or represents outlines so firmly drawn and so constantly subordinate to a special type. A knotty, angular, ungovernable-looking branch eight or ten feet thick may often be seen pushing out abruptly from the trunk, as if sure to throw the outline curves into confusion, but as soon as the general outline is approached it stops short, and dissolves in spreading, cushiony bosses of law-abiding sprays, just as if every tree were growing underneath some huge invisible bell-glass, against whose curves every branch is pressed and molded, yet somehow indulging so many small departures that there is still an appearance of perfect freedom.

The foliage of the saplings is dark bluish-green in color, while the older trees frequently ripen to a warm yellow tint like the libocedrus. The bark is rich cinnamon brown, purplish in younger trees, and in shady portions of the old, while all the ground is covered with brown burs and leaves, forming color masses of extraordinary richness, not to mention the flowers and underbrush that brighten and bloom in their season.

Walk the sequoia woods at any time of year, and you will say they are the most beautiful on earth. Rare and impressive contrasts meet you everywhere—the colors of tree and flower, rock and sky, light and shade, strength and frailty, endurance and evanescence. Tangles of supple hazel bushes, tree pillars rigid as granite domes, roses and violets around the very feet of the giants, and rugs of the low blooming chamaebatia where the light falls free. Then in winter the trees break forth in universal bloom, myriads of small four-sided conelets crowd the ends of the slender sprays, coloring the whole tree, and, when ripe, dusting all the air and the ground with golden pollen. The fertile cones are bright grass green, measuring about two inches in length by one and a half in thickness, and are made up of about forty firm rhomboidal scales densely packed, with from five to eight seeds at the base of each. A single cone, therefore, contains from two to three hundred seeds, about a fourth of an inch long by three-sixteenths wide, including a thin flat margin that makes them go glancing and wavering in their fall like a boy's kite. The irrepressible fruitfulness of sequoia may be illustrated by the fact that upon two specimen branches one and a half and two inches in diameter respectively I counted 480 cones clustered together like grapes. No other California conifer produces nearly so many seeds. Millions are ripened annually by a single tree, and the product of one of the small northern groves in a fruitful year would suffice to plant all the mountain ranges of the globe.

Nature takes care, however, that not one seed in a million shall germinate at all, and of those that do perhaps not one in ten thousand is suffered to live through the many vicissitudes of storm, drought, fire, and snow-crushing that beset their youth. . . .

Sequoia gigantea has hitherto been regarded as a lonely, companionless species not properly belonging to the present geological age, and therefore doomed to speedy extinction. The scattered groves are supposed generally to be the remnants of extensive ancient forests, vanquished, in the so-called struggle for life, by pines and firs, and now driven into their last fortresses of cool glens where moisture and general climate are specially favorable. These notions are grounded on the aspects and circumstances of the few isolated northern groups, the only ones known to botanists, where there are but few young trees or saplings growing up around the failing old trees to perpetuate the race.

The most notable tree in the well-known Mariposa Grove is the Grizzly Giant, some thirty feet in diameter, growing on the top of a stony ridge. When this tree falls, it will make so extensive a basin by the uptearing of its huge roots, and so deep and broad a ditch by the blow of its ponderous trunk, that even supposing that the trunk itself be speedily burned, traces of its existence will nevertheless remain patent for thousands of years. Because, being on a ridge, the root hollow and trunk ditch made by its fall will not be filled up by rain-washing, neither will they be obliterated by falling leaves, for leaves are constantly consumed in forest fires; and if by any chance they should not be thus consumed, the humus resulting from their 'decay would still indicate the fallen sequoia by a long straight strip of special soil, and special growth to which it would give birth.

I obtained glorious views in the broad forest-filled basin of the Fresno: innumerable spires of the yellow pine, ranking above one another on the braided slopes; miles of sugar-pine, with long arms outstretched in the lavish sunshine; while away toward the southwest, on the verge of the landscape, I discovered the noble dome-like crowns of sequoia swelling massively against the sky, singly or in imposing congregations. . . .

I pushed on southward across the wide corrugated basin of the San Joaquin in search of new groves or vestiges of old ones, surveying a wild tempest-tossed sea of pines from many a ridge and dome, but not a single sequoia crown appeared, nor any trace of a fallen trunk. The first grove found after leaving the Fresno is located on Dinky Creek, one of the northmost tributaries of King's River. It was discovered several years ago by a couple of hunters who were in pursuit of a wounded bear; but because of its remoteness and inaccessibility it is known only to a few mountaineers.

I was greatly interested to find a vigorous company of sequoias near the northern limit of the grove growing upon the top of a granite precipice thinly besprinkled with soil, and scarce at all changed since it came to the light from beneath the ice sheet toward the close of the glacial period—a fact of great significance in its bearings on sequoia history in the Sierra.

One of the most striking of the simpler features of the grove is a waterfall, made by a bright little stream that comes pouring through the woods from the north, and leaps a granite precipice. All the cañons of the Sierra are embroidered with waterfalls, yet each possesses a character of its own, made more beautiful by each other's beauty, instead of suffering by mere vulgar arithmetical contrast. The booming cataract of Yosemite, half a mile high, is one thing; this little woodland fairy is another. Its plain spiritual beauty is most impressively brought forward by the gray rocks and the huge brown trees, several of which stand with wet feet in its spray; and then it is decked with goldenrods that waver overhead, and with ferns that lean out along its white wavering edges, the whole forming a bit of pure picture of a kind rarely seen amid the sublimities of sequoia woods.

Hence, I led my mule down the cañon, forded the north fork of King's River, and climbed the dividing ridge between the north and middle forks. In making my way from here across the main King's River cañon I was compelled to make a descent of seven thousand feet at a single swoop, thus passing at once from cool shadowy woods to tropic sun glare. Every pine-tree vanished long ere I reached the river —scrubby oaks with bark white as milk cast their hot shadows on the sunburned ground, and not a single flower was left for company. Plants, climate, landscapes changing as if one had crossed an ocean to some far strange land. Here the river is broad and rapid, and when I heard it roaring I feared my short-legged mule would be carried away. But I was so fortunate as to strike a trail near an Indian rancheria that conducted to a regular ford about ten miles below the King's River Yosemite, where I crossed without the slightest difficulty, and gladly began climbing again toward the cool spicy woods. The lofty ridge forming the south wall of the great King's River cañon is planted with sugar-pine, but through rare vistas I was delighted to behold the well-known crowns of sequoia once more swelling grandly against the sky only six or seven miles distant. Pushing eagerly forward, I soon found myself in the well-known "King's River Grove," on the summit of the Kaweah and King's River divide. Then bearing off northwestward along the rim of the cañon, I discovered a grand forest about six miles long by two in width, composed almost exclusively of sequoia. *This is the northmost portion of the sequoia belt that can fairly be called a forest.* The species here covers many a hill and dale and gorge, and rocky ridge-top and boggy ravine, as the principal tree, without manifesting the slightest tendency toward extinction.

On a bed of gravelly flood soil fifteen yards square, once occupied by four large sugar-pines, I found ninety-four young sequoias—an instance of the present existence of conditions under which the sequoia is stronger than its rival in acquiring possession of the soil and sunshine.

Here I also noted eighty-six seedlings, from one to fifty feet high, upon an irregular patch of ground that had been prepared for their reception by fire. Bare virgin ground is one of the essential conditions for the growth of coniferous trees from the seed, and it is interesting to notice that fire, the great destroyer of tree life, also furnishes one of the conditions for its renewal. The fall of old trees, however, furnishes fresh soil in sufficient quantities for the maintenance of the forests. The ground is thus upturned and mellowed, and many trees are planted for every one that falls. Floods and avalanches also give rise to fresh soil beds available for the growth of forest trees in this climate, and an occasional tree may owe its existence and particular location to some pawing squirrel or bear. The most influential, however, of the natural factors concerned in the maintenance of the sequoia forests by the planting of seeds are the falling trees.

That sequoia is so obviously and remarkably grouped in twos and threes is no doubt owing to the restricted action of this factor as regards area. Thus when an old tree falls, a piece of ground forty or fifty feet in diameter will be cleared by the upturning roots, and a group of seedlings with an even start will speedily take its place. Out of this seedling thicket perhaps two or three may become trees, and then those groups called "Three Graces," "Faithful Couples," etc., will be formed. For even supposing they should stand twenty or thirty feet apart while young, by the time they are full grown they will touch and crowd and become "faithful." Also the branches on the inside of each will die for want of light, and the partial crowns be modeled into one, and the trunks, if close pressed, will appear as a forked specimen derived from one seed, leaning outward toward the top, on account of the outside of each being loaded with branches. . . .

Less than a mile from the southern extremity of this noble forest we enter the so-called "King's River Grove," extending southward to the Kaweah divide. Here during a former visit I heard the sound of axes, indicating a group of busy men preparing a section of one of the trees they had felled for exhibition at the Centennial. It was twenty-five feet in diameter at the base, and so fine was the taper, it measured ten feet in diameter at two hundred feet from the ground. The age, as counted by three different persons, is from 2125 to 2317, the fineness of the annual wood rings making accuracy in the count rather difficult.

Yet this specimen was by no means a very old-looking tree, and some are undoubtedly much older. A specimen observed by me in the New King's River Forest is probably over four thousand years old, as it measures thirty-five feet eight inches inside the bark, and is standing upon a dry hill-side where the growth has evidently been slow. . . .

I made my way across the river and up the opposite slopes into woods not a whit less noble. Brownie the meanwhile had been feeding luxuriously day after day in a ravine, among beds of leersia and wild wheat, gathering strength for new efforts. But way-making became more and more difficult—indeed impossible, in common phrase. But just before sundown I reached a charming camp ground, with new sequoias to study and sleep beneath. It was evidently a well-known and favorite resort of bears, which are always wise enough to choose homes in charming woods where they are secure, and have the luxury of cool meadow patches to wallow in, and clover to eat, and plenty of acid ants, wasps, and pine nuts in their season. The bark of many of the trees was furrowed picturesquely by their matchless paws, where they had stood up stretching their limbs like cats. Their tracks were fresh along the stream-side, and I half expected to see them resting beneath the brown trunks, or standing on some prostrate log snuffing and listening to learn the nature of the disturbance. Brownie listened and looked cautiously around, as if doubting whether the place were safe. All mules have the fear of bears before their eyes, and are marvelously acute in detecting them, either by night or day. No dog can scent a bear farther, and as long, therefore, as your mule rests quietly in a bear region, you need have no fears of their approach. But when bears *do* come into camp, mules tethered by a rope too strong to break are not infrequently killed in trying to run away. Guarding against this danger, I usually tie to an elastic sapling, so as to diminish the shock in case of a stampede, and perhaps thus prevent neck or rope from breaking.

The starry night circled away in profound calm, and I lay steeped in its weird beauty, notwithstanding the growing danger of being snow-bound, and feeling more than commonly happy; for while climbing the river cañon I had made a fine geological discovery concerning the formation and origin of the quartz sands of the great "dead river" deposits of the northern Sierra.

Two days beyond this bear dell I enjoyed a very charming meeting with a group of deer in one of nature's most sequestered gardens—a spot never, perhaps, neared by human foot.

The garden lies high on the northern cliffs of the south fork. The Kaweah goes foaming past two thousand feet below, while the sequoia forest rises shadowy along the ridge on the north. It is only about half an acre in size, full of golden-rods and eriogonae and tall vase-like tufts of waving grasses with silky panicles, not crowded like a field of grain, but planted wide apart among the flowers, each tuft with plenty of space to manifest its own loveliness both in form and color and wind-waving, while the plantless spots between are covered with dry leaves and burs, making a fine brown ground for both grasses and flowers. The whole is fenced in by a close-hedge-like growth of wild cherry, mingled with California lilac and glossy evergreen manzanita, not drawn around in strict lines, but waving in and out in a succession of bays and swelling bosses exquisitely painted with the best Indian summer light, and making a perfect paradise of color. I found a small silver fir near by, from which I cut plushy boughs for a bed, and spent a delightful night sleeping away all cañon-climbing weariness.

Next morning shortly after sunrise, just as the light was beginning to come streaming through the trees, while I lay leaning on my elbow taking my bread and tea, and looking down across the cañon, tracing the dip of the granite headlands, and trying to plan a way to the river at a point likely to be fordable, suddenly I caught the big bright eyes of a deer gazing at me through the garden hedge. The expressive eyes, the slim back-tipped muzzle, and the large ears were as perfectly visible as if placed there at just the right distance to be seen, like a picture on a wall. She continued to gaze, while I gazed back with equal steadiness, motionless as a rock. In a few minutes she ventured forward a step, exposing her fine arching neck and fore-legs, then snorted and withdrew.

This alone was a fine picture—the beautiful eyes framed in colored cherry leaves, the topmost sprays lightly atremble, and just glanced by the level sun rays, all the rest in shadow.

But more anon. Gaining confidence, and evidently piqued by curiosity, the trembling sprays indicated her return, and her head came into view; then another and another step, and she stood wholly exposed inside the garden hedge, gazed eagerly around, and again withdrew, but returned a moment afterward, this time advancing into the middle of the garden; and behind her I noticed a second pair of eyes, not fixed on me, but on her companion in front, as if eagerly questioning, "What in the world do you see?" Then more rustling in the hedge, and another head came slipping past the second, the two heads touching; while the first came within a few steps of me, walking with inimitable grace, expressed in every limb. My picture was being enriched and enlivened every minute; but even this was not all. After another timid little snort, as if testing my good intentions, all three disappeared; but I was true, and my wild beauties emerged once more, one, two, three, four, slipping through the dense hedge without snapping a twig, and all four came forward into the garden, grouping themselves most picturesquely, moving, changing, lifting their smooth polished limbs with charming grace—the perfect embodiment of poetic form and motion. I have oftentimes remarked in meeting with deer under various circumstances that curiosity was sufficiently strong to carry them dangerously near hunters; but in this instance they seemed to have satisfied curiosity, and began to feel so much at ease in my company that they all commenced feeding in the garden—eating breakfast with me, like gentle sheep around a shepherd —while I observed keenly, to learn their gestures and what plants they fed on. They are the daintiest feeders I ever saw, and no wonder the Indians esteem the contents of their stomachs a great delicacy. They seldom eat grass, but chiefly aromatic shrubs. The ceanothus and cherry seemed their favorites. They would cull a single cherry leaf with the utmost delicacy, then one of ceanothus, now and then stalking across the garden to snip off a leaf or two of mint, their sharp muzzle enabling them to cull out the daintiest leaves one at a time. It was delightful to feel how perfectly the most timid wild animals may confide in man. They no longer required that I should remain motionless, taking no alarm when I shifted from one elbow to the other, and even allowed me to rise and stand erect.

It then occurred to me that I might possibly steal up to one of them and catch it, not with any intention of killing it, for that was far indeed from my thoughts. I only wanted to run my hand along its beautiful curving limbs. But no sooner had I made a little advance on this line than, giving a searching look, they seemed to penetrate my conceit, and bounded off with loud shrill snorts, vanishing in the forest.

There is a wild instinctive love of animal-killing in everybody, inherited, no doubt, from savage ancestors, and its promptings for the moment have occasionally made me as excitedly blood-thirsty as a wolf. But far higher is the pleasure of meeting one's fellow-animals in a friendly way without any of the hunter's gross concomitants of blood and groans.

I have often tried to understand how so many deer, and wild sheep, and bears, and flocks of grouse—nature's cattle and poultry—could be allowed to run at large through the mountain gardens without in any way marring their beauty. I was therefore all the more watchful of this feeding flock, and carefully examined the garden after they left, to see what flowers had suffered; but I could not detect the slightest disorder, much less destruction. It seemed rather that, like gardeners, they had been keeping it in order. At least I could not see a crushed flower, nor a single grass stem that was misbent or broken down. Nor among the daisy, gentian, bryanthus gardens of the Alps, where the wild sheep roam at will, have I ever noticed the effects of destructive feeding or trampling. Even the burly shuffling bears beautify the ground on which they walk, picturing it with their awe-inspiring tracks, and also writing poetry on the soft sequoia bark in boldly drawn Gothic hieroglyphics. But, strange to say, man, the crown, the sequoia of nature, brings confusion with all his best gifts, and, with the overabundant, misbegotten animals that he breeds, sweeps away the beauty of wildness like a fire. . . .

The entire upper portion of the Tule basin is magnificently forested with sequoia, the finest portion being on the north fork. This, indeed, is, I think, the noblest block of sequoia in the entire belt, surpassing even the giant forest of the Kaweah. Southward from here I thought I could detect a slight falling off in the density and general thrift of the forest, without, however, noticing any further indication of approach to the southern limit. . . .

The ridge between the South Tule and Deer Creek is well planted with sequoia; but the trees are decidedly shorter and less irrepressible in aspect, and I began to feel confident that the southern limit of the species could not be very far distant. I was greatly interested here to find that the species had crossed over into the upper valley of the Kern, and planted colonies northward along the eastern slope of the western summit, or Greenhorn range. The western summit, like a branch axis, puts out from the main backbone of the Sierra at the head of King's River, trending southward, and enclosing the upper valley of the Kern on the west; and it is just where this lofty spur begins to break down on its approach to its southern termination that sequoia has been able to cross it.

Pushing on still southward over the divide between the north and south forks of Deer Creek, I found that the southern boundary was at length crossed, and a careful scrutiny of the woods beyond failed to discover a single sequoia, or any trace of its former existence; and now all that remained was to descend the range, and make a level way home along the plain.

It appears, then, from this general survey of the sequoia forest, that, notwithstanding the colossal dimensions of the trees, and their peculiarly interesting character, more than ninety per cent of the whole number of individuals belonging to the species have hitherto remained unknown to science. . . .

VIII

Nothing Beats a Good Story

The Town-Ho's Story

by HERMAN MELVILLE

OCTOBER, 1851

It is only in the past thirty years that Moby Dick *has become universally admired as one of the world's great pieces of literature. The book was poorly received when Harper & Brothers brought it out in the fall of 1851, despite the send-off which the magazine gave it by publishing this chapter and praising it in a review in the December issue. "Beneath the whole story," the review said, "the subtle, imaginative reader may perhaps find a pregnant allegory intended to illustrate the mystery of life. Certain it is that the rapid, pointed hints which are often thrown out, with the keenness and velocity of a harpoon, penetrate deep into the heart of things, showing that the genius of the author for moral analysis is scarcely surpassed by his wizard power of description." The magazine published three poems and eight other stories and essays by Melville, and recorded his death in its obituary column in the January, 1892 issue: "September 27th—In New York City, Herman Melville, aged seventy-three years."*

The Cape of Good Hope, and all the watery region round about there, is much like some noted four corners of a great highway, where you meet more travelers than in any other part.

It was not very long after speaking the Goney that another homeward-bound whaleman, the Town-Ho, was encountered. She was manned almost wholly by Polynesians. In the short gam that ensued she gave us strong news of Moby Dick. To some the general interest in the White Whale was now wildly heightened by a circumstance of the Town-Ho's story, which seemed obscurely to involve with the whale a certain wondrous, inverted visitation of one of those so-called judgments of God which at times are said to overtake some men. This latter circumstance, with its own particular accompaniments, forming what may be called the secret part of the tragedy about to be narrated, never reached the ears of Captain Ahab or his mates. For that secret part of the story was unknown to the captain of the Town-Ho himself. It was the private property of three confederate white seamen of that ship, one of whom, it seems, communicated it to Tashtego with Romish injunctions of secrecy, but the following night Tashtego rambled in his sleep, and revealed so much of it in that way, that when he was awakened he could not well withhold the rest. Nevertheless, so potent an influence did this thing have on those seamen in the Pequod who came to the full knowledge of it, and by such a strange delicacy, to call it so, were they governed in this matter, that they kept the secret among themselves so that it never transpired abaft the Pequod's mainmast. Interweaving in its proper place this darker thread with the story as publicly narrated on the ship, the whole of this strange affair I now proceed to put on lasting record.

For my humor's sake, I shall preserve the style in which I once narrated it at Lima, to a lounging circle of my Spanish friends, one saint's eve, smoking upon the thick-gilt tiled piazza of the Golden Inn. Of those fine cavaliers, the young Dons, Pedro and Sebastian, were on the closer terms with me; and hence the interluding questions they occasionally put, and which are duly answered at the time.

"Some two years prior to my first learning the events which I am about rehearsing to you, gentlemen, the Town-Ho, Sperm Whaler of Nantucket, was cruising in your Pacific here, not very many days' sail eastward from the eaves of this good Golden Inn. She was somewhere to northward of the Line. One morning upon handling the pumps, according to daily usage, it was observed that she made more water in her hold than common. They supposed a swordfish had stabbed her, gentlemen. But the captain, having some unusual reason for believing that rare good luck awaited him in those latitudes; and therefore being very averse to quit them, and the leak not being then considered at all dangerous, though, indeed, they could not find it after searching the hold as low down as was possible in rather heavy weather, the ship still continued her cruisings, the mariners working at the pumps at wide and easy intervals; but no good luck came; more days went by, and not only was the leak yet undiscovered, but it sensibly increased. So much so, that now taking some alarm, the captain, making all sail, stood away for the nearest harbor among the islands, there to have his hull hove out and repaired.

"Though no small passage was before her, yet, if the commonest chance favored, he did not at all fear that his ship would founder by the way, because his pumps were of the best, and being periodically relieved at them, those six-and-thirty men of his could easily keep the ship free; never mind if the leak should double on her. In truth, well nigh the whole of this passage being attended by very prosperous breezes, the Town-Ho had all but certainly arrived in perfect safety at her port without the occurrence of the least fatality, had it not been for the brutal overbearing of Radney, the mate, a Vineyarder, and the bitterly provoked vengeance of Steelkilt, a Lakeman and desperado from Buffalo."

"Lakeman!—Buffalo! Pray, what is a Lakeman, and where is Buffalo?" said Don Sebastian, rising in his swinging mat of grass.

"On the eastern shore of our Lake Erie, Don; but—I crave your courtesy—may be, you shall soon hear further of all that. Now, gentlemen, in square-sail brigs and three-masted ships, well nigh as large and stout as any that ever sailed out of your old Callao to far Manila; this Lakeman, in the land-locked heart of our America, had yet been nurtured by all those agrarian free-booting impressions popularly connected with the open ocean. For in their interflowing aggregate, those grand fresh-water seas of ours—Erie, and Ontario, and Huron, and Superior, and Michigan—possess an ocean-like expansiveness, with many of the ocean's noblest traits; with many of its rimmed varieties of races and of climes. They contain round archipelagoes of romantic isles, even as the Polynesian waters do; in large part, are shored by two great contrasting nations, as the Atlantic is; they furnish long maritime approaches to our numerous territorial colonies from the East, dotted all round their banks; here and there are frowned upon by batteries, and by the goat-like craggy guns of lofty Mackinaw; they have heard the fleet thunderings of naval victories; at intervals, they yield their beaches to wild barbarians, whose red painted faces flash from out their peltry wigwams; for leagues and leagues are flanked by ancient and unentered forests where the gaunt pines stand like serried lines of kings in Gothic genealogies; those same woods harboring wild Afric beasts of prey, and silken creatures whose exported furs give robes to Tartar Emperors; they mirror the paved capitals of Buffalo and Cleveland, as well as Winnebago villages; they float alike the full-rigged merchant ship, the armed cruiser of the State, the steamer, and the beech canoe; they are swept by Borean and dismasting blasts as direful as any that lash the salted wave; they know what shipwrecks are, for out of sight of land, however inland, they have drowned full many a midnight ship with all its shrieking crew. Thus, gentlemen, though an inlander, Steelkilt was wild-ocean born, and wild-ocean nurtured; as much of an audacious mariner as any. And for Radney, though in his infancy he may have laid him down on the lone Nantucket beach, to nurse at his maternal sea; though in after life he had long followed our austere Atlantic and your contemplative Pacific; yet was he quite as vengeful and full of social quarrel as the backwoods seaman, fresh from the latitudes of buck-horn handled Bowie-knives. Yet was this Nantucketer a man with some good-hearted traits; and this Lakeman, a mariner, who though a sort of devil indeed, might yet by inflexible firmness, only tempered by that common decency of human recognition which is the meanest slave's right; thus treated, this Steelkilt had long been retained harmless and docile. At all events, he had proved so thus far; but Radney was doomed and made mad, and Steelkilt—but, gentlemen, you shall hear.

"It was not more than a day or two at the furthest after pointing her prow for her island haven, that the Town-Ho's leak seemed again increasing, but only so as to require an hour or more at the pumps every day. You must know that in a settled and civilized ocean like our Atlantic, for example, some skippers think little of pumping their whole way across it; though of a still, sleepy night, should the officer of the deck happen to forget his duty in that respect, the probability would be that he and his shipmates would never again remember it, on account of all hands gently subsiding to the bottom. Nor in the solitary and savage seas far from you to the westward, gentlemen, is it altogether unusual for ships to keep clanging at their pump-handles in full chorus even for a voyage of considerable length; that is, if it lie along a tolerably accessible coast, or if any other reasonable retreat is afforded them. It is only when a leaky vessel is in some very out of the way part of those waters, some really landless latitude, that her captain begins to feel a little anxious.

"Much this way had it been with the Town-Ho; so when her leak was found gaining once more, there was in truth some small concern manifested by several of her company; especially by Radney the mate. He commanded the upper sails to be well hoisted, sheeted home anew, and every way expanded to the breeze. Now this Radney, I suppose, was as little of a coward, and as little inclined to any sort of nervous apprehensiveness touching his own person as any fearless, unthinking creature on land or on sea that you can conveniently imagine, gentlemen. Therefore when he betrayed this solicitude about the safety of the ship, some of the seamen declared that it was only on account of his being a part owner in her. So when they were working that evening at the pumps, there was on this head no small gamesomeness slily going on among them, as they stood with their feet continually overflowed by the rippling clear water; clear as any mountain spring, gentlemen—that bubbling from the pumps ran across the deck, and poured itself out in steady spouts at the lee scupper-holes.

"Now, as you well know, it is not seldom the case in this conventional world of ours—watery or otherwise; that when a person placed in command over his fellow-men finds one of them to be very significantly his superior in general pride of manhood, straightway against that man he conceives an unconquerable dislike and bitterness; and if he have a chance he will pull down and pulverize that subaltern's tower, and make a little heap of dust of it. Be this conceit of mine as it may, gentlemen, at all events Steelkilt was a tall and noble animal with a head like a Roman, and a flowing golden beard like the tasseled housings of your last viceroy's snorting charger; and a brain, and a heart, and a soul in him, gentlemen, which had made Steelkilt Charlemagne, had he been born son to Charlemagne's father. But Radney, the mate, was ugly as a mule; yet as hardy, as stubborn, as malicious. He did not love Steelkilt, and Steelkilt knew it.

"Espying the mate drawing near as he was toiling at the pump with the rest, the Lakeman affected not to notice him, but unawed, went on with his gay banterings.

" 'Ay, ay, my merry lads, it's a lively leak this; hold a cannikin, one of ye, and let's have a taste. By the Lord, it's worth bottling! I tell ye what, men, old Rad's investment must go for it! he had best cut away his part of the hull and tow it home. The fact is, boys, that swordfish only began the job; he's come back again with a gang of ship-carpenters, saw-fish, and file-fish, and what not; and the whole posse of 'em are now hard at work cutting and slashing at the bottom; making improvements, I suppose. If old Rad were here now, I'd tell him to jump overboard and scatter 'em. They're playing the devil with his estate, I can tell him. But he's a simple old soul—Rad, and a beauty, too. Boys, they say the rest of his property is invested in lookingglasses. I wonder if he'd give a poor devil like me the model of his nose.'

" 'Damn your eyes! what's that pump stopping for?' roared Radney, pretending not to have heard the sailors' talk. 'Thunder away at it!'

" 'Ay, ay, sir,' said Steelkilt, merry as a cricket. 'Lively, boys, lively, now!' And with that the pump clanged like fifty fire-engines; the men tossed their hats off to it, and ere long that peculiar gasping of the lungs was heard which denotes the fullest tension of life's utmost energies.

"Quitting the pump at last, with the rest of his band, the Lakeman went forward all panting, and sat himself down on the windlass; his face fiery red, his eyes bloodshot, and wiping the profuse sweat from his brow. Now what cozening fiend it was, gentlemen, that possessed Radney to meddle with such a man in that corporeally exasperated state, I know not; but so it happened. Intolerably striding along the deck, the mate commanded him to get a broom and sweep down the planks, and also a shovel, and remove some offensive matters consequent upon allowing a pig to run at large.

"Now, gentlemen, sweeping a ship's deck at sea is a piece of household work which in all times but raging gales is regularly attended to every evening; it has been known to be done in the case of ships actually foundering at the time. Such, gentlemen, is the inflexibility of sea-usages and the instinctive love of neatness in seamen; some of whom would not willingly drown without first washing their faces. But in all vessels this broom business is the prescriptive province of the boys, if boys there be aboard. Besides, it was the stronger men in the Town-Ho that had been divided into gangs, taking turns at the pumps; and being the most athletic seaman of them all, Steelkilt had been regularly assigned captain of one of the gangs; consequently he should have been freed from any trivial business not connected with truly nautical duties, such being the case with his comrades. I mention all these particulars so that you may understand exactly how this affair stood between the two men.

"But there was more than this: the order about the shovel was almost as plainly meant to sting and insult Steelkilt, as though Radney had spat in his face. Any man who has gone sailor in a whale-ship will undersιand this; and all this and doubtless much more, the Lakeman fully comprehended when the mate uttered his command. But as he sat still for a moment, and as he steadfastly looked into the mate's malignant eye and perceived the stacks of powder-casks heaped up in him and the slow match silently burning along toward them; as he instinctively saw all this, that strange forbearance and unwillingness to stir up the deeper passionateness in any already ireful being——a repugnance most felt, when felt at all, by really valiant men even when aggrieved——this nameless phantom feeling, gentlemen, stole over Steelkilt.

"Therefore, in his ordinary tone, only a little broken by the bodily exhaustion he was temporarily in, he answered him, saying that sweeping the deck was not his business, and he would not do it. And then, without at all alluding to the shovel, he pointed to three lads as the customary sweepers; who, not being billeted at the pumps, had done little or nothing all day. To this, Radney replied with an oath, in a most domineering and outrageous manner unconditionally reiterating his command; meanwhile advancing upon the still seated Lakeman, with an uplifted cooper's club hammer which he had snatched from a cask near by.

"Heated and irritated as he was by his spasmodic toil at the pumps, for all his first nameless feeling of forbearance the sweating Steelkilt could but ill brook this bearing in the mate; but somehow still smothering the conflagration within him, without speaking he remained doggedly rooted to his seat, till at last the incensed Radney shook the hammer within a few inches of his face, furiously commanding him to do his bidding.

"Steelkilt rose, and slowly retreating round the windlass, steadily followed by the mate with his menacing hammer, deliberately repeated his intention not to obey. Seeing, however, that his forbearance had not the slightest effect, by an awful and unspeakable intimation with his twisted hand he warned off the foolish and infatuated man; but it was to no purpose. And in this way the two went once slowly round the windlass; when, resolved at last no longer to retreat, bethinking him that he had now forborne as much as comported with his humor, the Lakeman paused on the hatches and thus spoke to the officer:

"'Mr. Radney, I will not obey you. Take that hammer away, or look to yourself.' But the predestinated mate coming still closer to him, where the Lakeman stood fixed, now shook the heavy hammer within an inch of his teeth; meanwhile repeating a string of insufferable maledictions. Retreating not the thousandth part of an inch; stabbing him in the eye with the unflinching poniard of his glance, Steelkilt, clenching his right hand behind him and creepingly drawing it back, told his persecutor that if the hammer but grazed his cheek he (Steelkilt) would murder him. But, gentlemen, the fool had been branded for the slaughter by the gods. Immediately the hammer touched the cheek; the next instant the lower jaw of the mate was stove in his head; he fell on the hatch spouting blood like a whale.

"Ere the cry could go aft Steelkilt was shaking one of the backstays leading far aloft to where two of his comrades were standing their mast-heads. They were both Canalers."

"Canalers!" cried Don Pedro. "We have seen many whale-ships in our harbors, but never heard of your Canalers. Pardon: who and what are they?"

"Canalers, Don, are the boatmen belonging to our grand Erie Canal. You must have heard of it."

"Nay, Señor; hereabouts in this dull, warm, most lazy, and heredi- tary land, we know but little of your vigorous North."

"Ay? Well, then, Don, refill my cup. Your chica's very fine; and, ere proceeding further, I will tell you what our Canalers are; for such information may throw side-light upon my story.

"For three hundred and sixty miles, gentlemen, through the entire breadth of the state of New York; through numerous populous cities and most thriving villages; through long, dismal, uninhabited swamps, and affluent, cultivated fields, unrivaled for fertility; by billiard-room and bar-room; through the holy-of-holies of great forests; on Roman arches over Indian rivers; through sun and shade; by happy hearts or broken; through all the wide contrasting scenery of those noble Mo- hawk counties; and especially by rows of snow-white chapels, whose spires stand almost like milestones, flows one continual stream of Venetianly corrupt and often lawless life. There's your true Ashantee, gentlemen; there howl your pagans; where you ever find them, next door to you; under the long-flung shadow, and the snug patronizing lee of churches. For by some curious fatality, as it is often noted of your metropolitan freebooters that they ever encamp around the halls of justice, so sinners, gentlemen, most abound in holiest vicinities."

"Is that a friar passing?" said Don Pedro, looking downward into the crowded plaza, with humorous concern.

"Well for our northern friend, Dame Isabella's Inquisition wanes in Lima," laughed Don Sebastian. "Proceed, Señor."

"A moment! Pardon!" cried another of the company. "In the name of all us Limeese, I but desire to express to you, sir sailor, that we have by no means overlooked your delicacy in not substituting present Lima for distant Venice in your corrupt comparison. Oh! do not bow and look surprised; you know the proverb all along this coast—'Corrupt as Lima.' It but bears out your saying, too; churches more plentiful than billiard-tables, and forever open—and 'Corrupt as Lima.' So, too, Venice; I have been there; the holy city of the blessed evangelist, St. Mark!—St. Dominic, purge it! Your cup! Thanks: here I refill; now, you pour out again."

"Freely depicted in his own vocation, gentlemen, the Canaler would make a fine dramatic hero, so abundantly and picturesquely wicked is he. Like Marc Antony, for days and days along his green-turfed, flowery Nile, he indolently floats, openly toying with his red-cheeked Cleopatra, ripening his apricot thigh upon the sunny deck. But ashore, all this effeminacy is dashed. The brigandish guise which the Canaler so proudly sports; his slouched and gayly-ribboned hat betoken his grand features. A terror to the smiling innocence of the villages through which he floats; his swart visage and bold swagger are not unshunned in cities. Once a vagabond on his own canal, I have received good turns from one of those Canalers; I thank him heartily; would fain be not ungrateful; but it is often one of the prime redeeming qualities of your man of violence, that at times he has as stiff an arm to back a poor stranger in a strait, as to plunder a wealthy one. In sum, gentlemen, what the wildness of this canal life is, is emphatically evinced by this; that our wild whale-fishery contains so many of its most finished graduates, and that scarce any race of mankind, except Sydney men, are so much distrusted by our whaling captains. Nor does it at all diminish the curiousness of this matter, that to many thousands of our rural boys and young men born along its line, the probationary life of the Grand Canal furnishes the sole transition between quietly reaping in a Christian corn-field, and recklessly ploughing the waters of the most barbaric seas."

"I see! I see!" impetuously exclaimed Don Pedro, spilling his chicha upon his silvery ruffles. "No need to travel! The world's one Lima. I had thought, now, that at your temperate North the generations were cold and holy as the hills. But the story."

"I left off, gentlemen, where the Lakeman shook the backstay. Hardly had he done so, when he was surrounded by the three junior mates and the four harpooners, who all crowded him to the deck. But sliding down the ropes like baleful comets, the two Canalers rushed into the uproar, and sought to drag their man out of it toward the forecastle. Others of the sailors joined with them in this attempt, and a twisted turmoil ensued; while standing out of harm's way, the valiant captain danced up and down with a whale-pike, calling upon his officers to manhandle that atrocious scoundrel, and smoke him along to the quarter-deck. At intervals, he ran close up to the revolving border of the confusion, and prying into the heart of it with his pike, sought to prick out the object of his resentment. But Steelkilt and his desperadoes were too much for them all; they succeeded in gaining the forecastle deck, where, hastily slewing about three or four large casks in a line with the windlass, these sea-Parisians entrenched themselves behind the barricade.

" 'Come out of that, ye pirates!' roared the captain, now menacing them with a pistol in each hand, just brought to him by the steward. 'Come out of that, ye cut-throats!'

"Steelkilt leaped on the barricade, and striding up and down there, defied the worst the pistols could do; but gave the captain to understand distinctly, that his (Steelkilt's) death would be the signal for a murderous mutiny on the part of all hands. Fearing in his heart lest this might prove but too true, the captain a little desisted, but still commanded the insurgents instantly to return to their duty.

" 'Will you promise not to touch us, if we do?' demanded their ringleader.

" 'Turn to! turn to!—I make no promise; to your duty! Do you want to sink the ship, by knocking off at a time like this? Turn to!' and he once more raised a pistol.

" 'Sink the ship?' cried Steelkilt. 'Ay, let her sink. Not a man of us turns to, unless you swear not to raise a rope-yarn against us. What say ye, men?' turning to his comrades. A fierce cheer was their response.

"The Lakeman now patrolled the barricade, all the while keeping his eye on the Captain, and jerking out such sentences as these: 'It's not our fault; we didn't want it; I told him to take his hammer away; it was boys' business: he might have known me before this; I told him not to prick the buffalo; I believe I have broken a finger here against his cursed jaw; ain't those mincing knives down in the forecastle there, men? look to those handspikes, my hearties. Captain, by God, look to yourself; say the word; don't be a fool; forget it all; we are ready to turn to; treat us decently, and we're your men; but we won't be flogged.'

" 'Turn to! I make no promises: turn to, I say!'

" 'Look ye, now,' cried the Lakeman, flinging out his arm toward him, 'there are a few of us here (and I am one of them) who have shipped for the cruise, d'ye see; now as you well know, sir, we can claim our discharge as soon as the anchor is down; so we don't want a row; it's not our interest; we want to be peaceable; we are ready to work, but we won't be flogged.'

" 'Turn to!' roared the Captain.

"Steelkilt glanced round him a moment, and then said: 'I tell you what it is now, Captain, rather than kill ye, and be hung for such a shabby rascal, we won't lift a hand against ye unless ye attack us; but till you say the word about not flogging us, we don't do a hand's turn.'

" 'Down into the forecastle then, down with ye, I'll keep ye there till ye're sick of it. Down ye go.'

" 'Shall we?' cried the ringleader to his men. Most of them were against it; but at length, in obedience to Steelkilt, they preceded him down into their dark den, growlingly disappearing like bears into a cave.

"As the Lakeman's bare head was just level with the planks, the Captain and his posse leaped the barricade, and rapidly drawing over the slide of the scuttle, planted their group of hands upon it, and loudly called for the steward to bring the heavy brass padlock belonging to the companionway. Then opening the slide a little, the Captain whispered something down the crack, closed it, and turned the key upon them—ten in number—leaving on deck some twenty or more, who thus far had remained neutral.

"All night a wide-awake watch was kept by all the officers, forward and aft, especially about the forecastle scuttle and fore hatchway; at which last place it was feared the insurgents might emerge, after breaking through the bulkhead below. But the hours of darkness passed in peace; the men who still remained at their duty toiling hard at the pumps, whose clinking and clanking at intervals through the dreary night dismally resounded through the ship.

"At sunrise the Captain went forward, and knocking on the deck summoned the prisoners to work; but with a yell they refused. Water was then lowered down to them, and a couple of handfuls of biscuit were tossed after it; when again turning the key upon them and pocketing it, the Captain returned to the quarter-deck. Twice every day for three days this was repeated; but on the fourth morning a confused wrangling, and then a scuffling was heard, as the customary summons was delivered; and suddenly four men burst up from the forecastle, saying they were ready to turn to. The fetid closeness of the air, and a famishing diet, united perhaps to some fears of ultimate retribution, had constrained them to surrender at discretion. Emboldened by this, the Captain reiterated his demand to the rest, but Steelkilt shouted up to him a terrific hint to stop his babbling and betake himself where he belonged. On the fifth morning three others of the mutineers bolted up into the air from the desperate arms below that sought to restrain them. Only three were left.

" 'Better turn to, now?' said the Captain with a heartless jeer.

" 'Shut us up again, will ye!' cried Steelkilt.

" 'Oh! certainly,' said the Captain, and the key clicked.

"It was at this point, gentlemen, that enraged by the defection of seven of his former associates, and stung by the mocking voice that had last hailed him, and maddened by his long entombment in a place as black as the bowels of despair; it was then that Steelkilt proposed to the two Canalers, thus far apparently of one mind with him, to burst out of their hole at the next summoning of the garrison; and armed with their keen mincing knives (long, crescentic, heavy implements with a handle at each end) run amuck from the bowsprit to the taffrail; and if by any devilishness of desperation possible, seize the ship. For himself, he would do this, he said, whether they joined him or not. That was the last night he should spend in that den. But the scheme met with no opposition on the part of the other two; they swore they were ready for that, or for any other mad thing, for anything, in short, but a surrender. And what was more, they each insisted upon being the first man on deck, when the time to make the rush should come. But to this their leader as fiercely objected, reserving that priority for himself; particularly as his two comrades would not yield, the one to the other, in the matter; and both of them could not be first, for the ladder would but admit one man at a time. And here, gentlemen, the foul play of these miscreants must come out.

"Upon hearing the frantic project of their leader, each in his own separate soul had suddenly lighted, it would seem, upon the same piece of treachery, namely: to be foremost in breaking out, in order to be the first of the three, though the last of the ten, to surrender; and thereby secure whatever small chance of pardon such conduct might merit. But when Steelkilt made known his determination still to lead them to the last, they in some way, by some subtle chemistry of villainy, mixed their before secret treacheries together; and when their leader fell into a doze, verbally opened their souls to each other in three sentences; and bound the sleeper with cords, and gagged him with cords; and shrieked out for the Captain at midnight.

"Thinking murder at hand, and smelling in the dark for the blood, he and all his armed mates and harpooners rushed for the forecastle. In a few minutes the scuttle was opened, and, bound hand and foot, the still struggling ringleader was shoved up into the air by his perfidious allies, who at once claimed the honor of securing a man who had been fully ripe for murder. But all three were collared, and dragged along the deck like dead cattle; and, side by side, were seized up into the mizen rigging, like three quarters of meat, and there they hung till morning. 'Damn ye,' cried the Captain, pacing to and fro before them, 'the vultures would not touch ye, ye villains!'

"At sunrise he summoned all hands; and separated those who had rebelled from those who had taken no part in the mutiny, he told the former that he had a good mind to flog them all around—thought, upon the whole, he would do so—he ought to—justice demanded it; but, for the present, considering their timely surrender, he would let them go with a reprimand, which he accordingly administered in the vernacular.

" 'But as for you, ye carrion rogues,' turning to the three men in the rigging—'for you, I mean to mince ye up for the try-pots'; and, seizing a rope, he applied it with all his might to the backs of the two traitors, till they yelled no more, but lifelessly hung their heads sideways, as the two crucified thieves are drawn.

" 'My wrist is sprained with ye!' he cried, at last; 'but there is still rope enough left for you, my fine bantam, that wouldn't give up. Take that gag from his mouth, and let us hear what he can say for himself.'

"For a moment the exhausted mutineer made a tremulous motion of his cramped jaws, and then painfully twisting round his head, said, in a sort of hiss, 'What I say is this—and mind it well—if you flog me, I murder you!'

" 'Say ye so? then see how ye frighten me'—and the Captain drew off with the rope to strike.

" 'Best not,' hissed the Lakeman.

" 'But I must'—and the rope was once more drawn back for the stroke.

"Steelkilt here hissed out something, inaudible to all but the Captain; who, to the amazement of all hands, started back, paced the deck rapidly two or three times, and then suddenly throwing down his rope, said, 'I won't do it—let him go—cut him down: d'ye hear?'

"But as the junior mates were hurrying to execute the order, a pale man, with a bandaged head, arrested them—Radney the chief mate. Ever since the blow, he had lain in his berth; but that morning, hearing the tumult on the deck, he had crept out, and thus far had watched the whole scene. Such was the state of his mouth, that he could hardly speak; but mumbling something about *his* being willing and able to do what the Captain dared not attempt, he snatched the rope and advanced to his pinioned foe.

" 'You are a coward!' hissed the Lakeman.

" 'So I am, but take that.' The mate was in the very act of striking, when another hiss stayed his uplifted arm. He paused: and then pausing no more, made good his word, spite of Steelkilt's threat, whatever that might have been. The three men were then cut down, all hands were turned to, and, sullenly worked by the moody seamen, the iron pumps clanged as before.

"Just after dark that day, when one watch had retired below, a clamor was heard in the forecastle; and the two trembling traitors running up, besieged the cabin-door, saying they durst not consort with the crew. Entreaties, cuffs, and kicks could not drive them back, so at their own instance they were put down in the ship's run for salvation. Still, no sign of mutiny reappeared among the rest. On the contrary, it seemed, that mainly at Steelkilt's instigation, they had resolved to maintain the strictest peacefulness, obey all orders to the last, and, when the ship reached port, desert her in a body. But in order to insure the speediest end to the voyage, they all agreed to another thing—namely, not to sing out for whales, in case any should be discovered. For, spite of her leak, and spite of all her other perils, the Town-Ho still maintained her mast heads, and her captain was just as willing to lower for a fish that moment, as on the day his craft first struck the cruising-ground, and Radney the mate was quite as ready to change his berth for a boat, and with his bandaged mouth seek to gag in death the vital jaw of the whale.

"But though the Lakeman had induced the seamen to adopt this sort of passiveness in their conduct, he kept his own counsel (at least till all was over) concerning his own proper and private revenge upon the man who had stung him in the ventricles of his heart. He was in

Radney the chief mate's watch; and as if the infatuated man sought to run more than half way to meet his doom, after the scene at the rigging, he insisted, against the express counsel of the Captain, upon resuming the head of his watch at night. Upon this, and one or two other circumstances, Steelkilt systematically built the plan of his revenge.

"During the night, Radney had an unseamanlike way of sitting on the bulwarks of the quarter-deck, and leaning his arm upon the gun-wale of the boat which was hoisted up there a little above the ship's side. In this attitude, it was well known, he sometimes dozed. There was a considerable vacancy between the boat and the ship, and down between this was the sea. Steelkilt calculated his time, and found that his next trick at the helm would come round at two o'clock, in the morning of the third day from that in which he had been betrayed. At his leisure, he employed the interval in braiding something very carefully in his watches below.

" 'What are you making there?' said a shipmate.

" 'What do you think? what does it look like?'

" 'Like a lanyard for your bag; but it's an odd one, seems to me.'

" 'Yes, rather oddish,' said the Lakeman, holding it at arm's length before him; 'but I think it will answer. Shipmate, I haven't enough twine—have you any?'

"But there was none in the forecastle.

" 'Then I must get some from old Rad'; and he rose to go aft.

" 'You don't mean to go a-begging to *him!*' said a sailor.

" 'Why not? Do you think he won't do me a turn, when it's to help himself in the end, shipmate?' and going to the mate, he looked at him quietly, and asked him for some twine to mend his hammock. It was given him—neither twine nor lanyard was seen again; but the next night an iron ball, closely netted, partly rolled from the pocket of the Lakeman's monkey-jacket, as he was tucking the coat into his hammock for a pillow. Twenty-four hours after, his trick at the silent helm—nigh to the man who was apt to doze over the grave always ready dug to the seaman's hand—that fatal hour was then to come; and in the foreordaining soul of Steelkilt, the mate was already stark and stretched as a corpse, with his forehead crushed in.

"But, gentlemen, a fool saved the would-be murderer from the bloody deed he had planned. Yet complete revenge he had, and without being the avenger. For by a mysterious fatality, Heaven itself seemed to step in to take out of his hands into its own the damning thing he would have done.

"It was just between daybreak and sunrise of the morning of the second day, when they were washing down the decks, that a stupid Teneriffe man, drawing water in the main-chains, all at once shouted out, 'There she rolls! there she rolls! Jesu! what a whale!' It was Moby Dick."

"Moby Dick!" cried Don Sebastian; "St. Dominic! Sir sailor, but do whales have christenings? Who call you Moby Dick?"

"A very white, and famous, and most deadly immortal monster, Don; but that would be too long a story."

"How? How?" cried all the young Spaniards, crowding.

"Nay, Dons, Dons—nay, nay! I can not rehearse that now. Let me get more into the air, sirs."

"The chicha! the chicha!" cried Don Pedro; "our vigorous friend looks faint; fill up his empty glass!"

"No need, gentlemen; one moment, and I proceed. Now, gentlemen, so suddenly perceiving the snowy whale within fifty yards of the ship— forgetful of the compact among the crew—in the excitement of the moment, the Teneriffe man had instinctively and involuntarily lifted his voice for the monster, though for some little time past it had been plainly beheld from the three sullen mast-heads. All was now a frenzy. 'The White Whale—the White Whale!' was the cry from captain, mates, and harpooners, who, undeterred by fearful rumors, were all anxious to capture so famous and precious a fish; while the dogged crew eyed askance, and with curses, the appalling beauty of the vast milky mass, that lit up by a horizontal spangling sun, shifted and glistened like a living opal in the blue morning sea. Gentlemen, a strange fatality pervades the whole career of these events, as if verily mapped out before the world itself was charted. The mutineer was the bowsman of the mate, and when fast to a fish, it was his duty to sit next him, while Radney stood up with his lance in the prow, and haul in or slacken the line, at the word of command. Moreover, when the four boats were lowered, the mate's got the start; and none howled more fiercely with delight than did Steelkilt, as he strained at his oar. After a stiff pull, their harpooner got fast, and, spear in hand, Radney sprang to the bow. He was always a furious man, it seems, in a boat. And now his bandaged cry was, to beach him on the whale's topmost back. Nothing loath, his bowsman hauled him up and up, through a blinding foam that blent two whitenesses together; till of a sudden the boat struck as against a sunken ledge, and keeling over, spilled out the standing mate. That instant, as he fell on the whale's slippery back, the boat righted, and was dashed aside by the swell, while Radney was tossed over into the sea, on the other flank of the whale. He struck out through the spray, and, for an instant, was dimly seen through that veil, wildly seeking to remove himself from the eye of Moby Dick. But the whale rushed round in a sudden maelstrom; seized the swimmer between his jaws; and rearing high up with him, plunged headlong again, and went down.

"Meantime, at the first tap of the boat's bottom, the Lakeman had slackened the line, so as to drop astern from the whirlpool; calmly looking on, he thought his own thoughts. But a sudden, terrific, downward jerking of the boat, quickly brought his knife to the line. He cut it; and the whale was free. But, at some distance, Moby Dick rose again, with some tatters of Radney's red woolen shirt, caught in the teeth that had destroyed him. All four boats gave chase again; but the whale eluded them, and finally, wholly disappeared.

"In good time, the Town-Ho reached her port—a savage, solitary place—where no civilized creature resided. There, headed by the Lakeman, all but five or six of the foremast-men deliberately deserted among the palms; eventually, as it turned out, seizing a large double war-canoe of the savages, and setting sail for some other harbor.

"The ship's company being reduced to but a handful, the Captain called upon the Islanders to assist him in the laborious business of heaving down the ship to stop the leak. But to such unresting vigilance over their dangerous allies was this small band of whites necessitated, both by night and by day, and so extreme was the hard work they underwent, that upon the vessel being ready again for sea, they were in such a weakened condition that the captain durst not put off with them in so heavy a vessel. After taking counsel with his officers, he anchored the ship as far off shore as possible; loaded and ran out his two cannon from the bows; stacked his muskets on the poop; and warning the Islanders not to approach the ship at their peril, took one man with him, and setting the sail of his best whale-boat, steered straight before the wind for Tahiti, five hundred miles distant, to procure a reinforcement to his crew.

"On the fourth day of the sail, a large canoe was descried, which seemed to have touched at a low isle of corals. He steered away from it; but the savage craft bore down on him; and soon the voice of Steelkilt hailed him to heave to, or he would run him under water. The Captain presented a pistol. With one foot on each prow of the yoked war-canoes, the Lakeman laughed him to scorn; assuring him that if the pistol so much as clicked in the lock, he would bury him in bubbles and foam.

" 'What do you want of me?' cried the Captain.

" 'Where are you bound? and for what are you bound?' demanded Steelkilt; 'no lies.'

" 'I am bound to Tahiti for more men.'

" 'Very good. Let me board you a moment—I come in peace.' With that he leaped from the canoe, swam to the boat; and climbing the gunwale, stood face to face with the Captain.

" 'Cross your arm, sir; throw back your head. Now, repeat after me. As soon as Steelkilt leaves me, I swear to beach this boat on yonder island, and remain there six days. If I do not, may lightnings strike me!

" 'A pretty scholar,' laughed the Lakeman. 'Adios, Señor!' and leaping into the sea, he swam back to his comrades.

"Watching the boat till it was fairly beached, and drawn up to the roots of the cocoa-nut trees, Steelkilt made sail again, and in due time arrived at Tahiti, his own place of destination. There, luck befriended him; two ships were about to sail for France, and were providentially in want of precisely that number of men which the sailor headed. They embarked; and so forever got the start of their former captain, had he been at all minded to work them legal retribution.

"Some ten days after the French ships sailed, the whale-boat arrived, and the Captain was forced to enlist some of the more civilized Tahitians, who had been somewhat used to the sea. Chartering a small native schooner, he returned with them to his vessel; and finding all right there, again resumed his cruisings.

"Where Steelkilt now is, gentlemen, none know; but upon the island of Nantucket, the widow of Radney still turns to the sea which refuses to give up its dead; still in dreams sees the awful white whale that destroyed him. . . ."

"Are you through?" said Don Sebastian, quietly.

"I am, Don."

"Then I entreat you, tell me if to the best of your own convictions, this your story is, in substance, really true? It is so passing wonderful!

Did you get it from an unquestionable source? Bear with me if I seem to press."

"Also bear with all of us, sir sailor; for we all join in Don Sebastian's suit," cried the company, with exceeding interest.

"Is there a copy of the Holy Evangelists in the Golden Inn, gentlemen?"

"Nay," said Don Sebastian; "but I know a worthy priest near by, who will quickly procure one for me. I go for it; but are you well advised? this may grow too serious."

"Will you be so good as to bring the priest also, Don?"

"Though there are no Auto-da-Fés in Lima now," said one of the company to another; "I fear our sailor friend runs risk of the archiepiscopacy. Let us withdraw more out of the moonlight. I see no need of this."

"Excuse me for running after you, Don Sebastian; but may I also beg that you will be particular in procuring the largest sized Evangelists you can. . . ."

"This is the priest; he brings you the Evangelists," said Don Sebastian, gravely, returning with a tall and solemn figure.

"Let me remove my hat. Now, venerable priest, further into the light, and hold the Holy Book before me that I may touch it.

"So help me Heaven, and on my honor, the story I have told ye, gentlemen, is, in substance and its great items, true. I know it to be true; it happened on this ball; I trod the ship; I knew the crew; I have seen and talked with Steelkilt since the death of Radney."

A Matter of Business

by SINCLAIR LEWIS

MARCH, 1921

Sinclair Lewis became in 1930 the first American to win the Noble Prize for literature. This story, about his favorite character, the American businessman, appeared just after his great triumph with Main Street. *Lewis was born in Sauk Center, Minnesota, in 1885, and was educated at Yale. He died in Rome in 1951.*

Candee's sleeping porch faced the east. At sunrise every morning he startled awake and became a poet.

He yawned, pulled up the gray camping blanket which proved that he had once gone hunting in Canada, poked both hands behind his neck, settled down with a wriggling motion, and was exceedingly melancholy and happy.

He resolved, seriously and all at once, to study music, to wear a rose down to business, to tell the truth in his advertisements, and to start a campaign for a municipal auditorium. He longed to leap out of bed and go change the entire world immediately. But always, as sunrise blurred into russet, he plunged his arms under the blanket, sighed, "Funny what stuff a fellow will think of at six A.M.," yawned horridly, and was asleep. Two hours afterward, when he sat on the edge of the bed, rubbing his jaw in the hope that he could sneak out of shaving this morning, letting his feet ramble around independently in search of his slippers, he was not a poet. He was Mr. Candee of the Novelty Stationery Shop, Vernon.

He sold writing paper, Easter cards, bronze book-ends, framed color prints. He was a salesman born. To him it was exhilaration to herd a hesitating customer; it was pride to see his clerks, Miss Cogerty and the new girl, imitate his courtesy, his quickness. He was conscious of beauty. Ten times a week he stopped to gloat over a print in which a hilltop and a flare of daisies expressed all the indolence of August.

But—and this was equally a part of him—he was delighted by "putting things over." He was as likely to speculate in a broken lot of china dogs as to select a stock of chaste brass knockers. It was he who had popularized Whistler in Vernon, and he who had brought out the "Oh My! Bathing Girl" pictures.

He was a soldier of fortune, was Candee; he fought under any flag which gave him the excuse. He was as much an adventurer as though he sat on a rampart wearing a steel corselet instead of sitting at a golden-oak desk wearing a blue-serge suit.

Every Sunday afternoon the Candees drove out to the golf club. They came home by a new route this Sunday.

"I feel powerful. Let's do some exploring," said Candee.

He turned the car off the Boulevard, down one of the nameless hilly roads which twist along the edge of every city. He came into a straggly country of market gardens, jungles of dead weeds, unpruned crab-apple trees, and tall, thin houses which started as artificial-stone mansions and ended as unpainted frame shacks. In front of a tar-paper shanty there was a wild-grape arbor of thick vines draped upon second-hand scantlings and cracked pieces of molding. The yard had probably never been raked, but it displayed petunias in a tub salvaged from a patent washing machine. On a shelf beside the gate was a glass case with a sign:

TOYS FOR THEE CHILRUN.

Candee stopped the car.

In the case were half a dozen wooden dolls with pegged joints—an old-man doll with pointed hat, jutting black beard, and lumpy, out-thrust hands; a Pierrot with a prim wooden cockade; a princess fantastically tall and lean.

"Huh! Hand-made! Arts-and-grafts stuff!" said Candee, righteously.

"That's so," said Mrs. Candee.

He drove on.

"Freak stuff. Abs'lutely grotesque. Not like anything I ever saw!"

"That's so," said Mrs. Candee.

He was silent. He irritably worked the air-choke, and when he found that it was loose he said, "Damn!" As for Mrs. Candee, she said nothing at all. She merely looked like a wife.

He turned toward her argumentatively. "Strikes me those dolls were

darn ugly. Some old nut of a hermit must have made 'em. They were
—they were ugly! Eh?"

"That's so," said Mrs. Candee.

"Don't you think they were ugly?"

"Yes, I think that's so," said Mrs. Candee, as she settled down to
meditate upon the new laundress who was coming tomorrow.

Next morning Candee rushed into his shop, omitted the report on
his Sunday golf and the progress of his game which he usually gave to
Miss Cogerty, and dashed at the shelf of toys. He had never thought
about toys as he had about personal Christmas cards or diaries. His
only specialty for children was expensive juveniles.

He glowered at the shelf. It was disordered. It was characterless.
There were one rabbit of gray Canton flannel, two rabbits of papier-
mâché, and nine tubercular rabbits of white fur. There were sixteen
dolls which simpered and looked unintelligent. There were one
train, one fire engine, and a device for hoisting thimblefuls of sand
upon a trestle. Not that you did anything with it when you had hoisted
it.

"Huh!" said Candee.

"Yes, Mr. Candee?" said Miss Cogerty.

"Looks like a side-street notions store. Looks like a racket shop.
Looks like a—looks like— Aah!" said Candee.

He stormed his desk like a battalion of marines. He was stern. "Got
to take up that bum shipment with the Fressen Paper Company. I'll
write 'em a letter that'll take their hides off. I won't type it. Make it
stronger if I turn the ole pen loose."

He vigorously cleared away a pile of fancy penwipers—stopping
only to read the advertisement on an insurance blotter, to draw one
or two pictures on an envelope, and to rub the enticing pale-blue
back of a box of safety matches with a soft pencil till it looked silvery
in a cross-light. He snatched his fountain pen out of his vest pocket.
He looked at it unrelentingly. He sharpened the end of a match and
scraped a clot of ink off the pen cap. He tried the ink supply by
making a line of O's on his thumbnail. He straightened up, looked
reprovingly at Miss Cogerty's back, slapped a sheet of paper on the
desk—then stopped again and read his mail.

It did not take him more than an hour to begin to write the letter
he was writing. In grim jet letters he scrawled:

FRESSEN COMPANY:
    GENTLEMEN,—I want you to thoroughly understand—

Twenty minutes later he had added nothing to the letter but a curlicue on the tail of the "d" in "understand." He was drawing the picture of a wooden doll with a pointed hat and a flaring black beard. His eyes were abstracted and his lips moved furiously:

"Makes me sick. Not such a whale of a big shop, but it's distinctive. Not all this commonplace junk—souvenirs and bum valentines. And yet our toys— Ordinary! Common! Hate to think what people must have been saying about 'em! But those wooden dolls out there in the country—they were ugly, just like Nelly said, but somehow they kind of stirred up the imagination."

He shook his head, rubbed his temples, looked up wearily. He saw that the morning rush had begun. He went out into the shop slowly, but as he crooned at Mrs. Harry McPherson, "I have some new light-weight English envelopes—crossbar lavender with a stunning purple lining," he was imperturbable. He went out to lunch with Harry Jason and told a really new flivver story. He did not cease his bustling again till four, when the shop was for a moment still. Then he leaned against the counter and brooded:

"Those wooden dolls remind me of— Darn it! I don't know what they do remind me of! Like something— Castles. Gypsies. Oh, rats! Brother Candee, I thought you'd grown up! Hey, Miss Cogerty, what trying do? Don't put those Honey Bunny books there!"

At home he hurried through dinner.

"Shall we play a little auction with the Darbins?" Mrs. Candee yawned.

"No. I— Got to mull over some business plans. Think I'll take a drive by myself, unless you or the girls have to use the machine," ventured Candee.

"No. I think I might catch up on my sleep. Oh, Jimmy, the new laundress drinks just as much coffee as the last one did!"

"Yes?" said Candee, looking fixedly at a candle shade and meditating. "I don't know. Funny, all the wild crazy plans I used to have when I was a kid. Suppose those dolls remind me of that."

He dashed out from dinner, hastily started the car. He drove rapidly past the lakes, through dwindling lines of speculative houses, into a world of hazel-nut brush and small boys with furtive dogs. His destination was the tar-paper shack in front of which he had seen the wooden dolls.

He stopped with a squawk of brakes, bustled up the path to the wild-grape arbor. In the dimness beneath it, squatting on his heels beside a bicycle, was a man all ivory and ebony, ghost white and out-landish black. His cheeks and veined forehead were pale, his beard was black and thin and square. Only his hands were ruddy. They were brick-red and thick, yet cunning was in them, and the fingers tapered to square ends. He was a medieval monk in overalls, a Hindu inde-cently without his turban. As Candee charged upon him he looked up and mourned:

"The chain, she rusty."

Now Candee was the friendliest soul in all the Boosters' Club. Squatting, he sympathized:

"Rusty, eh? Ole chain kind of rusty! Hard luck, I'll say. Ought to use graphite on it. That's it—graphite. 'Member when I was a kid—"

"I use graphite. All rusty before I get him," the ghost lamented. His was a deep voice, and humorless and grave.

Candee was impressed. "Hard luck! How about boric acid? No, that isn't it—chloric acid. No, oxalic acid. That's it—oxalic! That'll take off the rust."

"Os-all-ic," murmured the ghost.

"Well, cheer up, old man. Some day you'll be driving your own boat."

"Oh! Say!—" the ghost was childishly proud—"I got a phono-graph!"

"Have you? Slick!" Candee became cautious and inquisitive. He rose and, though actually he had not touched the bicycle, he dusted off his hands. Craftily: "Well, I guess you make pretty good money, at that. I was noticing—

"Reason I turned in, I noticed you had some toys out front. Thought I might get one for the kids. What do you charge?" He was resolving belligerently, "I won't pay more than a dollar per."

"I sharge fifty cent."

Candee felt cheated. He had been ready to battle for his rights and it was disconcerting to waste all this energy. The ghost rose, in sec-tions, and ambled toward the glass case of dolls. He was tall, fantastically tall as his own toy emperors, and his blue-denim jacket was thick with garden soil. Beside him Candee was rosy and stubby and distressingly neat. He was also uneasy. Here was a person to whom he couldn't talk naturally.

"So you make dolls, eh? Didn't know there was a toy maker in Vernon."

"No, I am nod a toy maker. I am a sculptor." The ghost was profoundly sad. "But nod de kine you t'ink. I do not make chudges in plog hats to put on courthouses. I would lige to. I would make fine plog hats. But I am not recognize. I make epitaphs in de monooment works. Huh!" The ghost sounded human now, and full of guile. "I am de only man in dose monooment works dat know what 'R.I.P.' mean in de orizhinal Greek!"

He leaned against the gate and chuckled. Candee recovered from his feeling of being trapped in a particularly chilly tomb. He crowed:

"I'll bet you are, at that. But you must have a good time making these dolls."

"You lak dem?"

"You bet! I certainly do. I—" His enthusiasm stumbled. In a slightly astonished tone, in a low voice, he marveled, "And I do, too, by golly!" Then: "You— I guess you enjoy making—"

"No, no! It iss not enjoyment. Dey are my art, de dolls. Dey are how I get even wit' de monooment works. I should wish I could make him for a living, but nobody want him. One year now—always dey stand by de gate, waiting, and nobody buy one. Oh, well, I can't help dat! I know what I do, even if nobody else don't. I try to make him primitive, like what a child would make if he was a fine craftsman like me. Dey are all dream dolls. And me, I make him right. See! Nobody can break him!"

He snatched the Gothic princess from the case and banged her on the fence.

Candee came out of a trance of embarrassed unreality and shouted: "Sure are the real stuff. Now, uh, the—uh— May I ask your name?"

"Emile Jumas my name."

Candee snapped his fingers. "Got it, by golly!"

"Pardon?"

"The Papa Jumas dolls! That's their name. Look here! Have you got any more of these in the house?"

"Maybe fifty." Jumas had been roused out of his ghostliness.

"Great! Could you make five or six a day, if you didn't do anything else and maybe had a boy to help you?"

"Oh, yez. No. Well, maybe four."

"See here. I could— I have a little place where I think maybe I could sell a few. Course you understand I don't know for sure. Taking a chance. But I think maybe I could. I'm J. T. Candee. Probably you know my stationery shop. I don't want to boast, but I will say there's no place in town that touches it for class. But I don't mean I could afford to pay you any fortune. But"—all his caution collapsed— "Jumas, I'm going to put you across!"

The two men shook hands a number of times and made sounds of enthusiasm, sounds like the rubbing of clothes on a washboard. But Jumas was stately in his invitation:

"Will you be so good and step in to have a leetle homemade wine?"

It was one room, his house, with a loft above, but it contained a harp, a double bed, a stove, a hen that was doubtful of strangers, a substantial Mamma Jumas, six children, and forty-two wooden dolls.

"Would you like to give up the monument works and stick to making these?" glowed Candee, as he handled the dolls.

Jumas mooned at him. "Oh, yez."

Ten minutes later, at the gate, Candee sputtered: "By golly! by golly! Certainly am pitching wild tonight. Not safe to be out alone. For first time in my life forgot to mention prices. Crazy as a kid—and I like it." But he tried to sound managerial as he returned. "What do you think I ought to pay you apiece?"

Craftily Papa Jumas piped: "I t'ink you sell him for more than fifty cent. I t'ink maybe I ought to get fifty."

Then, while the proprietor of the Novelty Stationery Shop wrung spiritual hands and begged him to be careful, Candee the adventurer cried: "Do you know what I'm going to do? I'm going to sell 'em at three dollars, and I'm going to make every swell on the Boulevard buy one, and I'm going to make 'em pay their three bones, and I'm going to make 'em like it! Yes, sir! And you get two dollars apiece!"

It was not till he was on the sleeping porch, with the virile gray blanket patted down about his neck, that Candee groaned: "What have I let myself in for? And are they ugly or not?" He desired to go in, wake his wife, and ask her opinion. He lay and worried, and when he awoke at dawn and discovered that he hadn't really been tragically awake all night, he was rather indignant.

But he was exhilarated at breakfast and let Junior talk all through his oatmeal.

He came into the shop with a roar. "Miss Cogerty! Get the porter and have him take all those toys down to that racket shop on Jerusalem Alley that bought our candlestick remainders. Go down and get what you can for 'em. We're going to have— Miss Cogerty, we're going to display in this shop a line of arts-and-crafts dolls that for artistic execution and delightful quaintness— Say, that's good stuff for an ad. I'll put a ten-inch announcement in the *Courier*. I'll give this town one jolt. You wait!"

Candee did not forever retain his enthusiasm for Papa Jumas dolls. Nor did they revolutionize the nurseries of Vernon. To be exact, some people liked them and some people did not like them. Enough were sold to keep Jumas occupied, and not enough so that at the great annual crisis of the summer motor trip to Michigan, Candee could afford a nickel-plated spotlight as well as slip covers. There was a reasonable holiday sale through the autumn following, and always Candee liked to see them on the shelf at the back of the shop—the medieval dolls like cathedral grotesques, the Greek warrior Demetrios, and the modern dolls—the agitated traffic policeman and the aviator whose arms were wings. Candee and Junior played explorer with them on the sleeping porch, and with them populated a castle made of chairs.

But in the spring he discovered Miss Arnold's batik lamp shades. Miss Arnold was young, Miss Arnold was pretty, and her lamp shades had many "talking points" for a salesman with enthusiasm. They were terra-cotta and crocus and leaf green; they had flowers, fruit, panels, fish, and whirligigs upon them, and a few original decorations which may have been nothing but spots. Candee knew that they were either artistic or insane; he was excited, and in the first week he sold forty of them and forgot the Papa Jumas dolls.

In late April a new road salesman came in from the Mammoth Doll Corporation. He took Candee out to lunch and was secretive and oozed hints about making a great deal of money. He admitted at last that the Mammoth people were going to put on the market a doll that "had everything else beat four ways from the ace." He produced a Skillyoolly doll. She was a simpering, star-eyed, fluffy, chiffon-clothed lady doll, and, though she was cheaply made, she was not cheaply priced.

"The Skillyoolly drive is going to be the peppiest campaign you ever saw. There's a double market—not only the kids, but all these Janes that like to stick a doll up on the piano, to make the room look dressy when Bill comes calling. And it's got the snap, eh?"

"Why don't you—? The department stores can sell more of these than I can," Candee fenced.

"That's just what we don't want to do. There's several of these fluff dolls on the market—not that any of them have the zip of our goods, of course. What we want is exclusive shops, that don't handle any other dolls whatever, so we won't have any inside competition, and so we can charge a class price."

"But I'm already handling some dolls—"

"If I can show you where you can triple your doll turnover, I guess we can take care of that, eh? For one thing, we're willing to make the most generous on-sale proposition you ever hit."

The salesman left with Candee samples of the Skillyoolly dolls, and a blank contract. He would be back in this territory next month, he indicated, and he hoped to close the deal. He gave Candee two cigars and crooned:

"Absolutely all we want is to have you handle the Skillyoolly exclusively and give us a chance to show what we can do. 'You tell 'em, pencil, you got the point!' "

Candee took the dolls home to his wife, and now she was not merely wifely and plump and compliant. She squealed.

"I think they're perfectly darling! So huggable—just sweet. I know you could sell thousands of them a year. You must take them. I always thought the Jumas dolls were hideous."

"They aren't so darn hideous. Just kind of different," Candee said, uncomfortably.

Next morning he had decided to take the Skillyoolly agency—and he was as lonely and unhappy about it as a boy who has determined to run away from home.

Papa Jumas came in that day and Candee tried to be jolly and superior.

"Ah there, old monsieur! Say, I may fix up an arrangement to switch your dolls from my place to the Toy and China Bazaar."

Jumas lamented: "De Bazaar iss a cheap place. I do not t'ink they lige my t'ings."

"Well, we'll see, we'll see. Excuse me now. Got to speak to Miss Cogerty about—about morocco cardcases—cardcases."

He consulted Miss Cogerty and the lovely Miss Arnold of the batik lamp shades about the Skillyoolly dolls. Both of them squeaked ecstatically. Yet Candee scowled at a Skillyoolly standing on his desk and addressed her:

"Doll, you're a bunch of fluff. You may put it over these sentimental females for a while, but you're no good. You're a rotten fake, and to charge two plunks for you is the darndest nerve I ever heard of. And yet I might make a thousand a year clear out of you. A thousand a year. Buy quite a few cord tires, curse it!"

At five Miss Sorrell bought some correspondence cards.

Candee was afraid of Miss Sorrell. She was the principal of a private school. He never remembered what she wore, but he had an impression that she was clad entirely in well-starched four-ply linen collars. She was not a person to whom you could sell things. She looked at you sarcastically and told you what she wanted. But the girls in her school were fervid customers, and, though he grumbled, "Here's that old grouch," he concentrated upon her across the showcase.

When she had ordered the correspondence cards and fished the copper address plate out of a relentless seal purse, Miss Sorrell blurted: "I want to tell you how very, very much I appreciate the Papa Jumas dolls. They are the only toys sold in Vernon that have imagination and solidity."

"Folks don't care much for them, mostly. They think I ought to carry some of these fluffy dolls."

"Parents may not appreciate them, and I suppose they're so original that children take a little time getting used to them. But my nephew loves his Jumas dolls dearly; he takes them to bed with him. We are your debtors for having introduced them."

As she dotted out, Candee was vowing: "I'm not going to have any of those Skillyoolly hussies in my place! I'm—I'll fight for the Jumas dolls! I'll make people like 'em, if it takes a leg. I don't care if I lose a thousand a year on them, or ten thousand, or ten thousand million tillion!"

It was too lofty to last. He reflected that he didn't like Miss Sorrell. She had a nerve to try to patronize him! He hastened to his desk. He made computations for half an hour. Candee was an irregular and temperamental cost accountant. If his general profit was sufficient he rarely tracked down the share produced by items. Now he found that, allowing for rent, overhead, and interest, his profit on Papa Jumas dolls in the last four months had been four dollars. He gasped:

"Probably could make 'em popular if I took time enough. But— four dollars! And losing a thousand a year by not handling Skillyoollys. I can't afford luxuries like that. I'm not in business for my health. I've got a wife and kids to look out for. Still, I'm making enough to keep fat and cheery on, entirely aside from the dolls. Family don't seem to be starving. I guess I can afford one luxury. I— Oh, rats!"

He reached, in fact, a sure, clear, ringing resolution that he would stock Skillyoolly dolls; that he'd be hanged if he'd stock Skillyoolly dolls; and that he would give nine dollars and forty cents if he knew whether he was going to stock them or not.

After the girls had gone out that evening he hinted to his wife: "I don't really believe I want to give up the Jumas dolls. May cost me a little profit for a while yet, but I kind of feel obligated to the poor old Frenchie, and the really wise birds—you take this Miss Sorrell, for instance—they appreciate—"

"Then you can't handle the Skillyoolly dolls?"

"Don't use that word! Skillyoolly! Ugh! Sounds like an old maid tickling a baby!"

"Now that's all very well, to be so superior and all—and if you mean that I was an old maid when we were married—"

"Why, Nelly, such a thought nev' entered my head!"

"Well, how could I tell? You're so bound and determined to be arbitrary tonight. It's all very well to be charitable and to think about that Jumas—and I never did like him, horrid, skinny old man!—and about your dolls that you're so proud of, and I still insist they're ugly, but I do think there's some folks a little nearer home that you got to show consideration for, and us going without things we need—"

"Now I guess you've got about as many clothes as anybody—"

"See here, Jimmy Candee! I'm not complaining about myself. I like pretty clothes, but I never was one to demand things for myself, and you know it!"

"Yes, that's true. You're sensible—"

"Well, I try to be, anyway, and I detest these wives that simply drive their husbands like they were pack-horses, but— It's the girls. Not that they're bad off. But you're like all these other men. You think because a girl has a new dancing frock once a year that she's got everything in the world. And here's Mamie crying her eyes out because she hasn't got anything to wear to the Black Bass dance, and that horrible Jason girl will show up in silver brocade or something, and Mamie thinks Win Morgan won't even look at her. Not but what she can get along. I'm not going to let you work and slave for things to put on Mamie's back. But if you're going to waste a lot of money I certainly don't see why it should go to a perfect stranger—a horrid old Frenchman that digs graves, or whatever it is—when we could use it right here at home!"

"Well, of course, looking at it that way—" sighed Candee.

"Do you see?"

"Yes, but—there's a principle involved. Don't know that I can make it clear to you, but I wouldn't feel as if I was doing my job honestly if I sold a lot of rubbish."

"Rubbish? Rubbish? If there's any rubbish it isn't those darling Skillyoolly dolls, but those wretched, angular Jumas things! But if you've made up your mind to be stubborn— And of course I'm not supposed to know anything about business! I merely scrimp and save and economize and do the marketing!"

She flapped the pages of her magazine and ignored him. All evening she was patient. It is hard to endure patience, and Candee was shaken. He was fond of his wife. Her refusal to support his shaky desire to "do his job honestly" left him forlorn, outside the door of her comfortable affection.

"Oh, I suppose I better be sensible," he said to himself, seventy or eighty times.

He was taking the Skillyoolly contract out of his desk as a cyclone entered the shop, a cyclone in brown velvet, white hair, and the best hat in Vernon—Mrs. Gerard Randall. Candee went rejoicing to the battle. He was a salesman. He was an artist, a scientist, and the harder the problem the better. Mechanically handing out quires of notepaper to customers who took whatever he suggested bored Candee as it would bore an exhibition aviator to drive a tractor. But selling to Mrs.

Randall was not a bore. She was the eternal dowager, the dictator of Vernon society, rich and penurious and overwhelming.

He beamed upon her. He treacherously looked mild. He seemed edified by her snort:

"I want a penholder for my desk that won't look like a beastly schoolroom pen."

"Then you want a quill pen in mauve or a sea-foam green." Mrs. Randall was going to buy a quill pen, or she was going to die—or he was.

"I certainly do not want a quill pen, either mauve or pea-green or sky-blue beige! Quill pens are an abomination, and they wiggle when you're writing, and they're disgustingly common."

"My pens don't wiggle. They have patent grips—"

"Nonsense!"

"Well, shall we look at some other kinds?"

He placidly laid out an atrocious penholder of mother-of-pearl and streaky brass which had infested the shop for years.

"Horrible! Victorian! Certainly not!"

He displayed a nickel penholder stamped, "Souvenir of Vernon," a brittle, red wooden holder with a cork grip, and a holder of chased silver, very bulgy and writhing.

"They're terrible!" wailed Mrs. Randall.

She sounded defenseless. He flashed before her eyes the best quill in the shop, crisp, firm, tinted a faint rose.

"Well," she said, feebly. She held it, wabbled it, wrote a sentence in the agitated air. "But it wouldn't go with my desk set," she attempted.

He brought out a desk set of seal-brown enamel and in the bowl of shot he thrust the rose quill.

"How did you remember what my desk set was like?"

"Ah! Could one forget?" He did not look meek now; he looked insulting and cheerful.

"Oh, drat the man! I'll take it. But I don't want you to think for one moment that I'd stand being bullied this way if I weren't in a hurry."

He grinned. He resolved, "I'm going to make the ole dragon buy three Jumas dolls—no, six! Mrs. Randall, I know you're in a rush, but I want you to look at something that will interest you."

"I suppose you're going to tell me that 'we're finding this line very popular,' whatever it is. I don't want it."

"Quite the contrary. I want you to see these because they haven't gone well at all."

"Then why should I be interested?"

"Ah, Mrs. Randall, if Mrs. Randall were interested, everybody else would have to be."

"Stop being sarcastic, if you don't mind. That's my own province." She was glaring at him, but she was following him to the back of the shop.

He chirped: "I believe you buy your toys for your grandchildren at the Bazaar. But I want to show you something they'll really like." He was holding up a Gothic princess, turning her lanky magnificence round and round. As Mrs. Randall made an "aah" sound in her throat, he protested. "Wait! You're wrong. They're not ugly; they're a new kind of beauty."

"Beauty! Arty! Tea-roomy!"

"Not at all. Children love 'em. I'm so dead sure of it that I want— Let's see. You have three grandchildren. I want to send each of them two Papa Jumas dolls. I'll guarantee— No. Wait! I'll guarantee the children won't care for them at first. Don't say anything about the dolls, but just leave 'em around the nursery and watch. Inside of two weeks you'll find the children so crazy about 'em they won't go to bed without 'em. I'll send 'em up to your daughter's house and when you get around to it you can decide whether you want to pay me or not."

"Humph! You are very eloquent. But I can't stand here all day. Ask one of your young women to wrap up four or five of these things and put them in my car. And put them on my bill. I can't be bothered with trying to remember to pay you. Good day!"

While he sat basking at his desk he remembered the words of the severe schoolmistress, Miss Sorrell, "Only toys in Vernon that have imagination and solidity."

"People like that, with brains, they're the kind. I'm not going to be a popcorn-and-lemonade seller. Skillyoolly dolls! Any ten-year-old boy could introduce those to a lot of sentimental females. Takes a real salesman to talk Jumas dolls. And— If I could only get Nelly to understand!"

Alternately triumphant and melancholy, he put on his hat, trying the effect in the little crooked mirror over the water cooler, and went out to the Boosters' Club weekly lunch.

Sometimes the Boosters' lunches were given over to speeches; sometimes they were merry and noisy; and when they were noisy Candee was the noisiest. But he was silent today. He sat at the long table beside Darbin, the ice-cream manufacturer, and when Darbin chuckled invitingly, "Well, you old Bolshevik, what's the latest junk you're robbing folks for?" Candee's answer was feeble.

"That's all right, now! 'S good stuff."

He looked down the line of the Boosters—men engaged in electrotyping and roofing, real estate and cigar making; certified accountants and teachers and city officials. He noted Oscar Sunderquist, the young surgeon.

He considered: "I suppose they're all going through the same thing —quick turnover on junk *versus* building up something permanent, and maybe taking a loss; anyway, taking a chance. Huh! Sounds so darn ridiculously easy when you put it that way. Of course a regular fellow would build up the long-time trade and kick out cheap stuff. Only—not so easy to chase away a thousand or ten thousand dollars when it comes right up and tags you. Oh, gee! I dunno! I wish you'd quit fussing like a schoolgirl, Brother Candee. I'm going to cut it out." By way of illustrating which he turned to his friend Darbin. "Frank, I'm worried. I want some advice. Will it bother you if I weep on your shoulder?"

"Go to it! Shoot! Anything I can do—"

He tried to make clear to Darbin how involved was a choice between Papa Jumas and the scent pots of the Skillyoolly. Darbin interrupted:

"Is that all that ails you? Cat's sake! What the deuce difference does it make which kind of dolls you handle? Of course you'll pick the kind that brings in the most money. I certainly wouldn't worry about the old Frenchman. I always did think those Jumas biznai were kind of freakish."

"Then you don't think it matters?"

"Why, certainly not! Jimmy, you're a good businessman, some ways. You're a hustler. But you always were erratic. Business isn't any jazz-band dance. You got to look at these things in a practical way.

Say, come on; the president's going to make a spiel. Kid him along and get him going."

"Don't feel much like kidding."

"I'll tell you what I think's the matter with you, Jimmy; your liver's on the bum."

"Maybe you're right," croaked Candee. He did not hear the president's announcement of the coming clam-bake. He was muttering, in an injured way: "Damn it! Damn it! Damn it!"

He was walking back to the shop.

He didn't want to go back; he didn't care whether Miss Cogerty was selling any of the *écrasé* sewing baskets or not. He was repeating Darbin's disgusted: "What difference does it make? Why all the fuss?"

"At most I'd lose a thousand a year. I wouldn't starve. This little decision—nobody cares a hang. I was a fool to speak to Nelly and Darbin. Now they'll be watching me. Well, I'm not going to let 'em think I'm an erratic fool. Ten words of approval from a crank like that Sorrell woman is a pretty thin return for years of work. Yes, I'll— I'll be sensible."

He spent the late afternoon in furiously rearranging the table of vases and candlesticks. "Exercise, that's what I need, not all this grousing around," he said. But when he went home he had, without ever officially admitting it to himself that he was doing it, thrust a Jumas doll and a Skillyoolly into his pocket, and these, in the absence of his wife, he hid beneath his bed on the sleeping porch. With his wife he had a strenuous and entirely imaginary conversation:

"Why did I bring them home? Because I wanted to. I don't see any need of explaining my motives. I don't intend to argue about this in any way, shape, manner, or form!" He looked at himself in the mirror, with admiration for the firmness, strength of character, iron will, and numerous other virtues revealed in his broad nose and square—also plump—chin. It is true that his wife came in and caught him at it, and that he pretended to be examining his bald spot. It is true that he listened mildly to her reminder that for two weeks now he hadn't rubbed any of the sulphur stuff on his head. But he marched downstairs—behind her—with an imperial tread. He had solved his worry! Somehow, he was going to work it all out.

Just how he was going to work it out he did not state. That detail might be left till after dinner.

He did not again think of the dolls hidden beneath his bed till he had dived under the blanket. Cursing a little, he crawled out and set them on the rail of the sleeping porch.

He awoke, suddenly and sharply, at sunup. He heard a voice— surely not his own—snarling: "Nobody is going to help you. If you want to go on looking for a magic way out—go right on looking. You won't find it!"

He stared at the two dolls. The first sunlight was on the Skillyoolly object, and in that intolerant glare he saw that her fluffy dress was sewed on with cheap thread which would break at the first rough handling. Suddenly he was out of bed, pounding the unfortunate Skillyoolly on the rail, smashing her simpering face, wrenching apart her ill-jointed limbs, tearing her gay chiffon. He was dashing into the bedroom, waking his bewildered wife with:

"Nelly! Nelly! Get up! No, it's all right. But it's time for breakfast."

She foggily looked at her wrist watch on the bedside table, and complained, "Why, it isn't but six o'clock!"

"I know it, but we're going to do a stunt. D'you realize we haven't had breakfast just by ourselves and had a chance to really talk since last summer? Come on! You fry an egg and I'll start the percolator. Come on!"

"Well," patiently, reaching for her dressing gown.

While Candee, his shrunken bathrobe flapping about his shins, excitedly put the percolator together and attached it to the baseboard plug, leaving out nothing but the coffee, he chattered of the Boosters' Club.

As they sat down he crowed: "Nelly, we're going to throw some gas in the ole car and run down to Chicago and back, next week. How's that?"

"That would be very nice," agreed Mrs. Candee.

"And we're going to start reading aloud again, evenings, instead of all this doggone double solitaire."

"That would be fine."

"Oh, and by the way, I've finally made up my mind. I'm not going to mess up my store with the Skillyoolly stuff. Going to keep on with the Jumas dolls, but push 'em harder."

"Well, if you really think—"

"And, uh— Gee! I certainly feel great this morning. Feel like a million dollars. What say we have another fried egg?"

"I think that might be nice," said Mrs. Candee, who had been married for nineteen years.

"Sure you don't mind about the Skillyoolly dolls?"

"Why, no, not if you know what you want. And that reminds me! How terrible of me to forget! When you ran over to the Jasons' last evening, the Skillyoolly salesman telephoned the house—he'd just come to town. He asked me if you were going to take the agency, and I told him no. Of course I've known all along that you weren't. But hasn't it been interesting, thinking it all out? I'm so glad you've been firm."

"Well, when I've gone into a thing thoroughly I like to smash it right through. . . . Now you take Frank Darbin; makes me tired the way he's fussing and stewing, trying to find out whether he wants to buy a house in Rosebank or not. So you—you told the Skillyoolly salesman no? I just wonder— Gee! I kind of hate to give up the chance of the Skillyoolly market! What do you think?"

"But it's all settled now."

"Then I suppose there's no use fussing— I tell you; I mean a fellow wants to look at a business deal from all sides. See how I mean?"

"That's so," said Mrs. Candee, admiringly. As with a commanding step he went to the kitchen to procure another fried egg she sighed to herself, "Such a dear boy—and yet such a forceful man."

Candee ran in from the kitchen. In one hand was an egg, in the other the small frying-pan. "Besides," he shouted, "how do we know the Skillyoollys would necessarily sell so darn well? You got to take everything like that into consideration, and then decide and stick to it. See how I mean?"

"That's so," said Mrs. Candee.

The Blue-Winged Teal

by WALLACE STEGNER

APRIL, 1950

A deeply moving story which has won wide acclaim. Mr. Stegner is an accomplished novelist and biographer, as well as short story writer. He also has given much help and encouragement to young writers as director of the Stanford University Creative Writing Center. He was born in Iowa in 1909.

Still in waders, with the string of ducks across his shoulder, he stood hesitating on the sidewalk in the cold November wind. His knees were stiff from being cramped up all day in the blind, and his feet were cold. Today, all day, he had been alive; now he was back ready to be dead again.

Lights were on all up and down the street, and there was a rush of traffic and a hurrying of people past and around him, yet the town was not his town, the people passing were strangers, the sounds of evening in this place were no sounds that carried warmth or familiarity. Though he had spent most of his twenty years in the town, knew hundreds of its people, could draw maps of its streets from memory, he wanted to admit familiarity with none of it. He had shut himself off.

Then what was he doing here, in front of this poolhall, loaded down with nine dead ducks? What had possessed him in the first place to borrow gun and waders and car from his father and go hunting? If he had wanted to breathe freely for a change, why hadn't he kept right on going? What was there in this place to draw him back? A hunter had to have a lodge to bring his meat to and people who would be glad of his skill. He had this poolhall and his father, John Lederer, Prop.

He stepped out of a woman's path and leaned against the door. Downstairs, in addition to his father, he would find old Max Schmeckebier, who ran a cheap blackjack game in the room under the sidewalk. He would find Giuseppe Sciutti, the Sicilian barber, closing his shop or tidying up the rack of *Artists and Models* and *The Nudist* with which he lured trade. He would probably find Billy Hammond, the night clerk from the Windsor Hotel, having his sandwich and beer and pie, or moving alone around a pool table, whistling abstractedly, practicing shots. If the afternoon blackjack game had broken up, there would be Navy Edwards, dealer and bouncer for Schmeckebier. At this time of evening there might be a few counter customers and a cop collecting his tribute of a beer or that other tribute that Schmeckebier paid to keep the card room open.

And he would find, sour contrast with the bright sky and the wind of the tule marshes, the cavelike room with its back corners in darkness, would smell that smell compounded of steam heat and cuechalk dust, of sodden butts in cuspidors, of coffee and meat and beer smells from the counter, of cigarette smoke so unaired that it darkened the walls. From anywhere back of the middle tables there would be the pervasive reek of toilet disinfectant. Back of the lunch counter his father would be presiding, throwing the poolhall light switch to save a few cents when the place was empty, flipping it on to give an air of brilliant and successful use when feet came down the stairs past Sciutti's shop.

The hunter moved his shoulder under the weight of the ducks, his mind full for a moment with the image of his father's face, darkly-pale, fallen in on its bones, and the pouched, restless, suspicious eyes that seemed always looking for someone. Over that image came the face of his mother, dead now and six weeks buried. His teeth clicked at the thought of how she had held the old man up for thirty years, kept him at a respectable job, kept him from slipping back into the poolroom-Johnny he had been when she married him. Within ten days of her death he had hunted up this old failure of a poolhall.

In anger the hunter turned, thinking of the hotel room he shared with his father. But he had to eat. Broke as he was, a student yanked from his studies, he had no choice but to eat on the old man. Besides, there were the ducks. He felt somehow that the thing would be incomplete unless he brought his game back for his father to see.

His knees unwilling in the stiff waders, he went down the steps, descending into the light shining through Joe Sciutti's door, and into the momentary layer of clean bay rum smell, talcum smell, hair tonic smell, that rose past the still-revolving barber pole in the angle of the stairs.

Joe Sciutti was sweeping wads of hair from his tile floor, and hunched over the counter beyond, their backs to the door, were Schmeckebier, Navy Edwards, Billy Hammond, and an unknown customer. John Lederer was behind the counter, mopping alertly with a rag. The poolroom lights were up bright, but when Lederer saw who was coming he flipped the switch and dropped the big room back into dusk.

As the hunter came to the end of the counter their heads turned toward him. "Well I'm a son of a bee," Navy Edwards said, and scrambled off his stool. Next to him Billy Hammond half stood up so that his pale yellow hair took a halo from the backbar lights. "Say!" Max Schmeckebier said. "Say, dot's goot, dot's pooty goot, Henry!"

But Henry was watching his father so intently he did not turn to them. He slid the string of ducks off his shoulder and swung them up onto the wide walnut bar. They landed solidly—offering or tribute or ransom or whatever they were. For a moment it was as if this little act were private between the two of them. He felt queerly moved, his stomach tightened in suspense or triumph. Then the old man's pouchy eyes slipped from his and the old man came quickly forward along the counter and laid hands on the ducks.

He handled them as if he were petting kittens, his big white hands stringing the heads one by one from the wire.

"Two spoonbill," he said, more to himself than to the others crowding around. "Shovelducks. Don't see many of those any more. And two, no three, hen mallards and one drake. Those make good eating."

Schmeckebier jutted his enormous lower lip. Knowing him for a stingy, crooked, suspicious little man, Henry almost laughed at the air he could put on, the air of a man of probity about to make an honest judgment in a dispute between neighbors. "I take a budderball," he said thickly. "A liddle budderball, dot is vot eats goot."

An arm fell across Henry's shoulders, and he turned his head to see the hand with red hairs rising from its pores, the wristband of a gray silk shirt with four pearl buttons. Navy Edwards' red face was close to his. "Come clean now," Navy said. "You shot 'em all sitting, didn't you, Henry?"

"I just waited till they stuck their heads out their holes and let them have it," Henry said.

Navy walloped him on the back and convulsed himself laughing. Then his face got serious again, and he bore down on Henry's shoulder. "By God you could've fooled me," he said. "If I'd been makin' book on what you'd bring in I'd've lost my shirt."

"Such a pretty shirt, too," Billy Hammond said.

Across the counter John Lederer cradled a little drab duck in his hand. Its neck, stretched from the carrier, hung far down, but its body was neat and plump and its feet were waxy. Watching the sallow face of his father, Henry thought it looked oddly soft.

"Ain't that a beauty, though?" the old man said. "There ain't a prettier duck made than a blue-wing teal. You can have all your wood ducks and redheads, all the flashy ones." He spread a wing until the hidden band of bright blue showed. "Pretty?" he said, and shook his head and laughed suddenly, as if he had not expected to. When he laid the duck down beside the others his eyes were bright with sentimental moisture.

So now, Henry thought, you're right in your element. You always did want to be one of the boys from the poolroom pouring out to see the elk on somebody's running board, or leaning on a bar with a schooner of beer talking baseball or telling the boys about the big German Brown somebody brought in in a cake of ice. We haven't any elk or German Browns right now, but we've got some nice ducks, a fine display along five feet of counter. And who brought them in? The student, the alien son. It must gravel you.

He drew himself a beer. Several other men had come in, and he saw three more stooping to look in the door beyond Sciutti's. Then they too came in. Three tables were going; his father had started to hustle, filling orders. After a few minutes Schmeckebier and Navy went into the card room with four men. The poolroom lights were up bright again, there was an ivory click of balls, a rumble of talk. The smoke-filled air was full of movement.

Still more people dropped in, kids in high school athletic sweaters and bums from the fringes of skid road. They all stopped to look at the ducks, and Henry saw glances at his waders, heard questions and answers. John Lederer's boy. Some of them spoke to him, deriving importance from contact with him. A fellowship was promoted by the ducks strung out along the counter. Henry felt it himself. He was so

mellowed by the way they spoke to him that when the players at the
first table thumped with their cues, he got off his stool to rack them
up and collect their nickels. It occurred to him that he ought to
go to the room and get into a bath, but he didn't want to leave yet.
Instead he came back to the counter and slid the nickels toward his
father and drew himself another beer.

"Pretty good night tonight," he said. The old man nodded and
slapped his rag on the counter, his eyes already past Henry and fixed
on two youths coming in, his mouth fixing itself for the greeting and
the "Well, boys, what'll it be?"

Billy Hammond wandered by, stopped beside Henry a moment.
"Well, time for my nightly wrestle with temptation," he said.

"I was just going to challenge you to a game of call-shot."

"Maybe tomorrow," Billy said, and let himself out carefully as if
afraid a noise would disturb someone—a mild, gentle, golden-haired
boy who looked as if he ought to be in some prep school learning to
say "Sir" to grownups instead of clerking in a girlie hotel. He was the
only one of the poolroom crowd that Henry half liked. He thought
he understood Billy Hammond a little.

He turned back to the counter to hear his father talking with Max
Schmeckebier. "I don't see how we could on this rig. That's the hell
of it, we need a regular oven."

"In my room in back," Schmeckebier said. "Dot old electric range."

"Does it work?"

"Sure. Vy not? I tink so."

"By God," John Lederer said. "Nine ducks, that ought to give us a
real old-fashioned feed." He mopped the counter, refilled a coffee cup,
came back to the end and pinched the breast of a duck, pulled out a
wing and looked at the band of blue hidden among the drab
feathers. "Just like old times, for a change," he said, and his eyes
touched Henry's in a look that might have meant anything from a
challenge to an apology.

Henry had no desire to ease the strain that had been between them
for months. He did not forgive his father the poolhall, or forget the
way the old man had sprung back into the old pattern, as if his wife
had been a jailer and he was now released. He neither forgot nor for-
gave the red-haired woman who sometimes came to the poolhall late
at night and waited on a bar stool while the old man closed up. Yet

now when his father remarked that the ducks ought to be drawn and plucked right away, Henry stood up.

"I could do ten while you were doing one," his father said.

The blood spread hotter in Henry's face, but he bit off what he might have said. "All right," he said. "You do them and I'll take over the counter for you."

So here he was, in the poolhall he had passionately sworn he would never do a lick of work in, dispensing Mrs. Morrison's meat pies and tamales smothered in chile, clumping behind the counter in the waders which had been the sign of his temporary freedom. Leaning back between orders, watching the Saturday night activity of the place, he half understood why he had gone hunting, and why it had seemed to him essential that he bring his trophies back here.

That somewhat disconcerted understanding was still troubling him when his father came back. The old man had put on a clean apron and brushed his hair. His pouched eyes, brighter and less houndlike than usual, darted along the bar, counting, and darted across the bright tables, counting again. His eyes met Henry's, and both half smiled. Both of them, Henry thought, were a little astonished.

Later, propped in bed in the hotel room, he put down the magazine he had been reading and stared at the drawn blinds, the sleazy drapes, and asked himself why he was here. The story he had told others, and himself, that his mother's death had interrupted his school term and he was waiting for the new term before going back, he knew to be an evasion. He was staying because he couldn't get away, or wouldn't. He hated his father, hated the poolhall, hated the people he was thrown with. He made no move to hobnob with them, or hadn't until tonight, and yet he deliberately avoided seeing any of the people who had been his friends for years. Why?

He could force his mind to the barrier, but not across it. Within a half-minute he found himself reading again, diving deep, and when he made himself look up from the page he stared for a long time at his father's bed, his father's shoes under the bed, his father's soiled shirts hanging in the open closet. All the home he had any more was this little room. He could not pretend that as long as he stayed here the fragments of his home and family were held together. He couldn't fool himself that he had any function in his father's life any more, or his father in his, unless his own hatred and his father's uneasy suspicion were functions. He ought to get out and get a job until he could go back to school. But he didn't.

Thinking made him sleepy, and he knew what that was, too. Sleep was another evasion, like the torpor and monotony of his life. But he let drowsiness drift over him, and drowsily he thought of his father behind the counter tonight, vigorous and jovial, Mine Host, and he saw that the usual fretful petulance had gone from his face.

He snapped off the bed light and dropped the magazine on the floor. Then he heard the rain, the swish and hiss of traffic in the wet street. He felt sad and alone, and he disliked the coldness of his own isolation. Again he thought of his father, of the failing body that had once been tireless and bull-strong, of the face before it had sagged and grown dewlaps of flesh on the square jaws. He thought of the many failures, the jobs that never quite worked out, the schemes that never quite paid off, and of the eyes that could not quite meet, not quite hold, the eyes of his cold son.

Thinking of this, and remembering when they had been a family and when his mother had been alive to hold them together, he felt pity, and he cried.

His father's entrance awakened him. He heard the fumbling at the door, the creak, the quiet click, the footsteps that groped in darkness, the body that bumped into something and halted, getting its bearings. He heard the sighing weight of his father's body on the other bed, his father's sighing breath as he bent to untie his shoes. Feigning sleep, he lay unmoving, breathing deeply and steadily, but an anguish of fury had leaped in him as sharp and sudden as a sudden fear, for he smelled the smells his father brought with him: wet wool, stale tobacco, liquor; and above all, more penetrating than any, spreading through the room and polluting everything there, the echo of cheap musky perfume.

The control Henry imposed upon his body was like an ecstasy. He raged at himself for the weak sympathy that had troubled him all evening. One good night, he said to himself now, staring furiously upward. One lively Saturday night in the joint and he can't contain himself, he has to go top off the evening with his girl friend. And how? A drink in her room? A walk over to some illegal after-hours bar on Rum Alley? Maybe just a trip to bed, blunt and immediate?

His jaws ached from the tight clamping of his teeth, but his orderly breathing went in and out, in and out, while the old man sighed into bed and creaked a little, rolling over, and lay still. The taint of perfume seemed even stronger now. The sow must slop it on by the cupful. And so cuddly. Such a sugar baby. How's my old sweetie tonight? It's been too long since you came to see your baby. I should be real mad at you. The cheek against the lapel, the unreal hair against the collar, the perfume like some gaseous poison tainting the clothes it touched.

The picture of his mother's bureau drawers came to him, the careless simple collection of handkerchiefs and gloves and lace collars and cuffs, and he saw the dusty blue sachet packets and smelled the faint fragrance. That was all the scent she had ever used.

My God, he said, how can he stand himself?

After a time his father began to breathe heavily, then to snore. In the little prison of the room his breathing was obscene—loose and bubbling, undisciplined, animal. Henry with an effort relaxed his tense arms and legs, let himself sink. He tried to concentrate on his own breathing, but the other dominated him, burst out and died and whiffled and sighed again. By now he had a resolution in him like an iron bar. Tomorrow, for sure, for good, he would break out of his self-imposed isolation and see Frank, see Welby. They would lend him enough to get to the coast. Not another day in this hateful relationship. Not another night in this room.

He yawned. It must be late, two or three o'clock. He ought to get to sleep. But he lay uneasily, his mind tainted with hatred as the room was tainted with perfume. He tried cunningly to elude his mind, to get to sleep before it could notice, but no matter how he composed himself for blankness and shut his eyes and breathed deeply, his mind was out again in a half-minute, bright-eyed, lively as a weasel, and he was helplessly hunted again from hiding place to hiding place.

Eventually he fell back upon his old device.

He went into a big dark room in his mind, a room shadowy with great half-seen tables. He groped and found a string above him and pulled, and light fell suddenly in a bright cone from the darker cone of the shade. Below the light lay an expanse of dark green cloth, and this was the only lighted thing in all that darkness. Carefully he gathered bright balls into a wooden triangle, pushing them forward until the apex lay over a round spot on the cloth. Quietly and thoroughly he chalked a cue: the inlaid handle and the smooth taper of the shaft were very real to his eyes and hands. He lined up the cue ball, aimed, drew the cue back and forth in smooth motions over the bridge of his left hand. He saw the balls run from the spinning shock of the break, and carom, and come to rest, and he hunted up the yellow 1-ball and got a shot at it between two others. He had to cut it very fine, but he saw the shot go true, the 1 angle off cleanly into the side pocket. He saw the cue ball rebound and kiss and stop, and he shot the 2 in a straight shot for the left corner pocket, putting drawers on the cue ball to get shape for the 3.

Yellow and blue and red, spotted and striped, he shot pool balls into pockets as deep and black and silent as the cellars of his consciousness. He was not now quarry that his mind chased, but an actor, a willer, a doer, a man in command. By an act of will or of flight he focused his whole awareness on the game he played. His mind undertook it with intent concentration. He took pride in little two-cushion banks, little triumphs of accuracy, small successes of foresight. When he had finished one game and the green cloth was bare he dug the balls from the bin under the end of the table and racked them and began another.

Eventually, he knew, nothing would remain in his mind but the clean green cloth traced with running color and bounded by simple problems, and sometime in the middle of an intricately-planned combination shot he would pale off into sleep.

At noon, after the rain, the sun seemed very bright. It poured down from a clearing sky, glittered on wet roofs, gleamed in reflection from pavements and sidewalks. On the peaks beyond the city there was a purity of snow.

Coming down the hill Henry noticed the excessive brightness and could not tell whether it was really as it seemed, or whether his plunge out of the dark and isolated hole of his life had restored a lost capacity to see. A slavery, or a paralysis, was ended; he had been for three hours in the company of a friend; he had been eyed with concern; he had been warmed by solicitude and generosity. In his pocket he had fifty dollars, enough to get him to the coast and let him renew his life. It seemed to him incredible that he had alternated between dismal hotel and dismal poolroom so long. He could not understand why he had not before this moved his legs in the direction of the hill. He perceived that he had been sullen and morbid, and he concluded with some surprise that even Schmeckebier and Edwards and the rest might have found him a difficult companion.

His father too. The fury of the night before had passed, but he knew he would not bend again toward companionship. That antipathy was too deep. He would never think of his father again without getting the whiff of that perfume. Let him have it; it was what he wanted, let him have it. They could part without an open quarrel, maybe, but they would part without love. They could part right now, within an hour.

Two grimy stairways led down into the cellar from the alley he turned into. One went to the furnace room, the other to the poolhall. The iron rail was blockaded with filled ashcans. Descent into Avernus, he said to himself, and went down the left-hand stair.

The door was locked. He knocked, and after some time knocked again. Finally someone pulled on the door from inside. It stuck, and was yanked irritably inward. His father stood there in his shirt sleeves, a cigar in his mouth.

"Oh," he said. "I was wondering what had become of you."

The basement air was foul and heavy, dense with the reek from the toilets. Henry saw as he stepped inside that at the far end only the night light behind the bar was on, but that light was coming from Schmeckebier's door at this end too, the two weak illuminations diffusing in the shadowy poolroom, leaving the middle in almost absolute dark. It was the appropriate time, the appropriate place, the stink of his prison appropriately concentrated. He drew his lungs full of it with a kind of passion, and he said, "I just came down to . . ."

"Who is dot?" Schmeckebier called out. He came to his door, wrapped to the armpits in a bar apron, with a spoon in his hand, and he bent, peering out into the dusk like a disturbed dwarf in an underhill cave. "John? Who? Oh, Henry. Shust in time, shust in time. It is not long now." His lower lip waggled, and he pulled it up, apparently with an effort.

Henry said, "What's not long?"

"Vot?" Schmeckebier said, and thrust his big head far out. "You forgot about it?"

"I must have," Henry said.

"The duck feed," his father said impatiently.

They stood staring at one another in the dusk. The right moment was gone. With a little twitch of the shoulder Henry let it go. He would wait a while, pick his time. When Schmeckebier went back to his cooking, Henry saw through the doorway the lumpy bed, the big chair with a blanket folded over it, the rolltop desk littered with pots and pans, the green and white enamel of the range. A rich smell of roasting came out and mingled oddly with the chemical stink of toilet disinfectant.

"Are we going to eat in here?" he asked.

His father snorted. "How could we eat in there? Old Maxie lived in the ghetto too damn long. By God I never saw such a boar's nest."

"Vot's duh matter? Vot's duh matter?" Schmeckebier said. His big lip thrust out, he stooped to look into the oven, and John Lederer went shaking his head up between the tables to the counter. Henry followed him, intending to make the break when he got the old man alone. But he saw the three plates set up on the bar, the three glasses of tomato juice, the platter of olives and celery, and he hesitated. His father reached with a salt shaker and shook a little salt into each glass of tomato juice.

"All the fixings," he said. "Soon as Max gets those birds out of the oven we can take her on."

Now it was easy to say, "As soon as the feed's over I'll be shoving off." Henry opened his mouth to say it, but was interrupted this time by a light tapping at the glass door beyond Sciutti's shop. He swung around angrily and saw duskily beyond the glass the smooth blond hair, the even smile.

"It's Billy," he said. "Shall I let him in?"

"Sure," the old man said. "Tell him to come in and have a duck with us."

But Billy Hammond shook his head when Henry asked him. He was shaking his head almost as he came through the door. "No thanks, I just ate. I'm full of chow mein. This is a family dinner anyway. You go on ahead."

"Got plenty," John Lederer said, and made a motion as if to set a fourth place at the counter.

"Who is dot?" Schmeckebier bawled from the back. "Who come in? Is dot Billy Hammond? Set him up a blate."

"By God his nose sticks as far into things as his lip," Lederer said. Still holding the plate, he roared back, "Catch up with the parade, for Christ sake, or else tend to your cooking." He looked at Henry and Billy and chuckled.

Schmeckebier had disappeared, but now his squat figure blotted the lighted doorway again. "Vot? Vot you say?"

"Vot?" John Lederer said. "Vot, vot, vot? Vot does it matter vot I said? Get the hell back to your kitchen."

He was, Henry saw, in a high humor. The effect of last night was still with him. He was still playing Mine Host. He looked at the two of them and laughed so naturally that Henry almost joined him. "I think old Maxie's head is full of duck dressing," he said, and leaned on the counter. "I ever tell you about the time we came back from Reno together? We stopped off in the desert to look at a mine, and got lost on a little dirt road so we had to camp. I was trying to figure out where we were, and started looking for stars, but it was clouded over, hard to locate anything. So I ask old Maxie if he can see the Big Dipper anywhere. He thinks about that maybe ten minutes with his lip stuck out and then he says, 'I t'ink it's in duh water bucket.'"

He did the grating gutturals of Schmeckebier's speech so accurately that Henry smiled in spite of himself. His old man made another motion with the plate at Billy Hammond. "Better let me set you up a place."

"Thanks," Billy said. His voice was as polite and soft as his face, and his eyes had the ingenuous liquid softness of a girl's. "Thanks, I really just ate. You go on, I'll shoot a little pool if it's all right."

Now came Schmeckebier with a big platter held in both hands. He bore it smoking through the gloom of the poolhall and up the steps to the counter, and John Lederer took it from him there and with a flourish speared one after another three tight-skinned brown ducks and slid them onto the plates set side by side for the feast. The one frugal light from the backbar shone on them as they sat down. Henry looked over his shoulder to see Billy Hammond pull the cord and flood a table with a sharp-edged cone of brilliance. Deliberately, already absorbed, he chalked a cue. His lips pursed, and he whistled, and whistling, bent to take aim.

Lined up in a row, they were not placed for conversation, but John Lederer kept attempting it, leaning forward over his plate to see Schmeckebier or Henry. He filled his mouth with duck and dressing and chewed, shaking his head with pleasure, and snapped off a bite of celery with a crack like a breaking stick. When his mouth was clear he leaned and said to Schmeckebier, "Ah, das schmecht gut, hey Maxie?"

"Ja," Schmeckebier said, and sucked grease off his lip and only then turned in surprise. "Say, you speak German?"

"Sure I speak German," Lederer said. "I worked three weeks once with an old squarehead brick mason that taught me the whole language. He taught me about sehr gut and nicht wahr and besser I bleiben right hier, and he always had his frau make me up a lunch full of kalter aufschnitt and gemixte pickeln. I know all about German."

Schmeckebier stared a moment, grunted, and went back to his eating. He had already stripped the meat from the bones and was gnawing the carcass.

"Anyway," John Lederer said, "es schmecht God damn good." He got up and went around the counter and drew a mug of coffee from the urn. "Coffee?" he said to Henry.

"Please."

His father drew another mug and set it before him. "Maxie?"

Schmeckebier shook his head, his mouth too full for talk. For a minute, after he had set out two little jugs of cream, Lederer stood as if thinking. He was watching Billy Hammond move quietly around the one lighted table, whistling. "Look at that sucker," Lederer said. "I bet he doesn't even know where he is."

By the time he got around to his stool he was back at the German. *"Schmeckebier,"* he said. "What's that mean?"

"Uh?"

"What's your name mean? Tastes beer? Likes beer?"

Schmeckebier rolled his shoulders. The sounds he made eating were like sounds from a sty. Henry was half sickened, sitting next to him, and he wished the old man would let the conversation drop. But apparently it had to be a feast, and a feast called for chatter.

"That's a hell of a name, you know it?" Lederer said, and already he was up again and around the end of the counter. "You couldn't get into any church with a name like that." His eyes fastened on the big drooping greasy lip, and he grinned.

"Schmeckeduck, that ought to be your name," he said. "What's German for duck? Vogel? Old Max Schmeckevogel. How about number two?"

Schmeckebier pushed his plate forward and Lederer forked a duck out of the steam table. Henry did not take a second.

"You ought to have one," his father told him. "You don't get grub like this every day."

"One's my limit," Henry said.

For a while they worked at their plates. Back of him Henry heard the clack of balls hitting, and a moment later the rumble as a ball rolled down the chute from a pocket. The thin, abstracted whistling of Billy Hammond broke off, became words:

> Now Annie doesn't live here any more.
> So you're the guy that she's been waiting for?
> She told me that I'd know you by the blue of your eyes . . .

"Talk about one being your limit," his father said. "When we lived in Nebraska we used to put on some feeds. You remember anything about Nebraska at all?"

"A little," Henry said. He was irritated at being dragged into reminiscences, and he did not want to hear how many ducks the town hog could eat at a sitting.

"We'd go out, a whole bunch of us," John Lederer said. "The sloughs were black with ducks in those days. We'd come back with a buggyful, and the women-folks'd really put us on a feed. Fifteen, twenty, thirty people. Take a hundred ducks to fill 'em up." He was silent a moment, staring across the counter, chewing. Henry noticed that he had tacked two wings of a teal up on the frame of the backbar mirror, small, strong bows with a band of bright blue half hidden in them. The old man's eyes slanted over, caught Henry's looking at the wings.

"Doesn't seem as if we'd had a duck feed since we left there," he said. His forehead wrinkled; he rubbed his neck, leaning forward over his plate, and his eyes met Henry's in the backbar mirror. He spoke to the mirror, ignoring the gobbling image of Schmeckebier between his own reflection and Henry's.

"You remember that set of china your mother used to have? The one she painted herself? Just the plain white china with the one design on each plate?"

Henry sat stiffly, angry that his mother's name should even be mentioned between them in this murky hole, and after what had passed. Gabble, gabble, gabble, he said to himself. If you can't think of anything else to gabble about, gabble about your dead wife. Drag her through the poolroom too. Aloud he said, "No, I guess I don't."

"Blue-wing teal," his father said, and nodded at the wings tacked to the mirror frame. "Just the wings, like that. Awful pretty. She thought a teal was about the prettiest little duck there was."

His vaguely rubbing hand came around from the back of his neck and rubbed along the cheek, pulling the slack flesh and distorting the mouth. Henry said nothing, watching the pouched hound eyes in the mirror.

It was a cold, skin-tightening shock to realize that the hound eyes were cloudy with tears. The rubbing hand went over them, shaded them like a hat brim, but the mouth below remained distorted. With a plunging movement his father was off the stool.

"Oh, God damn!" he said in a strangling voice, and went past Henry on hard, heavy feet, down the steps and past Billy Hammond, who neither looked up nor broke the sad thin whistling.

Schmeckebier had swung around. "Vot's duh matter? Now vot's duh matter?"

With a short shake of the head, Henry turned away from him, staring after his father down the dark poolhall. He felt as if orderly things were breaking and flying apart in his mind; he had a moment of white blind terror that this whole scene upon whose reality he counted was really only a dream, something conjured up out of the bottom of his consciousness where he was accustomed to comfort himself into total sleep. His mind was still full of the anguished look his father had hurled at the mirror before he ran.

The hell with you, the look had said. The hell with you, Schmeckebier, and you, my son Henry. The hell with your ignorance, whether you're stupid or whether you just don't know all you think you know. You don't know enough to kick dirt down a hole. You know nothing at all, you know less than nothing because you know things wrong.

He heard Billy's soft whistling, saw him move around his one lighted table—a well-brought-up boy from some suburban town, a polite soft gentle boy lost and wandering among pimps and prostitutes, burying himself for some reason among people who never even touched his surface. Did he shoot pool in his bed at night, tempting sleep, as Henry did? Did his mind run carefully to angles and banks and englishes, making a reflecting mirror of them to keep from looking through them at other things?

Almost in terror he looked out across the sullen cave, past where the light came down in an intense isolated cone above Billy's table, and heard the lugubrious whistling that went on without intention of audience, a recurrent and deadening and only half-conscious sound.

He looked toward the back, where his father had disappeared in the gloom, and wondered if in his bed before sleeping the old man worked through a routine of little jobs: cleaning the steam table, ordering a hundred pounds of coffee, jacking up the janitor about the mess in the hall. He wondered if it was possible to wash yourself to sleep with restaurant crockery, work yourself to sleep with chores, add yourself to sleep with columns of figures, as you could play yourself to sleep with a pool cue and a green table and fifteen colored balls. For a moment, in the sad old light with the wreckage of the duck feast at his elbow, he wondered if there was anything more to his life, or his father's life, or Billy Hammond's life, or anyone's life, than playing the careful games that deadened you into sleep.

Schmeckebier, beside him, was still groping in the fog of his mind for an explanation of what had happened. "Vere'd he go?" he said, and nudged Henry fiercely. "Vot's duh matter?"

Henry shook him off irritably, watching Billy Hammond's oblivious bent head under the light. He heard Schmeckebier's big lip flop and heard him sucking his teeth.

"I tell you," the guttural voice said. "I got somet'ing dot fixes him if he feels bum."

He too went down the stairs past the lighted table and into the gloom at the back. The light went on in his room, and after a minute or two his voice was shouting, "John! Say, come here, uh? Say, John!"

Eventually John Lederer came out of the toilet and they walked together between the tables. In his fist Schmeckebier was clutching a square bottle. He waved it in front of Henry's face as they passed, but Henry was watching his father. He saw the crumpled face, oddly rigid, like the face of a man in the grip of a barely controlled rage, but his father avoided his eyes.

"Kümmel," Schmeckebier said. He set four ice cream dishes on the counter and poured three about a third full of clear liquor. His squinted eyes lifted and peered toward Billy Hammond, but Henry said, on an impulse, "Let him alone. He's walking in his sleep."

So there were only the three. They stood together a moment and raised their glasses. "Happy days," John Lederer said automatically. They drank.

Schmeckebier smacked his lips, looked at them one after another, shook his head in admiration of the quality of his kümmel, and waddled back toward his room with the bottle. John Lederer was already drawing hot water to wash the dishes.

In the core of quiet which even the clatter of crockery and the whistling of Billy Hammond did not break into, Henry said what he had to say. "I'll be leaving," he said. "Probably tonight."

But he did not say it in anger, or with the cold command of himself that he had imagined in advance. He said it like a cry, and with the feeling he might have had on letting go the hand of a friend too weak and too exhausted to cling any longer to their inadequate shared driftwood in a wide cold sea.

Nobody Say a Word

by MARK VAN DOREN

JULY, 1951

Winner of the Pulitzer Prize for poetry and a teacher at Columbia University, Mark Van Doren long has been prominent in the literary world. He was born in Hope, Illinois, in 1894 and was educated at Urbana and at Columbia. Carl Van Doren was his brother. The sensitiveness of the poet is evident in this strangely gripping story.

After the children stopped asking she told them. "I don't know where your father is," she said quietly during supper on the sixth day. They were all at the table—neither of the girls had gone to the kitchen for anything, and their small brother hadn't bolted yet to resume his playing in the yard. They sat, paralyzed, and listened.

"I simply don't know." The strain of saying this was nothing to what it had been when Madie, the first evening he wasn't there, kept running to the door and reporting that he hadn't come in sight yet up the walk; or when Arthur, always a hard one to satisfy, had insisted every night when he went to bed: "Papa's on a business trip. He'll be back tomorrow." He would say it the next night as if he had never said it before, and Margaret learned soon enough to nod and say nothing, as if of course the child knew.

But the worst thing had been the anticipation of what Madie asked now. She was the directest of the three, though she wasn't the oldest. "What did he say, Mother, the last time he—what did he *say?*"

The worst thing was to have to answer, "Nothing," for in a way it wasn't true. George hadn't ever said: "I'm going, and I'm not coming back," but she had always known he would leave her, and so he didn't need to say so. He knew she knew.

But here was Madie looking at her, accusing her of holding something back. And a deep, sudden blush was her way of admitting that she had; only, what was there to tell, and how could it be told to these three? To Sarah most of all, who never had really asked. Sarah was the serious one who didn't like things to go wrong or change. No child does, said Margaret to herself; but the others had talked and Sarah hadn't—except, of course, with her strange large eyes. They had got larger every day, under the fine hair she insisted on combing straight back from her forehead. Young as she was, she knew the effect of that—knew it gave her authority, as if she weren't young after all; and in a sense she never had been.

"He didn't say anything," said Margaret, "about not—I mean, about not ever—"

"Not ever!" Madie was scowling in the odd way that made everybody love her. She looked near-sighted, though the doctor said she wasn't. She looked fierce; whereas she was the fondest of them all.

The words had given too much away. "Not ever" sounded—well, as fatal as the fact. And Margaret felt that she must have grown all at once very pale, for the children stared at her with a new intentness, and Arthur barely mumbled, "Papa's on a business trip —we know that," as if he had lost his confidence that this was so.

But Sarah's face had altered less, and her eyes not at all. Did Sarah understand that some men did what George had done? Some women, too? But the men. That father of five children, years ago when *she* was a child, that meek neighbor man, she forgot his name, who did so poorly and was so apologetic—"No force," her own father said—who disappeared one day and didn't come home for years. But he came home, and the town never knew how he made it up with his family: what he said to them, or they to him, or whether there was bitterness and quarreling. Not a sound or a sign from the house into which he walked one night and—well, what then? The next day he was in his leather shop as usual, and nobody had the nerve to ask him where he had been. He had so little nerve himself, it would have been torture on both sides.

Sarah had never heard of him, but she looked now as if she might have. Margaret was startled by the suspicion, yet there it was: Sarah's mind was on the same track as her own. She was even thinking—

Then she said it.

"When he does come—" Sarah closed her eyes a moment, imagining—"I know what we should do. Act just the same as if he never went anywhere. No talk, no questions. Not a word. I know."

Madie shook her brown hair out of her eyes. "I couldn't. I'd have to tell him I was glad."

Arthur merely stared down at his napkin.

They were all trying to help, they were all trying to seem undeserted, unafraid.

"You wouldn't have to tell him," Sarah said. "Wouldn't he know? *He'd* be glad. He'd like it best if none of us said a word."

At least, thought Margaret, motionless in her chair, it's confessed now. They realize he *did* desert me—and them. But me first of all. They are sorry for me. They are trying to be good children. And they are, they are.

Madie and Arthur, flying from their places across the table, reached her at the same moment. Neither one of them had ever seen her weep like this.

But Sarah didn't come.

What was she saying? She had been right—she really had, except of course that George would never—

What was she saying? The two others were so close about, it was almost impossible to hear.

"Listen! Mother, Madie, Arthur—listen! Nobody say a word."

For there was George.

Sarah must have seen him out of the back of her head; the hall door was behind her. Margaret, facing him with Madie and Arthur, started to her feet, but the two children clutched her closer and she sat down again, trembling. They hadn't looked up yet. When they did—

"Madie!" she managed to whisper. "You and Arthur—don't say anything. Don't go to him—not yet. Your father's come. He's here."

Now she had to clutch at them, they were so wild in her two arms. They all had to wait till Sarah spoke. Sarah hadn't been wrong about *one* thing. George couldn't stay away. And her heart struggled with itself, not knowing how the whole of her should feel. It was bad, it was good. She was still hurt, yet she was happy—in a strange way, as if she were asleep; in a bitter way, as if this new sweet taste—it might be so, it might—were the taste of poison.

The two children were quieter than she would have believed possible. They were minding her, they were waiting for Sarah. Or was it because George looked so terribly tired? Standing in the door, his shoulders drooping, he must have shocked them too. His eyes were the biggest thing about him. They seemed to want to look away; to close and stay closed; but they couldn't. They were for Margaret entirely, they saw no children there, no chairs, no table, no dishes, no clock.

"Hello," said Sarah, turning halfway round. "You're late. Was it a hard day at the shop?" It was scarcely her voice they heard. "Was Mr. Meeker mean, and kept you? Did somebody have an accident? You know, I was the one that set the table and I counted wrong. You go wash up, I'll fix a place." It was as if she were reciting from memory. "All of us helped get supper, even Arthur. He mashed the potatoes—partly."

But her father, if he listened to a single word, gave not a sign that he did. His dark eyes traveled for a moment, impartially, over the three young faces that separated him from Margaret, then returned to her where she sat, half guilty because of her silence, in her walnut armchair that matched his across the room. His stood against the wall, in shadow, as it had stood all week.

"Arthur," she said, "get Papa's chair for him." She spoke slowly, as if it were a deep wrong to mention only this. "Go on."

For the boy was staring at the man. A business trip, a business trip —he must be fighting the temptation to say those words and prove he had been right. A business trip. But he looked sidewise at Sarah and said nothing; then, embarrassed, ran to drag the armchair into place.

Madie's face burned with excitement, and her body shook all the way down; Margaret's arm felt the straight, strong back trembling as if in terror. But it wasn't terror. It was doubt that she ought to be where she was. It wasn't like Madie to keep this distance from someone she adored.

She only said: "Hello, Dad. We had a test in history today. I think I did all right. I'll tell you about it later. Miss Martingale—"

She stopped because he didn't seem to hear. He hadn't shifted a foot, he hadn't twitched a finger, since he came.

Margaret thought: He's a ghost, he isn't really there. It's like a game —all of us pretending to see him. It's like children who play family, and make up uncles and cousins. They're making up a father. That isn't him, that isn't George.

And suddenly she screamed—not loud, not long, but she knew she screamed. The sound was worse because it was so weak—she was ashamed, and reached for Arthur who had jumped away.

But he was already at his father's knees, and Madie, her face streaming tears, had hold of one of George's arms, which she embraced as if it had once been wounded in a war. It was veritable flesh. She hung upon it with all her weight.

Sarah came around the table, defeated, and stood while Margaret kissed her pale forehead. "All right, dear," said her mother. "It was a good thing to try, even if I broke down. You go over there with them. Quick, now."

For still George had not said a word. His hands strayed over two young heads, then three; but even while they did this they seemed to be thinking of the wife they had not touched. Never had touched, maybe, or else might never touch again. As if *she* were the ghost.

Margaret settled it. "All three of you," she said, standing straight up at last, "go somewhere else now. Outdoors, or anywhere. Don't stay long, I mean, but—oh, I don't need any help with Papa's supper. Madie—really—I don't need help."

"Are you sure?" asked Sarah. She was so responsible.

"Yes, dear. You take Arthur."

Sarah led them both out, never looking back, while Margaret waited for him to come close, to touch her flesh with his, to make one sound she could hear.

He didn't, soon enough. He was still all eyes, mournful and ashamed. He was still a man come out of a new grave.

So she went close to him.

One for the Collection

by ELIZABETH ENRIGHT

MAY, 1953

Miss Enright is a gifted writer of stories for both adults and children. She won the Newbery award for her Thimble Summer, *written while visiting the farm of her uncle, Frank Lloyd Wright. Her work has been published in* Harper's *from time to time since 1940. "One for the Collection" is a story brimming with hope.*

When I came up the basement steps I saw that it was going to be a fine day. I never know what the weather is till I come out, and I was glad to see it fine. The sun was still down low someplace but it was there, all right; the sky above the buildings was all lighted up with it. It was dead still, too; Sunday morning and the streets were empty; I felt as if I had the whole city to myself and I knew the park would be as empty as the streets and I could get on with my collecting undisturbed.

When I was young I never believed them when they said old age could be a pleasure. Never. At that I guess they didn't have in mind my kind of old age: their thoughts probably ran more to ideas of resignation or religion or taking things easy on the west coast of Florida; they surely didn't mean anything about living alone in a cellar room and prowling the city like a cat that has no owner. That wouldn't sound like happiness to anybody, it wouldn't have sounded like it to me. Yet now I am happy as I never was before; or maybe happy isn't just the right word.

It's more that I'm not bothered; and the reason I'm not bothered is that I have let go. I've let go of every single thing, just about, and I don't believe there are many people who can do that, either. But I have done it. You can't be happy much when you are young because there's so much love to bother you, different kinds, and with the love there's so much hate, and between the two of them there's pain, and you're pulled all this way and that way with feelings you don't know how to boss, or even understand. Then there are all the other things to fuss about, like having the children nicely dressed, and worrying when the wrinkles begin, and trying to keep money in the bank; oh, I tell you, I would not be young again for all the world! I don't want any of it back. My husband is dead, my children are grown and gone, I never see them. I've let them go. They wouldn't want me either if they saw me now. It's better this way; I'm free as a cat, I come and go, and no one interferes with my collecting. No one cares whether I wear my teeth or not, so I never wear them. They stay home where they belong in a tumbler of water, and they don't bother me.

Well, as I say, it was a lovely morning. It had rained hard the afternoon before; the metal trash basket on the corner had a broken-boned umbrella in it, but I had enough of those at home. I don't trouble much with the trash baskets on Sunday, anyway; too many empty bottles in them with not a drop left to encourage you.

No, the park was what I had my mind set on; and when I turned the corner there it was, like a piece of woods lifted out of the country and set down by magic in these streets. That's the way it always looks on early mornings in the spring. The leaves are so soft and clean still, and nobody is there.

Well, of course it just seems that way; in a park there's always *somebody*, and now as I crossed the street and entered it I saw the first person: a drunk left over from the night before lying on a bench, dead to the world.

I looked at him and thought once someone taught him how to walk and washed his face for him; he was new and valuable once.

"You get a good sleep," I said as I went by. "Enjoy your dreams, now, because when you wake up it won't be so rosy."

The next one I saw was Oley. When it's early like that Oley doesn't mind passing the time of day with me. Later when there are people around he won't, because I don't look respectable enough. I know that; I don't mind it. Vanity is something else I have let go of. When my mirror fell off the shelf and broke I threw it away and never got another. I haven't taken a good look at my face in years, and I guess it's just as well.

Oley was bumbling his big park barrow along the walk; his broom and rake were sticking out of it like a spoon and fork, and when he saw me he stopped.

"Hello, Ivy."

"Nice day," I said.

"Well, I don't know would I call it so nice," Oley said. "That rain and wind we had yesterday afternoon, look at all them twigs it's knocked down; it'll take the whole damn day to get 'em cleaned up and my back's been givin me trouble again——"

"Too bad," I said.

"——and I don't get no relief on Sundays, the other guy don't come at all, well, I told the fella if I don't get no relief on Sundays this year I'm goina take it up with City Hall or else I'm goina quit——"

"Oh, don't do that," I said.

"——and get me some other kinda job. I feel like quittin anyways, day in day out pickin up these damn twigs and these people's damn newspapers that they don't never put 'em in them waste containers like they oughta——"

"I guess it's disheartening," I said.

"——and walkin in dog messes all day long. Why don't they curb their dogs like they oughta? Let the street fellas take care of it. Why do they all hafta have dogs, anyways? They didn't use to have all these damn dogs when I was young."

Oley is always beefing. His conversation is like one long groan cut up into words. It's a pleasure to listen to anything so consistent.

"And take these kids today," he was saying. "Fresh! My God, I wonder what kinda mothers they got! Two of 'em there was one day, girls they was, these teen-agers up in one of the trees, they was! 'Hey you get down offa there,' I says. 'The park commissioner don't like for nobody to be climbin these trees,' I says. And they just sat there, kickin their legs. 'Come up and get us,' they says. 'Go hire a helicopter and come up and get us,' and they kept on laughin and screamin like a couple of fire engine sireens. Fresh! 'I wonder what kinda mothers you got!' I says to them. 'I'll call a cop,' I says."

"And did you?"

"Did I! Listen. Them cops they're never there when you need 'em. They're there daytimes to tell little kids to get off the grass and big kids not to throw no balls and stuff like that. But if there's a fight in the night or a purse taken or something like these fresh teen-agers, then where are they? No place. I never seen one when I needed him."

Grievance inhabits Oley like a tapeworm. I always heard it said of a tapeworm that unless you got its head you'd never be rid of it. But if you tried to get to the head of Oley's grievance you'd have to go so far back into his life and times that when you got hold of it you'd not only be rid of the grievance, you'd be rid of Oley.

I broke in on him finally. "It's a good day to hunt for things," I said. "The way the rain's washed off the top dust."

Oley picked up the handles of the barrow. "Okay, hop to it, Ivy. Help yourself. Let me know if you strike uranium." He gave me that look, that smile, that tells you you're a fool, or crazy. I've seen it often these last years. Sometimes there's a little kindness in it; there is in Oley's. Extract the kindness, I say, and never mind the rest.

I'm not the only queer one in this park. What about those old men who, rain or shine, come out three times a day to feed the pigeons? And while we're on the subject why is it only men that feed the pigeons? If women feed birds they tend to feed sparrows; I've often noticed it. And what about the woman who comes out early mornings with a dog that might be the oldest dog in the world? He's so old that he no longer looks like a dog but more like a queer little piece of furniture; his legs move just the way the legs of a table or chair would move if they could. His owner never speaks to anybody, just to him. "Are you cold, darling? Tell me. Should we have brought your little coat, dearest?" I think that animal keeps himself alive long beyond his span because he doesn't dare to die; what would become of her? And there's another lady, maybe my age, all tucked out in veils and ribbons, with a big bruise of rouge on each cheek, who comes into the park one step at a time on her high heels; one step at a time, so carefully and fearfully, as if she were walking a tightrope; and so she is, the very narrow tightrope of her balance, because she has not drawn a sober breath in years. Yes, and there's a little skinny fellow that flits along the paths sometimes, stopping now and then to scribble something on the walk with colored chalk. He looks so worried and hasty that you'd think he'd written something bad, but when you go to see you find that it says: "Jesus Saves." But he himself does not look saved. One who looks more saved than he is the fat man who brings a French horn with him on summer days and sits in the sun with the sweat standing out in sparkles on his bald head. He blows out his big purple cheeks and the horn baas noises like an operatic ram. There's never anyone around him but the children; nearby benches clear as soon as he sits down, but he doesn't care. That's the thing these people have in common: they don't care. They do what they want to do even if it's not a usual thing.

Now in my case I like to hunt for things, objects other people would not want: lost combs and keys and buttons and odd mittens, false pearls from broken strings, and bits of china if the pattern's pretty. Trash you would say, but never trash to me. The things I find are all surprises, presents given me because I'm watchful, and each has meaning for me though I can't explain it. It's as though they were signs or promises; clues left along the way to guide me. Sometimes I discover objects of a little value; dimes and pennies, once a dollar bill; a very old glass marble with a tiny horse inside, and two good fountain pens, and a camera, and a rosary with a silver cross. If it's something that will bring a few dollars I may sell it, but I'm just as pleased if it isn't worth a cent. It's a peculiar occupation, I will admit it's peculiar; but I am happy in my search. And it's healthy; it keeps me out of doors.

This particular morning, the one I'm talking about, was like many another, though prettier than most, it being May. There was a locust tree in flower, sweeter than perfume, and it kept dropping these little bonnet-shaped flowers onto the walk. There were dandelions in the grass, and some real country birds, on their way to someplace else, were up in the trees, singing. They made the pigeons and sparrows look like creatures that haven't had any education or advantages; even the stray blue jays seemed better off.

At first I didn't find much: a few marbles, there are always marbles in the spring, a handkerchief with the name Florence printed all over it, a nice long piece of string. The sun began to get into the park, now; the woman and the old dog made their appearance. They crawled along together, the two of them. "Look, darling, what a lovely day," she said. "Would you like to run a little on the grass?" As if he could run, poor thing; it's all he can do to lift his leg.

After they had gone the other dog owners began to come out, yawning and dawdling; one girl still walking in her sleep, almost, and wearing a nightgown under her coat.

When Angelo came, around nine, I stopped a while to talk to him. He's the nicest of the shoe-shiners, I know them all. He used to polish my shoes for nothing when I wore real shoes; but for a long time now I've favored these boy's sneakers with good thick rubber soles. They make softer walking.

Angelo said, "Shine?" anyway. That's his greeting, no matter if you're barefoot.

"Good morning, Angelo," I said. "How's your wife today?"

"Ah, she don' feela so good. Pain alla time. Pain leg, pain back, pain *head*. I don't know."

"Poor soul."

"Well, watcha goina do? Get old. Pain."

"Not you though."

"Me? Naw! No gotta time."

"Me either." We laughed together. Angelo has all his teeth; his original ones, as sound as when he was a boy in Sicily. His cheeks are like old leather, cured by the sun. He can't read or write, he blows his nose onto the air, he spends his days bowed over the dirty shoes of his inferiors, but he is a brave, tranquil man; he seems to know what he is here for.

I went on with my hunting. I crossed over onto the center grassplot, the largest one, where there are shrubs and cherry trees set out, and I was lucky. I found a broken string of beads; glass, with little cracked-up lights inside of them so that they looked like opals in the sun. Beautiful! I found a plastic Indian to give to some child on my block, and a torn scrap from a letter that said: "Sincerest regards, Irving." I did not put that into my collecting bag but into my pocket; as sort of a lucky piece. As though those sincere regards were really meant for me. I felt they were.

After a while I went to the diner near the Avenue to get a container of coffee. That's what I generally do if it's nice. Then I bring it back and sip it in the sun and dip a hard Italian roll into it till it gets soft. Chewing is a lost art as far as I'm concerned. Not mourned, either.

While I was sitting there eating my breakfast, Concetta Sanfillippo came by; she always comes on Sunday mornings pulling a child's express wagon that squawks with rust. She collects the Sunday papers that people leave around, I don't know why she does, I guess you'd say she was another of the queer ones. She's a skinny little old thing, more like an insect than a human. She talks to me in Italian and I talk to her in English and neither of us understands a word the other's saying, but we seem to be friends; at least what I say is friendly. That day we shouted and grinned as usual and Concetta went her way, and I sat on for a while and then went mine.

By now the children were in the park. No longer upholstered in snow suits, they were free at last. They ran and sprang and squirted drinking-fountain water at each other. They bounced their balls and smacked the air with jump ropes. I love to see the children; I love to hear them. I can appreciate them now without concern, the way I'd appreciate the daisies in a field, but I don't talk to them; I might frighten them. I never frighten the babies, though; they sit in their buggies and glance at me or stare and sometimes smile, too young to have opinions about age or clothes. Right now they are exactly what they seem to be and nothing else; they haven't yet pretended anything.

It's different with their mothers. When I go by a bench full of them the conversation stops as if a hearse had passed, and when it begins again, in a second, it's low and full of laughs and exclamation points. I don't resent those young women or their laughing. They don't understand yet about letting go; they're at the time of life when more and more is being given them, including trouble.

Now and then, since it was Sunday morning and early still, the drunks would wander in and out amongst the playing children on their way to somewhere else, maybe they didn't even know where. They looked as if they were made out of some different kind of material from the children. There's a brotherly resemblance, always, between those run-down men: their eyes seem puzzled and faded, and all their faces are a scalded red, as if sometime or other they'd gotten such a whiff of hell that they'd been scorched. They never linger in this part of the park; if they settle at all it's at the south end, where they roost along the benches like a row of torn old poultry.

I kept on searching for a good while, poking among the bushes with my stick; but I didn't dredge up much. Around eleven everything was bells; church bells from St. Michael's and Heavenly Host and Our Lady of Taormina, and other bells on the ice-cream wagons and toys. The air was all shaking and breaking with these sounds, it was like a great big fair or celebration. I don't often stay so late on Sundays; the place gets crowded and the hunting's no good then, but this was such a fine, lively day that I kept going.

Now over to the north side of the park, up on a high pedestal, there's a statue of some general or other. I never can recall his name, or which war it was that he enjoyed, though I see him almost daily. He's walking forward, supposed to be, with the wind blowing back a corner of his big stone coat and showing a military-looking thigh and knee. He's got white epaulettes of pigeon droppings, a fancy hat, and big mustache that points both east and west; he looks like an important, foolish man. I sometimes use his shade to sit in, but that's only in the late afternoon when it's grown long enough, because you can't get very close to him; he's got a plot of ground around him and a little fence. Every summer they plant flowers in the plot, and this time it was pansies. (I wonder how he'd like that, pansies all around him?) Ah, but they're lovely flowers with their bad-tempered little faces and their fine, rich colors. I bent over them to look closer and to breathe that queer half-bitter smell they have, and I guess it was the smell of them that brought to me the memory of my Grandma's pansy bed. For all of a sudden I saw it in my mind, and the green grass around it and myself down on my knees picking a bouquet; I was eight years old, about, wearing a white dress, and I could see my blue bead bracelet and my two long yellow plaits, and I knew that, like the drunks, I was made out of some other material from what I am now. . . . That's the one thing you can't let go of altogether—memory of the past. You think you've kicked it off the premises and then suddenly, because of some sound or sight or smell, it's back beside you in prime condition, to give you a pinch that hurts.

So as I was bending over, staring and remembering, the sun struck a sparkle from something lying deep among the pansy plants. I reached my hand down between them and what I picked up was a brooch about the size of a silver dollar, and caked with earth though it was I could tell that this was something valuable, not a toy or trash.

When I took it to the drinking fountain to wash it off I had to wait. The children were three deep around the place; you know how they are about water. The bigger ones were yelling for turns and pushing each other off the step, while the little ones, knowing their place, watched and waited. All of them were wet; their sleeves soaked to the elbows, their overalls covered with splash patches, and their faces, right up to the eyebrows, were dripping and shining. Every now and then a mother or nurse would run up and grab one and start scolding; but when the children noticed me beside them they gradually seeped away of their own accord. I suppose they thought I was a witch.

My hands were shaking as I held the brooch under the cold water, and then I dried it on my dress and took it off away from everyone to look at it. It was real, all right. It was like a little dish made out of diamonds and in the middle of it, green as a go-light, there was an emerald. I knew it was an emerald, though I had never looked at one before without a wall of glass between it and me.

As I turned it on my palm big stabs of light came out of it. It was worth thousands of dollars, I could tell that; not hundreds but thousands, though I could not guess how many. I had never held such a thing in my hand before, and as if its wealth might burn me, I dropped it into my bag.

I heard Concetta's wagon skrawking by and called to her. "Hey, Concetta," I said. "Lend me a paper for a second, will you?" She had a load of them by now and when I explained what I wanted by doing kind of a dance with my head and hands she gave me a big helping of the *Sunday Times.*

It took me a while to find the Lost and Found Column. I wonder why they call it Lost and Found, when it's all made up of Losts with never the mention of a Found? That day it was the same: a collection of laments and promises concerning everything from diamond bracelets to dogs answering to the name of Joe; but no one in all the city seemed to have mislaid a brooch. I guess it had been lost too long, or maybe it had come to town with the pansy plants; who knows?

"Okay, Concetta, thanks a lot," I said. "Grazia tante. Danke schoen."

After she had gone I reached in my collecting bag and brought out everything I'd found that morning. I put it all on the grass beside me; handkerchief and beads and brooch.

I saw that the toys were toys and nothing else, and the beads no longer looked like opals; they looked like rubbish. Crazy stuff to keep.

I picked up the brooch and watched its fiery lights and changes, and beneath what I was really seeing I could see myself with money in my hand; a lot of money, not just the little pension check that keeps me going. And what would I do with that money once I had it, I wondered. Well, I'm a woman; with cash in the bank there's no doubt that I'd think I needed a new dress, a coat. And then new shoes; and then I'd think I had to wear my teeth; learn how to make my peace with them all over again. And then I'd probably buy a looking glass and wash my face each day. I would remember about vanity and after that I would remember about pride.

It would follow then that I would want to show myself, respectable, to my children; I would meet the grandchildren I've never seen, and then of course I would remember about love. And once I remembered that and picked it up again I would be helpless. . . . And beyond these things, beyond all these things, I could see to the last chapter of my life: the clean quiet home and the other old women; all of us eating food prepared by dieticians, each of us boasting of a completed past, embroidered and trimmed up for competition. . . .

Oley's barrow, now full of twigs, stood neglected on the walk. Oley himself had crossed the grass plot to have a talk with Angelo. He had his rake in one hand; with the other he was making circles in the air, and I knew that each circle described a grievance. I walked over to the barrow and as I passed it by I hung the brooch upon a twig. The light struck dazzles from it, Oley could not miss it; he would only wonder how he'd ever overlooked it in the first place. . . .

Let him figure out a way to beef about this one, I said to myself; and because I knew, sure as shooting, sure as death and taxes and the rising sun, that he would somehow figure out a way, I got to laughing and laughed the whole way home. I felt comfortable again and happy. I wasn't bothered.

IX

Science and Philosophy

On Not Being Dead, as Reported

by ELMER DAVIS

APRIL, 1939

The late Elmer Davis had some strangely profound things to say about death in this article. It is illustrative of the wide range of subject matter he covered in his record of sixty-seven contributions to the magazine, more than any other free-lance writer. One of America's most distinguished journalists, he was also a CBS radio news broadcaster from 1939 to 1942, when his Hoosier voice and incisive comment did so much to bring the world-shaking events of those years into focus for millions of Americans. He was head of the Office of War Information from 1942 until V-J Day. He died in 1958, at the age of sixty-eight.

Twice it has been my fortune to be reported missing in a catastrophe, and probably dead. Each time I denied the story as soon as I heard of it, and seem to have been more generally believed than is usually the case when people have to contradict something that the papers have said about them; but if it happens again I shall fall back on that favorite formula of those whose misdeeds are unexpectedly brought to light, and refuse to dignify the rumor with a denial. For a third denial might not be wholly convincing, even to me; where there is smoke there is generally some fire; such an occurrence is bound to set you wondering if there may not be some truth in the story after all. And beyond that, to turn up alive after you have been reported dead is an unwarrantable imposition on your friends.

The first time it happened I was only twenty-six, and my repudiation of the canard was accordingly convinced and vigorous. I happened to be crossing from Holland to England on a steamer that was sub-marined and sunk—one of the most placid submarine sinkings on record, for the British Navy had time to get not only all the passengers but all their baggage off before she went under. (Indeed, the ship herself was raised after the war and put back into service, and there she is to this day, all ready to be sunk again in the next war.) But cross-channel communication was slow and uncertain in 1916; all that was known at first was that the ship had been sunk. Nothing had been heard about the passengers, so the Dutch public leaped to the conclusion which in those days was usually correct; and some days passed before my friends, and enemies, in Holland learned that I had not gone to the bottom after all.

My friends, I am afraid, took it in their stride; even before America was in the war anybody with an international acquaintance had become hardened to hearing the unexpected news of some friend's violent death any morning. When so many good men were being killed at the front every day there was no reason to waste any particular grief on a neutral who had accidentally got in the way of the war and been run over. The effect on my enemies was, in the long run, more deplorable.

They were not my enemies really—only a group of high-minded people who held with great fervor ideals on whose practicability I had been compelled to throw some doubt, in print; they were in fact the leaders and delegates of the Ford Peace Party, and they looked on me as one unsaved, who had not seen the light. Very likely there was more in that view than I would admit at the time. I still think the Ford Peace Party was a crazy enterprise; but an endeavor, however visionary and inadequate, to stop a war that was wrecking Europe appears in retrospect a little less crazy than most of the other purposes that were prevalent in Europe in 1916.

However, I was unable to see eye to eye with the leaders of this Children's Crusade, so it had sometimes come to black looks and harsh words. But when I was reported dead those who had thought so poorly of me were engulfed in a wave of Christian charity. "What a pity!" they said. "He was a young man of great promise." It was some years before I realized how callously inconsiderate it had been for me to turn up after that, alive and well, and just as unsaved as ever. Nobody who has risen to a noble gesture of generosity and forgiveness likes to be made to look foolish a couple of days later.

II

My alleged decease got no newspaper publicity that time, at least not in any newspaper that found me worthy of extended mention; so there was no opportunity to enjoy what might seem to the unthinking the rare privilege of reading my own obituary. But I know men who have had that privilege, and they tell me that it is anything but a pleasure.

You may be scandalized at the discovery that the papers thought you were worth no more than a paragraph or two when you would have supposed you rated at least half a column. Even if you get as much (or almost as much) space as you think you deserve, you are likely to find that the source material which the writer of the obituary discovered in the clippings in the newspaper morgue deals chiefly with what you had always regarded as trivial aspects of your career; or probably indeed with its scandalous aspects, if it has had any. This is natural; all the writer has found is some record of the occasions on which you said or did something that was news; and all of us except the great are most likely to become news by being conspicuously wicked, conspicuously unfortunate, or conspicuously ridiculous. Long years of industry and success in the hardware business, a lifetime of zealous and fruitful service to the church or the lodge, will pass all but unnoticed by the press. Whereas there are likely to be columns and columns in the newspaper files about the unfortunate occasion when that unbalanced woman to whom you had foolishly lent money, for no reason at all except disinterested benevolence, sued you for breach of promise, claiming that she never knew you were married.

For when a man dies the newspaper is compelled to function, to the best of its ability, as the Voice of History. Conscious enough of its own inadequacy, it must nevertheless do the best it can to represent the man not as he seemed to himself or to those who loved him (nor to those who hated him either); but the man as he was objectively, against his background, in proportion to his universe. How often when I was a young reporter have I called up a bereaved family for information about the deceased, to be told that he was one of Nature's noblemen and the kindest husband and father that ever lived. It takes a certain amount of tact in such moments to get what you want without having to explain that what you want is something worth putting in the paper, something that will place the man in his frame of reference. For most of us such an examination is likely to be deflationary; a man who has read his own obituary will never be quite the same again.

Not even if he is a man of consequence, who gets a creditable amount of space in the paper. Almost certainly, to run over this sketch of his life as seen by a stranger will be a melancholy exercise;

he will know that some of his achievements have been overestimated, he will be disgusted to find that the accomplishments in which he has taken most pride do not seem very important to an outsider; and here and there some phrase, set down in all innocence, will be a bitter reminder of some of the things he had always intended to do, and never got round to. Viewed objectively, compared with the history of the general run of men, it may be a respectable record; but its subject cannot view it objectively, he must compare it not with what other men have accomplished, but with what he intended to accomplish when he started out. Few men can make that comparison with any great satisfaction. Of the length and nature of my obituary, now in type in certain New York newspaper offices, I know nothing; all I can be sure of is that it is longer than I deserve, for it is a tradition of the trade that both newspapermen and ex-newspapermen always get more space than they are really worth on the obituary page. But whatever its length and implications, I have no regrets that I escaped reading it, by however narrow a margin, after the late New England hurricane.

III

It is not my purpose to tell you about the hurricane. No cataclysm of Nature, except possibly Noah's flood, ever afflicted a region populated by so many professional writers; and most of them were prompt to cash in on it, especially if they carried no wind insurance and had to compensate their losses somehow. Already I have read five magazine articles about it; an account of it will be the climactic chapter in two novels that are to be published before you read this, and God knows how many more in preparation. I can only hope that the novelists will remember from personal experience that the hurricane fell alike on the just and on the unjust, and will not use it as a *deus ex machina* which removes all the undesirable characters while the hero and heroine come through unscathed. For there have been novels in which hurricanes, earthquakes, volcanic eruptions, etc., displayed as sure a marksmanship and as careful a discrimination as the United States Marines.

Two gentlemen from upper New Hampshire have testified in *Harper's* that in that remote region, people were slow to realize the extent and gravity of the catastrophe. So, it must be confessed, were some of us on the Connecticut shore, right in the middle of things. When a hurricane is over you know that you are not dead; you realize it so vividly—especially if there had been some doubt about your survival, for a while—that it may not occur to you that people at a distance do not share your knowledge. It happened that no one was killed in the small community where I was living, that no one I knew personally was among the casualties in the near-by towns that suffered far more serious damage; and while we knew things had been pretty bad in our neighborhood, it took time to grasp the dimensions of the disaster, to perceive that when hundreds had been killed over a wide area, most of the millions who had not been killed were going to be worried about till definitely reported safe.

The process by which one is reported dead is simple and logical enough. One's friends call up the papers, asking, "What do you hear about X?" The wires being down, they have naturally heard nothing about X. Thus X is unreported, therefore X is missing; and a reading public unfamiliar with hurricanes draws the natural analogy from local and minor disasters, fires and train wrecks and so on, in which those at first reported missing usually turn out to be dead. So it happened that on the Saturday morning after the hurricane, when the yard had been cleaned up and the roads were open and we were ready to go back to town, the New York papers at làst got into the devastated area, and I learned that I was missing. But that was only the beginning.

It was due to the generosity of my friends in the trade that I was posted as missing on the front page, in a position and size of type about equivalent to that allotted, on the other side of the page, to the mobilization of the Czechoslovak army (nobody could have dreamed that day that the two pieces of news would turn out to be of equal inconsequence). But it is a thoroughly natural presumption that a man missing in large headlines must be more completely missing than somebody whose unreportedness is buried in the body of the story. So in that day's evening papers the possibility was verging on certainty; and one of the radio stations, I am told, went to the length of reporting that my corpse had been seen floating out to sea.

And that was the end of the story. Between the hurricane and Hitler, the papers and the broadcasting stations were overloaded that week; there was little time or space for the correction of misapprehensions. News is the unusual, the not-to-be-expected; so I suppose I have no right to complain if it was news that Davis was dead, but not news, not worth putting in the papers, that Davis was not dead after all. The implications, however, are by no means flattering; and it all entailed a good deal of inconvenience to my friends. My wife for some reason was not listed as missing—somewhat illogically, for a hurricane, like an air raid, is no respecter of women and children; my friends drew the natural conclusion that she was somewhere else and began to ask her about me by telephone and telegraph. But, believing that I was dead but not quite sure, they were driven to all sorts of circumlocutions; trying to find language that was neither callous enough to grieve her if she were a widow, nor ominous enough to alarm her if she did not yet know whether she was or not.

To the friends I met after I came back to town the inconvenience was of another and perhaps graver sort. On each man's face I could see a look of startled surprise, not altogether unmixed with resentment; for they had done their grieving for Davis, and it could not be but regarded as an imposition when they discovered that it was all a mistake, and that some day they would have it to do over again. My contemporaries are approaching the time of life when to hear of the unexpected death of a friend is as common as it was in war days; and if you have work to do you cannot spend too much time worrying about it. When you hear that good old X is dead you put in perhaps two minutes thinking hard about good old X, and hoping that he left enough for his widow to live on; after which you put him out of your mind and get down to business, so that you may leave enough for your widow to live on when your time comes. Now and then in later life you see some piece of news in the paper that he would have particularly appreciated or particularly detested; when your partner misses a slam that X would have made if he had been playing the hand; or when recurrently you have to try to find a job for his widow, in case he didn't leave enough for her to live on.

But that is about all, except in the rare instances of some personality so vivid that when it is gone the landscape never looks quite so bright again. (Such, in my experience, were Guy Holt, Don Marquis, and Max Swain; such, I gather, was Elinor Wylie to those who knew her well; and so indeed, as a personality rather than as an artist, William Shakespeare seems to have been remembered by his friends.) But most of us do not rate so much remembrance, except by those to whom our passing means a radical change in all the circumstances of life; this is the world of the living, and there would be no time to live if we spent too much time thinking about the dead. Two minutes

when the news is heard and an occasional passing recollection thereafter is about as much mourning as the average man can reasonably
expect from most of those who knew him; it is entirely intelligible if
my friends feel that they have done their mourning for me and owe
me no more grief at any later date, when the story can no longer be
denied.

IV

It appears also that practically all of my friends have read Mark
Twain, or at least heard him quoted; for they were few indeed who,
on seeing me reappear in the flesh, did not remark that the report
seemed to have been greatly exaggerated. Endeavoring to escape that
cliché, I contented myself with saying when comment was called for
that it was at least premature; but I begin to wonder if that is altogether true.

For if I remember correctly the science I once studied (and if it has
not since then been turned upside down, as other sciences have been),
from the biologist's point of view we start dying the moment we are
born—which is only another way of saying that every organism
exists in time as well as in space, that it is not quite the same at any
moment as it was the moment before. So, if I have an actuarial expectation of another quarter-century of life, about two-thirds of all
that will ever have been Davis has gone past already; from the time
angle, I am two-thirds dead.

I do not pretend to have any clear idea of what Time is (or Space
either); Sir Arthur Eddington's famous diagram of the Present as a
moving point between the infinite cones of the Past and the Future
may mean something to Eddington, but it does not help the layman
much. H. G. Wells, lately correcting in the *Saturday Review of Literature* the too extensive inferences that some people drew from the
concept of Time as the fourth dimension which he once presented in
The Time Machine, remarks that Time differs from other dimensions
in that you can travel along it in only one direction. (And, it might
be added, you must travel in that direction, at ever-increasing speed,
whether you like it or not. As Don Marquis said about being fifty, a
couple of years later you are sixty, and ten minutes after that you are
eighty-five.)

Wells adds that "we live in measurable bits of time," but very small
bits apparently, and quotes a suggestion of Sir Edwin Ray Lankester

that perhaps "our brain cells live for an instant as the blood and fresh oxygen pulse to them and then become inactive till the next heartbeat reawakens them." Maybe so; at any rate it is obviously an unwarranted simplification to speak of a personality. If the brain lives in each fresh heartbeat, a man who has lived seventy years is a sequence of something like two and a half billion transitory personalities, whose resemblance is sometimes close and sometimes remote. The conclusion is substantially true even if the premise be a little shaky, as almost anybody can testify when meeting an old friend after ten years' separation. He is not the man he used to be—maybe better, probably worse, but certainly not the same.

The photographer can abstract the outward appearance of a single one of these personalities from the rest, but only the outward appearance; we habitually talk as if we could manage a sort of psychic photography, grasping the personality as it is at the moment; but it will not look quite the same to any two observers, no outsider can penetrate very deep, and in any case what you are trying to photograph is changing under your eyes much more rapidly than its outward appearance. To take an obvious instance—a man may look pretty much the same, changed in expression no doubt but not in feature, the moment after he has been fired from a job he had held twenty years and expected to hold for the rest of his life, as he looked the moment before. But he is not the same and will never be the same again; even if he gets a better job and keeps it, the shock, the reminder of insecurity, the loss of prestige will have left permanent scars on all of his successive personalities thereafter.

Because our psychic mechanism is such that we must live for the most part in the present, we cannot manage this concept of the individual as a moving and changing picture; as a working hypothesis we must abstract the average of a comparatively few of his personalities and say, "That is the man." We used to omit his childhood from the excerpt, but the psychologists have taught us that that is a mistake; we still omit as a rule his old age, or the years after his activity has slowed down, for whatever reason; when we think of Napoleon we think of the average of all the Napoleons, say, from 1795 to 1815; but we leave the six years between Waterloo and his death out of account. Yet the fat and ailing gentleman who lived on St. Helena was Napoleon; not the Napoleon of 1796 or of 1807 (again one must simplify, for there were many Napoleons in each of those years), but certainly *a* Napoleon—and indeed a Napoleon who had considerable effect on the subsequent history of Europe. A good many of the second guesses by spinning which he whiled away his leisure on St. Helena were woven into the fabric—the ideal if not the real fabric—of the Second Empire.

A rough average of a period of months or years is likely to be not so very far wrong as a working hypothesis; but our craving for stability is apt to make us forget how soon even these provisional abstractions become outdated. Hitler has displayed an unusual continuity of purpose and fixity of ideas, but the post-Munich Hitler is not, cannot be, the pre-Munich Hitler; such a triumph as he won last September by the superior force of his personality must have its effect on what is loosely called the character of any man. It is nonsense to speak of the Lincoln of 1864; even with the crudest of abstractions there were half a dozen successive Lincolns in 1864. To be sure in Lincoln, as in most other individuals, there were certain characteristics that changed much more slowly, so slowly that we may think of them as permanent features of character. But of the manifestations of these traits the most that can truly be said is that some things are a little less impermanent than others.

v

We do not like to think of these matters, as a rule, because it is unpleasant to be reminded that we seem to be subject, like the rest of the cosmos, to the Second Law of Thermodynamics; that we are steadily running down. For a while, in some respects, the trend of the curve may be upward; the Shakespeare (an abstraction from innumerable momentary Shakespeares) who wrote *Hamlet* was not the Shakespeare who wrote *Love's Labour's Lost,* we say he was a better and greater Shakespeare, but it may not have seemed so to the self-observing mechanisms of that personality; he must have known that he was older, that he tired more easily; he had learned a good many things in the intervening years that could have been no fun for him to find out, however they broadened and deepened his understanding. But sooner or later for every man the curve turns downward, unless he escapes the misfortune of living too long by what may be the almost equally serious misfortune of dying too soon. (To this fairly obvious truth more attention might be paid by the income tax laws, which permit deductions for "the exhaustion, wear and tear, including obsolescence, of property used in the trade or business," unless that property happens to be a man's own energies and own brain.)

Somewhere in each human being's life there must be an optimum point, a moment when the average of all his successive personalities is higher than it ever was before, or will ever be again. But he can never identify that point himself; whether things to date have been good or bad, he usually hopes and very often believes that they are going to be better. Nor can outsiders discern that optimum point except in retrospect, and then none too confidently. Lincoln, almost alone among great men, seems to have died exactly at his peak; the average of all the Lincolns was higher on April 14, 1865, than it had ever been before—or might ever have been again if he had had to make the fight against Thad Stevens and the Radicals that Andrew Johnson made in vain. Yet who can be sure? Lincoln's prestige was enormous, his political shrewdness was exceptional, he would not have made Johnson's mistakes. If he had lived he might have won that fight, carried public opinion, North and South, with him on a decent scheme of Reconstruction. In that case the average of Lincoln would have stood even higher than it stands now.

Most people no doubt live too long—yet you cannot always be sure that even the elderly have lived long enough. It might have seemed to John Quincy Adams, leaving the White House in his sixty-second year—the first of Presidents, except his father, to be denied re-election—that he had passed his peak, that the average of all the John Quincy Adamses would never stand so high again; yet a good deal of the best of John Quincy Adams was still to come. Julius Caesar's average might be higher if he had died a year or two earlier, before he had been too much infected by Cleopatra's ideas—or it might be higher if he had lived another twenty years.

These examples from the great may seem remote from a discussion of the average man, but they have their bearing. When we say that X is dead we mean the average of all the X's—an average different for each observer, and none of them perhaps very close to the average that might be computed by Omniscience. But what the phrase really implies is that a moving picture has ended, that the succession of innumerable more or less different X's has stopped, there will never be any more of them. Going into the movie theater you ask the usher if the feature is over; no, he says, it is only half over. So when a middle-aged man says in a moment of weariness that he is half dead, he is telling the literal truth.

To say then that the report of my death was premature was to speak inexactly; it would have been more correct to say that it was two-thirds true, or perhaps even more. For at least two-thirds of all the Davises have passed on and are not coming back. (A good many men, and women, have tried sometimes to resurrect one of those vanished personalities, but without success; the best you can hope for is to find, as did the hero of *Conrad in Quest of His Youth,* something roughly similar, and approximately as satisfactory.) The young man who was mistakenly reported to have been drowned in 1916, himself an average impression created on the senses by the rapid succession of thousands of bits of film, is dead, and I cannot regret him very much; he was a good deal of an ass, he muffed some excellent opportunities—yet he had possibilities that his successors might have realized, and did not. Of those successors some few, I hope, were worth being remembered a little, and missed a little; but more than I like to think of are well buried, with no tears shed even by the current average who inherits what is loosely termed their identity.

To go away, said some Frenchman, is to die a little; true enough, but to stay where you are is also to die a little; in the midst of life we are in death, and the fear of dying (for there are people who fear dying in itself, aside from the pain and inconvenience of the final illness) ought to be mitigated by the reflection that we are dying all the time, and that most of the job has already been done. Few of the people I know are afraid of death, except as it might affect persons or institutions more or less dependent on them; which means that what they are afraid of is not death but the cessation of activity and usefulness. With regard to that not much can be said except that it is going to happen to us all some day, no matter how much we dislike the idea; and that to worry about it in advance is likely to make it happen all the sooner.

At any rate, the next time I am reported dead I shall not dignify the rumor with a denial. If it is not yet entirely true, people will find that out in due time.

The Functions of a Teacher

by BERTRAND RUSSELL

JUNE, 1940

A member of one of Britain's most famous families, a mathematician, philosopher, and storm center, Bertrand Russell has taught both in England and America. This article was published at a time when he was the center of an uproar resulting from his appointment to teach at the College of the City of New York. Religious leaders railed against him for his views on sex as expressed in various books. He was charged with being "a propagandist against religion and morality." A Brooklyn woman who said she had a daughter who might attend CCNY brought a taxpayer's suit, claiming he was an advocate of sexual immorality. This finally resulted in his ouster from the post. Lord Russell was born in 1872.

Teaching, more even than most other professions, has been transformed during the past hundred years from a small, highly skilled profession concerned with a minority of the population, to a large and important branch of the public service. The profession has a great and honorable tradition, extending from the dawn of history until recent times; but any teacher in the modern world who allows himself to be inspired by the ideals of his predecessors is likely to be made sharply aware that it is not his function to teach what he thinks, but to instill such beliefs and prejudices as are thought useful by his employers. In former days a teacher was expected to be a man of exceptional knowledge or wisdom, to whose words men would do well to attend. In antiquity teachers were not an organized profession, and no control was exercised over what they taught. It is true that they were often punished afterward for their subversive doctrines. Socrates was put to death and Plato is said to have been thrown into prison, but such incidents did not interfere with the spread of their doctrines. Any man who has the genuine impulse of the teacher will be more anxious to survive in his books than in the flesh. A feeling of intellectual independence is essential to the proper fulfillment of the teacher's functions, since it is his business to instill what he can of knowledge and reason-ableness into the process of forming public opinion. In antiquity he performed this function unhampered except by occasional spasmodic and ineffective interventions of tyrants or mobs. In the Middle Ages teaching became the exclusive prerogative of the Church, with the result that there was little progress either intellectual or social. With the Renaissance the general respect for learning brought back a very considerable measure of freedom to the teacher. It is true that the Inquisition compelled Galileo to recant and burnt Giordano Bruno at the stake, but each of these men had done his work before being pun-ished. Institutions such as universities largely remained in the grip of dogmatists, with the result that most of the best intellectual work was done by independent men of learning. In England especially, until near the end of the nineteenth century, hardly any men of first-rate emi-nence except Newton were connected with universities. But the social system was such that this interfered little with their activities or their usefulness.

In our more highly organized world we face a new problem. Some-thing called "education" is given to everybody, usually by the state, but sometimes by the churches. The teacher has thus become, in the vast majority of cases, a civil servant obliged to carry out the behests of men who have not his learning, who have no experience of dealing with the young, and whose only attitude toward education is that of the propagandist. It is not very easy to see how in these circumstances teachers can perform the functions for which they are specially fitted.

State education is obviously necessary, but as obviously involves certain dangers against which there ought to be safeguards. The evils to be feared are seen in their full magnitude in Germany and Russia. In each of these countries no man can teach unless he subscribes to a dogmatic creed which few people of free intelligence are likely to accept sincerely. Not only must he subscribe to a creed, but he must condone abominations and carefully abstain from speaking his mind on current events. So long as he is teaching only the alphabet and the multiplication table, as to which no controversies arise, official dogmas do not necessarily warp his instruction; but even while he is teaching these elements he is expected, in totalitarian countries, not to employ the methods which he thinks most likely to achieve the scholastic result, but to instill fear, subservience, and blind obedience by de-manding unquestioned submission to his authority. And as soon as he passes beyond the bare elements he is obliged to take the official view on all controversial questions. The result is that the young in Germany and Russia become fanatical bigots, ignorant of the world outside their own country, totally unaccustomed to free discussion, and not aware that their opinions can be questioned without wickedness. This state of affairs, bad as it is, would be less disastrous than it is if the dogmas instilled were, as in medieval Catholicism, universal and international; but the whole conception of an international culture is denied by the modern dogmatists, who preach one creed in Germany, another in Italy, another in Russia, and yet another in Japan. In each of these countries fanatical nationalism is what is most emphasized in the teaching of the young, with the result that the men of one country have no common ground with the men of another, and that no conception of a common civilization stands in the way of warlike ferocity.

The decay of cultural internationalism has proceeded at a continually increasing pace ever since the Great War. When I was in Leningrad in 1920 I met the Professor of Pure Mathematics, who was familiar with London, Paris, and other capitals, having been a member of various international congresses. Nowadays the learned men of Russia are very seldom permitted such excursions, for fear of their drawing comparisons unfavorable to their own country. In other countries nationalism in learning is less extreme, but everywhere it is far more powerful than it was. There is a tendency in England (and, I believe, in the United States) to dispense with Frenchmen and Germans in the teaching of French and German. The practice of considering a man's nationality rather than his competence in appointing him to a post is damaging to education and an offense against the ideal of international culture, which was a heritage from the Roman Empire and the Catholic Church, but is now being submerged under a new barbarian invasion, proceeding from below rather than from without.

In democratic countries these evils have not yet reached anything like the same proportions, but it must be admitted that there is grave danger of similar developments in education, and that this danger can be averted only if those who believe in liberty of thought are on the alert to protect teachers from intellectual bondage. Perhaps the first requisite is a clear conception of the services which teachers can be expected to perform for the community.

I agree with the governments of the world that the imparting of definite uncontroversial information is one of the least of the teacher's functions. It is of course the basis upon which the others are built, and in a technical civilization such as ours it has undoubtedly a considerable utility. There must exist in a modern community a sufficient number of men who possess the technical skill required to preserve the mechanical apparatus upon which our physical comforts depend. It is, moreover, inconvenient if any large percentage of the population is unable to read and write. For these reasons we are all in favor of universal compulsory education. But governments have perceived that it is easy in the course of giving instruction to instill beliefs on controversial matters and to produce habits of mind which may be convenient or inconvenient to those in authority. The defense of the state in all civilized countries is quite as much in the hands of teachers as in those of the armed forces. Except in totalitarian countries, the defense of the state is desirable, and the mere fact that education is used for this purpose is not in itself a ground of criticism. Criticism will arise only if the state is defended by obscurantism and appeals to irrational passion.

Such methods are quite unnecessary in the case of any state worth defending. Nevertheless, there is a natural tendency toward their adoption by those who have no first-hand knowledge of education. There is a widespread belief that nations are made strong by uniformity of opinion and by the suppression of liberty. One hears it said over and over again that democracy weakens a country in war, in spite of the fact that in every important war since the year 1700 the victory has gone to the more democratic side. Nations have been brought to ruin much more often by insistence upon a narrow-minded doctrinal uniformity than by free discussion and the toleration of divergent opinions. Dogmatists the world over believe that although the truth is known to them, others will be led into false beliefs provided they are allowed to hear the arguments on both sides. This is a view which leads to one or another of two misfortunes: either one set of dogmatists conquers the world and prohibits all new ideas, or, what is worse, rival dogmatists conquer different regions and preach the gospel of hate against each other, the former of these evils existing in the middle ages, the latter during the wars of religion, and again in the present day. The first makes civilization static; the second tends to destroy it completely. Against both the teacher should be the main safeguard.

It is obvious that organized party spirit is one of the greatest dangers of our time. In the form of nationalism it leads to wars between nations, and in other forms it leads to civil war. It should be the business of teachers to stand outside the strife of parties and endeavor to instill into the young the habit of impartial inquiry, leading them to judge issues on their merits and to be on their guard against accepting *ex parte* statements at their face value. The teacher should not be expected to flatter the prejudices either of the mob or of officials. His professional virtue should consist in a readiness to do justice to all sides, and in an endeavor to rise above controversy into a region of dispassionate scientific investigation. If there are people to whom the results of his investigation are inconvenient he should be protected against their resentment, unless it can be shown that he has lent himself to dishonest propaganda by the dissemination of demonstrable untruths.

The function of the teacher, however, is not merely to mitigate the heat of current controversies. He has more positive tasks to perform, and he cannot be a great teacher unless he is inspired by a wish to perform these tasks. Teachers are more than any other class the guardians of civilization. They should be intimately aware of what civilization is and desirous of imparting a civilized attitude to their pupils. We are thus brought to the question: what constitutes a civilized community?

II

This question would very commonly be answered by pointing to merely material tests. A country is civilized if it has much machinery, many motor cars, many bathrooms, and a great deal of rapid locomotion. To these things, in my opinion, most modern men attach much too much importance. Civilization, in the more important sense, is a thing of the mind, not of material adjuncts to the physical side of living. It is a matter partly of knowledge, partly of emotion. So far as knowledge is concerned, a man should be aware of the minuteness of himself and his immediate environment in relation to the world in time and space. He should see his own country not *only* as home, but as one among the countries of the world, all with an equal right to live and think and feel. He should see his own age in relation to the past and the future, and be aware that its own controversies will seem as strange to future ages as those of the past seem to us now. When taking an even wider view, he should be conscious of the vastness of geological epochs and astronomical abysses; but he should be aware of all this, not as a weight to crush the individual human spirit, but as a vast panorama which enlarges the mind that contemplates it.

On the side of the emotions, a very similar enlargement from the purely personal is needed if a man is to be truly civilized. Men pass from birth to death, sometimes happy, sometimes unhappy; sometimes generous, sometimes grasping and petty; sometimes heroic, sometimes cowardly and servile. To the man who views the procession as a whole, certain things stand out as worthy of admiration. Some men have been inspired by love of mankind; some by supreme intellect have helped us to understand the world in which we live; and some by exceptional sensitiveness have created beauty. These men have produced something of positive good to outweigh the long record of cruelty, oppression, and superstition. These men have done what lay in their power to make human life a better thing than the brief turbulence of savages. The civilized man, where he cannot admire, will aim rather at understanding than at reprobating. He will seek rather to discover and remove the impersonal causes of evil than to hate the men who are in its grip. All this should be in the mind and heart of the teacher, and if it is in his mind and heart he will convey it in his teaching to the young who are in his care.

No man can be a good teacher unless he has feelings of warm affection toward his pupils and a genuine desire to impart to them what he himself believes to be of value. This is not the attitude of the propagandist. To the propagandist his pupils are potential soldiers in an army. They are to serve purposes that lie outside their own lives, not in the sense in which every generous purpose transcends self, but in the sense of ministering to unjust privilege or to despotic power. The propagandist does not desire that his pupils should survey the world and freely choose a purpose which to them appears of value. He desires, like a topiarian artist, that their growth shall be trained and twisted to suit the gardener's purpose. And in thwarting their natural growth he is apt to destroy in them all generous vigor, replacing it by envy, destructiveness, and cruelty. There is no need for men to be cruel; on the contrary, I am persuaded that most cruelty results from thwarting in early years, above all from thwarting what is good.

Repressive and persecuting passions are very common, as the present state of the world only too amply proves. But they are not an inevitable part of human nature. On the contrary, they are, I believe, always the outcome of some kind of unhappiness. It should be one of the functions of the teacher to open vistas before his pupils, showing them the possibility of activities that will be as delightful as they are useful, thereby letting loose their kind impulses and preventing the growth of a desire to rob others of joys that they will have missed. Many people decry happiness as an end, both for themselves and for others; but one may suspect them of sour grapes. It is one thing to forego personal happiness for a public end, but it is quite another to treat the *general* happiness as a thing of no account. Yet this is often done in the name of some supposed heroism. In those who take this attitude there is generally some vein of cruelty based probably upon an unconscious envy, and the source of the envy will usually be found in childhood or youth. It should be the aim of the educator to train adults to be free from these psychological misfortunes, and not anxious to rob others of happiness, because they themselves have not been robbed of it.

As matters stand today, many teachers are unable to do the best of which they are capable. For this there are a number of reasons, some more or less accidental, others very deep-seated. Most teachers are overworked and are compelled to prepare their pupils for examinations rather than to give them a liberalizing mental training. The people who are not accustomed to teaching have no idea of the expense of spirit that it involves. Clergymen are not expected to preach sermons for several hours every day, but the analogous effort is demanded of teachers. The result is that many of them become harassed and nervous, out of touch with recent work in the subjects they teach and unable to inspire their students with a sense of the intellectual delights to be obtained from new understanding and new knowledge.

III

This, however, is by no means the gravest matter. In most countries certain opinions are recognized as correct, and others as dangerous. Teachers whose opinions are not correct are expected to keep silent about them. If they mention their opinions it is propaganda, while the mentioning of correct opinions is considered to be merely sound instruction. The result is that the inquiring young too often have to go outside the classroom to discover what is being thought by the most vigorous minds of their own time. There is a subject called civics, in which, perhaps more than in any other, the teaching is expected to be misleading. The young are taught a sort of copybook account of how public affairs are supposed to be conducted, and are carefully shielded from all knowledge as to how in fact they are conducted. When they grow up and discover the truth, the result is too often a complete cynicism in which all public ideals are lost; whereas if they had been taught the truth carefully and with proper comment they might have become men able to combat evils in which, as it is, they acquiesce with a shrug.

The idea that falsehood is edifying is one of the besetting sins of those who draw up educational schemes. I should not myself consider that a man could be a good teacher unless he had made a firm resolve never in the course of his teaching to conceal truth because it is what is called "unedifying." The kind of virtue that can be produced by guarded ignorance is frail and fails at the first touch of reality. There are in this world many men who deserve admiration, and it is good that the young should be taught to see the ways in which these men are admirable. But it is not good to teach them to admire rogues by concealing their roguery. It is thought that the knowledge of things as they are will lead to cynicism, and so it may do if the knowledge comes suddenly with a shock of surprise and horror. But if it comes gradually, duly intermixed with a knowledge of what is good, and in the course of a scientific study inspired by the wish to get at the truth, it will have no such effect. In any case to tell lies to the young, who have no means of checking what they are told, is morally indefensible.

The thing, above all, that a teacher should endeavor to produce in his pupils if democracy is to survive is the kind of tolerance that springs from an endeavor to understand those who are different from ourselves. It is perhaps a natural human impulse to view with horror and disgust all manners and customs different from those to which we are used. Ants and savages put strangers to death. And those who have never traveled either physically or mentally find it difficult to tolerate the queer ways and outlandish beliefs of other nations and other times, other sects and other political parties. This kind of ignorant intolerance is the antithesis of a civilized outlook, and is one of the gravest dangers to which our overcrowded world is exposed.

The educational system ought to be designed to correct it, but far too little is done in this direction at present. In every country nationalistic feeling is encouraged, and schoolchildren are taught, what they are only too ready to believe, that the inhabitants of other countries are morally and intellectually inferior to those of the country in which the schoolchildren happen to reside. Collective hysteria, the most mad and cruel of all human emotions, is encouraged instead of being discouraged, and the young are encouraged to believe what they hear frequently said rather than what there is some rational ground for believing. In all this the teachers are not to blame. They are not free to teach as they would wish. It is they who know most intimately the needs of the young. It is they who through daily contact have come to care for them. But it is not they who decide what shall be taught or what the methods of instruction are to be.

There ought to be a great deal more freedom than there is for the scholastic profession. It ought to have more opportunities of self-determination, more independence from the interference of bureaucrats and bigots. No one would consent in our day to subject the medical men to the control of non-medical authorities as to how they should treat their patients, except of course where they depart criminally from the purpose of medicine, which is to cure the patient. The teacher is a kind of medical man whose purpose is to cure the patient of childishness, but he is not allowed to decide for himself on the basis of experience what methods are most suitable to this end. A few great historic universities, by the weight of their prestige, have secured virtual self-determination, but the immense majority of educational institutions are hampered and controlled by men who do not understand the work with which they are interfering. The only way to prevent totalitarianism in our highly organized world is to secure a certain degree of independence for bodies performing useful public work, and among such bodies teachers deserve a foremost place.

The teacher, like the artist, the philosopher, and the man of letters, can perform his work adequately only if he feels himself to be an individual directed by an inner creative impulse, not dominated and fettered by an outside authority. It is very difficult in this modern world to find a place for the individual. He can subsist at the top as a dictator in a totalitarian state or a plutocratic magnate in a country of large industrial enterprises, but in the realm of the mind it is becoming more and more difficult to preserve independence of the great organized forces that control the livelihoods of men and women. If the world is not to lose the benefit to be derived from its best minds it will have to find some method of allowing them scope and liberty in spite of organization. This involves a deliberate restraint on the part of those who have power and a conscious realization that there are men to whom free scope must be afforded. Renaissance Popes could feel in this way toward Renaissance artists, but the powerful men of our day seem to have more difficulty in feeling respect for exceptional genius. The turbulence of our times is inimical to the fine flower of culture. The man in the street is full of fear and, therefore, unwilling to tolerate freedoms for which he sees no need. Perhaps we must wait for quieter times before the claims of civilization can again override the claims of party spirit. Meanwhile it is important that some should continue to realize the limitations of what can be done by organization. Every system must allow loopholes and exceptions; for if it does not it will in the end crush all that is best in man.

Who Are You?

by ALDOUS HUXLEY

NOVEMBER, 1944

Being his grandfather's grandson—and for that matter his brother's brother—Aldous Huxley shares a family interest in scientific ideas. Here he explores a scientific classification of Homo sapiens. Critic, essayist, and novelist, Mr. Huxley was born in England and educated at Oxford. His novels include Antic Hay, Point Counter Point, Brave New World, *and* The Genius and the Goddess (*which ran serially in* Harper's *magazine). Incidentally, the magazine for May, 1888 carried an engraving of Thomas Henry Huxley and said of him in an article, "His force has been felt in almost every direction of English progress."*

The most striking fact about human beings is that, in many respects, they are very unlike one another. Their bodies vary enormously in size and shape. Their modes of thought and speech and feeling are startlingly different. Startlingly different, too, are their reactions to even such basic things as food, sex, money, and power. Between the most highly gifted and those of least ability, and between persons endowed with one particular kind of talent or temperament and persons endowed with another kind, the gulfs are so wide as to be bridgeable only by the most enlightened charity.

These are facts which from time immemorial have been recognized, described in plays and stories, commented on in proverbs, aphorisms, and poems. And yet, in spite of their obviousness and their enormous practical importance, these facts are still, to a very great extent, outside the pale of systematic thought.

The first and indispensable condition of systematic thought is classification. For the purposes of pure and applied science, the best classification is comprehensive, covering as many of the indefinitely numerous facts as it is possible for thought to cover without becoming confused, and yet is simple enough to be readily understood and used without being so simple as to be untrue to the essentially complex nature of reality. The categories under which it classifies things and events are easily recognizable, lend themselves to being expressed in quantitative terms, and can be shown experimentally to be meaningful for our specifically human purposes.

Up to the present, all the systems in terms of which men have attempted to think about human differences have been unsatisfactory. Some, for example, have conspicuously failed to cover more than a part of the relevant facts. This is especially true of psychology and sociology as commonly taught and practiced at the present time. How many of even the best of our psychologists talk, write, think, and act as though the human body, with its innate constitution and its acquired habits, were something that, in an analysis of mental states, could safely be ignored! And even when they do admit, rather reluctantly, that the mind always trails its carcass behind it, they have little or nothing to tell us about the ways in which mental and physical characteristics are related.

Sociologists deal with abstractions even more phantasmally bodiless. For example, they will carry out laborious researches into the problems of marriage. But when we read the results, we are flabbergasted to find that the one factor never taken into account by the researchers is who the men and women under investigation actually *are*. We are told every detail about their social and economic background; nothing at all about their inherited psycho-physical constitution.

There are other classificatory systems which claim to be comprehensive, but in which the indispensable process of simplification has been carried so far that they are no longer true to the facts. The interpretation of all human activity in terms of economics is a case in point. Another type of oversimplification is to be found in such theories as those of Helvétius in the eighteenth century and of certain Behaviorists in the twentieth—theories which profess to account for everything that men do or are in terms of environment, education, or conditioned reflexes. At the other extreme of oversimplification we find some of the more rabid Eugenists, who attribute all the observable differences between human beings to hereditary factors, and refuse to admit that environmental influences may also play a part.

It may be remarked in passing that most of the hypotheses and classification systems we use in our everyday thinking are grossly oversimplified and therefore grossly untrue to a reality which is intrinsically complex. Popular theories about such things as morals, politics, economics, and religion are generally of the either-or, A-causes-B variety. But in any real-life situation there are almost always more than two valid and workable alternatives and invariably more than one determining cause. That is why the utterances of speech-making politicians can never, in the very nature of things, be true. In half an hour's yelling from a platform it is intellectually impossible for even the most scrupulous man to tell the delicately complex truth about any of the major issues of political or economic life.

We come now to the classification systems which attempt to cover the whole ground, but which have proved scientifically unsatisfactory because (though founded, as they often are, upon profound insights into the nature of human reality) they have made use of categories which could not be expressed in quantitative terms. Thus, for several thousands of years, the Hindus have been classifying human beings within the framework of four main psycho-physico-social categories. Because the caste system in India has become petrified into a rigidity that is untrue to the facts of life and therefore often unjust, the whole idea of caste is repellent to Western minds. And yet that special branch of applied psychology which deals with vocational guidance is concerned precisely with assigning individuals to their proper place in the natural caste system. The work of the specialists in "human engineering" has made it quite clear that individuals belong congenitally to one kind of caste, and that they hurt themselves and their society if, by some mistake, they get enrolled in another caste. Some time in the next century or two the empirical findings of the vocational guidance experts will be linked up with a satisfactory method of analyzing the total psycho-physical organism. When that happens society will be in a position to reorganize itself on the basis of a rejuvenated and thoroughly beneficent, because thoroughly realistic, caste system.

In the West, for more than two thousand years, men were content with a classification system devised by the Greek physician, Hippocrates. His theory was that one's innate psycho-physical constitution was determined by the relative predominance within one's body of one or other of the four "humors"—blood, phlegm, black bile, and yellow bile. (We still describe temperaments as "sanguine" or "phlegmatic"; we still talk of "choler" and "melancholia.") Humoral pathology persisted into the nineteenth century. Diseases were attributed to a derangement of the normal balance of the individual's humors, and treatment was directed to restoring the equilibrium. This relating of disease to inherited constitution was essentially realistic, and one of the things that modern medicine most urgently needs is a new and sounder version of the Hippocratic hypothesis—a classification of human differences in terms of which the physician may interpret the merely mechanical findings of his diagnostic instruments.

Finally we come to those classification systems which are unsatisfactory because the categories they make use of, although susceptible of being expressed in quantitative terms, have not, in practice, turned out to be particularly meaningful. Thus the anthropometrists have measured innumerable skulls, determined the coloring of innumerable heads of hair and pairs of eyes, but have told us very little of genuinely scientific or practical value about human beings. Why? Because, as a matter of empirical fact, these records and measurements could not be related in any significant way to human behavior.

And, not content with telling us very little by means of a colossal volume of statistics, the anthropometrists proceeded to confuse the whole issue by trying to think about human differences in terms of fixed racial types—the Nordic, the Alpine, the Mediterranean, and so forth. But the most obvious fact about all the existing groups of human beings, at any rate in Europe and America, is that each one of them exhibits a large number of individual variations. In certain areas, it is true, a single closely related set of such variations may be more common than in other areas. It is upon this fact that the whole theory of racial types has been built up—a system of classification which has proved extremely unfruitful as an instrument of pure and applied science, and, in the hands of the Nazi ideologists, extremely fruitful as an instrument of discrimination and persecution.

II

So much, then, for the classification systems which have proved to be unsatisfactory. Does there exist a more adequate system? This is a question which it is now possible, I think, to answer with a decided yes. A classification system more adequate to the facts and more potentially fruitful than any other devised hitherto has been formulated by Dr. W. H. Sheldon in two recently published volumes, *The Varieties of Human Physique* and *The Varieties of Temperament*.

Sheldon's classification system is the fruit of nearly fifteen years of research, during which he and his collaborators have made, measured, and arranged in order many thousands of standardized photographs of the male body, taken from in front, from behind, and in profile. A careful study of these photographs revealed that the most basic (first order) classification system in terms of which the continuous variations of human physique could adequately be described was based upon the discrimination of three factors, present to a varying degree in every individual. To these three factors Sheldon has given the names of *endomorphy, mesomorphy,* and *ectomorphy.*

Endomorphy is the factor which, when predominant, expresses itself in a tendency for anabolism to predominate over catabolism, which often results in soft and comfortable roundness of physique. At school the extreme endomorph is called Slob or Fatty. By middle life he or she may be so enormously heavy as to be practically incapable of walking. The endomorphic physique is dominated by its digestive tract. Autopsies show that the endomorphic gut is often more than twice as long and weighs more than twice as much as the intestine of a person in whom there is an extreme predominance of the ectomorphic constituent.

Predominant mesomorphy expresses itself in a physique that is hard and muscular. The body is built around strong heavy bones and is dominated by its extraordinarily powerful muscles. In youth, the extreme mesomorph tends to look older than his years, and his skin, instead of being soft, smooth, and unwrinkled, like that of the endomorph, is coarse and leathery, tans easily, and sets in deep folds and creases at a comparatively early age. It is from the ranks of extreme mesomorphs that successful boxers, football players, military leaders, and the central figures of the more heroic comic strips are drawn.

The extreme ectomorph is neither comfortably round nor compactly hard. His is a linear physique with slender bones, stringy unemphatic muscles, a short and thin-walled gut. The ectomorph is a lightweight, has little muscular strength, needs to eat at frequent intervals, is often quick and highly sensitive. The ratio of skin surface to body mass is higher than in endormorphs or mesomorphs, and he is thus more vulnerable to outside influences, because more extensively in contact with them. His body is built, not around the endomorph's massively efficient intestine, not around the mesomorph's big bones and muscles, but around a relatively predominant and unprotected nervous system.

Endomorphy, mesomorphy, and ectomorphy occur, as constituting components, in every human individual. In most persons the three components are combined fairly evenly, or at least harmoniously. Extreme and unbalanced predominance of any one factor is relatively uncommon.

For example, less than ten boys out of every hundred are sufficiently mesomorphic to engage with even moderate success in the more strenuous forms of athletics, requiring great strength and physical endurance. Hence the almost criminal folly of encouraging all boys, whatever their hereditary make-up to develop athletic ambitions. By doing this, educators condemn large numbers of their pupils to an unnecessary disappointment and frustration, plant the seed of neurosis among the unsuccessful, and foster a conspicuous bumptiousness and self-conceit in the extreme mesomorph. A rational policy with regard to athletics would be to tell all boys the simple truth, which is that very few of them can expect to excel in the more violent sports, that such excellence depends primarily on a particular inheritance of size and shape, and that persons of other shapes and sizes not suited to athletic proficiency have as good a right to realize their own *natural* capacities as the extreme mesomorph and can contribute at least as much to society.

In order to calculate the relative amounts of each component in the total individual mixture, Sheldon divides the body into five regions and proceeds to make a number of measurements in each zone. The records of these measurements are then subjected to certain mathematical procedures, which yield a three-digit formula. This formula expresses the amount of endomorphy, mesomorphy, and ectomorphy present within the organism, as measured on a seven-point scale of values. Thus the formula 7-1-1 indicates that the individual under consideration exhibits endomorphy in its highest possible degree, combined with the lowest degree of mesomorphy and ectomorphy. In practice, he would probably be extremely fat, gluttonous and comfort-loving, without drive or energy, almost sexless, and pathetically dependent on other people. How different from the well-balanced 4-4-4, the formidably powerful and aggressive 3-7-1, the thin, nervous, "introverted" 1-2-7!

The relationships between the components are such that only a certain number of the mathematically possible combinations can occur in nature. Thus it is obviously impossible for a human being to be a 7-1-7, or a 7-7-7, or a 1-7-7; for nobody can be simultaneously extremely round and soft and extremely hard and compact or extremely narrow, small-gutted, and stringy-muscled. Sheldon and his collaborators have found that, in terms of their seven-point scale of values for three components, seventy-six varieties of human physique can be clearly recognized. If a value scale of more than seven points were used, the number would of course be correspondingly greater. But they have found empirically that the seven-point scale provides an instrument of analysis sufficiently precise for most practical purposes.

The three-digit formula given by an analysis of the basic components tells some of the story, but not all. It needs to be supplemented by additional information in respect to three secondary components present in all individuals—the factor of *dysplasia* or disharmony; the factor of *gynandromorphy,* or the possession of characteristics typical of the opposite sex; and the factor of *texture,* whether fine or coarse, aesthetically pleasing or the reverse.

Dysplasia occurs when one region or feature of the body is more or less markedly in disharmony with the rest of the physique. We are all familiar, for example, with the big, barrel-chested man whose legs or arms taper off to an absurdly slender inefficiency. And who has not had to listen to the despairing complaints of the ladies to whom ironic nature has given an elegantly ectomorphic torso, with hips and thighs on the most amply endomorphic scale? Such disharmonies are significant and must be observed and measured, for they provide many clues to the explorers of human personality.

All persons exhibit characteristics of the opposite sex, some to a very slight degree, others more or less conspicuously. Again, the variations are significant. And the same is true of the factor of texture. Of two individuals having the same fundamental pattern one may be markedly fine-textured, the other markedly coarse-textured. The difference is one which cannot be neglected. That is why the basic formula is always supplemented by other descriptive qualifications expressing the amount of dysplasia, gynandromorphy, and fineness of texture observed in the individual under analysis.

III

So much for the varieties of physique and the methods by which they can be classified and measured. Inevitably two questions now propound themselves. First, is it possible for an individual to modify his basic physical pattern? Is there any system of dieting, hormone therapy, or exercise by means of which, say, a 1-1-7 can be transformed into a 7-1-1 or a 3-4-3? The answer would seem to be no. An individual's basic formula cannot be modified. True, an endomorph may be undernourished to the point of looking like a thing of skin and bones. But this particular thing of skin and bones will be measurably quite unlike the thing of skin and bones which is an undernourished, or even tolerably well nourished, ectomorph. Our fundamental physical pattern is something given and unalterable, something we can make the best of but can never hope to change.

The second question which naturally occurs to us is this: how closely is our fundamental psychological pattern related to our physical pattern? That such a relationship exists is a subject upon which every dramatist and storyteller, every observant student of men and women, has always been agreed. No writer in his senses would dream of associating the character of Pickwick with the body of Scrooge. And when the comic-strip artist wants to portray an athletic hero, he gives him the physique of Flash Gordon, not of Rosie's Beau. Further, men have always clearly recognized that individuals of one psycho-physical type tend to misunderstand and even dislike individuals whose basic psycho-physical pattern is different from their own. Here are the words which Shakespeare puts into the mouth of Julius Caesar:

> *Let me have men about me that are fat;*
> *Sleek-headed men and such as sleep o' nights.*
> *Yon Cassius has a lean and hungry look;*
> *He thinks too much; such men are dangerous.*

Translated into Sheldon's terminology, this means that the mesomorph is one kind of animal, the ectomorph another; and that their mutual incomprehension very often leads to suspicion and downright antipathy.

In a general way all this has been perfectly well known for the past several thousand years. But it has been known only in an intuitive, empirical way. No organized scientific thinking about the subject has been possible hitherto, because (in spite of some valuable work done in Europe and America) nobody had worked out a satisfactory classification system for describing temperamental differences.

Modern chemistry classifies matter in terms of a system of ninety-two first-order elements. In earlier times, men tried to do their thinking about matter in terms of only four elements—earth, air, fire, and water. But earth, air, and water are not first-order elements, but elaborate combinations of such elements; while fire is not an element at all, but something that happens to all kinds of matter under certain conditions of temperature. In terms of so inadequate a classification system it was impossible for scientific thought to go very far.

The problem of psychological analysis is identical in principle with that of the analysis of matter. The psychologist's business is to discover first-order elements, in terms of which the facts of human difference may be classified and measured. The failure of psychology—and it has conspicuously failed to become the fruitful Science of Man which ideally it should be—is due to the fact that it has done its analysis of human differences in terms of entities that were not first-order elements, but combinations of elements. Sheldon's great contribution to psychology consists in this: that he has isolated a number of genuine first-order elements of the basic psychological pattern which we call temperament, and has demonstrated their close correlation with the individual's basic physical pattern.

What follows is a summing up—necessarily rather crude and oversimplified—of the conclusions to which his research has led.

Endomorphy, mesomorphy, and ectomorphy are correlated very closely with specific patterns of temperament—endomorphy with the temperamental pattern to which Sheldon gives the name of *viscerotonia,* mesomorphy with *somatotonia,* and ectomorphy with *cerebrotonia.* Close and prolonged observation of many subjects, combined with an adaptation of the technique known as factor-analysis, resulted in the isolation of sixty descriptive or determinative traits—twenty for each of the main, first-order components of temperament. From these sixty, I select a smaller number of the more striking and easily recognizable traits.

Conspicuous among the elements of the viscerotonic pattern of temperament are relaxation in posture and movement, slow reaction, profound sleep, love of physical comfort, and love of food. With this love of food for its own sake goes a great love of eating in company, an almost religious feeling for the social meal as a kind of sacrament. Another conspicuous viscerotonic trait is love of polite ceremony, with which goes a love of company, together with indiscriminate amiability and marked dependence on, and desire for, the affection and approval of other people. The viscerotonic does not inhibit his emotions, but tends to give expression to them as they arise, so that nobody is ever in doubt as to what he feels.

Somatotonia, the temperament associated with the hard and powerful mesomorphic physique, is a patterning of very different elements. The somatotonic individual stands and moves in an assertive way, loves physical adventure, enjoys risk and loves to take a chance. He feels a strong need for physical exercise, which he hugely enjoys and often makes a fetish of, just as the viscerotonic enjoys and makes a fetish of eating. When in trouble, he seeks relief in physical action, whereas the viscerotonic turns in the same circumstances to people and the cerebrotonic retires, like a wounded animal, into solitude. The somatotonic is essentially energetic and quick to action. Procrastination is unknown to him; for he is neither excessively relaxed and comfort-loving, like the viscerotonic, nor inhibited and "sicklied o'er with the pale cast of thought," like the cerebrotonic. The social manner of the somatotonic is uninhibited and direct. The voice is normally unrestrained, and he coughs, laughs, snores and, when passion breaks through his veneer of civilization, speaks loudly. He is physically courageous in combat and enjoys every kind of competitive activity.

From a sociological point of view, the most significant of the somatotonic traits is the lust for power. The individual who is high in somatotonia loves to dominate, and since he is (when somatotonia is extreme) congenitally insensitive to other people's feelings, since he lacks the indiscriminate amiability and tolerance of viscerotonia and is devoid of cerebrotonic squeamishness, he can easily become a ruthless bully and tyrant. The somatotonic individual is always an extrovert in the sense that his attention is firmly fixed upon external reality, to such an extent that he is necessarily unaware of what is going on in the deeper levels of his own mind.

It should be noted that somatotonic extroversion is quite different from the extraversion of the viscerotonic; for while the latter is continually spilling the emotional beans and turning for support and affection to his fellows, the former tends to be insensitive to other people, feels little need to confide his emotions, and pursues his trampling course through external reality with an effortless callousness. For him the period of youth is the flower of life; he hates to grow old and often makes desperate efforts, even in advanced middle age, to live as actively as he did at twenty. The viscerotonic, on the other hand, is orientated toward childhood—his own and that of his offspring. He is the great family man. The cerebrotonic, on the other hand, looks forward, even in youth, to the tranquillity and the wisdom which, he hopes or imagines, are associated with old age.

With cerebrotonia we pass from the world of Flash Gordon to that of Hamlet. The cerebrotonic is the overalert, oversensitive introvert, who is more concerned with the inner universe of his own thoughts and feelings and imagination than with the external world to which, in their different ways, the viscerotonic and the somatotonic pay their primary attention and allegiance. In posture and movements, the cerebrotonic person is tense and restrained. His reactions may be unduly rapid and his physiological responses uncomfortably intense. It is the cerebrotonic who suffers from nervous indigestion, who gets stage fright and feels nauseated with mere shyness, who suffers from the various skin eruptions often associated with emotional disturbances.

Extreme cerebrotonics have none of the viscerotonic love of company; on the contrary, they have a passion for privacy, hate to make themselves conspicuous, and have none of the exhibitionistic tendencies displayed both by somatotonics and viscerotonics. In company they tend to be shy and unpredictably moody. When they are with strangers they fidget, their glances are shifting, sometimes furtive; their facial expression is apt to change frequently and rapidly. (For all these reasons no extreme cerebrotonic has ever been a good actor or actress.) Their normal manner is inhibited and restrained and when it comes to the expression of feelings they are outwardly so inhibited that viscerotonics suspect them of being heartless. (On their side, cerebrotonics tend to feel a strong repugnance for the viscerotonic's emotional gush and florid ceremoniousness.)

With self-conscious general restraint goes a marked restraint of voice and of all noise in general. To be compelled to raise the voice, as when speaking to the deaf, is, for the cerebrotonic, sheer torture. And it is also torture for him to have to endure noise made by other people. One of the best recipes for an unhappy marriage is to combine a high degree of noise-hating cerebrotonia with a high degree of loud-speaking, loud-laughing, loud-snoring and, in general, noise-making somatotonia. Cerebrotonics are extremely sensitive to pain, sleep poorly, and suffer from chronic fatigue; nevertheless they often live to a ripe old age—provided always that they do not permit themselves to be forced by the pressure of somatotonic public opinion into taking too much violent exercise. They do not easily form habits and are extremely bad at adapting themselves to an active routine, such as military life. They tend to look younger than their age and preserve a kind of youthful intensity of appearance far into middle life. Alcohol, which increases the relaxed amiability of viscerotonics and heightens the aggressiveness of the somatotonic, merely depresses the cerebrotonic and makes him feel thoroughly ill.

To determine the degree of viscerotonia, somatotonia, and cerebrotonia present in any given individual, Sheldon makes use of specially designed interviews, supplemented by a medical history and, where possible, by observation over a considerable period. The sixty traits are then assessed on a seven-point scale, in which *one* represents the minimum manifestation and *seven* the most extreme.

How do these temperamental assessments compare with the corresponding physical assessments of endomorphy, mesomorphy, and ectomorphy? The answer is that there is a high positive correlation. In some persons the correlation is complete, and the three-digit formula for temperament is identical with the three-digit formula for physique. More frequently, however, there is a slight deviation, as when a *four* in physical endomorphy is correlated with a *three* or a *five* in temperamental viscerotonia. Where there is a deviation, it is seldom of more than one point in any of the three components. Occasionally, however, the discrepancy between physique and temperament may be as much as two points; when this happens, the individual is under very considerable strain and has much difficulty in adapting himself to life. Deviations of more than two points do not seem to occur in the normal population, but are not uncommon among the insane.

The discrepancies between physique and temperament are probably due, in the main, to what the French philosopher, Jules de Gaultier, has called "bovarism." Mme. Bovary, the heroine of Flaubert's novel, was a young woman who consistently tried to be what in fact she was not. To a greater or less degree we are all bovarists, engaged from earliest childhood in the process of building up what the psychologists call a *persona,* to suit the tastes of the society surrounding us. The sort of *persona* we try to build up depends very largely upon our environment, physical and mental. Thus, in pioneering days, every Westerner tried to bovarize himself into the likeness of an Indian fighter. This was necessary, partly because people had to be tough, wary, and extroverted if they were to survive under frontier conditions, partly because local public opinion condemned and despised the introverted, the tender-minded, the aesthetes, and the abstract thinkers. Sheldon's researches show exactly how far bovarism can go without risk of compromising the individual's sanity; and the highly significant fact is that the borderline between normal and abnormal is reached pretty quickly. Hence the enormous psychological dangers inherent in such dogmatic and intolerant philosophies of life as Puritanism or Militarism—philosophies which exert an unrelenting pressure on those subjected to their influence, forcing a majority to try to change their fundamental psycho-physical constitution, to become something other than what they basically are.

Here a word of warning is necessary. Knowledge of an individual's constitutional make-up is not the same as complete knowledge of his character. Persons with the same temperamental formula may behave in very different ways and exhibit very different characters. Temperamentally similar individuals can make dissimilar uses of their constitutional endowments. It all depends on circumstances, upbringing, and the exercise of free will. Of three men with the same high degree of somatotonia one may become a suavely efficient executive, another a professional soldier of the explosive, blood-and-guts variety, and the third a ruthless gangster. But each in his own way will be aggressive and power-loving, daring and energetic, extroverted and insensitive to other people's feelings. And no amount of training, no effort of the will, will serve to transform them into relaxed and indiscriminately amiable viscerotonics, or into inhibited, hyperattentional, and introverted cerebrotonics.

IV

We are now in a position to consider a few of the things that constitutional analysis and appraisal can do for us. First and most important, it makes it possible for us to know who we and other people really are—of what psychological and bodily elements we and they are composed. Having determined the statics of physique and the closely related dynamics of temperament, we can begin to think in a genuinely intelligent and fruitful way about the environment and the individual's reaction to it. Moreover, to understand is to forgive; and when we realize that the people who are different from us did not get that way out of wickedness or perversity, when we understand that many of the profoundest of such differences are constitutional and that constitution cannot be changed, only made the best of, we may perhaps learn to be more tolerant, more intelligently charitable than we are at present.

Passing from the general to the particular, we find that constitutional appraisal has many important practical applications. In medicine, for example, the constitutional approach will undoubtedly prove helpful both in diagnosis and prognosis, in cure and prevention. To some extent, it is true, all physicians make use of the constitutional approach, and have been doing so for twenty-five centuries at least; but considering the importance of the subject, very little systematic research has been undertaken along these lines.

Education can never in the nature of things be one hundred per cent efficient. Teaching is an art and, in every field, bad artists vastly outnumber good ones. Great educators are almost as rare as great painters and composers. The best we can hope to do is to improve the system within which teachers of average ability do their work. In this improvement of the system, constitutional analysis is likely to prove extremely helpful. Ideally, there should be several educational systems, one adapted to each of the main varieties of human beings. Of the progressive education which in recent years has largely ousted from our schools the formal, suppressive type of training that was at one time universal, Dr. Sheldon makes the following significant remark: "This vigorous progressive education is actually as suppressive as was Christian education at its darkest. It suppresses the third instead of the second component. It is as suppressive to a young cerebrotonic to press him to join in the dance or in the swim, and to make noise and mix and socialize, as it is suppressive to a young somatotonic to make him sit still."

In the fields of history, sociology, and religion, the concepts of constitutional analysis may turn out to be extremely fruitful. From the constitutional point of view, civilization may be defined as a complex of devices for restraining extreme somatotonics from destroying society by their reckless aggressiveness. Of the great world religions one, Confucianism, has been pre-eminently viscerotonic; it has sought to tame somatotonia by inculcating ceremonious good manners, general amiability, and the cult of the family. Most of the other world religions—Buddhism, the higher forms of Hinduism, and, until recent years, Christianity—have been predominantly cerebrotonic. (The figure of Christ in traditional Christian art is almost always that of a man with a high degree of ectomorphy and therefore of cerebrotonia.) These cerebrotonic religions have tried to keep somatotonics in order by teaching them the virtues of self-restraint, humility, and sensitiveness. At the same time they tried to sublimate somatotonic aggressiveness, or to direct it into channels thought to be desirable, such as crusades and wars of religion. On their side, the somatotonics have often succeeded in modifying the cerebrotonic philosophies and institutions of the prevailing religion. For example, no cerebrotonic or viscerotonic would ever have thought of talking about the Church Militant.

v

In recent years there has been, in Sheldon's phrase, a great Somatotonic Revolution, directed against the dominance of cerebrotonic values as embodied in traditional Christianity. Thus, for traditional Christianity, it was axiomatic that the life of contemplation was superior to the life of action. Today the overwhelming majority even of Christians accept without question the primacy of action.

For traditional Christianity the important thing was the development of the right state of mind about the environment. Today, the important thing is not the state of the mind, but the state of the environment. We believe that men and women will be happy when they are surrounded with the right kind of gadgets. Our forefathers believed that they would be happy if they achieved what one of the greatest of Christian saints called "a holy indifference" to their material surroundings. The change is from a cerebrotonic point of view to the point of view of a somatotonic extrovert.

The Somatotonic Revolution has been greatly accelerated by technological advances. These have served to turn men's attention outward, and have encouraged the belief in a material apocalypse, a progress toward a mechanized New Jerusalem. Such beliefs have been carefully fostered by the writers of advertising copy—the most influential of all authors because they are the only ones whose works are read every day by every member of the population. In a world peopled by cerebrotonics, living an inward-turning life in a state of holy, or even unholy, indifference to their material surroundings, mass production would be doomed. That is why advertisers consistently support the Somatotonic Revolution.

It is hardly necessary to add that total war is another potent factor in creating and sustaining the Somatotonic Revolution. Nazi education, which was specifically education for war, aimed at encouraging the manifestations of somatotonia in those most richly endowed with it, and making the rest of the population feel ashamed of its tendencies towards relaxed amiability or restrained and inward-looking sensitivity. During the war the enemies of Nazism have had to borrow from the Nazi educational philosophy. All over the world millions of young men and even young women are now being educated to be tough, and to admire toughness beyond every other moral quality. Never has somatotonia been so widely or so systematically encouraged as at the present time. Indeed, most societies in the past systematically discouraged somatotonia, because they did not wish to be destroyed by the unrestrained aggressiveness of their most active minority. What will be the result of the present worldwide reversal of what hitherto has been an almost universal social policy? Time alone will show.

The Secret of Life

by LOREN C. EISELEY

OCTOBER, 1953

Loren C. Eiseley is known to the world of science as chairman of the Department of Anthropology at the University of Pennsylvania and curator of Early Man in the University Museum. But to the reading public he is known as a writer of rare ability, with an owl-eyed wonder about life in all its manifestations. A native of Nebraska, he has roamed widely over the world digging for the bones of our early ancestors. His most recent book is Darwin's Century.

I am middle-aged now, but in the autumn I always seek for it again hopefully. On some day when the leaves are red, or fallen, and just after the birds are gone, I put on my hat and an old jacket, reject the protests of my wife that I will catch cold, and start my search. I go carefully down the apartment steps and climb, instead of jump, over the wall. A bit further I reach an unkempt field full of brown stalks and emptied seed pods.

By the time I get to the wood I am carrying all manner of seeds hooked in my coat or piercing my socks or sticking by ingenious devices to my shoestrings. I let them ride. After all, who am I to contend against such ingenuity? It is obvious that nature, or some part of it in the shape of these seeds, has intentions beyond this field and has made plans to travel with me.

We, the seeds and I, climb another wall together and sit down to rest, while I consider the best way to search for the secret of life. The seeds remain very quiet and some slip off into the crevices of the rock. A woolly bear caterpillar hurries across a ledge, going late to some tremendous transformation, but about this he knows as little as I.

It is not an auspicious beginning. The things alive do not know the secret, and there may be those who would doubt the wisdom of coming out among discarded husks in the dead year to pursue such questions.

They might say the proper time is spring when one can consult the water rats or listen to little chirps under the stones. Of late years, however, I have come to suspect that the mystery may just as well be solved in a carved and intricate seed case out of which the life has flown, as in the seed itself.

In autumn one is not confused by activity and green leaves. The underlying apparatus, the hooks, needles, stalks, wires, suction cups, thin pipes, and iridescent bladders are all exposed in a gigantic dissection. These are the essentials. Do not be deceived simply because the life has flown out of them. It will return, but in the meantime there is an unparalleled opportunity to examine in sharp and beautiful angularity the shape of life without its disturbing muddle of juices and leaves. As I grow older and conserve my efforts, I shall give this season my final and undivided attention. I shall be found puzzling over the saw teeth on the desiccated leg of a dead grasshopper or standing bemused in a brown sea of rusty stems. Somewhere in this discarded machinery may lie the key to the secret. I shall not let it escape through lack of diligence or through fear of the smiles of people in high windows. I am sure now that life is not what it is purported to be and that nature, in the canny words of a Scotch theologue, "is not as natural as it looks." I have learned this in a small suburban field, after a good many years spent in much wilder places upon far less fantastic quests.

II

The notion that mice can be generated spontaneously from bundles of old clothes is so delightfully whimsical that it is easy to see why men were loath to abandon it. One could accept such accidents in a topsy-turvy universe without trying to decide what transformation of buckles into bones and shoe buttons into eyes had taken place. One could take life as a kind of fantastic magic and not blink too obviously when it appeared, beady-eyed and bustling, under the laundry in the back room.

It was only with the rise of modern biology and the discovery that the trail of life led backward toward infinitesimal beginnings in primordial sloughs, that men began the serious dissection and analysis of the cell. Darwin, in one of his less guarded moments, had spoken hopefully of the possibility that life had emerged from inorganic matter in some "warm little pond." From that day to this, biologists have poured, analyzed, minced, and shredded recalcitrant protoplasm in a fruitless attempt to create life from nonliving matter. It seemed inevitable, if we could trade life down through simpler and simpler stages, that we must finally arrive at the point where, under the proper chemical conditions, the mysterious borderline that bounds the inanimate must be crossed. It seemed clear that life was a material manifestation. Somewhere, somehow, sometime, in the mysterious chemistry of carbon, the long march toward the talking animal had begun.

A hundred years ago men spoke optimistically about solving the secret, or at the very least they thought the next generation would be in a position to do so. Periodically there were claims that the emergence of life from matter had been observed, but in every case the observer proved to be self-deluded. It became obvious that the secret of life was not to be had by a little casual experimentation, and that life in today's terms appeared to arise only through the medium of pre-existing life. Yet if science was not to be embarrassed by some kind of mind-matter dualism and a complete and irrational break between life and the world of inorganic matter, the emergence of life had, in some way, to be accounted for. Nevertheless, as the years passed, the secret remained locked in its living jelly, in spite of larger microscopes and more formidable means of dissection. As a matter of fact the mystery was heightened because all this intensified effort revealed that even the supposedly simple amoeba was already a complex, self-operating chemical factory. The notion that he was a simple blob, the discovery of whose chemical composition would enable us instantly to set the life process in operation, turned out to be, at best, a monstrous caricature of the truth.

With the failure of these many efforts science was left in the half-embarrassing position of having to postulate theories of living origins which it could not demonstrate. After having chided the theologist for his reliance on myth and miracle, science found itself in the unenviable position of having to create a mythology of its own; namely, the assumption that what, after long effort, could not be proved to take place today had, in truth, taken place in the primeval past.

My use of the term *mythology* is perhaps a little harsh. One does occasionally observe, however, a tendency for the beginning zoological textbook to take the unwary reader by a hop, skip, and jump from the little steaming pond or the beneficent chemical crucible of the sea, into the lower world of life with such sureness and rapidity that it is easy to assume that there is no mystery about this matter at all, or, if there is, that it is a very little one.

This attitude has indeed been sharply criticized by the distinguished British biologist Woodger, who remarked some years ago: "Unstable organic compounds and chlorophyll corpuscles do not persist or come into existence in nature on their own account at the present day, and consequently it is necessary to postulate that conditions were once such that this did happen although and in spite of the fact that our knowledge of nature does not give us any warrant for making such a supposition. . . . It is simple dogmatism—asserting that what you want to believe did in fact happen."

Yet unless we are to turn to supernatural explanations or reinvoke a dualism which is scientifically dubious, we are forced inevitably toward only two possible explanations of life on this planet. One of these, although not entirely disproved, is most certainly out of fashion and surrounded with greater obstacles to its acceptance than at the time it was formulated. I refer, of course, to the suggestion of Lord Kelvin and Svante Arrhenius that life did not arise on this planet, but was wafted here through the depths of space. Microscopic spores, it was contended, have great resistance to extremes of cold and might have come into our atmosphere with meteoric dust, or have been driven across the earth's orbit by light pressure. In this view, once the seed was "planted" in soil congenial to its development, it then proceeded to elaborate, evolve, and adjust until the higher organisms had emerged.

This theory has a certain attraction as a way out of an embarrassing dilemma, but it suffers from the defect of explaining nothing, even if it should prove true. It does not elucidate the nature of life. It simply removes the inconvenient problem of origins to far-off spaces or worlds into which we will never penetrate. Since life makes use of the chemical compounds of this earth it would seem better to proceed until incontrovertible evidence to the contrary is obtained, on the assumption that life has actually arisen upon this planet. The now widely accepted view that the entire universe in its present state is limited in time, and the apparently dangerously lethal nature of unscreened solar radiation are both obstacles which greatly lessen the likelihood that life has come to us across the infinite wastes of space. Once more, therefore, we are forced to examine our remaining notion that life is not coterminous with matter, but has arisen from it.

If the single-celled protozoans that riot in roadside pools are not the simplest forms of life, if, as we know today, these creatures are already highly adapted and really complex, though minute beings, then where are we to turn in the search for something simple enough to suggest the greatest missing link of all—the link between living and "dead" matter? It is this problem that keeps me wandering fruitlessly in pastures and weed thickets even though I know this is an old-fashioned naturalist's approach, and that busy men in laboratories have little patience with my scufflings of autumn leaves, or attempts to question beetles in decaying bark. Besides, many of these men are now fascinated by the crystalline viruses and have turned that remarkable instrument, the electron microscope, upon strange molecular "beings" never previously seen by man. Some are satisfied with this glimpse below the cell and find the virus a halfway station on the road to life. Perhaps it is, but as I wander about in the thin mist that is beginning to filter among these decaying stems and ruined spider webs, a kind of disconsolate uncertainty has taken hold of me.

I have come to suspect that this long descent down the ladder of life, beautiful and instructive though it may be, will not lead us to the final secret. In fact I have ceased to believe in the final brew or the ultimate chemical. There is, I know, a kind of heresy, a shocking negation of our confidence in blue steel microtomes and men in white in making such a statement. I would not be understood to speak ill of scientific effort, for in simple truth I would not be alive today except for the microscopes and the blue steel. It is only that somewhere among these seeds and beetle shells and abandoned grasshopper legs I find something that is not accounted for very clearly in the dissections to the ultimate virus or crystal or protein particle. Even if the secret is contained in these things, in other words, I do not think it will yield to the kind of analysis our science is capable of making.

Imagine, for a moment, that you have drunk from a magician's goblet. Reverse the irreversible stream of time. Go down the dark stair-well out of which the race has ascended. Find yourself at last on the bottom-most steps of time, slipping, sliding, and wallowing by scale and fin down into the muck and ooze out of which you arose. Pass by grunts and voiceless hissings below the last tree ferns. Eyeless and earless, float in the primal waters, sense sunlight you cannot see and stretch absorbing tentacles toward vague tastes that float in water. Still in your formless shiftings, the *you* remains, the sliding particles, the juices, the transformations are working in an exquisitely patterned rhythm which has no other purpose than your preservation, you, the entity, the ameboid being whose substance contains the unfathomable future. Even so does every man come upward from the waters of his birth.

Yet, if at any moment the magician bending over you should cry, "Speak! tell us of that road!" you could not: the sensations are yours but not—and this is one of the great mysteries—the power over the body. You cannot describe how the body you inhabit functions, nor picture nor control the flights and spinnings, the dance of the molecules that compose it, nor why they chose to dance into that particular pattern which is you, nor, again, why up the long stairway of the eons they dance from one shape to another. It is for this reason that I am no longer interested in final particles. Follow them as you will, pursue them until they become nameless protein crystals replicating on the verge of life. Use all the great powers of the mind and pass backward until you hang with the dire faces of the conquerors in the hydrogen cloud from which the sun was born. You will then have performed the ultimate dissection that our analytic age demands, but the cloud will still veil the secret and, if not the cloud, then the nothingness into which it now appears the cloud, in its turn, may be dissolved. The secret, if one may paraphrase a savage vocabulary, lies in the egg of night.

Only along the edges of this field after the frost there are little whispers of it. Once even on a memorable autumn afternoon I discovered a sunning black snake brooding among the leaves like the very simulacrum of old night. He slid unhurriedly away, carrying his version of the secret with him in such a glittering menace of scales, that I was abashed and could only follow admiringly from a little distance. I observed him well, however, and am sure he carried his share of the common mystery into the stones of my neighbor's wall, and is sleeping endlessly on in the winter darkness with one great coil locked around that glistening head. He is guarding a strange, reptilian darkness which is not night nor nothingness, but has, instead, its momentary vision of mouse bones or a bird's egg, in the soft rising and ebbing of the tides of life. The snake has diverted me, however. It was the dissection of a field that was to occupy us—a dissection in search of secrets—a dissection such as a probing and inquisitive age demands.

III

Every so often one encounters articles in leading magazines with titles such as "The Spark of Life," "The Secret of Life," "New Hormone Key to Life," or other similar optimistic proclamations. Only yesterday, for example, I discovered in the *New York Times* a headline announcing: "Scientist Predicts Creation of Life in Laboratory." The Moscow-dated dispatch announced that Academician Olga Lepeshinskaya had predicted that "in the not too distant future, Soviet scientists would create life." "The time is not far off," warns the formidable Madame Olga, "when we shall be able to obtain the vital substance artificially." She said it with such vigor that I had about the same reaction as I do to announcements about atomic bombs. In fact I half-started up to latch the door before an invading tide of Russian protoplasm flowed in upon me.

What finally enabled me to regain my shaken confidence was the recollection that these pronouncements have been going on for well over a century. Just now the Russian scientists show a particular tendency to issue such blasts—committed politically, as they are, to an uncompromising materialism and the boastfulness of very young science. Furthermore, Madame Lepeshinskaya's remarks as reported in the press had a curiously old-fashioned flavor about them. The protoplasm she referred to sounded amazingly like the outmoded *Urschleim* or *Urplasson* of Haeckel—simplified mucoid slimes no longer taken very seriously. American versions—and one must remember they are often journalistic interpretations of scientists' studies rather than direct quotations from the scientists themselves—are more apt to fall into another pattern. Someone has found a new chemical, vitamin, or similar necessary ingredient without which life will not flourish. By the time this reaches the more sensational press it may have become the "secret of life." The only thing the inexperienced reader may not comprehend is the fact that no one of these items, even the most recently discovered, is *the* secret. Instead, the substance is probably a part, a very small part, of a larger enigma which is well nigh as inscrutable as it ever was. If anything, the growing list of catalysts, hormones, plasma genes, and other hobgoblins involved in the work of life only serves to underline the enormous complexity of the secret. "To grasp in detail," says the German biologist von Bertalanffy, "the physico-chemical organization of the simplest cell is far beyond our capacity."

It is not, you understand, disrespect for the laudable and persistent patience of these dedicated scientists happily lost in their maze of pipettes, smells, and gas flames, that has led me into this runaway excursion to the wood. It is rather the loneliness of a man who knows he will not live to see the mystery solved, and who, furthermore, has come to believe that it will not be solved when the first humanly synthesized particle begins—if it ever does—to multiply itself in some unknown solution.

It is really a matter, I suppose, of the kind of questions one asks oneself. Some day we may be able to say with assurance, "We came from such and such a protein particle, possessing the powers of organizing in a manner leading under certain circumstances to that complex entity known as the cell, and from the cell by various steps onward, to multiple cell formation." I mean we may be able to say all this with great surety and elaboration of detail, but it is not the answer to the grasshopper's leg, brown and black and saw-toothed here in my hand, nor the answer to the seeds still clinging tenaciously to my coat, nor to this field, nor to the subtle essences of memory, delight, and wistfulness moving among the thin wires of my brain.

I suppose that in the forty-five years of my existence every atom, every molecule that composes me has changed its position or danced away and beyond to become part of other things. New molecules have come from the grass and the bodies of animals to be part of me a little while, yet in this spinning, light and airy if we could but see it, as the dance of a midge swarm in a shaft of sunlight, my memories hold, and the loved face of twenty years ago is before me still. Nor is that face, nor all my years, caught cellularly as in some cold precise photographic pattern, some gross, mechanical reproduction of the past. My memory holds the past and yet paradoxically knows, at the same time, that the past is gone and will never come again. It cherishes dead faces and silenced voices, yes, and lost evenings of childhood. In some odd, nonspatial way it contains houses and rooms that have been torn timber from timber and brick from brick. These have a greater permanence in that midge dance which contains them than ever they had in the world of reality. It is for this reason that Academician Olga Lepeshinskaya has not answered the kind of questions one may ask in an open field.

If the day comes when the slime of the laboratory for the first time crawls under man's direction, we shall have great need of humbleness. It will be difficult for us to believe, in our pride of achievement, that the secret of life has slipped through our fingers and eludes us still. We will list all the chemicals and the reactions. The men who have become gods will pose austerely before the popping flashbulbs of news photographers, and there will be few to consider—so deep is the mind-set of an age—whether the desire to link life to matter may not have blinded us to the more remarkable characteristics of both.

As for me, if I am still around on that day, I intend to put on my old hat and climb over the wall as usual. I shall see strange mechanisms lying as they lie here now, in the autumn rain, strange pipes that transported the substance of life, the intricate seed case out of which the life has flown. I shall observe no thing green, no delicate transpirations of leaves, nor subtle comings and goings of vapor. The little sunlit factories of the chloroplasts will have dissolved away into common earth.

Beautiful, angular, and bare the machinery of life will lie exposed, as it now is, to my view. There will be the thin, blue skeleton of a hare tumbled in a little heap, and crouching over it I will marvel, as I marvel now, at the wonderful correlation of parts, the perfect adaptation to purpose, the individually vanished and yet persisting pattern which is now hopping on some other hill. I will wonder, as always, in what manner "particles" pursue such devious plans and symmetries. I will ask once more in what way it is managed, that the simple dust takes on a history and begins to weave these unique and never recurring apparitions in the stream of time. I shall wonder what strange forces at the heart of matter regulate the tiny beating of a rabbit's heart or the dim dream that builds a milkweed pod.

It is said by men who know about these things that the smallest living cell probably contains over a quarter of a million protein molecules engaged in the multitudinous co-ordinated activities which made up the phenomenon of life. At the instant of death, whether to man or microbe, that ordered, incredible spinning passes away in an almost furious haste of those same particles to get themselves back into the chaotic, unplanned earth.

I do not think, if someone finally twists the key successfully in the tiniest and most humble house of life, that many of these questions will be answered, nor that the dark forces which create lights in the deep sea and living batteries in the waters of tropical swamps, nor the dread cycles of parasites, nor the most noble workings of the human brain, will be much if at all revealed. Rather, I would say that if "dead" matter has reared up this curious landscape of fiddling crickets, song sparrows, and wondering men, it must be plain even to the most devoted materialist, that the matter of which he speaks contains amazing, if not dreadful powers, and may not impossibly be, as Hardy said, "but one mask of many worn by the Great Face behind."

The Origins of Psychoanalysis — Personal Letters of Sigmund Freud

Translated by
ERIC MOSBACHER and JAMES STRACHEY

APRIL–MAY, 1954

Sigmund Freud's theory and technique of psychoanalysis have profoundly influenced Western man's thinking about himself. Freud first began to formulate this theory and develop this technique between 1887 and 1902, when he was from thirty-one to forty-five years old. During this period, his closest confidant was Wilhelm Fliess, a Berlin nose-and-throat specialist and biologist. Here are some of Freud's letters to Fliess, telling about his struggle and discovery. In the interest of space, the opening and closing salutations of the individual letters have been cut. While the first letters are addressed to "My dear Dr. Fliess" and signed "Dr. Sigmund Freud," this rapidly gives way to "Dear Wilhelm" from "Sigm."

MY DEAR DR. FLIESS,

Vienna, August 29, 1888

. . . I ADMIT unreservedly that you are right in what you say, and yet I cannot do as you suggest. To go into general practice instead of specializing, to use all the resources of general medicine and treat the patient as a whole, is certainly the only way which promises real satisfaction and material success; but for me it is too late for that now. I have not learned enough for general practice; there is a gap in my medical equipment which it would be hard to close. I was able to learn just enough to become a neuropathologist. And now I lack, not youth, but time and freedom to catch up. Last winter I was very busy, and that left me with just enough to live on with my large family, but with no time over for study. During the summer things were very bad; this left me with leisure enough, but with worries that sapped the inclination. Apart from that, the habit of research, to which I have sacrificed a good deal, dissatisfaction with what the student is offered, the need to go into detail and exercise the critical faculty, is an obstacle to the study of textbooks.

Vienna, April 19, 1894

AFTER YOUR kind letter I shall not restrain myself and spare you any longer, and I feel I have a right to write to you about my health. . . .

As everyone must have someone to be influenced by, to escape his own criticism, from that time on (three weeks ago today) I have had nothing lit between my lips, and I can now actually watch others smoking without envying them, and can conceive of life and work without it. I have only just reached this point, and the misery of abstinence has been unexpectedly great, but that is obvious, after all. . . .

Vienna, May 21, 1894

. . . I AM PRETTY well alone here in tackling the neuroses. They rather regard me as a monomaniac, while I have the distinct feeling that I have touched on one of the great secrets of nature. There is something comic about the incongruity between one's own and other people's estimation of one's work. Look at my book on the diplegias, which I knocked together almost casually, with a minimum of interest and effort. It has been a huge success. . . . But for the really good things, like the "Aphasia," the "Obsessional Ideas," which threaten to appear shortly, and the coming aetiology and theory of the neuroses, I can expect no more than a respectable flop. . . .

Vienna, June 12, 1895

. . . The construction of the "Psychology" looks as if it is going to come off, which would give me great cause for rejoicing. Of course I cannot say for certain yet. Saying anything now would be like sending a six-months female embryo to a ball. . . .

I have started smoking again, because I still missed it (after fourteen months' abstinence), and because I must treat that mind of mine decently, or the fellow will not work for me. I am demanding a great deal of him. Most of the time the burden is superhuman.

Vienna, October 8, 1895

. . . I am enclosing all sorts of things for you today, including two notebooks of mine. . . .

I wrote them in one breath since my return, and they contain little that will be new to you. I have a third notebook, dealing with the psychopathology of repression, which I am not ready to send you yet, because it only takes the subject to a certain point. From that point I had to start from scratch again, and I have been alternately proud and happy and abashed and miserable, until now, after an excess of mental torment, I just apathetically tell myself that it doesn't hang together yet and perhaps never will. What does not hang together yet isn't the mechanism—I could be patient about that—but the explanation of repression, clinical knowledge of which has incidentally made great strides.

Note that among other things I suspect the following: that hysteria is conditioned by a primary sexual experience (before puberty) accompanied by revulsion and fright; and that obsessional neurosis is conditioned by the same accompanied by pleasure.

But the mechanical explanation is not coming off, and I am inclined to listen to the still, small voice which tells me that my explanation will not do.

Missing you and your company came on rather late this time, but I felt it acutely. I am alone with my mind, in which so much is stirring, and for the time being stirring itself into a muddle. I am finding out the most interesting things, which I cannot talk about and for lack of leisure cannot get down on paper. I do not want to read, because it stirs up too many thoughts and stints me of the satisfaction of discovery. In short, I am a wretched recluse. . . .

Vienna, October 16, 1895

. . . I AM STILL all at sixes and sevens. I am practically sure I have
solved the riddle of hysteria and obsessional neurosis with the formula
of infantile sexual shock and sexual pleasure, and I am just as sure
that both neuroses are radically curable now—not just the individual
symptoms but the neurotic disposition itself. That gives me a kind of
flat satisfaction—at having lived some forty years not quite in vain;
but it is not real satisfaction, because the psychological gaps in the
new knowledge demand the whole of my interest.

I have entirely given up smoking again, so as not to have to reproach myself for my bad pulse, and to be rid of the horrid struggle
with the craving for a fourth or fifth cigar; better to struggle with the
craving for the first. Abstinence is probably another thing that is not
very conducive to mental satisfaction. . . .

Vienna, October 20, 1895

. . . I WAS OF COURSE tremendously pleased with your opinion of
the solution of hysteria and obsessional neurosis. Now listen to this.
One strenuous night last week, when I was in the stage of painful discomfort in which my brain works best, the barriers suddenly lifted,
the veils dropped, and it was possible to see from the details of neurosis all the way to the very conditioning of consciousness. Everything
fell into place, the cogs meshed, the thing really seemed to be a
machine which in a moment would run of itself. . . .

If I had waited a fortnight before setting it all down for you it
would have been so much clearer. But it was only in the process of
setting it down that I cleared it up for myself. . . .

You will not have any objection to my calling my next son Wilhelm!
If *he* turns out to be a daughter, *she* will be called Anna.

Vienna, November 8, 1895

YOUR LONG LETTER is a sign that you are well. May both the cause
and symptom persevere. As for my own health (so that I do not forget
to mention it and shall not have to mention myself again), I have been
incomparably better for the last fortnight. I was not able to maintain
complete abstinence [from smoking], for which my present burden of
theoretical and practical worries the increase in psychical hyperaesthesia was insupportable. . . .

Sunday, December 8, 1895

. . . WE LIKE TO THINK that the baby has brought a doubling of my practice. I have trouble in fitting everything in, and I can pick and choose and begin to dictate my fees. I am getting confident in the diagnosis and treatment of the two neuroses, and I think the town is gradually beginning to realize that something is to be had from me.

Have I already written and told you that obsessional ideas are invariably *self-reproaches,* while at the root of hysteria there is always *conflict* (sexual pleasure versus an accompanying unpleasure)? That is a new formula for expressing the clinical explanation. I have some beautiful mixed cases of the two neuroses at present, and hope to draw closer conclusions from them about the essential mechanisms involved. . . .

Vienna, March 16, 1896

. . . I HAVE A CASE of dipsomania I want to tell you about at our next meeting; it resolved itself very obviously in accordance with my theories. I keep on coming back to psychology; it is a compulsion from which I cannot escape. What I have is neither a million nor yet a penny, but a lump of ore containing an unknown amount of precious metal. On the whole I am satisfied with my progress, but I am met with hostility and live in such isolation that one might suppose I had discovered the greatest truths. . . .

June 30, 1896

. . . MY AGED FATHER (he is eighty-one) is in Baden in a very shaky condition with heart attacks, bladder weakness, and so on. Waiting for news, going to see him, etc., have been the only things to count in the last fortnight. In the circumstances I cannot undertake any plans that involve a day's journey from Vienna. My father's a tough fellow, and I hope he may yet be granted a spell of good health; if so I shall turn it to account for our meeting. . . .

October 26, 1896

. . . THE OLD MAN died on the night of the twenty-third, and we buried him yesterday. He bore himself bravely up to the end, like the remarkable man he was. He must have had meningeal hemorrhage at the last; there were stuporous attacks and inexplicable temperatures, hyperaesthesia, and muscular spasms, from which he would awake without temperature. The last attack ended with an edema of the lungs, and he had an easy death. It all happened in my critical period, and I am really down over it. . . .

Vienna, November 2, 1896

I FIND IT so difficult to put pen to paper at the moment that I have even put off writing to you to thank you for the moving things you said in your letter. By one of the obscure routes behind the official consciousness, the old man's death affected me deeply. I valued him highly and understood him very well indeed, and with his peculiar mixture of deep wisdom and imaginative light-heartedness he meant a great deal in my life. By the time he died his life had long been over, but at a death the whole past stirs within one.

I feel now as if I had been torn up by the roots. . . .

I recently heard the first reaction to my incursion into psychiatry. "Gruesome, horrible, old wives' psychiatry" were some of the things that were said. That was Rieger in Würzburg. I was extremely amused. And of all things about paranoia, which has become so clear!

I must tell you about a very pretty dream I had on the night after the funeral. I found myself in a shop where there was a notice up saying:

You are requested
to shut your eyes.

I recognized the place as the barber's to which I go every day. On the day of the funeral I was kept waiting, and therefore arrived at the house of mourning rather late. The family were displeased with me, because I had arranged for the funeral to be quiet and simple, which they later agreed was the best thing. They also took my lateness in rather bad part. The phrase on the notice board has a double meaning. It means "one should do one's duty toward the dead" in two senses— an apology, as though I had not done my duty and my conduct needed overlooking, and the actual duty itself. The dream was thus an outlet for the feeling of self-reproach which a death generally leaves among the survivors. . . .

January 24, 1897

. . . IN THE EXACTING standards insisted on by hysterics in love, in their humility before the loved one, or in their inability to marry because of unattainable ideals, I recognize the influence of the father-figure. The cause is, of course, the immense elevation from which the father condescends to the child's level. In paranoia compare the combination of megalomania with the creation of myths about the child's true parentage. . . .

Being absorbed in all this, I am left cold by the news that the board of professors have proposed my younger colleague in my specialty for the title of professor, thus passing me over, if the news is true. It leaves me quite cold, but perhaps it will hasten my final breach with the university. . . .

May 16, 1897

. . . No MATTER WHAT I start with, I always find myself back again with the neuroses and the psychical apparatus. It is not because of indifference to personal or other matters that I never write about anything else. Inside me there is a seething ferment, and I am only waiting for the next surge forward. I cannot bring myself to do the provisional summing up of the present position which you want; I think that what is stopping me is an obscure feeling that very shortly something vital will have to be added. On the other hand I have felt impelled to start writing about dreams, with which I feel on firm ground, and which you feel I ought to write about in any case. I was interrupted straight away by having hurriedly to prepare for the press an abstract of all my publications. The vote is going to take place any day. Now I have finished and can think about dreams again. I've been looking into the literature on the subject, and feel like the Celtic imp: "How glad I am that no man's eyes have pierced the veil of Puck's disguise." No one has the slightest suspicion that dreams are not non-sense but wish-fulfillment. . . .

A few days after my return a proud ship of mine ran aground. My banker, who had got furthest in his analysis, made off at a critical point, just before he should have produced the final scenes. This has no doubt damaged me materially also, and it has shown me that I do not yet know all the factors that are at work. But, refreshed as I was, I took it in my stride and told myself that obviously I must wait still longer for a complete cure. It must be possible, and it shall be done. . . .

Aussee, August 14, 1897

. . . AFTER A SPELL of good spirits here I am now having a fit of gloom. The chief patient I am busy with is myself. My little hysteria, which was much intensified by work, has yielded one stage further. The rest still sticks. That is the first reason for my mood. This analysis is harder than any other. It is also the thing that paralyzes the power of writing down and communicating what so far I have learned.

But I believe it has got to be done and is a necessary stage in my work.

Vienna, October 3, 1897

. . . OUTWARDLY VERY LITTLE is happening to me, but inside me something very interesting is happening. For the last four days my self-analysis, which I regard as indispensable for clearing up the whole problem, has been making progress in dreams and yielding the most valuable conclusions and evidence. At certain points I have the impression of having come to the end, and so far I have always known where the next night of dreams would continue. To describe it in writing is more difficult than anything else, and besides it is far too extensive. I can only say that in my case my father played no active role, though I certainly projected onto him an analogy from myself; that my "primary originator" (of neurosis) was [my childhood nurse] an ugly, elderly, but clever woman who told me a great deal about God and hell, and gave me a high opinion of my own capacities; that later (between the ages of two and two-and-a-half) libido toward my mother was aroused; the occasion must have been the journey with her from Leipzig to Vienna, during which we spent a night together and I must have had the opportunity of seeing her undressed (you have long since drawn the conclusions from this for your own son, as a remark of yours revealed); and that I welcomed my one-year younger brother (who died within a few months) with ill wishes and real infantile jealousy, and that his death left the germ of guilt in me.

I have long known that my companion in crime between the ages of one and two was a nephew of mine who is a year older than I am and now lives in Manchester; he visited us in Vienna when I was fourteen. We seem occasionally to have treated my niece, who was a year younger, shockingly. My nephew and younger brother determined, not only the neurotic side of all my friendships, but also their depth. My anxiety over travel you have seen yourself in full bloom.

I still have not got to the scenes which lie at the bottom of all this. . . . I cannot give you any idea of the intellectual beauty of the work.

The children arrive early tomorrow. The practice is still very bad. I fear that if it gets still worse it may interfere with my self-analysis. My recognition that difficulties of treatment derive from the fact that in the last resort one is laying bare the patient's evil inclinations, his will to remain ill, is growing stronger and clearer. We shall see.

October 15, 1897

MY SELF-ANALYSIS is the most important thing I have in hand, and promises to be of the greatest value to me, when it is finished. When I was in the very midst of it, it suddenly broke down for three days, and I had the feeling of inner binding about which my patients complain much, and I was inconsolable. . . .

I have found love of the mother and jealousy of the father in my own case too, and now believe it to be a general phenomenon of early childhood, even if it does not always occur so early as in children who have been made hysterics. (Similarly with the "romanticization of origins" in the case of paranoiacs—heroes, founders of religion.) If that is the case, the gripping power of *Oedipus Rex,* in spite of all the rational objections to the inexorable fate that the story presupposes, becomes intelligible, and one can understand why later fate dramas were such failures. Our feelings rise against any arbitrary, individual fate such as shown in the *Ahnfrau,** etc., but the Greek myth seizes on a compulsion which everyone recognizes because he has felt traces of it in himself. Every member of the audience was once a budding Oedipus in phantasy, and this dream-fulfillment played out in reality causes everyone to recoil in horror, with the full measure of repression which separates his infantile from his present state.

The idea has passed through my head that the same thing may lie at the root of *Hamlet.* I am not thinking of Shakespeare's conscious intentions, but supposing rather that he was impelled to write it by a real event because his own unconscious understood that of his hero. How can one explain the hysteric Hamlet's phrase, "So conscience doth make cowards of us all," and his hesitation to avenge his father by killing his uncle, when he himself so casually sends his courtiers to their death and despatches Laertes so quickly? How better than by the torment roused in him by the obscure memory that he himself had meditated the same deed against his father because of passion for his

* The title of a play by Grillparzer.

mother—"use every man after his dessert, and who should 'scape whipping?" His conscience is his unconscious feeling of guilt. And are not his sexual coldness when talking to Ophelia, his rejection of the instinct to beget children, and finally his transference of the deed from his father to Ophelia, typically hysterical? And does he not finally succeed, in just the same remarkable way as my hysterics do, in bringing down his punishment on himself and suffering the same fate as his father, being poisoned by the same rival?

My interest has been so exclusively concentrated on the analysis that I have not yet set about trying to answer the question whether, instead of my hypothesis that repression always proceeds from the female side and is directed against the male, the converse may hold good, as you suggested. But some time I shall tackle it. . . .

Vienna, November 14, 1897

"IT WAS November 12, 1897; the sun was in the eastern quarter, and Mercury and Venus in conjunction—" no, birth announcements do not begin like that any more. It was on November 12, a day under the influence of a left-sided migraine, on the afternoon of which Martin sat down to write a new poem and on the evening of which Oli lost his second tooth, when, after the terrible pangs of the last few weeks, a new piece of knowledge was born to me. Truth to tell, it was not entirely new; it had repeatedly shown and then withdrawn itself again, but this time it remained and saw the light of day. . . .

I have often suspected that something organic played a part in repression; I have told you before that it is a question of the attitude adopted to former sexual zones, and I added that I had been pleased to come across the same idea in Moll. Privately, I would not concede priority in the idea to anyone; in my case the suggestion was linked to the changed part played by sensations of smell; upright carriage was adopted, the nose was raised from the ground, and at the same time a number of what had formerly been interesting sensations connected with the earth became repellent—by a process of which I am still ignorant. ("He turns up his nose" = "he regards himself as something particularly noble.") Now, the zones which no longer produce a release of sexuality in normal and mature human beings must be the regions of the anus and of the mouth and throat. This is to be understood in two senses: first, that the appearance and idea of these zones no longer produce any exciting effect, and secondly, that the internal sensations arising from them no longer make any contribution to the libido like the sexual organs proper. In animals these sexual zones retain their power in both respects; where they do so in human beings, the result is perversion. We must suppose that in infancy sexual release is not so much localized as it becomes later, so that zones which are later abandoned (and possibly the whole surface of the body) stimulate to some extent the production of something that is analogous to the later release of sexuality. . . . Now, the release of sexuality (as you know, I have in mind a secretion, which we correctly perceive as an internal state of libido) comes about not only (1) through peripheral stimulation of the sexual organs and (2) through internal excitations arising from those organs, but also (3) from ideas (from memory traces)—that is to say, by deferred action. . . . Deferred action of this kind, however, operates also in connection with memories of excitation arising from the *abandoned* sexual zones. The consequence, however, is not a release of libido but a release of unpleasure, an internal sensation analogous to the disgust felt when an object is concerned.

To put it crudely, the current memory stinks just as an actual object may stink; and just as we turn away our sense organ (the head and nose) in disgust, so do the preconscious and our conscious apprehension turn away from the memory. This is *repression*. . . .

The choice of neurosis (the decision whether hysteria, obsessional neurosis, or paranoia is to emerge) probably depends on the nature (that is, the chronological relation) of the step in development which enables repression to occur, *i.e.,* which transforms a source of internal pleasure into one of internal disgust.

This is where I have got to, then—with all the obscurities involved. I have decided, then, henceforth to regard as separate factors what causes libido and what causes anxiety. I have also given up the idea of explaining libido as the masculine factor and repression as the feminine one. . . . The main value of my synthesis lies in its linking together the neurotic and normal processes.

My self-analysis is still interrupted. I have now seen why. I can only analyze myself with objectively acquired knowledge (as if I were a stranger); self-analysis is really impossible, otherwise there would be no illness. As I've come across some puzzles in my own case, it is bound to hold up the self-analysis.

January 16, 1898

. . . ALL SORTS OF little things are happening: dreams and hysteria are fitting in with each other even more neatly. These details are now standing in the way of the great problems touched on in Breslau. One must take it as it comes, and be glad that it does come. I send you herewith the definition of happiness (or did I tell you a long time ago?).

Happiness is the deferred fulfillment of a prehistoric wish. That is why wealth brings so little happiness; money is not an infantile wish. . . .

Vienna, January 3, 1899

. . . FIRST OF ALL I have accomplished a piece of self-analysis which has confirmed that phantasies are products of later periods which project themselves back from the present into earliest childhood; and I have also found out how it happens, again by verbal association.

The answer to the question of what happened in infancy is: nothing, but the germ of a sexual impulse was there. The whole thing would be easy and interesting to tell, but it would take many pages to write, so I shall keep it for the Easter congress. . . .

Vienna, May 28, 1899

. . . THE DREAMS HAVE SUDDENLY taken shape without any special reason, but this time for good. I have decided that all the efforts at disguise will not do, and that giving it all up will not do either, because I cannot afford to keep to myself the finest—and probably the only lasting—discovery that I have made. . . .

. . . So the dreams will be done. . . .

July 3, 1899

. . . THE AUTHOR OF the "extremely important book on dreams, which is still, unfortunately, insufficiently appreciated by scientists," greatly enjoyed himself for four days in Berchtesgaden *au sein de sa famille,* and only a remnant of shame prevented him from sending you picture postcards of the Konigsee. . . .

Vienna, January 8, 1900

THE NEW CENTURY—the most interesting thing about which for us is, I dare say, that it contains the dates of our death—has brought me nothing but a stupid review in the *Zeit* by Bürckhard, the former director of the Burgtheater (not to be confused with our old Jacob). It is unflattering, uncommonly lacking in understanding, and—most annoying of all—is to be continued in the next number.

I do not count on recognition, at any rate in my lifetime. . . .

March 8, 1902

I AM GLAD TO BE able to tell you that at last the long-withheld and recently really desirable professorship has been conferred on me. The *Wiener Zeitung* will next week announce the fact to the public, which I hope will take note of this seal of official approval. It is a long time since I have been able to send you any news with which pleasant anticipations could be associated.   Your

SIGM.

The Passionate State of Mind

by ERIC HOFFER

DECEMBER, 1954

Eric Hoffer, born in New York City in 1902, is one of the most extraordinary men writing today. He is a San Francisco long-shoreman who had no schooling and was almost totally blind from age seven to sixteen. He says that when his eyesight returned he was "seized with an enormous hunger for the printed word," and read everything within reach, both English and German. (His father was a German cabinetmaker; his mother died shortly before he lost his eyesight.) He has said he has no taste for owning more property than "I can pack on my back." His book The True Believer, *published in 1951, was praised by many reviewers as the best analysis of political fanaticism and mass movements ever written.*

There is in all passions a shrinking away from ourselves. The passionate pursuer has all the earmarks of a fugitive. Passions have their root in that which is crippled, blemished, or insecure within us. The passionate attitude is less a response to stimuli from without than an emanation of an inner dissatisfaction.

A poignant dissatisfaction, whatever be its cause, is at bottom a dissatisfaction with ourselves. It is surprising how much hardship and humiliation a man will endure without bitterness when he has not the least doubt about his worth, or when he is so integrated with others that he is not aware of a separate self.

It is strange how the moment we have reason to be dissatisfied with ourselves we are set upon by a pack of insistent, clamorous desires. Is desire somehow an expression of the centrifugal force that tears and pulls us away from an undesirable self? A gain in self-esteem reduces considerably the pull of the appetites, while a crisis in self-esteem is likely to cause a weakening or a complete breakdown of self-discipline.

Asceticism is sometimes a deliberate effort to reverse a reaction in the chemistry of our soul: by suppressing desire we try to rebuild and bolster self-esteem.

There is even in the most selfish passion a large element of self-abnegation. It is startling to realize that what we call extreme self-seeking is actually self-renunciation. The miser, health addict, glory chaser, and their like are not far behind the true believer in the exercise of self-sacrifice. Every extreme attitude is a flight from the self.

It is not love of self but hatred of self which is at the root of the troubles that afflict our world.

II

However much we guard ourselves against it, we cannot overcome the tendency to shape ourselves in the image other people have of us. The people we meet are the playwrights and stage managers of our lives: they cast us in a role, and we play it whether we will or not.

It is not so much the example of others we imitate as the reflection of ourselves in their eyes, and the echo of ourselves in their words.

The wisdom of others remains dull till it is writ over with our own blood. We are essentially apart from the world; it bursts into our consciousness only when it sinks its teeth and nails into us.

We almost always prove something when we act heroically. We prove it to ourselves and to others that we are not what we and they thought we were. Our real self is petty, greedy, cowardly, dishonest, and stewing in malice. And now in defying death and spitting in its eye we grasp at the chance of a grand refutation.

For all we know, the wholly harmonious individual might be without the impulse to push on, and without the compulsion to strive for perfection in any department of life. There is always a chance that the perfect society might be a stagnant society.

If it be true that the vigor of a society is proportionate to its capacity for enthusiasm, then the habit of insatiable desire can be as much a factor in maintaining social vigor as the dedication to ideals and holy causes.

A nation is "tired" when it ceases to want things fervently. It makes no difference whether this blunting of desire is due to satiety, reasonableness, or disillusion. To a tired nation the future seems barren, offering nothing which would surpass that which is and has been. The main effect of a real revolution is perhaps that it sweeps away those who do not know how to wish, and brings to the front men with insatiable appetites for action, power, and all that the world has to offer.

III

It is an evil thing to expect too much either from ourselves or from others. Disappointment with ourselves does not moderate our expectations from others; on the contrary, it raises them. It is as if we wished to be disappointed in our fellow men.

One does not really love mankind when one expects too much from them.

The remarkable thing is that we really love our neighbor as ourselves: we do unto others as we do unto ourselves. We hate others when we hate ourselves. We are tolerant toward others when we tolerate ourselves. We forgive others when we forgive ourselves. We are prone to torture and sacrifice others when we torture and sacrifice ourselves.

Perhaps our craving to change others is but a reflection of the craving to change ourselves. The self-dissatisfied are likely to be ardent reformers.

An uncompromising attitude is more an indication of inner uncertainty than of deep conviction. The implacable stand is directed more against the doubt within than the assailant without.

Rabid suspicion has nothing in it of skepticism. The suspicious mind believes more than it doubts. It believes in a formidable and ineradicable evil lurking in every person.

However unjust and unreasonable the attitude we assume toward others, we seem to set in motion an automatic process which works blindly to corroborate and justify that attitude. It is an awesome thing that when we expose people, however undeservedly, to prolonged hatred they tend to become hateful. Our prejudices, suspicions, and lies have this power to compel souls into a conforming pattern. It is as if the world, of its own accord, yields reasons for our unreasonable attitudes.

It has often been remarked that power corrupts. It is perhaps equally important to realize that weakness, too, corrupts. The most corrupt wielders of power are those who came up through the schools of weakness. Power usually corrupts the few, but weakness corrupts the many. Hatred, malice, rudeness, suspicion—are the fruits of weakness. The resentment of the weak does not spring from the injustice done to them but from the awareness of their own inadequacy and impotence. They do not crave justice but power. When it is in their power to do so, the weak destroy weakness wherever they see it. Woe to the weak when they are preyed upon by the weak! The self-hatred, too, of the weak is an instance of their hatred of weakness.

The sin of oppression is not in its injustice but in the sense of impotence it implants in the oppressed. It corrupts them absolutely.

Note also how perverse is the attitude of the weak toward their benefactors. They feel generosity as oppression; they want to retaliate. They say: "May the day come when you shall be weak, and we will send bundles to America."

IV

Some generations have patience and some are without it. This is perhaps the most crucial difference between eras. There is a time when the word "eventually" has the soothing effect of a promise, and a time when the word evokes in us bitterness and scorn.

In this godless age, as much as in any preceding religious age, man is still preoccupied with the saving of his soul. The discrediting of established religions by enlightenment did not result in a weakening of the religious impulse. A traditional religion canalizes and routinizes the quest for salvation. When such a religion is discredited, the individual must do his own soul-saving, and he is at it twenty-four hours a day. There is an eruption of fanaticism in all departments of life—business, politics, literature, art, science, and even in love-making and sport. The elimination of the sacerdotal outlet results thus in a general infection and inflammation of the social body.

A fateful process is set in motion when the individual is released "to the freedom of his own impotence" and left to justify his existence by his own efforts. The autonomous individual, striving to realize himself and prove his worth, has created all that is great in literature, art, music, science, and technology. The autonomous individual, also, when he can neither realize himself nor justify his existence by his own efforts, is a breeding cell of frustration, and the seed of the convulsions which shake our world to its foundations.

The individual on his own is stable only so long as he is possessed of self-esteem. The maintenance of self-esteem is a continuous task which taxes all of the individual's powers and inner resources. We have to prove our worth and justify our existence anew each day. When, for whatever reason, self-esteem is unattainable, the autonomous individual becomes a highly explosive entity. He turns away from an unpromising self and plunges into the pursuit of pride—the explosive substitute for self-esteem. All social disturbances and upheavals have their roots in crises of individual self-esteem, and the great endeavor in which the masses most readily unite is basically a search for pride.

Modern man is weighed down more by the burden of responsibility than by the burden of sin. We think him more a savior who shoulders our responsibilities than him who shoulders our sins. If instead of making decisions we have but to obey and do our duty, we feel it as a sort of salvation.

When a nation is subject to foreign domination its creativeness is as a rule meager. This is not due to a crippling of the "national genius" but to the fact that resentment against foreign rule so unites a nation that the potentially creative individual cannot attain the distinctness requisite for the full unfolding of his powers. His inner life is tinged and shaped by the feelings and preoccupations of the mass. Like the member of a primitive tribe, he exists not as an individual but as a member of a compact group.

Things are different in the case of resentment against domestic oppression. Provided the oppression is not of the thorough totalitarian brand, the individual may manifest his protest by asserting his distinctness and originality.

The conditions optimal for cultural creativeness seem to be a marked degree of individual differentiation; a modicum of economic well-being; absence of mass fervor whether religious, patriotic, revolutionary, business, or war; a paucity of opportunities for action; a milieu which recognizes and awards merit; and a degree of communal discipline.

The last point needs elucidation.

When people are free to do as they please, they usually imitate each other. Originality is deliberate and forced, and partakes of the nature of a protest. A society which gives unlimited freedom to the individual more often than not attains a disconcerting sameness. On the other hand, where communal discipline is strict but not ruthless—"an annoyance which irritates, but not a heavy yoke which crushes"—originality is likely to thrive. It is true that when imitation runs its course in a wholly free society it results in a uniformity which is not unlike a mild tyranny. Thus the fully standardized free society has perhaps enough of compulsion to challenge originality.

The Coming Ice Age:
A True Scientific Detective Story

by BETTY FRIEDAN

SEPTEMBER, 1958

In Thornton Wilder's The Skin of Our Teeth, *the Antrobuses heard people were burning pianos in Hartford. Coming generations might stock up on the item too. For the same wall of ice which threatened the Antrobuses is on its way back again, according to the chilling forecast of a couple of New York scientists. Betty Friedan graduated from Smith summa cum laude, and then studied for a year at the University of California. She is married, has three children, and writes an occasional article when she has time to research the subject properly.*

This is the story of two scientists, who started five years ago—with a single radiocarbon clue from the ocean bottom and a wild hunch—to track down one of the earth's great unsolved mysteries: What caused the ancient ice ages? Their search led over many continents and seas, to drowned rivers and abandoned mountain caves, into far-removed branches of science. It took them down through recorded history, from the stone tablets of primitive man to contemporary newspaper headlines.

These two serious, careful scientists—geophysicist Maurice Ewing, director of Columbia University's Lamont Geological Observatory, and geologist-meteorologist William Donn—believe they have finally found the explanation for the giant glaciers, which four times during the past million years have advanced and retreated over the earth. If they are right, the world is now heading into another Ice Age. It will come not as sudden catastrophe, but as the inevitable culmination of a process that has already begun in northern oceans.

As Ewing and Donn read the evidence, an Ice Age will result from a slow warming and rising of the ocean that is now taking place. They believe that this ocean flood—which may submerge large coastal areas of the eastern United States and western Europe—is going to melt the ice sheet which has covered the Arctic Ocean through all recorded history. Calculations based on the independent observations of other scientists indicate this melting could begin within roughly one hundred years.

It is this melting of Arctic ice which Ewing and Donn believe will set off another Ice Age on earth. They predict that it will cause great snows to fall in the north—perennial unmelting snows which the world has not seen since the last Ice Age thousands of years ago. These snows will make the Arctic glaciers grow again, until their towering height forces them forward. The advance south will be slow, but if it follows the route of previous Ice Ages, it will encase in ice large parts of North America and Europe. It would, of course, take many centuries for that wall of ice to reach New York and Chicago, London and Paris. But its coming is an inevitable consequence of the cycle which Ewing and Donn believe is now taking place.

The coming of another Ice Age is an event serious scientists have never been able to predict from observable Earth phenomena. For until Ewing and Donn postulated their new Theory of Ice Ages (it was first published in *Science* in June 1956 and a second report appeared in May 1958) the very nature of the problem seemed to defy the kind of scientific understanding which makes prediction possible.

Scientists know that the glaciers which stand quiet in the Arctic today once covered America with a wall of ice up to two miles thick—its southern boundary extending from Long Island across New York, Pennsylvania, Ohio, Illinois, Wisconsin, Iowa, and the Dakotas to the Missouri River, with extensions into the western mountain country . . . that it covered northern Europe, England, large parts of France and Germany . . . that it created the Great Lakes, the Hudson and St. Lawrence Rivers . . . that it moved mountains, crashed down forests, destroyed whole species of life.

They also know that it is cold enough at the Arctic for glaciers to grow today, but almost no snow has fallen there in modern times. What caused those snows that built the Ice Age glaciers until their own height forced them to march, and what caused them finally to retreat? And why has the earth been swinging back and forth between Ice Ages and climate like today's for a million years, when before then the entire planet enjoyed a temperate climate with no extremes of hot or cold? Scientists could answer these questions only in terms of sudden catastrophe—a volcanic eruption, the earth's movement into a cloud of cosmic dust—and unpredictable catastrophes are not the concern of contemporary science. Few scientists had even worked on the problem in recent years.

It was only by a combination of lucky circumstance and persistent curiosity that Ewing and Donn as a team began working steadily on the Ice Age Mystery. As Director of Lamont Geological Observatory, located on top of the New York Palisades over the Hudson River, Ewing teaches theoretical geophysics and directs research in earthquake seismology, marine geology and biology, and oceanography. Donn teaches geology at Brooklyn College and directs the research in meteorology at Lamont. Since the two men live twenty miles apart and were occupied all day, they would often meet at eleven at night in a deserted laboratory at Columbia University—midway between their homes—and work into the morning on the Ice Age trail.

The two men share the scientist's passion for pure search, no matter where it leads. Ewing, a tall and powerful Texan who speaks in a gentle voice, was white-haired before he was fifty, a fact his friends attribute to the pace at which he has lived his life as a scientist. For a quarter-century he has been leading expeditions over the ocean, often risking his life while pioneering new methods of investigating its secrets. In the early 1930s he founded a new science by dropping charges from a whale boat and using a seismograph to identify the different layers of earth beneath the ocean. In 1955 he was given the Navy Distinguished Service Award for devising the SOFAR (Sound Fixing and Ranging) method for rescuing men from ships and planes lost at sea.

Donn, New York City bred, is a slight, wiry meteorologist, who tames tidal waves with logarithms. His mastery of the complex relationship between sea and weather complemented Ewing's knowledge of the depths of the oceans.

The original bits of information which set the two scientists onto the trail of the Ice Age Mystery first came to light on the decks of the three-masted schooner *Vema* which Lamont Observatory uses for scientific exploration. In the summer of 1953, the ship traced a puzzling pattern on the ocean bottom which led from the Atlantic to the Gulf of Mexico and into the Caribbean Sea. The Columbia-Lamont crew were working with their newly perfected "deep sea corer," a device which can bring up primeval sediment undisturbed through as much as 4,000 fathoms of water (24,000 feet)—just as it was deposited thousands of years ago.

This "corer" is a sharp-edged steel tube, two-and-a-half inches in diameter and up to seventy feet in length. When it has been lowered from the ship to within fifteen feet of the sea bottom, a trigger trips the holding mechanism and the tube is punched by a weight into the sediment. The Lamont ocean expeditions have brought up cores as long as sixty feet—nearly two thousand of them—representing the successive deposits of thousands of years. As Ewing describes it,

"The entire record of the earth is there in the most undisturbed form it is possible to find anywhere—traces of the animals, rocks, and plants of successive ages preserved in the order in which they filtered down from the surface of the sea."

Only recently, radioactive isotope techniques have made it possible to deduce when the sediment was deposited, and other things about the world from which it came. Scientists can now measure the radiocarbon in a sample of ocean-bottom mud—and know how long it has lain there. Radioactive carbon ceases to be replenished when removed from the atmosphere, and decays at a known rate. Chemists therefore calculate from the ratio of radiocarbon to ordinary carbon in a fossil shell whether it has been decaying for a thousand, five, or ten thousand years.

In these cores of mud from the Caribbean, the equatorial Atlantic, and the Gulf of Mexico that summer, the Lamont expedition kept seeing a strange sharp line. "About a foot below the floor of the ocean the sediment suddenly changed from salmon pink to gray," Ewing said. "You could see it sharp as a razor when the cores were opened on the ship's deck. Others had reported this same line in the North Atlantic.

"When we put these cores to paleontological laboratory tests back at Lamont, we found out what that razor-sharp line meant: at a certain time the ocean suddenly changed from cold to warm. The pink sediment contained shells of minute warm-water animals; the gray sediment, cold-water animals."

Back at Lamont, measurement of radiocarbon showed that this sudden warming took place throughout the length and breadth of the vast Atlantic Ocean—eleven thousand years ago. The cores showed virtually no change in temperature for ninety thousand years—except for this one sudden increase. Donn, Lamont's meteorological expert, was as mystified as Ewing.

"What happened eleven thousand years ago to heat the ocean?" they kept asking themselves at odd moments over the next year or so. "What could change the climate of the whole ocean so abruptly?"

Neither Ewing nor Donn can say precisely when the hunch came. The problem continued to tantalize them, as they traveled about the country attending meetings and doing field work. On the way back from Chicago, they may have watched the ice break up in the Delaware River. They recall reading a newspaper item about a big gambling jackpot on which day the ice would go out in the Yukon. The chain of thought seems obvious now: water freezing—ice going out—this is a sharp, abrupt change, the only sudden change that *can* happen to a body of water.

But oceans don't freeze. Ocean currents dissipate the cold—except, of course, in the small Arctic Ocean which is almost entirely surrounded by land.

"What would happen if the ice went out of the Arctic Ocean as it does in the Yukon or the Delaware?" Ewing and Donn remember wondering, as they went over the problem again, one day at Lamont.

"Well, we figured, the Arctic Ocean would get warmer. Because water would flow more freely between it and the Atlantic, dissipating the cold. And of course, the Atlantic Ocean would get colder. But wait a minute . . . we saw it simultaneously. If the Arctic Ocean were open water, warmed by the Atlantic, warmer than the land around it, water would evaporate and fall as snow on the land. More snow on Greenland and northern Canada would make glaciers grow. Glaciers don't grow now because there is no open water in the Arctic to provide the moisture for snow.

"And suddenly we had the startling hunch that the Arctic Ocean *was open* during the Ice Age. And that it froze over only eleven thousand years ago. It was this freezing over of the Arctic Ocean which so suddenly warmed the Atlantic—and ended the Ice Age."

"That rather exciting ten minutes," they told me, "contradicted a whole lot of things we'd always taken for granted. Everyone has assumed that the Arctic Ocean, so covered with ice today, would be even colder and more completely frozen during an Ice Age.

"You get a lot of these wild ideas in our business. If one lasts five minutes you begin to take it seriously. The more we thought about this one, the more it added up. It explained so many things that have always puzzled us.

"For once you accept the radical idea that the Arctic was a warm open ocean at the time of the great continental glaciers, you can reconstruct a completely different weather pattern from the one we know today. As we worked it out, we could see a startling chain of cause and effect between the oceans and the glaciers themselves. We could see how the oceans would work as an actual 'thermostat' to keep the earth alternating between glacial ice ages and interglacial periods such as today.

"It all hinges on the fact that the North Pole is where it is—in the middle of the Arctic Ocean, which is almost completely surrounded by land except for a shallow 'sill' between Norway and Greenland opening into the Atlantic, and the insignificant Bering Strait. If the cold waters of the Arctic interchanged freely over this sill with the warm Atlantic water, the Arctic Ocean would not freeze over. Its moisture would build glaciers. (In the cold temperatures of the north, the moisture that evaporates from the open Arctic would all fall as snow—too much snow to melt in the short Arctic summer. When the rate at which snow accumulates exceeds the rate at which it melts, glaciers grow.) But as those glaciers grew, they would lock up so much ocean water that sea level would fall.

"We know that sea level was lowered between three hundred and four hundred feet at the peak of the last Ice Age. Now, most of that sill between Norway and Greenland is less than three hundred feet deep. At a certain point the glaciers would lower the sea level so much that the Arctic Ocean would be virtually cut off from the warmer Atlantic. The Arctic Ocean would then freeze over. And the glaciers, no longer fed by snow, would melt under the Arctic summer sun, restoring their water to the oceans. Then sea level would rise, until enough warm Atlantic water again flowed over that sill to melt the Arctic ice sheet, and start another glacial cycle."

Donn worked out a weather map of the world, with an open Arctic Ocean, warmer than surrounding lands. It showed a completely different storm pattern than exists today; more rain and snow in the Arctic, a wind pattern carrying more ocean moisture inland generally. It showed violent blizzards over eastern North America which would spread more snow on the glaciers. Summers would become more like winters as the glacial wall advanced southward. Donn's weather map with the open Arctic even showed that there would be rain in today's deserts.

But they needed more proof for their theory. They had to track down the circumstantial evidence of what happened eleven thousand years ago; they had to find geological witnesses to confirm their reconstruction of the crime.

They embarked on the painstaking examination of the records of past Arctic explorers. There was little relevant data. One day, going through dusty old volumes of the *National Geographic,* they found a photograph of an Arctic beach—a beach that could have been made only by long years of pounding waves. There must have been open sea in the Arctic to make that beach.

Ewing took to sea in the *Vema* again. In the Gulf of Mexico, the Ice Age trail seemed to peter out altogether in a bottomless plain of flat gray silt. The *Vema* took core after core below the Mississippi Delta without finding the crucial fossil lines.

"We couldn't even get to the bottom of it with our corers," Ewing recalls. "We were sure the Gulf must have changed from cold to warm just as the other oceans, but how could we prove it when there seemed to be no fossils at all in that endless gray layer? We suspected that the gray silt had come from the Mississippi and had spread over the floor of the Gulf by creeping along the bottom. If we could find a hill that stood well above the Gulf floor, the sediment on top of it would have come down undisturbed from the surface of the water and might contain the record of those temperature changes."

They nearly sailed over them—a cluster of hills rising a thousand feet off the ocean floor. There, instead of puzzling gray silt, they finally found the familiar, razor-sharp layers of glacial and interglacial fossils.

And that very gray silt which had obscured their trail turned out to be further proof that eleven thousand years ago was the date the Ice Age ended. For back at Lamont, radiocarbon measurement showed that the silt *stopped* sliding from the Mississippi just eleven thousand years ago. This meant that a great rise in sea level must have taken place at just that time. Drowned by the rising sea, the lower channels of the Mississippi River would retain their own sediment, losing the power to take it out to the deep central part of the Gulf. It was, almost certainly, the rise in sea level caused by the melting of the glaciers.

As the Lamont crew were pursuing this mystery in the sea, other scientists were unearthing new Ice Age clues on land. Atomic Energy Commissioner Willard F. Libby, the scientist who originated radiocarbon dating, found fossils of a forest at Two Creeks, Wisconsin, that had been first flooded and then overridden by the advancing ice. Radiocarbon dating proved that those trees, at one of the southern fingertips of the last glacial advance, were pushed over about eleven thousand years ago. (Previously, geologists thought the ice had disappeared long before that time.)

Then a series of dramatic clues were brought in by other geologists from caves in the cliffs above the dry Great Basin of Nevada and Utah. Several thousand feet above the basin are rock niches worn by the waves of glacial lakes—lakes created by the great rains that fell south of the Ice Age snows. Far below are caves, also worn by those waves, that were inhabited by man: the famous Fishbone Cave above the dry Winnemucca Lake in western Nevada and the Danger Cave above glacial Lake Bonneville in Utah.

The evidence showed that men moved into those caves shortly after the lake level suddenly dropped and exposed them. Remains were found of the nets and baskets they used to catch the fish of the now vanished glacial lakes. Radiocarbon dating showed that men were living in those caves—brought above the water when the great glacial rains and snows stopped—approximately eleven thousand years ago. And the time during which the glacial lakes dropped from those niches thousands of feet above on the cliffs, to the level of the lower caves, was dramatically short—only several hundred years. It was like the sudden change Ewing and Donn had observed in the ocean. The date was now established: eleven thousand years ago, plus or minus a few hundred years, the last Ice Age suddenly ended.

At the time the theory was constructed, there was no actual evidence from the Arctic Ocean itself to indicate it had ever been ice-free. Some months later Dr. A. P. Crary came back from the Arctic Ocean and sent his cores to Lamont. These cores indicated there had been minute animal life for thousands of years in the Arctic Ocean, which suddenly stopped—eleven millenniums ago. They also showed evidence of icebergs free to move in open water at the time Ewing and Donn think the Arctic was open.

Could men have lived on the shores of this ocean during the Ice Age? Were there human witnesses to the open Arctic sea?

"It was only by accident that we stumbled on a vital clue in a completely different branch of science," they told me. "We might have missed it altogether because of the compartmentalization of science."

One day a colleague of Donn's happened to remark over coffee that he'd overheard an anthropologist in the faculty room talking about some traces that had just been discovered of an ancient civilization around the Arctic.

Donn and Ewing started calling anthropologists. The evidence was uncertain, they learned, but some of it pointed strongly to well-established communities of man around the Arctic many thousands of years ago. In fact, the oldest flints showing man in America had been found recently in a band around the Arctic Circle, seldom straying south.

Anthropologists had been mystified. Even if a land bridge between Siberia and Alaska had existed then, why would man choose to use it to settle in the Arctic Circle, in the very heart of the intense polar cold, at temperature which was assumed to be even lower than today? Around that frozen Arctic Ocean, where would man have found the fish and game those flints suggested? Why would men have *stayed* there for centuries—unless, as Ewing and Donn now believe, the Arctic Ocean was open then, and its shores were a warm oasis compared with the glaciers to the South?

Ewing and Donn got another anthropologist out of bed late at night to question him further. He told them that, while anthropologists are still uncertain as to how and when man first *came* to America, they are pretty sure he suddenly started migrating south, in an explosive wave, about eleven thousand years ago.

Here, perhaps, were their human witnesses to the end of the Ice Age! The people who lived "beyond the north wind" on Arctic shores, behind the towering wall of ice, using their flint-tipped weapons on big game and fish that could not survive the old Arctic temperatures of today. These men evidently came to America from Siberia when the glaciers had taken enough water from the sea to uncover the Siberian land bridge. They stayed for some centuries around the warm Arctic because the glaciers kept them from straying south. Then, eleven thousand years ago, they suddenly fled. If the Arctic Ocean suddenly froze over, they couldn't eat. Nor could they go back to Siberia because the great rise in sea level at the end of the Ice Age would once more submerge the land bridge.

And just at the time when they could no longer stay in the Arctic, paths opened in the great ice wall south of them. The melting glaciers permitted men to go south at last—in such a rapid wave that they reached the tip of South America in a few thousand years.

So anthropologists are now reconstructing their own mysteries in the light of Ewing and Donn's Theory of Ice Ages—which California's authority on early man, Carl Sauer, calls "a major contribution to our understanding. . . . The old, simple belief that man waited at the threshold of the New World until the last ice sheet was gone has been proved wrong."

And, finally, human witnesses were tracked down in southern deserts. During this past year archaeologists have brought back new evidence that the Sahara desert was green and fertile and thriving with civilization when glaciers froze life in America and Europe. Ewing and Donn had deduced that an open Arctic Ocean would have caused rain in today's deserts. Now, from the caves of the Sahara, came ancient man's vivid drawings of the animals that he hunted on the once grassy desert.

One big question remained which the new theory did not seem to answer: What started off the first Ice Age cycle?

"We know that during the past million years, the world has swung back and forth between Ice Ages and weather like today's," Ewing and Donn told me. "Before then, the whole earth was much warmer. There were no zones of extreme heat or cold; palms and magnolias grew in Greenland, and coral around Iceland; subtropical plants thrived within eleven degrees of the North Pole. Why didn't the Arctic Ocean-glacier 'thermostat' work then? What suddenly turned it on one million years ago?

"The answer, we believe, is that until a million years ago, the North Pole was not in that landlocked Arctic Ocean at all, but in the middle of the open Pacific, where there was no land on which snow and ice could accumulate, and ocean currents dissipated the cold.

"The idea of wandering poles may seem fantastic. But recently discovered magnetic evidence leads to the geological inference that the whole earth can shift its surface crust with respect to the interior. As the earth's crustal zone 'slides' over the interior, different points on the surface can be at the North or South Pole.

"Such a shift in the earth's crust, it is now believed, did take place before the first Pleistocene Ice Age which began a million years ago. Before then, the magnetic record shows the North Pole in the middle of the Pacific, and the South Pole in the open southern Atlantic.

"An abrupt shift in the earth's crust carried the North Pole into the small and virtually landlocked Arctic, and the South Pole to the Antarctic continent, where the polar cold could not be dissipated by free ocean currents. That started the greatly contrasting zones of climate we know today—and the concentration of cold which finally froze the Arctic Ocean, to start the Ice Age cycles."

This would explain why the Ice Age glaciers have always marched from the Arctic. No ocean thermostat exists to turn on drastic glacial-interglacial cycles in the Antarctic. There, according to the theory, the Antarctic ice cap has been building up continually since the South Pole shifted to that continent a million years ago. With only minor changes caused by the slight warming and cooling of the Atlantic in the glacial-interglacial cycles. This is confirmed by evidence from elevated beaches, which seems to indicate that maximum sea level has been dropping successively lower in each glacial era.

And as long as the poles stay where they are, the Ice Age cycles must continue.

Ewing and Donn realized that their theory had startling implications for the future. They have the scientist's distaste for the sensational and carefully worked out the wording of the theory's formal conclusion: "The recent epoch can be considered as another interglacial stage." A number of scientists have tried to disprove their theory; so far they have been unsuccessful.

As Ewing and Donn read the glacial thermostat, the present inter-glacial stage is well advanced; the earth is now heading into another Ice Age. Certain signs, some of them visible to the layman as well as the scientist, indicate we may have been watching an Ice Age approach for some time without realizing what we were seeing.

Although scientists do not agree on its significance, they have observed an increasingly rapid warming and rising of the ocean in recent years. Warm water flowing north has driven the codfish off Cape Cod to Newfoundland; annual temperature has risen ten de-grees in Iceland and Greenland; down here winters are warmer; the Hudson River no longer freezes over as it used to. It is part of the Ewing-Donn paradox that the next Ice Age will be preceded by such a warming of climate.

"We suspect that the ocean is already warm enough to melt the Arctic ice sheet," Ewing and Donn told me. "For some time it has remained at the highest temperature ever reached in the four previous interglacial stages." As climate becomes warmer, more and more glacial melt-water pours into the sea. The Atlantic has already risen three hundred feet since the glaciers of the last Ice Age started to melt away. Up until twenty-five years ago the U. S. Geodetic Surveys indicated that sea level was rising six inches a century; in the past twenty-five years that rate has increased to two feet a century.

As sea level rises, more and more warm water pours over the Norway-Greenland sill, under the Arctic ice sheet. American, Russian, and Scandinavian scientists have observed a definite warming of the Arctic Ocean over the past fifty years, and a consequent thinning of the ice sheet. At an international conference on Arctic sea ice in March 1958, scientists estimated that Arctic ice covers an area 12 per cent smaller than it did fifteen years ago, and is 40 per cent thin-ner. A layman might surmise that if this trend continues the Arctic Ocean will be open and the Ice Age begin in another twenty years. Ewing and Donn are much more cautious about predictions.

"The rate at which our weather has been warming in recent years could be temporarily slowed down," they told me. "We don't know the exact rate at which the sea is now rising. We need long-term world-wide evidence which the International Geophysical Year may give us to assess accurately the changes that seem to be taking place in the ocean and the ice."

If the ocean continues to warm up at the present rate, Ewing and

Donn think it is conceivable that there will be open water in the Arctic within about a hundred years. If they are right, for the first time in the history of the world, the victims of an Ice Age are going to see it coming. Television cameramen will be ranging all over the far north, covering the break-up of the Arctic ice sheet, looking for the first dirty summer slush. For the Ice Age will dawn, not in crashing glacial terror but in slush; as Ewing and Donn describe it, on a summer vacation up north, you will simply see a lot of dirty slush, winter's snow that for the first time in thousands of years didn't quite melt.

In many parts of America, at that time, the worry may not be ice, but water. Many scientists have speculated on the ocean flood that will be caused if the melting of glacial icecaps continues. Antarctic scientist Laurence Gould recently warned that "the return of only a few feet of thickness of ice as melt-water to the oceans would have serious effects in many places; and if all the ice were melted into the sea, its level would rise from 150 to 200 feet. All the world's seaports and some of its most densely populated areas would be submerged."

Ewing and Donn don't know how much higher the sea is going to rise before it melts the Arctic ice sheet. They say the ocean has already risen to the point where, if certain recent storms had occurred at high tide, it would have flooded New York and Boston subways. Donn is now working at Lamont on studies of long and short period changes in world sea level.

The ocean flood that brings about the Ice Age will not resemble the flash floods that have caused havoc in the East in recent years. It will build up slowly, and it will not flow away. The cities, industries, and military bases that are concentrated on both sides of the Atlantic may have to be evacuated. (Fortunately, Pacific coastlines are higher.)

It will probably be possible to protect New York and Washington by levees. Parts or all of New Orleans, Amsterdam, Rotterdam, and other cities are now protected by levees from high water, Ewing and Donn point out. Evidently, New York is in no danger of becoming a lost Atlantis, drowned under the sea. If low-lying Brooklyn, Miami, Washington, New Orleans, or Amsterdam should become ghost cities, it will be because a decision will have been made long in advance of this slow-creeping flood to evacuate rather than build levees.

"According to our theory, with the melting of the Arctic ice sheet, the rise in sea level will stop," Ewing and Donn explained. Instead of adding water to the sea, the glaciers will begin taking it out.

For a long time after the ocean flood subsides, the only effect the Ice Age will have on us down here will be more rain. The new Arctic moisture that falls as snow on glaciers will increase both rain and snow here, swelling rivers and watering deserts. Then, gradually, our weather will cool. Icy winds will blow from the advancing glaciers; the great snows will fall farther and farther south. In several thousand years a two-mile ice sheet may cover the United States and Europe. If man finds no way to switch the glacial thermostat, there may well be a real estate boom in the Sahara.

X

An Eye on the Outside World

Hitler

by JOHN GUNTHER

JANUARY, 1936

Today he's like something out of a nightmare that never existed. Here, a sharply etched portrait by John Gunther brings the century's madman vividly to life again. The author had watched the convulsions of a tormented Europe as a correspondent of the Chicago Daily News *since 1924. Then in 1936 Gunther's* Inside Europe *was published. It was a smash hit—and the world became his beat. His books have sold in the millions; the latest is* Inside Russia Today. *He plans to cover at least one more area in his "Inside" series—Australasia.*

The union of theorist, organizer, and leader in one man is the rarest phenomenon on earth; therein lies greatness.—ADOLF HITLER.

Adolf Hitler, seemingly so irrational and self-contradictory, is a character of great complexity—not an easy nut to crack. To many he is meager and insignificant; yet he holds sixty-five million Germans, a fair share of whom adore him, in a thralldom compounded of love, fear, and nationalist ecstasy. Few men run so completely the gamut from the sublime to the ridiculous. He is a mountebank, a demagogue, a frustrated hysteric, a lucky misfit. He is also a figure of extreme veneration to millions of honest and not-even-puzzled Germans. What are the sources of his extraordinary power?

This paunchy, Charlie-Chaplin-mustached man, given to insomnia and emotionalism, who is head of the Nazi Party, commander-in-chief of the German army and navy, Leader of the German nation, creator, president, and chancellor of the Third Reich, was born in Austria in 1889. He was not a German by birth. This was a highly important fact, inflaming his early nationalism. He developed the implacable patriotism of the frontiersman, the exile. Only an Austrian could take Germanism so seriously.

His imagination is purely political. I have seen his early paintings, those which he submitted to the Vienna art academy as a boy. They are prosaic, utterly devoid of rhythm, color, feeling, or spiritual imagination. They are architect's sketches: painful and precise draftsmanship, nothing more. No wonder the Vienna professors told him to go to an architectural school and give up pure art as hopeless.

He went only to grade school, and by no stretch of generosity could he be called a person of genuine culture. He is not nearly so cultivated, so sophisticatedly interested in intellectual affairs as is, say, Mussolini. He reads almost nothing. The Treaty of Versailles was probably the most concrete single influence on his life; but it is doubtful if he ever read it in full. He dislikes intellectuals. He has never been outside Germany since his youth in Austria (if you except his war experiences in Flanders and the brief visit to Mussolini in Venice in 1934), and he speaks no foreign language except a few words of battered French.

To many who meet him Hitler seems awkward and ill-at-ease. This is because visitors, even among his subordinates, obtrude personal realities which interfere with his incessant fantasies. He has no poise. He finds it difficult to make quick decisions: capacity for quick decisions derives from inner harmony, which he lacks. He is no "strong, silent man."

Foreigners, especially interviewers from British or American newspapers, may find him cordial and even candid but they seldom have opportunity to question him, to participate in a give-and-take discussion. Hitler rants. He is extremely emotional. He never answers questions. He talks to you as if you were a public meeting, and nothing can stop the gush of words.

Some time ago, before signing the friendship pact with Poland, he received a well-known American publicist and editor. He did ask a question: What the American would think if, for example, Mexico and Poland and Texas were cut off from the United States by a "corridor" in Mexico. The American replied, "The answer to that is that Canada is not France." Hitler had intended the question rhetorically, and he was so shocked by the little interruption that it took him some time to get in full voice again—on another point.

For a time it was said commonly that Hitler's best trait was loyalty. He would never, the joke put it, give up three things: the Jews, his friends, and Austria. Nobody would make that joke today, now that Captain Roehm is dead. Nor would anyone of knowledge and discernment have made it even before June 30, 1934, because the scroll of Hitler's disloyalties was written in giant words.

One after another he eliminated those who helped him to his career: Drexler, Feder, Gregor Strasser. It is true that he has been loyal to some colleagues—those who never disagreed with him, who gave him absolute obedience. This loyalty is not an unmixed virtue, considering the unsavoriness of such men as Streicher, the Jew-baiter of Nuremberg. Nothing can persuade Hitler to give Goering up, or Streicher, or Rosenberg. Unsavoriness alone is not enough to provoke his draconian ingratitude.

His physical courage is a moot point. When his men were fired on in the Munich *Putsch* of 1923, he flung himself to the street with such violence that his shoulder was broken. Nazi explanations of this are two: (1) linked arm in arm with a man on his right who was shot and killed, he was jerked unwittingly to the pavement; (2) he behaved with the reflex action of the veteran front-line soldier, *viz.*, sensibly fell flat when the bullets came.

Hitler has told an acquaintance his own story of the somewhat mysterious circumstances in which he won the Iron Cross. He was a dispatch bearer. He was carrying messages across a part of No Man's Land which was believed to be clear of enemy troops when he heard French voices. He was alone, armed only with a revolver; so with great presence of mind he shouted imaginary orders to an imaginary column of men. The Frenchmen tumbled out of a deserted dugout, seven in all, hands up. Hitler alone delivered all seven to the German lines. Recounting this story privately, he told his interlocutor that he knew full well the feat would have been impossible, had the seven men been American or English instead of French.

Like that of all fanatics, his capacity for self-belief, his ability to delude himself, is enormous. Thus he probably is perfectly "sincere" when in a preposterous interview with the *Daily Mail* he says that the Nazi revolution cost only twenty-six lives. He believes absolutely in what he says—at the moment.

But his lies have been notorious. Hitler promised the authorities of Bavaria not to make a *Putsch;* and promptly made one. He promised to tolerate the Papen government; then fought it. He promised not to change the composition of his first cabinet; then changed it. He promised to kill himself if the Munich coup failed; it failed, and he is still alive.

II

Hitler, at forty-six, is not in first-rate physical condition. He has gained about twelve pounds in the past year, and his neck and midriff show it. His physical presence has always been indifferent; the extreme sloppiness with which he salutes is, for instance, notorious. The forearm barely moves above the elbow. He had lung trouble as a boy, and was blinded by poison gas in the war.

In August, 1935, it was suddenly revealed that the Leader had suffered a minor operation some months before to remove a polyp on his vocal cords—penalty of years of tub-thumping. The operation was successful. The next month Hitler shocked his adherents at Nuremberg by alluding, in emotional and circumlocutory terms, to the possibility of his death. "I do not know when I shall finally close my eyes," he said, "but I do know that the party will continue and will rule. Leaders will come and Leaders will die, but Germany will live. . . . The army must preserve the power given to Germany and watch over it." This speech led to rumors (quite unconfirmed) that the growth in Hitler's throat was malignant, and that he had cancer.

He takes no exercise, and his only important relaxation (though recently he began to like battleship cruises in the Baltic or North Sea) is music. He is deeply musical. Wagner is one of the cardinal influences in his life; he is obsessed by Wagner. He goes to the opera as often as he can. Sessions of the Reichstag, which take place in the Kroll Opera House, sometimes end with whole performances of Wagner operas—to the boredom of nonmusical deputies!

When he is fatigued at night then his friend and court jester Hanfstaengl may be summoned to play him to sleep, sometimes with Schumann or Verdi, more often with Beethoven and Wagner, for Hitler needs music as if it were a drug. Hanfstaengl is a demoniac pianist. I have heard him thump the keys at the Kaiserhof with such resonance that the walls shook. When Hanfstaengl plays he keeps time to his own music by puffing out his cheeks and bellowing like a trumpet. The effect is amazing. You cannot but believe that a trumpeter is hidden somewhere in the room. Hanfstaengl's popularity with Hitler is, however, believed to be waning.

Hitler cares nothing for books, nothing for clothes (he seldom wears anything but an ordinary brown-shirt uniform, or a double-breasted blue serge suit, with the inevitable raincoat and slouch hat), nothing for friends, and nothing for food and drink. He neither smokes nor drinks, and he will not allow anyone to smoke near him. He is practically a vegetarian. At the banquet tendered him by Mussolini he would eat only a double portion of scrambled eggs. He drinks coffee occasionally, but not often. Once or twice a week he crosses from the Chancellery to the Kaiserhof Hotel (the G.H.Q. of the Nazi Party before he came to power), and sits there and sips—chocolate.

This has led many people to speak of Hitler's "asceticism" but asceticism is not quite the proper word. He is limited in aesthetic interests, but he is no flagellant or anchorite. There is very little of the *austere* in Hitler. He eats only vegetables—but they are prepared by an exquisitely competent chef. He lives "simply"—but his flat in Munich is the last word in courtly sumptuousness.

He works, when in Berlin, in the palace of the Reichskanzler on the Wilhelmstrasse. He seldom uses the President's palace a hundred yards away on the same street, because when Hindenburg died he wanted to eliminate as much as possible the memory of Presidential Germany. The building is new, furnished in modern glass and metal, and Hitler helped design it. Murals of the life of Wotan adorn the walls. An improvised balcony has been built over the street, from which on public occasions the Leader may review his men. Beneath the hall—according to reports—is a comfortable bombproof cellar.

Hitler dislikes Berlin. He leaves the capital at any opportunity, preferring Munich or Berchtesgaden, a village in southern Bavaria, where he has an alpine chalet, Haus Wachenfeld. Perched on the side of a mountain, this retreat, dear to his heart, is not far from the Austrian frontier, a psychological fact of great significance. From his front porch he can almost see the homeland which repudiated him, and for which he yearns.

III

By a man's friends may ye know him. But Hitler has none. For years his most intimate associate, beyond all doubt, was Captain Ernst Roehm, chief of staff of the SA (*Sturm Abteilung*—storm troops—brown shirts), whom he executed on June 30, 1934. From one of the half-dozen men in Germany indisputably most qualified to know, I have heard it that Roehm was the *only* man in Germany, the single German out of sixty-five million Germans, with whom Hitler was on *Dufuss* (thee and thou) terms. Now that Roehm is dead there is no single German who calls Hitler "Adolf." Roehm was a notorious homosexual; but one should not deduce from this that Hitler is homosexual also.

The man who is closest to Hitler at present is his chief bodyguard, Lieutenant Brückner. The only two men who can see him at any time, without previous appointment, are Ribbentrop, his adviser in foreign affairs, and Schacht, the economics dictator. His chief permanent officials, like Dietrich, his press secretary, may see him daily, and so may Hess, the deputy leader of the party; but even Hess is not an *intimate* friend. Neither Goering nor Goebbels may see Hitler without previous appointment.

He is almost oblivious of ordinary personal contacts. A colleague of mine traveled with him in the same airplane, day after day, for two months during the 1932 electoral campaigns. Hitler never talked to a soul, not even to his secretaries, in the long hours in the air; never stirred, never smiled. My friend remembers most vividly that in order to sneak a cigarette when the plane stopped he had to run out of sight of the entourage. He says that he saw Hitler five or six hours a day during this trip, but that he is perfectly sure Hitler, meeting him by chance outside the airplane, would not have known his name or face.

He dams up his emotion to the bursting point, then is apt to break out in crying fits. A torrent of feminine tears compensates for the months of uneasy struggle not to give himself away. For instance, when he spent a whole night trying to persuade a dissident leader, Otto Strasser, from leaving the party, he broke into tears three times. In the early days he often wept when other methods to carry a point failed.

Hitler does not enjoy too great exposure of this weakness, and he tends to keep all subordinates at a distance. They worship him, but they do not know him well. They may see him every day, year in year out; but they would never dare to be familiar. Hanfstaengl told me once that in all the years of their association he had never called Hitler anything except "Herr Hitler" (*or* "Herr Reichskanzler" after the Leader reached power); and that Hitler had never called him by first name or his diminutive (Putzi), but always "Hanfstaengl" or "Dr. Hanfstaengl." There is an inhumanity about the inner circle of the Nazi party that is scarcely credible.

An old-time party member today would address Hitler as *"Mein Führer";* others as "Herr Reichskanzler." When greeted with the Nazi salute and the words "Heil Hitler," Hitler himself replies with "Heil Hitler." Speechmaking, the Leader addresses his followers as "My" German people. In posters for the plebiscites he asks, "Dost thou, German man, and thou, German woman . . . etc." It is as if he feels closer to the German people in bulk than to any individual German, and this is indeed true. The German *people* are the chief emotional reality of his life.

Let us now examine Hitler's relation to the imperatives which dominate the lives of most men.

He is totally uninterested in women from any personal sexual point of view. He thinks of them as housewives and mothers or potential mothers, to provide sons for the battlefield—other people's sons.

"The life of our people must be freed from the asphyxiating perfume of modern eroticism," he says in *Mein Kampf*, his autobiography. His personal life embodies this precept to the fullest. He is not a woman-hater, but he avoids and evades women. His manners are those of the wary chevalier, given to hand-kissing—and nothing else. Many women are attracted to him sexually, but they have had to give up the chase. Frau Goebbels formerly had evening parties to which she asked pretty and distinguished women to meet him, but she was never able to arrange a match. The rumor was heard for a time that the coy Leader was engaged to the granddaughter of Richard Wagner. It was nonsense. It is quite possible that Hitler has never had anything to do with a woman in his life.

Nor, as is so widely believed, is he homosexual. Several German journalists spent much time and energy, when such an investigation was possible, checking every lodging that Hitler in Munich days had slept in; they interviewed beer hall proprietors, coffee house waiters, landladies, porters. No evidence was discovered that Hitler had been intimate with anybody of any sex at any time. His sexual energies, at the beginning of his career, were obviously sublimated into oratory. . . .

IV

He was born and brought up a Roman Catholic. But he lost faith early and he attends no religious services of any kind. His Catholicism means nothing to him; he is impervious even to the solace of confession. On being formed, his government almost immediately began a fierce religious war against Catholics, Protestants, and Jews alike.

Why? Perhaps the reason was not religion fundamentally, but politics. To Hitler the overwhelming first business of the Nazi revolution was the "unification," the *Gleichschaltung* (co-ordination) of Germany. He had one driving passion, the removal from the Reich of any competition, of whatever kind. Catholicism, like Judaism, was a profoundly international (thus non-German) organism. Therefore— out with it.

The basis of much of the madness of Hitlerism was his incredibly severe and drastic desire to purge Germany of non-German elements, to create a one hundred per cent Germany for one hundred per cent Germans only. He disliked bankers and department stores—as Dorothy Thompson pointed out—because they represented non-German, international, financial and commercial forces. He detested socialists and Communists because they were affiliated with world groups aiming to internationalize labor. He loathed, above all, pacifists, because pacifists opposed war and were internationalist in basic views.

Catholicism he considered a particularly dangerous competitive force because it demands two allegiances of a man, and double allegiance was something Hitler could not countenance. Thus the campaign against the "black moles," as Nazis call priests. Thus the attacks on the Munich cardinal, Faulhauber; the anti-Catholic polemics of Rosenberg and Goebbels; the outrages of August, 1935.

Protestantism was—theoretically—a simple matter for Hitler to deal with because the Lutheran Church presumably was German and nationalist. Hitler thought that by the simple installation of an army chaplain, a ferocious Nazi named Mueller, as Reichsbishop, he could "co-ordinate" the Evangelical Church in Germany, and turn it to his service. The idea of a united Protestant Church appealed to his neat architect's mind. He was wrong. The church question has been an itching pot of trouble ever since.

It was quite natural, following the confused failure to Nazify Protestantism, that some of Hitler's followers should have turned to Paganism. The Norse myths are a first-class nationalist substitute. Carried to its logical extreme, Naziism in fact demands the creation of a new and nationalist religion.

Heiden has quoted Hitler's remark, "We do not want any other God than Germany itself." This is a vital point. *Germany* is Hitler's religion.

Vividly in *Mein Kampf* Hitler tells the story of his first encounter with a Jew. He was a boy of seventeen, alone in Vienna, and he had never seen a Jew in his life. The Jew, a visitor from Poland or the Ukraine in native costume, outraged the tender susceptibilities of the youthful Hitler.

"Can this creature be a Jew?" he asked himself. Then bursting on him, came a second question: "Can he possibly be a *German?*"

This early experience had a profound influence on him, forming the emotional base of his perfervid anti-Semitism. He was provincially mortified that any such creature could be one with himself, a sharer in Teuton nationality. Later he "rationalized" his fury on economic and political grounds. Jews, he said, took jobs away from "Germans"; Jews controlled the press of Berlin, the theater, the arts; there were too many Jewish lawyers, doctors, professors; the Jews were a "pestilence, worse than the Black Death."

No one can properly conceive the basic depth and breadth of Hitler's anti-Semitism who has not carefully read *Mein Kampf*. This book was written ten years ago. He changed it as edition followed edition, in minor particulars, and refuses to allow its publication—unexpurgated—abroad. Recently he sued a French publisher who tried to bring out an unabridged translation. In all editions the implacability of his anti-Jewish prejudice remains.

Any number of incidents outside the book may be mentioned. For instance, in the winter of 1934–35 he went four times to see a play called *Tovarich*, recounting sympathetically the plight of aristocratic Russian émigrés and sneering at the Bolsheviks. Before he first attended it, it is said, his secretaries telegraphed to Paris to ascertain if the author, Jacques Deval, was Aryan as far back as his grandparents. It would have been unthinkable for Hitler to have witnessed a play by even a partly Jewish author.

Long before he became chancellor, Hitler would not allow himself to speak to a Jew even on the telephone. A publicist as well known as Walter Lippmann, a statesman as eminent as Lord Reading, would not be received at the Brown House. An interesting point arises. Has Hitler since his youth actually ever been in the company of a Jew, ever once talked to one? Probably not.

v

Now we may proceed to summarize what might be called Hitler's positive qualities.

First of all, consider his single-mindedness, his intent fixity of purpose. His tactics may change; his strategy may change; his *aim,* never. His aim is to create a strong national Germany, with himself atop it. No opportunistic device, no zigzag in polemics, is too great for him; but the aim, the goal, never varies.

Associated with his single-mindedness is the quality of stamina. All dictators have stamina; all need it. Despite Hitler's lack of vigorous gesture and essential flabbiness, his physical endurance is considerable. I know interviewers who have talked to him on the eve of an election, after he had made several speeches a day, all over Germany, week on end; they found him fresh and even calm. "When I have a mission to fulfill, I shall have the strength for it," he said.

Like all dictators, he has a considerable capacity for hard work, for industry, though he is not the sloghorse for punishment that, for instance, Stalin is. He is not a good executive; his desk is usually high with documents requiring his decision which he neglects. He hates to make up his mind. His orders are often vague and contradictory. Yet he gets an immense amount of work done. "Industry" in a dictator or head of a state means, as a rule, ability to read and listen. The major part of the work of Hitler or Mussolini is perusal of reports and attention to the advice of experts and subordinates. During half their working time they are receiving information. Therefore it is necessary for a dictator (a) to choose men intelligently (many of Hitler's best men he inherited from the old civil service); and (b) to instill faith in himself in them. Hitler has succeeded in this double task amply. And when his men fail him he murders them.

Hitler's political sense is highly developed and acute. His calculations are shrewd and penetrating to the smallest detail. For instance, his two major decisions on foreign policy—Germany's departure from the League of Nations and the introduction of conscription—were deliberately announced on Saturday afternoon to ease the shock to opinion abroad. When he has something unpleasant to explain, the events of June 30th for instance, he usually speaks well after eight P.M., so that foreign newspapers can carry only a hurried and perhaps garbled account of his words.

He made good practical use of his anti-Semitism. The Jewish terror was, indeed, an excellent campaign maneuver. The Nazis surged into power in March, 1933, with an immense and unrealizable series of electoral pledges. They promised to end unemployment, rescind the

Versailles Treaty, regain the Polish corridor, assimilate Austria, abolish department stores, socialize industry, eliminate interest on capital, give the people land. These aims were more easily talked about than achieved. One thing the Nazis could do. One pledge they could redeem—beat the Jews.

Hitler bases most decisions on intuition. Twice, on supreme occasions, it served him well. In the spring of 1932 his most powerful supporters, chiefly Roehm, pressed him to make a *Putsch*. Hitler refused, *feeling* absolute surety that he could come to power legally. Again, in the autumn of 1932, after the Nazis had lost heavily in the November elections, a strong section of the party, led by Gregor Strasser, urged him to admit defeat and enter a coalition government on disadvantageous terms. Hitler, with consummate perspicacity, refused. And within three months he had reached power such as the maddest of his followers had never dreamed of.

Another source of Hitler's power is the impersonality I have already mentioned. His vanity is extreme, but in an odd way it is not personal. He has no peacockery. Mussolini must have given autographs and photographs to at least several thousand admirers since 1922. Those which Hitler has bestowed on friends may be counted on the fingers of two hands. His vanity is the more effective because it expresses itself in nonpersonal terms. He is the vessel, the instrument, of the will of the German people; or so he pretends. Thus his famous statement, after the June 30th murders, that for twenty-four hours he had been the supreme court of Germany.

Hitler is a man of passion, of instinct, not of reason. His "intellect" is that of a chameleon who knows when to change his color, of a crab who knows when to dive into the sand; his "logic" that of a panther who is hungry, and thus seeks food.

His brain is small and vulgar, limited, narrow, suspicious, but behind it is the lamp of passion, and this passion has such quality that it is immediately discernible and recognizable, like a diamond in the sand. The range of his interests is so slight that any sort of stimulus provokes the identical reflex: music, religion, economics mean nothing to him except exercise in nationalism.

Anthony Eden, when he visited Berlin in the spring of 1935 and talked with Hitler seven hours, was quoted as saying that he showed "complete mastery" of foreign affairs. This is, of course, nonsense. Hitler does not know one-tenth as much about foreign affairs as, say,

H. R. Knickerbocker, or Vernon Bartlett, or Frank H. Simonds, or H. F. Armstrong, or Mr. Eden himself. What Eden meant was that Hitler showed unflagging mastery of *his own view* of foreign affairs.

VI

Then there is oratory. This is probably the chief external explanation of Hitler's rise. He talked himself to power. The strange thing is that Hitler is a bad speaker. He screeches; his mannerisms are awkward; his voice breaks at every peroration; he never knows when to stop. Goebbels is a far more subtle and accomplished orator. Yet Hitler, whose magnetism across the table is almost nil, can arouse an audience, especially a big audience, to frenzy.

He knows of course all the tricks. At one period he was accustomed to mention at great length the things that "we Germans" (*wir*) had or did not have or wanted to do or could not do. The word *"wir"* drove into the audience with the rhythmic savagery of a pneumatic drill. Then Hitler would pause dramatically. That, he would say, was the whole trouble. In Germany the word *"wir"* had no meaning; the country was disunited; there was no "we."

Recently Hitler told a French interviewer about an early oratorical trick and triumph, fifteen years ago in a Communist stronghold in Bavaria. He was savagely heckled. "At any moment they might have thrown me out of the window, especially when they produced a blind war invalid who began to speak against all the things that are sacred to me. Fortunately I had also been blind as a result of the war. So I said to these people, 'I know what this man feels. I was even more bewildered than he at one moment—but *I* have recovered my sight!'"

Hitler's first followers were converts in the literal sense of the term. They hit the sawdust trail. Hitler might have been Aimee Semple McPherson or Billy Sunday. Men listened to him once and were his for life—for instance, Goebbels, Brückner, Goering, Hess.

VII

Hitler never flinched from the use of terror, and terror played a powerful role in the creation of the Nazi state. From the beginning he encouraged terror. The only purely joyous passage in *Mein Kampf* is the description of his first mass meeting, in which the newly organized SA pummeled hecklers bloody. The function of the SA was rough-house: first, rough-house with the aim of preserving "order" at public meetings; second, rough-house on the streets, to frighten, terrorize, and murder Communists.

He gave jobs, big jobs, to confessed and admitted terrorists and murderers, like Killinger and Heines. When a Communist was murdered at Potempa, in Silesia, in circumstances of peculiarly revolting brutality, Hitler announced publicly his spiritual unity with the murderers. When, in August, 1932, he thought that Hindenburg might appoint him chancellor, he asked for a three-day period during which the SA could run wild on the streets, and thus avenge themselves upon their enemies. And we cannot forget the 30th June, 1934.

Hitler's one contribution to political theory was the *Führer Prinzip* (Leader Principle). This means, briefly, authority from the top down, obedience from the bottom up, the reversal of the democratic theory of government. It was, as Heiden points out, a remarkably successful invention, since almost anybody could join the movement, no matter with what various aims, and yet feel spiritual cohesion through the personality of the leader. The Nazi movement gave wonderful play to diverse instincts and desires.

Then again, Germans love to be ruled. "The most blissful state a German can experience is that of being bossed," a friend of mine put it in Berlin. And Edgar Ansel Mowrer has recorded the shouts of Nazi youngsters on the streets, "We spit at freedom." A German feels undressed unless he is in uniform. The *Führer Prinzip* not only exploited this feeling by transforming the passive character of German docility, German obedience, into an active virtue; it gave expression also to the bipolar nature of obedience, namely that most men—even Germans—associate with a desire to be governed a hidden will to govern. The *Führer Prinzip* created hundreds, thousands, of sub-*Führers*, little leaders, down to the lowest storm-troop leader. It combined dignified submission with opportunity for leadership.

Mein Kampf, for all its impersonality, reveals over and over again Hitler's faith in "the man." After race and nation, personality is his main preoccupation. It is easy to see that the *Führer Prinzip* is simply a rationalization of his own ambition; the theory is announced on the implicit understanding that the "man" is Hitler himself. "A majority," he says, "can never be a substitute for the Man."

The Illusion of American Omnipotence

by D. W. BROGAN

DECEMBER, 1952

D. W. Brogan is a Scot who writes in the best tradition of a long line of European observers of the American scene. He was edu-cated at the University of Glasgow, Oxford, and got an M.A. in American history at Harvard. He has lectured at many American colleges and has written several books about us. As a citizen of a country which once shouldered the far-flung world responsibil-ities America now has, he is particularly fitted to comment, as he does here, on our attitude toward the sometimes maddening events which keep happening in the world and over which we have little control—but for which we often seek a scapegoat among our political leaders.

I am writing this on the Pacific Coast, before the election, but in the conviction that the result of the election will very little affect the prob-lem that I want to discuss. Even if the Republicans should make a clean sweep, even if the State Department is cleaned out, from the Secretary to the doorkeepers, even if the Pentagon is purged from the Joint Chiefs of Staff to the leaders of the rescue teams who find lost visitors, one problem of American policy will remain: the problem of the existence, in the American mind, of what I call the illusion of omnipotence. This is the illusion that any situation which distresses or endangers the United States can only exist because some Ameri-cans have been fools or knaves.

Such a situation may exist because of conditions about which the United States has, and will have, little to say. For America, powerful though she is, is not omnipotent. A great many things happen in the world regardless of whether the American people wish them to or not. I deeply regret this state of affairs; like Bertrand Russell, I would gladly settle for an American hegemony; but we are not representa-tive characters, and American hegemony not only does not exist, but it is not even universally expected or desired.

I should, perhaps, say that the illusion of omnipotence to which I refer is not shared by all Americans. Nothing could be sillier than to attribute to nearly 160,000,000 people one common attitude, or to assume, as many European intellectuals do, that there is such a thing as "what the American people are thinking." Nevertheless, the idea that I am trying to describe is expressed by Senators and columnists, by candidates, by preachers, by people overheard in taverns and club cars, in drugstores and restaurants—the idea that the whole world, the great globe itself, can be moving in directions annoying or dangerous to the American people only because some elected or nonelected Americans are fools or knaves. When something goes wrong, "I wuz robbed" is the spontaneous comment—the American equivalent of that disastrous French cry, *"Nous sommes trahis."*

It should also be said that I am not reproaching the American people, or even any important fraction of them, with the sort of mere arrogance that the British displayed in the nineteenth century, the arrogance that made the humiliation of the Boer War so refreshing to the rest of the world. There would be plenty of justification for reproach if the American people were as pleased with themselves today as the English were around the time of Queen Victoria's Diamond Jubilee. But except in the Tribune Tower and a few other strongholds of the spirit of Jefferson Brick, Americans are not overflowing with self-satisfaction.

It would not be surprising if they were self-satisfied. For twice, in a not very long lifetime, America has redressed the balance of history. But for American intervention in the first war, it would have ended in a draw. But for American intervention in the second (which began with Lend-Lease, not with Pearl Harbor), Hitler would have had, with his Axis partners, a free hand. One result of this would, in the long run, have been war with the United States; but that long-run consequence matters little in this context. What does matter is that what stopped the Second and the Third Reich was American power. By 1945—with the greatest fleet, the greatest air force, and one of the two greatest armies in the world—the United States had become a world power such as had never been seen before. Never had plowshares been beaten into swords so fast and on so large a scale.

And never were swords beaten back into plowshares as fast as in 1945. As a demonstration of power, and of pacific intention, the scenario was perfect. The crowd that formed a conga line round the

White House on V-J Day represented the American temper of August 1945 to perfection. So did Mr. Leo Crowley cutting off Lend-Lease; so did the immediate pressure to end all the controls and get the boys home. True, there was the atomic bomb—but the thought that there would soon be a world in which the atomic bomb would be a very present hope would have shocked nine Americans out of ten. The war had been won; the fascist menace had been destroyed. True, there was no such mood of high hope as in 1919; but the lesson of 1919 was not lost. America would not again take mere victory for enough, would not again walk out on the job.

And America has not walked out on the job. American policy since 1945 has, on the whole, been wise, far-seeing, magnanimous. Compare it with the policy of the years after the first war, with the policy of the years of Harding and Coolidge, and the growth in wisdom and responsibility is remarkable. Had there not been such a growth, the Kremlin would have won without firing a shot.

It is partly because the American people feel—rightly—that they have used their great power generously, that in 1952 they are perplexed, distressed, angry, and to some extent deluded. Why is it that, given the power, given the generosity of its use, the United States should be involved in the Korean mess? Why should so great a part of the world have passed into hostile hands? Why should the United States still be in danger, know the irritation of the draft in "peacetime," suffer, in Korea, one of the most humiliating of American military defeats, and nominate, for the Presidency, a soldier not merely or mainly as a reward, but because the times seem to call for a soldier in the White House?

It is my opinion that one reason for American distress is the American belief in American invulnerability and American omnipotence.

II

Belief in American invincibility is, on the whole, a good thing. A corresponding English belief in 1940, without nearly as much material justification for it, probably changed the history of the world. "The English always win, don't they?" asked my intelligent four-year-old son. The English won, but at a cost that has taken away the taste for victory. The Russians won too, but in the recent past they had lost. Probably the only people in the world who now have the historical sense of inevitable victory are the Americans. This belief, in its most extravagant, or McCormick, form, assumes that America doesn't need friends. In the less romantic, or Taft, form, it assumes that America doesn't need friends much. But even in the case of people who laugh at the Colonel and swear at the Senator, there is a lingering suspicion that there must be something grossly wrong when American policy suffers rebuffs; when, in despite of American opinion and interests, things go awry.

That grave mistakes have been made need not be doubted. As Mr. Walter Lippmann keeps on reminding his fellow-countrymen, one of the most obvious was the decision to exploit the victory at Inchon, regardless of the natural interest of the Chinese Communist government, of *any* Chinese government, in the arrival of a victorious American army on the Yalu. For that decision, Mr. Truman, Mr. Acheson, and General MacArthur are responsible, in that order. (For the actual military dispositions, General MacArthur is responsible, unless we are, belatedly, to blame Lincoln for the errors of General John Pope before Second Manassas.) That a naïve view of the world was displayed at Yalta, and long before Yalta, by many powerful Americans, is true. Eyes were kept on the conniving British Empire, as they are still kept by Colonel McCormick, Mr. George Sokolsky, and others— eyes which had better have been directed elsewhere. But even had those eyes been more prudently fastened upon Russia, even had American policy been controlled by a Richelieu or a Bismarck, some of the present disillusionment would have occurred all the same. For America, the most powerful nation in the world, was not omnipotent and a great many things in the world were going on and going their own way regardless of the views of the American people.

For great as is American power, it is not so great as to quell, by its mere existence, all opposition. In the good old days an English fleet could sail into the Bay of Naples and tell that able Bourbon, King Charles III, that he could be neutral or have his capital blown up around his ears. In the good old days before the "good neighbor" policy, the United States (or the United Fruit Company, if they could be distinguished) could lay down the law in the Caribbean. As Cleveland's Secretary of State said, the fiat of the United States was law in America, if the United States chose to insist.

But those days are gone. The United States could insist if she wanted to, but at excessive political cost. Even that American by-blow, the Republic of Panama, can defy Washington, up to the point where the safety of the United States is directly and indisputably involved. These facts are accepted. Yet a great many Americans, when China gets out of hand, or into the wrong hands, think this can only be because of some gross error or even crime on the part of the official rulers of America. Even so simple an explanation as that Chiang made the mistake denounced in all the military textbooks, and exemplified in the careers of Jefferson Davis and of Hitler, of commanding at long range and through favorites, is ignored. People feel that Chiang's defeat (a disaster for America, I freely admit) *must* have been due to American folly or American treason. People refuse to believe that it might have had other, more important causes, above all the one admirably described by Senator Tom Connally: "If he's a generalissimo, why doesn't he generalize?"

The Chinese situation is, at the moment, the most important of these American preoccupations and causes of bewilderment. But the sense of bewilderment is visible in some American attitudes toward Europe too. Why hasn't Marshall aid won over the French Communists— that is, ended a schism in French society going back to the Commune of 1871, if not to the Commune of 1793? Why hasn't it converted "Red Emilia," the Italian district that was in a violent revolutionary uproar in Wilson's first term? Why is it not certain that the inhabitants of the "People's Republic of Germany," after being fought over, and driven here and there, and after having had their social structure destroyed, following the disillusionments caused by the collapse of the Hohenzollerns, the Weimar Republic, and the Thousand-Year-Reich, will welcome slogans admirably designed for Cincinnati or Oakland? In such perplexities there is embedded, at the foundation perhaps, the illusion that the world must go the American way if the Americans want it strongly enough and give firm orders to their agents to see that it is done.

III

This illusion of omnipotence is best illustrated by the very common American attitude toward the Chinese Revolution. In this attitude— apparently the dominant one at the moment—there is a curious absence of historical awe and historical curiosity. The Chinese Revolution, an event of immense importance, is often discussed as if it were simply a problem in American foreign and domestic policy and politics. The Communist triumph in China is discussed as if it were simply the result of American action or inaction, the result of the mistakes, and worse than mistakes, of General Marshall, Secretary Acheson, President Roosevelt, and the Institute of Pacific Relations; and as if the Communists or the Russians would not have "captured" China had American policy been represented and controlled by Representative Judd—or even, perhaps, by Senators Cain and Jenner.

Is this not to display the belief in American omnipotence in very striking form? What is going on in China affects the oldest civilization now in existence. It affects about a fifth of the human race. It must have roots, deep roots, in the Chinese problem as seen by the Chinese. This is no matter of a regime imposed by Russia on a helpless small nation like Romania or Hungary. It is a historical phenomenon that may turn out to be more important than the Russian Revolution. It may well turn out, also, to be disastrous for us and for China. But the first thing to notice is the size of the phenomenon; to notice, for example, that there are five Chinese for every two Americans. What inherent necessity is there that the decision in China is, was, or ever will be in American hands?

It is not only a matter of scale. There is distance. China is six thousand miles from the Pacific Coast of America. How was and is American power to be effectively exercised in that distance? I anticipate one answer—that Russian power *is* being exercised, and that it was Russian power (in the absence of American power because of American folly and treason) that "took over" China. This is not demonstrated and in this crude and popular form is not probable. But even if it were true, Russia is not six thousand miles from China. Russia has had a common frontier with China for three hundred years, and as Russia's center of industrial gravity moves eastward, Russian power gets nearer China and can be more readily exercised there. In a straight contest for control of China between the United States and the U.S.S.R., with the Chinese regarded as vile bodies, the U.S.S.R. would hold the trumps. To ignore that is to show the attitude of mind of those who have complained that, at Yalta, F.D.R. "permitted" Russia to become a Pacific power. Russia was a Pacific power before the United States existed. And she was and is an Asiatic power, which the United States is not. Lake Baikal and Lake Superior are on different continents. Vladivostok and Peiping are not.

But the real lack of historical reference and realism is in the assumption that Russia "took over" China as she took over Poland.

Even if we assume that there is as united an opposition to Communist rule in China as I believe there is in Poland, the scale of the taking-over ought to impose reflection. By what miracle was it done? Could General Hurley or General Chennault have prevented it? Would a sounder understanding of what the Communists were have prevented the Communist triumph? If it would have, then China is a more tor-pid body, more open to mere manipulation, than it is pleasant to think. If so great an event as the Chinese Communist Revolution could have been prevented by a different American policy, China is "a corpse on the dissecting table," as Charles Gavan Duffy said of Ireland after the Famine. In that case, Mao and Stalin may dissect it and make a monster of it like Dr. Moreau in H. G. Wells' prophetic story. If it was taken over as easily as all that, it will be kept taken over even more easily.

There is some reason to believe and to hope that it is not quite as simple as this. We are in danger of being obsessed with the important and indisputable fact that world Communism is a real and potent force and that it is controlled from Moscow. We tend, therefore, to see the hand of Moscow everywhere and attribute to it an initiating and dominant role that may not always be justified. The Chinese Revolution, we should remember, has been going on longer than the Russian Revolution. Sun Yat-sen was the successful leader of a revo-lution when Lenin was an obscure and not too hopeful exile in Switzerland. But, I shall be told, that was a *different* Chinese Revolu-tion; that was the *good* Chinese Revolution, the one that deposed the Manchu dynasty and abolished the pigtail and the binding of feet; that was the revolution which was inspired and encouraged by Ameri-can missionaries and American-trained students. But isn't it a truism of history that when you start a revolution, you can't be sure where it is going and how far?

It wasn't Lenin who overthrew the Tsardom or Robespierre who stormed the Bastille. In a long, bloody, and profound revolution, the extreme party has many advantages. It may not win; it may not stay victorious; the Jacobins learned that. But it may destroy the old order, the old ruling classes, the rival revolutionary parties, Social Revolu-tionists or Girondins. It doesn't need, in a genuine revolutionary situa-tion, outside aid, outside doctrine, though it may get and benefit by both. The Chinese Communists got aid; they got doctrine. They prob-ably benefited by both (though in 1927 they might have done better without either). But to deny that the Chinese Communists are a large, native Chinese party is to fly in the face of all the evidence. Their leaders may be docile tools of Moscow, but that doesn't alter the fact that the Chinese Communist party which survived the Kuomintang war against it, which survived the "long march," is a formidable indigenous party. On the record, it seems to have been the most formidable indigenous party—the one that, had both the U.S.A. and the U.S.S.R. stayed out, might have won anyway.

Could it have been prevented from defeating the Kuomintang by the provision of "massive and controlled" American aid? I have already suggested that the Russians could play that game too, and their aid could have been both more massive and controlled than the American. But even assuming that they did not so react to open American intervention in a civil war against their political allies, in a neighboring country, how was the aid to be made massive and how was it to be controlled?

Does anyone think that a continuation of what arms aid had been given, or even a stepping-up of such aid, would have done the trick? The Washington wit who said that supplying arms to Chiang was simply a round-about way of Lend-Lease to the Chinese Communists was a jester, possibly frivolous; but he was not altogether wrong. Lend-Lease to Berlin, Lend-Lease to Russia was direct and massive aid to coherent, united, and combative governments. It was not aid to a divided party in a country torn and tired by a generation of foreign and domestic war. More aid to Chiang might have prolonged the war; it might have saved the situation south of the Yangtse; but would it have brought conquest of the Communists by Chiang's forces?

And how was American aid to be controlled—except by exercising a degree of American authority which would not only have inflamed the *amour propre* of the Generalissimo, but would have deprived the Kuomintang of its last political asset, its claim to be "nationalist," to represent the independence of China? Could the aid have been effective without active American participation—without keeping the Marines in China, without sending in more troops, without, in fact, involving the United States in a greater Korean war? Does anyone who remembers the temper of the American people in 1945, from the White House and Capitol to churches and bars, believe that such a policy was politically practicable?

I have been in America every year since 1944 with the exception of

1949. I have sometimes been twice in America in one year. I have been in all regions. At no time before the Korean war did I find anything like the resolution to make great sacrifices to save China which alone could have saved China.

IV

At first sight, the growing American distress at the continuance of the Korean war seems to show something very different from a sense of omnipotence. It shows, indeed, a sense of frustration, dismay, bewilderment. To find hundreds of thousands of American troops fighting in a remote country, seven years after "the end of the war," is baffling enough. To suffer over 120,000 casualties in such a situation is worse. The Korean war is already, in terms of losses, the third most serious war in American history. An American mother lamenting the fate of her son is a figure to inspire sympathy and understanding. It is natural that the American people should want, not on any terms but on some terms, an end to the Korean war.

But in addition to this common and natural sentiment, there is another American attitude that is less defensible and decidedly dangerous. It might be likened to the attitude of the prosperous and pompous citizen who, in a jam, firmly tells the cops, "You can't do that to me." Many, very many Americans, it seems to me, find it inconceivable that an American policy, announced and carried out by the American government, acting with the support of the American people, does not immediately succeed. If it does not, this, they feel, must be because of stupidity or treason. That the Chinese Communist government should defy—and successfully defy—the policy of the United States, seems to them to fly in the face of a truth which they hold to be self-evident.

Yet such situations exist and may well continue to exist. It is by no means certain that American forces will easily be withdrawn from Korea, or even that they may not have to take part in other wars of that kind. Mrs. Kathleen Norris can no more alter that fact than Senator Taft can really guarantee to keep the military budget to a fixed proportion of the total. In the great power vacuum created by the decline of Europe, the United States is forced, and will be forced, to do a great many disagreeable things—or to surrender. This is a new story for the United States, but it is an old one for Europe. What the American people are enduring now is what the French, the English, the Russian peoples, even the Spanish and Italian peoples, suffered in the process of extending or trying to retain their empires.

But, it will be objected, America is not trying to extend an empire; she is defending public order and morality in Korea. This is very different from the piratical adventures of the old world, from the French in Africa, the English in India, or the Russians in Samarkand or Armenia. Morally, this is true. But, just as the purity of the American cause does not win all American families to an acceptance of the Korean war as necessary and tolerable, so the moral turpitude of European enterprises added very little to the burden of empire. And that burden was heavy in terms of lives lost.

It has been calculated—and I do not think it is an improbable calculation—that the French conquest of Algeria cost the French 150,000 lives. (What it cost the Arabs, resisting civilization, no one has paused to compute.) I don't know what the British wars in India cost either in great battles, in minor battles, or in disease, but they cost plenty. Even the British peace, imposed on India, cost plenty to the 100,000 white troops permanently garrisoned in that remote, unhealthy land. Do you think it mattered to a French mother that her son, dead in Algeria, was an agent of imperialism? All she knew was that he had paid what Marshal Gouvion Saint-Cyr candidly called a blood tax. And the same story can be told of Indochina seventy years ago—and now. It is one of minor themes of a once-famous novel, Loti's *Pêcheur d'Islande.* "It's a long way to Carcassonne," said the soldier of the Grande Armée, dying in the snow on the retreat from Moscow; and it is a long time since Vergil made the dying Greek remember sweet Argos.

Morally justifiable—indeed, morally splendid—as the American action in Korea on behalf of the United Nations may be, and urgent as the need may be to find an honorable way out of the predicament in which she finds herself, what Americans are paying today is one of the normal prices of being a great power, of bearing the burdens as well as enjoying the advantages of power.

Again, I have no intention of minimizing the horror of the Korean war. I was in New York in December, 1950, when it was still not certain that the Marines would get out of the trap sprung on them in North Korea—when, indeed, it was not certain that many of them would ever get home. I felt passionately with the American people. And the situation is not purely American. In a year and a half, my eldest son will be in the army and may be in Malaya or Korea. It is a painful story. But it is an old one.

v

Another aspect of the "you can't do this to me" mentality—which, in turn, is an aspect of the illusion of omnipotence—can best be studied in the writings of Mr. David Lawrence of the *U. S. News & World Report*. To Mr. Lawrence the Korean war, the loss of American lives in it, is not merely painful but unendurable. It must be put an end to, and one of the methods suggested has a real interest —to me a pathological interest. If I understand Mr. Lawrence aright, in order to diminish Communist pressures on the Americans in Korea, Poles and Czechs are to be encouraged to acts of sabotage if not of active revolt, and a "resistance movement" is to be subsidized, with a view to diverting Russian or other Communist resources from Korea —that is, from the Americans in Korea.

This modest proposal deserves examination. Mr. Lawrence apparently does not pretend that the United States proposes to do anything more to liberate Poland and Czechoslovakia than to encourage and equip saboteurs. He does not pretend that such activities, in themselves, will bring down the Stalinist regime. They will, he hopes, cause such inconvenience that the heat will be off the Americans.

It is obvious that Mr. Lawrence does not know very much about resistance movements, or the means open to a totally ruthless government to repress resistance movements. He may have heard of Lidice, of Warsaw, even of Oradour-sur-Glane. But the meaning of those episodes is lost on him (and on many other Americans). To save the lives of Americans, to relieve this new and heavy but not intolerable pressure on American society, Poles and Czechs are to risk— for themselves and for their families and, if it comes to a pitch, for their countries—total destruction, the execution of hostages, the annihilation of whole villages, possibly the fate of the peoples of the three Baltic states, of whom we do not even know that, as nations, Lithuania, Estonia, and Latvia exist any longer.

These nations, and more especially the Poles, have undergone experiences that not one home-staying American in a hundred thousand, perhaps in a million, can really comprehend. The liberation of Poland, on these terms, might mean the end of Poland. And the Poles are not even promised liberation; merely the satisfaction of annoying the

Russians and relieving the Americans. If the United States were in mortal danger, patriotic Poles might be willing to take great risks to aid her, since in American survival "the only hope of freedom lies." But she is not in mortal danger; she is in what a Pole who has known first German, then Russian rule, can hardly regard as more than acute discomfort. To ask the Poles to act, at such risks, to diminish this discomfort is something pardonable only on the grounds of invincible ignorance. And it is something that Americans could hardly seriously recommend unless they saw in the situation a denial of one of "the Laws of Nature and of Nature's God," namely, the immunity of the United States from the common ills of this distressed world.

For it should be evident that only if the United States is willing, in a reasonably short time, to undertake, by general war, the liberation of the captive nations, has any American any business urging kinds of resistance which can pay only in the event of a general—and successful—war. Even were the United States to proclaim such a policy, the problem of encouraging resistance is not a simple one. It can be argued, for instance, that the damage done to France by the resistance movement there—from the torturing and burning of victims to the demoralization that some resistance methods fostered—was far more serious than any damage done to the German occupiers. The only justification for disregarding that calculation was a moral one: that if France took no part in her own liberation, she could not, in fact, be liberated; all that could be done was to expel the Germans, which was not the same thing. But even so, the appeals of General de Gaulle and others, and the organization from London of all sorts of resistance activities, were only just tolerable, because they were not only a means of saving English lives but also of saving French souls.

This is not to say that everything possible should not be done to keep alive hope, the Western tradition, the national tradition in the captive nations. A permanently hostile Poland or Czechoslovakia is a double weakness for the U.S.S.R., a possible future military weakness and a present propaganda weakness. But there is a world between the policy advocated by John Foster Dulles and that advocated by those Americans who say, "This can't go on." It may, and no amount of asserting that it can't will alter the fact.

When policies are advocated on the ground that they will "save the lives of American boys," the implication sometimes seems to be that only the lives of American boys really count. It is often forgotten, in this world of short memories, that one justification of Yalta, of the coaxing and bribing of Stalin to enter the Japanese war, was the saving of the lives of American boys. To save the lives of American boys is a high object of policy indeed. It is one of the marks of a democracy, or of a free government, that the military and political leaders can be held to account on that one point. As the Duke of Wellington pointed out, Napoleon could spend his conscripts as he liked, while Wellington might be summoned to the bar of the House of Commons if he threw away the lives of five hundred British soldiers. But that is a very different matter from giving the impression that American lives, as such, are of any special importance; that, as an American friend of mine put it in some unpublished verses:

> Clean-limbed American boys are not like any others.
> Only clean-limbed American boys have mothers.

Their lives are of special importance to Americans, but not to the people of other lands. And there would be widespread resentment over the thoughtless implication that it is the first duty of Poles or Czechs to save American lives.

These are hard sayings and they are negative sayings. But they may not be useless all the same. Only by constant vigilance, prudence, willingness to take the long view and to assess the situation, even in its most unpleasant, frustrating, and dangerous aspects, can American policy succeed—succeed in preserving the freedom of the United States and the freedom of other nations as a means to that end. There are no quick, sure recipes for security and power. The Kremlin hasn't got them; the White House will not have them either. This means that the American people will have to learn a great many new attitudes. (They learn fast, as the history of the world since 1939 shows.) They will have to learn that, even in election years, the world cannot be altered overnight by a speech or a platform. Only by accepting this depressing truth can American power, great, flexible, and beneficent as it is, be used to full advantage.

Russia and the West

by ARNOLD J. TOYNBEE

MARCH, 1953

*No living historian is better equipped than Professor Toynbee
of Britain to take the long view of what is happening between
Russia and the West. His ten-volumed,* A Study of History,
*completed in 1954, is a classic recognized as one of the great
intellectual works of all time. Professor Toynbee was born in
1889 and taught international history and Byzantine and modern
Greek language and literature at the University of London for
many years.*

In the encounter between the world and the West that has been
going on by now for four or five hundred years, the world, not the
West, is the party that, up to now, has had the significant experience.
It has not been the West that has been hit by the world; it is the
world that has been hit—and hit hard—by the West.

A Westerner who wants to grapple with this subject must try, for a
few minutes, to slip out of his native Western skin and look at the
encounter between the world and the West through the eyes of the
great non-Western majority of mankind. Different though the non-
Western peoples of the world may be from one another in race,
language, civilization, and religion, if any Western inquirer asks them
their opinion of the West, he will hear them all giving him the same
answer: Russians, Moslems, Hindus, Chinese, Japanese, and all the
rest. The West, they will tell him, has been the arch-aggressor of
modern times, and each will have their own experience of Western
aggression to bring up against him. The Russians will remind him
that their country has been invaded by Western armies overland in
1941, 1915, 1812, 1709, and 1610; the peoples of Africa and Asia
will remind him that Western missionaries, traders, and soldiers from
across the sea have been pushing into their countries from the coasts
since the fifteenth century. The Asians will also remind him that,

within the same period, the Westerners have occupied the lion's share of the world's last vacant lands in the Americas, Australia, New Zealand, and South and East Africa. The Africans will remind him that they were enslaved and deported across the Atlantic in order to serve the European colonizers of the Americas as living tools to minister to their Western masters' greed for wealth. The descendants of the aboriginal population of North America will remind him that their ancestors were swept aside to make room for the West European intruders and for their African slaves.

This indictment will surprise, shock, grieve, and perhaps even outrage most Westerners today. Dutch Westerners are conscious of having evacuated Indonesia, and British Westerners of having evacuated India, Pakistan, Burma, and Ceylon, since 1945. British Westerners have no aggressive war on their consciences since the South African War of 1899–1902, and American Westerners none since the Spanish-American War of 1898. We forget all too easily that the Germans, who attacked their neighbors, including Russia, in the first world war and again in the second world war, are Westerners too, and that the Russians, Asians, and Africans do not draw fine distinctions between different hordes of "Franks"—which is the world's common name for Westerners in the mass. "When the world passes judgment it can be sure of having the last word," according to a well-known Latin proverb. And certainly the world's judgment on the West does seem to be justified over a period of about four and a half centuries ending in 1945. In the world's experience of the West during all that time, the West has been the aggressor on the whole; and, if the tables are being turned on the West by Russia and China today, this is a new chapter of the story which did not begin until after the end of the second world war. The West's alarm and anger at recent acts of Russian and Chinese aggression at the West's expense are evidence that, for us Westerners, it is today still a strange experience to be suffering at the hands of the world what the world has been suffering at Western hands for a number of centuries past.

II

What, then, has been the world's experience of the West? Let us look at Russia's experience, for Russia is part of the world's great non-Western majority. Though the Russians have been Christians and are, many of them, Christians still, they have never been Western Christians. Russia was converted not from Rome, as England was, but from Constantinople; and, in spite of their common Christian origins, Eastern and Western Christendom have always been foreign to one another, and have often been mutually antipathic and hostile, as Russia and the West unhappily still are today, when each of them is in what one might call a "post-Christian" phase of its history.

This on the whole unhappy story of Russia's relations with the West did, though, have a happier first chapter; for, in spite of the difference between the Russian and the Western way of life, Russia and the West got on fairly well with one another in the early Middle Ages. The peoples traded, and the royal families intermarried. An English King Harold's daughter, for instance, married a Russian prince. The estrangement began in the thirteenth century, after the subjugation of Russia by the Tatars. The Tatars' domination over Russia was temporary, because the Tatars were nomads from the Steppes who could not ever make themselves at home in Russia's fields and forests. Russia's lasting losses as a result of this temporary Tatar conquest were, not to her Tatar conquerors, but to her Western neighbors; for these took advantage of Russia's prostration in order to lop off, and annex to Western Christendom, the western fringes of the Russian world in White Russia and in the western half of the Ukraine. It was not till 1945 that Russia recaptured the last piece of these huge Russian territories that were taken from her by Western powers in the thirteenth and fourteenth centuries.

These Western conquests at Russia's expense in the late Middle Ages had an effect on Russia's life at home, as well as on her relations with her Western assailants. The pressure on Russia from the West did not merely estrange Russia from the West; it was one of the hard facts of Russian life that moved the Russians to submit to the yoke of a new native Russian power at Moscow which, at the price of autocracy, imposed on Russia the political unity that she now had to have if she was to survive. It was no accident that this newfangled autocratic centralizing government of Russia should have arisen at Moscow; for Moscow stood in the fairway of the easiest line for the invasion of what was left of Russia by a Western aggressor. The Poles in 1610, the French in 1812, the Germans in 1941, all marched this way. Since an early date in the fourteenth century, autocracy and centralization have been the dominant notes of all successive Russian regimes. This Muscovite Russian political tradition has perhaps always been as disagreeable for the Russians themselves as it has certainly been distasteful and alarming to their neighbors; but unfortunately the Russians have learned to put up with it, partly perhaps out of sheer habit, but also, no doubt, because they have felt it to be a lesser evil than the alternative fate of being conquered by aggressive neighbors.

This submissive Russian attitude toward an autocratic regime that has become traditional in Russia is, of course, one of the main difficulties, as we Westerners see it, in the relations between Russia and the West today. The great majority of people in the West feel that tyranny is an intolerable social evil. At a fearful cost we have put down tyranny when it has raised its head among our Western selves in the forms of Fascism and National Socialism. We feel the same detestation and distrust of it in its Russian form, whether this calls itself Tsarism or calls itself Communism. We do not want to see this Russian brand of tyranny spread; and we are particularly concerned about this danger to Western ideals of liberty now that we Franks find ourselves thrown upon the defensive for the first time in our history since the second Turkish siege of Vienna in 1682–83. Our present anxiety about what seems to us to be a postwar threat to the West from Russia is a well-justified anxiety in our belief. At the same time, we must take care not to allow the reversal in the relation between Russia and the West since 1945 to mislead us into forgetting the past in our natural preoccupation with the present. When we look at the encounter between Russia and the West in the historian's instead of the journalist's perspective, we shall see that, over a period of several centuries ending in 1945, the Russians have had the same reason for looking askance at the West that we Westerners feel that we have for looking askance at Russia today.

During the past few centuries, this threat to Russia from the West, which has been a constant threat from the thirteenth century till 1945, has been made more serious for Russia by the outbreak, in the West, of a technological revolution which has become chronic and which does not yet show any signs of abating.

When the West adopted firearms, Russia followed suit, and in the sixteenth century she used these new weapons from the West to conquer the Tatars in the Volga valley and more primitive peoples in the Urals and in Siberia. But in 1610 the superiority of the Western armaments of the day enabled the Poles to occupy Moscow and to hold it for two years, while at about the same time the Swedes were also able to deprive Russia of her outlet on the Baltic Sea at the head of the Gulf of Finland. The Russian retort to these seventeenth-century Western acts of aggression was to adopt the technology of the West wholesale, together with as much of the Western way of life as was inseparable from Western technology.

It was characteristic of the autocratic centralizing Muscovite regime that this technological and accompanying social revolution in Russia at the turn of the seventeenth and eighteenth centuries should have been imposed upon Russia from above downward, by the fiat of one man of genius, Peter the Great. Peter is a key figure for an understanding of the world's relations with the West not only in Russia but everywhere; for Peter is the archetype of the autocratic Westernizing reformer who, during the past two and a half centuries, has saved the world from falling entirely under Western domination by forcing the world to train itself to resist Western aggression with Western weapons. Sultans Selim III and Mohammed II and President Mustafa Kemal Atatürk in Turkey, Mehemet Ali Pasha in Egypt, and "the Elder Statesmen," who made the Westernizing revolution in Japan in the eighteen-sixties, were, all of them, following in Peter the Great's footsteps consciously or unconsciously.

Peter launched Russia on a technological race with the West which Russia is still running. Russia has never yet been able to afford to rest, because the West has continually been making fresh spurts. For example, Peter and his eighteenth-century successors brought Russia close enough abreast of the Western world of the day to make Russia just able to defeat her Swedish Western invaders in 1709 and her French Western invaders in 1812; but, in the nineteenth-century Western industrial revolution, the West once more left Russia behind, so that in the first world war Russia was defeated by her German Western invaders as she had been defeated, two hundred years earlier, by the Poles and the Swedes. The present Communist autocratic government was able to supplant the Tsardom in Russia in consequence of Russia's defeat by an industrial Western technology in 1914–17; and the Communist regime then set out, from 1928 to 1941, to do for Russia, all over again, what the Tsar Peter had done for her about 230 years earlier.

For the second time in the modern chapter of her history Russia was now put, by an autocratic ruler, through a forced march to catch up with a Western technology that had once more shot ahead of hers; and Stalin's tyrannical course of technological Westernization was eventually justified, like Peter's, through an ordeal by battle. The Communist technological revolution in Russia defeated the German invaders in the second world war, as Peter's technological revolution had defeated the Swedish invaders in 1709 and the French invaders in 1812. And then, a few months after the completion of the liberation of Russian soil from German-Western occupation in 1945, Russia's American-Western allies dropped in Japan an atom bomb that announced the outbreak of a third Western technological revolution. So today, for the third time, Russia is having to make a forced march in an effort to catch up with a Western technology that, for the third time, has left her behind by shooting ahead. The result of this third event in the perpetual competition between Russia and the West still lies hidden in the future; but it is already clear that this renewal of the technological race is another of the very serious difficulties now besetting the relations between these two ex-Christian societies.

III

Technology is, of course, only a long Greek name for a bag of tools; and we have to ask ourselves: What are the tools that count in this competition in the use of tools as means to power? A power-loom or a locomotive is obviously a tool for this purpose, as well as a gun, an airplane, or a bomb. But all tools are not of the material kind; there are spiritual tools as well, and these are the most potent that Man has made. A creed, for instance, can be a tool; and, in the new round in the competition between Russia and the West that began in 1917, the Russians this time threw into their scale of the balances a creed that weighed as heavily against their Western competitors' material tools as, in the Roman story of the ransoming of Rome from the Gauls, the sword thrown in by Brennus weighed against the Roman gold.

Communism, then, is a weapon; and, like bombs, airplanes, and guns, this is a weapon of Western origin. If it had not been invented by a couple of nineteenth-century Westerners, Karl Marx and Friedrich Engels, who were brought up in the Rhineland and spent the best part of their working lives in London and in Manchester respectively, Communism could never have become Russia's official ideology. There was nothing in the Russian tradition that could have led the Russians to invent Communism for themselves; and it is certain that they would never have dreamed of it if it had not been lying, ready-made, there in the West, for a revolutionary Russian regime to apply in Russia in 1917.

In borrowing from the West a Western ideology, besides a Western industrial revolution, to serve as an anti-Western weapon, the Bolsheviki in 1917 were making a great new departure in Russian history; for this was the first time that Russia had ever borrowed a creed from the West. But it was a creed particularly well suited to serve Russia as a Western weapon for waging an anti-Western spiritual warfare. In the West, where Communism had arisen, this new creed was heresy. It was a Western criticism of the West's failure to live up to her own Christian principles in the economic and social life of this professedly Christian society; and a creed of Western origin which was at the same time an indictment of Western practice was, of course, just the spiritual weapon that an adversary of the West would like to pick up and turn against its makers.

With this Western spiritual weapon in her hands, Russia could carry her war with the West into the enemy's country on the spiritual plane. Since Communism had originated as a product of uneasy Western consciences it could appeal to other uneasy Western consciences when it was radiated back into the Western world by a Russian propaganda. And so now, for the first time in the modern Western world's history since the close of the seventeenth century, when the flow of Western converts to Islam almost ceased, the West has again found itself threatened with spiritual disintegration from inside, as well as with an assault from outside. In thus threatening to undermine Western civilization's foundations on the West's own home ground, Communism has already proved itself a more effective anti-Western weapon in Russian hands than any material weapon could ever be.

Communism has also served Russia as a weapon for bringing into the Russian camp the Chinese quarter of the human race, as well as other sections of that majority of mankind that is neither Russian nor Western. We know that the outcome of the struggle to win the allegiance of these neutrals may be decisive for the outcome of the Russo-Western conflict as a whole, because this non-Western and non-Russian majority of mankind may prove to hold the casting vote in a competition between Russia and the West for world power. Now

Communism can make a twofold appeal to a depressed Asian, African, and Latin American peasantry when it is the voice of Russia that is commending Communism to them.

The Russian spokesman can say to the Asian peasantry first: "If you follow the Russian example, Communism will give you the strength to stand up against the West, as a Communist Russia can already stand up against the West today." The second appeal of Communism to the Asian peasantry is Communism's claim that it can, and that private enterprise neither can nor would if it could, get rid of the extreme inequality between a rich minority and a poverty-stricken majority in Asian countries. Discontented Asians, however, are not the only public for whom Communism has an appeal. Communism also has an appeal for all men, since it can claim to offer mankind the unity which is our only alternative to self-destruction in an atomic age.

It looks as if, in the encounter between Russia and the West, the spiritual initiative, though not the technological lead, has now passed, at any rate for the moment, from the Western to the Russian side. We Westerners cannot afford to resign ourselves to this, because this Western heresy—Communism—which the Russians have taken up, seems to the great majority of people in the West to be a perverse, misguided, and disastrous doctrine and way of life. A theologian might put it that our great modern Western heresiarch Karl Marx has made what is a heretic's characteristic intellectual mistake and moral aberration. In putting his finger on one point in orthodox practice in which there has been a crying need for reform, he has lost sight of all other considerations and therefore has produced a remedy that is worse than the disease.

The Russians' recent success in capturing the initiative from us Westerners by taking up this Western heresy called Communism and radiating it out into the world in a cloud of anti-Western poison gas does not, of course, mean that Communism is destined to prevail. Marx's vision seems, in non-Marxian eyes, far too narrow and too badly warped to be likely to prove permanently satisfying to human hearts and minds. All the same, Communism's success, so far as it has gone, looks like a portent of things to come. What it tells us is that the present encounter between the world and the West is now moving off the technological plane onto the spiritual plane.

The Order of the Turkish Bath

by GEOFFREY FLAVELL

SEPTEMBER, 1956

Americans take more baths than the citizens of any other country, but their quick showers and hurried tubs have little in common with "The Bath" of ancient civilizations, still an important feature of life in some parts of the Mediterranean area. Geoffrey Flavell, a distinguished London surgeon, has written this humorous report on his introduction to "The Bath" in North Africa during the war, when he commanded a surgical division in the RAF. As a surgeon he specializes in the heart and lungs, and is the author of a textbook on thoracic surgery. He writes frequently on travel, food, and wine, and his many interests include military history, archaeology, and modern pictures.

Wherever the bones of Rome are found among the tawny Maghrebian hills, at Dougga and Sbeitla in Tunisia, Timgad near Batna, Djemila near Setif, Volubilis in Morocco, and a hundred lesser, lonelier sites, the greatest surviving monument is invariably the bath. Timgad was a remote provincial garrison town in the Aures mountains, then as now a hotbed of Berber-Numidian insurrections; yet the ruins of fifteen thermae are to be seen there, four of them vast, columned, domed, sumptuous with marble and mosaics. Throughout the Empire the practice held, and the status of a city was judged by the splendor of its baths. The Roman forum itself will still fit into a corner of the Baths of Caracalla, the Museo Nazionale occupies but a room or two of those of Diocletian, and these were rivaled by the magnificences of Titus, Domitian, and Trajan. Who went to them? Everyone.

Patricians first installed private baths in their villas as Renaissance princes did chapels; but to bathe privately vitiated the pleasure of the bath. The thermae were social institutions, compendiums of club, casino, café, causerie, gymnasium, and bath. In them business was transacted, bets made, intrigues fostered, plots hatched, love affairs begun, and the body pleasured, purged, scraped, massaged, exercised, and oiled. One baking day in Timgad, alone save for the hares which infested the ruins, I brushed the sand from a pavement stone and read, scratched there by an ancient hand on some equally hot and idle afternoon, the words *"Venari lavari, ludere ridere, occ est vivere"*—"To hunt and bathe, to play and laugh, that's the life!"

The skin is a sense organ and is derived from the same delicate substance as the retina of the eye, the intricately entwined cochlea of the ear, the pulsing brain itself: it deserves culture and indulgence. Almost the only purpose for which a Roman gentleman did not go to the baths was to wash. He left such perversions to Nordic savages, and rightly. Instead, like Catullus in the great pleasure dome at Sermione, he disrobed in the apodyterium, drifted languidly to be tempered in the tepidarium, heated in the caldarium, steamed in the sudatorium, chilled in the frigidarium, exercised in the ephebeum, oiled in the alipterium, and eventually chatted to in the exedra. Such were the polysyllabic ablutions of a Roman citizen, be he Numidian, Syrian, or Gaul; and such, more or less, they remain in those enchanting survivals of the thermae, built sometimes of their very stones, the hammams of North Africa.

Why Islam alone has so vividly preserved the Roman bath in the "Turkish" bath is obscure. I am unaware of any such cult among the Byzantines from whom the Arab invaders of the seventh century imbibed most of their architecture, decoration, and jewelry. But it is perfectly possible that the Crusaders wrecked as many thermae in Byzantium as they looted churches. More probably, however, the institution, already strongly implanted in the Roman provinces, continued to flourish where civilization itself survived; in short, in Islam until the fourteenth century—for the European Middle Ages were those called by Michelet "the thousand years without a bath."

Two unexpected factors, apart from the Moslem rule of ritual cleanliness, may be added. Contrary to Western beliefs, the Prophet is a puritanical master, at any rate in North Africa, who forbids the pleasure of wine to all, and to the strict even coffee and tobacco; while the visual and plastic arts are reduced by the ban on human representation to mere repetitive geometry, and Arabic music, though the mother of flamenco, has its limitations. With sensual pleasure at so many entrances shut out, the senses of the skin and smell alone remain to be indulged; and so in high and popular use we find perfumes, women, and the hammam.

The other preservative element is the democratic nature of Mohammedanism. Pasha and fellah are brothers in the mosque and in the hammam. At Mecca, on the pilgrimage, all finery is stripped away; sultans and peasants are wrapped in an equal linen cloth. In the warm womb of the hammam they have not even that. Naked as they were born, all men lie in the hot darkness, artificial impediments to conversation cast aside. There is no first or second class at the bathhouse.

The first hammam I ever sampled was at Blida, some forty miles from Algiers. It was a flyblown little town, but it lay at the foot of a mountain where there was skiing in wintertime, and from whose summit the tomb of Cleopatra's daughter was clearly visible at Castiglione. It was perfectly possible, therefore, to roll in the snow and an hour later bathe in a warm sea: as one may do, for example, in the Lebanon but in few other places in the world. Perhaps these extremes suggested the hammam; or perhaps that, mingling business with pleasure, the Colonel and I had been inspecting the town brothel, a resort much favored by military personnel of all ranks, but with little to recommend it beyond a most amiable madam. There is something about this honest and useful trade which seems in later life to promote good humor. At any rate the hammam was conveniently close, and as the Colonel was now a prey to great anxiety concerning both his health and his pension (two subjects which constantly, and with some reason, preoccupied him), I remembered the advice of St. Augustine concerning baths—*"anxietatem pellat ex animo"*—and prescribed a visit. The excellent sense of the Saint (himself born in the Maghreb at Souk Ahras, and later to be bishop of Bône), who prayed "to be made chaste and continent . . . but not yet," and who knew, clearly at first hand, that a visit to the thermae soothed the soul of its *Angst,* could not more opportunely have come to mind.

Beyond the small vestibule was an airy peaceful room of arches almost completely encircled by a wide divan a few inches high upon which cushions were strewn and where lay a number of silent white enshrouded figures. In a corner four men, similarly wrapped, played cards and drank coffee while on the floor nearby three disconsolate hens flapped with their legs tied together. This clearly was the "exedra" or "xystus," a place for recovery and recreation.

Around the walls were many niches for the deposit of clothes, a simple arrangement echoed in the recently excavated ritual baths of Artemis at Cyrene. To one of these the Colonel, with profound misgiving, entrusted his khaki drill and his splendid scarlet hat; we were given each a pair of wooden pattens which clattered on the stone-flagged floor and, girded with an exiguous towel soon to be abandoned, we teetered after the custodian toward a heavy iron-studded door in the farther wall. Counterweighted, it opened ponderously upon creaking hinges, and we were thrust into its gulf like Carthaginian victims into the fiery maw of Moloch.

Inside it was almost as hot, and at first appeared to be in total darkness. A voice beside me gasped, "I'm getting out of here!" and through the steaming murk I was just able to discern the Colonel's white and tubby figure turn too quickly back toward the door and crash to the flags as he fell over his pattens. Had he not been still dazed when we picked him up, I doubt if we would have got him further; but my eyes were beginning to accommodate to the gloom and I could now see that we stood in a stone hall filled with steam. It was almost empty, but in its embrasures stood troughs, also of stone, at which one or two naked men washed with soap.

"My God," said the Colonel, "if I'd known what it was going to be like I'd never have come. I don't believe my heart will stand this heat. What if anyone should see us? Do you suppose they keep tabs on places like this?"

"This is the tepidarium," I replied, breaking into a heavy sweat. "It is time to move on to the next room."

The door through which we now passed was as heavy as the first and so low that we had to stoop beneath its arch. As it swung open, a blast of heat gushed out at us. It reminded me of the day the sirocco blew at Guelma and the birds fell dead; but it was much hotter. I pushed the Colonel through as a sort of screen, and half expected him to melt. Indeed he began to deliquesce, little rivulets of steaming sweat coursing down his folds and wrinkles; but the essential form remained. We now stood, a little out of breath, in a much bigger hall surmounted by a flattish dome mistily seen in the darkness and supported on low vaults. The obscurity increased its scale, so that it resembled a Piranesi prison, or one of the antechambers of Hell. Scattered over the floor, in those attitudes of limp abandon achieved only by the corpse, lay an extraordinary naked throng, the victims, it seemed, of some hideous but bloodless massacre—strangled, perhaps, by order of the Emir.

I saw the Colonel's mouth opening and closing, shaping words whose substance was filched by the heat before it reached his lips, so that he seemed speaking on the other side of a thick glass screen. All at once he wilted to the floor, flung out both his arms, and lay like a plump white sea beast on a fishmonger's slab. Beside him stretched a black meharist, nearby a Berber goum, and a spahi lay beyond. The door seemed a long way off, and I lay down too. The floor itself covered a hypocaust built exactly in the Roman fashion, the hot air being driven along its channels by a kind of primitive bellows or punka fan made of palm branches on a wooden frame. This was hinged to the mud-brick furnace door, outside the building, and worked by hand. Some paving stones were thus hotter than others depending on where the flues ran, and I crawled limply to the coolest. It was exceedingly hot.

A sensation of abandonment now pervaded me, similar to that to which I succumb on rickety funiculars—frightening though one's predicament is there is nothing to be done about it; others are in a like boat; and maybe we shall all get out at the other end in safety. For I cannot pretend the Colonel's fears of heart failure had left me altogether unmoved, and I was conscious of an alarming beat in my temples and in the pit of my stomach. It rapidly became, however, much too hot to worry at all about anything.

The quality of an hammam depends wholly upon the skill of the *kayyās*. "Masseur" is much too emasculate a word to describe his function, though of course he massages expertly. More important is his age-old craft of joint manipulation which leaves that of fashionable blind chiropractors far behind.

When my turn came the heat had done its work, and my muscles were a flaccid pulp. First, squatting beside me, the *kayyās* took my fingers, limp and unresisting, and gently cracked them at every phalangeal joint, not merely by pressing backwards upon them, but by pulling each in its long axis. I was only mistily aware as he lay with his foot in my armpit, grasped a wrist, and glided my humerus up and down in its socket in exactly the maneuver osteopaths employ when they are working on arthritic patients under anesthesia. In like manner the femur was swiveled in its acetabulum; and my neck stretched like a hanging man's. Then he flopped me over onto my belly, stood barefooted in the small of my back, and seizing my hands and feet arched my trunk into a backward bow. I could feel my intervertebral discs clunk back into place as he stamped on them with his heels. Nothing hurt at all. Massage, starting at the extremities and working toward the heart, followed; and finally he produced a strigil, the image of one the Etruscans used, and scraped me vigorously, pausing now and then to show me proudly the debris of desquamation with a *"Comme tu es sale!"*

The Colonel was muttering "bloody wonderful!" as I got him to his feet and into the cold-room; but there was no time for words as the icy douche descended, and we gasped for breath as blood and consciousness flooded back. In another moment, wrapped each in a vast *burnous* of towel, we lay, feeling better than we had ever felt before, on the long dais in the outer room. A sense of great well-being, of having shed ten years of time, our anxieties purged, our pains departed, glowed within us. As we sipped our coffee the Colonel began to unfold a terrible plan for a night in the Kasbah.

It was the first of many hammams, some good in that the *kayyās* was good, some bad in that he was clumsy, but all similar in structure and in atmosphere. In each village or oasis they were the centers of pleasure and of society, certain days being set aside for women who gaggled to them in chattering veiled droves. They soon became the only sovereign cure for the Colonel's hangovers, and we spent delightful hours in them in strange and remote places: in almond-blossomed Tlemcen, delicious academe of the Maghreb, city of Averroës and Avicenna; in Ghardaia, whose spoken name is like the sand sighing over Saharan wastes, which is the fantastic stronghold of the Mozabites; in El Golea among the November roses and the sad Italian generals; in Touggourt after the feast of the Prophet's birthday; in Fez, where I broke open my wound; and in the gardens of Hamilcar, in Megara, on the outskirts of Carthage. The very catalogue of their names evokes for me the dust, the acid tang of oleanders, the fragrance of dried dung and of sandalwood, of *kebab* sizzling over the charcoal, of frankincense, and the smell of love and wild myrtle on the lion pelt of the hills.

In the seventh century Sidi Okbar, the Conqueror, drove the Visigoths from Africa and rode weeping on his horse into the Atlantic because it seemed no lands were left to conquer in the West. Behind his lances came what learning and sophistication the world had left in it—poetry and paper-making, the art of medicine, astronomy and the compass, silks and fountains, carpets and the bath; and when the great Ommayad caliphs swept instead north through Spain, and crossed the Pyrenees, and almost battered on the gates of Paris before Charles Martel turned them back at Tours, all these things, some lost since the last lights of Rome had flickered out, came back to reillumine Europe.

The other day I wandered in the alleys of Gerona, from which the Moors were driven a thousand years ago; and saw before me in the wall an ancient door, like other doors I knew in Kairouan or in Bou Saada. I opened it and found within a familiar columned court; a little fountain jet, dry now; the domed, succeeding rooms; the troughs; the furnaces, all cold, but calcined by the pleasant heat of long ago. This little lost hammam is the only surviving Islamic structure in Gerona.

The Moors remained in Andalusia much longer, to the end of the fifteenth century. So it is no surprise to find there a rich hammam beneath the marble pavements of the Alhambra. Were its fires rekindled it could be used again, as it was used in the last days by poor Boabdil and his laughing odalisques before they fled forever to die in exile under the almond trees of Tlemcen. They are all dead now, the splendid Almohades, the Fatimites, the Almoravides; and the Sa'adian sultans lie in Marrakech in their tombs of lace. The great empire they built is ruined and distraught, civilization has ebbed away from their lands. But after the heat of the desert or the terrors of the police, simple men may still turn gratefully in at the hammam.

A bath today in England is a puritan pinchbeck thing, a mere enamel coffin; and after you have played with hydrodynamics, Archimedes-like, and made a desert island of your abdomen, and at last extracted the plug with a great toe and felt the pleasant suspension of your body slowly subside into the galloping suction of the sink, only deflation remains.

Coffin-like? Perhaps it is that which redeems them. For since the days of Agamemnon, when a man in his bath might perish at the hands of an adulterous Clytemnestra, to those of Marat, when the fatal dagger was wielded by a mere political theorist, to our own modern degeneracy, when young men so frequently asphyxiate themselves with complicated caliphonts, the Angel of Death stands over the bath. Hammams are djin-haunted. And I am at one with Seneca, who, when his veins had been opened by Nero's order, elected to lie in his bath tasting to the end the crimsoned pleasures of a warm and happy enervation. I, too, would wish to die in my bath.

XI

Fighting Words

The Second Division at Shiloh

by DANIEL McCOOK

MAY, 1864

It was April, 1862. In southwestern Tennessee, the peach orchards were in full bloom. One of them was destined to become hallowed ground as a focal point in one of the bloodiest battles of the Civil War—Shiloh. (The orchard is still there, though the trees are several generations removed.) Here is a firsthand description of the swirling fighting there along the Tennessee River. Daniel McCook, from Carrollton, Ohio, was a captain and assistant adjutant general of the Second Division. About a month after this article appeared, he was mortally wounded in the Battle of Kenesaw Mountain, during Sherman's march on Atlanta. He died July 17, 1864.

The highest romance in military life centers in a succoring army. The sturdy heart of England throbbed responsive to the tread of Bulow's legions—the fortunes of consular France rested on Dessaix's eagles—the hopes and fears of the loyal North marched with Buell's columns, surging to the red field of Shiloh.

Sunday morning, April 5, 1862, came beautiful and bright. The soft spring sunshine bathed valley and hill in mellow splendor. Our Division was early on the march. As its head was debouching out of the valley of Indian Creek heavy indistinct mutterings, as of distant thunder, came from a southwesterly direction. The air was calm, the sky cloudless—it could be no April storm—it must mean battle. When this became evident to the men, a shout, stern, defiant, and eager, broke along the lines, filling the distant woods, and rolling grandly from front to rear. A halt was ordered; three days' rations and sixty additional rounds of ammunition a man were issued, and all baggage was taken off to be left behind. Terrill's battery galloped to the front, to be dragged by hand, if need be, over impassable places. Soon the troops were again in motion. Over fields where the road was impracticable or blocked by other troops, across swamps and morasses, through streams breast-high, the Division pushed for twenty-two miles, till just at nightfall it arrived at Savannah.*

I had been ordered forward to the river, to prepare for the embarkation of the troops. Every thing was in confusion. I could find no General to whom to report. Generals Grant and Buell had gone by steamboat to Pittsburg Landing; General C. F. Smith, the commander of the army, was lying upon his death-bed; General Nelson, with his Division, had already gone, without orders, by land to the battle-field, ten miles distant. Guides reported this route impracticable in the darkness. Steamboats were landing and pushing out without any apparent object; officers were hurrying hither and thither, confused and excited; skulkers from the battle-field were relating deeds of personal prowess, mingled with tales of disaster to our arms; artillery was rumbling, bands playing, drums beating, trains, empty and loaded, choked and jammed in the streets. Above and through all this din swelled the awful cadence of the distant battle. Through the discordant crowd, like a crimson thread, flowing in rapidly augmenting numbers from the steamboats to the hospitals, came the wounded, calm, quiet, and uncomplaining. It was the carnival of rumor, rumor direful, rumor hopeful; but toward night we settled sadly into the clear conviction that our army had sustained a reverse.

As the afternoon waned the sky became overcast. Lightning, red and lurid, flashed in the west, while the thunder, surly and threatening, added its deep bass to the battle's roar. The bivouac fires were gleaming brightly as I returned in the settling gloom to the Division, encamped upon the outskirts of the village, with embarking orders. Crittenden's Division must go first. We waited impatiently for our time. As it grew darker the roar of the battle ceased; only now and then a throb of sound breaking the silence. The two armies rested to renew the battle on the morrow. Ours sad and defeated; theirs hopeful and exultant.

Some time after dark the gun-boats opened fire, slow and measured. This told us that our cause was not altogether desperate—that fresh

* "The army of the Ohio" was organized by General D. C. Buell into six divisions of infantry, of three brigades each. The First Division was commanded by General Geo. H. Thomas; the Second, by A. M'D. M'Cook; Third, by O. M. Mitchell; Fourth, by Wm. Nelson; Fifth, by T. L. Crittenden; Sixth, by T. J. Wood. Subsequently, when General Rosecrans took command, its name was changed to that of Army of the Cumberland, and it was reorganized into three *corps d'armée*. The Fourteenth, Twentieth, and Twenty-first, commanded respectively by Generals Thomas, M'Cook, and Crittenden.

troops might restore the battle. The command to "fall in" was hailed with cheers loud and defiant. Standing in column of company, sweeping the broad road from side to side, that splendid division, nine thousand bayonets strong, high in hope, health, and discipline, with the moon scudding the clouds, lighting up the bronzed faces of the men, and glimmering on their muskets, presented a spectacle I shall never forget. Before we reached the river the storm burst, the April rain coming down in torrents. In the gloom, blinded by lightning flashes, the troops stumbled and groped their way down the slippery banks to the spectral steamboats. Although standing in the streets like drenched cattle nearly all night long, the men took their India-rubber blankets from their manly shoulders to wrap up and preserve their trusty rifles and priceless ammunition from the storm.

That night was an agony of rumor—rumors of defeat, of panic, of men rushing into the river, of the annihilation of our army, of terms of surrender proposed and discussed. But two facts gave us comfort. Nelson, though panting and breathless, after surmounting obstacles of every kind, had arrived in time to take part in the last struggle of the evening; and the enemy had just, at dark, been repulsed within twenty feet of Sherman's semicircle of blazing batteries. We hugged the hopes these facts suggested to our dripping bosoms with delicious pleasure. All that long and miserable night, at short intervals, we heard the solemn thunder of that gun-boat cannon swelling high above the howling storm—a nation's minute-gun.

Before morning one brigade and two regiments of another were embarked. With the latter, on the steamer *Tigress*, the General and Staff went. Weary and heart-sick, I clambered into an upper berth, and, although the rain dripped through the leaky roof in rivulets, I soon slept. I awoke with a start, fearing I had slumbered too long. Day was just breaking. The boat was still under way. There was no tumult of battle. Even the gun-boat had ceased firing with the approach of light. Hope—that main-stay of the soldier in his darkest moods—began to whisper, "No battle today; the enemy have fallen back." The rain was falling in mist; the fog clung to the dank forests, veiling their recesses in obscurity; the steel-gray sky was cold, cheerless, and depressing. Upon the right bank, as we went up, and here and there a soldier in our uniform, without arms, could be seen wandering listlessly along the shore. Soon we saw squads of our cavalry on picket, an assurance that the disorganization of our army was not complete.

As we were eating our breakfast upon the boiler deck a fierce rattle of musketry came from a point of woods above the landing, which was now in plain sight. Soon it grew into the full volume of a well-sustained infantry fight. As we neared the shore, mingled with these crashes of musketry came the strains of the Sixteenth Infantry band, performing a gem from *Il Trovatore*—death and rejoicing borne to us upon the same wave of sound. At the landing-place confusion was worse than confounded. Rations, forage, and ammunition were trampled into the mire by an excited and surging crowd. Officers were rushing about, endeavoring to collect the stragglers of their commands and lead them into the rapidly-increasing battle. Trains were huddled together in sheltered places; ambulances, with their bleeding loads, were coming to the steamboats; sutlers, camp-followers, and even women were adding their voices to the Babel of sound. Thousands of soldiers, panic-stricken, were hiding under the bank, and, not satisfied with their own infamy, were discouraging our troops newly arrived. How we loathed them! Yet the glory of Raymond, Jackson, Blackwater, and Vicksburg gleams upon the bayonets of these same men; and I am convinced now we thought too harshly of them then. Providence, in His inscrutable ways, permitted these men, thirty months later, to pay the debt of Shiloh with compound interest, when, gathering from the plains and savannas of the Southwest, they marched with eager feet to our relief in beleaguered Chattanooga, and with their brawny shoulders helped bear our banners up the blazing lights of Mission Mountain. But at Pittsburg Landing, that memorable day, only the long ranks of dead ranged for recognition or burial at the hospital on the hill-side were calm and free from distracting panic.

The First Brigade, after pushing its way through the throng at the river with the point of the bayonet, was already forming on the crest of the hill. Now and then we heard the pattering sound of bullets, stragglers from the leaden storm above, falling upon the roofs of the boats. Our horses were quickly disembarked, and with the First Brigade in columns closed in mass, leaving orders for the rest of the Division to follow as soon as landed, we moved toward the point indicated by the firing. Directly we saw evidences of close and terrible fighting. Artillery horses dead, cannon dismounted, caissons abandoned, muskets broken, accouterments torn and bloody, appeared everywhere. The first dead soldier we saw had fallen in the road; our artillery had crushed and mangled his limbs, and ground him into the mire. He lay a bloody, loathsome mass, the scraps of his blue uniform furnishing the only distinguishable evidence that a hero there had died. At this sight I saw many a manly fellow gulp down his heart, which swelled too closely into his throat. Near him lay a slender rebel boy—his face in the mud, his brown hair floating in a bloody pool. Soon a dead Major, then a Colonel, then the lamented Wallace, yet alive, were passed in quick and sickening success. The gray gloaming of the misty morning gave a ghostly pallor to the faces of the dead. The disordered hair, dripping from the night's rain, the distorted and passion-marked faces, the stony, glaring eyes, the blue lips, the glistening teeth, the shriveled and contracted hands, the wild agony of pain and passion in the attitudes of the dead—all the horrid circumstances with which death surrounds the brave when torn from life in the whirlwind of battle, were seen as we marched over the field, the beseeching cries of the wounded from their bloody and miry beds meanwhile saluting our ears and cutting to our hearts. Never, perhaps, did raw men go into battle under such discouraging auspices as did this Division. There was everything to depress, nothing to inspirit; and yet determination was written upon their pale faces. They knew too well that defeat was death, with that foaming river at their backs. Their hope was in God, the justice of their cause, and in their own stout hearts.

In a deserted camp, where two long lines of muskets stood stacked —evidences of disaster and surrender the day before—the battalions were deployed. The quiet obedience and intelligent execution of all orders gave an earnest of what those regiments were yet to do that day. Nelson, upon the far left, was heavily engaged. Mendenhal, of Crittenden's Division, was thundering nearer. Sharp skirmishing in the dense wood beyond an open field in our immediate front showed the rebels to be there also. In this field was a peach-orchard in full bloom —spring's scarlet offering to the heroic dead. Further to the left was a group of farm-buildings. In a few moments our skirmishers were driven out of the woods to the edge of the field, then over it, under cover of our lines. Then the enemy began to show themselves in serried front. The command "Ready!" ran along our line. The ominous click of three thousand musket-locks was the response. All stood awaiting the shock. Soon that dingy gray line had become well defined; three flags floated not three hundred yards distant, sinister with star and bar. For what was our commander waiting? Perhaps to decoy the rebels into the open field. They, also wary, halted, and prepared to fire. Then came a deafening crash, the flame from our avenging muskets leaping almost half-way across the field. The sound had scarcely reached its full volume when it was answered by another. Then the roar of battle swelled over all, seemingly filling the firmament. Still, under all this noise, we could hear the *spitz, spitz, sping* of the hurtling bullets, and their crackling sound among the undergrowth, until the air darkened with missiles. The line swept back and forth like an undulating thread; there it shrank for a moment; here it bowed toward the enemy. At one time a company of regular recruits gave way in a body; but all the officers of the battalion joined, and with their sabers drove it back into line.

The brigade had been engaged an hour—it seemed to me but a few minutes—when the rebel line began to waver. How the cheer that then went up lingers in my memory still! It was the first pæan of victory raised by the "Army of the Cumberland." But the exultation was premature. The rebels were only relieving their regiments. The battle waxed hotter as their fresh men opened fire. They planted a battery under cover of the houses, and began enfilading our line with canister. Where was Terrill to answer this new and annoying enemy? He had been taken by mistake to General Nelson. His bell-toned Napoleons were already ringing loud and clear far to the left. Upon the bayonet, that right arm of infantry, we must therefore rely.

"Cease firing—fix bayonets!" rang from wing to wing. As the bristling shafts of steel were fixed onto the smoking barrels with a deadly clang, the blood rushed to the heart, a sickly pallor overspread the faces of the men—a pallor not from fear, but intense determination. The men needed no further command. With an impulse higher than all discipline they rushed forward, a tumultuous tide. Over the field, through the orchard, into the woods around the houses, like an avalanche they dashed, overthrowing the battery, and grinding the rebel line to powder. Through a belt of woods, over another field, they pressed on, driving the broken rebels, until, beaten and panting, they took refuge under cover of their reserves upon the further side of "Sherman's Drill-Ground."

This was the first decided success of the day; our advance threatened the rebel line of retreat. Nelson was bravely holding his own, with Terrill's help; while Crittenden, though stoutly fighting, was calling for reinforcements.

As we passed through the orchard, lying with his shoulders propped against a peach-tree, I saw the mangled form of one of my best-loved classmates dressed in rebel uniform. The mist gathered in his silken beard showed he had died the day before. The pitiless rain had fallen on his upturned face all night. A smile beautified his features, while his eyes seemed gazing far to the southward, as if there an anxious mother were waiting for words of hope from that war-swept field. A cannon-ball had partly severed a branch of the tree. Flower-laden, it fell in scarlet festoons about his head—a fitting pall for his gallant, pure-hearted, yet erring nature. In the lull that followed this contest, while our troops were re-forming their broken ranks, I found leisure to wrap his body in a blanket, and to place it where the artillery and cavalry would not trample his already shattered form—determined that if God spared me and gave us the victory I would pay the last sad offices of respect to his memory.

We had changed direction to the left, following the refluent rebel force. This exposed our right flank. The wily Beauregard was not slow in taking advantage of this fact. Massing three batteries and a full division of infantry, he launched them against our right. Athwart our line at nearly right angles they came with fierce determination, yelling and exultant. Their eighteen guns, hurling death into our ranks, elicited no response, for we had no artillery to reply. All eyes turned to that long line of advancing, flashing steel. The Second Brigade, which had just landed from the boats, was placed upon our right flank, the men lying on their faces in the edge of the field, concealed by the dense undergrowth. A regiment was thrown forward to seize a point of water-oaks, which shouldered out into the open field. In "column in mass" it attempted the perilous mission, dashing on at the double-quick. But reaching the range of rebel fire, a tornado of canister, round-shot, shrapnel, and bullets staggered it. It attempted to deploy, to answer fire with fire. Human flesh and blood could no more endure. It came recoiling back, leaving a mosaic of blue bodies to mark its rugged path. This encouraged the rebels, who swept steadily onward, furious for their prey, contemptuously returning with straggling shots the fire the First Brigade had opened upon them. Little did they think of the reception prepared for them. The Second Brigade, four regiments, 2,700 strong, which had not fired a shot, were lying in the thicket at the field's edge. Nearer and still nearer came the advancing column, until within half-musket range. Still all was silent on our right. Fearing some guile, they threw a few shells into the wood. But this developed nothing. Obviously reassured, they began wheeling upon their right regiment as a pivot, in order to more completely envelop the flank of the First Brigade. This maneuver insured their destruction, for it turned their own flank to the ambushed thicket. The men of the Second Brigade quietly fixed bayonets while lying down.

"Up—one volley—and at them!" Struck as by a thunder-bolt, that blow followed by a storm of bayonet-thrusts, the proud column went rolling backward, followed by our men. When the smoke lifted the field was clear of "gray backs." We had won the field and the Corinth road by one volley.

But still our men kept pressing the enemy back, back into the deep wood beyond, until their blue coats were lost in its bosky recesses as they streamed onward. We heard a cry of disappointment and surprise from part of our line; the musketry began to swell from the woods in deeper chorus. We could hear the voices of our officers checking their men. Midway our line became entangled in a swamp. The Thirty-fourth Illinois dashed in with their muskets held high over their heads, but the water, running up to their belts, drove them back; they could not afford to lose their ammunition. The regiments to the right and left dared not advance until it passed this obstacle, for our disjointed line would have been at the mercy of the enemy's "offensive return." This check gave them a moment to rally. Their consummate commander, knowing that any further advance on this road would cut his army off from retreat, concentrated all his available force for an overwhelming attack upon our line at this point. At others the battle virtually ceased. Far in the "dim aisles" the gray mass of the enemy could be seen marshaling for the final struggle. In three lines of triple steel they came at last—no stratagem this time—dogged, determined fighting, with stern and desperate purpose. The soldiers of both armies seemed to comprehend the importance of the crisis. Our men felt assured that if they could quickly reach Shiloh church, whose dusky gable, with its yellow flag, they saw through the vistas of the forest, a surrender of the enemy would make a fitting close to the glory of the day. The rebels believed that if they could regain the Corinth road, and rout the right, victory again would crown their standard. Each man clutched his musket more firmly, awaiting the shock. It came in awful grandeur. Full twenty thousand muskets bellowed in competing echoes. The wood seemed swept by fire. Our men bravely breasted the storm, but the odds were fearful. The ammunition of the First Brigade was rapidly giving out; soon the last cartridge was expended. The Third Brigade, the only Union reserve on the field, must go in. But it was only twelve o'clock, and the power of the rebels yet unbroken. By right of companies, under a galling fire, the First Brigade retired, and the Third took its place. This movement was supposed by the rebels to mean retreat. A yell, wild and hopeful, rose from their lines—their muskets cracked more deadly still. Their artillery enfilading our front was making fearful havoc. A battery, more impudent than the rest, pushed up to the further edge of the swamp, dashing canister into the faces of the Thirty-fourth Illinois, fighting up to its knees in water. That battery well knew it was protected from the avenging bayonets of our men by that impassable sheet of water. Their lines, constantly relieved by fresh regiments, were firing more rapidly than ours. There was difficulty in procuring ammunition. The First Brigade, so sorely needed, must lie idle. Kirk and Gibson, brigade commanders, were both wounded; Bass had gone back to die; Levanway had dyed the waters of the swamp with his life's-blood. But no man wavered. In the breach of that awful field stood the throbbing hearts of those two brigades, the only bulwark between our army and destruction.

Suddenly—far to our extreme left, above the horrid tumult—we heard something rushing as a great wind. Bursting from the woods over the field to our support Mendenhal dashed in—his horses full of foam and smoke, the clay flying in tangents from his swiftly whirring wheels. He galloped into battery on the rebel flank. Soon his roaring Rodmans added their sonorous music to the medley. Like a whirlwind Terrill followed. His Virginian blood was up. "Nearer, nearer; give them double canister into their very faces!" he shouted to his drivers. The rebels did not take this tamely, but turned with fierce rage upon the batteries. A Missouri regiment came down on Terrill. Pitilessly he hurled a storm of fire and iron into their faces. But steadily and with even tread they still advanced. All the cannoneers were killed at one piece. Terrill and a corporal worked the gun alone, until an unknown but gallant infantry sergeant volunteered to help. Terrill, grimly standing at the vent, shouted, "Canister! canister!" Quick as light the sergeant flew to the caisson. Loaded with three charges he came back to the gun, when, struck full in the forehead, he fell dead, his body rolling to the feet of the corporal. He, brave fellow, faltered not, but drove the three charges home. Terrill's quick eye for a moment swept along the smoke-grimed piece. Then came a blinding flash, a stunning crack. Prone in their breast the iron tempest struck the advancing regiment, blowing some from the very muzzle of the gun. They staggered, reeled; then Missouri's pride and chivalry broke, and like a shattered wave ebbed back, sweeping the supporting regiments with them. Our battery, our Division was saved. Surely, in the annals of this conflict, that sergeant's deed must ever stand ablaze with glory!

The Seventy-seventh Pennsylvania regiment, the only venture the Keystone State had on the field that day, dashed in after the recoiling rebel regiments. The First Brigade, with replenished boxes, came up at the run. The whole Division charged, sweeping over lines and guns. Through Hurlburt's, Prentice's, and Sherman's camps, we drove the enemy past the old church, over the stream beyond. Our first battle was won. The intellect of Beauregard was no match for the genius of Grant. Three divisions of infantry, with twelve pieces of artillery, routed the entire rebel army, restored our fortunes in the West, and turned defeat into victory; capturing of their artillery, and recapturing of ours twenty pieces. That night, in the pelting rain, upon the bloody ground, without tents or blankets, the Division slept, hungry, exhausted, and sad; for nine hundred manly forms, one-tenth of our entire number, lay dead or dying, and maimed.

To me a mournful task remained unperformed. Far over the field— for we had driven the rebels five miles—I must ride to bury my friend. Darkness almost impenetrable had settled in the woods, only relieved here and there by the flickering glimmer of the ambulance lanterns, as the surgeons were gathering up the wounded. In the midst of conflict the soul is racked by all the horrible impressions that mutilated and mangled humanity can excite. But these emotions were nothing compared with the deep revulsion which the silence and gloom a night after battle suggested. Our jaded horses sank above the fetlocks in the miry roads. Progress was slow, often impeded by the dead blocking the way. It was the saddest ride—the saddest night of my life.

The houses near the peach orchard were already filled with wounded. There we found a spade, and with it hollowed out a grave. No matter how. He sleeps under a spreading oak and in a soldier's grave—with a miniature—a fair, girlish face—resting on his breast.

Since that sanguinary day the blood of our Division has been sprinkled like water upon four other fields; but soldiers and officers refer to Shiloh as the most terrible of them all. Even the memories of that awful struggle by the Southern "River of Death" grow dim at the recollection of Shiloh—our first and bloodiest battle.

How We Fight at Atlanta

by HENRY O. DWIGHT

OCTOBER, 1864

Here is a detailed, realistic account of some refinement in the art of war developed during our civil conflict. It even mentions massed artillery fire, whose advantage the Japanese had not entirely learned as recently as World War II. Henry O. Dwight was born in Constantinople, the son of missionary parents, and was at Ohio Wesleyan University when the war broke out. He enlisted as a private, became an officer and was an aide to a division commander in the Army of the Tennessee. After the war he returned to Constantinople as a missionary himself. He died in 1917.

Here in the trenches before Atlanta, on this fifteenth day of August, I propose to give you some idea of the actual manner in which we fight. With us the pomp and show of war has become a matter of poetry rather than of fact. We need no gay dress or nodding plumes to inspire a soldier's pride. Practical utility is what we look at in matters of dress and equipment. Look at most of the pictures. Two-thirds of the pictures in books and papers represent the soldiers with enormous knapsacks neatly packed; officers leading the charge in full dress uniform, with their sabers waving in the most approved style. Now this makes a pretty picture; but let me tell you that soldiers don't put on their well-packed knapsacks to double-quick over a half-mile of open ground in the hot sun at the *pas du charge*. Limited transportation soon exhausts an officer's stock of white collars. The most elegant dress uniform will become torn and spotted, and the brightly polished boots will become soiled with mud, when one is reduced to marching in line-of-battle through swamps, thickets, and brier patches, and then sleeping night after night on the bare ground with only heaven's clouds for an over coat. Know ye, then, ladies all, yonder pretty-looking officer, with his spotless dress, resplendent with gold lace, will present a very different spectacle after a few months of campaigning. Dusty, ragged, and unshaven, his appearance is far more in accordance with his surroundings, far more becoming the earnest fighting man that you really suppose he is, than if he were arrayed as you formerly saw him, or as the pictures represent him to be.

Of course, in a war like this, upon which we all entered with the art yet to learn, the science has been progressive. Each succeeding year has developed new phases, and under such schooling our soldiers are indeed veterans; men whom practice has perfected in all the mysteries of military life. Each soldier knows that where he used to lie upon his arms all the time, in the face of the enemy, only seeking cover from the shape of the ground, he must now make a strong fortification, to enable him to hold his position, and must arrange it to stop pieces of shell from the flank as well as bullets from the front. Had the army been as experienced at Shiloh as it is now, Beauregard would have come up and broken his army to pieces on our fortifications, instead of finding our whole army lying exposed to his attacks on the open field. At Fort Donelson, too, where we had to attack fortifications, we ourselves had no sign of a work upon which we could fall back after each day's repulse; nor did the enemy seem to realize the value of his own works, for instead of quietly waiting the attack, he threw away his army by fighting outside his works.

It is now a principle with us to fight with movable breast-works, to save every man by giving him cover, from which he may resist the tremendous attacks in mass of the enemy. Thus at least we fight in Georgia, in the Atlanta campaign.

Wherever the army moves, either in gaining the enemy's work, or in taking up a new line of attack, the first duty after the halt is to create defensive fortifications—rude, indeed, but effective in enabling us to hold our ground against any force. In forming these field-works every man is to some extent his own engineer. The location of the line is selected by the officers, and each regiment fortifies its own front, each company its own ground.

Generally the situation will not allow finishing the works at once, for the enemy will probably attack soon after you take position, which is on a commanding hill or some similar point. So you cause a hasty barricade to be constructed. The front rank take all the guns and remain on the line, while the rear rank goes off in double-quick to collect rails, logs, rocks, anything that can assist in turning a hostile bullet. These they place on the front of the front rank, and in five minutes there is a hasty barricade, bullet-proof and breast-high, along your whole line; not a mere straight work, but one varied with its salients and re-entering angles, taking every advantage of the ground, and cross-firing on every hollow. You can do this after the enemy forms to charge you, while he is feeling you with artillery. Thus it takes just five minutes to prepare for an assault; and you can hold your line against an attack by three times your number—and that, too, with but slight loss to yourself—if your men be veteran soldiers.

It may be that when your barricade is done you have yet time. Shovels and picks are always carried by your men, and to work they go to complete the frail works. A ditch is speedily made on the inside to stand in. The earth is thrown on the outside of the barricade, and the ditch deepened, so that, standing inside, your head will be protected by the parapet. Thus you speedily have a pretty substantial earth-work, with a step inside to stand on when firing, and a ditch to stand in while loading. If you are in the woods, you want to give range to your rifles, and have all the thick undergrowth and small trees cut away for fifty paces in front. By felling these all the same way, the bushy tops all turning outward, and trimming off the smaller twigs and leaves, and tangling the tops together, you have a formidable abattis, through which it shall be next to impossible for a line to advance alone, let alone against the showers of bullets from your men at short range. This done, you can be making any amount of additions to your work as you have time, all tending to make it impregnable. Even after you have pronounced the job finished, your men will fuss and dig and tinker about the works to make them sure protection. They have no notion of taking a position, and then having it taken from them by a sudden assault. They will cut huge logs eighteen inches through, and place them on the parapet to protect the head while they shoot through a space left between the log and the parapet. They have also an ingenious plan for preventing these "head-logs" from being an injury to the service. Experience has taught them that a cannon-ball will sometimes strike one of these huge logs, and throw it off the parapet on to the troops inside. As a preventive, skids, or stout poles, are placed at equal distances along the rifle-pits, extending from the parapet across the ditch. The logs being knocked off the top of the breast-work are supposed to roll along these skids, over the heads of the soldiers in the ditch, until they lodge safely on the bank beyond.

The men will also amuse themselves with devising some new entanglement or snare to annoy the advance of the enemy. They drive palisades—stakes set in the ground with their sharpened points directed outward at an angle of forty-five degrees, and so close together that a man cannot pass between them. In front of the palisade they place a strong wire so arranged that it cannot be seen but will trip all comers. They will then imagine how astounded will be the rebels in charging the works to be suddenly tripped up and to fall forward on the sharp palisades.

Your main works being completed you can rest secure, only putting in an embrasure for a howitzer or two here or there. These howitzers are a fine thing to repel an attack, for they throw nearly a bucketful of small balls at a charge. Your skirmish line has, in the mean time, fortified itself sufficiently for protection, and can hold an attacking column long enough for you to form line in the main works before the enemy can get there.

One reads in the papers of the assaults on earth-works, of the repulses, and yet one does not know what is contained in those words—"Assault repulsed." You make up your mind to assault the enemy's works. You have formed line of battle, with a second and third line behind you for support. You march forth filled with the determination to accomplish the object, yet feeling the magnitude of the undertaking. Two hundred yards brings you to the picket-line, and here the opposition commences. You dash across the space between the two lines, you lose a few men; and the enemy's pickets, after making as much noise as possible, run back to their main works. By this time the enemy are sure you are really coming, and open on you with artillery, besides a pretty heavy fire of musketry. This artillery throws the shell screaming through your ranks, producing more moral than physical effect, or throws shrapnel which, bursting in front, scatter myriads of small bullets around. You commence to lose men rapidly. The ball is opened. "Forward, double-quick!" again; and while the whole line of the enemy open fire from behind their works, your men, mindless of this—mindless of the death intensified, the bullets and the shells, they dash on with wild cheers. The abattis with its tangled intricacy of sharpened branches snares your line. Tripping, falling, rising to fall again, the men struggle through this abattis. You get through this abattis, though the minutes are drawn out interminably, and though in each step are left brave men to pay for the ground. You get through a part of you and still rush on: the firing grows more fierce, the men grow more desperate. Your three lines have been almost reduced to one, and you strike another line of abattis. In this abattis are the palisades, which must be uprooted by force before a man can pass. You stumble, fall, tear your flesh on these stakes, and must stop to pull them up—stop, when every instant is an hour—stop, when you are already gasping for breath; and here open up the masked batteries, pouring the canister into that writhing, struggling, bleeding mass—so close that the flame scorches, that the smoke blinds from those guns. Is it any wonder that your three lines are torn to pieces, and have to give back before the redoubled fire of an enemy as yet uninjured comparatively? And then the slaughter of a retreat *there!* Oftentimes it is preferable to lie down and take the fire there until night rather than lose all by falling back under such circumstances.

This war has demonstrated that earth-works can be rendered nearly impregnable on either side against direct assault. An attack on fortified lines must cost a fearful price, and should be well weighed whether the cost exceeded not the gain. This, then, is what an assault means—a slaughter-pen, a charnel-house, and an army of weeping mothers and sisters at home. It is inevitable. When an assault is successful, it is to be hoped that the public gain may warrant the loss of life requisite. When it is repulsed tenfold is the mourning.

It was a long time before the men could appreciate the value of these field-works. They would grumble and growl, recalling instances without number where the most charming little traps, the most elegant cross-fires, had been prepared with great labor, and had never been attacked. I saw some men most beautifully satisfied as to the necessity for defensive works the other day. On the twenty-second of July, before Atlanta, while these men were engaged in grumbling over some newly-finished works which the enemy would not charge, Hardee struck the Seventeenth Corps in flank and rear. His furious onset crushed the flank, and the Second Brigade of the Third Division, to which these grumblers belonged, found themselves suddenly forming the unprotected left of the corps and attacked from the rear in those very works they grumbled so about building. When this attack was made they jumped the works to the front, or outside, and fought that way. This attack repulsed, they jumped back and repulsed an attack from the outside, or real front. Thus they fought, looking for all the world like a long line of these toy-monkeys you see which jump over the end of a stick. Thus they fought for four long hours, cut off from all commanders, corps, division, and brigade, cut off from ammunition-trains, and only cheered by the noble example of General Giles A. Smith, whose command, broken by the first onset—all except one brigade— had rallied behind the works of the Third Division. Firing to front and rear, and to either flank, they held their works, only changing front by jumping over the parapet as five assaults were made upon them, successively from front, rear, or flank, until the rebel onset was checked long enough to make sure the safety of the immense wagon-trains already saved by the Sixteenth Corps.

The next works of these men I saw, and seeing them, laughed. Experience had taught the utility of fortifications, and they fortified not only the front, but facing the rear and every way, so that they could hold out if surrounded. They were not going to be caught without ammunition either; for each company had its little powder-magazine in a safe place, well stored with ammunition gathered from the battle-field. No grumbling was heard about building the works. All the spare time of the men was devoted to finishing up their pet works, standing off and regarding the effect of each addition with something of the same paternal feeling that an artist exhibits in regarding the power of each master-stroke in finishing his picture.

We hear a great deal about hand-to-hand fighting. Gallant though it would be, and extremely pleasant to the sensation newspapers to have it to record, yet, unfortunately for gatherers of items, it is of very rare occurrence. This year's campaigns have probably seen more of it than any other of the war. When men can kill one another at six hundred yards they generally would prefer to do it at that distance than to come down to two paces. Still as each army grows wiser in military matters, the fighting must naturally become closer and more desperate, and those who have the firmest endurance, the greatest self-control, must win. This war is not one between mere military machines as soldiers are in Europe, but of rational, thinking beings, fighting with the highest of motives on our side, and with the belief that theirs is the highest of motives on the part of the enemy. When such men are thrown in deadly personal contact with each other the strife is deadly indeed. On the twenty-second of July, in that part of the battle to which

I have already alluded, it chanced that I saw hand-to-hand fighting in that same Second Brigade aforementioned. A man was actually well-nigh dismembered, the rebels pulling his feet, to take him prisoner, and our boys pulling his head to save him. Men were bayoneted, knocked down with the butts of muskets, and even fists were used in default of better weapons in that deadly strife. Officers used their dress swords, which they had hitherto considered as mere playthings for the parade, to hack down a troublesome enemy. A rebel colonel, who had laid hold of the colors of the Twentieth Ohio Regiment, was bayoneted by the color-guard, who at the same instant saved the colors of the Seventy-eighth Ohio, their bearer, shot through the heart, having dropped the precious flag among the enemy. Men begged for more cartridges as they would for bread, and made every one count, as the horrible sight in the ditch testified the next morning.

So much for hand-to-hand fighting. While there are thousands of such brave men in the field our country can never go to ruin, and the honor of our flag will be upheld against traitors, enemies, at home or abroad.

In a protracted attack like that on Petersburg or Atlanta, although not actually a siege, still the operations have to be carried on more or less after the principles of one. The works are more solid, more substantial, than mere field-works. The men make their bunks right behind the works so as to be protected from the pieces of shell and bullets. The parapets are made thicker and higher to resist the heavy artillery fire of the enemy, and batteries are erected at commanding points to keep up a constant fire upon the enemy. These batteries are made very strongly, and are often casemated, or roofed with a heavy bomb-proof of logs and earth. It is amusing to watch the operations of these batteries. They are arranged with the most consummate skill, so far as regards position, etc. No sooner does a rebel battery dare to speak than you will hear a volley from all the guns that can see it, and a dozen or more shells of every shape and size will strike exactly in the embrasure of the hostile fort. This practice of concentration of fire renders the enemy exceedingly chary of using his guns unless he thinks he has us at an advantage.

Sharp-shooters play an important part in the operations of our army. Hiding themselves in a good position they soon build a little pit, digging with the bayonet and tin cup, if they cannot stand up to use a spade, from which they annoy the enemy most immensely. Their keen eyes readily detect the slightest portion of an enemy exposed, and they generally mark it with a quick bullet. Many a trick is resorted to by them to induce the enemy so to expose himself. Sometimes they will all raise a tremendous shout, and when the enemy bob up to see what is going on they give them a telling volley, and then roll over and kick up their heels with joy. Nothing short of an actual attack in force will dislodge these sharp-shooters; and it is rarely that one of them is killed. They take the same pride in their duty that a hunter does in the chase, and tally their victims in three separate columns—the "certainly," the "probably," and the "possibly" killed—thinking no more of it than if it were not men they hunt so diligently. The enemy also have efficient sharp-shooters who climb high trees and with their long-range rifles soon make themselves felt in our camps.

Besides the fighting population of our camps, there is a population constitutionally opposed to warfare—cooks, ambulance nurses, stretcher-bearers, shirks, and sometimes surgeons, who all come under the class technically called *bummers*. These are treated by the fighting men with a sort of cool contempt, no matter whether necessity or inclination keeps them to the rear, and they have a hard time. Frequently the rear of the army is a much more dangerous locality than the front line, for the missiles passing over the front line must fall somewhere, and often demoralize whole hosts of "bummers," who build miniature fortifications to live in, and collect together in crowds; for misery loves company. Any favorable ravine thus peopled immediately becomes denominated "Bummer's Roost." Here they spend their days in cooking for their nurses, if they are cooks, or attending to their own business, if their object be to escape duty and danger. Among them originate all sorts of marvelous reports of immense success or terrible disaster. They always know just what General Sherman said about the situation at any given time; and from them start many of the wild stories which penetrate the columns of our best papers.

To watch these cooks, freighted with the precious coffee for the men in the trenches, as they go out to the front three times a day, is amusing. From continually dodging the passing shells or stray bullets their forms become bent and stooping. As they approach the line, the men in the trenches commence shouting, "Hey, bummer! Run quick, bummer!" "A man was killed just there, bummer!" With such encouragements the coffee at last reaches its destination, and being distributed among the eager men the bummer is soon at liberty to hurry back to the "Roost."

The Decision to Use the Atomic Bomb

by HENRY L. STIMSON

FEBRUARY, 1947

Debate over whether we should have used the atomic bomb against Japan to bring World War II to a speedy end will go on for many years, but the man who had to make that fateful decision had a powerful argument in its favor. That man was Henry L. Stimson, who, as Secretary of War from 1940 to 1945, was given special responsibility for the development, production, and use of the bomb. In this article, perhaps the most important historical document the magazine ever published, he told for the first time the full story behind the decision. Mr. Stimson died in 1950.

In recent months there has been much comment about the decision to use atomic bombs in attacks on the Japanese cities of Hiroshima and Nagasaki. This decision was one of the gravest made by our government in recent years, and it is entirely proper that it should be widely discussed. I have therefore decided to record for all who may be interested my understanding of the events which led up to the attack on Hiroshima on August 6, 1945, on Nagasaki on August 9, and the Japanese decision to surrender, on August 10. No single individual can hope to know exactly what took place in the minds of all of those who had a share in these events, but what follows is an exact description of our thoughts and actions as I find them in the records and in my clear recollection.

It was in the fall of 1941 that the question of atomic energy was first brought directly to my attention. At that time President Roosevelt appointed a committee consisting of Vice President Wallace, General Marshall, Dr. Vannevar Bush, Dr. James B. Conant, and myself. The function of this committee was to advise the President on questions of policy relating to the study of nuclear fission which was then proceeding both in this country and in Great Britain. For nearly four years thereafter I was directly connected with all major decisions of policy on the development and use of atomic energy, and from May 1, 1943, until my resignation as Secretary of War on September 21, 1945, I was directly responsible to the President for the administration of the entire undertaking; my chief advisers in this period were General Marshall, Dr. Bush, Dr. Conant, and Major General Leslie R. Groves, the officer in charge of the project. At the same time I was the President's senior adviser on the military employment of atomic energy.

The policy adopted and steadily pursued by President Roosevelt and his advisers was a simple one. It was to spare no effort in securing the earliest possible successful development of an atomic weapon. The reasons for this policy were equally simple. The original experimental achievement of atomic fission had occurred in Germany in 1938, and it was known that the Germans had continued their experiments. In 1941 and 1942 they were believed to be ahead of us, and it was vital that they should not be the first to bring atomic weapons into the field of battle. Furthermore, if we should be the first to develop the weapon, we should have a great new instrument for shortening the war and minimizing destruction. At no time, from 1941 to 1945, did I ever hear it suggested by the President, or by any other responsible member of the government, that atomic energy should not be used in the war. All of us of course understood the terrible responsibility involved in our attempt to unlock the doors to such a devastating weapon; President Roosevelt particularly spoke to me many times of his own awareness of the catastrophic potentialities of our work. But we were at war, and the work must be done. I therefore emphasize that it was our common objective, throughout the war, to be the first to produce an atomic weapon and use it. The possible atomic weapon was considered to be a new and tremendously powerful explosive, as legitimate as any other of the deadly explosive weapons of modern war. The entire purpose was the production of a military weapon; on no other ground could the wartime expenditure of so much time and money have been justified. The exact circumstances in which that weapon might be used were unknown to any of us until the middle of 1945, and when that time came, as we shall presently see, the military use of atomic energy was connected with larger questions of national policy.

The extraordinary story of the successful development of the atomic bomb has been well told elsewhere. As time went on it became clear that the weapon would not be available in time for use in the European Theater, and the war against Germany was successfully ended by the use of what are now called conventional means. But in the spring of 1945 it became evident that the climax of our prolonged atomic effort was at hand. By the nature of atomic chain reactions, it was impossible to state with certainty that we had succeeded until a bomb had actually exploded in a full-scale experiment; nevertheless it was considered exceedingly probable that we should by midsummer have successfully detonated the first atomic bomb. This was to be done at the Alamogordo Reservation in New Mexico. It was thus time for detailed consideration of our future plans. What had begun as a well-founded hope was now developing into a reality.

On March 15, 1945 I had my last talk with President Roosevelt. My diary record of this conversation gives a fairly clear picture of the state of our thinking at that time. I have removed the name of the distinguished public servant who was fearful lest the Manhattan (atomic) project be "a lemon"; it was an opinion common among those not fully informed.

> The President . . . had suggested that I come over to lunch today. . . . First I took up with him a memorandum which he sent to me from —— who had been alarmed at the rumors of extravagance in the Manhattan project. —— suggested that it might become disastrous and he suggested that we get a body of "outside" scientists to pass upon the project because rumors are going around that Vannevar Bush and Jim Conant have sold the President a lemon on the subject and ought to be checked up on. It was rather a jittery and nervous memorandum and rather silly, and I was prepared for it and I gave the President a list of the scientists who were actually engaged on it to show the very high standing of them and it comprised four Nobel Prize men, and also how practically every physicist of standing was engaged with us in the project. Then I outlined to him the future of it and when it was likely to come off and told him how important it was to get ready. I went over with him the two schools of thought that exist in respect to the future control after the war of this project, in case it is successful, one of them being the secret close-in attempted control of the project by those who control it now, and the other being the international control based upon freedom both of science and of access. I told him that those things must be settled before the first projectile is used and that he must be ready with a statement to come

out to the people on it just as soon as that is done. He agreed to that. . . .

This conversation covered the three aspects of the question which were then uppermost in our minds. First, it was always necessary to suppress a lingering doubt that any such titanic undertaking could be successful. Second, we must consider the implications of success in terms of its long-range postwar effect. Third, we must face the problem that would be presented at the time of our first use of the weapon, for with that first use there must be some public statement.

I did not see Franklin Roosevelt again. The next time I went to the White House to discuss atomic energy was April 25, 1945, and I went to explain the nature of the problem to a man whose only previous knowledge of our activities was that of a Senator who had loyally accepted our assurance that the matter must be kept a secret from him. Now he was President and Commander-in-Chief, and the final responsibility in this as in so many other matters must be his. President Truman accepted this responsibility with the same fine spirit that Senator Truman had shown before in accepting our refusal to inform him.

I discussed with him the whole history of the project. We had with us General Groves, who explained in detail the progress which had been made and the probable future course of the work. I also discussed with President Truman the broader aspects of the subject, and the memorandum which I used in this discussion is again a fair sample of the state of our thinking at the time.

MEMORANDUM DISCUSSED WITH

PRESIDENT TRUMAN APRIL 25, 1945

1. Within four months we shall in all probability have completed the most terrible weapon ever known in human history, one bomb of which could destroy a whole city.

2. Although we have shared its development with the U.K., physically the U.S. is at present in the position of controlling the resources with which to construct and use it and no other nation could reach this position for some years.

3. Nevertheless it is practically certain that we could not remain in this position indefinitely.

a. Various segments of its discovery and production are widely known among many scientists in many countries, although few scientists are now acquainted with the whole process which we have developed.

b. Although its construction under present methods requires great scientific and industrial effort and raw materials, which are temporarily mainly within the possession and knowledge of U.S. and U.K., it is extremely probable that much easier and cheaper methods of production will be discovered by scientists in the future, together with the use of materials of much wider distribution. As a result, it is extremely probable that the future will make it possible for atomic bombs to be constructed by smaller nations or even groups, or at least by a larger nation in a much shorter time.

4. As a result, it is indicated that the future may see a time when such a weapon may be constructed in secret and used suddenly and effectively with devastating power by a wilful nation or group against an unsuspecting nation or group of much greater size and material power. With its aid even a very powerful unsuspecting nation might be conquered within a very few days by a very much smaller one. . . .*

5. The world in its present state of moral advancement compared with its technical development would be eventually at the mercy of such a weapon. In other words, modern civilization might be completely destroyed.

6. To approach any world peace organization of any pattern now likely to be considered, without an appreciation by the leaders of our country of the power of this new weapon, would seem to be unrealistic. No system of control heretofore considered would be adequate to control this menace. Both inside any particular country and between the nations of the world, the control of this weapon will undoubtedly be a matter of the greatest difficulty and would involve such thoroughgoing rights of inspection and internal controls as we have never heretofore contemplated.

7. Furthermore, in the light of our present position with reference to this weapon, the question of sharing it with other nations and, if so shared, upon what terms, becomes a primary question of our foreign relations. Also our leadership in the war and in the development of this weapon has placed a certain moral responsibility upon us which we cannot shirk without very serious responsibility for any disaster to civilization which it would further.

8. On the other hand, if the problem of the proper use of this weapon can be solved, we would have the opportunity to bring the world into a pattern in which the peace of the world and our civilization can be saved.

* A brief reference to the estimated capabilities of other nations is here omitted; it in no way affects the course of the argument.

9. As stated in General Groves' report, steps are under way looking towards the establishment of a select committee of particular qualifications for recommending action to the executive and legislative branches of our government when secrecy is no longer in full effect. The committee would also recommend the actions to be taken by the War Department prior to that time in anticipation of the postwar problems. All recommendations would of course be first submitted to the President.

The next step in our preparations was the appointment of the committee referred to in paragraph (9) above. This committee, which was known as the Interim Committee, was charged with the function of advising the President on the various questions raised by our apparently imminent success in developing an atomic weapon. I was its chairman, but the principal labor of guiding its extended deliberations fell to George L. Harrison, who acted as chairman in my absence. It will be useful to consider the work of the committee in some detail. Its members were the following, in addition to Mr. Harrison and myself:

James F. Byrnes (then a private citizen) as personal representative of the President.

Ralph A. Bard, Under Secretary of the Navy.

William L. Clayton, Assistant Secretary of State.

Dr. Vannevar Bush, Director, Office of Scientific Research and Development, and president of the Carnegie Institution of Washington.

Dr. Karl T. Compton, Chief of the Office of Field Service in the Office of Scientific Research and Development, and president of the Massachusetts Institute of Technology.

Dr. James B. Conant, Chairman of the National Defense Research Committee, and president of Harvard University.

The discussions of the committee ranged over the whole field of atomic energy, in its political, military, and scientific aspects. That part of its work which particularly concerns us here relates to its recommendations for the use of atomic energy against Japan, but it should be borne in mind that these recommendations were not made in a vacuum. The committee's work included the drafting of the statements which were published immediately after the first bombs were dropped, the drafting of a bill for the domestic control of atomic energy, and recommendations looking toward the international control of atomic energy. The Interim Committee was assisted in its work by a Scientific Panel whose members were the following: Dr. A. H. Compton, Dr. Enrico Fermi, Dr. E. O. Lawrence, and Dr. J. R. Oppenheimer. All four were nuclear physicists of the first rank; all four had held positions of great importance in the atomic project from its inception. At a meeting with the Interim Committee and the Scientific Panel on May 31, 1945 I urged all those present to feel free to express themselves on any phase of the subject, scientific or political. Both General Marshall and I at this meeting expressed the view that atomic energy could not be considered simply in terms of military weapons but must also be considered in terms of a new relationship of man to the universe.

On June 1, after its discussions with the Scientific Panel, the Interim Committee unanimously adopted the following recommendations:

(1) The bomb should be used against Japan as soon as possible.

(2) It should be used on a dual target—that is, a military installation or war plant surrounded by or adjacent to houses and other buildings most susceptible to damage, and

(3) It should be used without prior warning [of the nature of the weapon]. One member of the committee, Mr. Bard, later changed his view and dissented from recommendation (3).

In reaching these conclusions the Interim Committee carefully considered such alternatives as a detailed advance warning or a demonstration in some uninhabited area. Both of these suggestions were discarded as impractical. They were not regarded as likely to be effective in compelling a surrender of Japan, and both of them involved serious risks. Even the New Mexico test would not give final proof that any given bomb was certain to explode when dropped from an airplane. Quite apart from the generally unfamiliar nature of atomic explosives, there was the whole problem of exploding a bomb at a predetermined height in the air by a complicated mechanism which could not be tested in the static test of New Mexico. Nothing would have been more damaging to our effort to obtain surrender than a warning or a demonstration followed by a dud—and this was a real possibility. Furthermore, we had no bombs to waste. It was vital that a sufficient effect be quickly obtained with the few we had.

The Interim Committee and the Scientific Panel also served as a channel through which suggestions from other scientists working on the atomic project were forwarded to me and to the President. Among the suggestions thus forwarded was one memorandum which questioned using the bomb at all against the enemy. On June 16, 1945, after consideration of that memorandum, the Scientific Panel made a report, from which I quote the following paragraphs:

> The opinions of our scientific colleagues on the initial use of these weapons are not unanimous: they range from the proposal of a purely technical demonstration to that of the military application best designed to induce surrender. Those who advocate a purely technical demonstration would wish to outlaw the use of atomic weapons, and have feared that if we use the weapons now our position in future negotiations will be prejudiced. Others emphasize the opportunity of saving American lives by immediate military use, and believe that such use will improve the international prospects, in that they are more concerned with the prevention of war than with the elimination of this special weapon. We find ourselves closer to these latter views; *we can propose no technical demonstration likely to bring an end to the war; we see no acceptable alternative to direct military use.* [Italics mine]

> With regard to these general aspects of the use of atomic energy, it is clear that we, as scientific men, have no proprietary rights. It is true that we are among the few citizens who have had occasion to give thoughtful consideration to these problems during the past few years. We have, however, no claim to special competence in solving the political, social, and military problems which are presented by the advent of atomic power.

The foregoing discussion presents the reasoning of the Interim Committee and its advisers. I have discussed the work of these gentlemen at length in order to make it clear that we sought the best advice that we could find. The committee's function was, of course, entirely advisory. The ultimate responsibility for the recommendation to the President rested upon me, and I have no desire to veil it. The conclusions of the committee were similar to my own, although I reached mine independently. I felt that to extract a genuine surrender from the Emperor and his military advisers, they must be administered a tremendous shock which would carry convincing proof of our power to destroy the Empire. Such an effective shock would save many times the number of lives, both American and Japanese, that it would cost.

The facts upon which my reasoning was based and steps taken to carry it out now follow.

The principal political, social, and military objective of the United States in the summer of 1945 was the prompt and complete surrender of Japan. Only the complete destruction of her military power could open the way to lasting peace.

Japan, in July, 1945, had been seriously weakened by our increasingly violent attacks. It was known to us that she had gone so far as to make tentative proposals to the Soviet government, hoping to use the Russians as mediators in a negotiated peace. These vague proposals contemplated the retention by Japan of important conquered areas and were therefore not considered seriously. There was as yet no indication of any weakening in the Japanese determination to fight rather than accept unconditional surrender. If she should persist in her fight to the end, she had still a great military force.

In the middle of July, 1945, the intelligence section of the War Department General Staff estimated Japanese military strength as follows: in the home islands, slightly under 2,000,000; in Korea, Manchuria, China proper, and Formosa, slightly over 2,000,000; in French Indo-China, Thailand, and Burma, over 200,000; in the East Indies area, including the Philippines, over 500,000; in the by-passed Pacific islands, over 100,000. The total strength of the Japanese Army was estimated at about 5,000,000 men. These estimates later proved to be in very close agreement with official Japanese figures.

The Japanese Army was in much better condition than the Japanese Navy and Air Force. The Navy had practically ceased to exist except as a harrying force against an invasion fleet. The Air Force had been reduced mainly to reliance upon Kamikaze, or suicide, attacks. These latter, however, had already inflicted serious damage on our seagoing forces, and their possible effectiveness in a last ditch fight was a matter of real concern to our naval leaders.

As we understood it in July, there was a very strong possibility that the Japanese government might determine upon resistance to the end, in all the areas of the Far East under its control. In such an event the Allies would be faced with the enormous task of destroying an armed force of five million men and five thousand suicide aircraft, belonging to a race which had already amply demonstrated its ability to fight literally to the death.

The strategic plans of our armed forces for the defeat of Japan, as they stood in July, had been prepared without reliance upon the atomic bomb, which had not yet been tested in New Mexico. We were planning an intensified sea and air blockade, and greatly intensified strategic air bombing, through the summer and early fall, to be followed on November 1 by an invasion of the southern island of Kyushu. This would be followed in turn by an invasion of the main island of Honshu in the spring of 1946. The total U. S. military and naval force involved in this grand design was of the order of 5,000,000 men; if all those indirectly concerned are included, it was larger still.

We estimated that if we should be forced to carry this plan to its conclusion, the major fighting would not end until the latter part of 1946, at the earliest. I was informed that such operations might be expected to cost over a million casualties, to American forces alone. Additional large losses might be expected among our allies, and, of course, if our campaign were successful and if we could judge by previous experience, enemy casualties would be much larger than our own.

It was already clear in July that even before the invasion we should be able to inflict enormously severe damage on the Japanese homeland by the combined application of "conventional" sea and air power. The critical question was whether this kind of action would induce surrender. It therefore became necessary to consider very carefully the probable state of mind of the enemy, and to assess with accuracy the line of conduct which might end his will to resist.

With these considerations in mind, I wrote a memorandum for the President, on July 2, which I believe fairly represents the thinking of the American government as it finally took shape in action. This memorandum was prepared after discussion and general agreement with Joseph C. Grew, Acting Secretary of State, and Secretary of the Navy Forrestal, and when I discussed it with the President, he expressed his general approval.

July 2, 1945

Memorandum for the President

PROPOSED PROGRAM FOR JAPAN

1. The plans of operation up to and including the first landing have been authorized and the preparations for the operation are now actually going on. This situation was accepted by all members of your conference on Monday, June 18.

2. There is reason to believe that the operation for the occupation of Japan following the landing may be a very long, costly, and arduous struggle on our part. The terrain, much of which I have visited several times, has left the impression on my memory of being one which would be susceptible to a last ditch defense such as has been made on Iwo Jima and Okinawa and which of course is very much larger than either of those two areas. According to my recollection it will be much more unfavorable with regard to tank maneuvering than either the Philippines or Germany.

3. If we once land on one of the main islands and begin a forceful occupation of Japan, we shall probably have cast the die of last ditch resistance. The Japanese are highly patriotic and certainly susceptible to calls for fanatical resistance to repel an invasion. Once started in actual invasion, we shall in my opinion have to go through with an even more bitter finish fight than in Germany. We shall incur the losses incident to such a war and we shall have to leave the Japanese islands even more thoroughly destroyed than was the case with Germany. This would be due both to the difference in the Japanese and German personal character and the differences in the size and character of the terrain through which the operations will take place.

4. A question then comes: Is there any alternative to such a forceful occupation of Japan which will secure for us the equivalent of an unconditional surrender of her forces and a permanent destruction of her power again to strike an aggressive blow at the "peace of the Pacific"? I am inclined to think that there is enough such chance to make it well worthwhile our giving them a warning of what is to come and a definite opportunity to capitulate. As above suggested, it should be tried before the actual forceful occupation of the homeland islands is begun and furthermore the warning should be given in ample time to permit a national reaction to set in.

We have the following enormously favorable factors on our side— factors much weightier than those we had against Germany:

Japan has no allies.

Her navy is nearly destroyed and she is vulnerable to a surface and underwater blockade which can deprive her of sufficient food and supplies for her population.

She is terribly vulnerable to our concentrated air attack upon her crowded cities, industrial and food resources.

She has against her not only the Anglo-American forces but the rising forces of China and the ominous threat of Russia.

We have inexhaustible and untouched industrial resources to bring to bear against her diminishing potential.

We have great moral superiority through being the victim of her first sneak attack.

The problem is to translate these advantages into prompt and economical achievement of our objectives. I believe Japan is susceptible to reason in such a crisis to a much greater extent than is indicated by our current press and other current comment. Japan is not a nation composed wholly of mad fanatics of an entirely different mentality from ours. On the contrary, she has within the past century shown herself to possess extremely intelligent people, capable in an unprecedentedly short time of adopting not only the complicated technique of Occidental civilization but to a substantial extent their culture and their political and social ideas. Her advance in all these respects during the short period of sixty or seventy years has been one of the most astounding feats of national progress in history—a leap from the isolated feudalism of centuries into the position of one of the six or seven great powers of the world. She has not only built up powerful armies and navies. She has maintained an honest and effective national finance and respected position in many of the sciences in which we pride ourselves. Prior to the forcible seizure of power over her government by the fanatical military group in 1931, she had for ten years lived a reasonably responsible and respectable international life.

My own opinion is in her favor on the two points involved in this question:

a. I think the Japanese nation has the mental intelligence and versatile capacity in such a crisis to recognize the folly of a fight to the finish and to accept the proffer of what will amount to an unconditional surrender; and

b. I think she has within her population enough liberal leaders (although now submerged by the terrorists) to be depended upon for her reconstruction as a responsible member of the family of nations. I think she is better in this last respect than Germany was. Her liberals yielded only at the point of a pistol and, so far as I am aware, their liberal attitude has not been personally subverted in the way which was so general in Germany.

On the other hand, I think that the attempt to exterminate her armies and her population by gunfire or other means will tend to produce a fusion of race solidity and antipathy which has no analogy in the case of Germany. We have a national interest in creating, if possible, a condition wherein the Japanese nation may live as a peaceful and useful member of the future Pacific community.

5. It is therefore my conclusion that a carefully timed warning be

given to Japan by the chief representatives of the United States, Great Britain, China, and, if then a belligerent, Russia by calling upon Japan to surrender and permit the occupation of her country in order to insure its complete demilitarization for the sake of the future peace.

This warning should contain the following elements:

The varied and overwhelming character of the force we are about to bring to bear on the islands.

The inevitability and completeness of the destruction which the full application of this force will entail.

The determination of the Allies to destroy permanently all authority and influence of those who have deceived and misled the country into embarking on world conquest.

The determination of the Allies to limit Japanese sovereignty to her main islands and to render them powerless to mount and support another war.

The disavowal of any attempt to extirpate the Japanese as a race or to destroy them as a nation.

A statement of our readiness, once her economy is purged of its militaristic influence, to permit the Japanese to maintain such industries, particularly of a light consumer character, as offer no threat of aggression against their neighbors, but which can produce a sustaining economy, and provide a reasonable standard of living. The statement should indicate our willingness, for this purpose, to give Japan trade access to external raw materials, but no longer any control over the sources of supply outside her main islands. It should also indicate our willingness, in accordance with our now established foreign trade policy, in due course to enter into mutually advantageous trade relations with her.

The withdrawal from their country as soon as the above objectives of the Allies are accomplished, and as soon as there has been established a peacefully inclined government, of a character representative of the masses of the Japanese people. I personally think that if in saying this we should add that we do not exclude a constitutional monarchy under her present dynasty, it would substantially add to the chances of acceptance.

6. Success of course will depend on the potency of the warning which we give her. She has an extremely sensitive national pride and, as we are now seeing every day, when actually locked with the enemy will fight to the very death. For that reason the warning must be tendered before the actual invasion has occurred and while the impending destruction, though clear beyond peradventure, has not yet reduced her to fanatical despair. If Russia is a part of the threat, the

Russian attack, if actual, must not have progressed too far. Our own bombing should be confined to military objectives as far as possible.

It is important to emphasize the double character of the suggested warning. It was designed to promise destruction if Japan resisted, and hope, if she surrendered.

It will be noted that the atomic bomb is not mentioned in this memorandum. On grounds of secrecy the bomb was never mentioned except when absolutely necessary, and furthermore, it had not yet been tested. It was of course well forward in our minds, as the memorandum was written and discussed, that the bomb would be the best possible sanction if our warning were rejected.

The adoption of the policy outlined in the memorandum of July 2 was a decision of high politics; once it was accepted by the President, the position of the atomic bomb in our planning became quite clear. I find that I stated in my diary, as early as June 19, that "the last chance warning . . . must be given before an actual landing of the ground forces in Japan, and fortunately the plans provide for enough time to bring in the sanctions to our warning in the shape of heavy ordinary bombing attack and an attack of S-1." S-1 was a code name for the atomic bomb.

There was much discussion in Washington about the timing of the warning to Japan. The controlling factor in the end was the date already set for the Potsdam meeting of the Big Three. It was President Truman's decision that such a warning should be solemnly issued by the U.S. and the U.K. from this meeting, with the concurrence of the head of the Chinese government, so that it would be plain that *all* of Japan's principal enemies were in entire unity. This was done, in the Potsdam ultimatum of July 26, which very closely followed the above memorandum of July 2, with the exception that it made no mention of the Japanese Emperor.

On July 28 the Premier of Japan, Suzuki, rejected the Potsdam ultimatum by announcing that it was "unworthy of public notice." In the face of this rejection we could only proceed to demonstrate that the ultimatum had meant exactly what it said when it stated that if the Japanese continued the war, "the full application of our military power, backed by our resolve, will mean the inevitable and complete destruction of the Japanese armed forces and just as inevitably the utter devastation of the Japanese homeland."

For such a purpose the atomic bomb was an eminently suitable weapon. The New Mexico test occurred while we were at Potsdam, on July 16. It was immediately clear that the power of the bomb measured up to our highest estimates. We had developed a weapon of such a revolutionary character that its use against the enemy might well be expected to produce exactly the kind of shock on the Japanese ruling oligarchy which we desired, strengthening the position of those who wished peace, and weakening that of the military party.

Because of the importance of the atomic mission against Japan, the detailed plans were brought to me by the military staff for approval. With President Truman's warm support I struck off the list of suggested targets the city of Kyoto. Although it was a target of considerable military importance, it had been the ancient capital of Japan and was a shrine of Japanese art and culture. We determined that it should be spared. I approved four other targets including the cities of Hiroshima and Nagasaki.

Hiroshima was bombed on August 6, and Nagasaki on August 9. These two cities were active working parts of the Japanese war effort. One was an army center; the other was naval and industrial. Hiroshima was the headquarters of the Japanese Army defending southern Japan and was a major military storage and assembly point. Nagasaki was a major seaport and it contained several large industrial plants of great wartime importance. We believed that our attacks had struck cities which must certainly be important to the Japanese military leaders, both Army and Navy, and we waited for a result. We waited one day.

Many accounts have been written about the Japanese surrender. After a prolonged Japanese cabinet session in which the deadlock was broken by the Emperor himself, the offer to surrender was made on August 10. It was based on the Potsdam terms, with a reservation concerning the sovereignty of the Emperor. While the Allied reply made no promises other than those already given, it implicitly recognized the Emperor's position by prescribing that his power must be subject to the orders of the Allied Supreme Commander. These terms were accepted on August 14 by the Japanese, and the instrument of surrender was formally signed on September 2, in Tokyo Bay. Our great objective was thus achieved, and all the evidence I have seen indicates that the controlling factor in the final Japanese decision to accept our terms of surrender was the atomic bomb.*

The two atomic bombs which we had dropped were the only ones we had ready, and our rate of production at the time was very small. Had the war continued until the projected invasion on November 1, additional fire raids of B-29's would have been more destructive of life and property than the very limited number of atomic raids which we could have executed in the same period. But the atomic bomb was more than a weapon of terrible destruction; it was a psychological weapon. In March, 1945 our Air Force had launched its first great incendiary raid on the Tokyo area. In this raid more damage was done and more casulties were inflicted than was the case at Hiroshima. Hundreds of bombers took part and hundreds of tons of incendiaries were dropped. Similar successive raids burned out a great part of the urban area of Japan, but the Japanese fought on. On August 6 one B-29 dropped a single atomic bomb on Hiroshima. Three days later a second bomb was dropped on Nagasaki and the war was over. So far as the Japanese could know, our ability to execute atomic attacks, if necessary by many planes at a time, was unlimited. As Dr. Karl Compton has said, "it was not one atomic bomb, or two, which brought surrender; it was the experience of what an atomic bomb will actually do to a community, *plus the dread of many more,* that was effective."

The bomb thus served exactly the purpose we intended. The peace party was able to take the path of surrender, and the whole weight of the Emperor's prestige was exerted in favor of peace. When the Emperor ordered surrender, and the small but dangerous group of fanatics who opposed him were brought under control, the Japanese became so subdued that the great undertaking of occupation and disarmament was completed with unprecedented ease.

In the foregoing pages I have tried to give an accurate account of my own personal observations of the circumstances which led up to the use of the atomic bomb and the reasons which underlay our use of it. To me they have always seemed compelling and clear, and I cannot see how any person vested with such responsibilities as mine

* Report of United States Strategic Bombing Survey, "Japan's Struggle to End the War"; "If the Atomic Bomb Had Not Been Used," by K. T. Compton, *Atlantic Monthly,* December, 1946; unpublished material of historical division, War Department Special Staff, June, 1946.

could have taken any other course or given any other advice to his chiefs.

Two great nations were approaching contact in a fight to a finish which would begin on November 1, 1945. Our enemy, Japan, commanded forces of somewhat over 5,000,000 armed men. Men of these armies had already inflicted upon us, in our breakthrough of the outer perimeter of their defenses, over 300,000 battle casualties. Enemy armies still unbeaten had the strength to cost us a million more. *As long as the Japanese government refused to surrender,* we should be forced to take and hold the ground, and smash the Japanese ground armies, by close-in fighting of the same desperate and costly kind that we had faced in the Pacific islands for nearly four years.

In the light of the formidable problem which thus confronted us, I felt that every possible step should be taken to compel a surrender of the homelands, and a withdrawal of all Japanese troops from the Asiatic mainland and from other positions, before we had commenced an invasion. We held two cards to assist us in such an effort. One was the traditional veneration in which the Japanese Emperor was held by his subjects and the power which was thus vested in him over his loyal troops. It was for this reason that I suggested in my memorandum of July 2 that his dynasty should be continued. The second card was the use of the atomic bomb in the manner best calculated to persuade that Emperor and the counselors about him to submit to our demand for what was essentially unconditional surrender, placing his immense power over his people and his troops subject to our orders.

In order to end the war in the shortest possible time and to avoid the enormous losses of human life which otherwise confronted us, I felt that we must use the Emperor as our instrument to command and compel his people to cease fighting and subject themselves to our authority through him, and that to accomplish this we must give him and his controlling advisers a compelling reason to accede to our demands. This reason furthermore must be of such a nature that his people could understand his decision. The bomb seemed to me to furnish a unique instrument for that purpose.

My chief purpose was to end the war in victory with the least possible cost in the lives of the men in the armies which I had helped to raise. In the light of the alternatives which, on a fair estimate, were open to us I believe that no man, in our position and subject to our responsibilities, holding in his hands a weapon of such possibilities for accomplishing this purpose and saving those lives, could have failed to use it and afterwards looked his countrymen in the face.

As I read over what I have written, I am aware that much of it, in this year of peace, may have a harsh and unfeeling sound. It would perhaps be possible to say the same things and say them more gently. But I do not think it would be wise. As I look back over the five years of my service as Secretary of War, I see too many stern and heart-rending decisions to be willing to pretend that war is anything else than what it is. The face of war is the face of death; death is an inevitable part of every order that a wartime leader gives. The decision to use the atomic bomb was a decision that brought death to over a hundred thousand Japanese. No explanation can change that fact and I do not wish to gloss it over. But this deliberate, premeditated destruction was our least abhorrent choice. The destruction of Hiroshima and Nagasaki put an end to the Japanese war. It stopped the fire raids, and the strangling blockade; it ended the ghastly specter of a clash of great land armies.

In this last great action of the Second World War we were given final proof that war is death. War in the twentieth century has grown steadily more barbarous, more destructive, more debased in all its aspects. Now, with the release of atomic energy, man's ability to destroy himself is very nearly complete. The bombs dropped on Hiroshima and Nagasaki ended a war. They also made it wholly clear that we must never have another war. This is the lesson men and leaders everywhere must learn, and I believe that when they learn it they will find a way to lasting peace. There is no other choice.

Merrill's Marauders: The Truth about an Incredible Adventure

by CHARLTON OGBURN, JR.

JANUARY, 1957

Here is one of the most amazing stories to come out of World War II (or any other war). It is the story of the Burma campaign —how it was bungled by Washington and the theater command, and how it was finally saved by the heroism, good humor, and incredible endurance of a handful of foot soldiers. The grandeur and misery of the campaign are told here with restraint and wit by Charlton Ogburn, Jr., who was a lieutenant with that small and fearsome band. Mr. Ogburn was with the State Department for eleven years after the war, and resigned in order to write. He has published two books, The White Falcon, *a juvenile, and* The Bridge, *a novelette.*

To us, the war looked different. To nearly everybody else, the American performance in World War II looked like a monumental achievement in planning, organization, and command. The United States had to create armies, fleets, and air forces more or less from a standing start. It had to move them to half a dozen major fronts, strung halfway around the globe. It had to supply them—plus its hard-pressed allies—across two oceans. Finally, it had to use this power effectively against powerful, wily, and desperate enemies, who appeared to be in a fair way to conquer the rest of the world. All this America succeeded in doing; and at the end one got the impression of a nation overflowing with the capabilities that count in modern war.

Not everyone, however, got this impression at all times and places. Indeed, less than eighteen months before the final victory the American effort in one particularly vast theater seemed alarmingly thin. There—at the end of our longest line of communications—our combat ground forces consisted of only one regimental-sized unit. The nearest American combat infantry force was three thousand miles away. At one stage, the fate of operations over a huge area hinged on the ability of a few hundred of those infantrymen to stay on their feet another few days—a task which at that moment struck most of us as all but impossible.

When a campaign unexpectedly comes to such a pass, a military man might (I suppose) suspect that there had been a miscalculation somewhere. Such an inference might also be drawn from an investigation report made a little later, which recorded an "almost complete breakdown of morale in the major portion of the unit."

The infantrymen involved had, for their part, no doubt about it. Their impression was that things had somehow got off on the wrong foot, and had stayed on that foot—or worse feet—ever since.

The story of Galahad—the code name given the organization during its operations, to the intemperate amusement of its more literary members—throws some light on how not to run an army.

It also throws some light on other things less easy to define. For Galahad, in spite of everything, did not give an altogether unsatisfactory account of itself. It marched some five hundred miles over jungle-covered hills and fought five major and thirty minor engagements (by the War Department's reckoning) in a campaign that saw the enemy cleared from an area the size of Connecticut. At the end, after it had been pulled back for recuperation, the proportion of its survivors who were AWOL or in the guardhouse was, to say the least, abnormally high. The rest were dispirited or embittered. Yet, as a cloudy day is sometimes redeemed at sunset, a glow was cast upon its last days by an order conferring upon it the Distinguished Unit Citation—which amounted to a decoration for superior performance of duty for every man in its ranks.

I might have had some premonition about the organization from the haphazard way in which I fell into it. It came about as a result of a remark I chanced to drop in the mess line after a cold night in Mississippi in September, 1943—for nights can be cold in early autumn, even in the deep South, when you are sleeping on the ground. I said that I wished I could be sure of doing my fighting in a warm climate. As it happened, my neighbor in the line was a lieutenant in the Adjutant General's section. The consequences illustrate the frightening role that pure accident can play in one's life.

"Do you?" he said. "Maybe it could be arranged. We've had orders from Washington asking for volunteers with jungle training—I don't know what for. Probably for a jungle-training center in Panama or some place. Why don't I send your name in?"

"I don't see how I could claim to have had any jungle training," I ventured.

"Oh, well. You could say that Mississippi is like a jungle in spots. In fact, isn't life itself really a jungle?"

A few days later it was rumored that the call for volunteers was not, after all, entirely routine and innocuous. I do not know who started the rumor. Perhaps it was someone who had read all the way through the orders from Washington. The lieutenant in the Adjutant General's section surely had not done so. That I deduced when, ten days later, I found myself at the San Francisco Port of Embarkation and learned that I had volunteered for "a dangerous and hazardous mission."

What else the mission might be, no one in the barracks where I was quartered with other junior officers had any idea. Later that evening, however, several of us were given the qualification cards of a thousand other officers and enlisted men who had volunteered, and were detailed to form a battalion out of them by reveille. Another battalion was to be formed, we heard, from the cards of another thousand who had volunteered from the Caribbean Defense Command. I was to remember later a remark by a fellow lieutenant in the detail:

"This is one way to form an organization—on the docks. If they try to use it before it's had a chance to grow together, we'll find out how good the method is."

After working most of the night, we held a formation in the morning of the men that went with the cards. In any body of troops, I suppose, the ones who are likely to give trouble stand out. It was certainly true of this one. I thought I had never seen a less tractable-looking assemblage.

I glanced at the round-faced, youthful officer beside me—Captain Senff. "The only thing stupider than volunteering is asking for volunteers," he allowed amiably in the accents of North Carolina. "We've got the misfits of half the divisions in the country."

That night, when I had charge of the orderly room for a two-hour stint, I got to see some of them individually. The post MPs brought in a steady procession of them—more accurately an unsteady procession. They were not only drunk but AWOL, for since we were sailing the next day we had been confined to the area. . . .

A headquarters was set up in the main saloon of our transport, which turned out to be the *SS Lurline* traveling incognito. It was here that I was brought up in my turn to be presented to our acting commander.

"Quite a distinction for us," he observed, "having a Signal Corps officer for a communications platoon leader."

I thought it time to unburden myself of a fact that had been bothering me; I explained that I had been in field-wire and message center but knew nothing of radio.

Colonel Charles N. Hunter was a highly competent professional—a West Pointer, with the true soldier's capacity to eliminate the human factor from a situation. My smile of disarming candor manifestly failed.

"Then, Lieutenant," he stated with a singularly direct gaze, "you had better learn."

Radio turned out to be, for all practical purposes, the only communications equipment we were to have. Fortunately, my platoon happened to include some highly competent operators and repairmen.

What surprised me most about the men with whom I found myself was that, among the wilder and rougher types, there were so many sober and normal-seeming Americans. It was hard to believe, however, that a call for volunteers for a hazardous mission would bring out a cross-section of the population, and I wondered what it was that set these men apart. In the course of a forty-two-day voyage, I began to form some idea.

Whatever else they might be—adventurers, idealists, drunkards, journalists, wealthy ne'er-do-wells, old army types, cotton speculators, American Indians (we had three or four), Niseis, Southern farm boys, and Northern slum products—they were individualists with little taste for being told what to do, and scant patience with the routine and monotony of training camps. Each had something egging him on. In some it was a nomadic instinct that is never reconciled to the settled life. In the two youngest members of my platoon—Eve, the fresh-looking, blond boy from the Middle West who turned out to have the blessed gift of a Way with Mules; and my radio technician, an intent New Yorker of Italian parentage—it was perhaps the simple high-mindedness of youth. In the oldest member—a quiet, steady, slow-smiling New Englander who was to outlast many of his juniors, a house-builder in civilian life—it seemed to be the unresting conscience that goes with craftsmanship.

Then there were the junior officers with whom I shared a stateroom. Winnie Steinfield was a young doctor for whom frontiers had a powerful attraction—any frontiers—and whose instinct was to go beyond them. (He was to cross the ultimate one ten years later in a small boat in a storm off the coast of Maine.) Lieutenant Scott had been a fire marshal and a dedicated hunter who was drawn irresistibly by the chance to pursue the toughest game of all. Phil Weld, whose family had given Harvard its boathouse, was, I suspected, in the *Lurline* for fundamentally the same reason that his forebears had been in the *Mayflower*—though with a gayer and not perceptibly reverent spirit.

Finally, there was Lieutenant Caldwell, the Tennessean, whose explanation of why he was there, although probably not the true one, won him great admiration. He had been taking a junior officers' course at an infantry training school and his class, as he recalled in his dry drawl, "had had an exercise in weapons placement out in some ol' piney hills." Young Caldwell, it appeared, had taken the occasion to catch up on his sleep and accordingly was somewhat at a loss when he was called upon, along with the others, to submit a written terrain evaluation.

"So Ah just put down 'About ten dollars an acre.' They gave me the choice of joining up with you fellows or standing a court-martial. And so, ol' gallant Caldwell—here he is."

Our battalion commander was a puzzler to me. Lieutenant Colonel Lloyd Osborne had fought through the Philippines debacle and, escaping, had reached Australia after a voyage of over fifty days in an open boat. What his condition then was, I hesitate to surmise. When he boarded the *Lurline* he weighed all of 120 pounds, and he resembled an assistant professor of mathematics. It finally came out that he had a characteristic that must be rare among those who have actually been through war: he liked fighting. Months later during a period of tranquillity unusual at that time, he was to make a lasting impression upon me by observing plaintively, "I don't see much chance of any contact with the enemy, but of course we *could* cross the ridge and have a fight with B battalion." He gave a mild laugh, and of course he was joking, but all the same . . . the idea *had* occurred to him.

This shipload of soldiers had no designation. We were not even classified as, for example, an infantry regiment. We were just two battalions of something or other. This tended to be disconcerting, even to an assortment of individuals with little in common but an aversion to conformity. In a way, it was as if we did not really exist.

We had no idea where we were going. On a map of the world I had bought in San Francisco (to be prepared for any place), I plotted our course as best I could across the empty, endless Pacific on the basis of guesses as to our speed and direction. I was greatly pleased to find I was only a few hundred miles off when we made our first landfall at Noumea, New Caledonia. Partly there and partly at Brisbane, Australia, we picked up a third battalion, this one composed of veterans of the Southwest Pacific campaign.

By that time, we had been issued a booklet that gave us an idea of what was in store. It was an account of Brigadier Wingate's force of British, Gurkas, and Indians—the renowned Chindits—and of the extraordinary march they had made the year before halfway across Burma and back. . . .

Our destination was a desolate area of central India, where we were to have two months' training in infantry weapons and guerrilla tactics. . . . We heard that the decision to form our organization had been taken at the conference President Roosevelt and Prime Minister Churchill had held in Quebec. We got the impression that the two Chiefs of State were the last, as well as the first, to have any precise idea of how we were to be used. As far as we could tell, it had not even been settled whether we were to be under direct British or American control. While the issue remained in doubt, we profited from His Britannic Majesty's patronage by being issued a rum ration. It was not enough to make the desert bloom—but the evidence that a military command could be human did something for our spirits, and the rum itself helped counteract the effects of the tea our pirate cooks boiled in twenty-gallon drums.

Admiral Lord Louis Mountbatten, Commander of the Southeast Asia Command, paid us a visit. . . . General Joseph W. Stilwell—who was Mountbatten's Deputy as well as Commanding General of the Chinese Army in India—never came to see us at all, although eventually we were to be placed under his operational control. If we had not been the only American infantry between New Guinea and North Africa, I suppose we should not particularly have expected him to appear. As it was, our feelings of being detached from the known world were deepened.

This was also the beginning of our suspicion that Stilwell was interested exclusively in the Chinese army he had trained, of which two divisions were then being deployed in northern Burma, our destination. From the record that was later written, it is clear that he had reason to be preoccupied with his Chinese divisions and his relations with the Generalissimo in Chungking. All the same, it is hard to believe that his headquarters could not have avoided conveying an impression that finally—when the end was near—provoked our commanding officer to charge that favoritism was being displayed toward the Chinese at our expense.

We trained hard, but it seemed that every time we were beginning to form up into teams we would be reorganized. Presumably the plans for our employment were being changed. I was to learn later in life that, perhaps because we are so good at organizing, we tend as a nation to meet any new situation by *re*organizing; and a wonderful method it can be for creating the illusion of progress while producing confusion, inefficiency, and demoralization. During our reorganizations, several commanding officers were tried out on us, which added to the discontinuity. Meanwhile, Colonel Hunter, whom everyone respected, held the organization together.

We still lacked a designation of any kind. The authorities, in their preoccupation with Tables of Organization, would doubtless have been surprised to learn what an unsettling effect this had on the men. The British seem to have a better understanding of these matters. They recognize that a name like the Sixth Inniskilling Dragoons or the Queen's Own Cameron Highlanders, and the history that goes with it, can do something for an organization that a mobile snack-bar cannot. (Not that we had a mobile snack-bar either.) Perhaps the British awareness of the importance to an organization of a sense of corporate identity also leads them to avoid reorganizations.

On the night of Christmas Eve, the men cut loose, or, as Winnie Steinfield expressed it, they "sought release through an externalization of inner tensions." A rifle shot rang out, then another. The example was picked up all over the camp. Within minutes it sounded as if every weapon in our considerable armory of small arms was being discharged—rifles, carbines, Tommy guns, Browning automatics. Tracer-bullets from machine guns were crisscrossing on their way to the horizon like red-hot bees. Magnesium flares hung over the scene, casting their white glare upon it while colored signal lights zoomed into the firmament.

Officers sent out by the enraged battalion headquarters to apprehend the miscreants were later found—by officers sent out to find *them* —dancing about like satyrs, firing their revolvers into the sky. . . .

One day we were assembled and informed that we finally had an appellation. The United States Army had outdone itself to find a name to make hearts beat faster; it was going to send us into battle as the 5307th Composite Unit (Provisional). After the last formation that day, I heard a Pfc in the next platoon addressing the ranks in a fair imitation of his sergeant's voice: "Listen, you monkeys. The Army has bestowed a great honor upon you, and it ain't one you deserve. I don't know what 'composite' means, but no one who'd ever seen what lousy soldiers you gold-bricks make would call you even provisional."

We had been told that five hundred mules were on their way to us from the United States, and meanwhile we had been lent a few British mules to practice with. It was not until almost the end of our training period that our own animals began to arrive. The mules, augmented by a few saddle horses, were to be our sole means of transport—and, to understate it, one of our major preoccupations. Half our men had never seen a mule before and not one in fifty had ever touched one— or had any burning desire to do so.

The true inwardness of the situation was brought home to me at the outset of our first practice river-crossing. I had the job of taking the lead mule across (my whimsical battalion commander, Colonel Osborne, had learned that I had been a book reviewer before rallying to the colors). I found myself offshore in the Betwa River, fighting cheek-to-jowl with a mule whose head was as big as my torso, trying to launch him toward the opposite bank. (The technique, as I discovered, was to keep the animal turning in circles until he tired of trying to head back, and struck out across the river. Thereupon, it was advisable to slip down his back and cling to his tail; if once he got away from you the brute would leave you behind no matter how you struggled to catch up.) Coasting along—alone but for the straining mule in the broad waters of an exotic Indian river with the shore of the Princely State of Gwalior on the other side—it struck me that I had come a long, long way.

The mules were evidently one of the two things we had been waiting for. The other—a commanding general—now also arrived. Because of the warmth of his personality, the evidence he gave of genuine interest and confidence in us, and his convincing air of knowing his business, Brigadier General Frank D. Merrill, our new commander, instantly made a favorable impression that was to grow stronger with time. He told us that we should not have long to wait. Soon thereafter we were piled into a couple of trains. After ten days, including two in a river boat on the Brahmaputra, we reached the end of the line near Ledo, Assam, at the northeast corner of India.

At eight o'clock in the evening of February 6, 1944, we were scheduled to set off on our long march into Burma, but at that time, amid scenes of turmoil such as various artists have considered characteristic of Hades, we were still being issued mules and pack-saddles. In fact, at precisely H-Hour the occupants of the bamboo edifice housing the First Battalion headquarters were clinging to the rafters, while an overwrought saddle horse down below was kicking it to pieces. It was not until after midnight that the chaos of that last evening was converted into a long and only dimly visible column and, in a sudden and impressive silence, we set off down the Ledo Road.

By prodigious efforts on the part of American engineer units, an unreckoning use of equipment, and the toil of what must have been thousands of native laborers, this amazing road had been pushed 120 miles over precipitous, forested hills. It ran from the end of the Indian road net to the northwestern tip of the central valley of Burma, which was also the point of farthest Japanese advance. The plan was to extend the Ledo south and east across the country, through the northern Burmese railhead at Myitkyina, to a juncture with the famous Burma Road that led into China. The object was to open a supply route for China-based operations against the Japanese. Chiang Kai-shek's armies and the United States air force in China were at that time dependent for supplies upon what could be flown in from India over the Hump. The task of the 5307th was to spearhead the two Chinese divisions that—operating from Indian bases under Stilwell's command—were trying to push the Japanese southward to make possible the advance of the Ledo Road.

The first night of our march we kept going until well after dawn, and we resumed in the afternoon. . . .

Two or three days later, after winding slowly up the longest grade of that toilsome road, we reached the 4,300-foot saddle of Pangsau Pass. On the other side of it lay Burma. To the west, on the far horizon, more nearly resembling a stratum of cloud than mountains, were the snowy ridges of the Himalayas. Behind, stretching down into the valley—the only time I ever saw it in full view—was a long line of heavy-laden men and animals that in time acquired the name of Merrill's Marauders. This designation—said to have been coined by a newspaperman—made an instant appeal to the troops. The same could not be said of the official code name that was bestowed upon us at this time, though there were those who maintained that it required inspiration of a high order to think of the name Galahad for an organization like the 5307th.

Our arrival at the end of the Ledo Road after a march of eleven days marked the beginning of a campaign of three months' duration during which we had no contact with the world except by radio and plane and never saw a road or motorcar except those possessed by the Japanese. Whatever came to us in that time came by air; all our supplies, including even the grain for the animals, were kicked out of planes a couple of hundred feet up. The breakables sailed down on parachutes and too often came to rest in the top of a tree seventy feet high.

The terrain of northern Burma is divided into corridors by parallel ridges running north and south. It greatly favored the Japanese, for in those defiles a battalion could hold off a division. These Chinese were finding it hard going. What we were to do was to go wide around the Japanese right flank—over the ranges, through the nearly impenetrable forest, across the rivers—and undercut their defenses by attacking without warning from the rear. This maneuver the 5307th carried out four times, to such effect that the commander of the Japanese Eighteenth Division, which held the area, is said to have believed that the three battalions of Americans actually amounted to two divisions.

The strategy of which we were a part was well understood by all of us; for it was characteristic of the organization that most of the privates in it had managed to add a map to their belongings and insisted upon being kept informed not only of how their platoon's mission fitted into the company's, but what place the battalion had in the grand plan of the Southeast Asia Command. The maps gave us the only vista we had, for the actual terrain made us virtually blind. Except when we crossed a few acres of open ground where the local hill people—the Kachins—had a cluster of bamboo huts, or descended into the main valleys where our objectives lay, we moved through matted forest and ten-foot *kunai* grass that shut out even the sky.

On every trail the Japanese had outposts or patrols. Sometimes the first evidence of their presence came when they opened fire on the head of the column. Again, we would find signs of them—fresh tracks —and the whisper would be passed down the line from man to man, "Take a five-yard interval."

Off in the forest a band of monkeys would set up a din of whooping, humorless laughter. Breaking out of the silence, it was incredible and unnerving. Then it would abruptly cease, and that was perhaps even more unnerving. The column would halt while the scouts were sent out. The only sound then would be the soft stomping of the mules and the clink of a harness ring—and the questioning, plaintive, four-note whistle of a bird in a treetop. *"Whee-oo,* WHEE-*oo,"* it went, at ten-second intervals. There was always that bird. I have only to whistle its call now to bring the whole mood back, including the earthy, faintly acrid smell of the jungle floor.

In the breathless stillness, the first rattle of firing was incredibly loud. It had the effect of a horrible moral shock. It was as if the pleasant trappings of the earth, the blue sky, the shimmering leaves of the bamboo, the trickly little stream, were all whisked away and you saw a death's-head leering into your face.

After the first burst, the silence would close in again like the well-oiled door of a cage. Then explosions would follow one upon another as the Japanese brought their grenade-throwers to bear.

From the head of the column, the order would be passed back, "Weapons platoon forward!" Then, a minute later, coming up from the rear: "Clear the trail."

You got the mules into the dense growth alongside to let the mortar crews move through. Their heavily laden mules were the biggest of all, without doubt the biggest that ever came out of Missouri. From up front would come bursts of automatic-rifle and machine-gun fire and then the detonations of mortars. From the middle of the column you could never be sure whose they were unless they began to hit around you.

"Medics forward!"

The wounded who could still stand were mounted on horses. Litter patients were sent to the rear to be picked up by the Chinese regiment that was following behind and would provide bearers to carry them until our advance had reached a paddy field on which the little liaison planes could land. A detail remained behind to bury the rifleman killed in the first burst and to erect a bamboo cross.

"Column's moving!"

You picked your way around a couple of dead Japanese lying like dolls on the trail and pushed on.

And so it went, from one place name on the map to another: Lanem Ga, Tanja Ga, Wesu Ga, Lagang Ga, Janpan, Auche, Warong, Manpin, Sharaw, Weilangyang, Hsamshingyang, Tingkrukawng, Ritpong, Namkwi. . . .

The major engagements came when we descended from the hills. The first indication the Japanese would have of our arrival would come when they ran into an American roadblock of battalion strength far behind the front on their main supply route. Their reaction was habitually violent. They would attack in waves. The number that were killed by the 5307th is not known, but the toll at Walawbum, Shadúzup, and Nhpum Ga alone was estimated at 1,700.

In order to achieve surprise, we often had to leave the trails altogether and hack our way through solid vegetation. One stretch of four miles once took us two days. That was on the way to Shadúzup—a mission the First Battalion, to which I belonged, had by itself. Altogether it took us two weeks to cover the whole distance of fifty miles. The last day we waded down a river—a tributary of the Mogaung—through water which was sometimes waist-high.

We reached the Mogaung itself, on which Shadúzup was located, at dusk. From a hill overlooking the river, we could see the Japanese bathing and washing their cooking pots. Peering out through the trees, we must have resembled a band of Iroquois gazing down upon an unsuspecting encampment of settlers; certainly we were wild enough looking by then. Before dawn, the battalion crept down from the hill, silently forded the Mogaung, and fell upon the Japanese with Tommy guns and bayonets.

The Japanese speedily collected themselves and counterattacked all day in a vain effort to dislodge us. For thirty-six hours they poured artillery shells into our positions—whinnying, high-trajectory 70s that you could hear coming for an eternity, whip-lash 75s, and thundering 150s. For all too-brief intervals Mustang fighter planes from India would come overhead and keep the Japanese batteries quiet. But most of the time, having no artillery of our own, we had to sit and take it—until the Chinese regiment we were spearheading could come up with its pack howitzers and take over from us.

At night we were helpless. We could only make ourselves small and pull our helmets down over our ears. Toward dawn of the last night, just after a shell had turned a tree into a shower of sparks a few feet from the foxhole where I crouched with the brassy taste of fear in my mouth—every time a shell burst it was as if a dry cell had been touched to my tongue—a clear voice, ringing out of the darkness, spoke for all of us:

"Where the hell are those other five thousand, three hundred and six composite units?"

The next morning I was impressed when one of the more profane stalwarts of the communications platoon confessed that he had spent much of the night praying.

"And you see," said I, "your prayers were answered."

"Not by a damn sight they ain't been! What I was praying for was a shell fragment in the fleshy part of the leg."

This wistful jest was heard with growing frequency as the campaign progressed. The prospect of being spared merely to endure more of it seemed less and less satisfactory. Not to know, from one instant to the next, week after week, when the silence would explode around you created a suspense difficult to describe. It made everyone look alike, for all faces—and they were equally emaciated to begin with—wore habitually the same expression of furtive intentness, of the strain of trying to exercise a sixth sense. Every time a twig crunched underfoot it jarred your nerves because of the way it echoed inside your helmet; the echo made it sound as if it came from off to the side, from where an ambush would be.

Maybe some kinds of danger are stimulating and ennobling, but if so, this was not one of them. You felt it as sordid, debasing, evil, a steady contamination. It was corrosive, like an acid eating at the heart and nerves. Every minute was an enemy to be outlived; the weeks were lifetimes. The number of mental breakdowns in the organization mounted to several score.

In other parts of the Army, men might talk of women. We talked of food. We were perpetually famished. K rations, on which we depended, were calculated merely to prevent starvation. We never received enough in one air-drop to carry us to the next; three days' rations had to do for four days or even five. However short on food we might be, we had to march. No matter what, the column had to go on. Jungle sores appeared on our bodies, the result, probably, of the lesions left by the leeches that fastened on us during the night. Many of the men could hardly walk (they had to anyway) because the sand that seeped into our shoes from our continual river crossings wore the skin off the soles of the feet. Dysentery and fevers were epidemic and left wraiths in their wake. Those with dysentery could eat nothing while the disease raged, which was for about a week, except the little cubes of chocolate we were issued as "B rations." This was a windfall for the others, of course, who were able to trade off their chocolate for real food—cans of pork and egg yolk and "cheese units"—that the dysentery sufferers could not get down or carry, weak as they were.

Fighting the enemy took it out on the unit, fighting disease and the hills took out still more, but maybe what took out most of all was the battle of the mules.

The mules had become as worn out as the men. When the monsoon rains began to turn the surface of the trails to butter, the only way the animals could mount the steep slopes was by galloping up on momentum. They would go bounding up like huge rabbits, the exhausted muleteers struggling to keep up. When they slipped and fell—which was often—they could not rise until they had been unloaded. Then they could not be reloaded except at the top of the hill, which meant that their two-hundred-pound packs had to be manhandled up the slope by men already burdened with heavy packs of their own. The muleteers became virtually dehumanized. Sometimes the struggling animals reached the crest only to topple over and go crashing down the precipitous flanks of the ridge, as like as not breaking their backs or stabbing themselves to death on broken bamboo. In any event, the column had to push on.

The world beyond the hills of northern Burma was something we could think of only with incredulity. We kept moving through a kind of green limbo, as if we had become detached from the human race. How could we ever explain what it was like? The danger and the hardship were not the important things, we would tell ourselves, and we would all nod wisely. In my first letter when I got out, I wrote anxiously that it was not all bad. There was lots of joking and laughter.

What were the jokes? One would say, "Whenever I close my eyes,

I see a tenderloin steak . . . French fries—" And another would interrupt, "You're lucky. Whenever I close mine, I see a mule's behind. Also when I don't." That was about the way the jokes were, but, like everything else, they were part of something that seemed terribly significant, something we felt we had to communicate, that we must explain when we got back. Life could never be the same for those who had learned what we had learned. We had learned it during the long talks on quiet evenings around the embers of a fire in a shallow pit, over which we heated water to make cocoa with the shavings of a hoarded chocolate bar, when the murmured conversation would range over the day's events and what life is for, while the Burmese hills stood black and silent around us. We learned it when the firing began and each of us read in the face of the man next to him the same undisguised, horribly anxious fear he himself was struggling with, something each shared yet each was utterly alone with. When we got out, we would tell what it was.

It is sometimes this way in a dream. You see life in a new and queer perspective or bathed in a strange and revealing illumination. The mysterious design of things is made clear and you understand . . . it is so simple and unmistakable . . . it is on the tip of your tongue, you have almost got it . . . and then you wake up and it is gone and there is only the tantalizing flavor of the dream left. So it was with us. Only last month I ran into a former major of the Third Battalion, and it was the same as it had been among us when we first got out. There was the same exchange of puzzled, questioning glances: can *you* say what it was? And you never can.

Because the Area Command back in Assam was the origin of the orders that kept us moving, we had a natural and wholesome antipathy toward it. This was not improved when, in the course of the campaign, the Command responded to a list of recommended promotions we sent in by suggesting that we interest ourselves less in promotions and more in fighting. . . .

Another memorable message reached us in the midst of one of our most arduous treks, when we had been unable for several days to reach India by our radio; the vegetation had been so dense that the bamboo refused to fall when we cut it and we could not clear a space for our antennas. Finally it thinned out and we were able to spot a liaison plane quartering over the jungle, obviously looking for us. I flagged it from a tiny clearing and it dropped a message. The message inquired acidly when we were going to conclude our scenic tour of northern Burma and get to Shadúzup.

It was after Nhpum Ga, however, that the unit developed a real and smoldering hostility toward the Command that was never to be extinguished.

Nhpum Ga was a village of a few huts on top of a hill where our Second Battalion had been ordered to stand and block a Japanese advance. What had happened was that while my battalion, the First, had been going around the Japanese flank to Shadúzup, the Second had been sent even farther around, down the valley of the Chindwin, to strike the Japanese still deeper in the rear. As it turned out, the Japanese were just then preparing to mount precisely the same kind of offensive up the same valley to outflank the Chinese. With this offensive the outnumbered Americans collided head-on. After killing, at point-blank range, some two hundred of the enemy who charged it through the *kunai* grass, the battalion was ordered to pull back twenty miles and hold the valley.

It arrived at Nhpum Ga under artillery bombardment and in a state of exhaustion. It was promptly surrounded and for two weeks fought for its life. Even drinking water had to be dropped by plane. The First Battalion was ordered to move to the scene by forced marches. Not until we of the First arrived, ravenously hungry (we had not been able to get our last food-drop) to augment the Third Battalion—which was holding an airstrip five miles further up the valley—was a force able to break through to the battle-torn hilltop where so long the men of the Second had been fighting back to back among a litter of dead horses and mules. Fifty-seven had been killed; three hundred wounded.

By that time, the 5307th had lost about seven hundred men, mostly wounded or sick, of its original three thousand. The rest were as good as finished. What had kept them going toward the end was the promise—the original source of which was never determined—that after the Nhpum Ga operation they would be pulled back to rest and reorganize before being sent back into combat the next dry season.

Then the blow fell. Far from being brought back—the 5307th was to be sent on a tougher mission than any it had yet had. It was to lead an advance to Myitkyina, an important Japanese base on the Irrawaddy far to the southeast.

Between General Stilwell's headquarters and us there was, not unnaturally, a difference of perspective. To Stilwell, Myitkyina (which is pronounced *Mitch*inah) was a vital objective. If it could be taken, planes flying the Hump would before very long be able to refuel there from the pipeline that was being laid along the Ledo Road and hence the volume of supplies they could carry to China would be substantially increased. Our costly victory at Nhpum Ga was later called by the official Army history—in the volume entitled *Stilwell's Command Problems*—"one of the hardest-fought American engagements in Burma." But it was, the history added, "from the perspective of China-Burma-India Theater headquarters a battle between a few battalions. Farther south, around Imphal, whole divisions were grappling for a prize that might change the course of the war in Asia." (It was at this time that the Japanese offensive against India, which had carried over the mountains of the Burmese frontier almost into the Indian lowlands, was just beginning to lose its impetus.)

Stilwell, it must be acknowledged, had a good deal to worry about. The Imphal offensive threatened, among other things, to cut the railroad to Assam that supplied his forces. The British had never been in sympathy with a campaign in north Burma, and Stilwell suspected the Generalissimo in Chungking of going behind his back to order the Chinese divisions in Burma to go slowly and avoid losses. As *Stilwell's Command Problems* also makes clear, he was concerned, too, by the Generalissimo's refusal to launch the offensive into north Burma across the Salween from China, which Stilwell considered so important, or to release another division from China for the offensive against Myitkyina.

The official history further points out, however, that as a result of Nhpum Ga, "the fighting edge of the most mobile and most obedient force that Stilwell had was worn dull. From this fact were to flow consequences of great magnitude."

What the 5307th felt was that while Myitkyina was doubtless important, so was Shanghai, and—to begin with—no one really believed the unit was to be sent against the one any more than against the other. When it appeared that in fact it was to be sent against Myitkyina, not a soul doubted that the Area Command was either wholly ignorant of (or wholly indifferent to) the organization's condition— or was out of its mind. General Merrill had had a heart attack during the siege of Nhpum Ga and was reported seriously ill. We felt helpless in the absence of anyone to represent us back in Assam, where, it was rumored, jealousy among Stilwell's subordinates of the renown General Merrill had achieved was a factor in the situation. Doubting that it would be able to make Myitkyina even if there were no Japanese in the way, the 5307th was convinced that someone had blundered. Unlike the Light Brigade, it did not scruple to reason why. It reasoned why with bitterness, though without much strength, of which it had little left. Worst of all, it felt betrayed.

There was no alternative, however, but to go on. After two weeks at Nhpum Ga, it backtracked twenty miles up the valley to a rendezvous with two untried Chinese regiments that were to make up the main strength.

I have two memories in particular of that historic encounter. One is of Lieutenant Weld, still retaining an air of Beacon Street and the Cape though clad only in soiled and ragged underwear, jovially panhandling for rice among the Chinese troops. (Phil was tall and active and required more food than the rest of us. To keep going, he would salvage the so-called dextrose tablets from the K rations that the rest of us would throw away unless we were positively starving; these objects had the appearance and consistency of the little tiles on bathroom floors and tasted just as you would expect them to.) The other memory is of being summoned by Colonel Hunter to the lean-to serving as headquarters for the operation, where he sat with the commander of the Chinese force. I was reminded for some reason of Marco Polo and Kublai Khan, though not for long.

"The walkie-talkies the General has received don't work," said Colonel Hunter. "See if you can fix them."

I had a horrible feeling that upon the outcome of my efforts would depend the future psychological balance of power between the two commanders and I felt faint. I prayed harder than I had prayed the last night at Shadúzup. There was only one thing I knew about walkie-talkies: if you inserted the two batteries head-and-head and tail-and-tail—which would seem the natural thing to do—the set would not function: head and tail was the ordained arrangement. I opened the first set . . . and I was saved. They were in the wrong way. There was nothing else the matter.

General Merrill was sufficiently recovered to return and take command of End Run, as the Myitkyina operation was termed—with a double meaning not intended. The 5307th, as usual, was split up for the trek into its three battalions, though it was now reduced to half its original strength. To our battalion, the First, was attached the Chinese 150th Regiment, to the Second the Chinese 88th, and to the Third three hundred Kachin levees. The three columns thus formed moved separately, though in proximity, toward Myitkyina. The Americans marched with what habitually served them in place of morale, a sort of what-the-hell-did-you-expect-anyhow? attitude. More than that, we had, to sustain us, the explicit promise that when we had performed this last task we should be flown back to a well-appointed rest camp in India. However, for the first time there began to be stragglers, men physically incapable of keeping up with the column in the heat—which had become intense—and indifferent to the danger of prowling Japanese.

It was sixty-five miles to Myitkyina and the terrain that had to be crossed was the worst so far, including as it did the saw-toothed Kumon range. The trail over the hills, which crossed the highest pass at six thousand feet, had not been used in years and in some places had to be redug out of the sheer slopes. In addition, the rains were becoming harder and more frequent. The mules simply sat down now for the steeper descents, sliding fifty yards at a stretch in the oily mud. Going up, steps had to be cut in the trails to give them a foothold. Even so, the surface was so treacherous that the losses from the animals slipping and plunging to their death down the mountainsides had become serious. One column lost twenty of its mules in a stretch of a few miles. . . .

At the outset of the march to Myitkyina, a new enemy attacked, and in a way it did more damage than any other, for it was mysterious and unforeseen. It was a fever no one could identify, and it struck without warning, felling its victims virtually where they stood. Before it finished with us, 149 men succumbed and had to be evacuated. Many of them died later in the hospitals of Assam, where eventually the fever was identified as an unfamiliar kind of typhus. One of the fatalities was the other lieutenant in my platoon. He left behind him a silence of which I was acutely aware, one that he had filled for so many weeks with repeated renditions of the first lines of a ditty that went something like, "I want a paper dolly just to call my own." There was still the bird that went *"Whee-oo,* WHEE-*oo,"* however. . . .

The Kumon range was the most formidable natural barrier on the route of march. However, even after we had put it behind us, the toll from disease and exhaustion continued to mount. So, of course, did the toll of battle casualties as the dazed, half-demented columns plodded on.

The end was near for me, however. One night we camped in an abandoned village on an open elevation. The battalion headquarters, if it could be so called, occupied a *basha* raised on posts about five feet above the ground. In addition to Colonel Osborne, the battalion commander, Colonel Hunter, who commanded the column, was there, so that altogether my ignominious fate did not lack for an adequate audience. We had a fire going on a dirt hearth—which, as I realized with misgivings, must have made our shelter stand out for some little distance around like a jack-o'-lantern. I had taken off my shoes on entering so as not to track mud onto the floor. Then there came that awful rattle of firing that was always the preliminary. Obviously, a body of Japanese—Heaven knew of what size—had struck the perimeter. In a moment the mortars had opened up and were thundering all around us. It is possible, even probable, that I led the exodus from the shack. I did not take time to put on my shoes before jumping, and I landed on a gaping cheese can. It laid my heel open nearly to the bone. I stumbled on out of the circle of light and hit the ground. Lying there in the dark amid the whine of bullets and in a drizzle of rain, holding my heel together to try to stay the flow of blood, I said to myself with an objective distinctness I still remember that this was assuredly the low point of my life so far.

The battle quickly subsided. It turned out that we had been mortared chiefly by the Chinese regiment we had with us which, as time went on, gave increasing evidence of being made up largely of trigger-happy children. The Japanese were dispersed, our casualties were treated, the medics taped up my heel, and in the morning we set off—for Myitkyina.

The indulgence accorded to invalids of having their packs put on the mules was granted to me, and by improvising a crutch I was able to hobble along for nearly a week. But the heel was infected and growing worse, and since I was of little use to anybody, I was included with about thirty others who were left behind for evacuation at an abandoned clearing that looked as if it would serve as a landing strip. It barely did serve. Two planes were lost in taking off, and in addition we had to beat off an attack by a Japanese patrol—fortunately a small one. At length, however, the operation was completed, and that night, after flying in hours over ground it had taken months to cross on foot, I was back in India lying in a real bed after a meal of real food under a real roof and was almost out of my mind with the luxury of it. But best of all was the news that came a few days later. Two battalions of the 5307th had in one last dash reached the airfield at Myitkyina, taking the Japanese completely by surprise, and had secured the approaches.

The hospital began rapidly to fill up as the DC-3s shuttling between Myitkyina and Ledo brought back the wounded, sick, and exhausted. There was elation in the wards as the long stream of white-faced, incredulous-looking refugees swelled. The final success had been achieved, and the campaign at last was over.

This was the first elation the unit ever knew and the last, and it was short-lived.

News arrived that an attempt to take the town of Myitkyina unaccountably had failed. Later we heard the details. . . .

The Japanese in the town were well dug in and in addition were protected by the roads that, elevated above the level of the paddy fields, served as earthworks. The defense, moreover, was favored by the heavy monsoon rains that had turned some of the surroundings into lakes.

An attack by a battalion of the 5307th on May 21 was pushed back to its starting point and one by the Chinese a few days later did no better. The evacuation of the disabled members of the 5307th was now running at between seventy-five and one hundred a day. The last action fought by a Marauder battalion, as such, was on May 27. The men were then so worn out that some of them were not even able to stay awake to defend themselves, and the battalion commander lost consciousness three times while directing the engagement. By the end of May, only two hundred of the three thousand men with which the 5307th had gone into combat were considered fit to remain at Myitkyina. To be considered unfit and warranting evacuation, a man at that time had to run a fever of 102 degrees or better for three consecutive days.

"The earlier optimism," *Stilwell's Command Problems* notes, "was replaced by a brief period of extreme alarm, caused by the rapid disintegration of Galahad and the Chindits' evacuation of the block they had placed across the railway near Hopin. Only twelve men were left in the Second Battalion of Galahad, while the Chinese 150th Regiment was down to 600 men. American reinforcements of any men who could hold a rifle were rushed in from every possible source." . . .

Before we had ever set out for Myitkyina, we were convinced that Stilwell's headquarters was overreaching itself. What we thought the results would be, I do not remember. I am sure, however, that we never anticipated quite what sort of reckoning there would be. Receiving only fragmentary information, we were not, in the first couple of weeks, aware of the dimensions of the reckoning as it unfolded. We had barely digested the news that the evacuation of the 5307th could not be completed, when we learned that orders had been issued that any of us who could walk were to be sent back to Myitkyina. We were stunned. As the official history was to put it, "This order was in sharp contrast to the men's expectation that after reaching Myitkyina they would have a long period of recuperation." It was indeed.

On the heels of this order, the convalescent camp was combed and two hundred were adjudged sufficiently recovered to be sent back in. Of these, fifty were pronounced unfit for any kind of service upon arrival at Myitkyina and were returned. (The remaining 150 were among the veterans assigned to the new battalions who shared in the six Distinguished Service Crosses earned at Myitkyina by members of the 5307th.)

Then began a time when the Marauders, who had done so much fighting, were themselves fought over. On one side was Stilwell's headquarters, which was placing "extremely heavy moral pressure, just short of outright orders . . . on medical officers to return to duty or keep in the line every American who could pull a trigger." On the other were the medical officers themselves—the unit's own and the local hospital authorities—who were determined not to certify as fit for combat men who were broken physically and mentally.

General Stilwell was later reported to have been appalled at the overzealous interpretation given his instructions by his subordinates. On this point I cannot testify. On one occasion when these subordinates succeeded in loading several hundred convalescents into trucks, the medical officers took after the convoy in Jeeps, intercepted it and forced it to return.

In the end, the doctors won. The pressure at Myitkyina was progressively relaxed, and thereafter no more wholesale movements of troops from the 5307th back to combat were attempted. And at long last, yielding to mounting pressure, the town fell. In the meantime, the 5307th had been totally wrecked.

It happened that I was picked—I forget why, but perhaps it was because I had been designated adjutant of the rest camp, for some reason—to write a report for the Army's morale division explaining what had happened.

I could testify from my own experience that it was impossible for men to make any kind of recovery when release from the hospital automatically meant return to combat while they were still suffering nervous and physical exhaustion. I found myself with a strange debility that sometimes made me feel I could not get out of my chair. It was like being drugged. It could not be explained by the cut in my heel, which had largely been cured, or by the malaria from which I had just recovered, and I concluded it must be mental, the result of the all-pervasive fear of being sent to Myitkyina.

The only thing to do—for the frightening ailment seemed to be growing—was to take the bull by the horns. So I got myself flown to Myitkyina—and was sent back again by Colonel Osborne, who said his purpose was to get the 5307th out of the place, not reassembled there. (The Myitkyina airfield, surrounded by trenches and red, green, blue, and white nylon supply-drop parachutes strung up as tents, resembled a fair grounds in hell.)

That was only part of it, however. To begin with, the 5307th was a volatile compound. What had held it together through the long campaign was danger, isolation, and impatience to get a detested job done. Toward the end, it kept going on promises, first the promise of a respite after Nhpum Ga, then the promise of a comfortable rest camp with real shower baths after Myitkyina. The default on the first promise left an ineradicable mark. The results of the second did not matter so much. The rest camp turned out to consist of mud-floored huts surrounding a few overgrown cow pastures, and the showers were two old oil drums and some lengths of rusty pipe that were dumped off the back of a truck one day with the injunction that we could make anything we wanted to out of them. It was merely annoying to reflect that the base-area troops a few miles away, who had yet to spend a night out of their beds, had finished, concrete shower-stalls which no one had suggested they share with us. The effect was more serious when some of our early evacuees who had been on furlough brought back stories of electric fans and refrigerators that rear-echelon officers at

New Delhi had abstracted out of the supply line for their offices or even private use—which explained why our sick and injured had in many cases to swelter in airless wards, without cold drinks.

Above all, when I wrote the report, my mind went back to an observation made by Tom Senff, the officer beside whom I had stood at our first formation. On this last occasion we were watching the column trudging into a bivouac area one evening on the way to Myitkyina. The way the men looked, they made you think of gaunt-faced, fanatic-eyed, and for the most part bearded Indian holy men.

"They look as if it were the end of war for them, don't they?" he said. "But, you know, all they need is a pat on the back, a little recognition of what they've done—maybe a parade—and they'd be back in here next season ready to do it all over again."

What happened was just the opposite. At the end, they were made to feel inadequate and shamed.

Many swallowed their feelings—and many did not. With the first general releases from the hospital, the building where the men's private belongings had been stored was ransacked and the contents either stolen or destroyed in sheer wanton violence. The signs of demoralization multiplied. The rest camp, as it filled up, was little better than a shambles and at night was enlivened by gunfire—for no one had seen fit to challenge the men on the retention of their side arms. Almost all the unit's officers were either at Myitkyina or in the hospital, and the policy of the local MPs was—wisely, I think—to keep out of the way as much as possible. Back pay and stolen articles were converted into beer or, which was much worse, a product of the Assam Distilleries labelled "Bull-Fight Brandy," which had been proscribed by the military authorities because it turned men into maniacs who would as soon assault an officer as look at him. (I had myself to swing a chair at two of them who were trying to demolish the little Red Cross building one night.)

Work details were impossible to assemble and discipline impossible to enforce; there was nothing with which to threaten the rebellious except the guardhouse, and this would have appealed to most of them as a luxurious alternative to Burma. AWOLs were wholesale, and as furloughs began to be granted, the MPs in Calcutta had their hands full. Those in the rest camp lived like bands of castaway pirates, gambling and pitching empty beer cans out the windows. Inspecting officers arrived from various echelons and went away with pursed lips.

However, either for reasons of pity or apprehension, no effort was made to impose discipline from the outside. I doubt very much if it could have been done.

Thievery was rampant, in fact was one of the worst problems. In an innocent effort to combat it by stimulating the organization's pride, I procured a two-foot square of sheet metal and some oil paints from an ordnance depot and spent a couple of days laboriously constructing a large replica of our dramatic and colorful insignia. This insignia, which local Indian tailors were beginning to reproduce for us on shoulder-patches, was one by which we set particular store since we had designed and conferred it upon ourselves (no one else had appeared likely to confer one upon us). I hung my handiwork from a telephone pole outside the orderly room. All day, as word of the ornament spread, groups of soldiers came to gaze up at it and stop by to express their extravagant admiration of it. It was stolen the first night and never recovered.

No doubt, with General Merrill's recovery and the return of Colonel Hunter from Myitkyina, the 5307th could have been pulled back together again—with an effort. But by then a new regulation had been issued by the Army authorizing the return to the United States of all those with over two years' foreign duty. This applied to two-thirds of the 5307th's strength. Of the remainder, those who were still fit were incorporated in a larger force that, the following winter, was to complete the task the Marauders had begun and reach the Burma Road. I myself was ordered back to the United States for another kind of duty.

The 5307th Composite Unit (Provisional) never even had a final formation. It simply trickled away. But before then, we had had our moment. At the high point of our delinquencies, the Distinguished Unit Citation was bestowed upon us from Washington. The order read:

> After a series of successful engagements in the Hukawng and Mogaung Valleys of North Burma in March and April 1944, the unit was called on to lead a march over jungle trails through extremely difficult mountain terrain against stubborn resistance in a surprise attack on Myitkyina. The unit proved equal to its task and after a brilliant operation of 17 May 1944 seized the airfield at Myitkyina, an objective of great tactical importance in the campaign, and assisted in the capture of the town of Myitkyina on 3 August 1944.

As far as we were concerned, the Army had made it up to us.

When I left, carrying in a suitcase what remained unfilched of my possessions, there appeared to be nobody around to say good-by to, except a lieutenant outside the orderly room. I think it must have been young Caldwell of Tennessee, for I seem to recall that he wore the broad-brimmed, flat-crowned hat Caldwell had found in a bazaar and habitually wore with the courtliness of a Southern planter. I seem also to recall that the wave of the hand with which he indicated the area of the camp was languid and majestic, in the Caldwellian manner.

"The time will come," he observed, "when you will feel you were with the Green Mountain Boys and Mad Anthony Wayne's Indian fighters and Morgan's Raiders. And being as big an idiot as I am, you will wonder how anyone as fearful and unworthy as you could have been included in such a glorious company."

Young Caldwell was wise beyond his years.

Index of Authors